Pre-Columbian Art at Dumbarton Oaks, Number 3

ANCIENT MEXICAN ART AT DUMBARTON OAKS

Pre-Columbian Art at Dumbarton Oaks, Number 3

ANCIENT MEXICAN ART AT DUMBARTON OAKS
Central Highlands, Southwestern Highlands, Gulf Lowlands

Susan Toby Evans
EDITOR

DUMBARTON OAKS RESEARCH LIBRARY AND COLLECTION
WASHINGTON, D.C.

Printed in Korea at Tara Printing

LIBRARY OF CONGRESS CATALOGING-IN-PUBLICATION DATA

Ancient Mexican art at Dumbarton Oaks : central highlands, southwestern highlands, Gulf lowlands / editors, Susan Toby Evans, Joanne Pillsbury, Jeffrey Quilter.

p. cm. — (Pre-Columbian art at Dumbarton Oaks ; no. 3)

Includes bibliographical references and index.

ISBN 978-0-88402-345-6 (hardcover : alk. paper)

1. Indian art—Mexico—Catalogs.
2. Indians of Mexico—Antiquities—Catalogs.
3. Mexico—Antiquities—Catalogs.
4. Robert Woods Bliss Collection of Pre-Columbian Art—Catalogs.
5. Dumbarton Oaks—Catalogs.
6. Art, Mexican.

I. Evans, Susan Toby, 1945–
II. Pillsbury, Joanne.
III. Quilter, Jeffrey, 1949–
IV. Dumbarton Oaks.

F1219.3.A7.A4825 2010

972′.01—dc22

2009035272

GENERAL EDITORS: Jeffrey Quilter and Joanne Pillsbury

MANAGING EDITOR: Sara Taylor

ART DIRECTOR: Kathleen Sparkes

DESIGN AND COMPOSITION: Melissa Tandysh

JACKET ILLUSTRATION: Teotihuacan black limestone mask, Terminal Formative and Early Classic periods, PC.B.053

www.doaks.org/publications

CONTENTS

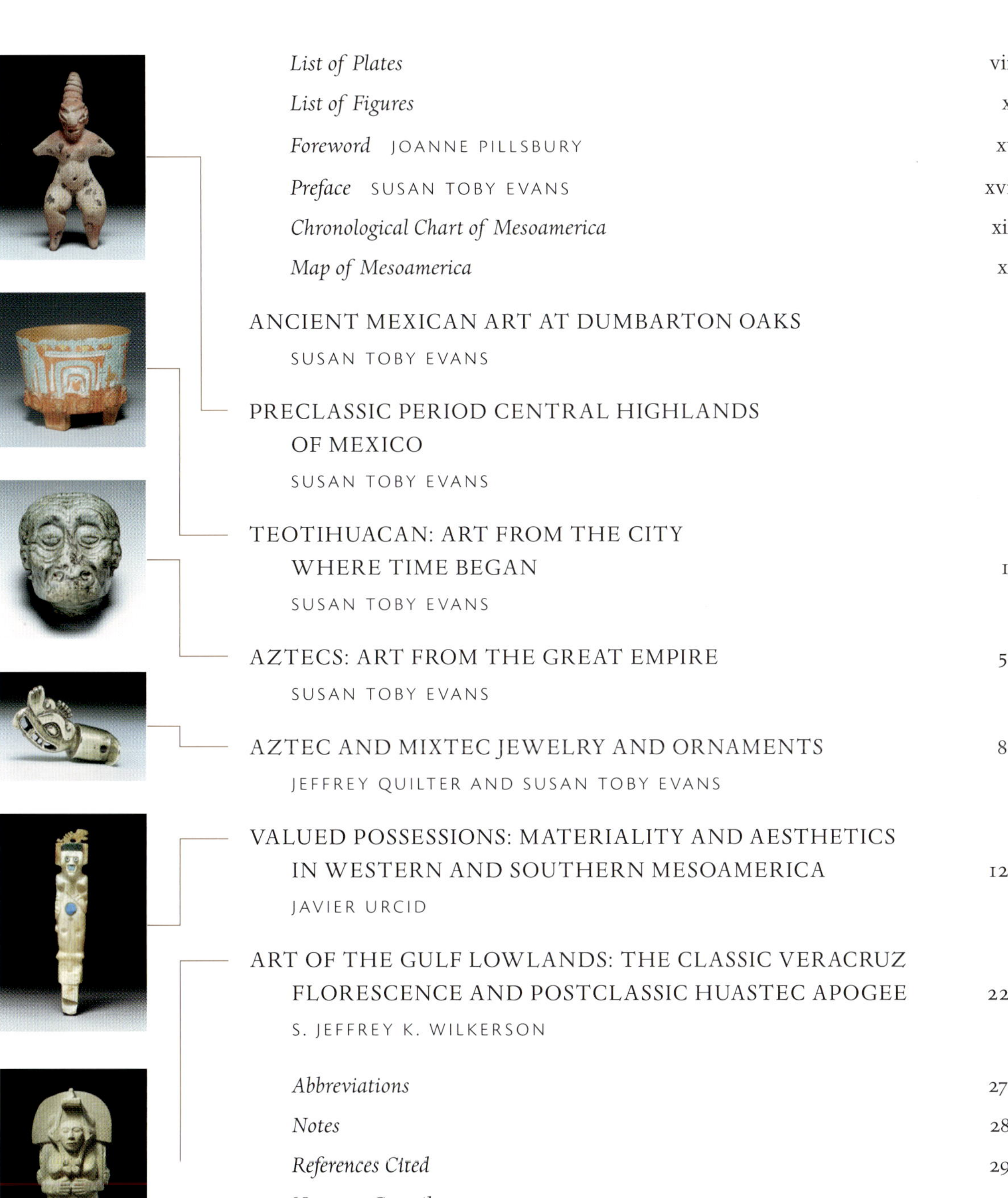

FIGURES

The objects in this catalogue represent the work of artists from many different eras, working in regions now encompassed by the modern country of Mexico. The oldest works, a ceramic figurine and a figurine fragment from an area that is now part of Mexico City, were created more than two thousand years ago. Most of the collection antedates the arrival of Europeans to the region in 1519, although one object made of obsidian—a material much valued in the pre-Hispanic period—was incorporated into a Franciscan portable altar in the early colonial period.

The geographic range represented in the collection is equally broad, with works from the central Basin of Mexico, coastal Veracruz and adjacent regions, Oaxaca, and other areas of western and southern Mexico. In some cases, we are able to associate with certainty objects to cultures we now know as Aztec (also called Mexica) or Teotihuacan, whereas in other cases such identification is impossible, particularly with small, exquisitely crafted portable objects that may have circulated widely.

The Dumbarton Oaks collection of ancient art from the Central Highlands, Southwestern Highlands, and Gulf Lowlands of Mexico is notable for several reasons. The collection includes singular objects of historic importance as well as fine examples of well-known types. At the time Robert Woods Bliss was establishing his collection, little was known about what the individuals who commissioned and created these objects thought about the meanings of specific materials. Yet Bliss's choices echo some ancient hierarchies of valued materials, especially those that were difficult to obtain and work, such as greenstone, shell, and gold. Luminous color and radiance captured the eye as easily in 1950 as in antiquity, although many associated meanings undoubtedly of importance in the ancient world still elude us today. Bliss eschewed other materials that were of profound importance in pre-Hispanic Mexico—such as featherwork—perhaps in part due to the scarcity of such objects on the market in the twentieth century, as he did collect feather objects from the Andes. He collected ancient Mexican ceramics and wooden objects sparingly, focusing on a few objects of exceptional importance. In this sense the collection remains a personal, rather than comprehensive, selection of rare and finely crafted works.

The formation of this collection had a significant impact on the development of the field of Pre-Columbian studies. Robert Bliss was perhaps the first to establish a collection of Pre-Columbian objects selected on the basis of aesthetic criteria. Rather than view the objects as pieces of ethnographic interest installed in the context of a natural history museum, Robert Bliss felt that Pre-Columbian art was worthy of display alongside Western art, and his collection was first shown at the National Gallery of Art in Washington, D.C., and subsequently (after 1963) in the purpose-built gallery designed by Philip Johnson at Dumbarton Oaks. In concert with the creation of the collection, a small program of scholarly activities was initiated, including the publication of the first catalogue of the Pre-Columbian collection in 1947.

In the years since, the focus of activities in the Pre-Columbian Program at Dumbarton Oaks has gradually shifted away from collecting objects to the scholarly study of the cultures of the ancient Americas. Through a program of fellowships, project grants, scholarly meetings, publications, and research projects, Dumbarton Oaks has become a center for advanced research for scholars internationally. The research library has grown to more than 32,000 volumes, and both scholars and the public alike are able to enjoy the exhibitions in the newly renovated museum. The present catalogue is part of the publications program, and it is intended to foster the dissemination of research. Some of the objects in this catalogue are well known to both the scholarly world and the public, whereas others have received little attention before the creation of this catalogue. It is hoped that this publication will become a springboard for future research and discussions, as our knowledge of and ideas about the art of these regions evolve over time.

The preliminary work on a catalogue of the collection of objects from the central, southwestern, and Gulf Coast regions of Mexico began in the early 1990s, under the direction of Elizabeth Boone, then director of Pre-Columbian Studies. Over the course of the years, Janet Berlo, John Pohl, and Emily Umberger were among the numerous scholars who contributed their time to study of the collection. The present volume was organized by Elizabeth's successor, Jeffrey Quilter. At Jeffrey's invitation, Susan Toby Evans was invited to edit a multiauthored catalogue, with contributions from scholars actively engaged in archaeological research in the regions where the objects in this collection were thought to have been produced. The resulting essays and entries reflect the robust diversity of anthropological approaches to the study of ancient American objects and the cultures in which they were created. Dumbarton Oaks remains grateful to Jeffrey and Susan for their tireless efforts in shaping this catalogue, and to the authors Jeffrey Quilter, Nicholas Saunders, Jeffrey Wilkerson, and Javier Urcid, who contributed many hours to researching and writing on the collection.

As Susan Evans notes in her Preface, a project of this scale and duration involved the contributions of many individuals. I join Susan in thanking all of them, and I particularly reiterate thanks to Patricia Alexander, Emily Gulick, Reiko Ishihara, Grace Morsberger, Juan Antonio Murro, Patricia Sarro, Kathy Sparkes, and Sara Taylor for their assistance in the preparation of this catalogue over the past two years. We are grateful to Joe Mills for the splendid object photography throughout the publication. We thank Justin Kerr for his fine photographs of two objects shown in Plates 17 and 19. Miriam Doutriaux's careful attention to many aspects of this catalogue has enhanced and refined it greatly. I also thank the two anonymous external reviewers of the manuscript for contributing their expertise to this project. I remain indebted to them for their careful and detailed reviews and for their insights into this collection. Finally, I thank Lisa Trever for her outstanding contributions to the final editorial stages of this project.

Joanne Pillsbury
Director of Studies, Pre-Columbian Program
Dumbarton Oaks

PREFACE

> In the Edwardian world of spacious living when the accumulating of possessions was regarded in Europe as an innocuous but "distinguished" pastime, I became aware of Pre-Columbian stone and gold work. The first few objects acquired in Paris thirty-five years ago were an antidote to the insidious charm of the XVIII Century and opened vistas I soon became eager to explore.
>
> Robert Woods Bliss (1947: 5)

Thus Robert Woods Bliss recalled the period during which he began to collect Pre-Columbian objects. At that time, Pre-Columbian objects were displayed as part of natural history collections rather than art. Robert and Mildred Bliss instead established the perspective that would continue informing this collection throughout their lives, and they would share it with scholars and with the public, first through a long-term exhibition at the National Gallery of Art in Washington, D.C., by lending various objects to museums around the world, and finally by providing the collection with an architecturally distinguished home, the Philip Johnson Wing of Dumbarton Oaks in Washington, D.C.

The Bliss Collection of Pre-Columbian Art has been further shared through the publication of catalogues that range from the 1947 version in which Ambassador Bliss wrote the statement above, to the comprehensive 1957 and 1963 editions, and to the recent volumes (Boone 1996; Taube 2004b) that focus on particular regions. This volume continues this new series and presents works from the Central Highlands of Mexico—the broad set of mountains and valleys that surround present-day Mexico City—and from the adjacent areas to the west, south, and east. These include the Gulf of Mexico Lowlands and the region extending from Morelos to Puebla and Oaxaca.

In terms of chronological range, the objects presented here include those from the Preclassic period, Mesoamerica's earliest era of village agriculture, through the Classic period (AD 250 or 300–900), the Postclassic period (AD 900–1521), and into the Early colonial period, which begins with the conquest of the Aztec Empire by the Spaniards in AD 1521 and continues into the early seventeenth century. Culturally, the collection incorporates the distinctive artistic traditions of Classic Teotihuacan and Late Classic Gulf Lowlands centers, as well as marvelous examples of Postclassic artisanship typical of the Mixteca-Puebla style and monumental sculptures that the Aztecs used to intimidate their allies and enemies.

Although the collection is eclectic in terms of materials and styles, Robert and Mildred Bliss were drawn to particular types of objects, and Robert Bliss was well known for his interest in small, polished stone sculptures. Over the course of decades of collecting, they brought together a distinguished set of artifacts.

It is essential for us today to understand the Blisses in their era, in which objects from the ancient cultures of the Americas held little interest for most collectors and were not well known to the general public. Research into archaeologically and ethnographically known cultures was expanding, however, and these early collectors of ancient American art did much to foster interest in the field, both through the dissemination of information on the collection through exhibitions and publications, and later through the establishment of scholarly programs at Dumbarton Oaks.

Three successive directors of Pre-Columbian Studies at Dumbarton Oaks have overseen the production of this new series of catalogues: Elizabeth Boone, Jeffrey Quilter, and Joanne Pillsbury. All of them have encouraged scholars to understand the objects from a variety of perspectives. The present catalogue includes contributions from anthropologists who have studied and thought about the collection in different ways, highlighting the possibilities inherent in the study of such a collection. My own scholarly focus is the Basin of Mexico, the region immediately surrounding modern Mexico City, and for objects from other regions I have been fortunate to have as co-authors Jeffrey Quilter, who contributed articles about the collection's personal adornments made of gold and other precious substances; Javier Urcid, who wrote essays on materials in the Mixteca-Puebla tradition; and S. Jeffrey K. Wilkerson, who analyzed sculptures from the Gulf Lowlands, particularly those pertaining to the ancient ball game. Nicholas Saunders described the obsidian mirror or altar (PC.B.078, Plate 24), which may date to the colonial period.

It would be impossible to produce a volume of such topical diversity without the generous participation of colleagues who offered information, advice, and skills. Elizabeth Benson, Dumbarton Oaks's first director of the Pre-Columbian Studies program, provided important historical background as well as good advice on how to interpret various objects. Elizabeth Boone, Benson's successor and expert on the culture of the Aztecs, offered essential guidance from an art-historical perspective. Boone's successor, Jeffrey Quilter, gave me the opportunity to edit this volume, and helped enormously in the organization of the overall project, intellectually and logistically. Joanne Pillsbury, the present director of Pre-Columbian Studies, has been invaluable in helping this project toward completion and maintaining a commitment for the new series of catalogues of the Bliss Collection.

Staff members at Dumbarton Oaks have been vital to the successful completion of this catalogue. Bridget Gazzo was tireless in the pursuit of obscure references. James Carder, Miriam Doutriaux, Juan Antonio Murro, Loa Traxler, and Jennifer Younger generously shared their expertise about archives and images. Jai Alterman, Emily Gulick, Pete Haggerty, Kristy Keyes, and Hector Paz offered important logistical and material support; Marlene Chazan has ably administered our budget. Further clerical support was given by Wendy Fultz, Kim Miller, and Diane Snyder of the Department of Anthropology, Pennsylvania State University.

I have been fortunate in being able to call on my colleagues for help. Barbara Stark included a sample from an incense burner in the Bliss Collection (PC.B.052, Plate 74) in the neutron activation analysis of a set of materials from the Gulf Lowlands, establishing a general provenience for that object. Rae Beaubien examined a Teotihuacan mask (PC.B.056, Plate 14) with fiber impressions, and the advice given by her and by Mary Frame and Barbara Stark led me to examine the role of textiles at Teotihuacan. Kenneth Hirth and Gerardo Gutiérrez Mendoza supplied information on the jade disks (PC.B.133, Plate 4) and provided valuable suggestions. I was able to consult notes on the collection that were made by Janet Catherine Berlo and by Emily Umberger, whose knowledge of Aztec sculpture was essential to the study of the Fire Serpent (PC.B.069, Plate 19). Wendy Grossman generously shared research pertaining to the birth figure (PC.B.071, "Tlazolteotl," Plate 25) and its popularity with Parisian Surrealists, and Sandra Stelts of Penn State University's library gave me access to a facsimile of the Codex Borbonicus image of Tlazolteotl. Dorothy Hosler examined many of the metal objects (PC.B.090–PC.B.092, PC.B.100–PC.B.110; Plates 40, 36, 37, 27, 28, 30, 29, 31, 39, 38, 34, 32, 33, and 35, respectively) and offered important insights. Sue Bergh, Susan Boyd, Heather McCune Bruhn, Staffan Brunius, Michael Glascock, Annabeth Headrick, Frances Karttunen, Mary Miller, Patricia Sarro, Karl Taube, and David Webster readily discussed objects and issues pertaining to them.

To complete this project, Dumbarton Oaks offered me hospitality as well as access to its incomparable library of Pre-Columbian materials. My various research trips permitted me to discuss aspects of the project with Dumbarton Oaks fellows and readers William Barnes, Linda Brown, Patrick Hajovsky, and Sarah Jackson.

Finally, it has been a privilege to be a part of the Dumbarton Oaks community and to see its campus transformed by the addition of the new library and the renovation of the Main Building and its collections facilities. This project was completed under the guidance of the director of Dumbarton Oaks Edward Keenan and his successor, Jan Ziolkowski, and their support for the catalogue series of the Bliss Collection of Pre-Columbian Art is very much appreciated.

Chronological Chart of Mesoamerica

YEAR	RELATIVE CHRONOLOGY	CENTRAL HIGHLANDS OF MEXICO	OAXACA, MIXTECA	GULF COAST	WEST MEXICO, GUERRERO	MAYA HIGHLANDS / PACIFIC COAST	LOWLAND MAYA
1519	Late Postclassic	Aztec *Tenochtitlan* *Cholula*	Mixtec independent kingdoms *Mitla*	*Cempoala*	Tarascan *Tzintzuntzan*	Maya independent city-states *Mixco Viejo* *Iximché*	*Tulum* *Mayapán*
1200	Early Postclassic	Toltec *Tula* *Cholula*	*Coixtlahuaca* *Yagul*			*Utatlán*	*Chichén Itzá* Tepeu phase
900	Terminal Classic	*Xochicalco* *Cacaxtla*		*El Tajín*			*Uxmal* and Puuc sites
	Late Classic	*Tula Chico* *Cholula*	*Monte Albán* IIIb	Classic Veracruz *Remojadas*	*Guachimontón*	*Cotzumalhuapa*	*Palenque* *Tikal* *Yaxchilán*
600	Early Classic	*Teotihuacan*	*Monte Albán* IIIa	*Cerro de las* *Mesas*		*Kaminaljuyu* Esperanza phase	Tzakol phase *Copán* *Tikal* *Uaxactún*
300 AD	Protoclassic	*Cholula* *Teotihuacan*	*Monte Albán* II	*El Pital*	Shaft tombs	*Kaminaljuyu* Miraflores phase	Chicanel phase *El Mirador* *Nakbé* *Cerros* *San Bartolo*
BC 300	Late Preclassic	*Cuicuilco* *Ticoman* *Zacatenco*	*Dainzú*	*Tres Zapotes*	*Chupícuaro*	*Santa Leticia* *Monte Alto* *Pijijiapan* *Xoc*	Mamom phase
600	Middle Preclassic	*Tlapacoya*	Guadalupe	*La Venta* *Río Pesquero* *La Merced*	*Oxtotitlan Cave* *Juxtlahuaca Cave*	*Takalik Abaj*	
900	Early Preclassic	*Tlatilco* *Las Bocas*	San José Tierras Largas	*San Lorenzo* B San Lorenzo A Chicharras Bajío Ohochi	*Teopantecuanitlan* *Xochipala* *El Opeño* Capacha	Cuadros phase Cherla phase Ocós phase	
1500	Early Preclassic		*San José Mogote* Espiridón	*El Manatí*		Locona phase Barra *Paso de la Amada*	
2000			Martinez		*Matanchén*	Chantuto B	
2500	Archaic	Abejas	Blanca				
3000							

Note: Selected cultures and phases are noted, and selected site names are indicated in italics.

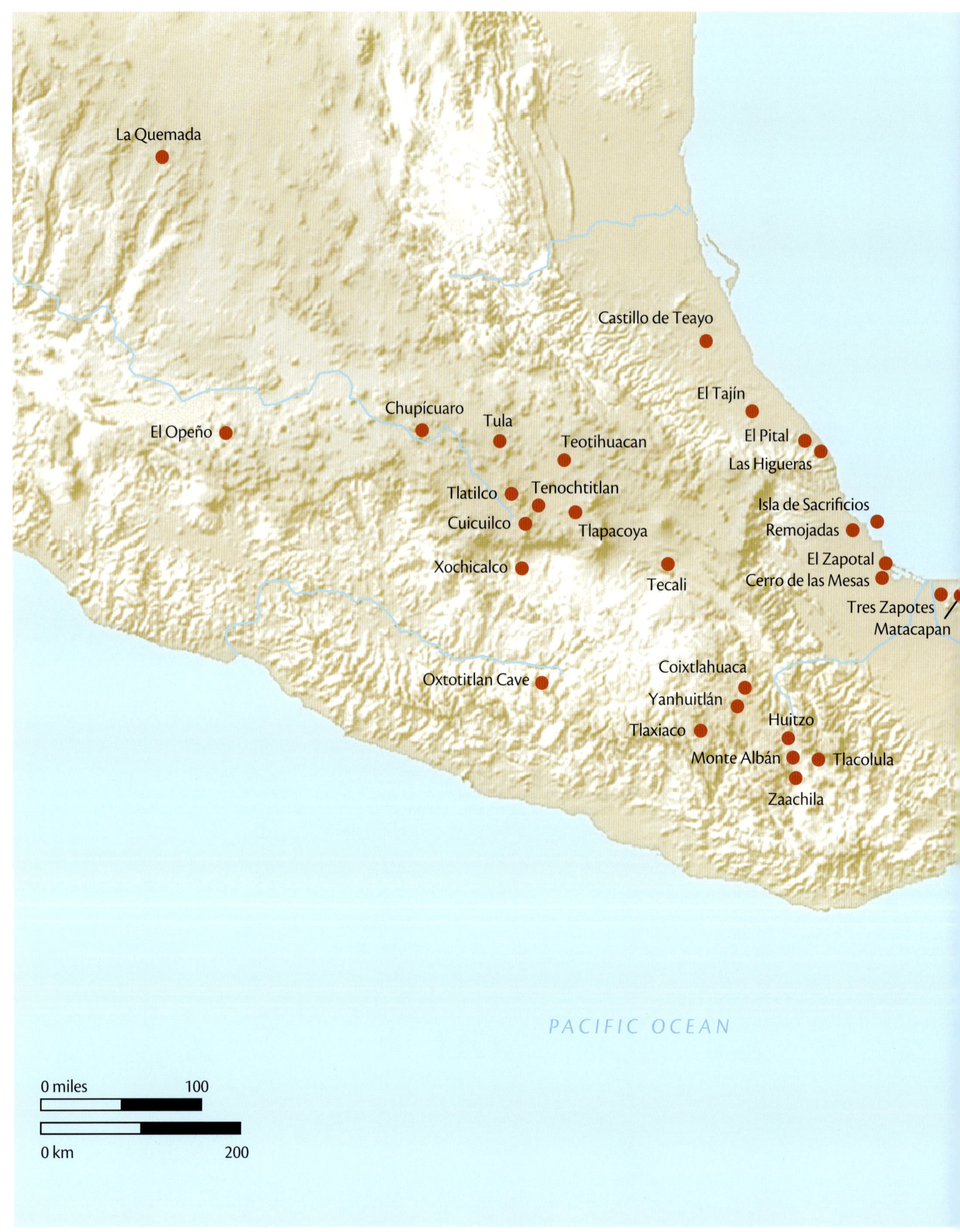

fig. 1 Map of Mesoamerica, showing locations of major sites mentioned in the text.

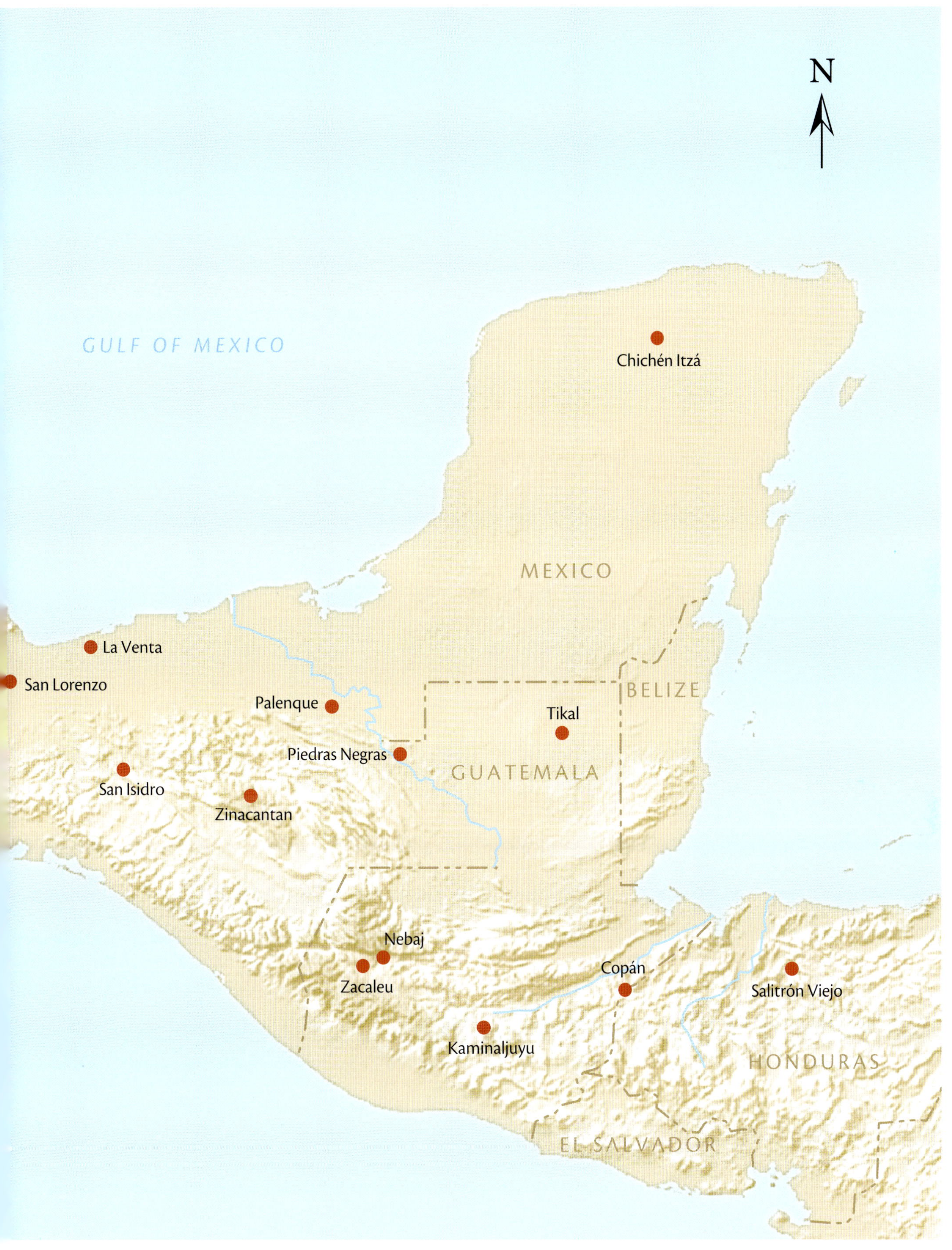
N
GULF OF MEXICO
Chichén Itzá
MEXICO
La Venta
San Lorenzo
BELIZE
Palenque
Tikal
Piedras Negras
GUATEMALA
San Isidro
Zinacantan
Nebaj
Zacaleu
Copán
Salitrón Viejo
Kaminaljuyu
HONDURAS
EL SALVADOR

ANCIENT MEXICAN ART AT DUMBARTON OAKS

SUSAN TOBY EVANS

> I saw the things which have been brought to the king from the new land of gold [Mexico], a sun all of gold a whole fathom broad, and a moon all of silver of the same size, . . . all kinds of wonderful objects of human use. . . . All the days of my life I have seen nothing that rejoiced my heart so much as these things, for I saw amongst them wonderful works of art, and I marveled at the subtle *ingenia* of men in foreign lands.
>
> Albrecht Dürer[1]

Five hundred years ago, a sustained and permanent contact was begun between the Old World and the New. By 1519 Spanish soldiers were marveling at the wealth and extent of the Aztec Empire, and by the summer of 1521 they began to control it on behalf of Spain. A few Europeans, like Dürer, would admire the precious objects from New Spain and value them enough to save them, but most examples of *art mobilier* were either reduced to their component materials for reuse or were destroyed as works of the devil.

It was not until the early twentieth century that finely crafted objects from ancient Mexico and Central America were appreciated as art by those in Europe and the Americas. Members of the intelligentsia were viewing the world through two different but complementary perspectives: art and science. The latter emphasized systematic knowledge about peoples of the world through the emerging discipline of anthropology, whereas the former stressed the study of objects through more humanistic disciplines.

Scientific collections of representative artifacts from ancient Mexico were being established at museums and universities by the early twentieth century, but the aesthetic qualities of these objects were not widely appreciated. In 1912 Robert Bliss, living in Paris as a U.S. diplomat, began to collect Pre-Columbian pieces. As Elizabeth Boone noted in an essay on Robert Bliss's development as a collector, he was primarily concerned with these objects "as works of art" (Boone 1996: 3). Over time, Robert and Mildred Bliss would form a landmark collection of materials from Middle America and South America.

Since Robert Bliss began his collection, the Pre-Columbian world has been rediscovered through archaeology, ethnohistory, and art history, and today we understand much more about the different cultures of the ancient Americas. We know that geography strongly shaped cultural expression, and in Middle America, topography created two major environmental regions with an area of strong overlap: a western block of semiarid highlands, mountains, and valleys that extended down into the hot lowlands of the Pacific and Gulf of Mexico coasts and the Isthmus of

Tehuantepec, and an eastern block that stretched from the Isthmus through the Maya Lowlands and Highlands and into Central America (see Figure 1).

The earliest settled villages, dating from the Early Preclassic period (see the Chronological Chart of Mesoamerica, page xix), reflect this broad division, and ancient Mesoamerica's first complex culture, that of the Olmec, arose in the Isthmus of Tehuantepec overlap zone.[2] Olmec culture was one of several important regional developments, and even areas lacking monumental construction at this time, such as the Basin of Mexico, produced objects of rare beauty and inspired concept.

By the end of the Preclassic period, the Basin of Mexico would see the rise of Teotihuacan, America's first great city. Teotihuacan dominated the Central Highlands region in the Early Classic period. Its influence extended to the Southwestern Highlands—heartland of the city of Monte Albán—and to the Gulf Lowlands and across the Isthmus of Tehuantepec into the Maya region. Teotihuacan's monumentality, population size, and range of influence were remarkable for any premodern culture, but there is still much that we do not understand about it. Teotihuacan's fall from greatness began in the sixth century AD, the middle of the Classic period. By the Late Classic period, cultural hegemony in western Mesoamerica had become regionalized.

The lowlands along the Gulf of Mexico emerged as a newly important region for the development of society and art. Olmec culture had flourished in the southern Gulf Lowlands, but by the Late Classic period, cultural focus had moved north. The Huastecs, who spoke a Mayan language, became a dominant ethnic group. Their culture produced distinctive sculptures of standing figures as well as smaller-scale works that represented equipment used in ritual ball games.

As the Classic period drew to a close and the Postclassic period began, the area linking the Central and Southwestern Highlands became a focus for artistic development. This Mixteca-Puebla region lent its name to the decorative style that would influence all of western Mesoamerica throughout the Postclassic period. Not only were Mixteca-Puebla artistic traditions masterful and assured, but they were also expressed in a variety of media: lapidary and metal jewelry, wood carving, and mosaics were among their notable achievements. Artisans from this region were sought after by rulers in other regions, who brought them to their own capitals, gaining prestige by establishing workshops to produce high-quality elite goods.

The Late Postclassic period was dominated by Aztec culture, and the Basin of Mexico once again became the principal region in western Mesoamerica. "Aztec" encompasses a set of ethnic groups that harkened back to a semimythical homeland called "Aztlán," which means "place of whiteness" or "place of the [white] heron." This was an island in a lake, and the new Aztec capital, Tenochtitlan-Tlatelolco, was a second Aztlán, an island homeland for the Mexica Aztecs. The Mexica name would become immortalized after European contact, when their city became Mexico City, and their old empire became known as Mexico. Their empire extended throughout much of the Central Highlands, the Southwestern Highlands, and into the Gulf Lowlands, and was built through aggressive violence. The Aztecs advertised their fierceness in monumental sculpture, awing the viewer with brutal themes.

The Bliss Collection of Pre-Columbian Art from the land of the ancient Mexica—the old Aztec Empire—comprises a varied sampling of the best that the ancient cultures of western Mesoamerica had to offer. These objects present us with a treasury of artistic masterpieces, and help us to understand and appreciate the ancient peoples whose genius and skill produced such works.

PRECLASSIC PERIOD CENTRAL HIGHLANDS OF MEXICO

SUSAN TOBY EVANS

In the Basin of Mexico nearly 5,000 years ago, someone fashioned a small piece of clay into a simple figure of a pregnant woman. This figurine, from the Late Archaic site of Tlapacoya/Zohapilco (Niederberger Betton 2000: 176), is perhaps the oldest surviving example from Mesoamerica, and it illustrates a tradition that would soon be found all over Mesoamerica and would persist for millennia. The figurine's theme of fertility dominated Mesoamerica's iconography as Early Preclassic cultures were transformed: hunter-foragers began to experiment with maize farming and with extended periods of occupation at some sites, in places fertile enough to support farming villages.

By 3,000 years ago, there were many villages but no major ceremonial center in the Basin of Mexico, indicating a lack of complex hierarchies of authority, either involving individuals living in a community or communities interacting in this region. Settlements of roughly equal size were clustered in the southern and western basin, where modest irrigation systems near streams and rivers made farming more secure (Nichols and Frederick 1993: 126).

Another Early Preclassic site, Cuicuilco, was in the southern Basin of Mexico. Long after Tlatilco was abandoned, Cuicuilco gained size and power, and by the Late Preclassic period it had a conical pyramid 20 m high, the first monumental architecture in the basin. Its sphere of influence is poorly understood but may have extended over a broad area, perhaps encompassing Chupícuaro, 200 km to the northwest (Florance 1985: 45).

With the growth of Cuicuilco in the southern basin, the region would have had an urbanized settlement, a natural product of increasing population in the basin and surrounding areas. We look to earlier sites to understand the background for the later development of complex societies, and Tlatilco is one of the best known of these Early Preclassic sites. Contemporaneous with Cuicuilco, Chupícuaro's remains represent the cultures of the Late Preclassic period in the Central Highlands. Both Tlatilco and Chupícuaro were excavated as salvage operations, with little or no architecture associated with the remains, which came largely from burial contexts.

Almost nothing remains of Tlatilco but a cemetery, with virtually no surviving architecture. The mortuary remains are exceptional, however, and include many skeletons. They revealed that life was difficult, with high infant mortality and a fairly low life expectancy 35 years for those surviving to adulthood. Adult bones show the effects of hard work and also of iron-deficiency anemia and arthritis. Nearly 70 percent of the population had been subject to cranial remodeling, and a few individuals had deliberately altered the shape of their teeth, for cosmetic reasons. Others experienced more fatal interference; human sacrifice is evidenced by decapitation and dismemberment, and there are possible instances of cannibalism (García Moll and Salas Cuesta 1998: 25).

Grave goods, including tools and adornments, comprise a wide selection of Tlatilco's material culture repertoire. Ceramic items include elegant animal-effigy vessels, pottery vessels, roller stamps, and figurines (Covarrubias 1943; García Moll 1999; García Moll et al. 1991; Moedano Koer 1957; Piña Chán 1958; Porter 1953; Romano 1967). These grave goods show that, although communities in the Basin of Mexico seem not to have been ranked in a political hierarchy, individuals differed in terms of status, as indicated by variations in the quality and quantity of burial materials. Some of these materials indicate a strong affinity with Olmec styles from the Gulf Lowlands. Olmec culture was complex and hierarchical, and from its centers, such as San Lorenzo and La Venta, sprang long-distance trade in commodities and ideas. Possibly, some people raised in Olmec ethnic traditions migrated to the Central Highlands (Tolstoy 1989b: 296).

The 3,000-year-old cemetery site of Tlatilco is perhaps most famous for its figurines, most of them whole and relatively undamaged, and most depicting nude young women. In general, Mesoamerican figurines were sacred objects, not toys, and they were used in personal and household rituals as opposed to state ceremonies. Exactly how they functioned, however, is not clear, in spite of their ubiquity throughout the culture area. They may have been thought to promote fertility or possibly were regarded as companions for the dead.

At Tlatilco, small solid figurines of nude young women were found in graves of individuals of both sexes and all ages, with some intriguing patterns of association.[3] They were found with about 20 percent of the skeletons, and although half of these burials contained only one figurine, others had many more: one individual was buried with 22 figurines. Children were slightly more likely to be accompanied by this type of figurine than were adult women, who were slightly more likely to have them than were adult men. There was no clear-cut association of certain artifacts with males or females "perhaps because mourners of the opposite sex contributed grave goods to the deceased or because sex roles at Tlatilco were flexible" (Tolstoy 1989a: 112). This lack of associative patterns for the figurines makes it difficult to determine their function and role in the larger culture.

Tlatilco was uncovered in the 1930s by clay-mining operations, and its artifacts, sold in markets in nearby Mexico City, were noticed by Miguel Covarrubias, whose interest in contemporary and ancient native cultures had led to a pioneering recognition of the importance of Olmec culture. He saw that some Tlatilco pieces echoed Olmec stylistic and iconographic themes and were similar to artifacts found at other nearby sites, such as Gualupita (Vaillant and Vaillant 1934). Covarrubias promoted the systematic investigation of Tlatilco, and projects there continued over many decades.

Chupícuaro, like Tlatilco, is known to us through a set of cemeteries, excavated in the 1940s before being flooded when a dam was built along the Lerma River. Chupícuaro's ceramic figurines and vessels, with distinctive red-on-buff and black-on-red geometric designs dating from 650 to 100 BC (Braniff 1998: 102) and widely distributed, were found in the Tula region, the Basin of Mexico, Morelos, Michoacán, West Mexico, and in the far north, at La Quemada (McBride 1969). The large area over which these remains have been found attests to active long-distance trade in the Central Highlands at this time, perhaps directed from Cuicuilco, the largest settlement in this region during the Late Preclassic period.

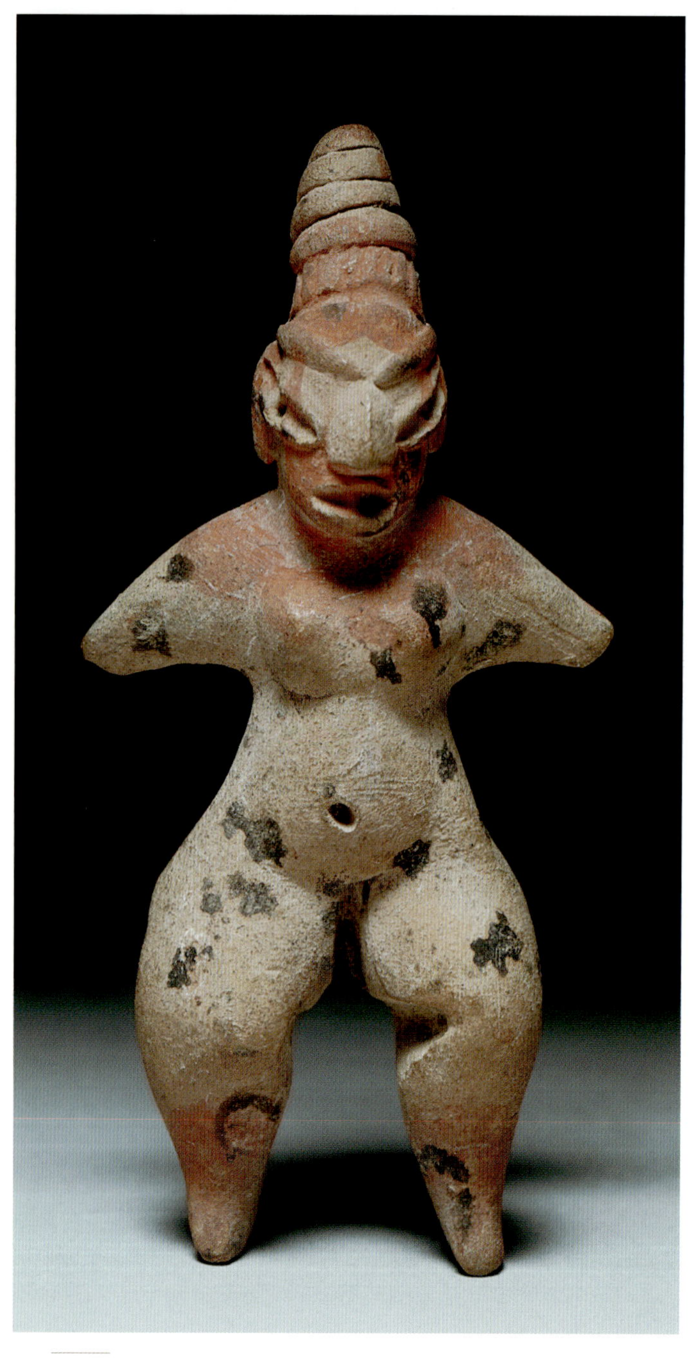

plate 1

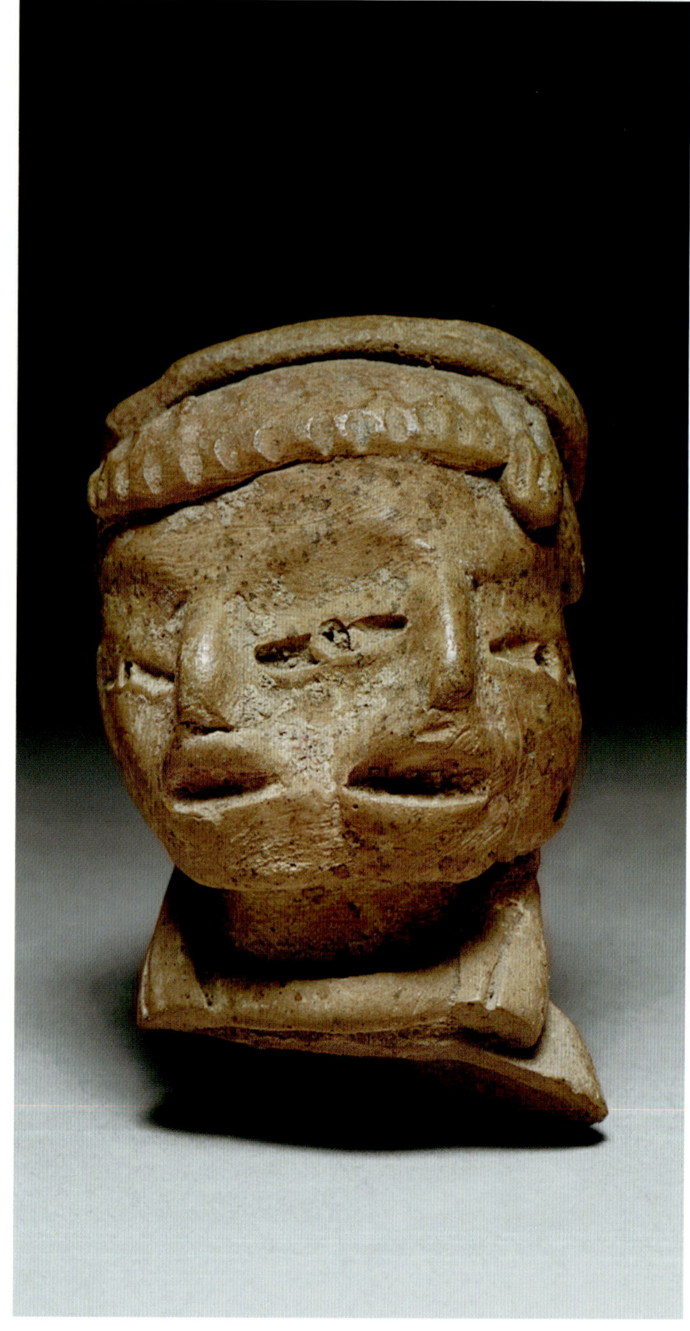

plate 2

PLATE 1
Tlatilco
Middle Preclassic period, 1500–500 BC
Ceramic
H. 9.5 cm (3¾"); W. 4.6 cm (1¾"); D. 2.0 cm (¾")
PC.B.141

PLATE 2
Tlatilco
Middle Preclassic period, 1500–500 BC
Ceramic
H. 4.2 cm (1⅝"); W. 2.5 cm (1"); D. 2.5 cm (1")
PC.B.142

ACQUISITION HISTORY:
Gifts of Samuel K. Lothrop, 1953

BIBLIOGRAPHY:
PC.B.141: Bliss 1957: 233, cat. no. 1, pl. I, top left; Dumbarton Oaks 1963: 9, cat. no. 43
PC.B.142: Bliss 1957: 233, cat. no. 2, pl. I, top center; Dumbarton Oaks 1963: 9, cat. no. 44

Tlatilco figurines in the Bliss Collection are represented by PC.B.141 (Plate 1), an entire solid figurine of a nude young woman, and PC.B.142 (Plate 2), a two-faced head from a solid figurine. Both are hand-modeled, with details added by filleting, punching, gouging, and incising the clay (Covarrubias 1957: 24).

PC.B.141 is a standing figure with short, outstretched arms, small breasts, and substantial legs. Typical of Tlatilco figurines, its facial features have been modeled and appliquéd, as has the headdress, either representing long hair fashioned into a coil atop the head or an adornment, such as a hank of fiber. Incisions detail her navel and the cleft of her crotch. Painted marks are common on figurines of this type; this one has red paint on the face, headdress, and shoulders, and black paint on the lower legs.

PC.B.142's headdress or hairstyle features a fillet around the upper part of the head, with streamers of hair or adornment coming forward around the neck. The double face itself seems to have been appliquéd onto the head, and the incised features of the faces have similar expressions. Traces of red paint are found in the groove of the right hair strand and on the right side of the nose.

These two figurines are of the same type (type D) according to the figurine typology for Early Preclassic materials in the Basin of Mexico that began to be established in 1902, when Zelia Nuttall discerned a much earlier cultural presence than that of the Aztecs (Vaillant 1935: 289). Over the years, such figurines were classified according to an alphanumeric typology.[4] Among these types, D has become iconic for this period and region, and its female figurines became well known in the early twentieth century as "pretty ladies":[5] "with small breasts, short arms, slim waists, and large bulbous legs" (Covarrubias 1957: 24). They vary in posture; some seem to be dancing; others carry a baby or a dog. Typically, they have elaborate hairdos, but clothing, where present, is limited to short skirts. Designs painted on their bodies suggest that the roller stamps also found at these sites may have been used to apply temporary tattoos.

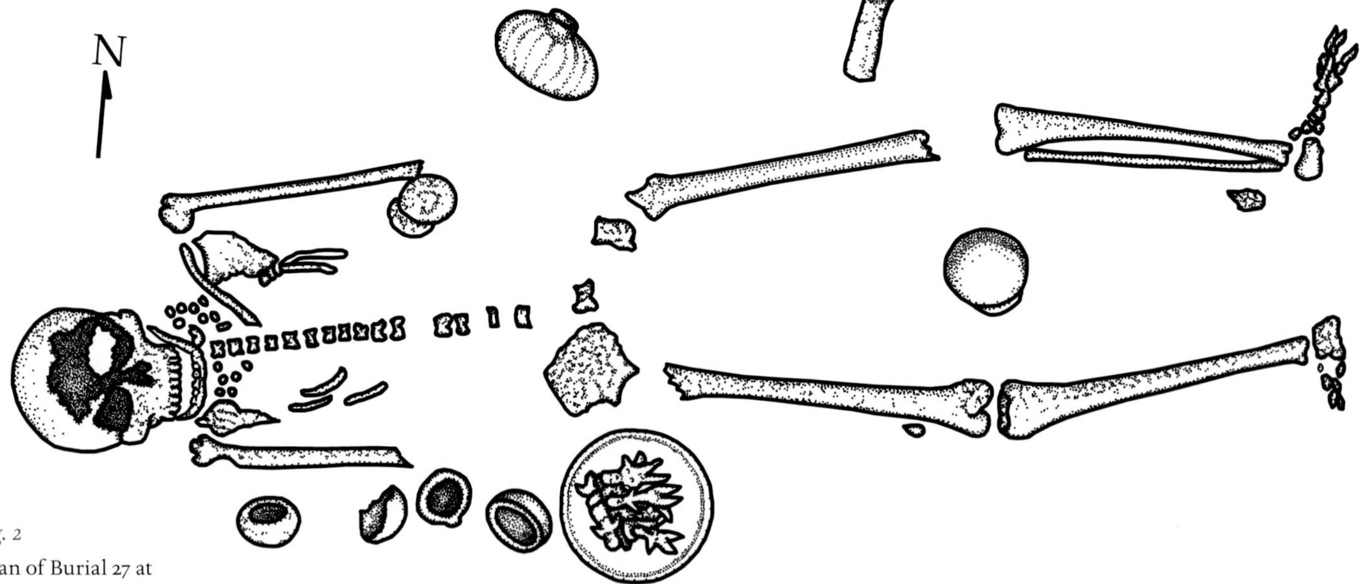

fig. 2
Plan of Burial 27 at the site of Tlatilco. Next to the extended skeleton's right hip is a bowl of figurines. Drawing by Susan Toby Evans (after García Moll et al. 1991: 93 [no scale], see also 33–34, 182–185).

At the site of Tlatilco, the 21 individuals whose graves contained Type D1 and/or D2 figurines ranged in age from neonate to mature adult. Burials of children and women had a slightly higher proportion of figurines. Figure 2 indicates how the figurines would have been placed relative to the interred individual.

The double-faced figurine head, PC.B.142, is of a type that is well known but uncommon in the corpus. The examples of bicephalic and dual-face figurines at Tlatilco are too few to indicate a pattern of association with particular types of individuals. Certainly no human skulls with three eye openings, two nasal openings, and two mouths have been found. These figurines have long intrigued scholars. Covarrubias suggested that the double face, or double head, might suggest duality, a basic organizing principle of the Mesoamerican spiritual world, and he noted that Pablo Picasso used a similar fractured view to depict faces (Covarrubias 1950: 157), a point also made by Samuel Lothrop, who linked such depictions to animation: "As in a Picasso drawing, two mouths, two noses and three eyes suggest motion. The Hindu deity Siva also is shown with three eyes, representing insight into the past, present and future" (Lothrop in Bliss 1957: 233, cat. no. 2). Mesoamericans revered the expression of life and movement; the principle of animism informed their spiritual values, so it is probable that such depictions suggest "a supernatural significance" (Pasztory 1998a: 27).[6]

STE

CHUPÍCUARO FIGURINE

PLATE 3
Chupícuaro
Late Preclassic period, 500 BC–AD 200
Polychrome ceramic
H. 6.2 cm (2⅜"); W. 3.8 cm (1½"); D. 1.8 cm (⅝")
PC.B.140

ACQUISITION HISTORY:
Gift of Alan Sawyer, 1961

BIBLIOGRAPHY:
Dumbarton Oaks 1963: 9, cat. no. 45; Evans 2004: 212, fig. 8.5; Evans 2008: 212, fig. 8.5

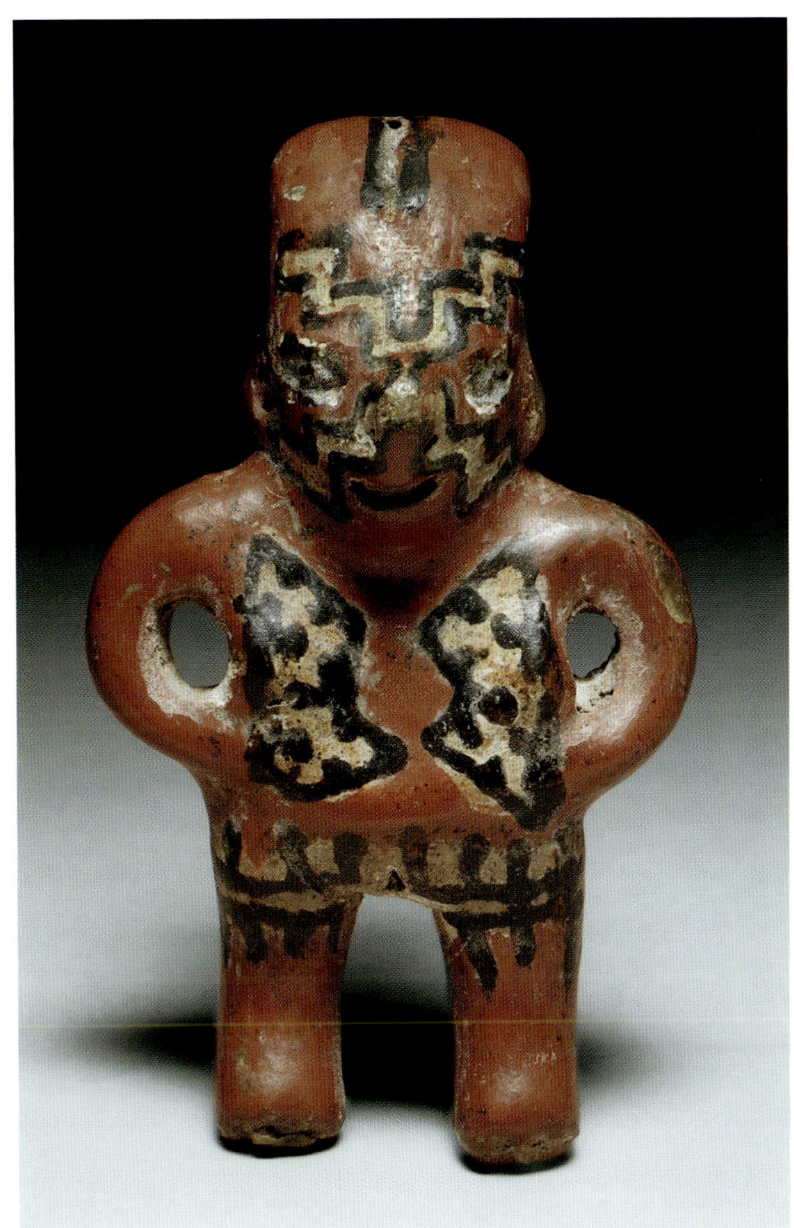

plate 3

The Chupícuaro-style figurine PC.B.140 is a highly burnished small solid female with breasts and a definite cleft in the crotch.[7] Its black and cream geometric designs on a deep red background are common to Chupícuaro pottery and are stylistically similar to those of West Mexico. For this reason, Chupícuaro is usually considered as part of the West Mexican sphere of cultural influence, in spite of its proximity to Guanajuato, near the Basin of Mexico.

Remains at the site of Chupícuaro included about 400 skeletons, some apparently the victims of sacrifices. They also included the skeletons of dogs, thought by Mesoamericans to guide the spirits of the dead in the underworld. Many of the graves included cut-stone hearths, possibly used in conducting funerary rituals. Figurines were important grave goods, as were ceramic vessels and musical instruments of various types: ceramic flutes and whistles, and rasps made from human femurs. Although little is known about the culture in general, these remains indicate the rich cultural life of the people of Chupícuaro.

STE

TEOTIHUACAN: ART FROM THE CITY WHERE TIME BEGAN

SUSAN TOBY EVANS

The Basin of Mexico's history was marked by the rise of civilizations associated with two great cities: Teotihuacan—which became an important center in the Late Preclassic period and became the largest urban settlement in Mesoamerica in the Early Classic period (AD 300–600)—and Tenochtitlan/Mexico City—formally established by the Aztecs in AD 1325, conquered by the Spaniards in 1521, and adopted as the latter's colonial capital—which later became the capital of the independent nation of Mexico.

Teotihuacan's rise to prominence was well under way by 100 BC, as its culture was becoming dominant in the Basin of Mexico. Teotihuacan was America's first great city. It grew to enormous size—more than 100,000 people during the Early Classic period—in the Basin of Mexico's relatively arid northeast arm. Who designed this huge, impressive city? Who built it? What was Teotihuacan society like, and what role was played by its distinctive artistic works? Besides its monumental pyramids and palaces, the site's aesthetic energies were expressed through murals and portable art, such as decorated ceramic vessels and carved stone masks.

Legends recorded in the sixteenth century describe Teotihuacan as the place where gods sacrificed themselves to set the sun and the moon in motion, and the city was thus the place where time began. Even with this important cosmological basis, the city required a strong agricultural base to grow large and powerful. Teotihuacan was situated at the base of Cerro Gordo, an eroded volcanic cone. Teotihuacan seems to have exploded into substantial existence about 2,000 years ago, though its earliest settlement probably dates to the Middle Preclassic period, when population pressure in the southern and western Basin of Mexico prompted colonization of regions like the Teotihuacan Valley, marginal for maize cultivation because of low annual rainfall. Abundant water, however, bubbled from springs that emerged from beneath Cerro Gordo's lower piedmont.

So copious were these springs that they created something of a bog as the water flowed southwest into Lake Texcoco, and when this swampy zone was channeled in a drained-field pattern, it became exceptionally productive. As often happens in human history, the need to wrest crops from a marginal environment prompted intensification, resulting in higher yields that permitted higher and denser populations and coinciding with the emergence of more complex social organization. And because the city's life depended on water from springs and from storms, water became the object of highest veneration.

At Teotihuacan, the trend toward greater societal complexity was heightened by an influx of population from around Cuicuilco in the southern basin, and possibly even from Puebla, because several volcanoes in these regions became active in the several hundred years before and after the turn of the millennium. Although these events suggest reasons for Teotihuacan's development, we know little of the city's history in detail. Unlike Maya rulers, the leaders of Teotihuacan did not record the important events of their reigns on carved portrait stelae that detailed their names and achievements. We can, however, reconstruct three general historical periods on the basis of archaeological evidence at Teotihuacan and related communities, and from materials analysis and interpretation of art works and glyph systems.

The first period began several centuries before the Common Era and ended after the massive influx of population. The town's established residents would have become de facto patrons of the new immigrants, providing work and leadership. Old Teotihuacanos may have established proprietary claims on the most valuable land, irrigated by the springs. During this initial urban stage, Teotihuacanos laid the groundwork for a city that glorified its setting and claimed for itself the role of the place where time began. The Street of the Dead was the site's north-south axis, and construction began on the Pyramid of the Moon at the northern end of this ceremonial avenue (Millon 1992: 384).

By the beginning of the second period, ca. AD 1, construction had begun on the Pyramid of the Sun, built over a cave whose west-facing aperture viewed an important calendric horizon marker associated with the origin of time (Millon 1993: 35, n. 7). Between AD 150 and 200, the Teotihuacanos built the third and last large pyramid, embellished with repeated motifs of the Feathered Serpent and serving as a funerary monument to the important person entombed beneath it. They dedicated the pyramid with the sacrifice of about 260 individuals (Cabrera 1993a: 106).

The material and human cost of this funerary monument may have spurred a subsequent change in government or governmental policy. Until that time, much of the population had been living in a disorderly array of residences—a shanty town—surrounding the civic-ceremonial zone, the Street of the Dead and its pyramids. Replacing these with well-built residential compounds was the focus of the third phase in Teotihuacan's urbanization process, which continued for the next several hundred years.

This building boom included the new city palace known as the Street of the Dead Complex, a massive example of the apartment compounds that were being built across the city. Some of these were clearly the domain of affluent extended families: the Street of the Dead Complex, Tetitla, Yayahuala, and Zacuala. Others, such as Oztoyahualco and Tlajinga, were far more modest. All were arranged following a gridded plan.[8] This differs radically from the layouts of many ancient communities, with their accretions of jumbled buildings and narrow winding passageways that indicate evolved communities rather than designed ones. Teotihuacan's grid marked out spatial and temporal chords that linked pivotal features in the landscape and also indicated important calendric points in the solar year and in the count of the ages.

The city's construction as a gridded expanse of residential architecture coincided with the layout and construction of walkways and drainage canals that channeled water and sewage around the compounds (Angulo 1987b). These residential and hydrological programs suggest the strong hand of centralized government (Nichols et al. 1991: 128). They also coincided with a new reverence for water from the earth, from springs. Imagery venerating the Feathered Serpent, associated with water from the sky (Miller and Taube 1993: 141), remained part of the city's iconography, but there was a new emphasis on the jaguar, honored for its association with water from springs.

Much of the Feathered Serpent imagery on this third temple-pyramid was covered by a façade that was, essentially, a building mask. The mask was one of Teotihuacan's strongest ideological and iconographic themes; it appeared as sculpted pieces and as ceramic and painted—and architectural—representations of masks. Sometimes the masks themselves had masks, for example, face masks wearing butterfly-shaped mouth masks.[9] Some archaeological cultures are difficult to understand because they are relatively unexplored (for example, the Harrapan civilization of the Indian subcontinent), but Teotihuacan seems to project enigma as a personality trait—one mask may be insufficient to block our view, so two must be deployed. As Pasztory (1993e: 54) notes, more masks survive from Teotihuacan than from any other Mesoamerican culture. This phenomenon is in part due to particular cultural values, of which we have a very incomplete understanding. One might say that our difficulty in interpreting Teotihuacan stems from the ways that society masked itself.

Teotihuacan's de-emphasis on individual personality and apotheosis of the expressionless mask and stylized uniform costumes may have been a deliberate program highlighting community above the person or family (Pasztory 1992: 288). Much of the artistic evidence for this utopian community-focused program dates from after the defacement of the Temple-Pyramid of the Feathered Serpent, probably as a ritual termination, and possibly resulting from an internal power struggle (Millon 1992: 346; Sugiyama 1998, 2005).

The coincidence of these political events with apparent changes in artistic style lends credence to the argument that there was a radical shift in Teotihuacan's ethos, but in truth we have very little in the way of comparative art or residential architecture that predates this shift (Millon 1992: 371). One of the most characteristic objects associated with Teotihuacan is a type of stone mask, more correctly termed a face plaque (PC.B.053–PC.B.056, Plates 12–15). But the only mask for which we have good context comes from the North Palace of the Ciudadela—that is, the building adjacent to the Temple-Pyramid of the Feathered Serpent—in a context that would have been in active use at the time before the Temple-Pyramid was defaced. On a stucco floor were found the mask (Jarquín and Martínez 1982: 110, Elemento no. 193) and carved stone features from the pyramid's north façade, which had apparently been wrenched from the façade and thrown down on the still-extant palace roof. A layer of ash and carbon covered the floor (Jarquín and Martínez 1982: 101).

Teotihuacan's period of greatest extent as a city and greatest influence abroad took place during the Early Classic period—ca. AD 300–500. In the late fourth century, emissaries from the city appeared at the Maya site of Tikal and for a brief time seemed to control that important center's politics. Teotihuacan's authority was felt at other Maya centers, such as Copán, but this influence did not constitute a "Teotihuacan empire"—rather, the Maya used Teotihuacan's icons for their prestige value. More direct Teotihuacan influence was found at Kaminaljuyu in the Guatemala Highlands and at Matacapan in the south-central Gulf Lowlands.

Teotihuacan interest in the Gulf Lowlands may have been spurred by a need for a source of cotton cloth (Hall 1997: 133), which, by the Classic period, had come into widespread use.[10] Preclassic figurines found at Tlatilco were costumed in tattoos and head wraps; in contrast, Teotihuacanos, as shown in murals and some figurines, seem all but immobilized by layers of skirts and tunics. The difference in clothing is not explained by climate—Tlatilco and Teotihuacan are only about 25 miles (about 40 km) apart. This change was prompted by a revolution in fiber processing and textile production, and we see the effects reflected in the Classic art of the Maya as well, in which men and women wear clothes that appear to have been woven (Mahler 1965).[11]

There is no direct evidence for weaving at Teotihuacan, and ceramic spindle whorls do not appear there until the end of the Classic period. In the south-central Gulf Lowlands, however, thread was being produced using ceramic spindle whorls as early as the end of the Terminal Preclassic period, when "there was a substantial increase in cotton production in the region" (Stark 2001: 225).[12] It seems possible that spinning technology in any form was absent from Teotihuacan until the end of the Classic period, and the reason may pertain to cultural patterns associated with women's roles as spinners and weavers. Spinning is a skill best learned in childhood, when the motion becomes reflexive. Thus the practice of spinning would best be imported into Teotihuacan through the immigration of adult women spinners from, say, the south-central Gulf Lowlands, who would teach their daughters the skills they learned as children. We know of many patterns of influence between Teotihuacan and other regions, but this one has not been documented.

Another, ideological piece of negative evidence bears on the issue of whether Teotihuacan women spun (and wove). Teotihuacan art depicts women of very high rank, perhaps even a Teotihuacan Goddess, who may be specific to—and coterminous with—the site of Teotihuacan and may be closely related to features of the city's natural environment (Berlo 1992). She does not seem ancestral to the family of female deities of the Postclassic Central Highlands, who shared with mortal women a fundamental identity as textile artisans. The Teotihuacan Goddess's character touched on textile arts only with rare visual references to spiders (Taube 1983), in contrast to the spinning and weaving gear that later Central Mexican goddesses incorporated into their costumes.

At ca. AD 500 another great change in Teotihuacan history transformed the city again, from the New World's largest urban center, with international influence, into a more insular community. Arson along the Street of the Dead was committed by foreigners or Teotihuacanos (Wolfman 1990: 301). By the end of the Classic period (ca. AD 900), the city's population had dropped to 20,000–30,000.[13]

Important vestiges of the city's art remain as testament to Teotihuacan's greatness. The Bliss Collection includes objects representative of two of these traditions: lapidary work and painting. The former includes jadeite disks (PC.B.133, Plate 4) and masks (PC.B.053–PC.B.056 and PC.B.058, Plate 21), and the latter includes a mural (PC.B.062, Plate 5) and ceramic vessels (PC.B.063–PC.B.068, Plates 6–11). Teotihuacan lapidaries, like those elsewhere in Mesoamerica, used techniques including fracturing, grinding, sawing, grooving, incising, drilling, and polishing (Turner 1992: 95–102). Teotihuacan technological style was controlled, its forms standardized and expressing little individual variation in style (Turner 1992: 109).

Such standardization was evident in painting as well. Writing in 1967, George Kubler said that "the entire repertory of pictorial expression at Teotihuacan supports the view that painters and sculptors were seeking forms of logographic clarity and simplicity . . . combining and compounding associative meanings in a quest for viable forms of writing" (1967: 5). Kubler's prescience was confirmed by recent research interpreting designs on murals and vessels and uncovering evidence of glyph forms (Taube 2000b).

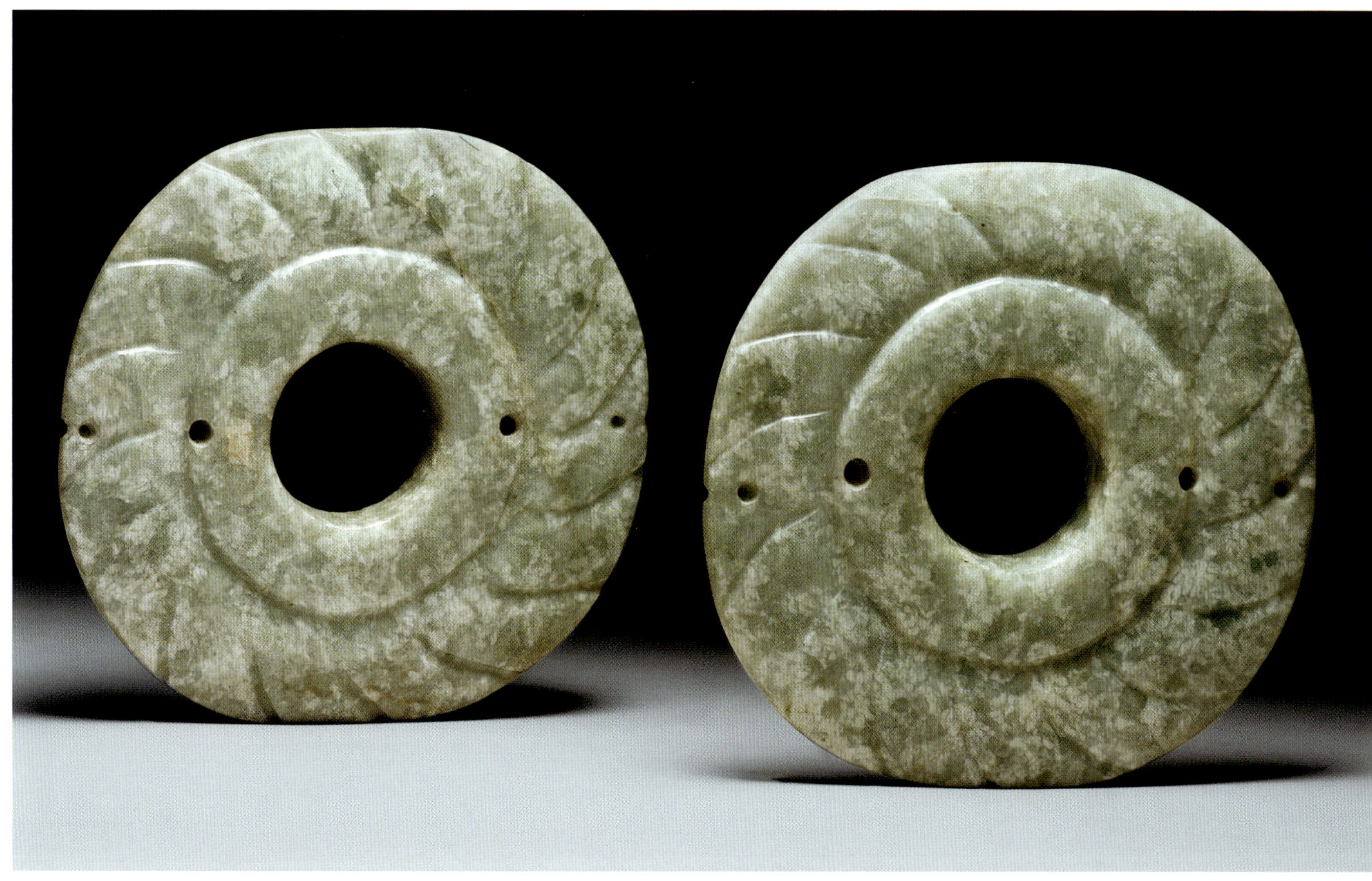

plate 4

PAIR OF JADEITE DISKS

PLATE 4
Teotihuacan
Middle to Late Classic period, AD 400–900
Jadeite
PC.B.133a: D. 1.1 cm (½"); Diam. 12.0 cm (4¾")
PC.B.133b: D. 0.9 cm (⅜"); Diam. 11.8 cm (4⅝")
PC.B.133a and PC.B.133b

ACQUISITION HISTORY:
Acquired before 1957

EXHIBITION HISTORY:
Indigenous Art of the Americas, National Gallery of Art, Washington, D.C., May 1948–July 1962 (NGA 385)

BIBLIOGRAPHY:
Bliss 1957: 247, cat. no. 91, pl. LVII; Dumbarton Oaks 1963: 31, cat. no. 156

These disks aptly introduce the Bliss Collection's objects in the style of Classic period Teotihuacan: they embody preciousness in substance, form, and meaning. Made of costly jadeite, their form is an ancient Mesoamerican glyph symbol for jade that echoes the concentric circles made by droplets of precious blood or water, a shape that came to symbolize preciousness in abstract aspects, such as religious sanctity and political power. The Bliss Collection specimens are not merely iconographic representations of such disks; they *are* jadeite disks, chalchihuitls (the term in Nahuatl, the Aztec language, for "precious green stones"). The disk motif is common; flat jadeite disks, themselves, however, are very rare.

The disk motif recurs in other Teotihuacan objects in the Bliss Collection. It appears in the mural (PC.B.062, Plate 5) and on the ceramic vessels (PC.B.063–PC.B.068, Plates 6–11). In fact, the disk motif permeates Mesoamerican iconography from the Preclassic period into the colonial period, occurring in personal adornment, architecture, and texts, and consistently conveying the sense of transcendent value.

The raw material, jadeite, almost certainly came from the Motagua Valley of Guatemala, the only verified source of jadeite in Mesoamerica. The color is light grayish green. Measuring nearly five inches across and roughly half an inch thick, each disk weighs about half a pound. The slightly conical central perforations were probably established by drilling, then enlarged by cord-sawing with an abrasive, such as quartzite or jadeite sand. Four smaller holes on either side of the central perforation are biconical, drilled from each side using a solid pointed object and abrasive. Continuing the line of holes are semicircular scars of additional holes, drilled from the back side on the outer edges of each disk.

Both surfaces of the disks were polished, the plain backs less so than the decorated front sides. The decoration consists of two concentric fields: a simple inner circle and an outer circle with sixteen curved arcs, suggesting feathers. These designs may have been executed by the "grooving" technique, which results in polished round troughs (Proskouriakoff 1974: 9). The technique was used extensively by the Early Classic Maya, and was later superseded by methods that produced sharper, more standardized curves.

More than a dozen similar examples of flat perforated disks are known from systematic investigations at three sites in and beyond Mesoamerica. At Salitrón Viejo, the dominant site in the Cajón region of eastern Honduras, six disks and half-disks were recovered from dedication caches dated to AD 400–600 in monumental architecture (Hirth 2001; Hirth and Hirth 1992, 1993). From Cerro de las Mesas in the south-central Gulf Lowlands, six whole disks came from an offering cache that probably dates to no earlier than the Middle Classic period (several others from Cerro de las Mesas appear to have been reworked earspool flares [Drucker 1955: 54]). Finally, the remains of seven "large flat rings" were among the jades dredged from the Cenote of Sacrifice at Chichén Itzá in the early years of the twentieth century. Stratigraphic context in the cenote was largely unreconstructable, but Proskouriakoff (1974) hypothesized that, based on style, four of the disks dated from the Late Classic and the other three were Early Postclassic "Toltec" style. The Classic period examples from Cerro de las Mesas, Salitrón Viejo, and Chichén Itzá are most similar to the Bliss Collection pair.

What role did these polished stone disks play in their society, and what was their ideological significance? The three sets of provenienced Classic disks have in common a final function as offerings, cached precious materials in either a sacred monumental structure or a sacred body of water. The architectural dedication episodes probably took place in the Middle Classic at sites influenced by Central Mexico. Caching these precious objects would remove them from circulation, ending their use life in active social contexts. Unfortunately, Chichén's cenote offers little insight into the circumstances of dedication, but Cerro de las Mesas and Salitrón Viejo provide good—and similar—contexts, in monumental structures but not associated with mortuary materials.

The use life that ended as an offering would have begun as the unfinished jadeite reached a specialized lapidary workshop. Like other objects of high value, polished stone disks would have been produced by artisans specializing in luxury goods, and strong evidence indicates that such artisans customarily were nobles, and even royals. We have long known this to have been true for the Aztecs; it seems to have been the case among the Classic Maya as well: at Copán, a lapidary workshop that produced pendants for high-status individuals was located in a noble compound (Widmer 1997).

Objects like these disks may have been made for members of the noble household, as part of a tribute requirement, as a gift to a high-status individual, or as part of a special ceremony. Possibly, flat jade disks went directly from workshop to dedicated cache. However, the pattern of small drilled holes in the Bliss Collection examples and others suggests that they were displayed, and their

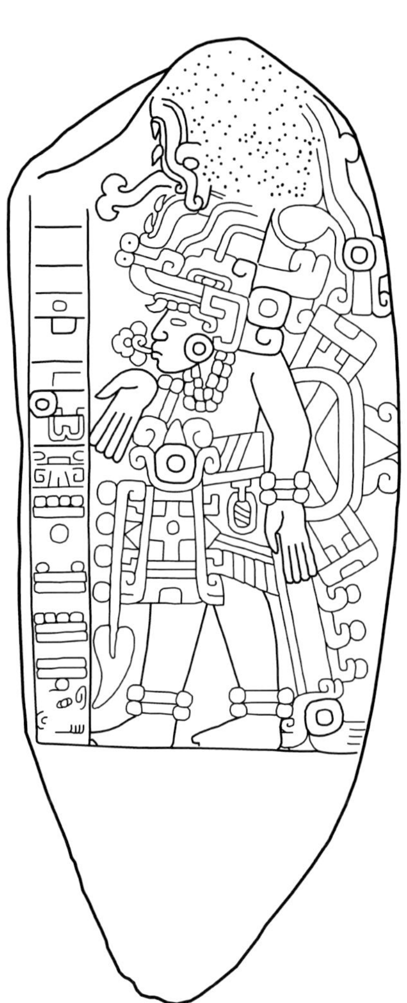

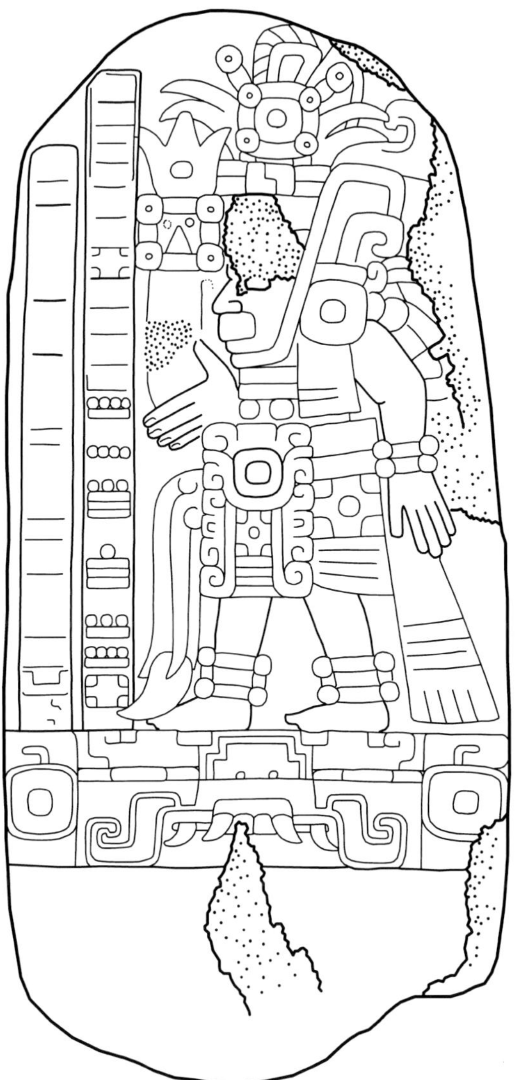

fig. 3
Stela 6 (left) and Stela 8 (right) from Cerro de las Mesas. Drawing by Susan Toby Evans (after Stirling 1943: fig. 11).

depiction as a common motif in Mesoamerican art indicates that they would have provided important public demonstration of high status.

The disks are too heavy to have been used as backing disks in an earspool assembly. They may have been pendants, or fastened to fabric (Proskouriakoff 1974: 88) or to a wooden superstructure that an individual may have worn. Cerro de las Mesas Stelae 6 and 8 (Figure 3) illustrate disks on figures and on the panels indicating dates AD 468 and 533, respectively (Miller 1991: 30). Each figure, probably a lord, wears a loincloth with a concentric circle at the waist, with a "*kan* cross" below (Miller 1991: 31). In Mayan, *k'an*, the glyph for "preciousness," placed the cross in the concentric circles of the disk.

The disk motif or glyph occurred widely, beginning in the Early to Middle Preclassic period (for example, Oxtotitlan Cave, Painting 1-d [Grove 1970: 17, fig. 13]), contemporaneous with the Olmec horizon, and even in these Middle Preclassic contexts it had already acquired a rich and varied significance. By then, jade was widely traded and largely reserved for the elites, mediators between the gods and the farmers. Rulers prayed for rain and oversaw irrigation projects to ensure the fertility of the land, and they made blood sacrifices that acknowledged humankind's debt to the gods. Thus the disk, the form of concentric rings of blood or water, bore meanings of ritual sanctity and royal authority. Mesoamericans knew that the same image would project different meanings, a consistent and complex cognitive package reinforced through metaphor and metonym.

The chalchihuitl concept included green stones (including jades), water, and blood. The blue-green chalchihuitl was linked to water, an essential component of settled life: "rain was the jewel, the precious commodity, and chalchihuitl itself represented, through its own color, the idea of vegetation; . . . dedicated to the rain gods, the best . . . sacrifice for those gods" (Seler 1991: III: 126–127 [1901]). As vegetation, chalchihuitls have been interpreted as symbolizing its most essential Mesoamerican form, maize, with designs incised on celts from Offering 2 at the Olmec site of La Venta. Teotihuacan was a core area for use and elaboration of the disk as a symbol of preciousness in the Classic period. In addition to their other meanings, concentric circles represented mirrors, which served as divining and impression-management devices in the practice of shamanism. Rimmed disks encircled by plumes are extremely common in the art of Teotihuacan (Taube 1992: 170), occurring in murals (see Plate 5 below), on sculpture and vessels, and included as adornos (decorations) on *incensarios* (incense burners). In the friezes on the original façade of the Temple-Pyramid of the Feathered Serpent, headdresses bear double concentric circles above the eye and are framed on each side by a cluster of feathers (Sugiyama 1992: 207, fig. 2), suggesting the feathered mirror frame.

Feather-framed mirrors are part of costumes in Teotihuacan's art, appearing on headdresses and also as back devices on the net jaguars of Tetitla, as depicted on the Bliss Collection's Net-Jaguar Mural (PC.B.062). In the Spider Woman murals in the Tetitla compound, a mirror with a feathered frame in the headdress appears (Taube 1983: fig. 4).[14] The feathered disk frame also adorns Teotihuacan's ballcourt markers, such as the La Ventilla ballcourt marker and those depicted in Tepantitla Mural 2 (Taube 1983: fig. 26).

Concentric circles are interpreted as a shorthand expression for the Storm God (Langley 1992: 248–252, figs. 4–8) and occur as roundels in the Tassel Headdress and other costume elements (C. Millon 1973). In the Early Classic period, the disk motif in use outside Teotihuacan came to imply that city's influence, for example, the "raindrop" symbol of the Guatemala Highlands, interpreted as a Teotihuacan iconographic element (Borhegyi 1965: 24). In Maya Copán, Central Mexican motifs including disks are common on Structure 26 (Fash and Fash 2000: 456, fig. 14.9.c). At Tikal, the feathered disk appears on El Marcador, a three-foot-high carved stone ballcourt marker found in a Mexican-style residential compound. On this monument, the feathered disk framed the insignia of Spearthrower Owl, the enigmatic force behind the Teotihuacan intrusion into Tikal's politics in AD 378, and the Maya text on the standard describes Spearthrower Owl's accession to "rulership" in 374 (Martin and Grube 2000: 31). Where he ruled is unknown, but it might have been in Teotihuacan itself.

STE

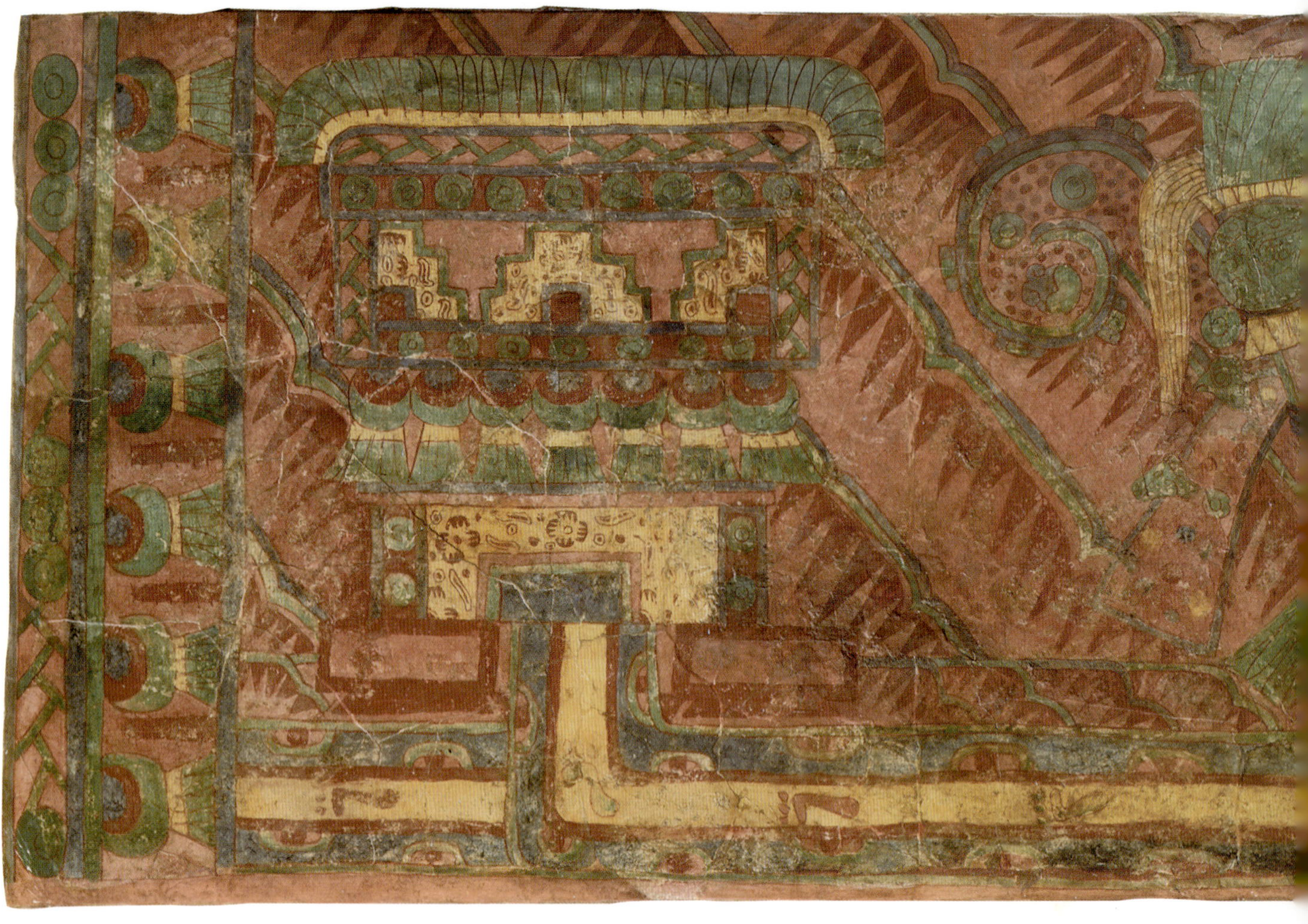

plate 5

NET-JAGUAR MURAL

PLATE 5

Teotihuacan; Tetitla apartment compound, Room 12
Middle Classic period, AD 400–600
Fresco
H. 72.7 cm (28⅝"); W. 2.12 m (83⅝")
PC.B.062

ACQUISITION HISTORY:

Purchased from Earl Stendahl, 1941

EXHIBITION HISTORY:

Indigenous Art of the Americas, National Gallery of Art, Washington, D.C., April 1947–July 1962 (NGA 341)

BIBLIOGRAPHY:

Rodríguez 1940: 28, 29; Bliss 1947: 25–26, 55, 124, 125, cat. no. 124; Marquina 1951: 105 (Fot. 32 bis); Villagra Caleti 1951: 157–158, fig. 6; Christensen 1955: 204; Bliss 1957: 238, cat. no. 33, pls. XXV–XXVI; Covarrubias 1957: 142; Dumbarton Oaks 1963: 2, cat. no. 7; Sejourné 1966a: 50–51, fig. 13, and motif embossed on cover; Willey 1966: I: 112, fig. 3-45; Kubler 1967: 5, 6, 9, 10, fig. 15; Von Winning 1968a: 33–35, Abb. 2; Kubler 1972: 25–26, fig. 7; Miller 1973: 151, fig. 317; Nicholson 1976: 163–164, fig. 2; Grey 1978: pl. 4; Miller 1986: 76, fig. 52; Von Winning 1987: 43, fig. 3a; Pasztory 1993e: 60–61, fig. 7; Fuente 1995: 299, 305, pl. 61, fig. 19.35; Lombardo de Ruíz 1995: 45, 46, fig. 136, 54, lám. 13; Anawalt 1996: 200, fig. 19; Pasztory 1997: 134, 182–185, fig. 11.1; Scott 1999: 71, fig. 3.18; Evans 2004: 260, fig. 9.24; Pasztory 2005: 139; Evans 2008: 260, fig. 9.24; Vila Llonch 2008f: 198–199; Evans 2009: 72–73

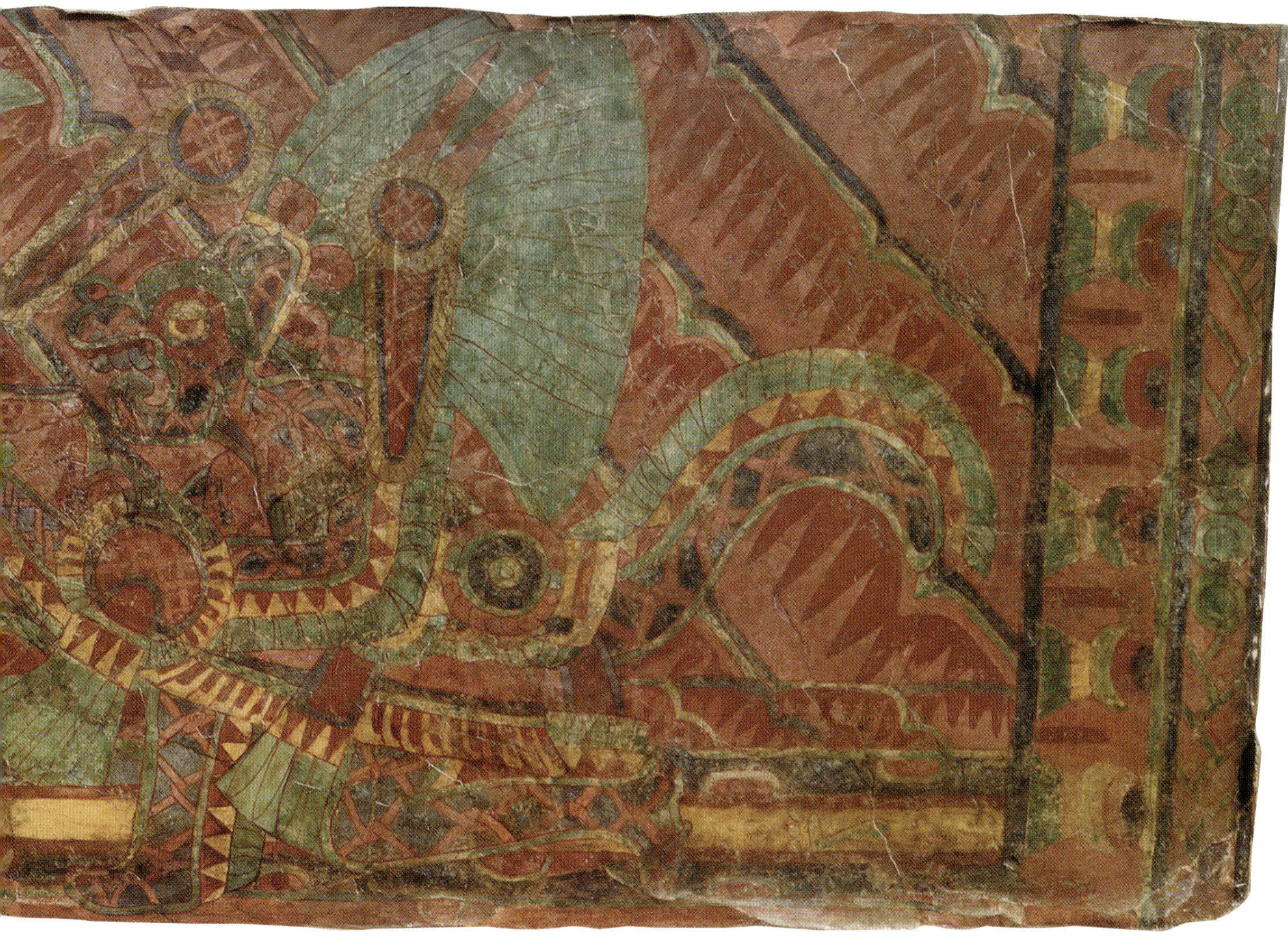

Mural 8 (PC.B.062) from Teotihuacan's Tetitla apartment compound is one of a unified set of eight images framing a doorway and extending along the walls of Room 12, part of the compound's largest and most impressive set of rooms, the Patio 13 complex. In a city famed for its dazzling murals, Mural 8 is one of the finest. It depicts a kneeling figure dressed in a net-jaguar costume, facing an elaborate temple from which water emerges in a set of canalized streams flanking a causeway (Figure 4). The background's diagonal motifs of broad panels in two shades of red are offset by ribbons of color. The mural's borders include mat motifs, tassels, and concentric disks indicating precious chalchihuitls.

Mural painting was Teotihuacan's major art form, art for the living found on temples, palaces, public buildings, habitations, and shrines (Millon 1972: 1). Mural painting reached its apogee in the Classic period, after the city's apartment compounds were built but before violence gutted the fine buildings along the Street of the Dead. Walls of patios and chambers of apartment compounds were covered with repeated motifs featuring stylized figures that served as armatures for constellations of impressive symbols.

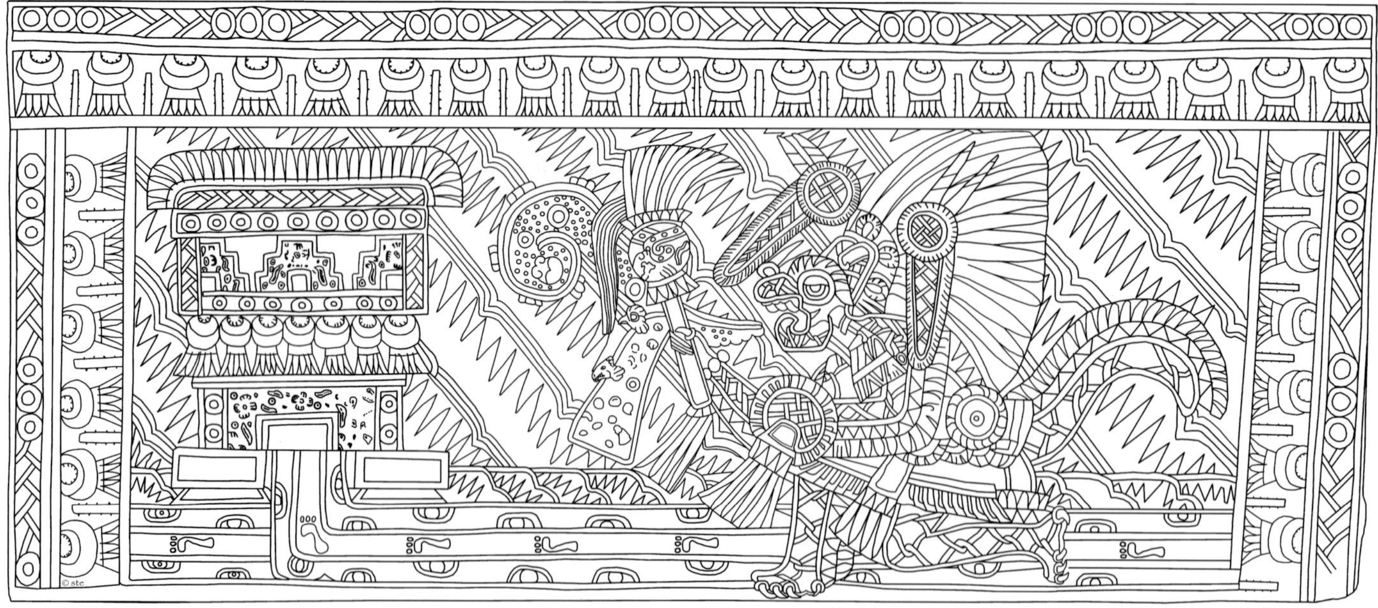

fig. 4
Reconstruction drawing of Mural 8 in the Tetitla apartment compound, Teotihuacan, with border details from other similar murals. Drawing by Susan Toby Evans.

The muralists produced their designs with rich saturated colors by applying pigments directly onto a thin layer of wet lime plaster (Bone 1988: 232), which covered a smooth substrate of volcanic ash sediment mixed with mud. This substrate covered the walls and moldings around room features, such as doorways. Pigments, painted in layers, followed designs scratched into the damp lime plaster. Lighter colors delineated details, and then larger areas took on medium hues. "Finally the image was sharpened by the used of dark red—occasionally this was almost a black—to outline the design" (Bone 1988: 233).

Red was derived from "specular hematite with ilmenite inclusions . . . [that] make the mural surface sparkle" (Bone 1988: 233). Light green was finely ground malachite, and yellow was achieved through the use of limonite. The blue pigment in Teotihuacan's murals has not been identified (Bone 1988: 233). In Tetitla compound's Mural 8 these colors have survived in relatively good condition. Their relative intensity is so similar that it makes the mural's pattern less clear to modern eyes accustomed to contrasts in the intensity of hue.

To understand the mural, we must understand its context in the Tetitla compound (Figure 5), located about 500 m (about 545 yards) due west of the Street of the Dead Complex, which was probably the royal palace (Sanders and Evans 2006). Tetitla measures about 66 m by 63 m (216 feet by 206 feet), with about 140 rooms, patios, porticos, corridors, and closets, grouped around half a dozen patios, all within an outer wall pierced by a few entryways. Clearly an affluent residence, Tetitla's internal variety suggests use by an extended family household, possibly formed when at least three separate structures were incorporated within one wall (Angulo 1987a: 302) during the period of residential construction, when the city's grid was laid out and roads and drainage canals were established along the lines of the grid (Nichols and Frederick 1993; Nichols et al. 1991). The Patio 13 complex, site of Mural 8, may have housed the household head and his or her immediate family.

Tetitla has undergone considerable archaeological investigation: the Patio 13 complex was explored by Pedro Armillas, Carlos Margain, and Agustín Villagra Caleti in the 1940s (Armillas 1950: 55–56; Villagra Caleti 1954). Mural 8 was first published in 1940 (Rodríguez 1940). Further excavations at Tetitla in 1951 by Frank Moore (1966) and by Laurette Séjourné (1966a, 1966b) in 1963 and 1964 uncovered the compound and revealed its interior composition and its wealth of murals. The Teotihuacan Mapping Project dug a stratigraphic pit in the Patio 13 complex (Millon 1992: 348). In Clara Millon's chronology of Teotihuacan mural painting, Mural 8 and its associates represent a mature expression of this art form, and she attributed Mural 8 to "Period 4" of six phases (Millon 1972: 10). The murals have been thoroughly described by Fuente (1995); the compound's burials are detailed by Sempowski (1994: 67–76).

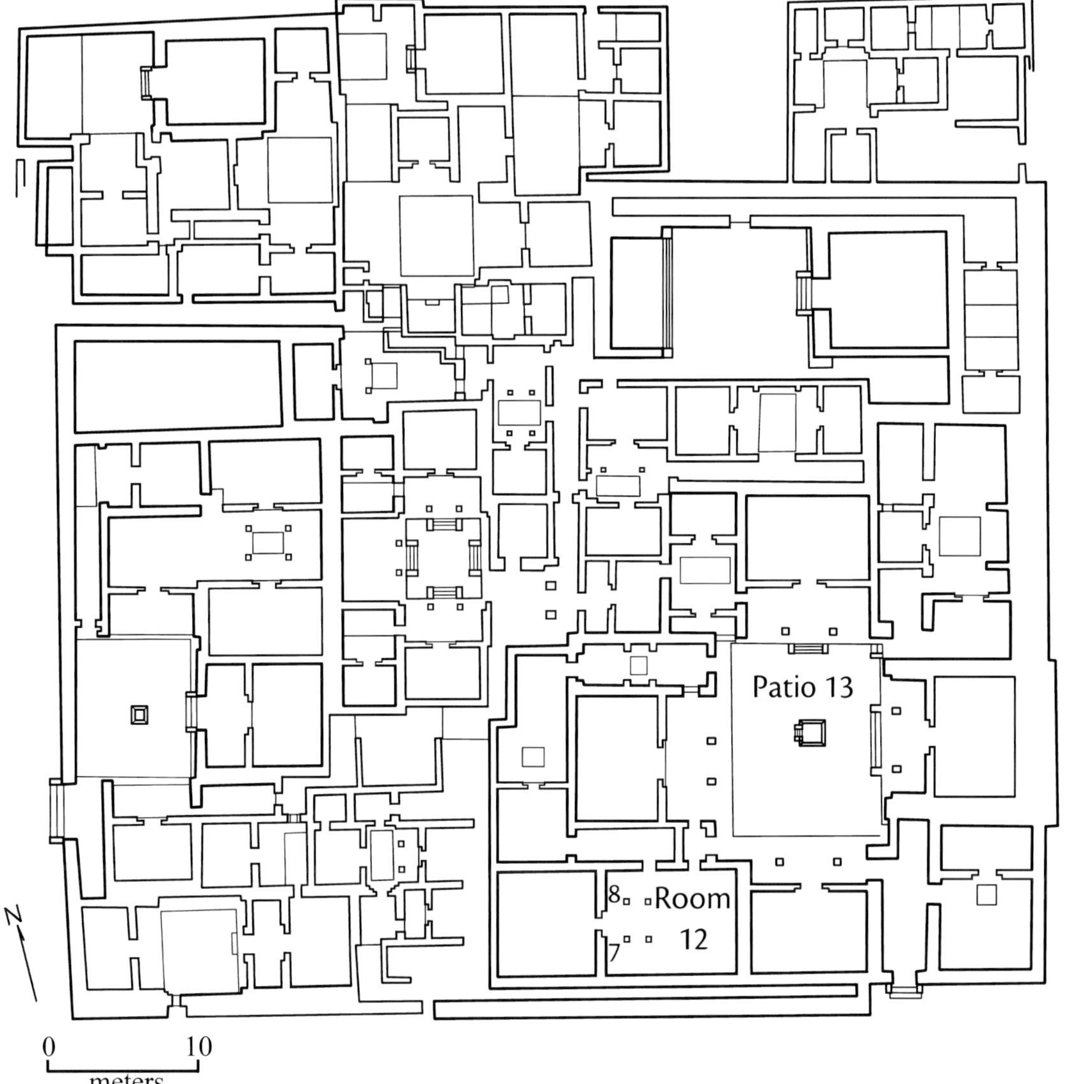

fig. 5
Plan of the Tetitla apartment compound, Teotihuacan, showing location of the Patio 13 complex in the lower right. Room 12 is at the bottom, second from the exterior entryway, and Mural 8 was on the north side of the west wall. Drawing by Susan Toby Evans (after Miller 1973: Plan XIII).

Tetitla is rich in murals, having more than any other compound at Teotihuacan (Miller 1973: 119). It was a cosmopolitan place; Villagra Caleti (1954: 70) saw a resemblance to Maya glyphs in several designs. Indeed Maya stylistic traits in depictions of individuals and elements of costume gave Tetitla almost the character of an "International House," according to Millon (1972: 11–12). Above the Net-Jaguar Murals, one of the Maya texts indicates a date in "the mid-fifth and sixth centuries A.D." (Taube 2003: 281, 286), suggesting continuing interaction with the Maya region long after Teotihuacan's influence at Tikal.[15]

The murals in the Patio 13 complex, including Room 12's Murals 7 and 8, are rich in symbolism, expressing broad themes that include the power of the Teotihuacan polity and its established religion as expressed in the costumes and headdresses of the abstract, human, and jaguar figures; the jaguar; bounty and preciousness; the chalchihuitl disk motif; architectonic designs; and sacrifice.

Enough survives of Room 12's west wall to reconstruct a partial decorative program consisting of Mural 7 and Mural 8 on either side of a doorway edged by a border of twined motifs.[16] These netlike motifs surrounded jade jewels of both simple and complex form (Taube 2003: 298).[17] Through this doorway the viewer would have seen, along the bottom of the west wall of Room 12, "Light-red circles [-20 in or 0.5 m in diameter] on a dark-red ground" (Miller 1973: 156, fig. 328), all that remains of Mural 5 on that wall.

Kubler (1972: 19) wrote that the jaguar figures in Room 12 and elsewhere at Teotihuacan "appear to be more clever" than jaguars anywhere else in the Mesoamerican world. Men dress up as jaguars, and jaguars wear netted garments.[18]

Physiologically, Mural 8's jaguar figure looks like a feline (the Dumbarton Oaks mural's clawless feet have been incorrectly restored), but some have interpreted it as a jaguar-garbed human on the basis of posture: kneeling, rather than in the quadrupedal feline poses of other Teotihuacan jaguars.[19] The head, however, has no human features, and at Teotihuacan these would be visible through apertures in masks. Whatever its internal identity, this figure projects the powerful iconography of the jaguar, the most revered of all animals in Mesoamerica (Pasztory 1976: 235, 237–238), venerated for its beauty and grace as well as its strength and stealth (Evans 2008: 163).

Jaguar figures are common in Teotihuacan murals, and net jaguars are found along the Street of the Dead, at Atetelco and Zacuala; at Tetitla they cluster in the Patio 13 complex. The net motif has its own associations, among them water, fertility, and the Ollin (movement) sign, which, as a divinatory mirror, is personified by the net jaguar (Taube 1983: 127). The net jaguar was Tezcatlipoca's representative (Séjourné 1962b: 88–90, fig. 102; Taube 1983: 127) and may be related to the Teotihuacan Goddess in her avatar as Spider Woman (Taube 1983: 111).

The net jaguar wears a red kilt bordered with colored plaques and half-circles edged with plumes, and a drape with geometric designs. The back, tail, and arms are edged by a "red-on-yellow sawtooth design . . . one of the most common signs associated with the female deity" (Millon 1988: 227), bordered by a set of light green plumes. The figure's headdress features long and short green plumes and red forms. In its left hand it holds a shield with a basketry design on a red background. Similar designs adorn the two red circular ornaments near its face. The right arm, upraised, has a bracelet of jade beads and holds a plumed standard resembling a rattle or timbrel (Cook de Leonard 1971: 223).

In front of the figure are two scrolls; the upper one seems to extend from its mouth and would be a breath or sound scroll. Its outer bands of green and blue are ornamented by five trios of conjoined green and blue rectangles. Many Teotihuacan sound scrolls are edged with tabs or other symbols; their meaning is poorly understood, but their variety and patterns of occurrence deserve closer study. Inside the scroll are two green chalchihuitl disks and another form, blue and green, similar to the Postclassic Central Mexican glyph for the heart or the stone. These elements and about four dozen red dots are scattered over a light red field. Near the figure's mouth another part of the scroll bears a half dozen dark red dots against a light red ground, with an upper border of bands of green and blue, and a lower scalloped edge. The dots on the two parts of the sound scroll may represent seeds, extending the themes of preciousness and fertility.

The other scroll descends in a curved, square-ended fall of precious objects, much like the hand-scattering falls in other Teotihuacan murals. It contains at least one chalchihuitl disk, other small blue and green objects that may represent precious stones (see Villagra Caleti 1971: 144), and a bird head and other animal head carved from precious stones.

The figure kneels on the border of the painting, not on the causeway that approaches the temple and continues on to the left. The causeway is inscribed with footprints, a common and ancient motif in Mesoamerican art, occurring in Olmec art on La Venta Monument 13 (Drucker 1952: 203, fig. 61). The footprints on Murals 7 and 8 feature a break in the rhythm of the steps, repeating the right footstep—a pattern also found in Room 12's Mural 4 (Fuente 1995: lám 64 [p. 300]). This could indicate a kind of choreography, a ritualized pattern of movement appropriate to approaching the temple (see also Boone 2000: 65–67).

On either side of the causeway are wide blue lines with eyes (or eye-shaped bubbles [Angulo 1996: 75]) that echo the net jaguar's eye. At Teotihuacan the eye represented a freshwater spring (Lombardo de Ruíz 1995: 25). The doorway of the temple is filled in with the same blue, implying that spring water is emerging from the temple. Placing a temple at a water source is widespread among world cultures, marking the preciousness of the source and laying claim to it for the political institution legitimizing the religious one. Today one of Teotihuacan's only active springs is in the walled compound of the parish church of San Juan Teotihuacan, begun in 1557–58 and probably overlying an even earlier colonial church that may in turn overlie a Pre-Columbian temple.

The mural's temple is a rarity in Teotihuacan mural painting, which seldom depicts architecture. Most such representations are abstract, sometimes reduced to triangular roof merlons that were widely used in Teotihuacan (Pasztory 1988b: 183). The temples shown in Tetitla's Net-Jaguar Murals are one-room buildings raised on platforms of talud and tablero design, not unlike the shrines found in many Teotihuacan apartment compounds (see Séjourné 1966a: 127, fig. 55). The temple's yellow wall, scattered with black rosettes, represents jaguar skin, and the building's sides feature chalchihuitl disks. This same combination of features and colors runs horizontally above and below the jaguar rosette merlons in the building's roof comb. This element is separated from the building by a line of plumed tassels, and the sides of the roof comb display a mat design; the building is topped with green plumes.

Three elements that border the building—chalchihuitl, mat, and tassel—are repeated in the border around the whole mural. The mural border is a "jade-marked mat . . . entirely consistent with Mesoamerican concepts of rulership" and, with the plumed tassels, appears as "a horizontal throne with hanging tassels," common in Classic Maya art (Taube 2003: 293). The element between the tassels closely resembles the rostrum or "bill" of the sawfish, which had sacred associations with primordial fertility.[20]

The major elements—the net jaguar and the temple with its causeway and canals—are set against a dramatic diagonal background. Broad bands of light and dark red mesh in a zigzag (or "saw-tooth" [Von Winning 1977: 14]) pattern. They are divided from each other by a set of narrow ribbons of light red, green, and blue, similar to the water flows in the mural's foreground. They probably represent irrigation channels bringing water to the dark and light red fields, based on the mural's theme of water as an object of veneration at a time when the city depended on the canals that systematized the use of water from its springs.

The Net-Jaguar Mural is "one of the most complex and quintessentially 'Teotihuacan' murals" (Pasztory 1997: 183). At the same time, it is unique in the proportions of the central figures and their placement in front of the background, creating "the illusion of a figure existing in space . . . by the use of staggered planes, a rare concept in two-dimensional pre-Columbian art" (Millon 1972: 10).

Mural 8 is a truly exceptional technical example of Teotihuacan's most important artistic tradition. What story does it tell? A central theme is power: control of expensive foreign sumptuary goods, land, and water. Painted when the city threw its energies into construction and drainage, it expresses the value of channeled water as an essential resource as Teotihuacan's population grew and the city could not be sustained by agricultural areas watered by rainfall alone. The strong iconographic associations of jaguars with water from the earth, vegetation, militarism, and rulership, all indicate a reverence for control of the springs, possibly in opposition to the Feathered Serpent's domain of rainfall (Lombardo de Ruíz 1995: 25–26). The mural can be read as a combination of tropes: power, majesty, and mystery; Mural 8 places this net jaguar into the dynamic history of Teotihuacan. The city sought riches and knowledge from foreign parts. It sought to divine the future and to house and feed its people. The net jaguar casts chalchihuitls at a water temple adorned with them, and in the background, water from springs, earth's blue-green bounty, pulses across the fields.

STE

TEOTIHUACAN FRESCOED VESSELS

Ceramic vessels are among the most important material clues to an ancient culture. Clay may be traced to a source; temper indicates local or even individual preferences. Vessel form indicates style and function, which in turn identifies activities and even activity areas, and the presence or influence of particular cultures and phases within or beyond their periods of dominance. Surface finishing is another cultural signature, with characteristic colors, design motifs, and techniques. Furthermore, clay vessels are durable, and even potsherds retain characteristics of material, form, and surface treatment.

Teotihuacan was famed for stuccoed and painted bowls and vases, many of them in a cylindrical footed form known as "cylinder tripods." Of the six stuccoed and painted Teotihuacan-style vessels in the Bliss Collection, five are cylindrical vases with tripod supports, and the sixth is a bowl. All are unmistakably Teotihuacan in form, proportions, and motifs, although expressing a variety of iconographic devices and artistic styles. Cylinder tripod vessels have become a diagnostic of contact with Teotihuacan culture wherever they were found in the Mesoamerican world. The form was borrowed and altered by the Maya, who made taller versions decorated in recognizably Maya style. The examples from Teotihuacan have stockier proportions, and their motifs are typical of the city's symbolic vocabulary. These stuccoed and painted vessels "were a Teotihuacan invention . . . many of the subjects and designs represented are related to or abbreviations of mural paintings" (Pasztory 1988a: 65, 67).

These portable versions of the murals use the same palette—what Kidder et al. (1977 [1946]: 232) somewhat disparagingly described as "the rather monotonous Teotihuacan red or pink, green, and a little yellow"—and simplify major muralistic themes in an abstracted form of the bordered mural. In the case of the vessels, the borders are relatively more obtrusive, framing a central register showing "alternating motifs such as elaborately plumed headdresses, and other regalia" commonly in the context of human figures, "the most frequently depicted subject associated with cylindrical tripod vessels" (Conides 1997: 40).

Cylinder tripods were Teotihuacan's "primary ceremonial vessel form . . . the fanciest objects deposited in burials" (Pasztory 1993a: 236). Yet they were found in less than 20 percent of the nearly 400 burials in the Teotihuacan apartment compounds (Rattray 1992, 1997; Sempowski 1994). The proportion of burials with cylinder tripods in any compound correlates directly with that compound's status.[21] The designs on these vessels may have been markers of particular statuses, "high-ranking members of Teotihuacan society who were affiliated with specific, socially defined institutions within the city" (Conides 1997: 39). The single cylinder tripod found at the low-status Tlajinga compound, for example, may indicate that the individual had achieved a status in a social network beyond the compound (Conides 1997: 41–42). Vessels were buried with adult males and females in roughly equal numbers but were scarce when the only remains were those of children (Sempowski 1994: 248, 249).

Burials with cylinder tripods date from the Early Tlamimilolpa phase (AD 200–300) through Metepec phase (AD 650–750), with greatest representation during Xolalpan phases (AD 400–650), particularly Late Xolalpan (AD 550–650), which accounted for nearly 40 percent of the cylinder tripods found. Some of these may have been curated from earlier times, but it is clear that cylinder tripods were products of the mature Teotihuacan state. Stucco painting and plano-relief, found on the Bliss Collection cylinder tripods, are typical of decorative techniques characteristic of such vessels "in the more complex grave offerings" (Sempowski 1994: 254). These objects would have had important roles in ceremonies and also in gift exchange, accompanying an ambassador on a diplomatic mission, or a deceased individual on the journey to the underworld.

STE

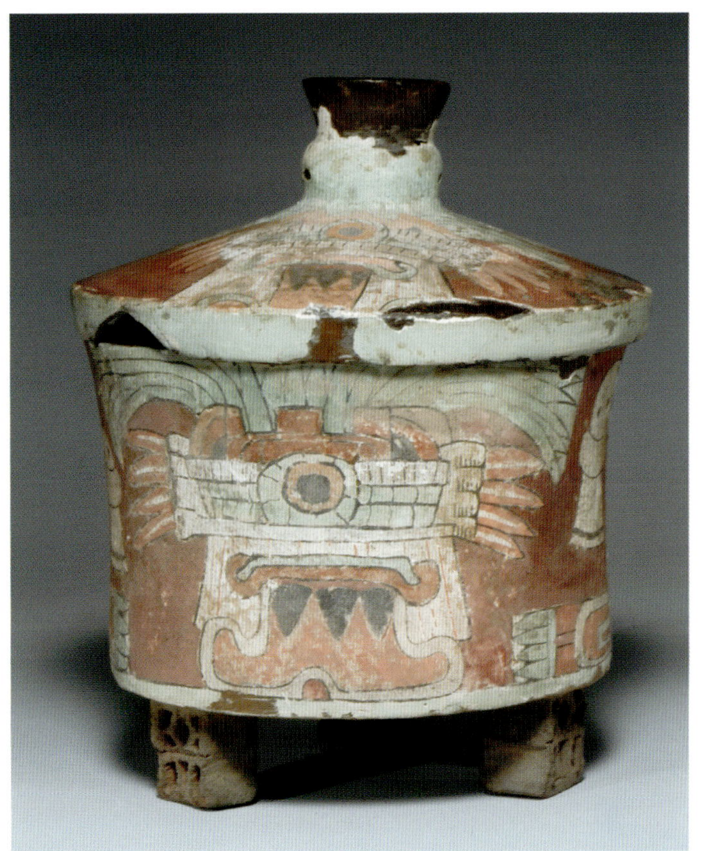

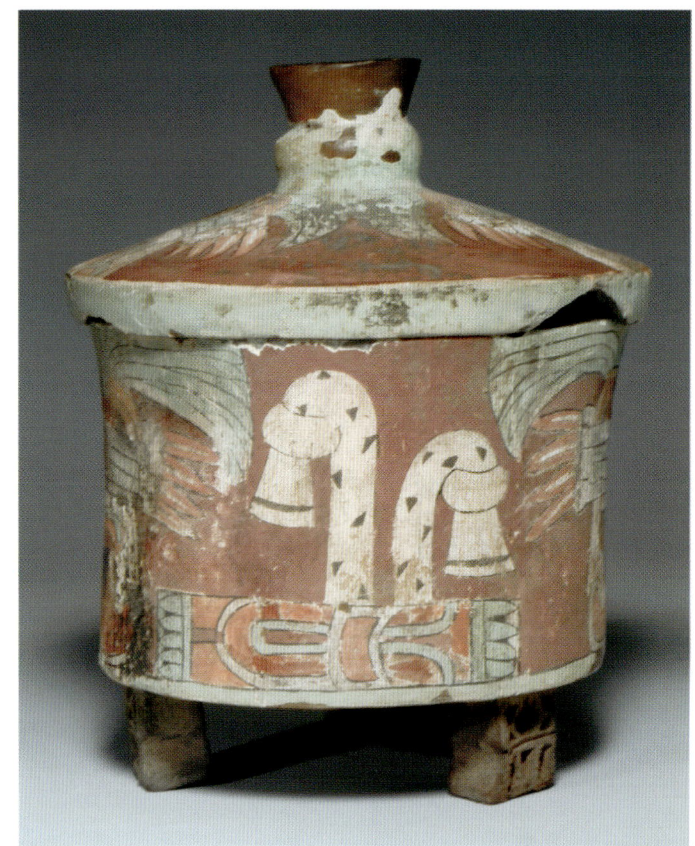

plate 6a *plate 6b, side view*

JAR WITH LID

PLATE 6
Teotihuacan
Classic period, AD 200–750
Frescoed brownware ceramic
H. (overall) 20.9 cm (8¼")
Lid: H. 7.7 cm (3"); Diam. 18.3 cm (7¼")
Pot: H. 14.0 cm (5½"); Diam. 17.0 cm (6⅝")
PC.B.063

ACQUISITION HISTORY:
Purchased from Earl Stendahl, 1954

EXHIBITION HISTORY:
Indigenous Art of the Americas, National Gallery of Art, Washington, D.C., July 1954–July 1962 (NGA 637)

BIBLIOGRAPHY:
Bliss 1957: 239, cat. no. 44, pl. XXXI; Becker-Donner 1962: pl. 3; Ishida 1962: 164, fig. 41; Dumbarton Oaks 1963: 2–3, cat. no. 8; Willey 1966: I: 114, fig. 3-49, top; Von Winning 1977: 29, fig. 15a (motif only); Grey 1978: pl. 3; Davies 1983: fig. 7; Miller 1986: 79, fig. 55; Sempowski 1992: 40, fig. 6; Taylor 2000: fig. 8

Vessel PC.B.063 is a cylindrical vase with three rectangular openwork supports and a slightly convex lid with a knob shaped like a topknot. The lid overhangs the edge of the vessel, much like a roofline overhanging the wall of a house (Conides and Barbour 1999: 412). This object, the only lidded Teotihuacan vessel in the Bliss Collection, demonstrates these proportions. The vessel was examined by conservators in 1992, who reported that it and the lid had numerous cracks, had been

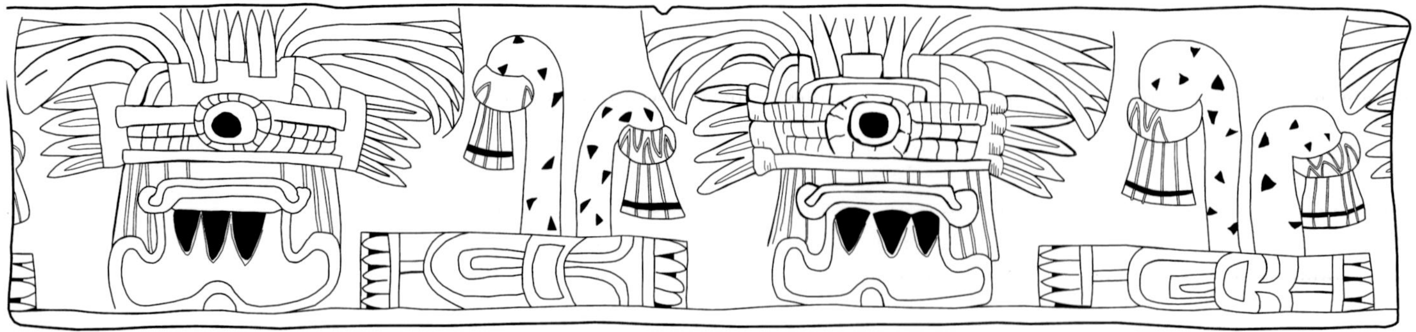

fig. 6
Rollout drawing of design on Teotihuacan frescoed jar with lid PC.B.063. Drawing by Susan Toby Evans.

"heavily restored," and areas had been overfilled and overpainted (Art Conservation Technical Services n.d.a). The supports may not be original to the vessel.

The vessel and lid have designs in black and white, blue-green, and orange-red against a dark red background. Application of designs seems careful and unhurried. Of all the Bliss Collection Teotihuacan vessels, this one most resembles Teotihuacan murals in formality of the presentation of its designs. The vessel's exterior bears two repetitions of two designs (Figure 6): a fanged mouth surmounted by a headdress (this motif is also used twice on the vessel's lid) and a set of two upright crooks atop a horizontal knot.

The fanged mouth is a costumed abstraction, frontal view, consisting of a top panache of green feathers; a middle headdress with a concentric circular element with side extensions of rows of squarish plaques; and a bottom section, the mouth. These motifs are outlined in black. The meaning of this set of motifs is complex. Particular costume elements signified an official role or status in Teotihuacan society (C. Millon 1973; see Millon and Rattray 1972). In the case of this frontal motif, the feathers in the panache, from the rare tropical quetzal bird, were imported to Teotihuacan at great cost and used in costumes of the highest authorities. The midsection of the headdress reiterates the message of preciousness and power with its three rows of jade beads. The central element is almost certainly a jade disk inscribed with a feather edge, seemingly a portrait of one of the Bliss Collection jade disks, in this case with a centermost inset possibly representing a polished obsidian mirror.

The lower section of this frontal abstract is a fanged mouth, the upper lip framed by a *bigotera* (moustache) and the black teeth dramatically staged against a wide bifurcated orange-red tongue, a recurrent set of symbols that Langley (1986: 73) has termed "mouth fanged." Long associated with the Aztec storm god Tlaloc, its ancestral form is the Teotihuacan Storm God (Langley 1992: 248–259).

This frontal abstraction brings together symbols of preciousness: feathers, jades, mirrors, and the sanctity of storms and rainwater. The other set of symbols is less accessible. The upper pair of crooked figures is similar to those labeled by Langley (1986: 230) as an "aspergillum," a term used in Western contexts to denote a brush-like device used to sprinkle holy water.[22] In the case of PC.B.063's aspergilla, the white material is rendered as undifferentiated with black triangular flecks. Almost invisible white lines trace large triangles along the horizontal "knot" of each. The composition of a rounded white form with black flecks and a loose knot suggests a hank of unprocessed cotton.

These black and white aspergilla emerge out of a bundle, a type of rectangle that Von Winning (1977: 29, fig. 15a) identifies as a "firewood bundle." Green projections at either end suggest a bundle of feathers or reeds, or a bundle decorated by them. The bow binding the bundle (Langley 1986: 236, 237) is much like the decoration at the neck of the net jaguars in Tetitla's Room 12 (see Plate 5) and is also a common element in Storm God insignia (Langley 1992: figs. 1, 4, 5, 7; 1993: fig. 6b). If the aspergillum design is a hank of cotton, then these motifs are high-status, high-cost goods brought from distant warm regions. Cotton was probably imported into Teotihuacan as woven cloth, but diplomatic and trading parties would have also brought back samples of this precious material in unprocessed form. Combined with long green feathers, secured with a bow knot of a type worn by net jaguars, the set of images conveys the sense of sanctity and preciousness.

The combined suggested meanings of these two sets of images reiterate divinity and power, based on Teotihuacan's local resources and foreign influence. This vessel's abstract motifs honor the rainfall that watered crops, and they honor the city's long-distance trade in feathers, jade, and cotton. This capacity in turn was founded on Teotihuacan's prestige as a source of knowledge, a place where mirrors served as divinatory devices that were memorialized in its monumental architectural façades (Taube 1992) as well as in abstract motifs, such as those on this vessel. Teotihuacan's power to intimidate was conveyed by the image of fangs and a serpent's bifurcated tongue.

STE

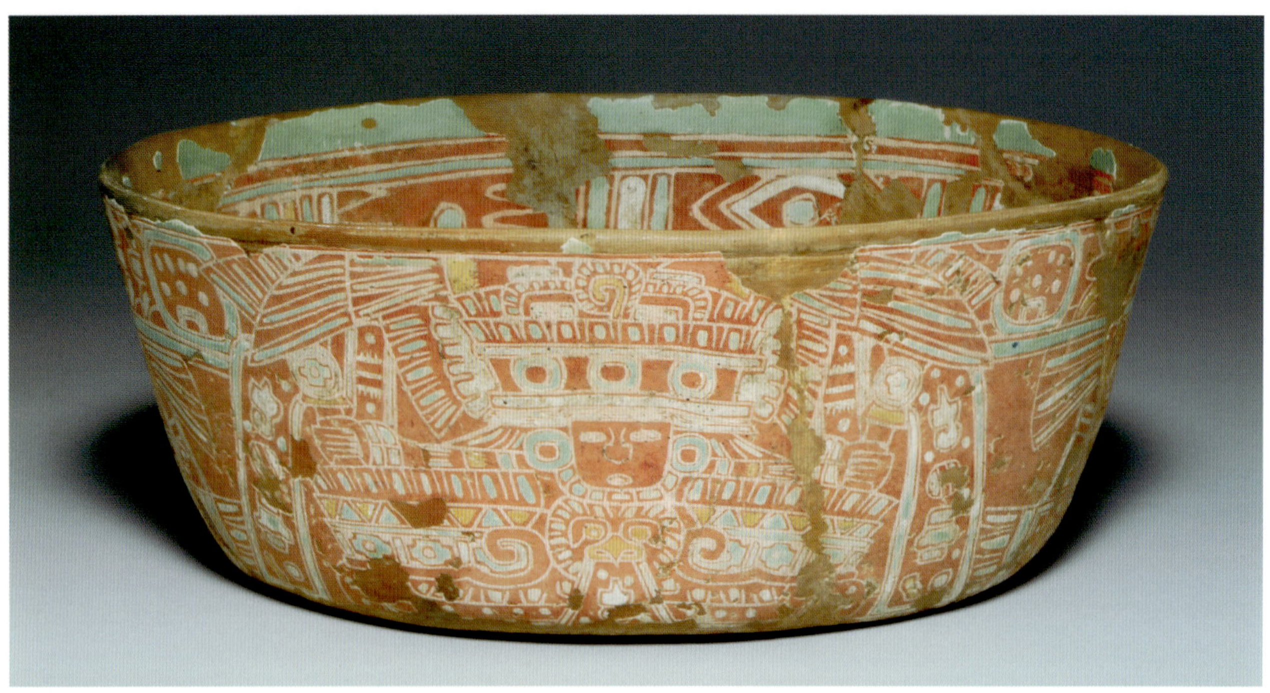

plate 7a

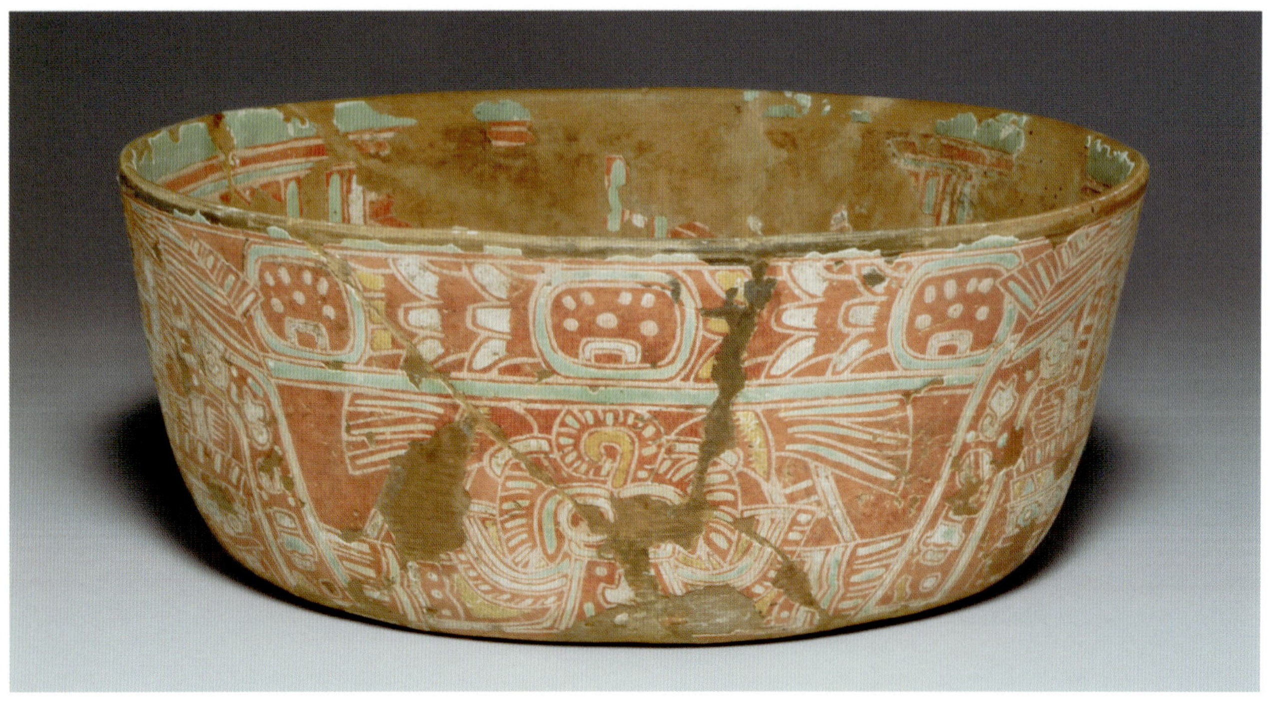

plate 7b, back view

PLATE 7
Teotihuacan
Classic period, AD 200–750
Frescoed orangeware ceramic
H. 9.0 cm (3½"); Diam. 24.5 cm (9⅝")
PC.B.064

ACQUISITION HISTORY:
Acquired before 1957

EXHIBITION HISTORY:
Indigenous Art of the Americas, National Gallery of Art, Washington, D.C., April 1947–July 1949, February 1954–July 1962 (NGA 365)

BIBLIOGRAPHY:
Bliss 1957: 240, cat. no. 49, pl. XXXIV; Von Winning 1961: 130 (refers to PC.B.064 but is actually discussing PC.B.066); Dumbarton Oaks 1963: 3, cat. no. 9; Berlo 1992: 141, fig. 14

The only bowl among the Bliss Collection's Teotihuacan vessels, PC.B.064 is decorated inside and out, but the poor condition of the stucco complicates interpretation of its exterior motifs and makes understanding the interior design program nearly impossible. A conservation report notes that the bowl consisted of 14 fragments and that the remaining surface decoration was in extremely fragile condition (Art Conservation Technical Services n.d.e). The conservators further noted that the colors had faded somewhat. The vessel's palette is dominated by the medium-light red background, accented by filled bands of medium blue-green and highlighted by yellow and white, with motifs outlined in white. Of the other Bliss Collection vessels, cylinder vase PC.B.067 (Plate 10) has a palette most similar to that of bowl PC.B.064.

The outside designs consist of two sets of two alternating figures: a richly costumed frontal human figure and a frontal abstract in a similar pose. These are thought to represent "two major motifs . . . a butterfly [and] . . . a deity whose headdress is crowned by a butterfly design" (Lothrop in Bliss 1957: 240, cat. no. 49). On the interior, remaining fragments on the base of the vessel suggest a frontal figure with an elaborate headdress. Around the interior side is a wide upper band with alternating abstract motifs, and below that, isolated symbols are arrayed against the red background.

The frontal human figure on the exterior set of figures is among the clearest images on the vessel, and Berlo (1992) has interpreted it as an image of the Teotihuacan Goddess.[23] The figure's face is uncovered, and it wears large ear spools of the same size as the three disks arrayed across the lower part of the headdress. Above this is a horizontal line of rectangular plaques, and from the middle of this line rises a curved element, framed by eyes; these all seem to be edged with smaller plaques. This set of elements closely resembles the curved "proboscis" framed by eyes found on vessel PC.B.066 and linked by Caso to the butterfly (see discussion for Plate 9).

Also found in PC.B.064's other exterior motif, and possibly in the design on the bottom of the interior, this curved element resembles part of the "reptile eye" glyph, specifically, the reptile eyebrow. Stylized feathers extend from either side of the headdress, and from the junction of a set of shorter and longer feathers there extend matched vertical panels with a horizontal sawtooth design, much like Langley's "serrated" comb and bar (1986: 241), framed by the dots with which this design is sometimes associated. This set of motifs echoes similar designs on the upper band of the interior.

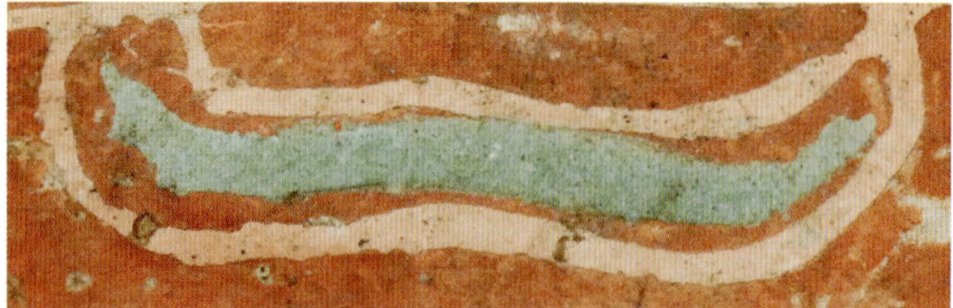

plate 7c, interior side detail, bigotera

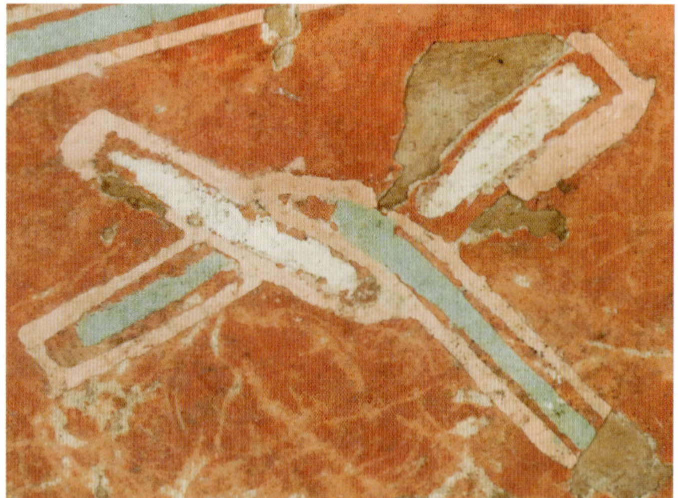

plate 7d, interior side detail, interlaced bands

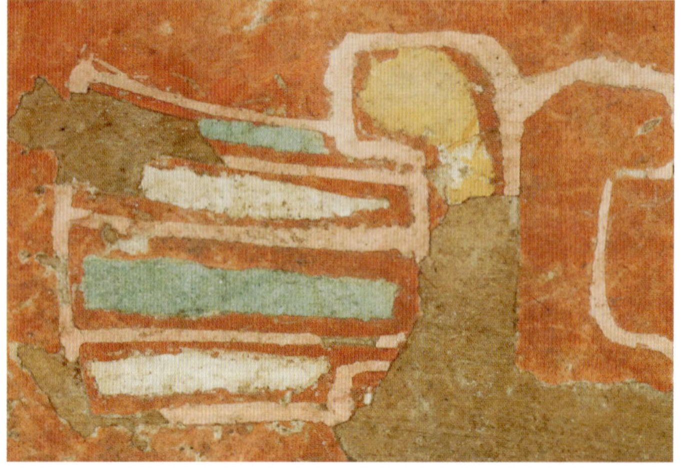

plate 7e, interior side detail, nose pendant

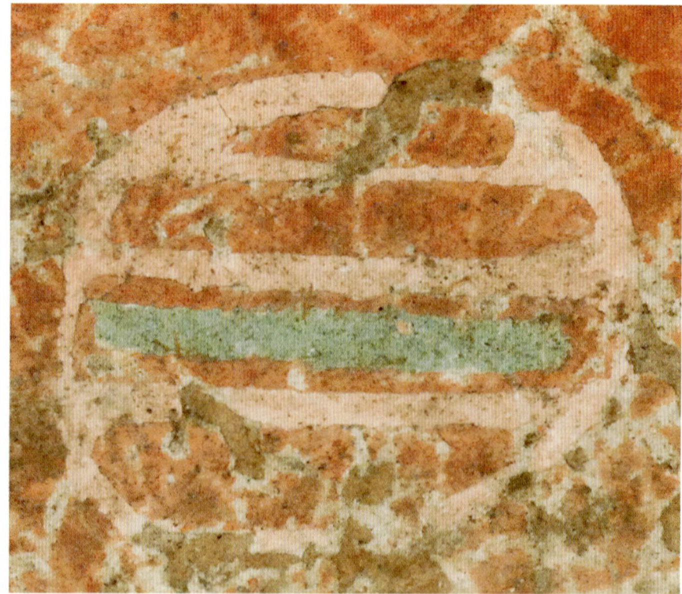

plate 7f, interior side detail, medallion with transverse bars

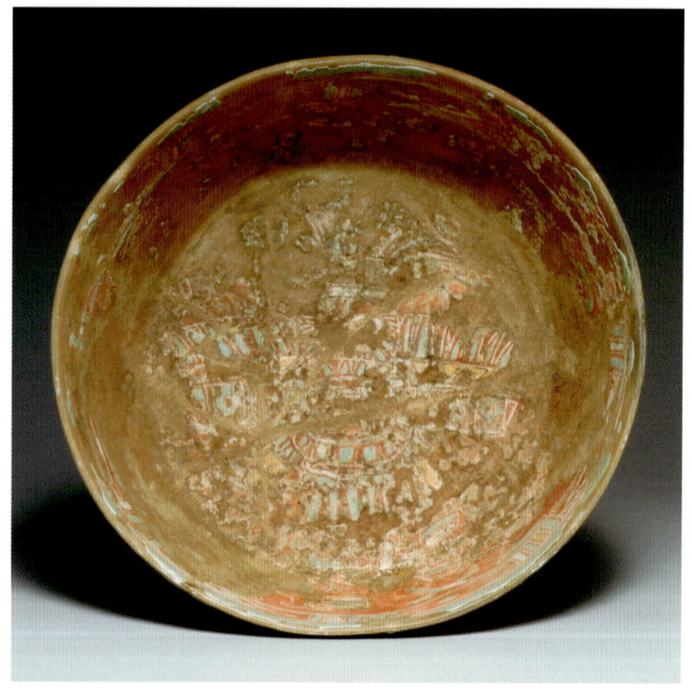

plate 7g, interior view

From just below the figure's ears, its arms stretch out horizontally, its hands holding what may be rattle handles. A "quincross" symbol (Langley 1986: 279), similar to the Maya *kan* cross, marks the rattles. It shares with the Central Mexican disk motif the connotations of preciousness and is also associated with Storm God insignia (Langley 1992: 249, 252). The falls from the rattles bear symbols for conch shells, medallions with transverse bars (Langley 1986: 233–234); a three-part element that may represent an ornament and its plug; and a few smaller designs, one resembling Langley's "Pod A" (1986: 316).

Below the figure's head is an avian head pectoral, possibly an owl, and from its beak, a falling panel contains the quincross symbol and several dots. Parallel to, and below the arms, are three horizontal lines of elements. A single scroll on either side abuts its curl against the avian head. The alternating figure is an abstraction, a constellation of several elements presented in the human figure. Atop the "head" is the curved element that tops the human's headdress. From either side of this extend stylized tufts of long feathers, and from them fall panels with the comb and bar design found on the human figure's upper panels. Damage to the figure's midsection prevents detailed interpretation of this part of the abstract, but there may be a face with features suggestive of butterfly imagery, and clearly visible are the quincross, rounded rows of plaques and at the bottom, extended horizontal panels ending with feather tufts.

Above this figure is a partial upper border for the bowl, three medallions separated by a flowing set of flowers (see Langley 1986: 254, Floral Chain A, or see Cabrera 1996: 19, for a "capa o lienzo con plumas" on murals at the Gran Conjunto of Teotihuacan). The medallions are clear expressions of the "RM" sign (Langley 1986: 281), a variant of the "reptile eye" (RE) that lacks the curl element. Kubler (1967: 6) believed that both RE and RM always seem to label the shape with which it is included to contribute to the process of naming and ranking the shape. The RM sign may be associated with militarism, because it commonly occurs with butterfly imagery, thought to invoke notions of the dead spirits of warriors (Langley 1986: 98–102). The sign may also pertain to calendrics (Langley 1986: 145–148).

The wide upper band of the interior wall bears what appears to be a simple repetition of two design motifs—rhombus with dots and serrated comb and bars—but much of the painted surface has been lost. There are eight separate motif instances, and the rhombus (Rh) and comb and bars (C&B) alternate as follows, beginning with the part of the band above the nose pendant on the lower band (see below), and continuing clockwise: Rh, C&B, Rh, C&B, Rh, Rh, C&B?, C&B. The arrhythmia is interesting, because the artist could easily have painted consistently alternating motifs. Like the arrhythmic footprints in the Net Jaguar Murals of the Tetitla compound (PC.B.062, Plate 5), this pattern suggests a deliberate ordering whose purpose we cannot at present determine, but which may be related to prompts in the expression of an invocation.

The rhombus with dot has ancient associations with fire (Langley 1986: 252 cites Séjourné's and Von Winning's research) and is commonly part of the costume of the Old Fire God (whom the Aztecs knew as Huehueteotl), often appearing on the rim of his hat (see Miller and Taube 1993: 93). The oldest monumental stela in the Basin of Mexico, dating from about 3,000 years ago, is a tall narrow pillar found near the monumental pyramid of Cuicuilco (Pérez Campa 1998), a cult center for worship of the Old Fire God. The only designs carved onto this stela are about twenty dotted rhombuses. The comb and bar motif has also been interpreted by Von Winning as having associations with fire; according to Langley (1986: 241), Von Winning regarded it as an abstraction of a bundle of sticks and further suggested that it might suggest the "binding of the years."

The lower band of the interior wall is heavily damaged but has a few recognizable elements. Among them are the *bigotera* "moustache" (Plate 7c; Langley 1986: 235–236) (or possibly the "U" motif [Langley 1986: 299]); interlaced bands (Plate 7d; Langley 1986: 232; Taube 1983: 127 isolates this as part of the net complex related to mirrors); nose pendant G (Plate 7e; Langley 1986: 278); and a medallion with transverse bars (Plate 7f). It should be noted that the last three elements are among the 11 design elements that Langley has isolated as "the Core cluster," a small group of signs whose patterns of association display remarkable consistency (Langley 1986: 103–104). Given the poor condition of the inner wall of the vessel, it is impossible to do more than point to the coincidence of these few elements and those of the Core cluster.

The bottom of the vessel's interior has an extremely fragmentary figure that is difficult to interpret or even to orient correctly with certainty (Plate 7g). The central horizontal elements form three lines that are in the same top-to-bottom order as those on the human frontal figure on the bowl's exterior: a top row of plaques, a middle row of triangles, and a lower row of quincrosses. Running up and down the central portion of this composition is a series of semicircular sets of plaques or truncated feathers that could serve as the outline to a visage or as a necklace or pectoral. This central set of features is topped by the fragmentary remains of a feather panache.

STE

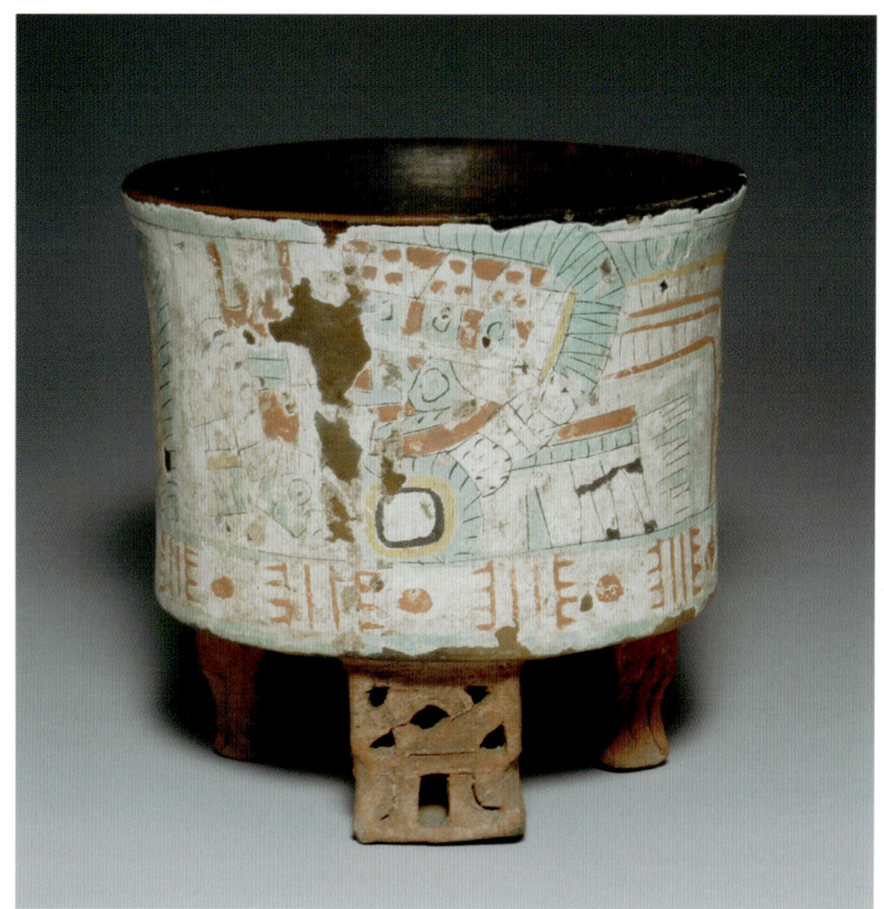

plate 8a

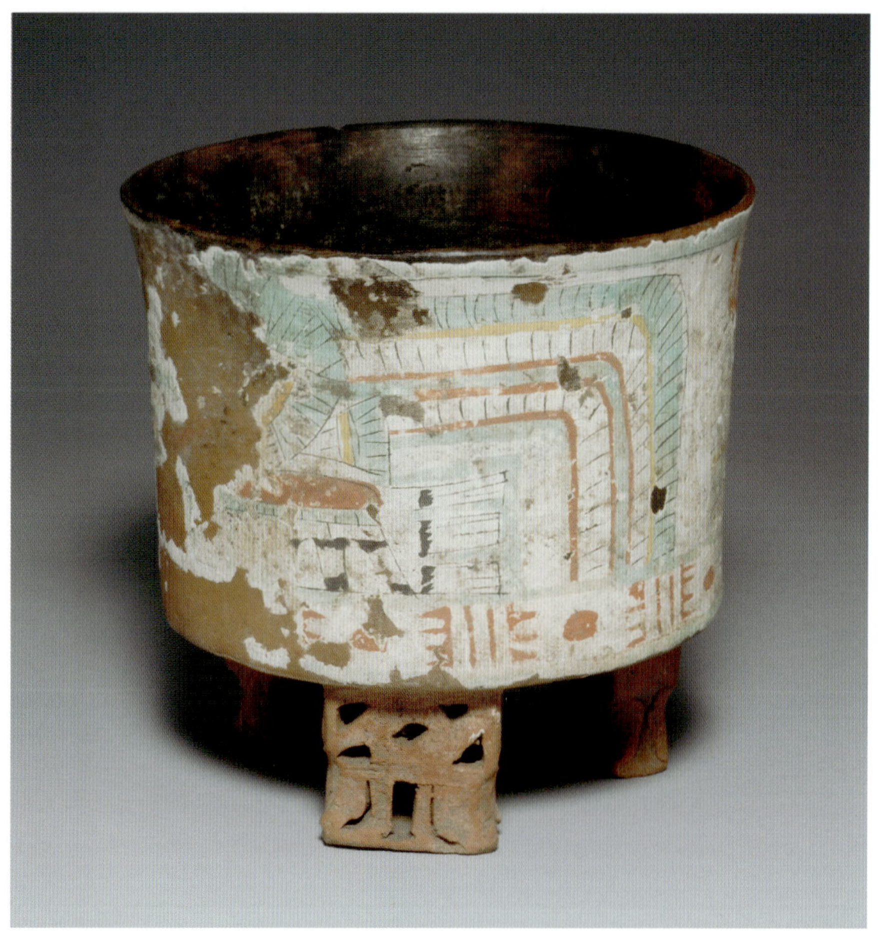

plate 8b, back view

PLATE 8
Teotihuacan
Classic period, AD 200–750
Frescoed brownware ceramic
H. 13.9 cm (5½"); Diam. 14.0 cm (5½")
PC.B.065

ACQUISITION HISTORY:
Purchased from Earl Stendahl

EXHIBITION HISTORY:
Indigenous Art of the Americas, National Gallery of Art, Washington, D.C., April 1947–November 1952, February 1954–July 1962 (NGA 79)

BIBLIOGRAPHY:
Kidder et al. 1977 [1946]: fig. 176c; Bliss 1947: 26, 57, cat. no. 126; Christensen 1955: 206, pl. 18; Bliss 1957: 240, cat. no. 46, pl. XXXIII, top; Dumbarton Oaks 1963: 3, cat. no. 10; Willey 1966: I: 114, fig. 3-49, bottom

Cylinder tripod vase PC.B.065 is one of four such vessels (PC.B.065–PC.B.068) that Kidder et al. (1977 [1946]) suggest came from a single grave. If these vessels were interred together, then it is possible that they have something more in common besides a general form. PC.B.068 (Plate 11) has a dramatic diagonal plano-relief carved design, whereas the others have designs painted on stucco. Alone among the Bliss Collection vessels, PC.B.067 (Plate 10) is embossed with adornos around its base. Most similar in terms of style and content of design, palette, and technique of artistic expression are PC.B.065 and PC.B.066 (Plate 9): "the two were doubtless a pair" (Kidder et al. 1977 [1946]: fig. 176 caption).

PC.B.065 is brownware with large and tall feet that have two openwork design fields, the upper resembling "interlaced bands" (Langley 1986: 232) and the lower suggesting a trilobe (Langley 1986: 296–297). The vase has suffered extensive loss of stucco and paint in the crucial areas of the heads of the two identical figures. There is also considerable loss in some parts of the border. PC.B.065's background is white, with designs in yellow, blue green, pale pink-beige, and red that are defined by thin black lines, seemingly sketched in quickly by a sure hand.

Below a narrow blue-green upper border, the vessel's central register is dominated by two identical figures, left-facing profiles that seem to be human, although much simplified (Figure 7). They may be abstractions, or humans wearing masks. Above the face is a headdress with a horizontal base of three or four blue-green plaques with central dots, against a red background, surmounted by three (or four) conical features in white, each with three red dots. Around the headdress is a curving line of short blue-green feathers, the "feather fringe" motif identified by Langley (1986: 259). Extending back from this element is an elaborate feather fringe, larger than the figure itself and having three main rows of feathers or plaques, separated by narrow bands of color. This fringe surrounds a smaller structure extending from the figure's back, consisting of sketchy white motifs against a blue-green background, and black and white plume shapes extending down from a horizontal double bar of red and blue-green.

On the figure's chest is a roundel of four concentric circles, the outermost being blue-green and almost certainly representing a feather frame, or a chalchihuitl incised with a feather design (PC.B.133, Plate 4). Concentric yellow and black frames enclose a white circle. This probably represents a mirror (see Langley 1986: 318), yet the object emerging from its upper right has the position of a dart (though its shape is

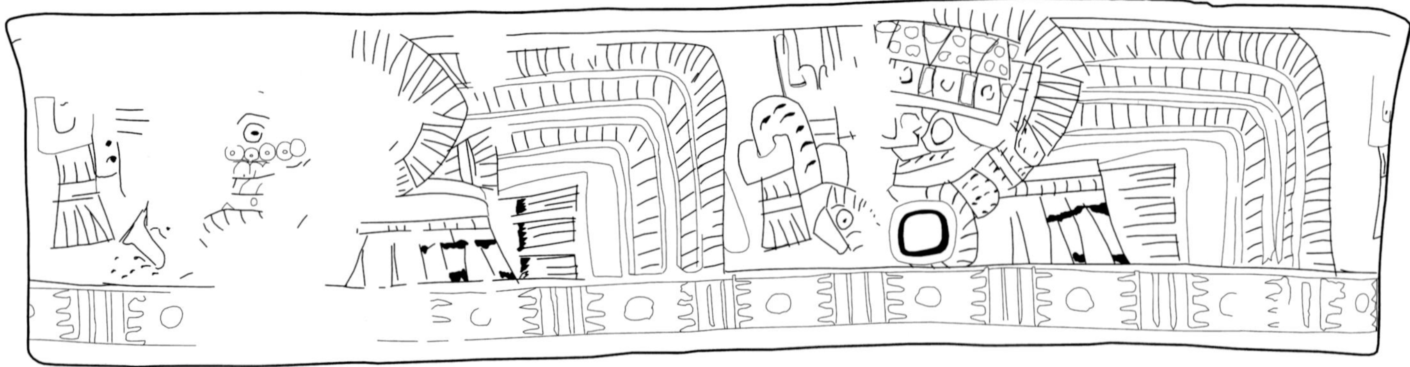

fig. 7
Rollout drawing of design on Teotihuacan frescoed jar PC.B.065. Drawing by Susan Toby Evans.

amorphous and its design problematic), which would suggest that it may be a shield, and that these figures might represent warriors.

Damage to the area in front of the face on both figures has rendered difficult the interpretation of the sketchy shapes in those areas. The crook shape of the aspergillum (Langley 1986: 230) dominates this area, and to its left are two faint pink-beige drops, one above the other, each with an eye on the side (Langley 1986: 248), perhaps signifying water or blood. To the right of (and appearing to be somewhat behind) the aspergillum are two vertical scrolls, forms that some scholars label "flames" (Langley 1986: 254), each with a vertical blue-green bar. Below these are rounded rectangular forms in blue-green and red, and below these is a set of shapes that may describe a left-looking avian head in profile or may be entirely unrelated to each other. The basal band's white field is bounded by narrow blue-green lines and presents a simple repetition of nine serrated comb and bar groups in red, separated by red dots (Langley 1986: 241), similar to the basal band motif shown for a vessel found at Kaminaljuyu, Guatemala (Kidder et al. 1977 [1946]: fig. 177c).

STE

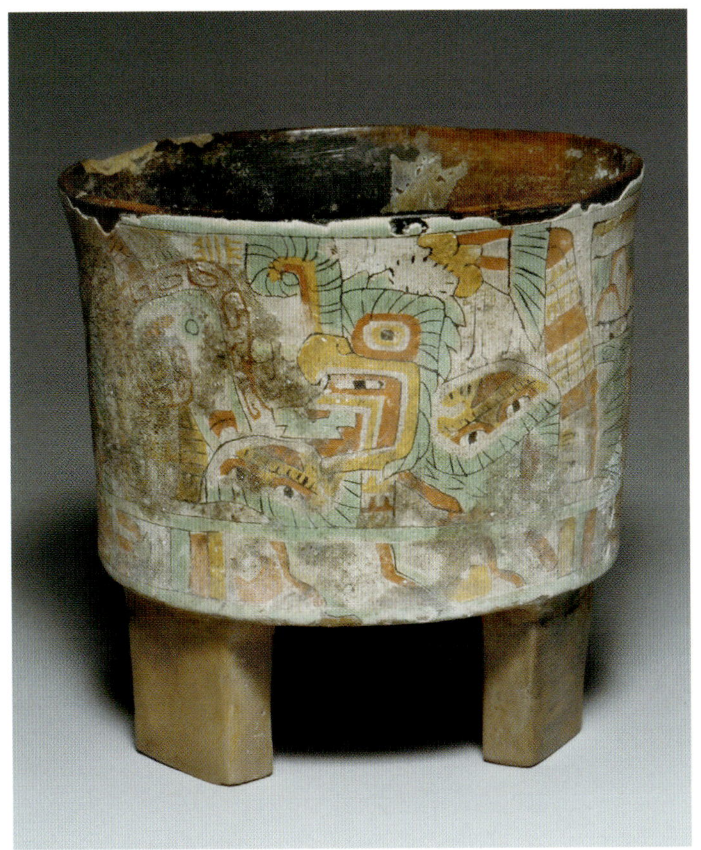

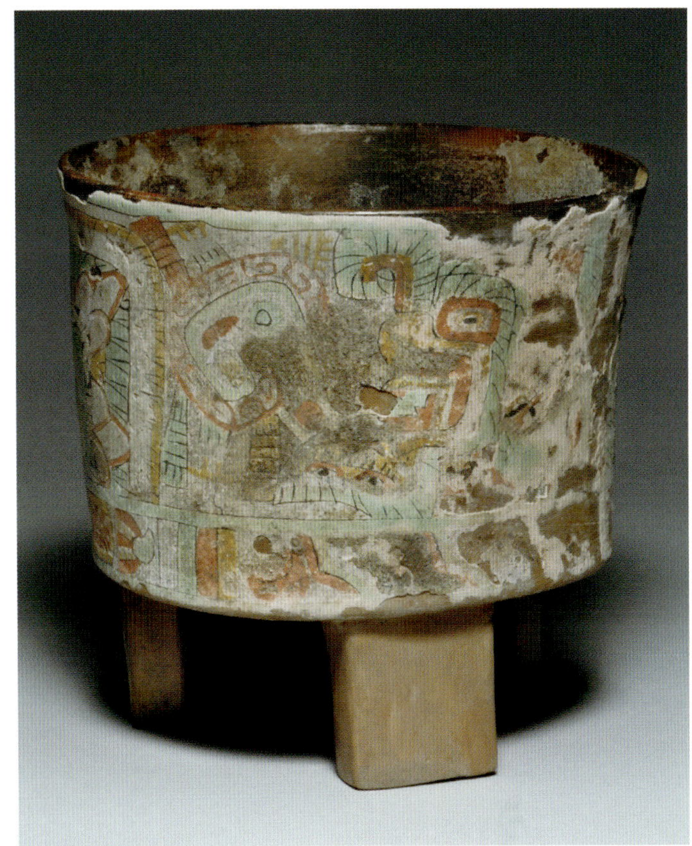

plate 9a *plate 9b, back view*

JAR

PLATE 9
Teotihuacan
Classic period, AD 200–750
Frescoed brownware ceramic
H. 10.6 cm (4⅛"); W. 14.0 cm (5½")
PC.B.066

ACQUISITION HISTORY:
Purchased from Earl Stendahl

EXHIBITION HISTORY:
Indigenous Art of the Americas, National Gallery of Art, Washington, D.C., April 1947–November 1952, February 1954–July 1962 (NGA 78)

BIBLIOGRAPHY:
Kidder et al. 1977 [1946]: figs. 101b, 176b; Bliss 1947: 26, cat. no. 125; Bliss 1957: 239–240, cat. no. 45, pl. XXXII; Von Winning 1961: 130; Dumbarton Oaks 1963: 3, cat. no. 10; Alcina Franch 1979: fig. 262; Conides and Barbour 1999: 412, fig. 1

Teotihuacan cylinder vessel PC.B.066 seems like a sister to PC.B.065 (Plate 8), with a similar palette and design program and such a marked likeness of drawing style that the two may have been the products of the same workshop, possibly even the same artist.[24] Both vessels reveal a "'reserved space' technique, i.e., the incorporation into the design of parts of the uncolored background" (Kidder et al. 1977 [1946]: 220). Like the other vessels, PC.B.066 has sustained some damage: its missing feet have been recently replaced, paint and stucco have flaked off, and some areas

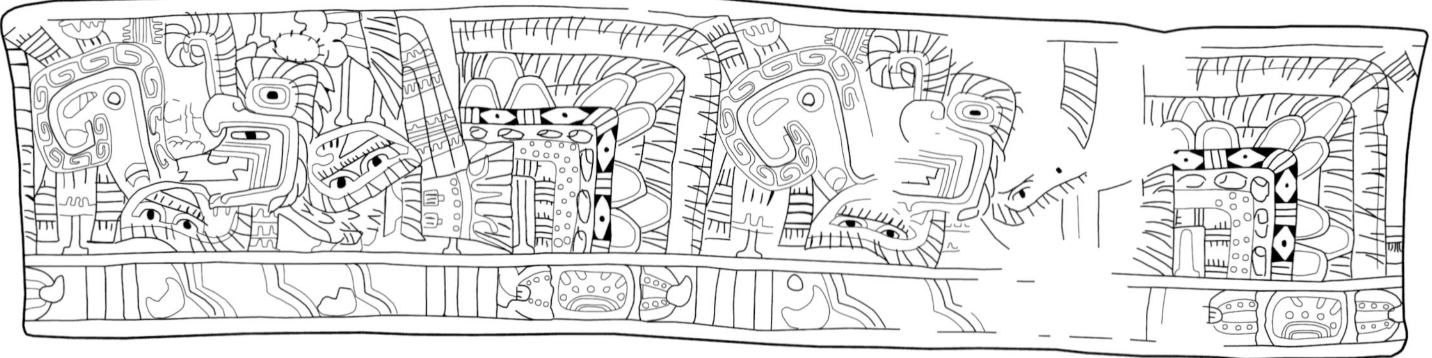

fig. 8
Rollout drawing of design on Teotihuacan frescoed jar PC.B.066. Drawing by Susan Toby Evans.

show a dark incrustation (Art Conservation Technical Services n.d.b). Yet the motifs remain fairly clear.

The decorative field is similar to that of PC.B.065: a narrow blue-green band at the top, a central register comprising three-quarters of the vessel's height for the two identical horizontally arrayed figures and their accoutrements, and a lower decorated band. The figures are left-facing profiles wearing masks and costumes with avian and butterfly attributes (Figure 8).

The face is painted red; the yellow rectangular area extending over the nose and cheek probably represents face paint. Covering the mouth is a blue-green Teotihuacan-style nose ornament, a device that scholars have associated with butterflies and with talud and tablero architecture.

From the mouth area emerges a scroll with a red-on-white scrolled edge (Langley 1986: 287), a motif related to torrents of water (Angulo 1996: 75). The area it encloses is outlined in black and has a white background with a blue-green band abutting the black line. Each scroll contains four or five objects that are difficult to define, given the damage and the sketchy style of rendering. The clearest, a blue-green concentric disk in the upper right section, is almost certainly a chalchihuitl symbol of preciousness. Other shapes, red and yellow, are on the periphery; there is room for a fifth object in the middle, but both scrolls are damaged in this area. Each scroll has six appendages around its outer edge, shapes of the comb and bar type, including a serrated comb and bar (Langley 1986: 241) that some scholars regard as symbolic of bundles, such as of firewood.

The human figure is elaborately costumed. The face peers out through the headdress's wide-open beak, which is topped by a curling feathered scroll extending upward, a motif often identified as a diagnostic of the reptile eye (being the eyebrow), although Séjourné (1962a) pointed out that it resembles more closely a butterfly's proboscis. The headdress-mask's eye is a black dot surrounded by concentric yellow, white, and red circles and by two tiers of feathers. On top, a white puffball secures to the headdress a yellow trilobe, from which emerges a long three-tiered tuft of feathers.

Extending from either side of the base of this headdress are wing-shaped feather banners, each decorated with red-rimmed half-eyes. More multi-tiered feather tufts extend to the back of the figure, seeming to overlap the large feathered panel behind it. This panel, probably a feathered banner that is part of the figure's costume, is almost square and nearly as large as the figure.

This profile figure resembles a full-face figure on a cylindrical tripod from Kaminaljuyu that Alfonso Caso identified as "a goddess . . . [with] symbolic representations of the butterfly. The staring eyes, pointed wings, feathered tassels, and curling proboscis . . . are all matched in representations of butterflies at Teotihuacan" (Kidder et al. 1977 [1946]: 220, fig. 207h). Unlike the Kaminaljuyu example, PC.B.066's face is framed by an open beak.

In addition to wide outer bands of blue-green and yellow feathers, the panel features three sets of "triple mountains" (Langley 1986: 274). These rest on a black and white band of four rhomboid eyes separated by white bars. Next to this band is an inner one of blue-green on which are sketched seven ovoids that could represent beans, which were used in divination by Pre-Columbian peoples. Further inside this square is a band of white with yellow dots, and then a red band decorated with the serrated comb and bar design. This frames the panel's innermost motif, a vertical flattened droplet drawn in black against white.

On some Teotihuacan vessels, the decorative band is related to larger motifs in a thematic fashion but is not painted so that its design is integrated into that of the main panel. On PC.B.066, however, each of the principal motifs is related to a particular design sequence on the band below it, and these design sequences are separated by sets of four vertical bars in white, yellow, red, and blue-green.

The costumed figure is above a set of three wavy diagonals, narrow red and blue-green bands separated by a black line, against a white background. In each background zone floats an object similar in shape to those in the sound scrolls.[25] The costumed figure's background panel is above a complex motif whose central element is the "RM" variant of the reptile eye glyph. PC.B.066 was cited by Von Winning (1961) in his broad study of this important Teotihuacan symbol.

On either side of the RM glyph is a compound design, a red and white striped partial oval with a curved shape extending from its end, probably a knife (Langley 1986: 272). The shape is also similar to the stylized curve of a spear thrower hook and resembles the weapon held by a figure in the Red Tlalocs mural at the Tepantitla compound (Pasztory 1974: 11–12, fig. 14).

STE

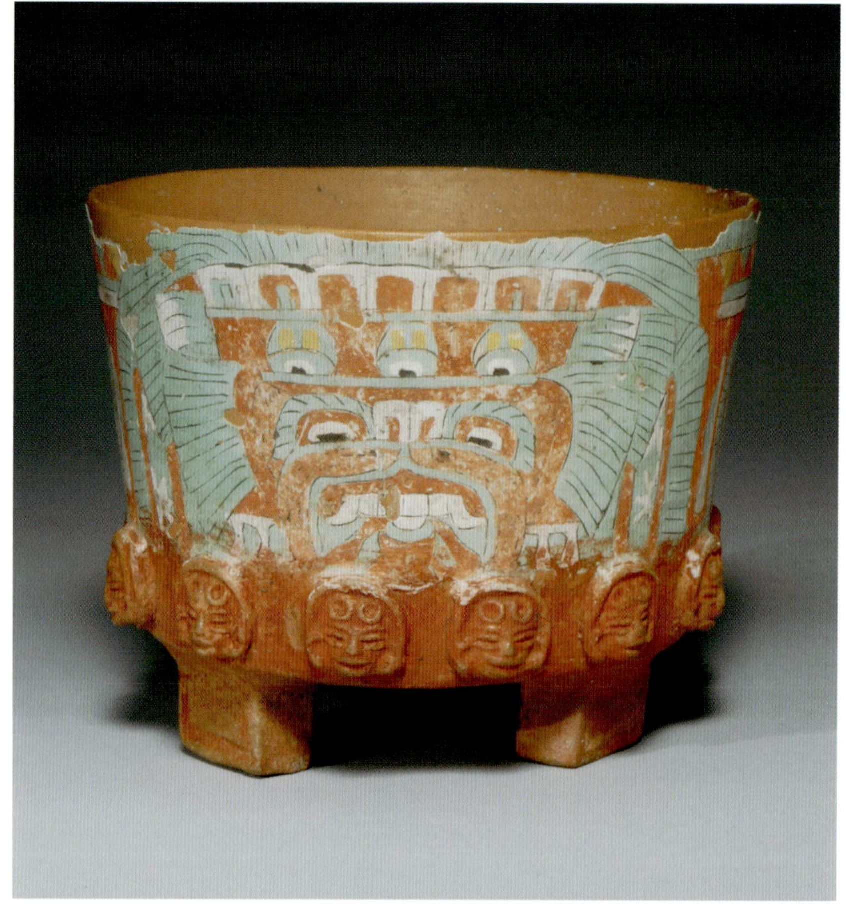

plate 10a

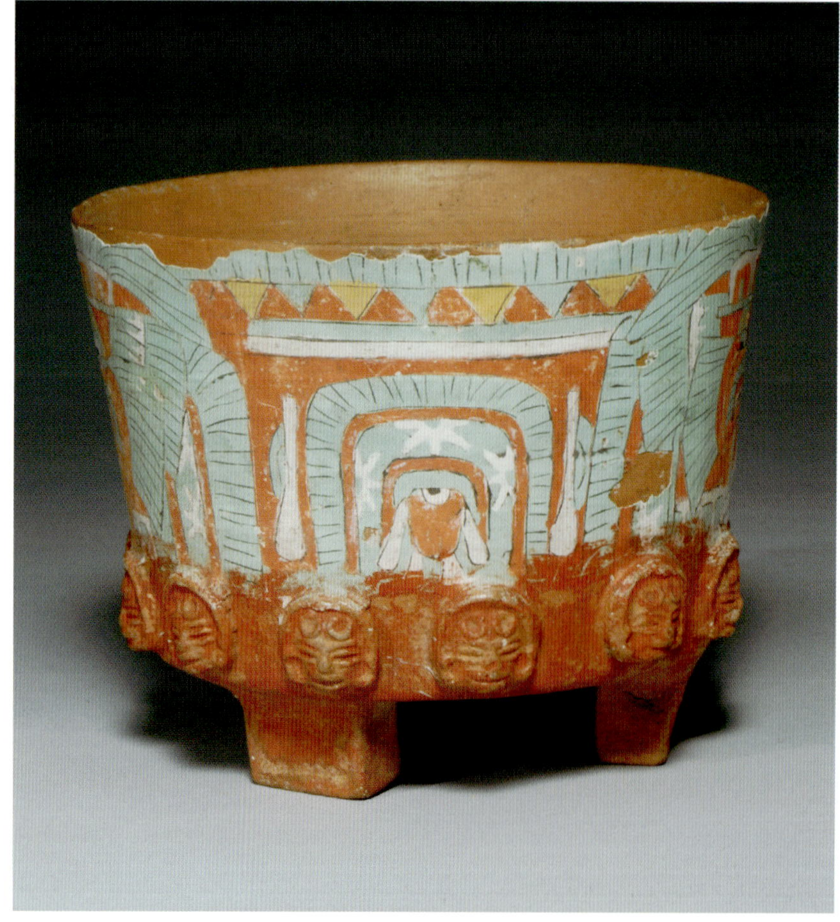

plate 10b,
side view

PLATE 10
Teotihuacan
Classic period, AD 200–750
Frescoed orangeware ceramic
H. 10.5 cm (4⅛"); Diam. 13.2 cm (5¼")
PC.B.067

ACQUISITION HISTORY:
Purchased from Earl Stendahl

EXHIBITION HISTORY:
Indigenous Art of the Americas, National Gallery of Art, Washington, D.C., April 1947–November 1952, February 1954–July 1962 (NGA 81)

BIBLIOGRAPHY:
Kidder et al. 1977 [1946]: fig. 176a; Bliss 1947: 26, 126, cat. no. 127; Bliss 1957: 240, cat. no. 48, pl. XXXIII, bottom right; Séjourné 1959: 164, fig. 133; Becker-Donner 1962: pl. 3; Ishida 1962: 164, fig. 42; Dumbarton Oaks 1963: 3, cat. no. 11; Grosses modernes Lexikon 1982; Stuart 1988: 115; Vila Llonch 2008g: 200–201

PC.B.067 is one of the set of four cylinder tripod vessels that Kidder et al. (1977 [1946]) believe to have come from one grave. As was the case for vessels PC.B.065 (Plate 8) and PC.B.066 (Plate 9), the primary design field for the vase's exterior decoration presents two copies of a major and a minor figure, and with the upper edge band it comprises three-quarters of the surface. The lower register is not, however, painted with a design but is studded with a set of 12 identical adornos, appliquéd clay emblems that resemble figurine faces.

Many Teotihuacan cylinder tripods are decorated with adornos. For PC.B.067, the adorno is a bas-relief head of an individual with narrowed or closed eyes, ear spools, and two perforated disks on its forehead.[26] The face is set in a nearly circular raised cartouche that extends from the base of one ear spool over the top of the head to the base of the other ear spool. Kidder et al. (1977 [1946]: caption for fig. 176) note about this piece that the "outer surface of feet, faces, spaces between faces, [were] treated with cinnabar, applied after stucco of upper wall, as in places it is daubed over the latter." The conservation report, however, indicates that this overlap was probably only circumstantial, that there was no stucco over the faces or in the lower register (Art Conservation Technical Services n.d.c).

PC.B.067's painted designs feature a simple and dramatic use of the standard palette: important elements of the composition are rendered in blue-green against the red background, with minor accents of black, white, and yellow. The dominating motif is a frontal face in a feathered headdress, and the abstract secondary design echoes the shape at a smaller scale (Figure 9). The vase has a partial upper border that takes up about one-quarter of the vertical space. Its three horizontal levels begin, at the top, with a continuous blue-green band with curving vertical black lines, suggesting an abstraction of a feather panache. Below this is a sawtooth pattern, and the bottom level has two lines, blue-green and white. This upper border is obscured where the artist has extended the principal design up to the edge of the vessel, but it is visible above the secondary abstract design.

This main motif is a frontal animal face with claws. It wears a headdress with a lower horizontal rectangle in red containing three eye-like shapes, their black pupils and white sclerae surrounded by

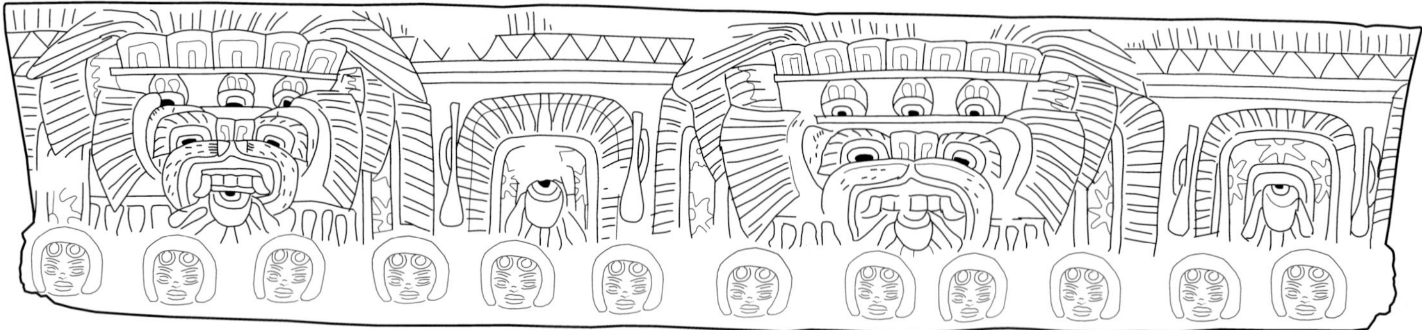

fig. 9
Rollout drawing of design on Teotihuacan frescoed jar PC.B.067. Drawing by Susan Toby Evans.

blue-green and surmounted by blue-green ovals, each with two yellow rounded shapes. Above this is another horizontal rectangle comprised of rectangular plaques edged in white. These horizontal rectangular headdress elements are framed by blue-green feather panaches, some edged in white; they have blue falls with white "half stars" (Langley 1986: 261) that probably represent cut conch shells. The mouth of the animal face is in a style Langley terms "Fangs A" (1986: 252); from it emerges what is probably a pattern of blood droplets, partially obscured by the appliquéd adornos and their red coating. White paws with blue claws frame the mouth.

The secondary motif takes several themes from the main motif and simplifies them into a miniature abstracted version of the larger picture. Central to the motif is an eye oriented opposite to those in the face and headdress; the pattern of white drops falling from the eye's red matrix echo the blood droplets falling from the animal mouth. Narrow bands of red set off the three wider arches of blue. The outermost of these is a sketchy version of the feather panache, and its proportions conform to the Teotihuacan muralistic standards for these features. The smaller interior blue arch is decorated with white "half stars." The secondary motifs are separated from the main motifs by vertical "drop eyes" (Langley 1986: 248), which may convey the sense of sweet (potable) water (Angulo 1996: 76).

STE

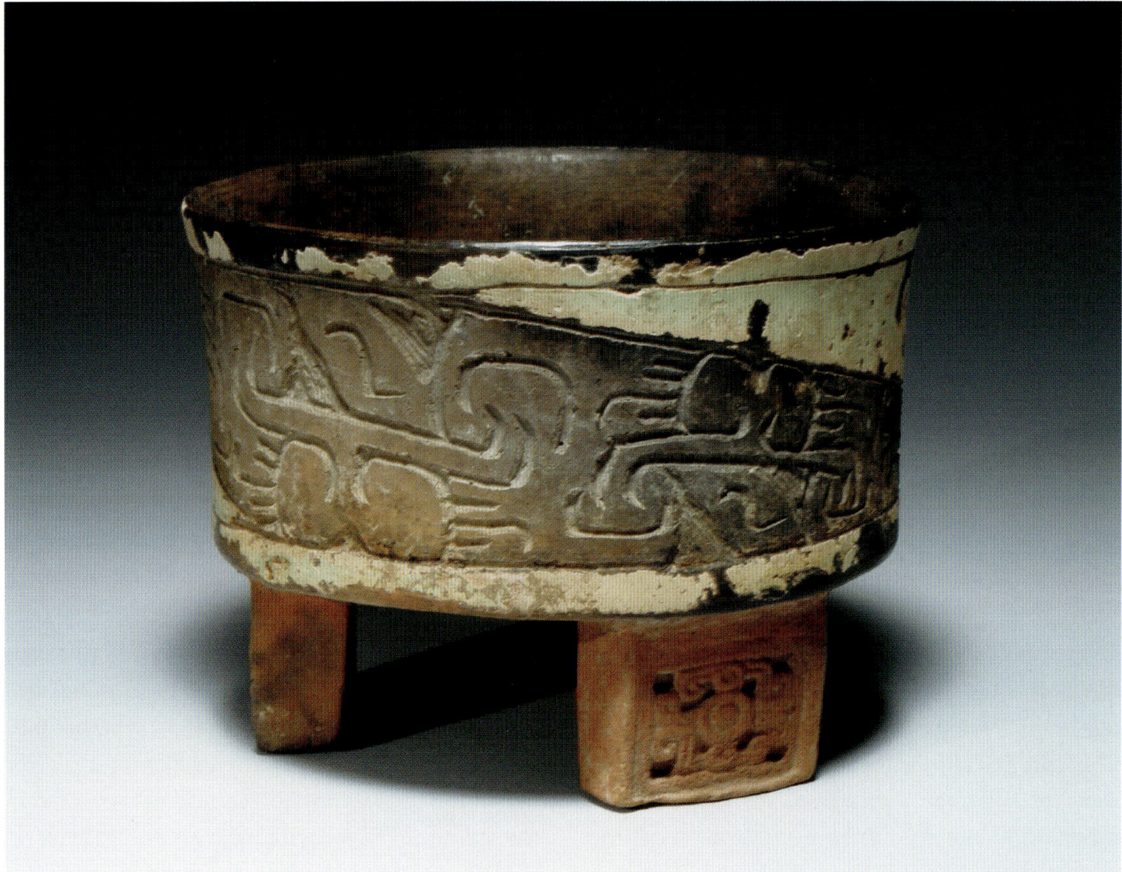

plate 11

JAR

PLATE 11
Teotihuacan
Classic period, AD 200–750
Frescoed brownware ceramic
H. 11.3 cm (4¼"); Diam. 15.5 cm (6⅛")
PC.B.068

ACQUISITION HISTORY:
Purchased from Earl Stendahl

EXHIBITION HISTORY:
Indigenous Art of the Americas, National Gallery of Art, Washington, D.C., April 1947–July 1949, February 1954–July 1962 (NGA 80)

BIBLIOGRAPHY:
Kidder et al. 1977 [1946]: fig. 176d; Bliss 1947: 26, 127, cat. no. 128; Bliss 1957: 240, cat. no. 47, pl. XXXIII, bottom left; Dumbarton Oaks 1963: 3, cat. no. 12

Unlike the other vases in the Bliss Collection, PC.B.068 has no painted scene. Rather, it belongs to another class of decorated cylinder tripod vessels associated with Teotihuacan, those with diagonal friezes of plano-relief design, often abstract and curvilinear, against a plain background. The conservation report (Art Conservation Technical Services n.d.d) notes that the plain field was stuccoed and then painted green. The plano-relief design field had no stucco or paint coating. The feet, which bear a curvilinear motif similar to that of the plano-relief design, had been painted red, with no stucco layer. The feet have an "impressed design, made on each with [the] same stamp, an

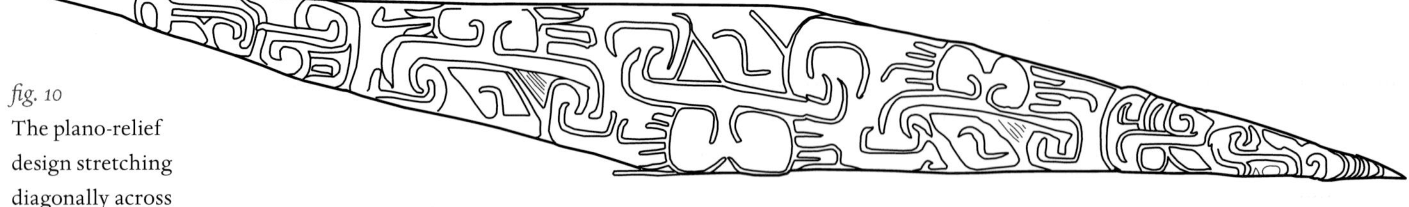

fig. 10
The plano-relief design stretching diagonally across Teotihuacan frescoed jar PC.B.068 shows similarities with motifs from the Gulf Lowlands. Drawing by Susan Toby Evans.

implement so boldly carved that deeper parts of its print give false impressions of openwork" (Kidder et al. 1977 [1946]: fig. 176d).

The plano-relief design is an "elongated rhombus . . . [with an] Incised design drawn while [the] clay [was] still soft, but after polishing, for distinct 'burrs' remain along edges of many lines" (Kidder et al. 1977 [1946]: fig. 176d). This design is difficult to interpret. The vase has been described as having a "principal motif, one unit of which appears on the left side of the illustration, [and] represents the upper jaw and snout of an animal—as attested by effigy vessels modeled in the round from Oaxaca" (Lothrop in Bliss 1957: 240, cat. no. 47). The designs are reversed and repeated (Figure 10), and they seem to express the scroll pattern so commonly associated with contemporaneous art of the Gulf Lowlands.

A comparable vessel with an even more elaborate program of scroll motifs in a diagonal rhombus was found in salvage excavations at San Francisco Mazapa, adjacent to Teotihuacan (Berrin and Pasztory 1993: 256, no. 145, INAH 10-213195), and a much cruder example was purchased at Teotihuacan by Linné (2003b: 94, fig. 177). Although opinions may differ as to whether particular life forms are represented here, it is clear that the motifs strongly resemble those found in the sculpture of the Gulf Lowlands, for example, at the site of El Tajín.

STE

TEOTIHUACAN MASKS

> The great stone masks that have been discovered at Teotihuacan . . . are justly renowned for their severe beauty. They undoubtedly must be counted among the elite of art productions achieved by the people of ancient America. (Linné 2003a: 137)

Teotihuacan's life-sized stone masks, long appreciated for their restrained aesthetic, remain one of the most enigmatic categories of objects from Teotihuacan. They represent a significant investment of labor and valuable materials, and yet their role is not altogether clear. The mask is "frequently seen as the masterpiece of the Teotihuacan style of lapidary art, [but it] was highly standardized. It was not a portrait mask" (Turner 1992: 109). Dozens, if not hundreds, of these masks exist.

Nor could these pieces have functioned as masks in the common modern sense of being positioned over a living person's face—few of them have been carved on the back to accommodate facial features, and they are too heavy to have been worn, even with the support of a headdress framework. Possibly, however, "at least some of them were tied on to the outside of bundles containing dead persons" (Linné 2003a: 138). With the addition of a mask, the mortuary bundle would have been given an active face.

The use of masks in ancient Mesoamerica goes far beyond the occasional masquerade experienced in modern Euro-American culture. In Mesoamerica, masks are, to this day, an important component of costumes worn in traditional festivals and permit an individual to take on roles in plays and processions. In ancient Mexico, the meanings of masks would have been far more complex, because their ritual roles would have been thought to transform the wearers into different beings with different powers.

Thus ancient masks signal this other dimension—a transcendence of everyday life, a conversation with another world. Teotihuacan masks are presumed to have functioned in this way. When attached to the mortuary bundles of important persons, they would have animated the bundles, which were probably displayed, "set up in temples to be venerated as spirits" (Pasztory 1998a: 69), and they may have been consulted as oracles (Headrick 1999).

The manner of display is suggested by figurines that represent funerary bundle figures. This type consists of an almost conical body, surmounted by a mask-like face or head (Taube 2000a: 306–307). One of these, found in the north side of the Ciudadela, had a removable mask, and the figurine "was part of an offering found in a tomb . . . a funerary bundle figure" (Cabrera 1990: 98).

Mask use in a ritual setting is also suggested by the "theater censer," an elaborate ceramic composite artifact in which a masked figure, its face conforming to the proportions of the Teotihuacan mask, is displayed in a setting perhaps representing a shrine or temple. Limited archaeological evidence supports this hypothesis: only a few stone masks have been found in archaeological context at Teotihuacan in the past 50 years,[27] and they "came from the major temples of the state near the Street of the Dead. The censers made in the cheaper medium of clay may have been entire miniature household temples with the deity represented only by a mask" (Pasztory 1993e: 54). The theater censer figure's mask-like face often wears another mask over the mouth and is thus a masked mask, a distillation of the city's enigmatic quality.

Teotihuacan life-sized stone masks are among the most famous artifacts associated with this culture, and in addition to the dozen or so masks or mask fragments found in context, there are many unprovenienced examples. The proportions and style of these masks are also known from the often much smaller ceramic masks and figurine faces and heads, and even from masks made of wood. All display a highly standardized style: the face is usually about as wide as it is long. The upper part of the head is somewhat squared. The forehead forms a smooth plane above an expressionless and often nearly horizontal brow line. The eyes are open and seem alert, but are also without emotional expression, even where there are lapidary insets representing the iris and sclera. The nose is prominent and fairly narrow. The lips are full, and the mouth is slightly open and also expressionless, including the mouths that still bear inset teeth made of shell. The lower part of the face is oval, with a rounded chin. The masks have ear-like projections that are blocky vertical rectangles. The back of the mask is usually not hollowed out, thus rendering it unsuitable for accommodating the features of an individual wearing it.

Stone masks varied considerably as to the type of material used, which included various greenstones (such as jadeite) and also calcite and andesite. Thus there is a range of color and hardness. Stone and shell of contrasting color were used to make the insets representing parts of the eye and the teeth.

STE

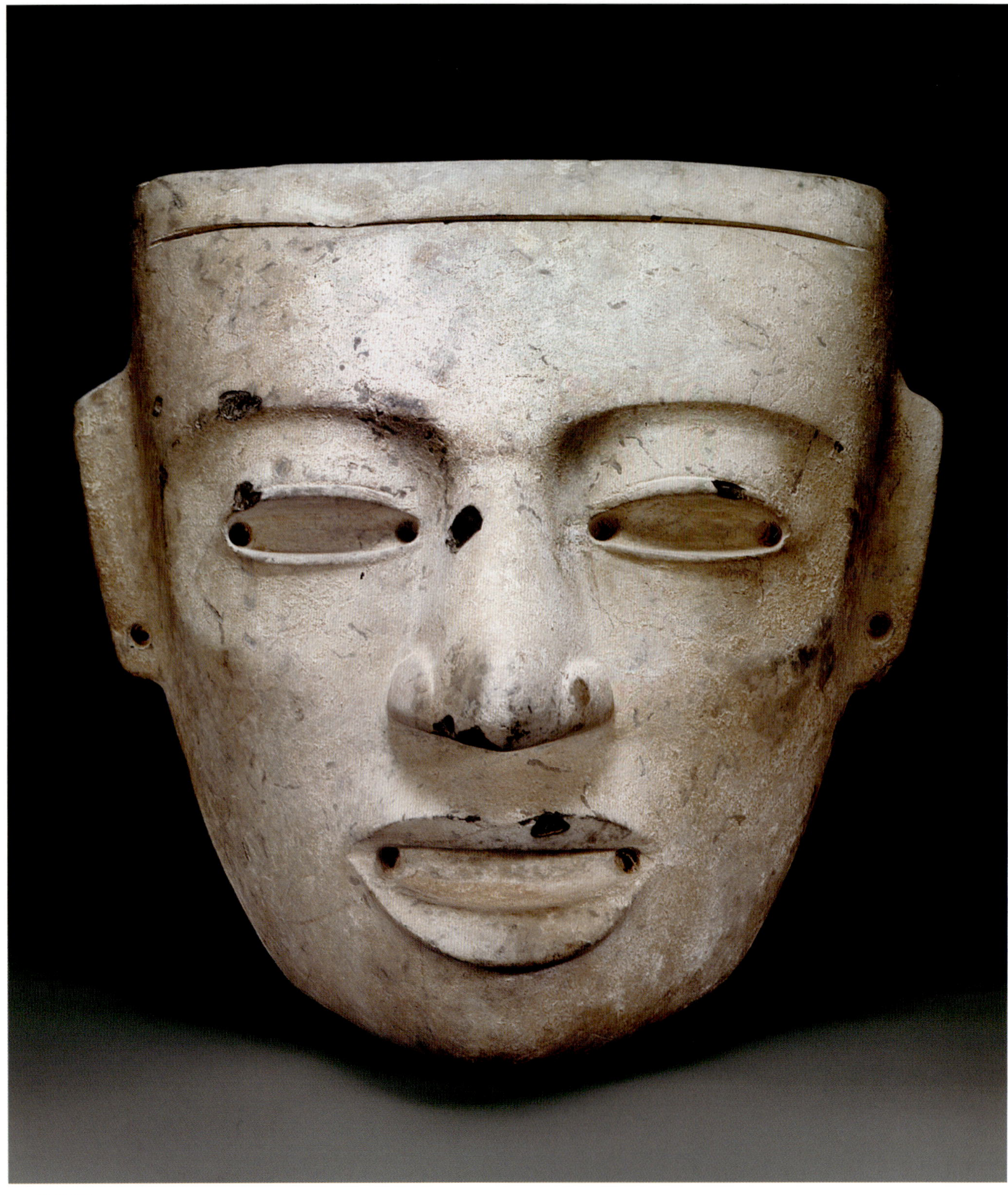

plate 12

PLATE 12
Teotihuacan
Terminal Formative and Early Classic periods, AD 0–600
Black limestone
H. 25.0 cm (9⅞"); W. 25.5 cm (10"); D. 14.5 cm (5¾")
PC.B.053

ACQUISITION HISTORY:
Purchased from William Spratling, 1940

EXHIBITION HISTORY:
Ancient American Art, Santa Barbara Museum of Art, Santa Barbara, Calif., April–June 1942; M. H. de Young Memorial Museum, San Francisco, July–August 1942; Museum of Art, Portland, Ore., September–October 1942; *Indigenous Art of the Americas*, National Gallery of Art, Washington, D.C., April 1947–July 1949, February 1954–July 1962 (NGA 52)

BIBLIOGRAPHY:
Santa Barbara Museum of Art 1942: cat. no. 154; Bliss 1947: 25, 122, cat. no. 120; *Artes de México* 1957: pl. 20; Bliss 1957: 238, cat. no. 34, fig. 12, pl. XXVII; *Natural History* 1958: 128–129; Dumbarton Oaks 1963: 1, cat. no. 1; Willey 1966: 115, fig. 3-51; Grey 1978, pl. 5; Davies 1983, pl. 11

Mask PC.B.053 is a classic example of this Classic art form. Its proportions are balanced and elegant; its features conform to established standards. A band along the top of the forehead is etched by a linear incision parallel to the top of the mask. The ears have been drilled through, and drilling also is present at the sides and top, where the hole extends from the upper edge of the mask to the back, not through the forehead. The back has been finished flat and is slightly concave. Cavities drilled into the corners of the eyes and mouth are of the same size, and the insets that would have enlivened the eyes and mouth are missing. The underside of the nose is flat. The mask's color, once the black of its stone, has aged to a soft gray.

STE

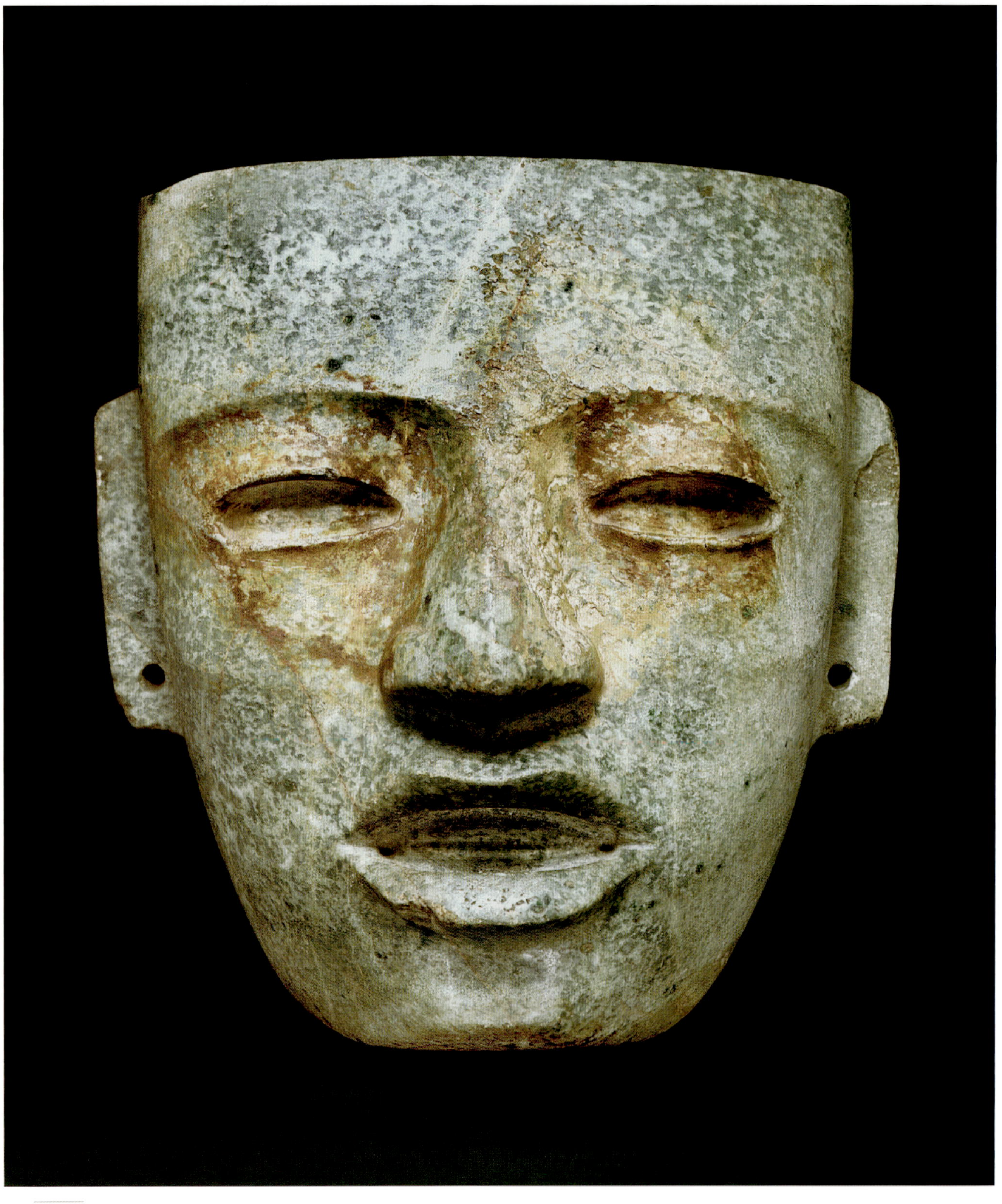

plate 13

PLATE 13
Teotihuacan
Terminal Formative and Early Classic periods, AD 0–600
Green serpentine
H. 21.6 cm (8½"); W. 20.5 cm (8⅛"); D. 10.5 cm (4⅛")
PC.B.054

ACQUISITION HISTORY:
Purchased from Joseph Brummer, 1937

EXHIBITION HISTORY:
Ancient American Art, Santa Barbara Museum of Art, Santa Barbara, Calif., April–June 1942; M. H. de Young Memorial Museum, San Francisco, July–August 1942; Museum of Art, Portland, Ore., September–October 1942; *Indigenous Art of the Americas*, National Gallery of Art, Washington, D.C., April 1947–July 1962 (NGA 50); *Teotihuacan: City of the Gods*, M. H. de Young Memorial Museum, San Francisco, May–October, 1993

BIBLIOGRAPHY:
Santa Barbara Museum of Art 1942: cat. no. 201; Bliss 1947: 25, 53, cat. no. 121; Bliss 1957: 239, cat. no. 36, pl. XXVIII; Dumbarton Oaks 1963: 2, cat. no. 2; Pasztory 1988a: 63, fig. III.15; Pasztory 1992: 294, fig. 11; Turner 1992: 90, fig. 1a; Berrin and Pasztory 1993: 186, plate opposite p. 186; Braun 1993: photo on p. 109; Pasztory 1997: 130; Pasztory 1998a: 65, fig. 44; Seipel 1998: 225, cat. no. 77, fig. 1; Headrick 2007: 55, fig. 3.8, cover; Vila Llonch 2008h: 202–203

Like PC.B.053 (Plate 12), mask PC.B.054 exemplifies what we have come to accept as the strict format of the Teotihuacan mask tradition: the serene, expressionless face, achieved through a series of smooth planes and gentle repetitive curves. The eyes and mouth lack the inserts of lapidary stone and shell that would have made the mask somewhat less abstract. The ears are elongated rectangular protuberances, drilled through toward the lower edge, perhaps to allow adornment with jewelry or to permit the mask to be secured to a framework or mortuary bundle.

The original green color of the stone has been altered around the eyes, apparently from a yellow residue that results from the decay of iron pyrite, which may have formed part of the lapidary inserts of the eyes (Pasztory 1993b: 186). Our aesthetic appreciation is engaged by the high level of artisanship and by the balanced beauty of its proportions.[28]

STE

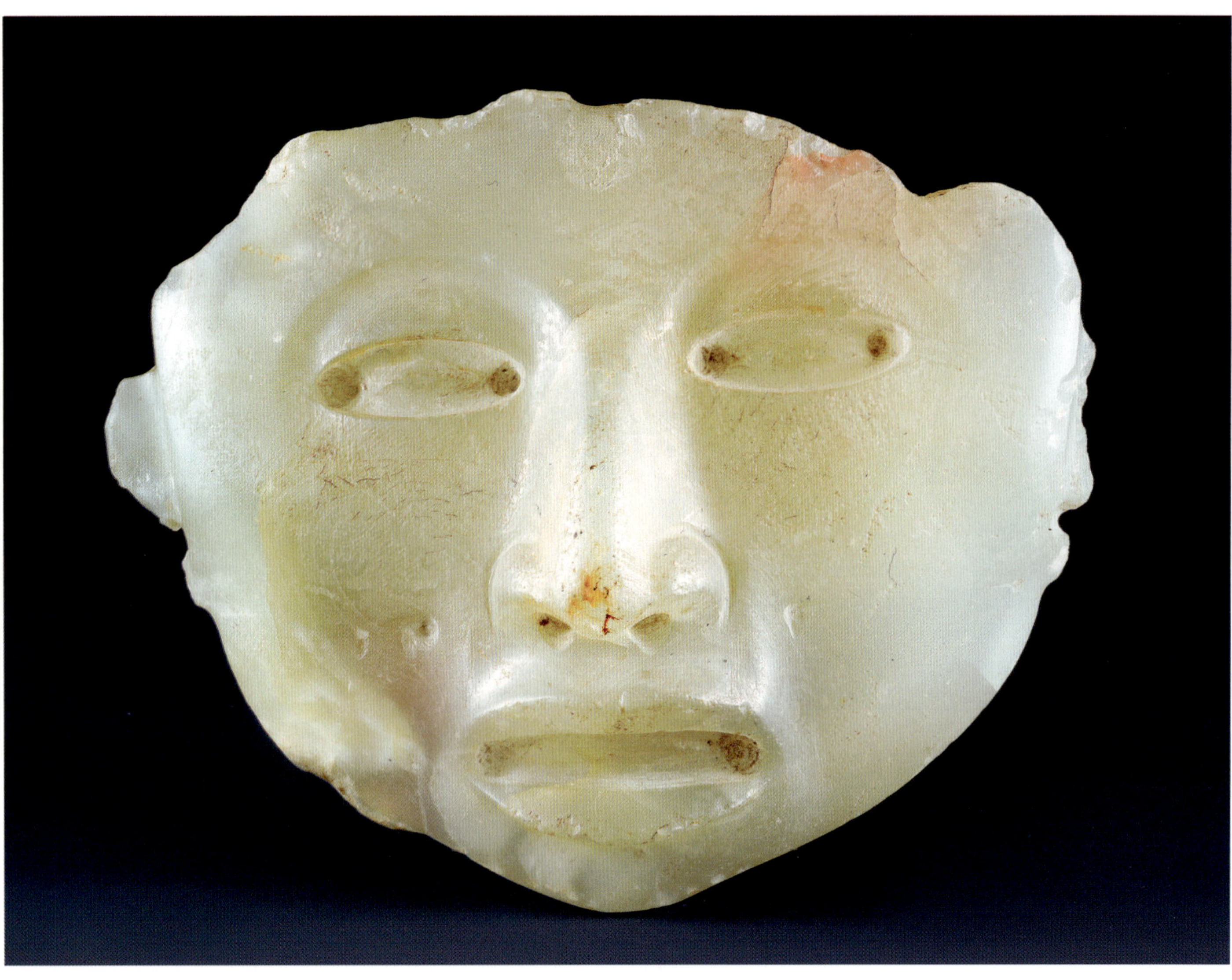

plate 14

MASK

PLATE 14
Teotihuacan
Terminal Formative and Early Classic periods, AD 0–600
Onyx
H. 11.8 cm (4⅝"); W. 15.0 cm (5⅞"); D. 5.3 cm (2⅛")
PC.B.056

ACQUISITION HISTORY:
Purchased at Sotheby's, June 9, 1937; formerly in the collection of Jean Holland

EXHIBITION HISTORY:
Ancient American Art, Santa Barbara Museum of Art, Santa Barbara, Calif., April–June 1942; M. H. de Young Memorial Museum, San Francisco, July–August 1942; Museum of Art, Portland, Ore., September–October 1942; *Indigenous Art of the Americas*, National Gallery of Art, Washington, D.C., April 1947–May 1948, February 1954–July 1962 (NGA 44)

BIBLIOGRAPHY:
Sotheby's 1937: no. 179, pl. IV; Santa Barbara Museum of Art 1942: cat. no. 149; Bliss 1947: 20, 98, cat. no. 93; Read 1956: pl. 149; *Artes de México* 1957: pl. 8; Bliss 1957: 239, cat. no. 38, pl. XXX; Dumbarton Oaks 1963: 2, cat. no. 4

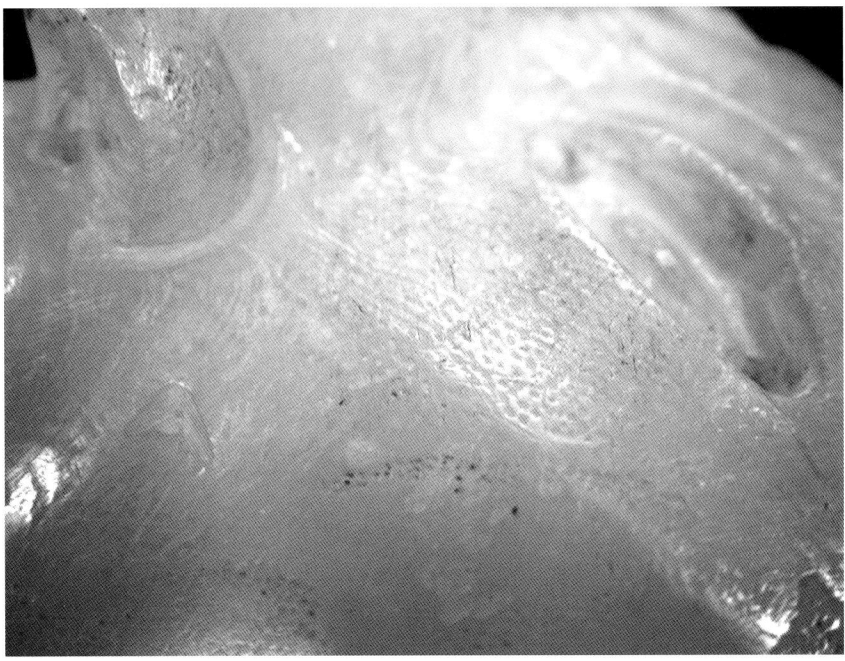

fig. 11
The fiber impression on the surface of Teotihuacan onyx mask PC.B.056 is clearly visible in this close-up. Photograph by William Barnes.

Mask PC.B.056 is not a perfect work of art. Unlike masks PC.B.053 (Plate 12) and PC.B.054 (Plate 13), PC.B.056 is broken, and its surface has been chipped and eroded. Yet its proportions and features are quite clearly good examples of the genre, and its flaws make it one of the most interesting of the Teotihuacan objects in the collection.

The mask is made of a type of calcite known as Mexican onyx; the material may have come from the mining area near the present-day town of Tecali in Puebla, Mexico. Although onyx is an admirably durable material for the production of architectural elements and portable art, it is vulnerable to erosion and less resistant to water than is plaster (Rae Beaubien, personal communication, 23 August 2002).

This mutability of onyx has made the mask's front surface a welter of erosion scars, with several areas on the forehead, around the eyes, the nose, and the cheeks repeating the same pattern of textile impressions. The mask has no textile impressions on its back surface. These erosion patterns indicate the coincidence of three probable circumstances: the mask was immersed in water (or at least kept damp) for a long time, the mask's front was wrapped in textiles, and its back was not. These circumstances would occur if the mask had been affixed to a bundle, and then the whole thing wrapped in textiles.

The fabric is a plain weave with approximately 30 x 25 threads per square inch (Figure 11), comparable to a medium grade of modern cheesecloth (28 x 24 threads per square inch). We do not know whether the fabric that impressed mask PC.B.056 was cotton or a bast fiber, such as maguey (*Agave*; century plant). Maguey was grown in the Central Highlands, but cotton would have been imported from a tropical region, such as the Gulf Lowlands.

Mask PC.B.056 provides valuable and intriguing evidence about textiles: it gives an idea of the kind of fabric that would have been used in binding a precious stone mask to an important bundle, probably a mummy bundle. This evidence also reminds us that there is much that we do not understand about the lives of the Teotihuacanos, and one of those areas of enigma pertains to the production of the cloth that was so clearly in abundant use.

STE

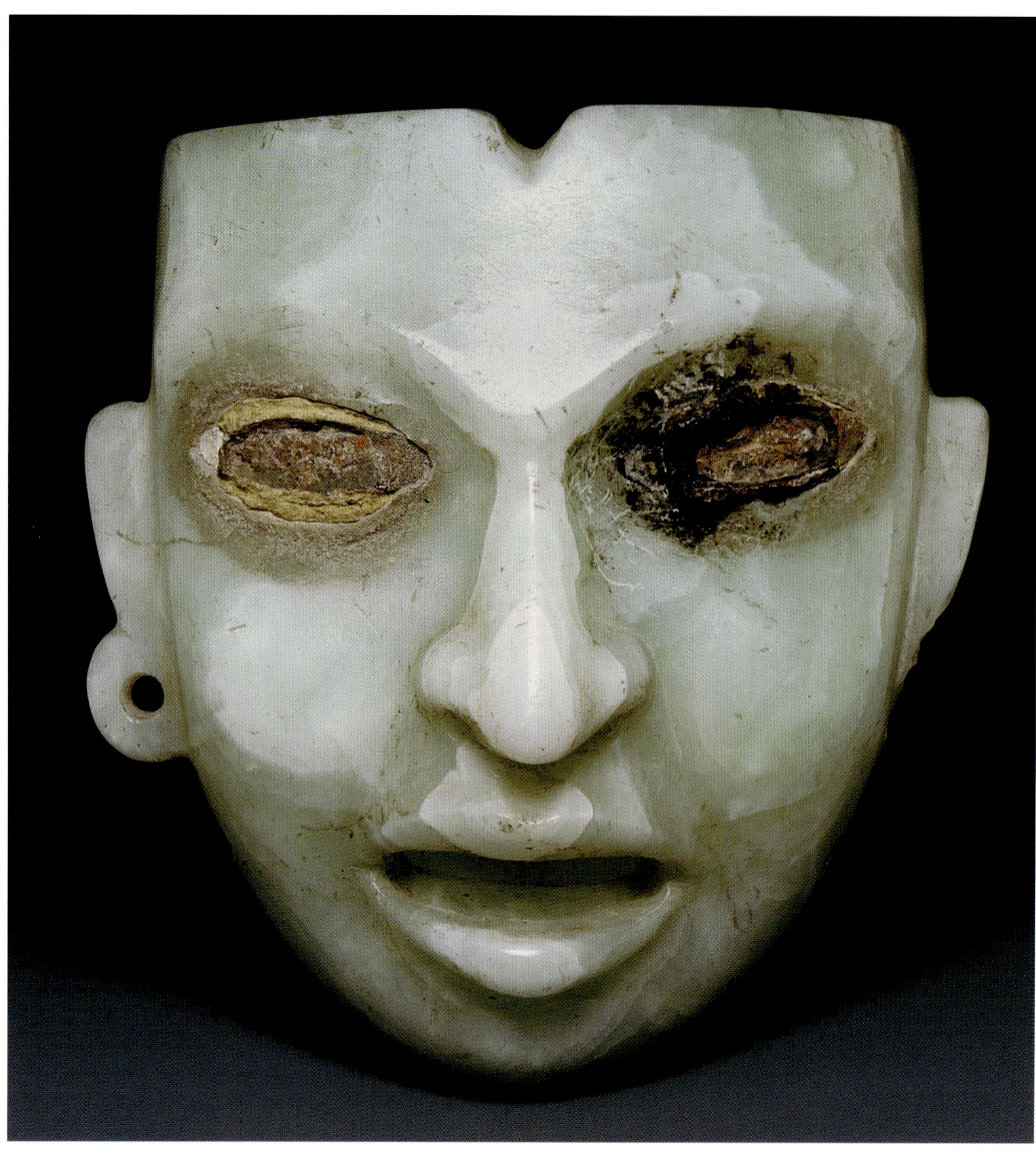

plate 15

MASK

PLATE 15
Teotihuacan style
Classic or Postclassic period, AD 0–1520
Onyx
H. 18.0 cm (7⅛"); W. 17.2 cm (6¾"); D. 7.2 cm (2⅞")
PC.B.055

ACQUISITION HISTORY:
Purchased from Earl Stendahl, 1948

EXHIBITION HISTORY:
Indigenous Art of the Americas, National Gallery of Art, Washington, D.C., May 1948–July 1954, January 1956–July 1962 (NGA 392); *Teotihuacan: City of the Gods*, M. H. de Young Memorial Museum, San Francisco, May–October 1993

BIBLIOGRAPHY:
Bliss 1957: 239, cat. no. 35; Fabbri and Gibelli 1965: 50, photo; Dumbarton Oaks 1963: 2, cat. no. 3; Alcina Franch 1983: pl. 62; Berrin and Pasztory 1993: plate on p. 14, 188; Headrick 1999: 74–76, fig. 10

Mask PC.B.055's pale green onyx marble surface is highly polished, but what first commands attention is the corroded surface in the eye cavities, probably the remains of inserts of iron pyrite (Pasztory 1993c: 188). Several other features of PC.B.055 set it apart from Teotihuacan-style masks that conform more closely to an aesthetic program of standardized features. One unusual feature is the high polish, achieved either in antiquity or perhaps much more recently.

The second non-Teotihuacan feature is a set of anomalies, the most important of which pertain to facial expression rather than to violation of strict tenets regarding form. Compared to other Teotihuacan-style masks, PC.B.055 presents some definite departures from the norm. The notched forehead is unusual in such masks, more commonly associated with Olmec examples, but some Teotihuacan face depictions have this notch. The notch is also explicable as the result of reworking a mask that had a hole in the middle of the upper forehead and was broken, such that the flaw could be corrected by making the mask vertically shorter. Furthermore, one of the only masks found in context has a slight but definite shallow depression at top center (Cabrera 1993b: 186).

If the top of the mask had been broken and reworked, however, then the original mask would have been abnormally elongated. Most Teotihuacan masks are roughly equal in their horizontal and vertical dimensions, and PC.B.055, even in its present form, is remarkably long for a Teotihuacan mask. Another anomaly is the ear, which has a circular ear lobe (proper right on the mask—the left "ear lobe" is broken); it is common for the ears on these masks to be long rectangles.

These features—height to width proportions, shape of the ear—differ from the norm for Teotihuacan masks. The greatest difference, however, is in the overall impression conveyed by the facial features, rather more difficult to quantify, but obvious as a constellation of attributes. In contrast to typical Teotihuacan masks, PC.B.055 is more expressive. The brows are deeply arched, and the nose is far more substantially modeled.

In fact, a review of this mask cited these very characteristics as making it valuable: "In contrast to the absolute abstraction of many masks, in which the character of the face seems to be reduced to simple geometric motifs, this example from the Bliss Collection has the almost pathetic intensity of a portrait; the suffering lips, partly open as if in the instant before death, grant it a human reality"[29] (Fabbri and Gibelli 1965: 50).

The topic of subjectiveness in Mesoamerican portraiture is worthy of a far more intensive examination than can be offered here. However, I can assert that although subjective portraiture is *not* a characteristic of Teotihuacan art, it is found elsewhere in art of the Classic period (as in certain Maya portraits), and there are also examples in other time periods and other regional traditions. PC.B.055 may represent an anomalous style of mask from Teotihuacan, or it may represent an homage to the Teotihuacan mask, rendered by an artisan working in another culture.[30]

STE

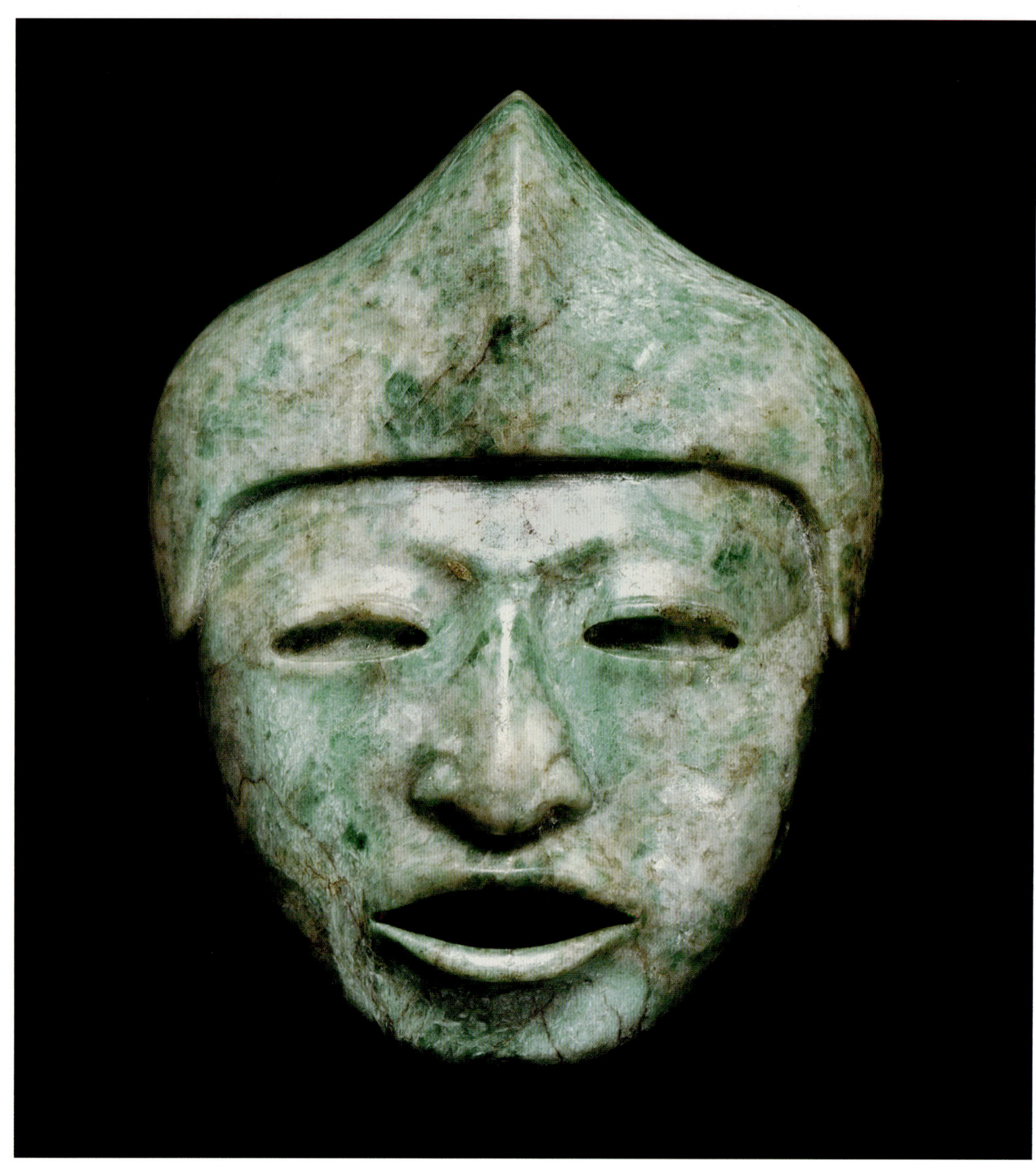

plate 16

PLATE 16
Teotihuacan
Terminal Formative and Early Classic periods, AD 0–600
Jadeite
H. 7.0 cm (2¾"); W. 5.5 cm (2⅛"); D. 1.9 cm (¾")
PC.B.059

ACQUISITION HISTORY:
Purchased from Ernest Brummer, 1947

EXHIBITION HISTORY:
An Exhibition of Pre-Columbian Art, Fogg Art Museum, Cambridge, January–March 1940; Art of the Americas, Cleveland Museum of Art, Cleveland, Ohio, November 1945–January 1946; *Ancient American Gold and Jade*, Taft Museum, Cincinnati, Ohio, October–November 1950; *Indigenous Art of the Americas*, National Gallery of Art, Washington, D.C., May 1948–April 1962 (NGA 378)

BIBLIOGRAPHY:
Kelemen 1937: pl. 2, left; Peabody Museum of Archaeology and Ethnology and Fogg Art Museum 1940: cat. no. 165; Kelemen 1943: 302, pl. 247.c and on cover, and illustrated on dust jacket of 1956 edition; Cleveland Museum of Art 1946: picture book no. 2: 28; Taft Museum 1950: cat. no. 17 and frontispiece; Bliss 1957: 239, cat. no. 37, pl. XXIX; Gump 1962: 191; Dumbarton Oaks 1963: 2, cat. no. 6; Benson 1993

Teotihuacan masks come in several sizes that are worked in several different media. Best known are the life-sized renditions worked in stone. There are also countless examples of the same type of face but measuring about one inch across and made of clay. Some wooden masks also survive (see below). PC.B.059 is an unusual case, a stone mask of standard proportions but unusual size, less than three inches tall, including its pointed hat. The size thus distinguishes this example from the typical stone mask; other distinctive features are the notable delicacy of the carving and the perforation of the mask at the mouth.

There are two comparable examples of small masks in Teotihuacan style. One is made of wood, and measures 3 inches by 4 inches (Pasztory 1993d: 193, photo on p. 84). The other, of stone, was found by Sigvald Linné during his excavations at the Xolalpan compound in Teotihuacan in 1932 (Linné 2003a: 138, fig. 275). This mask has been reconstructed from a fragment, with reconstructed dimensions of 2⅜ inches high by 2¼ inches wide by 1¼ inches deep—roughly comparable to PC.B.059. Thus we can assume that this small mask is an atypical example of the larger tradition, but it is not unique.

The unusual features of this piece, combined with its fine material and high quality of artisanship, make it enormously attractive. It is an object that inspires a kind of affectionate loyalty, and was apparently long in the possession of the early twentieth-century collector Joseph Brummer, who "refused to part with it during his lifetime" (Lothrop in Bliss 1957: 239, cat. no. 37). Joseph Brummer had acquired it in Paris, and the object was reputed to have belonged to the widow of Porfirio Díaz, president of Mexico until the Mexican Revolution of 1911, when he fled into exile in Paris and died in 1915. It would have had intrinsic appeal for Robert Bliss, whose taste in Pre-Columbian objects favored polished stone pieces of small size and elegant design.

STE

AZTECS:
ART FROM THE GREAT EMPIRE

SUSAN TOBY EVANS

The greatest empire to arise in Mesoamerica was that of the Aztecs, who ruled over a broad swath of the Middle American subcontinent for a few short decades, and then saw their domain absorbed into Spain's growing realm. The Aztecs included the Mexica, who settled on swampy islands in Lake Texcoco some time after the fall of Tula and established there the city of Tenochtitlan-Tlatelolco, which later became Mexico City.

The dedication of the city is thought to have occurred in ca. AD 1325, and by the 1370s the Tenochca Mexica had petitioned for and received a noble from the prestigious Culhua lineage to rule them and found their dynastic line. Until ca. AD 1430, the Mexica were vassals of a neighboring group, the Tepanecs, who had built up a confederation of tributary city-states in the Basin of Mexico. In ca. 1430, the Mexica joined forces with another disaffected city-state, Texcoco, and together they vanquished the Tepanecs and took over the confederation.

From this modest beginning, the Aztec Empire grew, and after the 1450s it expanded vigorously outside the Basin of Mexico. The ruling dynasties grew increasingly wealthy, and their cities became beautiful and elaborate. Ritual precincts and palaces were enlarged, and the objects that adorned them were increasingly refined in material and execution. All this culture change took place over the course of 90 years, and even though the Mexica could not have known how short their career was to be, they strove to burnish their reputation by drawing on the artistic and ideological traditions of the Toltecs and (more distantly in terms of continuity) of Teotihuacan. They sought artisans conversant with the sophisticated styles developed in the Mixteca-Puebla region southeast of the Basin of Mexico.

Sculpture was the most important plastic art form in the heartland of Aztec society, and the empire's rulers oversaw an era of "production of major works of sculpture such as the world has rarely seen. . . . In Tenochtitlan alone, the number of monumental pieces of outstanding sculptural quality . . . is formidable, and these represent but a fraction of the total pieces which must have been on display when the Spaniards entered the city in the fall of 1519" (Nicholson 1971a: 115). Many Aztec sculptures were systematically destroyed in the early years following the conquest.

The most monumental of these, such as the statue of the goddess Coatlicue,[31] are massive indeed and represent the most ambitious and complex projects attempted by Aztec sculptors. There are also much smaller pieces that are impressive,[32] and many sculptures survive that are unprepossessing in design and crude in execution; clearly, there was a great range in size and quality.

Aztec-style sculptures in the Bliss Collection vary in scale, but all pieces exhibit a high standard of quality. There are three serpent sculptures, two of them very large coiled snakes (PC.B.069 and PC.B.070, Plates 19 and 17, respectively) and the third (PC.B.077, Plate 18) a finely executed serpent head. The magnificent mask of the god Tezcatlipoca (PC.B.072, Plate 20) is one of most sensitive works in all of Aztec sculpture. The sculpted head of an old man (PC.B.058, Plate 21) recalls Mesoamerican culture's long-term veneration of the Old Fire God, and another sculpted head, a skull (PC.B.081, Plate 22), evokes the cultural preoccupation with death. Another death's head appears on the side of a cup (PC.B.080, Plate 23), in much the same style as the "pulque cups" found in excavations at the Templo Mayor of Tenochtitlan.

Themes of life and death motivate the design of these sculptures. The Aztecs revered serpents, because they regularly emerge anew from their old skins, a life-after-death scenario.[33] Death was inevitable, but fertility (human or agricultural) was not—and thus the Aztecs also honored fertility in sculpture. Two pieces in the Bliss Collection that honor the Aztec tradition of this theme are small (about 8 inches high) polished greenstone sculptures: one is a woman in childbirth (PC.B.071, Plate 25), and the other, a crouching rabbit (PC.B.079, Plate 26).

It is likely many of these pieces date to the last 70 years or so before European intrusion into the Aztec world, and two pieces (the Fire Serpent, PC.B.069, and the Tezcatlipoca mask, PC.B.072) bear glyph dates that may indicate AD 1507, the last of the great New Fire Ceremonies that were arguably the most important events in Aztec ritual life. Most of the other pieces are in a style consistent with this last phase of the Late Postclassic period, particularly from the later fifteenth and early sixteenth centuries, when the wealth of an empire flowed into Tenochtitlan and Texcoco, and master artisans executed the prestigious works that adorned the temples and palaces of their cities. The woman in childbirth (PC.B.071) and the crouching rabbit (PC.B.079), both Aztec in style, may have been produced or heavily altered in the late nineteenth or early twentieth century.

The Aztec-style sculptures in the Bliss Collection reflect the mature phase of this genre in their themes and generally in their design. This Aztec sculptural tradition had developed under the patronage of the Tepanecs, before the Mexica and their allies claimed the Tepanec domain (Nicholson 1971a: 113–114). The Aztecs so revered Toltec traditions that they looted Tula for relics, but more importantly they imitated the massive blocky forms of Toltec sculptural style (Umberger 1987: 72). However, Aztec sculpture was more realistic, with more standardized iconography.

Aztec sculpture was also highly influenced by the designs that came from the Mixteca-Puebla area, with its famed and far-reaching artistic influence. Mixteca-Puebla style expresses "particular precision in the delineation of symbols and motifs, plus their considerable standardization. . . . an almost Disneyesque, caricaturelike stylistic quality" (Nicholson 1973: 73). Aztec sculptural style can be thought of as a subtradition of Mixteca-Puebla style, one that was distinguished by "a greater degree of depictive 'realism' and literalness" (Nicholson 1973: 73). For example, Aztec "relief style" closely imitates Mixteca-Puebla "pictorial style of the paper and skin books" (Nicholson 1971a: 119).

However, the Aztecs developed their own distinctive sculptural style: many Mesoamerican cultures have sculpted serpents, but this subject became a signature for the Aztecs, who focused on the rattlesnake. The Aztecs developed the three-dimensional coiled serpent as their "most famous and successful method of representation" which was, however, "apparently unknown or extremely rare before Aztec times" (Nicholson 1971a: 129).[34]

The coiled posture is associated with an aggressive attack position characteristic of Aztec serpent sculpture (Uriarte 1982: 256). In fact, snakes can strike from many postures, and Aztec coiled serpents includes tall coils with extended heads and others that are more casually arranged. The two complete coiled serpents in the Bliss Collection, both exceptional examples of this genre, display a marked contrast in their iconographic programs. One (PC.B.070) has the elegance that comes from a strong simple design, masterfully executed on a large scale. From its size and shape, we can tentatively attribute the serpent head (PC.B.077) to this category as well. The other, the Fire Serpent (PC.B.069), is the simple coiled rattler's counterpart, a serpent who served as the god Huitzilopochtli's fantastic weapon of destruction, and while maintaining the same coiled shape it bears a complicated design embellishing its head, body, tail, and clawed legs.

These serpents are the first objects in Aztec style discussed in the essays that follow. Next I turn to heads and masks, beginning with the Tezcatlipoca mask. Two small sculptures in Aztec style, the woman in childbirth and the rabbit, are then described. The final essay in this section discusses a colonial period composite object, an obsidian mirror in its frame (PC.B.078, Plate 24).

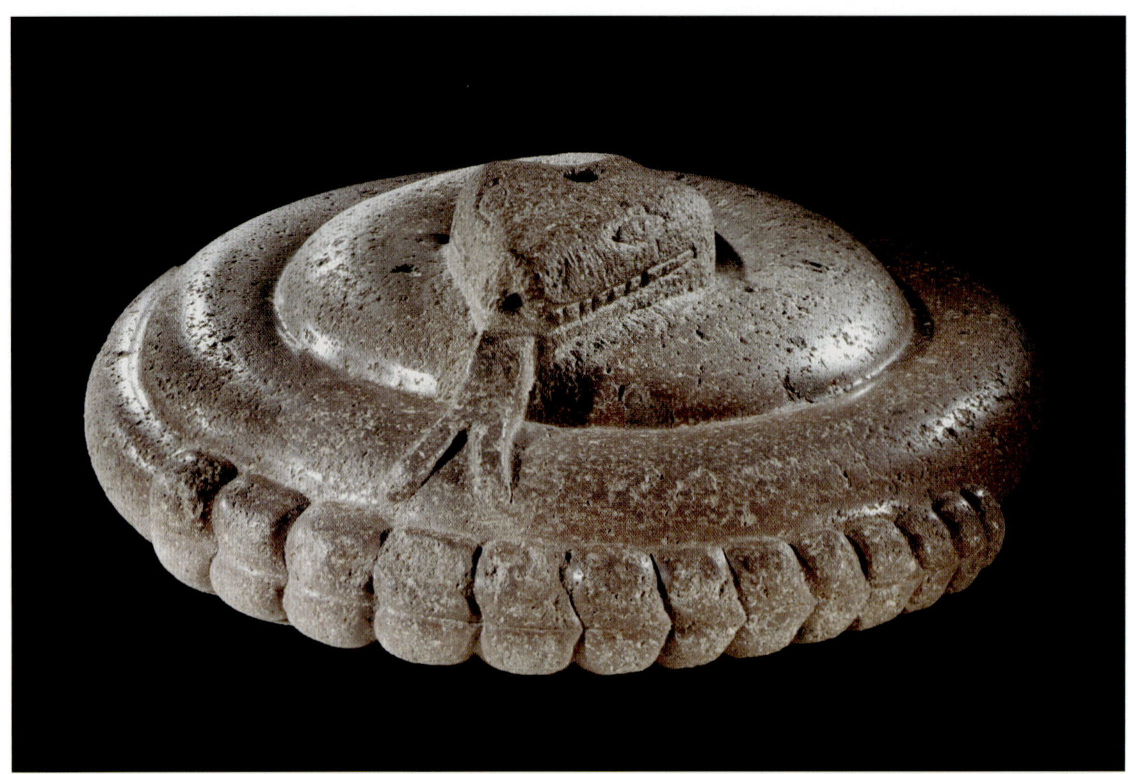

plate 17a
Photograph
by Justin Kerr.

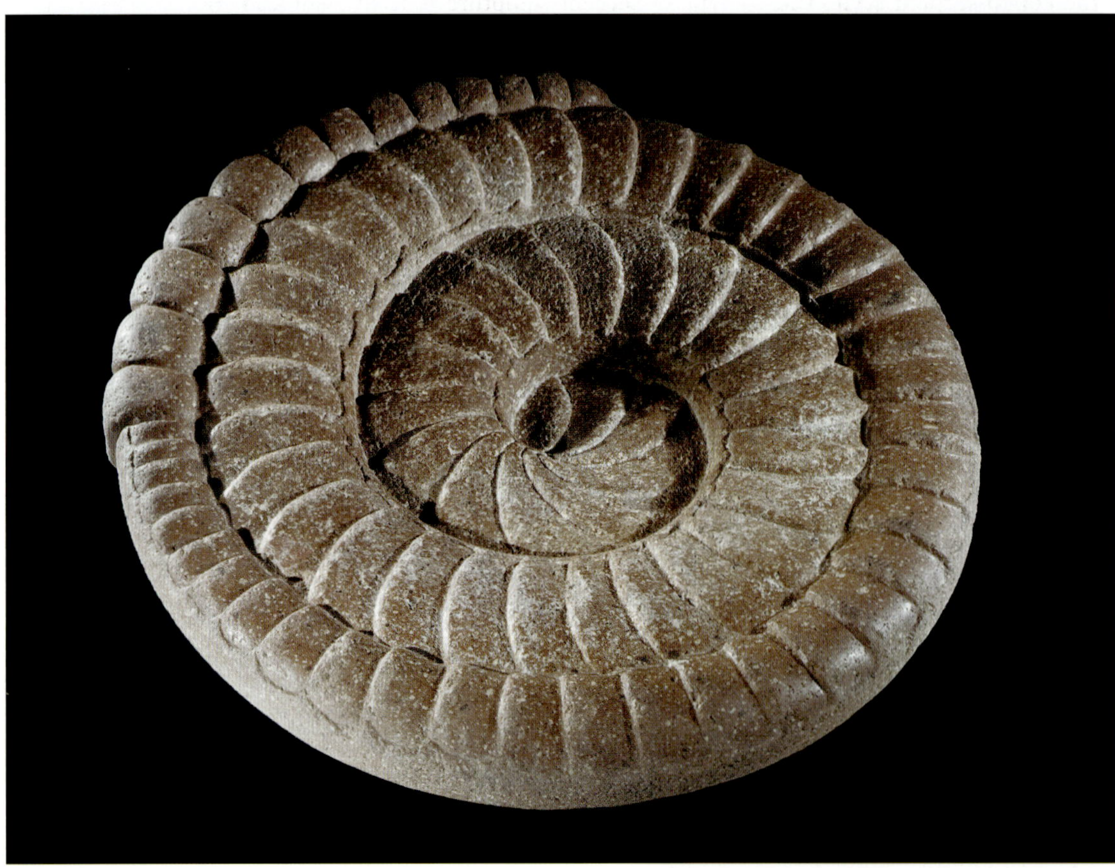

plate 17b,
bottom view.
Photograph
by Justin Kerr.

PLATE 17
Aztec
Late Postclassic period, AD 1200–1520
Rhylolite porphyry
H. 18.3 cm (7¼"); Diam. 60.6 cm (23¾")
PC.B.070

ACQUISITION HISTORY:
Purchased from Earl Stendahl, 1946

EXHIBITION HISTORY:
Indigenous Art of the Americas, National Gallery of Art, Washington, D.C., April 1947–July 1962 (NGA 208); *The Story of Time,* National Maritime Museum, London, December 1999–September 2000

BIBLIOGRAPHY:
Bliss 1947: 23, 112–113, cat. no. 109; Bliss 1957: 242, cat. no. 54, pl. XL, pl. XLI, top; Dockstader 1961: 37; Ishida 1962: 208, fig. 135; Dumbarton Oaks 1963: 23, cat. no. 105; Guirand 1968: 433; Graves 1977: 433; Boone 1982: 158, fig. 11; Kubler 1984: fig. 9; Gutiérrez Solana 1987: 97, pl. 49; Smith 1996: 266, fig. 10.8; Pasztory 1998a: 94–95, figs. 67, 68; Lippincott 1999: 67, cat. no. 057; *Washington Post* 2003: G9

Having pioneered the coiled-serpent style, the Aztecs executed it in a wide range of sizes and proportions. The Coiled Rattlesnake, PC.B.070, exemplifies a flat type. At 2 feet across and about 7 inches high, it is an impressive piece; its overall form is satisfying and nicely crafted.

"Top and bottom it is shaped to represent the living venomous reptile of the countryside with its typical arrow-shaped head poised to strike" (Lothrop in Bliss 1957: 242, cat. no. 54). Comprising a low coil of three or four levels, the serpent's body winds counterclockwise from its flattened head, which is not extended. The head, with shallowly carved eyes and teeth, bears a cylindrical vertical hole on its top, possibly for incense, and a smaller cylindrical horizontal hole at the base of the nose, just above the bifid tongue. This tongue thrusts down from the closed mouth, past two levels of its coiled body, almost touching the set of 13 rattles that form the front quarter of the circumference of the base. This circumference measures about 6 feet, and thus the uncoiled serpent would be about 11 feet long, more than twice as long as most very large living rattlesnakes. This type of serpent sculpture is fairly well known, and other similar examples are found at The Field Museum in Chicago[35] and in the Museo Nacional de Antropología in Mexico City.[36]

The practice of carving the underside of a sculpture as carefully as the visible top part is characteristic of Aztec artisanship (Plate 17b), suggesting that the indigenous attitude valued "all relevant surfaces of certain sacred images whether perceptible to a human observer or not" (Nicholson with Quiñones Keber 1983: 130). Ancient peoples of Mesoamerica perceived a vibrant and interactive world around them, and their intent in producing sculptures had only partially to do with impressing the humans who saw them. To the Aztecs and others, sentience was not an exclusively human trait but also characterized the spiritually charged earth. This sculpture is a telling example of the contrast between modern concepts of art and the traditional world's production of aesthetically masterful pieces whose complicated significance challenges the outsider's understanding.

PC.B.070 bears 13 rattles, as do the examples from The Field Museum and the Museo

Nacional.[37] Although other serpent sculptures have different numbers of rattles, a count of 13 is an important symbolic and divinatory element in Aztec iconography (Gendrop and Díaz 1994: 101). The Aztec divinatory almanac links day names to numbers in groups of 13 (Sahagún 1979c [1569]); in Aztec cosmology, the upper world has 13 levels.

Although many pieces of major Aztec sculpture express the fantastic and hybrid features of the culture's complex iconographic program, the Bliss Collection's Coiled Rattlesnake is a good example of the strong strain of naturalism that characterized some of the most beautiful pieces. Using PC.B.070 as an example, Boone (1982: 158) writes, "Certainly all Aztec art can not be labeled naturalistic, but it would seem that naturalism was tolerated and often sought within the Aztec aesthetic, as is evidenced also by the creation of sensitively rendered sculptures of serpents."

STE

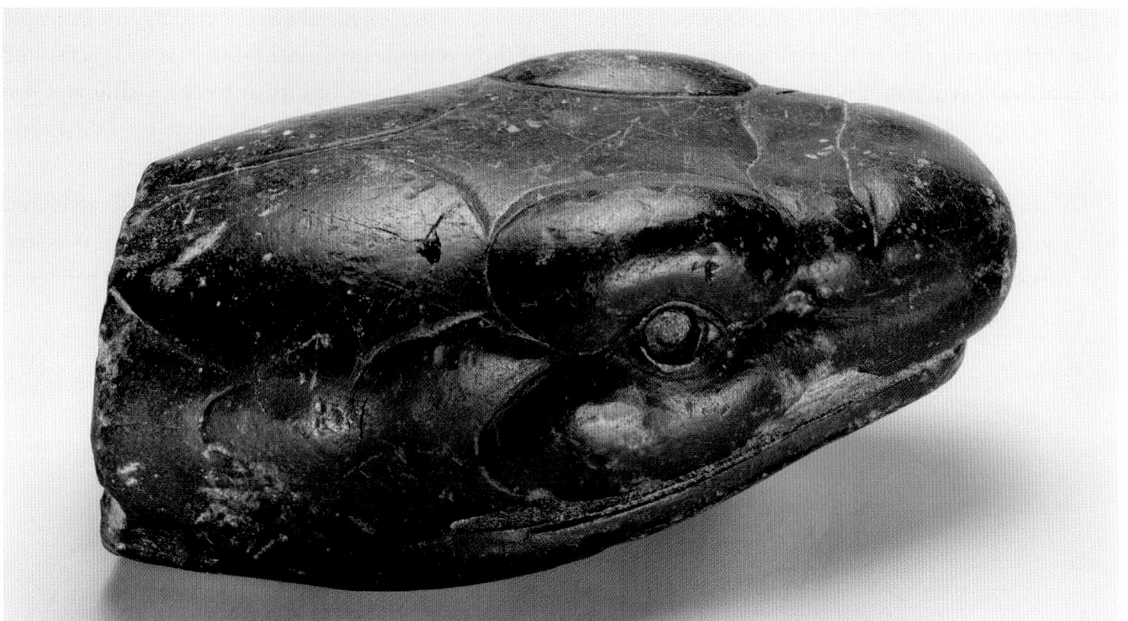

plate 18

HEAD OF A SNAKE

PLATE 18
Aztec
Late Postclassic period, AD 1200–1520
Serpentine
H. 5.9 cm (2¼"); W. 8.2 cm (3¼"); D. 15.4 cm (6")
PC.B.077

ACQUISITION HISTORY:
Purchased from Robert Stolper, 1960

EXHIBITION HISTORY:
Indigenous Art of the Americas, National Gallery of Art, Washington, D.C., August 1960–April 1962 (NGA 760); *Die Azteken und ihre Vorläufer: Glanz und Untergang des Alten Mexico*, Roemer- und Pelizaeus-Museum, Hildesheim, Germany, June–November 1986; Haus der Kunst, Munich, December 1986–March 1987; Oberösterreichisches Landesmuseum, Linz, Austria, April–August 1987; Louisiana Museum of Modern Art, Humlebæk, Denmark, August–November 1987; Musées royaux d'Art et d'Histoire, Brussels, December 1987–March 1988; National Archaeological Museum, Athens, May–July 1988; Société du Palais de la Civilisation, Montreal, July–October 1988

BIBLIOGRAPHY:
Bliss 1957: 242, cat. no. 55, pl. XLI; Dumbarton Oaks 1963: 23, cat. no. 106; Boone 1986f: cat. no. 156; Louisiana Museum 1987: 74, cat. no. 149

This sensitively rendered serpent head probably represents a rattlesnake, with its characteristic lance shape to accommodate the venom-producing glands on either side of the skull (Fergus 2000: 421). The polished stone surface has been incised, detailing the scales on the head and outlining the supraorbital ridges.

The head comprises three broken fragments, rejoined almost invisibly, because the breaks are crisp and show no signs of wear or erosion. The head was probably part of a coiled serpent sculpture. A complete coiled serpent sculpture at the Hamburgisches Museum für Völkerkunde measures 9 inches high and 9½ inches long, and the head, about 5 inches long and extending from the body at about a 40° angle, is similar in size and proportions to PC.B.077.[38]

PC.B.077's balance of form and quality of carving reveal it to have been the work of a master artisan. It "is among the most realistically carved of all the Aztec serpents" (Boone 1986f: cat. no. 156), and it is not significantly flawed by recent minor reworking in the area of the mouth.

STE

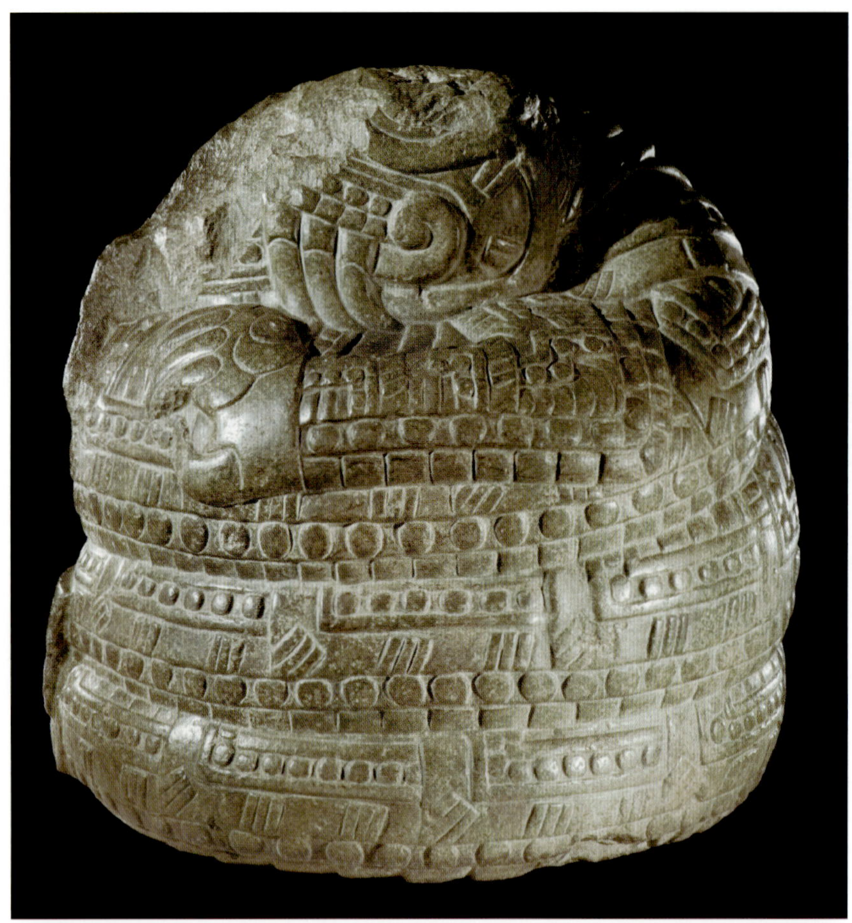

plate 19a, Photograph by Justin Kerr.

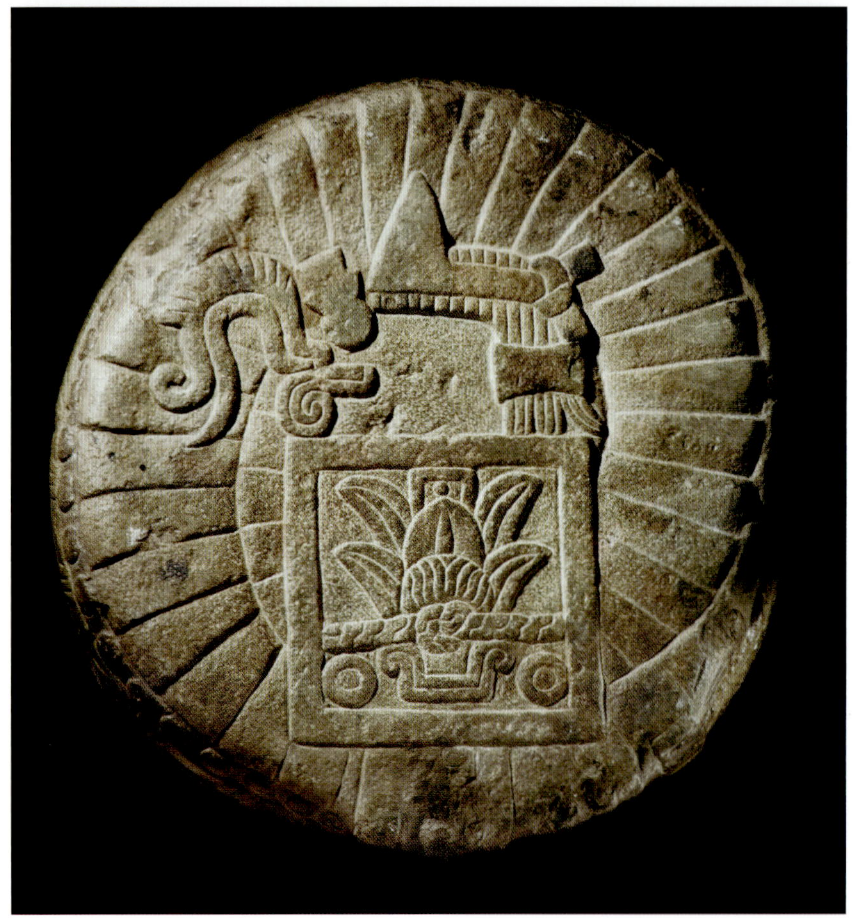

plate 19b, bottom view. Photograph by Justin Kerr.

XIUHCOATL OR FIRE SERPENT

PLATE 19
Aztec
Late Postclassic period, AD 1500–20
Quartz-diorite
H. 43.4 cm (17⅛"); Diam. 45.4 cm (17⅞")
PC.B.069

ACQUISITION HISTORY:
Purchased from William Spratling, 1940

EXHIBITION HISTORY:
American Museum of Natural History, March 1941–June 1942, November 1942–February 1947; *Ancient American Art*, Santa Barbara Museum of Art, Santa Barbara, Calif., April–June 1942; M. H. de Young Memorial Museum, San Francisco, July–August 1942; Museum of Art, Portland, Ore., September–October 1942; *Indigenous Art of the Americas*, National Gallery of Art, Washington, D.C., April 1947–July 1962 (NGA 342); *The Story of Time*, National Maritime Museum, London, December 1999–September 2000; *The Aztec Empire*, Guggenheim Museum, New York, October 2004–February 2005; Guggenheim Museum, Bilbao, Spain, March–September 2005

BIBLIOGRAPHY:
Palacios 1935: 264, figs. 15, 16; Santa Barbara Museum of Art 1942: cat. no. 110; Bliss 1947: 23, 114–115, cat. no. 110; Christensen 1955: 241, 208, fig. 196; *Artes de México* 1957: pl. 3; Bliss 1957: 242, cat. no. 56, fig. 14, bottom, pl. XLII; Robertson 1959: 106–107; Dumbarton Oaks 1963: 23, cat. no. 107; Willey 1966: 162, fig. 3-117, right; Kubler 1984: figs. 10, 11; Gutiérrez 1987: 140, 148, pl. 83; Alcina Franch 1992: 198; Lippincott 1999: 90, cat. no. 083; Traxler 2004a: 35, cat. no. 144; Izeki 2008: 44, 112, fig. 6.17; Vila Llonch 2008b: 190–191

This compact and elaborate sculpture is one of the most important works in the Bliss Collection because of the quality of its execution and the subject of its design. It is a Fire Serpent, whose Nahuatl (Aztec) name, "Xiuhcoatl," means "Turquoise Snake," a hybrid, dragon-like creature whose "origins are probably connected with the celestial dragons of Classic Lowland Maya civilization . . . whose sectioned bodies bore stellar and other celestial symbols" (Nicholson with Quiñones Keber 1983: 47). The word "*xihuitl* signifies 'year,' 'turquoise,' and 'grass' in Nahuatl" (Miller and Taube 1993: 188–189) and invokes associations of preciousness in much the same way as does the word "chalchihuitl."

The Xiuhcoatl represents Tenochca tribal ascendancy, because it was the weapon with which their patron god Huitzilopochtli slew his enemies. Furthermore, the Fire Serpent served the sun and sometimes was thought to have carried it on its trip across the sky (Gutiérrez Solana 1982: 259). It was also associated with Xiuhtecuhtli, the fire god (Pasztory 1983: 83), and sometimes with Tezcatlipoca, supreme deity (Nicholson with Quiñones Keber 1983: 47).

The piece is a blocky mass just under 18 inches across and high. It was once taller, its characteristic crest having been broken off just above the enormous set of fangs, three on each side, which curve from the jaw. We can reconstruct the head's basic

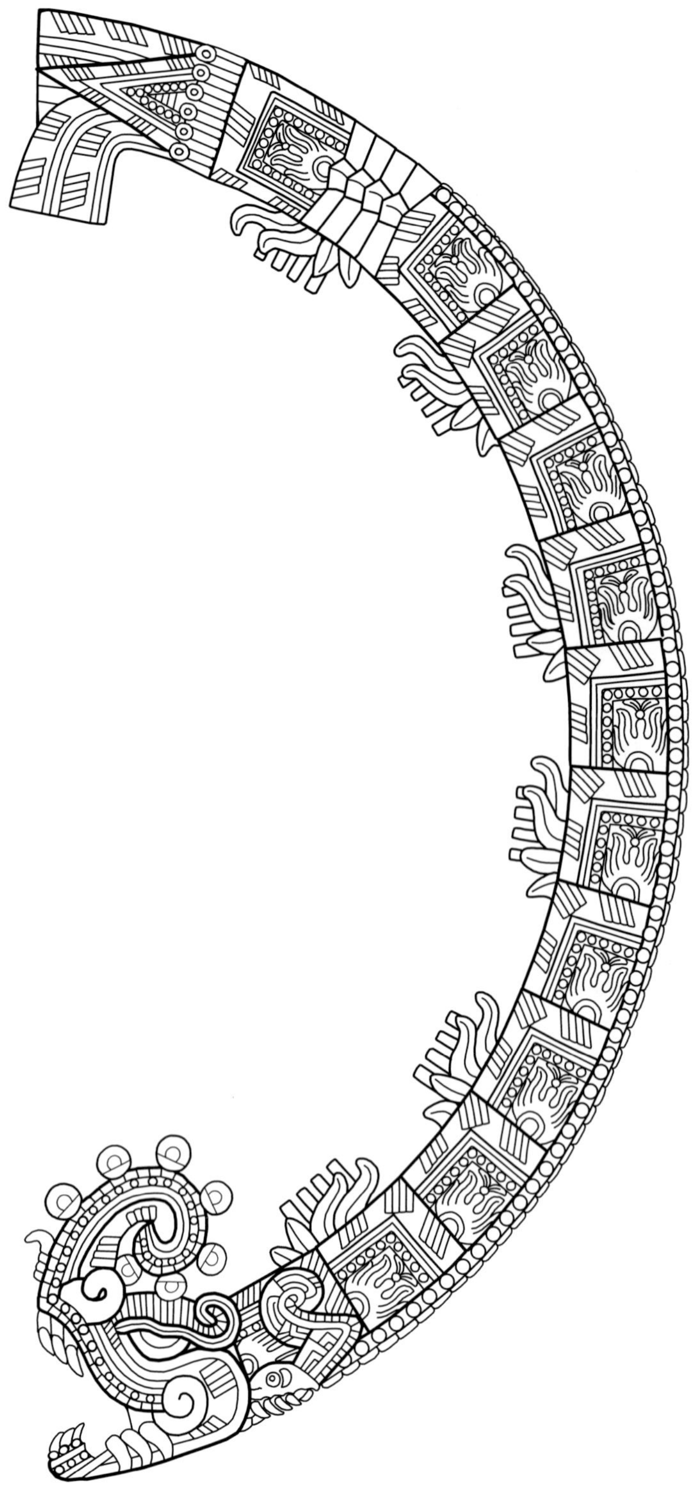

fig. 12
One of two Fire Serpents that together encircle the central motifs of the Aztec Calendar Stone, found in Mexico City. Drawing by Susan Toby Evans (after Pasztory 1983: 83).

features from other examples. Fire Serpent heads were clearly ophidian and so distinctive that they were frequently depicted by themselves, and this practice marks a continuous sculptural tradition extending back to Teotihuacan via Tula.[39] The Xiuhcoatl head typically bears "a peculiar extended snout that curves back on itself and is edged with circular eye symbols, i.e., the eyes of night, the stars" (Nicholson with Quiñones Keber 1983: 47).

Fire Serpents have nonophidian features, such as the arms and claws on PC.B.069. Below the head are three levels of coiled snake, with scales abstracted into a series of square emblems depicting a standardized set of elements. In the case of PC.B.069, the coils of the serpent overlap and obscure the details of these emblems, but other examples of Fire Serpents show the design more clearly. Perhaps the most famous examples are on the Calendar Stone, a great cylinder whose circular flat plane is divided concentrically, with two Fire Serpents comprising the outer ring (Figure 12).[40] On PC.B.069, each square has in its outer rank a set of diagonal triple bars, and inside a frame one side of the set of dots is visible. These, in turn, enclose a flame motif, which on PC.B.069 is obscured.

One of the most significant diagnostic features of the Fire Serpent is its tail. Knotted paper strips precede the trapeze and ray year symbol (*xihuitl*), which suggests "the first element in the creature's name" (Nicholson with Quiñones Keber 1983: 47). On PC.B.069, the stylized paper strips are at the base of the exterior, directly below the damaged face. This motif is an ancient iconographic symbol for sacrifice.[41]

The underside of PC.B.069 (Plate 19b) bears a rich symbolic combination of a date glyph and a name glyph against the background of the serpent's coils. The date glyph, 2 Acatl (reed), occurs in a cartouche, and thus is a year date corresponding to AD 1507, in which the last Pre-Columbian New Fire Ceremony was held. An additional piece of iconographic evidence related to the transition to a new 52-year cycle is the knotted rope over the date glyph, suggesting the Binding of the Years. Above this date is a name glyph of Tenochtitlan's *tlatoani* at that time, Motecuzoma II (reigned ca. 1502–20).[42]

The Fire Serpent sculpture at Dumbarton Oaks stands as one of the most iconographically

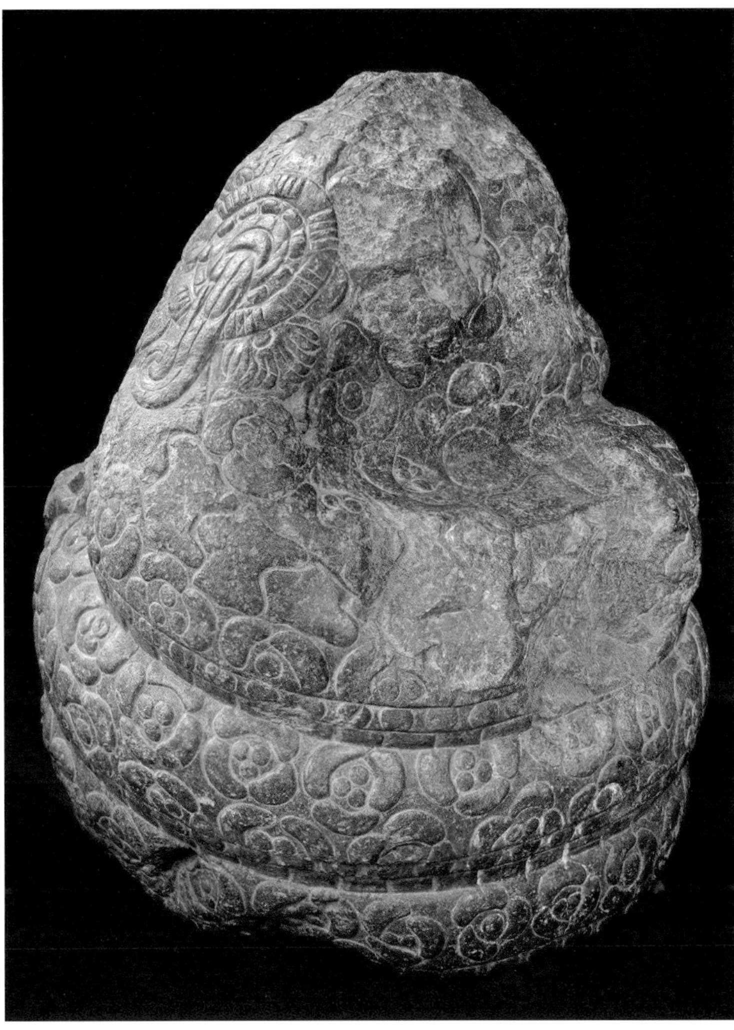

fig. 13
Now in Berlin's Ethnologisches Museum, this Fire Serpent is similar to Dumbarton Oaks sculpture PC.B.069, but the skin is covered by a design of rosettes rather than a geometric pattern. Bildarchiv Preussischer Kulturbesitz/Art Resource, N.Y.

potent and aesthetically balanced sculptures that survive from the Aztec world. Similar pieces are now in the Museo Nacional de Antropología, Mexico City, and in the Ethnologisches Museum of the Staatliche Museen, Berlin (Figure 13).[43] These sculptures may have adorned the temple precincts of their associated deities, or perhaps they were placed in contexts of rulership so that Tenochtitlan's kings could associate themselves with the strength of Huitzilopochtli's power-charged serpent.[44]

STE

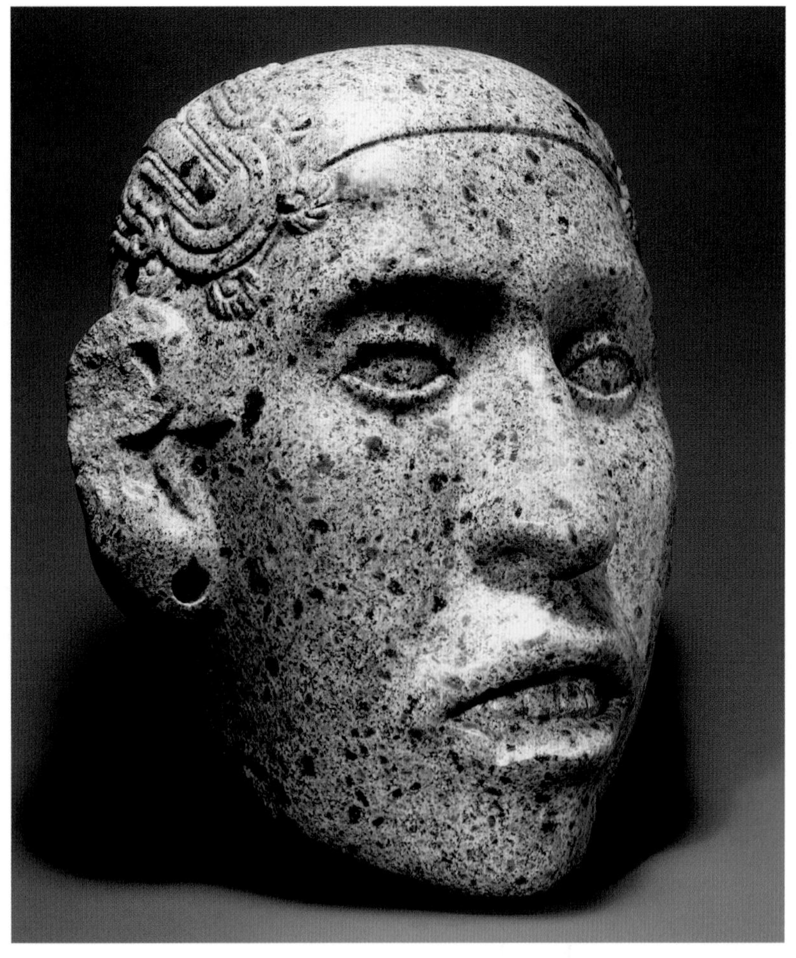

plate 20a

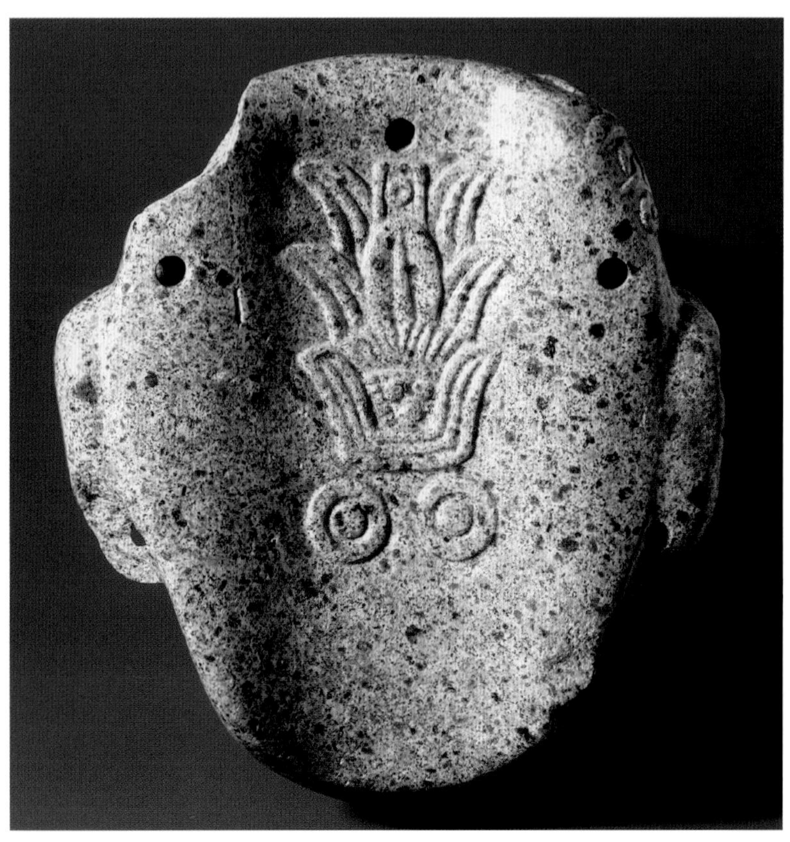

plate 20b, back view

MASK OF THE GOD TEZCATLIPOCA

PLATE 20
Aztec
Late Postclassic period, AD 1502–20
Greenstone
H. 18.5 cm (7¼"); W. 16.3 cm (6⅜"); D. 8.8 cm (3½")
PC.B.072

ACQUISITION HISTORY:
Purchased from Earl Stendahl, 1948

EXHIBITION HISTORY:
Alter Ego—Masks, Their Art and Use, Museum for the Arts of Decoration, Cooper Union, New York, Spring 1951; *Indigenous Art of the Americas,* National Gallery of Art, Washington, D.C., March 1947–July 1962 (NGA 398); *Art of Aztec Mexico: Treasures of Tenochtitlan,* National Gallery of Art, Washington, D.C., September 1983–April 1984; *Circa 1492: Art in the Age of Exploration,* National Gallery of Art, Washington, D.C., December 1991–February 1992

BIBLIOGRAPHY:
Cooper Union Museum for the Arts of Decoration 1951: cat. no. 20; Christensen 1955: 209, 244, fig. 201; Bliss 1957: 242, fig. 14, upper, 243, cat. no. 57, pl. XLIII; Robertson 1959: 107; Vaillant 1962: pl. 59; Dumbarton Oaks 1963: 23, cat. no. 108; Soustelle 1967a: 242, illus. no. 169; Graves 1977: 432; Alcina Franch 1979: fig. 315; Nicholson with Quiñones Keber 1983: 105–106 text and photo, color pl. p. 9, cat. no. 35; Kubler 1984: 14–15; figs. 7, 8; García Moll et al. 1990: 151; Coe 1991a: 548, cat. no. 364; Miller 1991: 35, fig. 6; Voyages of the Mind 1991: cover; Gendrop and Díaz 1994: 116, fig. 154; Olivier 1997: frontispiece; Olivier 2003: frontispiece; Vila Llonch 2008c: 192–193

Slightly smaller than life size, the mask PC.B.072 is a compellingly human countenance, and one of the most beautiful of Aztec sculptures. It "ranks with the very finest of its class" (Nicholson with Quiñones Keber 1983: 106) and is clearly "one of the most sensitively carved depictions of the human countenance known in Aztec art" (Coe 1991a: 548).

It is highly polished and made from a mottled, fine-grained stone, permitting the sculptor to produce one of the most naturalistic human faces among those depicted in Aztec style. It is an elegantly simple design, a handsome young man wearing a close-fitting headdress with two identical emblems, one above each temple.[45] Each emblem is a "smoking mirror," the symbol of the great god Tezcatlipoca, "the omniscient archsorcerer" (Nicholson with Quiñones Keber 1983: 106).[46] This representation of the diviner's tool is "composed of the circular rim, four edging balls of eagle down (a sacrifice symbol), and smoke volutes issuing from its center" (Nicholson with Quiñones Keber 1983: 105).[47] Although mirrors have been widely depicted in Mesoamerican art, the emblem design of the smoking mirror, as a motif, is found "only in Aztec art" (Umberger 1987: 75).

The back of the mask (Plate 20b) features a date glyph in bas-relief, 2 Acatl (reed), which is probably the day of Tezcatlipoca's birth, according to documentary and iconographic sources (Caso 1959: 90–91; Coe 1991a: 548).[48] Several scholars have posited that this glyph refers to the year 2 Acatl, as was depicted on the underside of the Fire Serpent PC.B.069 (Plate 19b), and AD 1507 was a 2 Acatl year[49] but "missing here is the square frame that usually surrounds Aztec years" (Coe 1991a: 548). Also, in contrast to the 2 Acatl date on PC.B.069, this one lacks the rope thought to bind the years.

Unlike many other Mesoamerican masks that rely on inlays to animate the eyes and mouth, PC.B.072's features are carved, which contributes to its realism, from the modern perspective. Nor were the eyes or mouth perforated. The mask has five perforations, visible in the back view. The upper perforations may have been used to suspend the mask, and those at the bases of the ears would have held ornaments.

A provenience in the southern Basin of Mexico has been suggested for PC.B.072, which is certainly possible.[50] Stylistically, the face bears much in common with Late Postclassic sculpture from Castillo de Teayo (Veracruz).[51] A mask so beautifully made would have had a special purpose, possibly fitted over the head of a body in a mortuary bundle (Coe 1991a: 548). If the Bliss Collection mask served such a purpose, then it may have covered the face of "a member of the royal family or even the *tlatoani* himself, for Tezcatlipoca was patron of the royal line" (Coe 1991a: 548).

STE

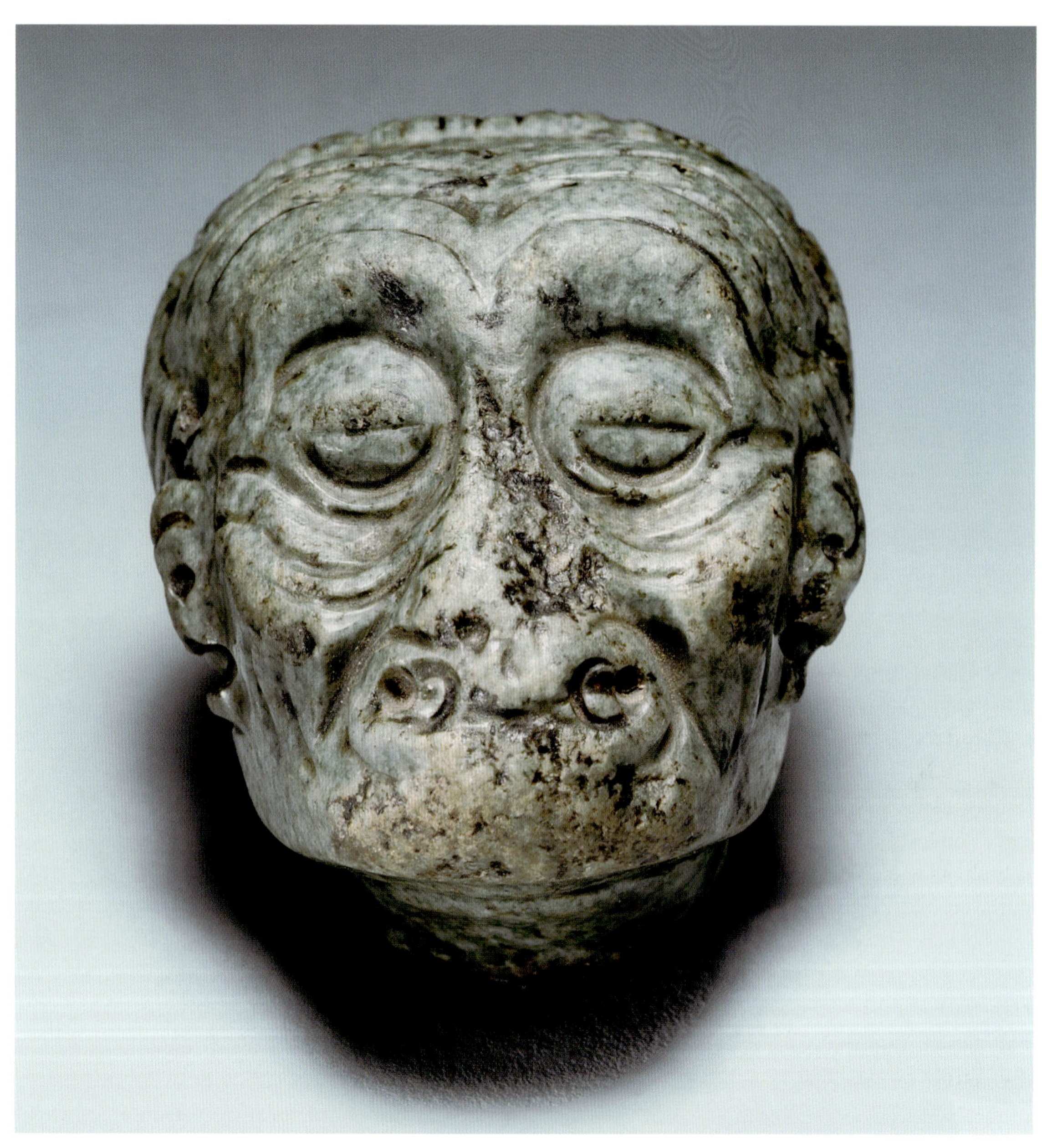

plate 21

HEAD OF THE OLD FIRE GOD HUEHUETEOTL

PLATE 21
Aztec
Late Postclassic period, AD 1200–1520
Greenstone
H. 6.4 cm (2½"); W. 5.3 cm (2⅛"); D. 5.1 cm (2")
PC.B.058

ACQUISITION HISTORY:
Acquired before 1957

EXHIBITION HISTORY:
Indigenous Art of the Americas, National Gallery of Art, Washington, D.C., January 1954–July 1962 (NGA 555)

BIBLIOGRAPHY:
Bliss 1957: 239, cat. no. 40, pl. XXX, center left; Dumbarton Oaks 1963: 2, cat. no. 5; Nicholson 1967: 52

This small greenstone head has been worked by grooving and polishing. It shows what may be areas of breakage, as from a larger object of which the head was once part. Its shape is almost that of a skull, but the details of the eyes, skin, and hair indicate that it represents a living individual. The head's dimensions are nearly as wide and deep as it is high, its ovoid shape derived from the contours of the cranium and the pointed chin.

The eyes are the focal point of this face. A circular outer rim defines each eye, and in these circles, horizontal crescents show that the eyes are half-closed, suggesting the bleary gaze of someone barely awake. The eyes resemble the Aztec graphic shorthand of the half-closed eye as a star. Surrounding the circular eyes are concentric half-circles. Four sets above the eyes indicate eyebrows and a wrinkled forehead. The high forehead ends with a cap-like hairline; the rest of the hair is drawn into a bun at the back of the head.

Below the eyes, several other half-circles portray sagging skin on the cheeks. The nose has been damaged; similar objects have a sharp beaked nose. The crescent of the mouth contains several isolated teeth, deliberately indicating tooth loss as a sign of age. The ears are small and close to the head.

This very old individual is thought to portray the Central Mexican deity Huehueteotl, the Old Fire God. This deity was conceptualized as an old man and had been revered in Central Mexico since at least the Preclassic period. The figure lacks Huehueteotl's characteristic headdress, however, and thus could represent one of the venerated Central Mexican elder goddesses, such as Toci. Whatever the sex, the figure's combination of half-closed eyes, wrinkled face, and nearly toothless mouth show without doubt that this piece depicts the face of a very old person.

STE

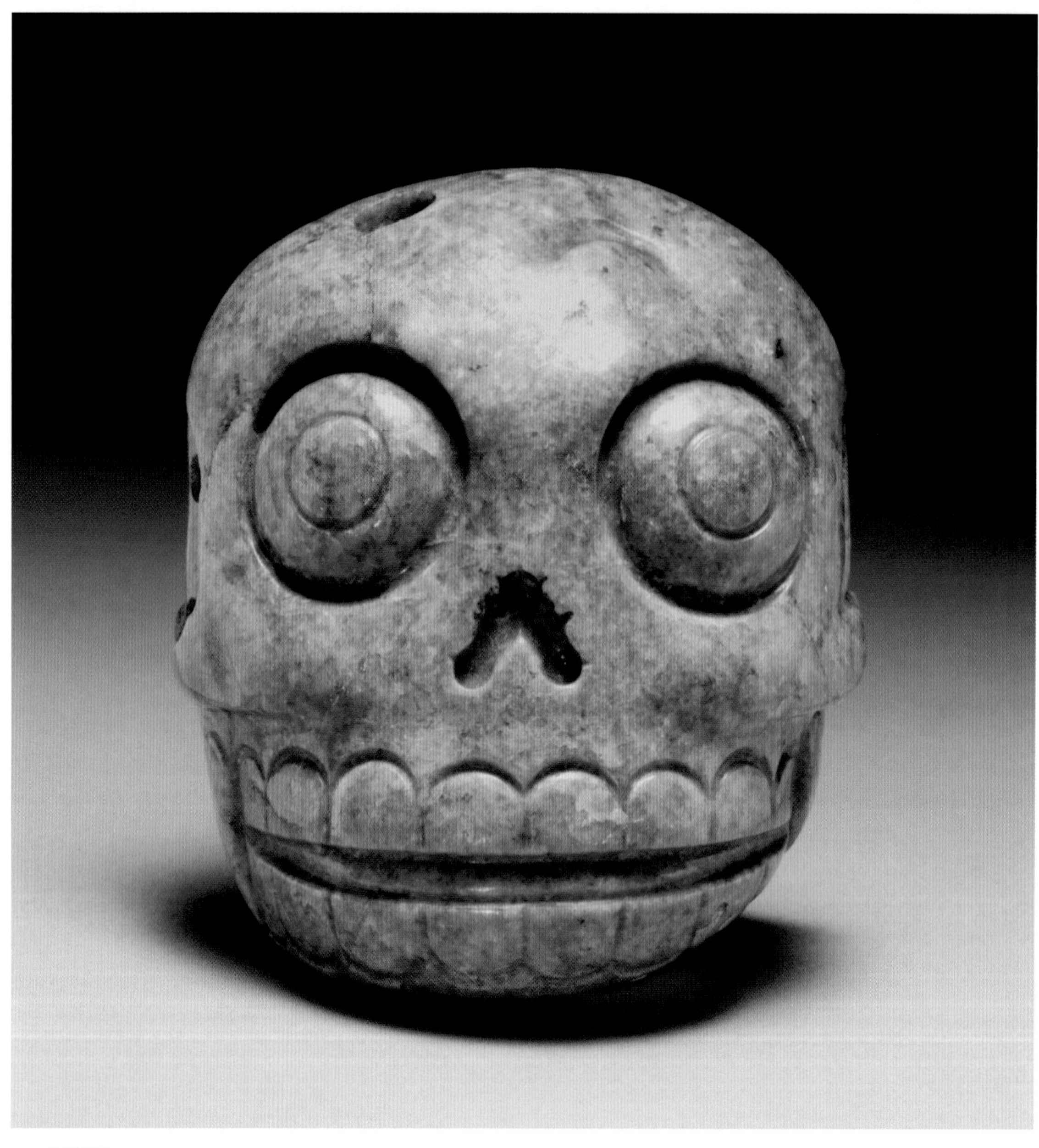

plate 22

JADEITE SKULL

PLATE 22
Aztec
Late Postclassic period, AD 1200–1520
Jadeite
H. 7.1 cm (2¾"); W. 6.4 cm (2½"); D. 4.8 cm (1⅞")
PC.B.081

ACQUISITION HISTORY:
Acquired before 1957

EXHIBITION HISTORY:
Indigenous Art of the Americas, National Gallery of Art, Washington, D.C., May 1948–July 1949, November 1952–July 1962 (NGA 386)

BIBLIOGRAPHY:
Bliss 1957: 244, cat. no. 63, pl. XLVIII, bottom right; Charlot 1958: 49; Dumbarton Oaks 1963: 24, cat. no. 111; Willey 1966: 162, fig. 118, bottom

The subject of this small sculpture is death, which was a rather lively part of Aztec culture. Skeletons and death transformations were important themes in sculpture: consider the skull racks where the remains of sacrificial victims were curated in Tenochtitlan's Templo Mayor precinct, or the great goddess Coatlicue, decapitated and with snakes emerging from her severed neck.

This spherical piece is worked to emphasize circular shapes, and the focal point of the face is the eyes, incised into the sculpture as two concentric rings. The central ones, delineating the irises, are much shallower than the outer rings that mark the skull's orbital cavities. That the eyes are detailed seems not in keeping with a true representation of a skull, but in Aztec art, human skulls were decorated with insets of lapidary materials to indicate iris and sclera.

The mouth is an incised horizontal line, and the upper and lower teeth are semicircles extended with straight lines. The lapidarian may have established the outlines of these semicircles and of the concentric circles of the eyes by drilling with a hollow reed and sand, and then continued working them by grooving.

STE

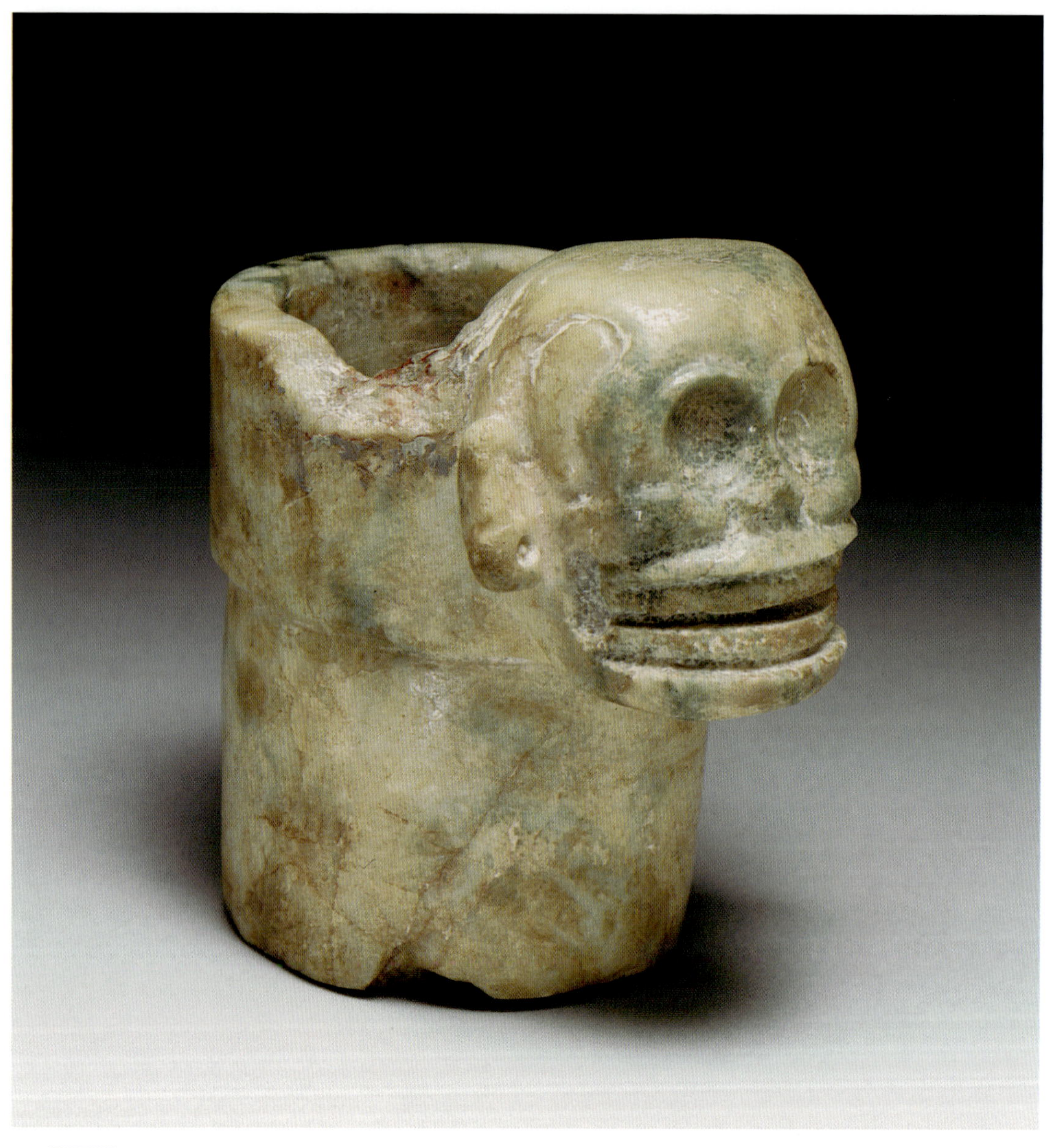

plate 23

PLATE 23

Aztec

Late Postclassic period, AD 1200–1520

Jadeite

H. 7.8 cm (3"); W. 5.4 cm (2⅛"); D. 7.9 cm (3⅛")

PC.B.080

ACQUISITION HISTORY:

Purchased from Earl Stendahl, 1944

EXHIBITION HISTORY:

Indigenous Art of the Americas, National Gallery of Art, Washington, D.C., April 1947–July 1949, November 1952–July 1962 (NGA 186); *The Aztec Empire*, Guggenheim Museum, New York, October 2004–February 2005; Guggenheim Museum, Bilbao, Spain, March–September 2005

BIBLIOGRAPHY:

Bliss 1947: 13, 77, cat. no. 45; *Artes de México* 1957: pl. 4; Bliss 1957: 244, cat. no. 64, pl. XLVIII, below; Charlot 1958: 49; Dumbarton Oaks 1963: 24, cat. no. 114; Murro 2004b: 47, cat. no. 204

A sculpted skull adorning the side of a cup, PC.B.080 represents a type of vessel that is sometimes referred to as a "pulque cup," pulque being a beer made from agave sap. A similar example was found as part of Offering 20 at the Templo Mayor (Matos 1990: 74–75). The Templo Mayor cup is about twice as tall as the Dumbarton Oaks example and is far more elaborately decorated, with not just a skull but also a full figure thought to represent Mictlantecuhtli, lord of the land of the dead. Matos notes that "its feet and hands have skins while its face is totally denuded of flesh" (1990: 74). In fact, the Templo Mayor cup, like PC.B.080, has ears—apparently this state of being partially defleshed was typical of Aztec skeletal figures. The context in which the Templo Mayor example was found is thought to date to ca. AD 1469 (Solís 1991: 546).

PC.B.080 may have had more elaborate accoutrements at one time, but the piece was broken and reworked, apparently in antiquity. The cup has two design fields: a lower one forming a slightly narrower cylinder than the upper field, on which the skull forms a protuberance. The eye holes, surrounded by a raised rim, are conical and detailed by circular pupils, similar to the Templo Mayor example presented by Matos. Round cavities define the sides of the mouth, which is formed by three parallel horizontal lines, simple grooves that express the death's head grin. On the face's temples appear incised marks, each in the shape of an elongated bean, possibly indicating "that this is a representation of a mask" (Murro 2004b: 47). The ears are naturalistic in shape, with cylindrical depressions in the enlarged lobes.

The class of vessels to which PC.B.080 belongs is extensive and varied. The two other vessels from Templo Mayor that display a figure or a skull on the side are lidded funerary urns (Matos 1990: 68). Both contained charred bones. Another similar vessel is the "Bilimek pulque vessel," which was 14½ inches tall and richly carved with a tapestry of iconographically significant designs (see Nicholson with Quiñones Keber 1983: 62–63; Taube 1993). The Bilimek vessel's face shows another alternative in the variety of skull fleshiness: only the mouth seems defleshed. However, the vessel's complex imagery is replete with references to death and to the souls of dead warriors (Taube 1993). Unlike other known examples, in which the head is placed toward the top of the vessel, the Bilimek face is below center. The Bliss Collection example, PC.B.080, is simple and small but conforms well to the known parameters of the examples of these vessels that have been found in context.

STE

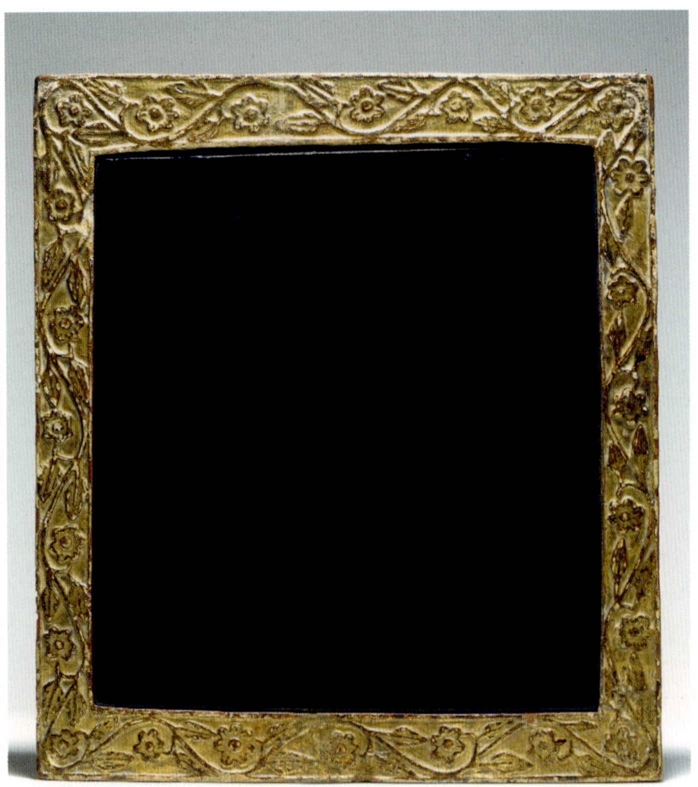

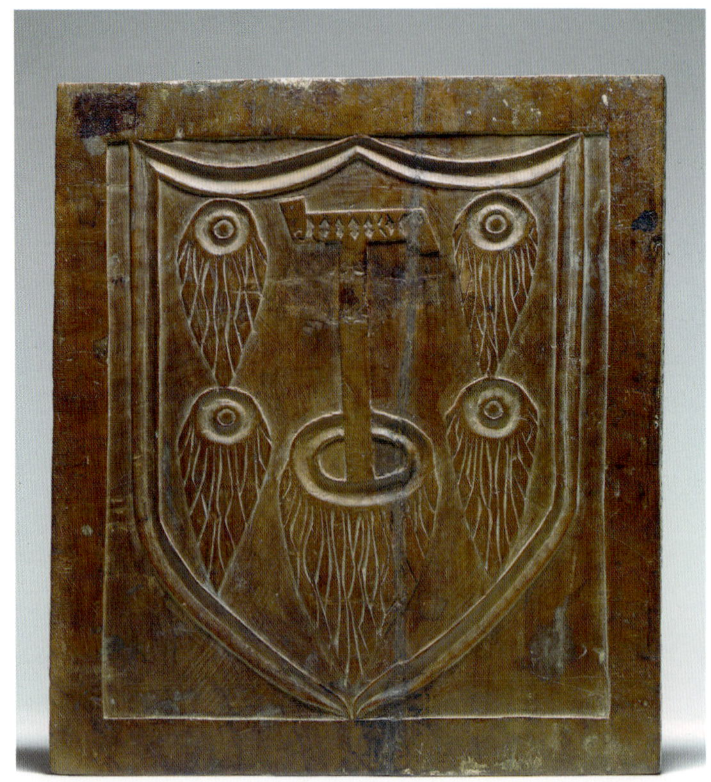

plate 24a *plate 24b, back view*

OBSIDIAN MIRROR OR PORTABLE ALTAR

PLATE 24

Aztec and Spanish colonial
Late Postclassic and colonial periods, AD 1500–1600
Obsidian and wood
Mirror: H. 25.5 cm (10"); W. 23.4 cm (9¼")
Frame: H. 31.5 cm (12⅜"); W. 28.5 cm (11¼"); D. 2.8 cm (1⅛")
PC.B.078

ACQUISITION HISTORY:

Purchased in Madrid, 1961

EXHIBITION HISTORY:

Die Azteken und ihre Vorläufer: Glanz und Untergang des Alten Mexico, Roemer- und Pelizaeus-Museum, Hildesheim, Germany, June–November 1986; Haus der Kunst, Munich, December 1986–March 1987; Oberösterreichisches Landesmuseum, Linz, Austria, April–August 1987; Louisiana Museum of Modern Art, Humlebæk, Denmark, August–November 1987; Musées royaux d'Art et d'Histoire, Brussels, December 1987–March 1988; National Archaeological Museum, Athens, May–July 1988; Société du Palais de la Civilisation, Montreal, July–October 1988; *Aztecs*, Royal Academy of Arts, London, September 2002–April 2003; Ethnologisches Museum, Berlin, May–August 2003; Art and Exhibition Hall of the Federal Republic of Germany, Bonn, September 2003–January 2004; *The Aztec Empire*, Guggenheim Museum, New York, October 2004–February 2005

BIBLIOGRAPHY:

Boone 1986d: cat. no. 354; Louisiana Museum 1987: 83, cat. no. 298; Saunders 2002: 484, cat. no. 335; Saunders 2004b: 77, cat. no. 362; Solís 2004: 350, bottom, 369, no. 198; Vila Llonch 2008a: 188–189

This rectangular block of obsidian is set in a gilt wood surround that is decorated in a floral style of the early colonial period. Carved into the back of the surround is the Franciscan emblem showing Christ's stigmata in a shield, which dates it to the sixteenth century (García Granados 1940–42). Framed pieces of polished obsidian are rare, with one rectangular example in the Museum für Völkerkunde in Vienna (Eggebrecht 1986: fig. 353) and a disk-shaped item in the American Museum of Natural History (Coe 1991b).

PC.B.078 and other examples of Pre-Columbian polished obsidian surfaces have traditionally and problematically been called mirrors, due in part to their polished reflective surfaces and to the Aztec use of obsidian disks as divinatory mirrors, such as one formerly owned by the Elizabethan alchemist Dr. John Dee and now in the British Museum (Tait 1967). This potentially misleading functional attribution also has been assigned by museums to these objects.

There is little unambiguous evidence, however, that large square or rectangular examples are Pre-Columbian or that they had a similar descrying function. In a survey of 21 such objects, only one appears to be possibly Pre-Columbian, with a dated inscription engraved on its surface and interpreted as "9 Panquetzaliztli, 4 Acatl" (9 December 1438).[52] Because a polished obsidian surface casts a dark, distorted, and sometimes indistinct image, rectangular examples probably were not used in colonial times as ornamental or vanity mirrors, especially considering the availability of European glass mirrors. Instead, such objects may have served as portable altars (*aras*); some were commissioned by Spanish mendicant priests from native obsidian workers.[53] In a shortage of suitably consecrated European alternatives, such items would have served as liturgical instruments for the conversion of native peoples.

During early colonial times, *aras* were typically rectangular, measuring 12 inches by 14 inches and fitted into a special cavity in a larger stone slab (*mensa*), which formed the altar (McAndrew 1965: 353). The ara, removable and thus portable, was the most sacred part of the altar: it symbolically represented Christ and formed the surface on which the chalice and other paraphernalia were placed during a religious service. *Aras* were indispensable to a mendicant priest's equipment and, together with a chalice, chasuble, cross, alb, and candlesticks, fit into a small wooden chest that could be strapped to a donkey.

So admiring were the Spanish of these obsidian *aras* that one was installed in the main altar of San José de los Naturales, the *atrio* of San Francisco in Mexico City in 1564 (McAndrew 1965: 379). Many of these objects were sent back to Spain.[54] The Dumbarton Oaks piece may have been among them. The wood-framed example in Vienna[55] may have been a gift from Charles V to his brother Ferdinand as one of the many Mexican curiosities that he gave to his brother.

Although Spaniards admired obsidian artifacts, particularly *aras*, they seem not to have perceived obsidian's iconographic associations, including its identification with the supreme Aztec deity Tezcatlipoca (Saunders 2001: 221–224). This god, the patron of Aztec royalty, wielded his eponymous possession, the obsidian mirror, itself a metaphor for rulership and power, and the Nahuatl term *itztli* (obsidian) was associated with Tezcatlipoca (Ruíz de Alarcón 1984 [1629]: 229). Spaniards identified Tezcatlipoca as the Devil incarnate (Burkhart 1988: 70), but they failed to recognize obsidian's significance. Torquemada (1943 [1615]) recorded that Tezcatlipoca's name meant "shiny resplendent mirror," and Aztec informants spoke of Tezcatlipoca as the omnipresent god who makes the black mirror shine (Zantwijk 1985: 128). Obsidian mirrors as descrying implements were an important feature of native religious ritual, as were obsidian blades used in sacrifice. Not recognizing these clues, the Spaniards made the most sacred representation of Christ from polished obsidian, the embodiment of the Aztec god who epitomized the paganism that Christian conversion sought to eradicate.

Tezcatlipoca's associations with sacrifice, blood, and obsidian drew an ironic parallel between Aztec belief and Christian crucifixion imagery, which is embodied in the Dumbarton Oaks piece. The Franciscan stigmata emblem carved on the back of the wood surround associated Christ's bloody death with obsidian as the divine substance of Tezcatlipoca. For the Aztecs, sacrificial blood was the precious substance chalchihuitl, and it may be significant that the circles representing the stigmata from which the blood flows are executed in a form characteristic of the Aztec way of representing chalchihuitl.

NJS

TWO SCULPTURES IN AZTEC STYLE

Two of the most famous sculptures in the Bliss Collection are the Female Figure in the Act of Childbirth (PC.B.071, Plate 25), often identified as the Aztec goddess Tlazolteotl, and Rabbit (PC.B.079, Plate 26). They have been attributed to Aztec culture of the Late Postclassic period, but this attribution is complicated by the unique style of the pieces and the stoneworking techniques involved in their manufacture and finishing. These matters have been the focus of curiosity since these sculptures came to light, and scholars have wondered whether they might be of recent manufacture or reworking.

The acceptance of an unprovenienced work as authentically ancient may depend on the extent to which the style of the piece conforms to our understanding of the iconography, conventions, and range of variation among known examples from a given culture. Scholars may be asked whether an object is authentic based only on stylistic characteristics, and over time a researcher can develop a sense of what to expect in the range of style exhibited by pieces with impeccable provenience. One also learns to be cautious about dismissing highly unusual objects that lack provenience, because at times they turn out to have near-twins found in well-documented contexts.

Until recently, Aztec archaeological contexts have been relatively rare, compared to the wealth of Aztec documentary resources. The contexts of monumental sculptures were well documented, and from them scholars could interpret other similar but unprovenienced large works. For much smaller sculpture, however, there was no adequate sample of provenienced objects, leading to the uncertain practice of interpreting small unprovenienced pieces from features of other small unprovenienced sculptures thought to represent Aztec style. Therefore, many scholars who wrote about the Tlazolteotl and Rabbit sculptures before the early 1980s did not have the benefit of comparing them with examples of Aztec small sculpture from good contexts.

For the world of Aztec sculpture, 1978 was a watershed year, marking the beginning of the systematic recovery of materials from the Templo Mayor in Mexico City. Any of the illustrated volumes about these finds[56] show the kinds of small sculptures that the Aztecs treasured. These included some deity representations; some Mezcala figures, thought to be from Guerrero, with their typical minimalist severity; and Mixtec *penate* (votive) figures bearing proportions of chess pieces and averaging 4¾ inches high. There were miniature representations of animals, such as fish and turtles, and objects in the shape of musical instruments and abstract symbols.

Long before this repertoire provided a genuine sample of small Aztec sculpture, however, several specialists of Aztec art thought that "Tlazolteotl" (PC.B.071) was disquietingly unlike other known Aztec pieces and bore evidence of modern techniques and sensibilities. Gordon Ekholm, Curator of Mexican Archaeology at the American Museum of Natural History and an advisor to Robert Bliss, noted that the piece was an unusual and awkward size for Aztec sculpture. It and "Rabbit" (PC.B.079) are both about 8 inches tall—too large to wear, too small to be an architectural element or to serve as a monumental sculpture.

There are other unprovenienced objects in this general size category, ranging from 4¾ to 12¼ inches.[57] There is, however, an object in the Museum für Völkerkunde in Vienna that is similar to Tlazolteotl in terms of its posture. This Monster Deity is possibly Pre-Columbian, but it cannot be authenticated.[58] Made of wood and adorned with shell and other precious materials, it squats with its hands clasped around its lower legs just below the knees, and a mosaic face protrudes from its rounded abdomen. The figure is blocky, with a broad base on which to rest, and it is only 3½ inches tall.

Objects of the same general size as Tlazolteotl and Rabbit that come from documented contexts include animal representations from the Templo Mayor: a lizard and a feline face in Guerrero style (Matos 1990: 130–131). Human figures include standing males and a female, rendered in a style much cruder than either of the Bliss Collection sculptures.[59] Thus although it appears there are provenienced sculptures of the same general size as Tlazolteotl and Rabbit, when they are compared to Tlazolteotl, the anthropomorphic pieces, whether deities or mortals, are less refined in technique, sculpted in shallow relief, and their subjects are clothed or wear insignia. With regard to Rabbit, well-documented examples of animals of this size are rare, indeed, and very different in style from PC.B.079.

Another approach to understanding the uniqueness of these pieces is physical analysis. Close examination of the surface can determine whether modern methods were employed in shaping or finishing. Dumbarton Oaks initiated testing involving microscopic analysis of the scars made on the surface of PC.B.071 and PC.B.079 by the manufacturing process (Walsh 2008a). These scars were then compared with those made on the surfaces of objects of known provenience and with experimental marks made by modern tools. This analysis indicated that the manufacturing scars on both sculptures most closely resemble those made by modern tools.

Traditional Mesoamerican methods of stone sculpting involved chipping, sawing, cleaving, and grinding, using tools made of stone, bone, and hollow reed, plus sand and string. Objects made using such methods and tools bear scars that are much less regular than are the scars made using modern rotary tools. Modern tools are standardized in size and leave marks of consistent dimensions, bearing regular striations. Similarly, surface buffing using modern tools tends to leave a higher shine; scarring from abrasives is less obvious and more regular. Furthermore, modern polishing tools can reach into deep-relief spaces. Ancient stoneworkers tended to expend less energy on such crevices, so ancient objects tend to exhibit a range of degrees of polishing on their surfaces.

The analysis revealed that Tlazolteotl and Rabbit bear manufacturing and polishing scars like those made using modern tools, with distinctive regularity of groove size and striations. Surfaces are highly polished, even in areas that would be difficult to reach using traditional methods. These preliminary findings indicate that these objects may have been manufactured in modern times, or that they are ancient sculptures that have been very heavily reworked using modern tools.

STE

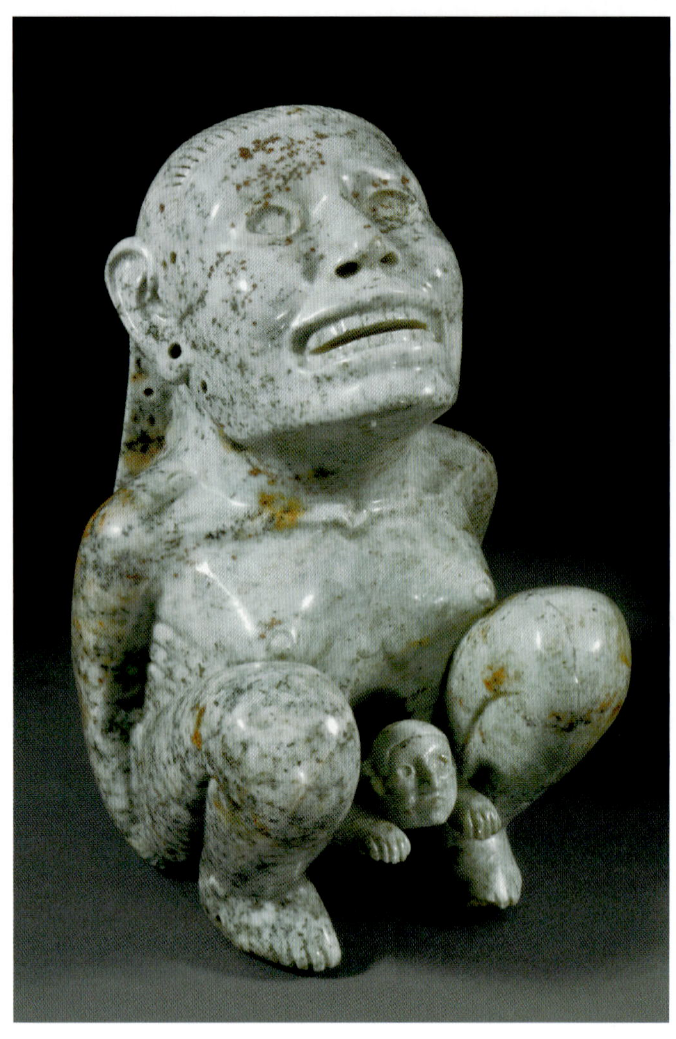

plate 25a

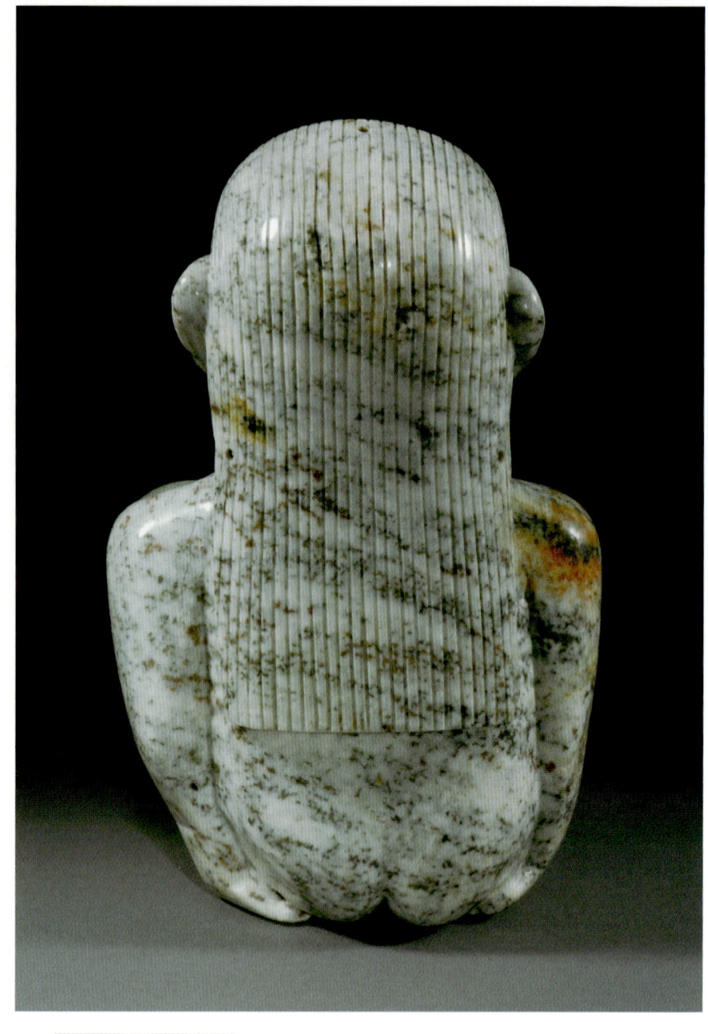

plate 25b, back view

FEMALE FIGURE IN THE ACT OF CHILDBIRTH

PLATE 25
Aztec style
Probably nineteenth century
Aplite
H. 20.2 cm (8"); W. 12.0 cm (4¾"); D. 14.9 cm (5⅞")
PC.B.071

ACQUISITION HISTORY:
Purchased from Ernest Brummer, 1947; in the possession of Charles Ratton during the 1940s; in the possession of Dr. Ribemont-Dessaignes after 1902, possibly until 1940; in the possession of Augustin Damour after 1883, until his death in 1902; previously in the possession of Mr. Wan

EXHIBITION HISTORY:
Ancient American Gold and Jade, Taft Museum, Cincinnati, Ohio, October–November 1950; *Art Méxicain du Précolombien à nos jours*, Musée national d'Art moderne, Paris, May–July 1952; *Mexikansk Konst från Forntid till Nutid*, Liljevalches Konsthall, Stockholm, 1952; *Exhibition of Mexican Art from Pre-Columbian Times to the Present Day*, Tate Gallery, London, March–April 1953; *Kunst der Mexikaner*, Kunsthaus, Zürich, January–March 1959; Wallraf-Richartz Museum, Cologne, 1959; *Mexicaanse Kunst*, Haags Gemeente-Museum, The Hague, 1959; *Kunst aus Mexico und Mittelamerika*, Akademie der Künste, Berlin, October–November 1959; *Präkolumbische Kunst aus Mexico und Mittelamerika*, Künstlerhaus, Vienna, December 1959–February 1960; *The Imagination of Primitive Man*, Nelson Gallery, Kansas City, Mo., 1962; *Indigenous Art of the Americas*, National Gallery of Art, Washington, D.C., May 1948–July 1962 (NGA 374); *The Arts of Latin America*, UNESCO Traveling Exhibition, Paris, 1977; *Aztecs*, Royal Academy of Arts, September 2002–April 2003; Ethnologisches Museum, Berlin, May–August 2003; Art and Exhibition Hall of the Federal Republic of Germany, Bonn, September 2003–January 2004

BIBLIOGRAPHY:
Hamy 1899: 11; Hamy 1906; Kelemen 1943: 307–308, pl. 254b; Pijoán 1946: pl. X; Seymour 1949: 70; *Art Digest* 1950: 12; Taft Museum 1950: cat. no. 32; Liljevalchs Konsthall 1952: cat. no. 665 I, pl. 48; Musée national d'Art moderne 1952: I: cat. no. 624, pl. 48; Rubín de la Borbolla et al. 1952: 33, pl. 26; Tate Gallery 1953: cat. no. 631; Linné 1956: 100; Westheim 1956: fig. 68; Bliss 1957: 240–241, cat. no. 52, pls. XXXVI, XXXVII; Covarrubias 1957: 327, pl. LXII; Universidad Nacional Autónoma de México 1957: pls. 1, 2; Mason 1958: 123–124, pls. XXXVI, XXXVII; *Natural History* 1958: 132; Von Hagen 1958: 81; Akademie der Künste 1959: cat. no. 1034, pl. 117; *Art International* 1959: 45; *Die Weltkunst* 1959: 9; Haags Gemeentemuseum 1959: cat. no. 29, pl. 29; Kunsthaus Zürich 1959: cat. no. 687, pl. VI; Künstlerhaus Wien 1959: cat. no. 947, pl. 82; Peterson 1959: 261; Rautenstrauch-Joest-Museum für Völkerkunde and Wallraf-Richartz-Museum 1959: cat. no. 132, pl. 132; *Time* Magazine 1959: 26; Coloquio Internacional Sobre Estados Depressivos 1960: 1; Disselhoff and Linné 1960: 81; Oertwig and Friese 1960: pl. 51; Piña Chán 1960: 121, fig. 38; Ishida 1962: 176, fig. 73; Kubler 1962: 56, pl. 21; William Rockhill Nelson Gallery of Art and Mary Atkins Museum of Fine Arts 1962: cat. no. 249; Vaillant 1962: pl. 57; Dumbarton Oaks 1963: 23, cat. no. 109; Fabbri and Gibelli 1965: 103; Reed 1966: 95; Nicholson 1967: 101; Soustelle 1967a: 199, 200; Anton 1973: pl. 69; *Artes de México* 1973: 54, fig. 129; Campbell 1974: 411; Zenner 1974: 160, pl. 50; Preble 1976: 18, fig. 18; Stingl 1976: opp. p. 17; Anton 1977: pl. 70; Westheim 1977: pl. 123; Alcina Franch 1979: 358, pl. 145; Herrera 1979: 28; Breslow 1980: 37; Chicago 1981; López Portillo et al. 1981: photo p. 302; Feldman 1982: 38; Marx 1982: 11; Pasztory 1982: fig. 8; Alcina Franch 1983: pl. 145; Davies 1983: fig. 29; Zantwijk 1983: 75; Kubler 1984: pl. II; Sjöö and Mor 1987: 169; Berdan 1989: 82; Fichner-Rathus 1989: 9; Weigle 1989: cover; Alcina Franch et al. 1992: 358, pl. LXXXVI; Benson 1993: 21–25, fig. 6; Braun 1993: 100; Gendrop and Díaz 1994: 151, fig. 219; Gilboa 1994: 5–6, figs. 5, 8; Clendinnen 1995: 174–175, unnumbered pl.; Comisarenco 1996: fig. 1; Smith 1996: 217, fig. 9.4; Graham 1997: 104; Hansen 1997: 91; Kausch 1998: 31, fig. 16; Paxson 1998: 167; Vuille 1998: cover; Chicago and Lucie-Smith 1999: 54; Lindauer 1999: 92; Mirkin 1999: fig. 1; Thompson 1999: 174; Struble 2000: cover; Townsend 2000: 123, fig. 85; McElvaine 2001: 120; Blade 2002: 32; Bories and Coe 2002: 155; Matos and Solís 2002: 341, color pl. on p. 340; Traxler 2002e: 479, cat. no. 320; Dean and Leibsohn 2003: 28, fig. 12; Kassner 2003: 128; Matos 2003: 1, 16; Shlain 2003: 10; Berrelleza 2004: 33, Incas, Mayas, Azteken 2004: 104; Rademacher 2004: 104; Pasztory 2005: 214, fig. 17.7; Boardman 2006: 294, fig. 507; Carpenter 2007: 24, fig. 8; Lozano and Coronel Rivera 2007: 539; Nakagawa 2007: 195; Grossman 2008: 114–116, 131–133, figs. 1, 2, 11; Schulz 2008: 164–167; Walsh 2008a; Walsh 2008b; Gilboa 2009: 99, fig. 46

This compelling small sculpture is one of the most famous pieces in the Bliss Collection. Its image has been featured in major exhibitions, graced book pages (and at least one book cover), and been reinterpreted in popular artistic media. It has been esteemed as an icon of fertility, and even played a featured role in one of the most popular films of all time when it was the object of Indiana Jones's attentions in the opening scenes of *Raiders of the Lost Ark*.[60] It has been regarded as "among the finest pieces of world art" (Peterson 1959: 261). Other authors claim it "to be one of the best examples of Aztec art,"[61] to be a rare example of birth-giving in art (Chicago 1981), and that it "possibly inspired [Frida] Kahlo's painting . . . entitled *Childbirth*" (Breslow 1980: 37).[62]

In spite of its charisma, some questioned the piece's authenticity. Gordon Ekholm believed that PC.B.071 is seriously anomalous in terms of its size, perfect condition, techniques of shaping, degree of polishing, the grooves of the hair and their placement, placement of the ears, placement of the drill holes, smoothing of the eye sockets, and the shape of the figure, rendering it "unique in the corpus of Aztec sculpture in hard stone. Full roundedness of this kind does occur in softer stones but hard stones are mainly carved only in relief. This is more reminiscent of European carving, and I expect that that is what it is. It was done by someone who knew the rudiments of Aztec iconography, but not the limitations of Aztec technique" (Ekholm n.d.: 4).

Ekholm based these opinions on his own wide range of experience and also on that of Junius Bird, Elizabeth Easby, F. E. Ross, and Carlos Gay. In June 1963 Gay (n.d.: 1–2) sent a long letter to Ekholm in which he said, "I do not think the piece is right for the following reasons," describing stylistic features of the woman and the baby that are neither Aztec nor Mixtec.

Furthermore, Gay had never seen this type of stone used in Pre-Columbian art.[63] He noted that when Aztec lapidaries used hard stone, they produced shallow relief sculptures, not three-dimensional ones. He believed that mechanical tools had been used in PC.B.071's manufacture. Highly polished pieces occurred among Pre-Columbian stone sculptures, but Tlazolteotl's high polish extended to areas that were less accessible. "Out of context the sculpture appears to be a common lapidary work, void of true artistic merits, created by a late nineteenth century artist acquainted with Aztec iconography and ancient techniques, but clearly betraying an academic training opposed to any Pre-Columbian artistic tradition" (Gay n.d.: 3).

In fact, the very complicated issues of Aztec iconography are largely avoided by the creator of this piece, who depicted the figure not only unclothed, but without any accoutrements and insignia. The figure's nudity is itself highly anomalous in Aztec art. Possibly the least important reason is Aztec prudishness; they commented denigratingly about other ethnic groups—the Tarascans, the Huastecs—who went about unclothed. More significant for this study is the Aztec artistic convention of labeling figures by including signature elements of costume and insignia. For example, even though the circular sculpture of Coyolxauhqui at the foot of the stairs of the Templo Mayor shows the degraded and murdered deity stripped of her clothing, she is wearing elaborate paraphernalia associated with her identity and fate. An Aztec sculpture of an important deity would certainly include such signatures.

Nudity is fascinating to modern people, however, as is the birth-giving pose[64] and grimace of effort; these features suggest (but do not prove) that this sculpture may have been made, or reworked, to appeal to a modern audience. In these respects, PC.B.071 contrasts strongly with the best-documented and most detailed depiction of the goddess in the Codex Borbonicus (Figure 14), a pre-conquest or early sixteenth-century Central Mexican document (Glass with Robertson 1975: 97). It shows a deity impersonator wearing the skin of a sacrificed female impersonator of the goddess and ritually re-enacting the goddess giving birth to the maize god Centeotl or the goddess Xochiquetzal.[65] Coincidentally, Ernest Hamy, a founder of the Museé d'Ethnographie du Trocadéro in Paris, was responsible for the first publication of the Borbonicus (Codex Borbonicus 1899). Hamy later (1906) published a commentary on the birth-giving sculpture and titled it the goddess Ixcuina. As Sullivan (1982) pointed out, this is a secondary name of the Aztec goddess Tlazolteotl.

Like many Aztec deities, Tlazolteotl has an extraordinarily complicated identity, overlapping with many other major female deities (Nicholson 1971b: 420–422; Sullivan 1982: 7). Tlazolteotl is a gender-neutral name, meaning "filth deity," and various sources applied it to both males and females. In fact, Tlazolteotl is famous as the filth eater,[66] the purifier, the confessor, and for the Aztecs, there was only one confession in a lifetime. Sahagún's informants described her as one who both gave and took away sin.[67] They mentioned her overlapping identity with Ixcuina, a weaving goddess with a multiple identity as four sisters. As Tlazolteotl-Ixcuina, she was "filth god–Lady Cotton," associated with spinning, weaving, and fertility. Sullivan called her "the Great Genetrix . . . Great Spinner and Weaver" (Sullivan 1982: 30). Yet her role with regard to motherhood was as a fertility goddess at a grandiose scale, not as the patroness of childbirth.[68]

A related deity with multiple identities, Teteo innan/Tlalli iyollo/Toci was patroness of midwives and of sweatbaths, in which women prepared for childbirth. Pregnant women typically cried out to "Ticitl, the mother of the gods, Tonan, Yoalticitl" (Sahagún 1969 [1569]: 153), another set of female deities whose identities overlapped those of Tlazolteotl-Ixcuina. And in labor, they were exhorted to "imitate the brave woman Ciuacoatl" (Sahagún 1969 [1569]: 160), the Serpent Woman whom Diego Durán described as "the main goddess" (Durán 1971 [1574–79]: 210), who was the special patron of the *cihuateteo*—women who had died in childbirth (see Klein 1993 for an extended discussion).

The Borbonicus Tlazolteotl is in squatting pose, a "figure with arms and legs outstretched in frog fashion" (Covarrubias 1954: 34). In contrast, the birth-giving sculpture is squatting, her legs parallel to each other. However, unlike other Aztec sculptures in squatting pose (and which are male), if PC.B.071 rests on its feet and buttocks, it also must sit on its hands as well, which is awkward, especially for birthing. On exhibit, the sculpture is propped up. Known examples of female Aztec sculptures either stand or sit with their legs folded under them, knees forward.[69] The figure has numerous holes in various parts of its body.[70] These may have been used to add decorative elements, or possibly for suspension, a hypothesis that has not been empirically tested.

Although anomalies in the style and form of the Bliss Collection's Tlazolteotl have long raised serious questions as to its true age, the piece has acquired a cultural identity transcending issues of authenticity. It has become an icon, a rare rendering of the power and pain of childbirth, and because the sculpture was identified as the Aztec deity Tlazolteotl, it has redefined Tlazolteotl's role as a special patroness of childbirth. The sculpture's style was recognized by early twentieth-century artists as primitive, and while it was in the possession of Paris art dealer Charles Ratton, it was admired by Surrealists André Breton[71] and Man Ray (Grossman 2008). A glance at the sculpture's bibliography reveals its popularity as an exhibition piece and with writers on feminist issues. Pasztory (1998b: 159) once noted that "before they are unmasked, forgeries are intensely loved." It is likely that this image will continue to be widely admired, and that the object has much to teach us about the influence of images.

STE

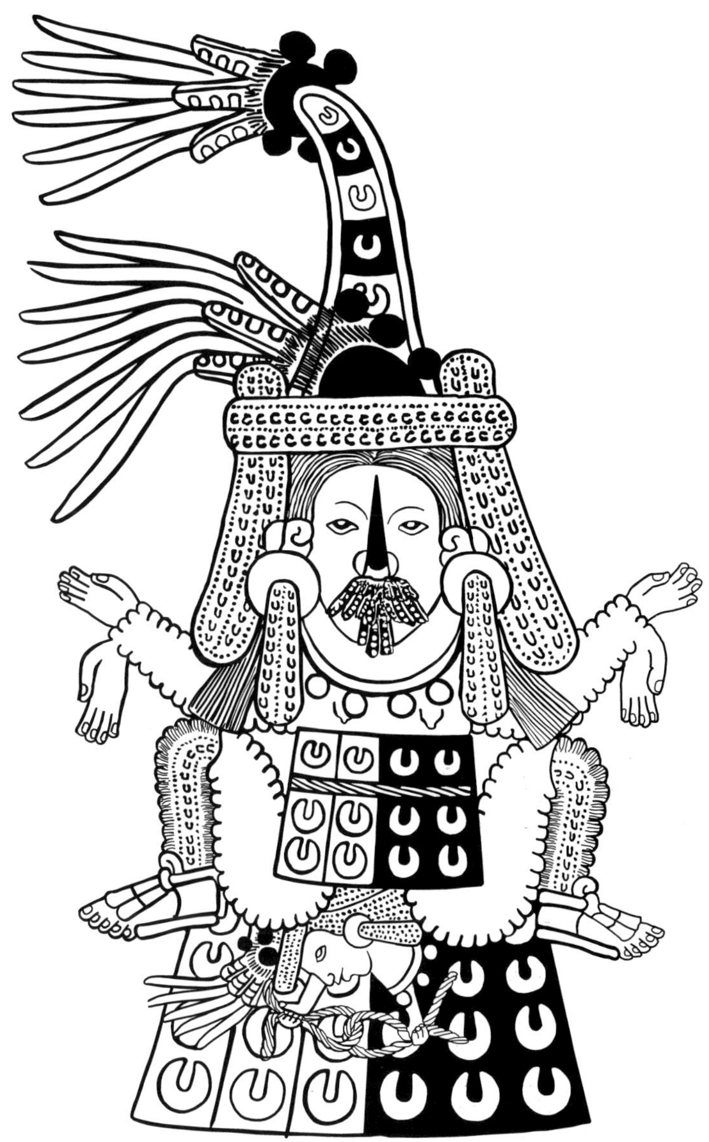

fig. 14
This image from the Codex Borbonicus, a pre-conquest or early sixteenth-century Central Mexican document (Glass with Robertson 1975: 97), shows an impersonator of the goddess Tlazolteotl in squatting position. Drawing by Susan Toby Evans (after Codex Borbonicus 1899: 13).

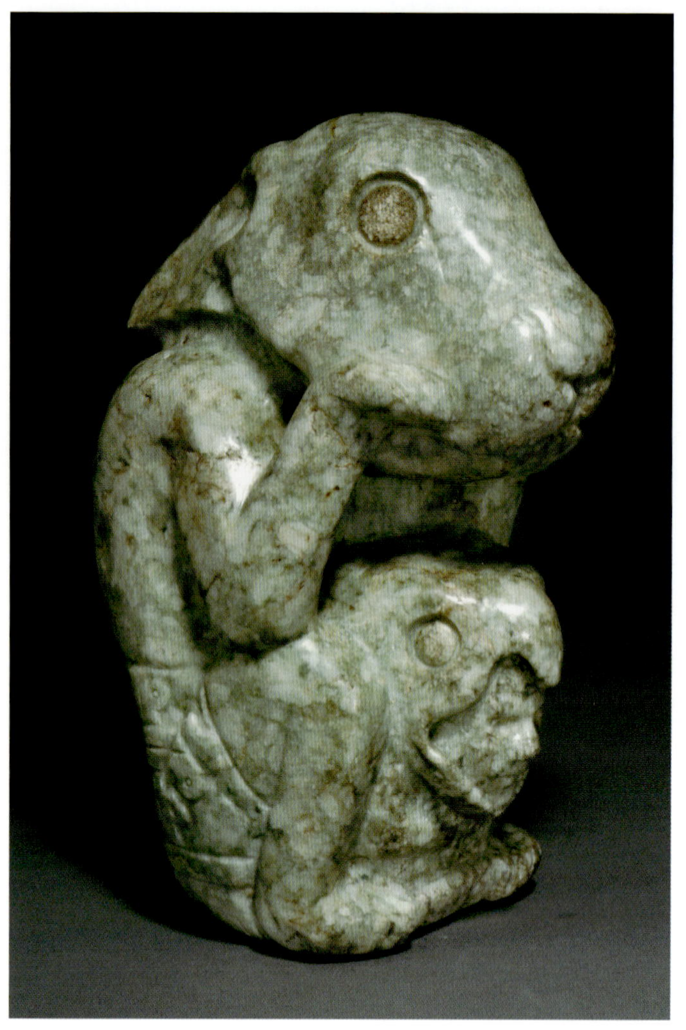

plate 26a

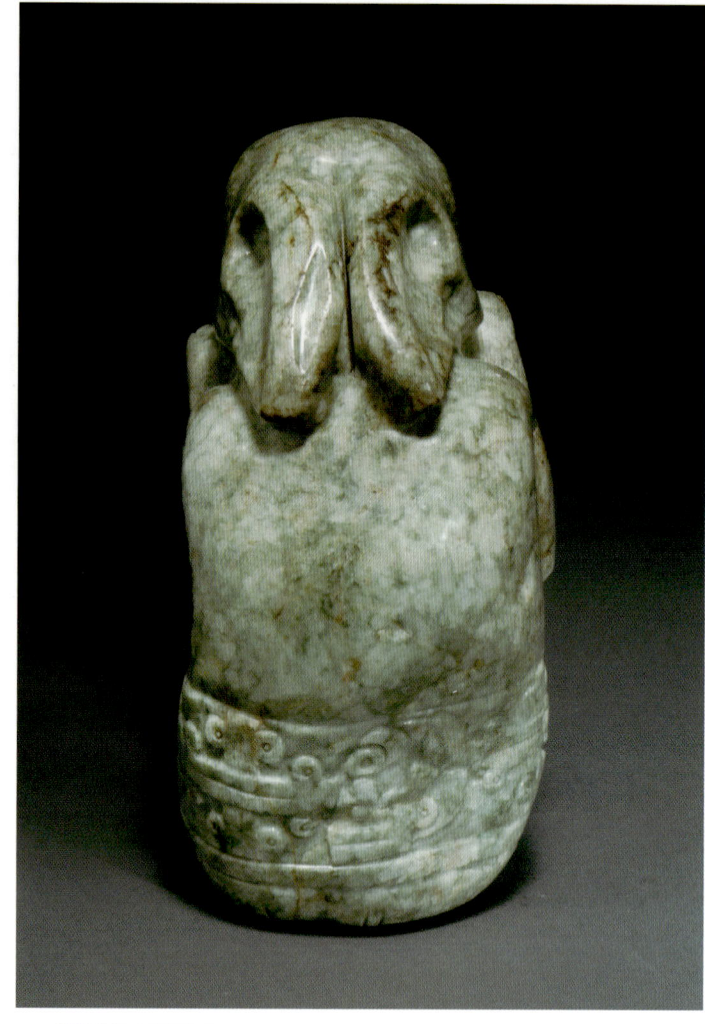

plate 26b, back view

PLATE 26
Aztec style
Probably nineteenth century
Jadeite
H. 18.1 cm (7⅛"); W. 9.15 cm (3⅝"); D. 13.2 cm (5¼")
PC.B.079

ACQUISITION HISTORY:
Purchased from Ernest Brummer, 1947; formerly in the collection of Joseph Brummer

EXHIBITION HISTORY:
An Exhibition of Pre-Columbian Art, Fogg Art Museum, Cambridge, January–March 1940; Art of the Americas, Cleveland Museum of Art, Cleveland, Ohio, November 1945–January 1946; *Indigenous Art of the Americas*, National Gallery of Art, Washington, D.C., May 1948–July 1952 (NGA 373); *Art Méxicain du Précolombien à nos jours*, Musée national d'Art moderne, Paris, May–July 1952; *Mexikansk Konst från Forntid till Nutid*, Liljevalches Konsthall, Stockholm, 1952; *Treasures in America*, Virginia Museum of Fine Arts, Richmond, 1961

BIBLIOGRAPHY:
Peabody Museum of Archaeology and Ethnology and Fogg Art Museum 1940: cat. no. 32; Cleveland Museum of Art 1946: picture book no. 2: 20; Liljevalchs Konsthall 1952: cat. no. 665g; Musée national d'Art moderne 1952: I: cat. no. 622; Rivet 1954: pl. 71; Christensen 1955: 209, 241, fig. 197; Bliss 1957: 241–242, cat. no. 53, pls. XXXVIII, XXXIX; Covarrubias 1957: pl. LXII; Mason 1958: 123–124; *Natural History* 1958: 135; Virginia Museum of Fine Arts 1961: 92; Von Hagen 1961: pl. 1; Gump 1962: 186, pl. 18; Vaillant 1962: pl. 58; Dumbarton Oaks 1963: 23–24, cat. no. 110; Soustelle 1967b: 233, fig. 159; Krickeberg 1969: 101, cat. no. 61, pl. XXVII; Westheim 1977: pl. 113; Alcina Franch 1979: fig. 309; Davies 1983: fig. 28; Pasztory 1983: 253–254, pl. 45; Kubler 1984: 13–15, pl. 1, fig. 6; Alcina Franch et al. 1992: 84, pl. XIV; Werness 2004: 340

The small Aztec-style rabbit sculpture (PC.B.079) is usually paired with PC.B.071 ("Tlazolteotl," Plate 25) for several reasons. Neither has a documented provenience, and both were acquired from the same dealer at the same time. They are about the same size; both are made of unusual mottled green stone and are deeply sculpted and highly polished. Both bear an unconventional iconographic program featuring the emergence of a smaller figure from the lower part of the body of the main figure.[72] Furthermore, both figures touch on similar iconographic themes. Tlazolteotl was an Aztec fertility goddess, and rabbits are universally associated with fertility because of their own high levels of fecundity. Another association of rabbits with human fertility is made by the traditional cultures of the Americas (and Asia), who perceived a "rabbit in the moon"—the image of a rabbit made by shadows on the surface of the rising full moon—and recognized the lunar cycle as a temporal counterpart to the human menstrual cycle. Moreover, in Aztec society both Tlazolteotl and rabbits were associated with filth.[73] Tlazolteotl was the goddess who consumed filth, the deeds by which people had tainted their lives. Rabbits, in Mesoamerica, were associated with drunkenness (Anawalt 1993); the gods of pulque (the native beer) were the Centzon Totochtin, the Four Hundred Rabbits.

PC.B.079 rests on its haunches with its paws upraised, framing the lower part of its face. It has large round eyes with rough centers and deeply sculpted ears that lie back against the head and the curve of the upper back. Its broad belt has a design of alternating skulls and crossbones.[74] Protruding from its abdomen is a bird head with large round eyes with roughened centers. The bird's open beak reveals a human face in high relief, interpreted by some scholars as a warrior wearing an eagle helmet.

Martial imagery seems at odds with Aztec views of rabbits. The association with drunkenness is familiar to Mesoamericanists, but less well known is the careful respect that Aztecs had for rabbits. Among their list of bad omens is "the rabbit when it entered someone's house. . . . now his house would be laid waste" (Sahagún 1979a [1569]: 167). The reasons for the impending disaster seem to pertain to competitive husbandry rather than to military overthrow. The Aztecs honored hard work and vigilance with regard to the family's resources, however modest, and a house should be busy with activity, not so vacant and quiet that a timid rabbit would feel safe making a foray into it.

This view of rabbits is substantiated by the personality profile of those born under the divinatory almanac sign 1 Rabbit, who "were ample providers, good workers, and rich. . . . diligent, careful and vigilant. . . . Everything frightened him. . . . Perhaps they might thus snare or snatch something of his goods and property" (Sahagún 1979a [1569]: 127). This type of individual was well respected in Aztec society but hardly conforms to the militant warrior image. This is a hard-working, hard-worrying family man: Sahagún's informants devoted two long paragraphs to all the bad things that those born under 1 Rabbit feared might happen to that hard-won prosperity.

As subjects of Aztec sculpture in the round, rabbits are unusual and thus scarce in surveys of Aztec sculpture (Nicholson 1971a: 129; Pasztory 1983: 234–235); most occur in bas-relief and are dated. A comparable rabbit sculpted in the round is also unprovenienced, nearly twice as tall as PC.B.079, much less detailed, and bears no iconographic paraphernalia (Solís and Velasco 2002: 159, 417).

Sculpture PC.B.079 "has the slightly irregular surface modeling often found on greenstone carving, which makes it appear lively rather than rigid" (Pasztory 1983: 253). The artist has not made an entirely symmetrical rendering but has worked with the somewhat uneven character of the stone, and the effect is more similar to the naturalistic style of Aztec sculptures of animals than is the rendition of the birthing figure PC.B.071.

STE

AZTEC AND MIXTEC JEWELRY AND ORNAMENTS

JEFFREY QUILTER AND SUSAN TOBY EVANS

Elites in ancient Mexico had a highly developed taste for adornment with luxurious materials worked in interesting and ideologically significant forms. Jewelry of worked and polished stone was an ancient tradition in Mesoamerica, but in the Central Highlands objects of metal occurred in the Late Classic and Postclassic periods, with AD 650 as "the earliest secure date for a metal object found in West Mexico," where the metalworking traditions of Central Mexico had their start (West 1994: 9). Although the "Initial period" of metalworking (AD 650–1200/1300) was devoted to copper products, in the Early Postclassic the repertoire was extended to gold and silver and their alloys, and knowledge of metalworking spread into Central Mexico (Hosler 2003: 159). The Aztecs called gold *tecuitlatl*, "its name comes from *teotl* [god] and *cuitlatl* [excrement], because it is wonderful, yellow, good, fine, precious. It is the wealth, the riches, the lot, the possession, the property of the rulers, our lords" (Sahagún 1963 [1569]: 233).

Scientific reconstruction of the timing of metalworking in Central Mexico accords nicely with culture histories recorded by contact-era chroniclers. These emphasize the ruined city of Tula as a place "where the streets were paved with gold . . . and palaces were made of jade, silver, and shell" (Torquemada 1975–83 [1615] Lib. VI, Cap. XXIV: 81–82). The city was under the patronage of the great culture hero Topiltzin Quetzalcoatl, who "introduced great riches, jade, turquoise, gold, silver, redshell" (Codex Chimalpopoca 1992: 29). The term for the city's inhabitants, "Tolteca," became synonymous with artisans of the highest order. Sixteenth-century Aztecs, writing about the god Quetzalcoatl (with whom the culture hero Topiltzin Quetzalcoatl was conflated), noted that "the Tolteca, his vassals, were highly skilled. Nothing was difficult when they did it, when they cut the green stone and cast gold . . . these [crafts] . . . proceeded from Quetzalcoatl—all the crafts work, the learning" (Sahagún 1978 [1569]: 13).

By the Late Postclassic, "gold" had become synonymous with wealth and power. The Mexica Aztec's patron deity had prophesized to them: "we shall conquer nations, . . . become lords of gold and silver, of jewels and precious stones . . . of the insignia [that distinguish lords and chieftains]" (Durán 1994 [1581]: 40–43) and the recitation of precious materials, in that order, became something of a stock phrase for the Aztecs as they recounted their history, it was a "metaphor for power" (Heyden, note 1 in Durán 1994: 43).

In the mid-fifteenth century, Tenochtitlan emperor Motecuzoma I sent envoys to find the Aztec place of origin, bearing the message that, although the Mexica had started in poverty, "'now

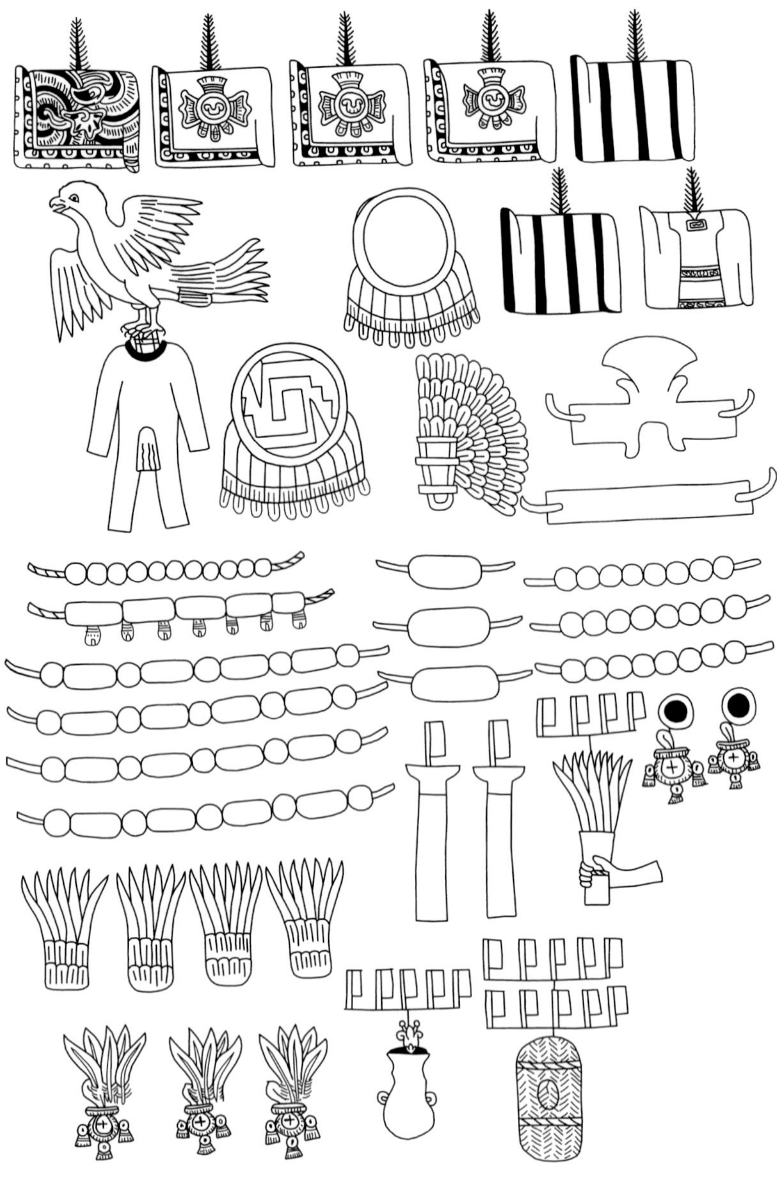

fig. 15
The Aztecs required gold as tribute in various forms and recorded tributes in documents like the Codex Mendoza. This page shows that finished gold products such as diadems and lip plugs were among the goods demanded of towns in the south-central Gulf Lowlands. Drawing by Susan Toby Evans (after Codex Mendoza 1992: fol. 46r).

the city . . . is prosperous. Tenochtitlan is . . . the leader and queen of all the cities, all of which pay obedience to her. For now the Aztecs have found the mines of gold and silver and precious stones'" (Durán 1994 [1581]: 218). It was true that Tenochtitlan had found sources of gold, but the Aztecs did not mine it—that was a Spanish colonial era innovation. Instead, those who sent gold to the Aztec Empire as tribute (Figure 15) found it in veins in the earth or panned it from river sands (Sahagún 1963 [1569]: 233). The Aztecs tried to secure access to the mineral riches of northern Guerrero, leading to chronic military hostilities with the Tarascan Empire (Pollard and Smith 2003: 87). When Cortés wished to know the sources of gold, Motecuzoma II sent out pairs of his men, accompanied by pairs of Spaniards, to four gold-producing provinces, including the Mixteca region (Cortés 1986 [1519–26]: 92–93).

The Mixtec of Oaxaca became the foremost Late Postclassic gold workers, refining the lost-wax technique of gold casting by which most three-dimensional objects were made. In the lost-wax technique, a wax model of the object is enclosed in a mold and the wax is melted out, replaced with liquid metal, which takes the shape of the original wax model (Hosler 2003: 160). Simple items were cast in open molds and then cold-worked by hammering and smoothing (Hosler 2003: 159–160). Mixtec metalworkers used both techniques, combining technical skill and innovation with mastery of design.[75]

The Aztecs classed the different grades of gold workers according to artisanship: "Some were called smiths. These had no office but to beat gold, to thin it out; to flatten it with a stone. . . . And some were called finishers . . . the real master craftsmen" (Sahagún 1959 [1569]: 69). At any level of mastery, there were good and bad practitioners. "The good goldworker [is] skilled . . . careful in his work—a purifier [of gold]. . . . The bad goldworker . . . lets ashes enter . . . [into the gold. He is] a pilferer . . . a thief, a looter" (Sahagún 1961 [1569]: 25).

An Aztec gold worker, describing his craft, wrote: "Thus I make things beautiful . . . I make things give off rays" (Sahagún 1963 [1569]: 234). Qualities of brilliance and sound were far more important to Mesoamericans than were gold's rarity and imperviousness, the traits valued by Europeans. Metallic objects could multiply light and produce different tones; thus they had life, they were animated, and these qualities made such objects sacred to Mesoamericans.

Their sanctity made the objects essential to rituals and indispensable to the lords. By the mid-fifteenth century, Motecuzoma I established sumptuary laws restricting access to gold and elite materials (Durán 1994 [1581]: 208–209). At about this time, long-distance merchants based in Tlatelolco, Tenochtitlan's sister city, began dealing in "gold lip and ear plugs . . . and necklaces with radiating pendants, and fine turquoise" (Sahagún 1959 [1569]: 2). Gold and greenstone jewelry and metal bells were among the most important traded commodities in the Postclassic world (Smith 2003: 118); gold-dust–filled feather quills became one of the period's standard exchange media (Berdan 2003: 94).

Mixteca-Puebla style in jewelry and imagery spread widely over the Central Highlands and into western Mexico (Nicholson 1973). Because of shared technologies and design preferences, Aztec and Mixtec gold ornaments are virtually indistinguishable and share a number of stylistic conventions. First, cast objects tend to have relatively compact and dense central sections with more intricate work around their perimeters, a formal characteristic that may be due to the nature of the casting technique but is also shared with southern Central American gold jewelry. Fine, wire-like decorations exemplify false filigree technique, presumably adopted from Colombia: although the pieces appear to be made of wires soldered together, they were, in fact, cast whole. Another trait that may reflect southern influence is the shape of the clapperless bells or tinklers that are commonly suspended below larger ornaments. Although southern Central American tinklers are usually rounder, both they and the Mixtec-Aztec examples shared narrow, curved rectangular slits as sound holes.

Mixtec-Aztec gold jewelry is distinctive in its use of linked sections, especially in necklaces, pendants, and ear ornaments. A large decorative item, usually round in contour, serves as the upper element from which are suspended a series of rows of small elements, commonly tinklers or bells, successively linked by wire rings or similar connectors. This technique allowed for increased light reflection of the various parts and movement of the piece with the wearer; it also maximized the sound effect (Hosler 1994) as pieces of jewelry tinkled against one another.

Many objects that have been assumed to be parts of necklaces or ear ornaments were in fact not designed to function in these ways. Although the parts often appear in multiples, they commonly have no holes for suspension on a cord. Supposed ear ornaments lack posts to insert in pierced ear lobes. These ornaments may have been sewn onto cloth backings or other materials to serve decorative purposes.

Ear spools and labrets were intended for particular body locations, and most Mixtec-Aztec jewelry items were made for the face, neck, and upper chest. The ears were the vehicles for hearing, and the mouth for speaking and breathing, of great social significance in societies in which the highest political authority was the "Great Speaker," the Hue Tlatoani, and in which breath was seen as an emanation of the soul (Taube 2004a: 72). Ornaments hanging from a hole in the nasal septum (*narigueras* in Spanish) linked the two orifices of breath, especially when gold plates moved with speech. *Narigueras* were powerful symbols of rank, and among the Mixtec, piercing the septum was the critical ceremony conferring royal power.

A noble Aztec or Mixtec would have been impressive, wearing large ear spools, a jangling *nariguera*, and a dramatic labret protruding from below the lips. The detailed ornamentation of gold work would have been most admired from relatively close range, such as in group meetings among peers. Sumptuary laws would have made any set of adornments and clothing into a coded status message, signifying fine distinctions of birth and achievement.

The jewelry from Central and West Mexico in the Bliss Collection includes many of the precious materials and kinds of ornaments favored by Postclassic elites. The objects command our admiration for their beauty and our respect as fragments of a lost world of high civilization in Mesoamerica. Although the courtly rituals, warrior dances, oratory, and other celebrations in the ancient palaces of Postclassic Mexico are no more, the study of these objects offers us today glimpses into that past and the people who made and wore these ornaments.

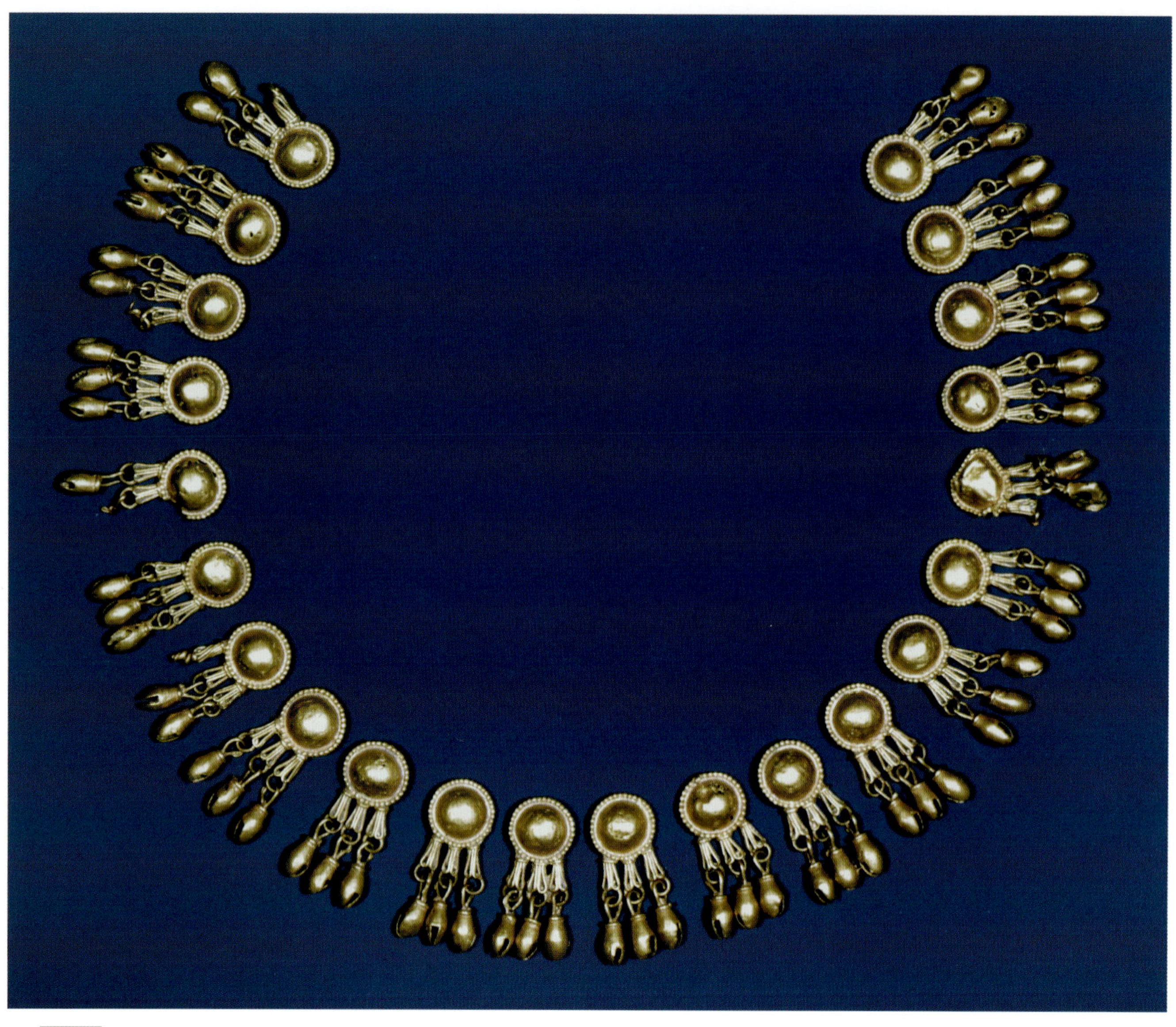

plate 27

PLATE 27
Mixteca-Puebla
Postclassic period, AD 900–1520
Cast gold
Each bead: H. 3.0 cm (1³⁄₁₆"); W. 3.1 cm (1¼")
PC.B.100

ACQUISITION HISTORY:
Purchased as two lots.[76] Ten pendants purchased at Sotheby's on 9 June 1937; formerly in the collection of Jean Holland. Twelve additional pendants purchased from John Wise, 1940

EXHIBITION HISTORY:
An Exhibition of Pre-Columbian Art, Fogg Art Museum, Cambridge, January–March 1940 (before purchase of second half of material); *Twenty Centuries of Mexican Art*, Museum of Modern Art, New York, May–September 1940; *Special Exhibit of Latin American Silver*, Pan American Union, Washington, D.C., October–November 1941; *Ancient American Art*, Santa Barbara Museum of Art, Santa Barbara, Calif., April–June 1942; M. H. de Young Memorial Museum, San Francisco, July–August 1942; Museum of Art, Portland, Ore., September–October 1942; Art of the Americas, Cleveland Museum of Art, Cleveland, Ohio, November 1945–January 1946; *Indigenous Art of the Americas*, National Gallery of Art, Washington, D.C., April 1947–March 1952, February 1954–July 1962 (NGA 1); *Ancient American Gold and Jade*, Taft Museum, Cincinnati, Ohio, October–November 1950; *Art Méxicain du Précolombien à nos jours*, Musée national d'Art moderne, Paris, May–July 1952; Mexikansk Konst frän Forntid till Nutid, Liljevalches Konsthall, Stockholm, 1952; *Art of Aztec Mexico: Treasures of Tenochtitlan*, National Gallery of Art, Washington, D.C., September 1983–April 1984

BIBLIOGRAPHY:
Sotheby's 1937; Wenham 1937: 258; Peabody Museum of Archaeology and Ethnology and Fogg Art Museum 1940: cat. no. 230; Bliss 1947: 20, 49, cat. no. 90; *Art Digest* 1950; Liljevalchs Konsthall 1952: cat. no. 665e; Musée national d'Art moderne 1952: I: cat. no. 526, pl. 38; Bliss 1957: 247, cat. no. 97, pl. LIX; Mason 1958: pl. LIX; Dumbarton Oaks 1963: 26, cat. no. 127; Willey 1966: I: 164; Burchwood 1972: pl. 24; Nicholson with Quiñones Keber 1983: 157, cat. no. 72; Berdan 1989; Solís and Carmona 1995: cat. no. 157; Smith 1996

Each of these 22 composite objects consists of a gold alloy oval with a flattened edge, a form that resembles the Late Postclassic warrior shield. From one side of each object, three elongated bells are suspended. The overall three-tiered form is typically Mixtec-Aztec in style, although the wire-like middle sections, from which hang the tinklers, are less common than other treatments.

These composite objects are arrayed in a necklace-like fashion, though it would have been necessary to mount them on a backing to wear them as a necklace or on two separate backings for them to function as bracelets. Alternatively, they may have ornamented a piece of clothing or leggings, or even a shield or banner. The presence of the bells in the design means that movement would have activated the sound and the reflective quality of the gold.

Although these objects were definitely reserved for royals, nobles, and high-status commoners (such as long-distance merchants), they could be purchased at markets in large cities. At the Tlatelolco market, largest in Tenochtitlan-Tlatelolco, the Spaniards found "every kind of merchandise . . . provisions as well as ornaments of gold and silver" (Cortés 1986 [1519–26]: 101).

JQ AND STE

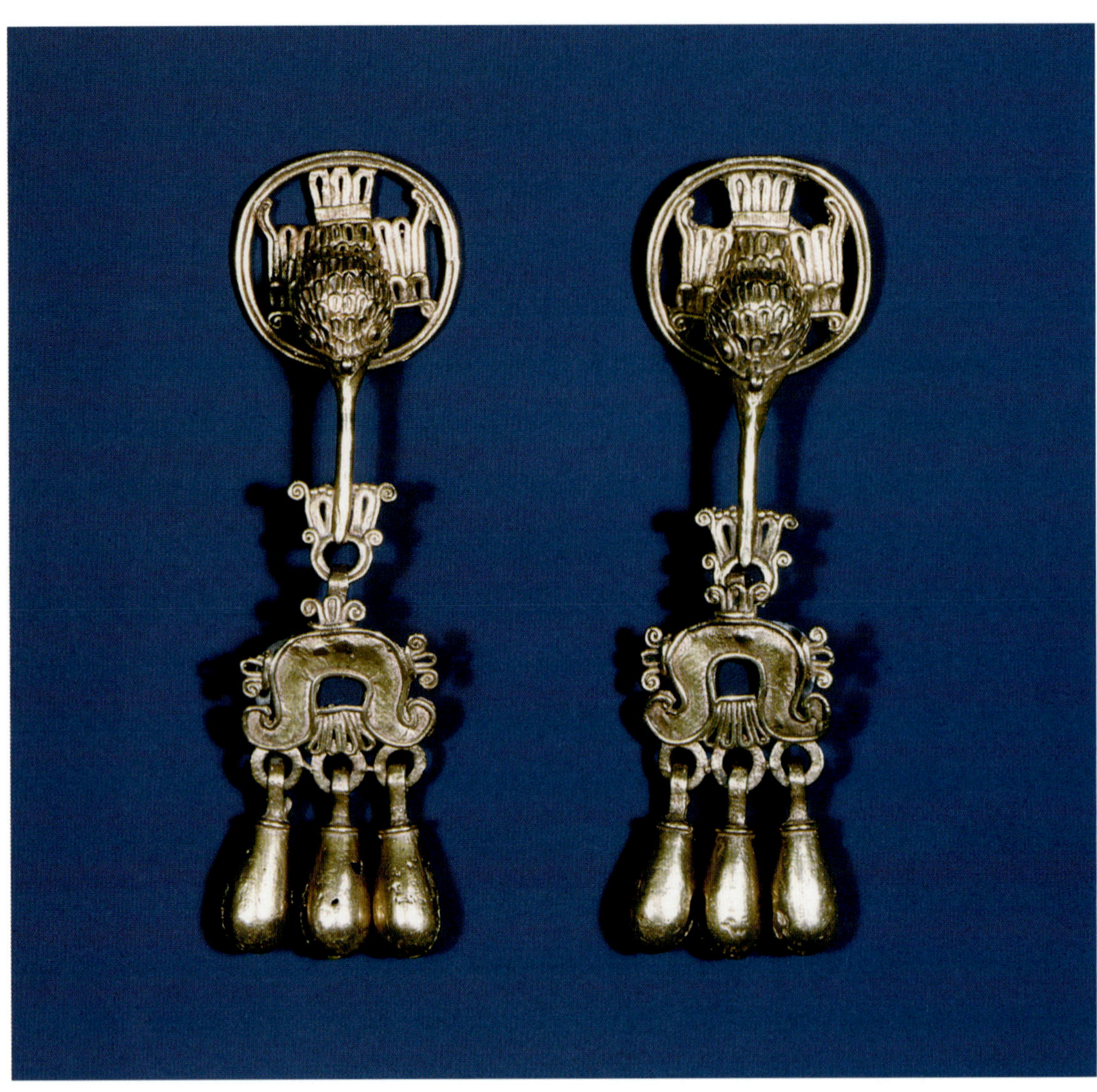

plate 28

EAR ORNAMENTS

PLATE 28
Mixtec
Postclassic period, AD 900–1520
Cast gold
H. 6.03 cm (2⅜"); W. 1.91 cm (¾"); D. 0.95 cm (⅜")
PC.B.101

ACQUISITION HISTORY:
Purchased in two lots.[77] One ornament purchased at Sotheby's on 9 June 1937; formerly in the collection of Jean Holland. The other ornament purchased from John Wise, 1940

EXHIBITION HISTORY:
An Exhibition of Pre-Columbian Art, Fogg Art Museum, Cambridge, January–March 1940 (before purchase of second half of material); *Twenty Centuries of Mexican Art*, Museum of Modern Art, New York, May–September 1940; Special Exhibit of Latin American Silver, Pan American Union, Washington, D.C., October–November 1941; *Ancient American Art*, Santa Barbara Museum of Art, Santa Barbara, Calif., April–June 1942; M. H. de Young Memorial Museum, San Francisco, July–August 1942; Museum of Art, Portland, Ore., September–October 1942; Art of the Americas,

EXHIBITION HISTORY: *(Continued)*
Cleveland Museum of Art, Cleveland, Ohio, November 1945–January 1946; *Indigenous Art of the Americas*, National Gallery of Art, Washington, D.C., April 1947–July 1962 (NGA 91); *Ancient American Gold and Jade*, Taft Museum, Cincinnati, Ohio, October–November 1950; *Art Méxicain du Précolombien à nos jours*, Musée national d'Art moderne, Paris, May–July 1952; Mexikansk Konst frän Forntid till Nutid, Liljevalches Konsthall, Stockholm, 1952; *Art of Aztec Mexico: Treasures of Tenochtitlan*, National Gallery of Art, Washington, D.C., September 1983–April 1984

BIBLIOGRAPHY:
Sotheby's 1937: no. 166, pl. III; Wenham 1937: 258, fig. 1a; Peabody Museum of Archaeology and Ethnology and Fogg Art Museum 1940: cat. no. 230; Greenwood 1942: cat. no. 25; Santa Barbara Museum of Art 1942: cat. no. 97; Bliss 1947: 20, 49, cat. no. 90; Taft Museum 1950: cat. no. 191–192; Liljevalchs Konsthall 1952: cat. no. 665e; Musée national d'Art moderne 1952: I: cat. no. 526; Bliss 1957: 248, cat. no. 98, pl. LIX; Mason 1958: pl. LIX; Dumbarton Oaks 1963: 26, cat. no. 127; Willey 1966: I: 164; Burchwood 1972: pl. 24; Nicholson with Quiñones Keber 1983: 156, cat. no. 71; Berdan 1989: 68; Smith 1996: 104, fig. 4.9

Each of these gold ornaments has, as its most prominent motif, a hummingbird head. The hummingbird head unites the three tiers of the design: body at top and, suspended from the bird's beak, a curving ornament from which dangle three elongated bells. These objects are assumed to have been worn on the ears or near them, probably supported by cloth backings.

The hummingbird's simplified, downward-facing body is wrought in cast gold false filigree, a design mimicking the use of gold wire and a common feature of Mixtec-style gold pieces. The false filigree's looping pattern imitates the feathers of the bird's body, wings, and tail, a form that had been "modeled in wax and cast in a single flow of metal" (Lothrop in Bliss 1957: 248, cat. no. 98). The body is enclosed by a double circle of gold filigree. The hummingbird head emerges from the body out of a collar of looping false filigree "feathers" and this feather motif covers the bird's downward-facing, three-dimensional head. The stylized object suspended from its beak possibly represents a butterfly (Bliss 1947: 20) or a butterfly nose ornament turned upside-down (Nicholson with Quiñones Keber 1983: 152–153).

The bottom tier of this design consists of three bells.[78] The hummingbird's long beak gives greater play to the bells, enhancing the sound effect. The long beak adds drama to the overall composition by separating the head and body from the lower part of the composition. These features reveal how the artist has used the design elements to advantage.

To the Aztecs, the hummingbird was revered for its association with the Mexica tribal patron deity, Huitzilopochtli, "Hummingbird on the Left" or "Hummingbird to the South," who oversaw their journey to Tenochtitlan from their mythic homeland, Aztlán. In establishing Tenochtitlan, the Mexica honored Huitzilopochtli with one of the two temples atop the pyramid of the Templo Mayor in the main ritual precinct of Tenochtitlan. Few sculpted images of this deity survive, and in the documentary sources he is often depicted as a priest or impersonator wearing a hummingbird helmet and a costume appropriate to the god (Boone 1989).

The ornaments are comparable to gold ornaments made using the lost wax technique that have been found among the magnificent Mixtec offerings of Tomb 7 at Monte Albán (Caso 1969: 107–109, láms. 12, 13). A similar pair of ear ornaments is at The Metropolitan Museum of Art, New York (accession no. 1978.412.200. a, b [Solís 2004: 238, 362, no. 128]); they are in the shape of eagle heads in a gold roundel, with three bells descending from the beak.

STE AND JQ

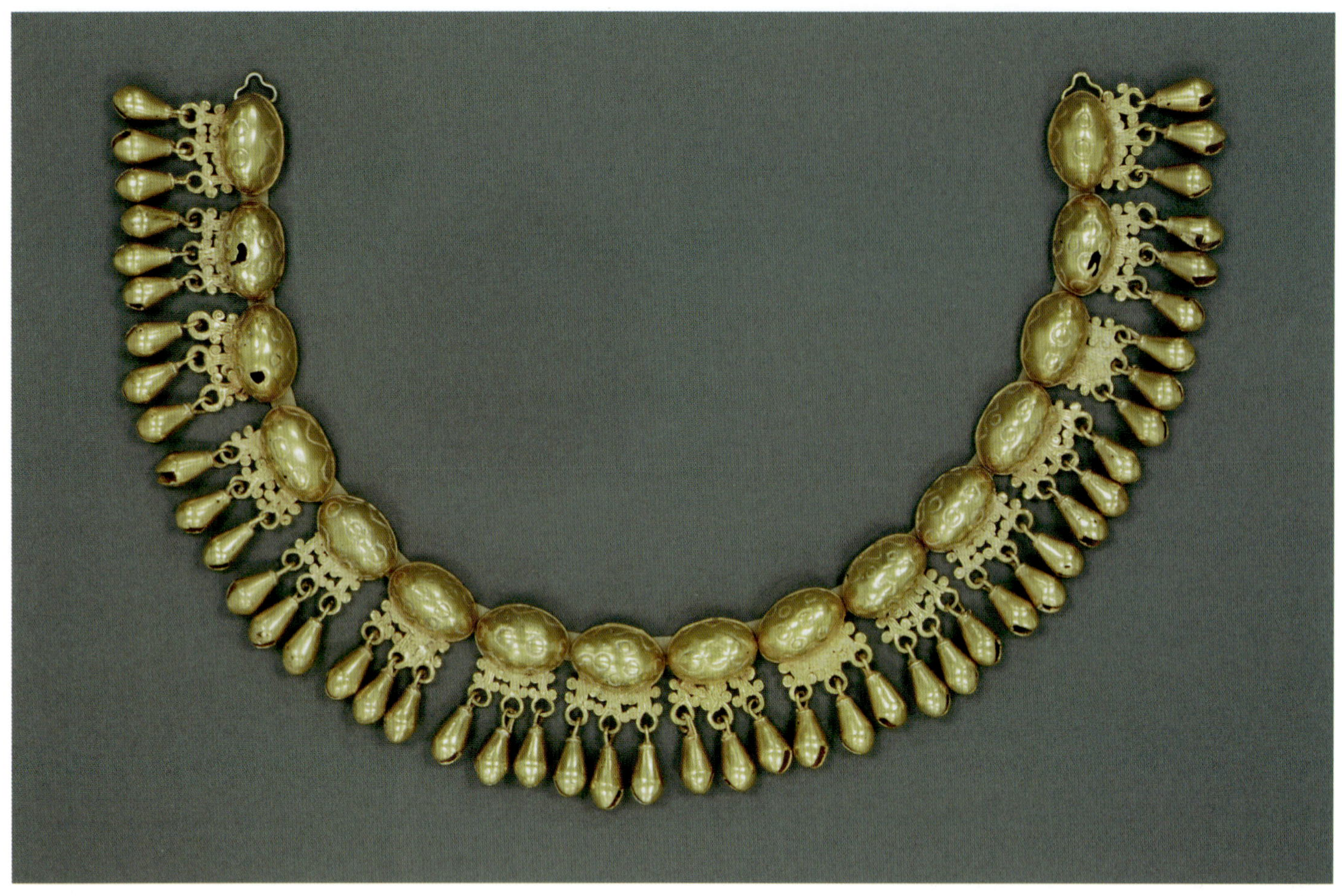

plate 29

TURTLE SHELL GOLD ORNAMENTS

PLATE 29
Mixtec-Aztec
Late Postclassic period, AD 1200–1520
Cast gold
L. (overall) 39.5 cm (15¾")
Each bead: H. 3.7 cm (1½"); W. 1.35 cm (½"); D. 0.6 cm (¼")
PC.B.103

ACQUISITION HISTORY:
Purchased from Earl Stendahl, 1960

EXHIBITION HISTORY:
Indigenous Art of the Americas, National Gallery of Art, Washington, D.C., July 1960–April 1962 (NGA 755); *Art of Aztec Mexico: Treasures of Tenochtitlan*, National Gallery of Art, Washington, D.C., September 1983–April 1984; *The Aztec World*, The Field Museum, Chicago, October 2008–April 2009

BIBLIOGRAPHY:
Dumbarton Oaks 1963: 27, cat. no. 129; Nicholson with Quiñones Keber 1983: 159, cat. no. 74; Solís and Carmona 1995: cat. no. 159

These 16 stylized turtle shells were probably sewn onto a cloth backing to be worn as a collar or necklace. The typical three-tier design mode of gold objects has been contracted in this example, with the second tier consisting only of volutes extending as a flange from the lower edge of the shells and terminating in loops for the suspension of teardrop-shaped tinklers.

The design field of the shells consists of ovals flanked by zigzags on the long sides of each shell. This form is highly conventionalized, only vaguely referencing the plates of a real turtle shell. The volutes that transform into rings for the suspension of the tinklers may be water motifs, apt for turtles and perhaps linking the idea of the sounds of water with the sounds of the tinklers.

Nicholson (with Quiñones Keber 1983: 159–160, citing Saville 1920: 67) notes that an undated list of treasure sent back to Spain after the conquest includes necklaces with either turtle shell or turtle elements; one of the necklaces consisted of 48 pieces. Similar necklaces were found in Tomb 7 at Monte Albán by Alfonso Caso (1969: 170–171, láms. 51, 52), one with 14 carapace-shaped beads, each bearing 3 elongated bells, and the other having 16 carapaces with zigzag designs and flattened edges, and 4 bells suspended from each shell. Caso wrote that these necklaces made of turtle shell–shaped beads "seemed to be very much in vogue when the Spaniards arrived," because they figured in the inventories of jewels sent to the king of Spain, and one of them was represented in a manuscript known as the Memorial de los indios de Tepetlaóztoc, or the Codex Kingsborough (1969: 170).

JQ

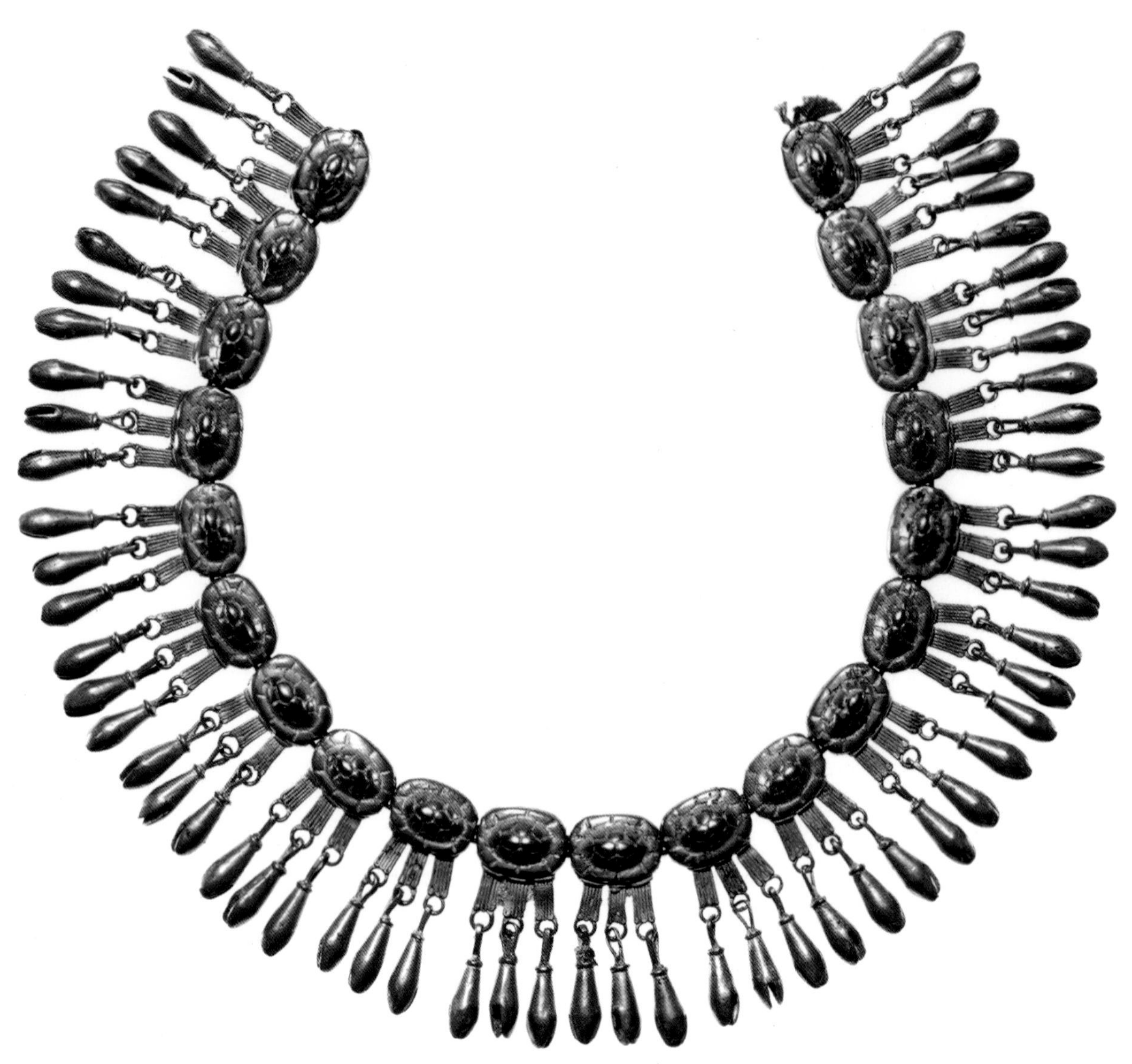

plate 30

TURTLE SHELL GOLD ORNAMENTS

PLATE 30
Mixtec-Aztec
Postclassic period, AD 900–1520
Cast gold
Overall ornament: L. 26.3 cm (10⅜")
Each bead: H. 3.7 cm (1½"); W. 1.35 cm (½"); D. 0.6 cm (¼")
PC.B.102

ACQUISITION HISTORY:
Purchased from Earl Stendahl, 1962

EXHIBITION HISTORY:
Die Azteken und ihre Vorläufer: Glanz und Untergang des Alten Mexico, Roemer- und Pelizaeus-Museum, Hildesheim, Germany, June–November 1986; Haus der Kunst, Munich, December 1986–March 1987; Oberösterreichisches Landesmuseum, Linz, Austria, April–August 1987; Louisiana Museum of Modern Art, Humlebæk, Denmark, August–November 1987; Musées royaux d'Art et d'Histoire, Brussels, December 1987–March 1988; National Archaeological Museum, Athens, May–July 1988; Société du Palais de la Civilisation, Montreal, July–October 1988

BIBLIOGRAPHY:
Dumbarton Oaks 1963: 26, cat. no. 128; Boone 1986c: cat. no. 263; Louisiana Museum 1987: 13, 82, cat. no. 278

This necklace of 20 turtle shell ornaments resembles PC.B.103 (Plate 29) and the cast gold turtle shell necklaces found in Tomb 7 at Monte Albán, in that the cast gold turtle shells have carapace motifs like those on living turtle species. Alfonso Caso enlisted the help of a biologist to identify the possible model for Tomb 7's gold carapaces, and he suggested genus *Cinosternum* and species *hirtipes* (Caso 1969: 170–171), a turtle now known as *Kinosternon hirtipes*, the Mexican rough-footed mud turtle.

To the Aztecs, the turtle (*ayutl*) was respected for its role in the cosmos. The jagged surface of the earth was thought to be the back of a turtle or crocodilian animal, rendered as an earth monster. Perhaps for this reason, the turtle shell was a popular motif for jewelry.

Like the composite design of PC.B.103, that of PC.B.102 includes elongated bells, in this case suspended from long and simple false filigree attachments. This design would have enhanced their capacity to make sound and reflect light. The variety in the size and shape of metal bells known from Postclassic contexts may seem, from the modern perspective, simply to reflect a relatively primitive state of mass production in the manufacturing process. In fact, the presence of bells of the same or different sizes and shapes in a single composition, such as a set of matched ornaments, was a deliberate choice. Pitch varied by size and shape, so the sound effect of any set of bells would be distinctive. Worn as ankle bracelets in a dance, the coordinated effect of several dancers would be subtle but discernible to the trained ear. Small bells imitated the sound of rain, thus suggesting fertility, and the wearer's perceived power over agricultural fertility might be enhanced by the use of these ornaments (Hosler 2003: 162). In combination with icons of the earth monster, the design composition emphasizes the fertility of the earth.

STE

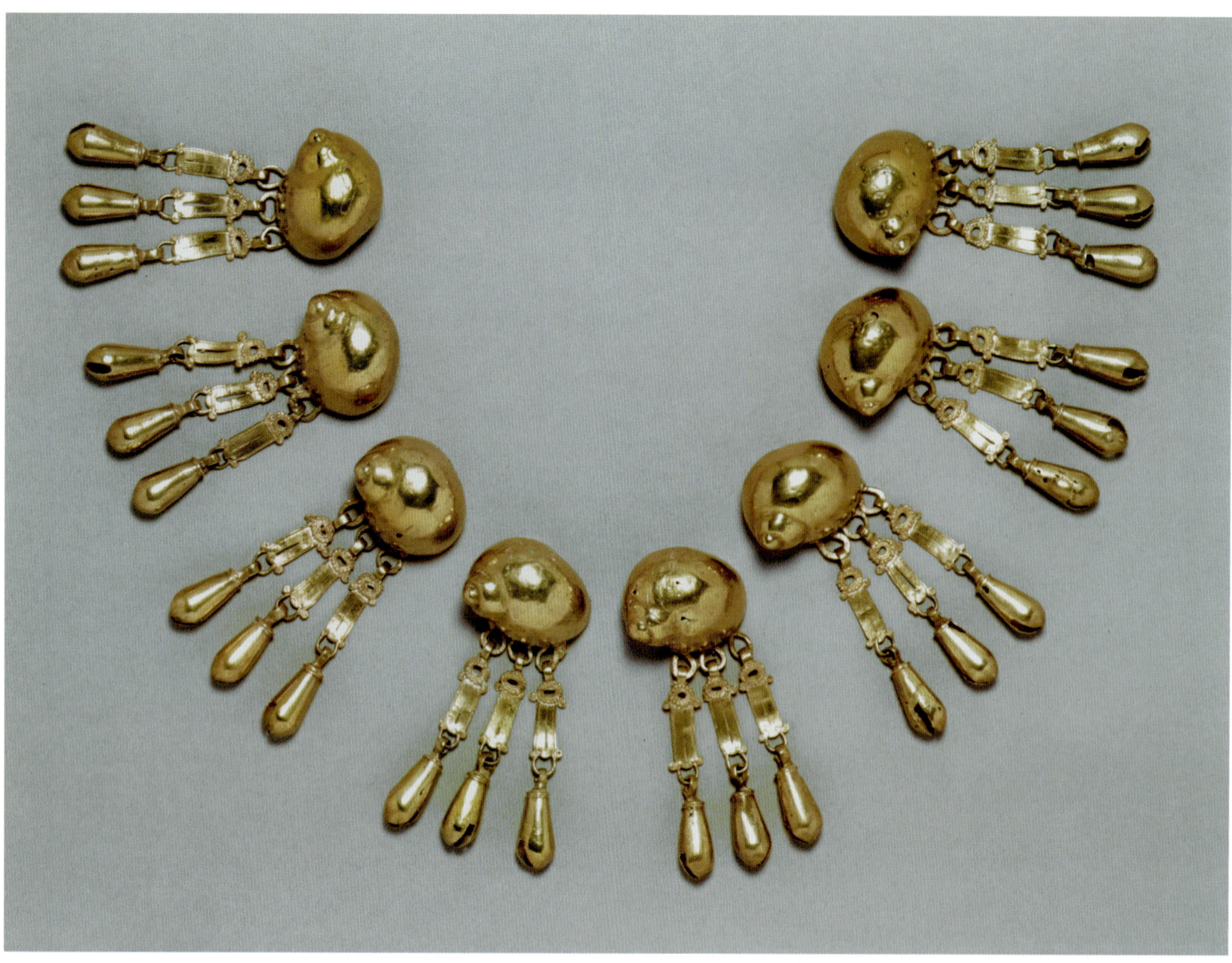

plate 31

SNAIL SHELL ORNAMENTS

PLATE 31
Mixtec-Aztec
Late Postclassic period, AD 1200–1520
Cast gold
Each bead assemblage: H. 8.0 cm (3⅛")
Each bead: W. 3.1 cm (1¼"); D. 2.3 cm (⅞")
PC.B.104

ACQUISITION HISTORY:
Purchased from Earl Stendahl, 1958, reportedly found in Chiapas

EXHIBITION HISTORY:
Präkolumbische Kunst aus Mexico und Mittelamerika, Haus der Kunst, Munich, October–December 1958; *Kunst der Mexikaner,* Kunsthaus, Zürich, January–March 1959; *Kunst aus Mexico und Mittelamerika,* Akademie der Künste, Berlin, October–November 1959; *Präkolumbische Kunst aus Mexico und Mittelamerika,* Künstlerhaus, Vienna, December 1959–February 1960; Historisches Museum, Frankfurt am Main, May–September 1960; *Arte Precolumbiana del Messico e dell'America Centrale,* Palazzo delle Esposizioni, Rome, November–December 1960; *Art of Aztec Mexico: Treasures of Tenochtitlan,* National Gallery of Art, Washington, D.C., September 1983–April 1984;

EXHIBITION HISTORY: *(continued)*
Die Azteken und ihre Vorläufer: Glanz und Untergang des Alten Mexico, Roemer- und Pelizaeus-Museum, Hildesheim, Germany, June–November 1986; Haus der Kunst, Munich, December 1986–March 1987; Oberösterreichisches Landesmuseum, Linz, Austria, April–August 1987; Louisiana Museum of Modern Art, Humlebæk, Denmark, August–November 1987; Musées royaux d'Art et d'Histoire, Brussels, December 1987–March 1988; National Archaeological Museum, Athens, May–July 1988; Société du Palais de la Civilisation, Montreal, July–October 1988; *Aztecs*, Royal Academy of Arts, London, September 2002–April 2003; Ethnologisches Museum, Berlin, May–August 2003; Art and Exhibition Hall of the Federal Republic of Germany, Bonn, September 2003–January 2004; *The Aztec Empire*, Guggenheim Museum, New York, October 2004–February 2005; Guggenheim Museum, Bilbao, Spain, March–September 2005

BIBLIOGRAPHY:
Haus der Kunst München 1958: cat. no. 241, ill. opp. p. 80; Akademie der Künste 1959: cat. no. 848, ill. opp. p. 96; Kunsthaus Zürich 1959: cat. no. 652, pl. VII; Künstlerhaus Wien 1959: cat. no. 764, ill. opp. p. 80; Centro di Azione Latina 1960: cat. no. 135; Historisches Museum Frankfurt am Main 1960: cat. no. 130, pl. 10; Dumbarton Oaks 1963: 27, cat. no. 130; Nicholson with Quiñones Keber 1983: 158, cat. no. 73; Boone 1986b: cat. no. 262; Louisiana Museum 1987: 82, cat. no. 277; Solís and Carmona 1995: cat. no. 158; Matos and Solís 2002: 248, cat. no. 178; Traxler 2002d: 443, cat. no. 178; Heinken 2003: 37; Solís 2004: 242, top, 363, no. 133, cat. no. 178; Traxler 2004b: 42, cat. no. 178

These gold snail shells were probably sewn to a cloth backing to be worn as a necklace or similar multi-item ornament, similar to the manner of display of the gold turtle shells (PC.B.103, Plate 29). Each piece of the ensemble consists of a typical Mixtec-Aztec three-piece unit comprised of a shell with rings on its lower edge, ribbon-and-rosette elements with links, and, lowest, tear-shaped tinklers. The three tiers of ornaments are complemented by three separate ribbon-tinkler units hanging from each shell.

Slight differences in each of these ornaments suggest that real snail shells were used to make the molds for casting, but the species has not been determined.[79] Casting flaws, mostly holes, are found on both the shells and the tinklers.

The form of the small snail shells on which this necklace is based may be a reference to larger oceanic conch shells, which would have been awkward to wear around the neck. Such shells were popular motifs in ancient Mexico, emblematic of the primordial waters of the underworld and those on which the earth floats. Wearing snail shell jewelry was a special prerogative of rulers (Sahagún 1979b [1569]: 28). Shells are associated with Tlaloc at the Aztec Templo Mayor and with Quetzalcoatl in the Classic and Postclassic periods. The symbolic referents of these ornaments therefore may be to general notions of origins and fertility rather than to a specific deity. Worn by a high-ranking man or woman, such a necklace would have not only broadcast the owner's access to precious metals but also marked the owner as connected to such origins and thus of great importance.

JQ

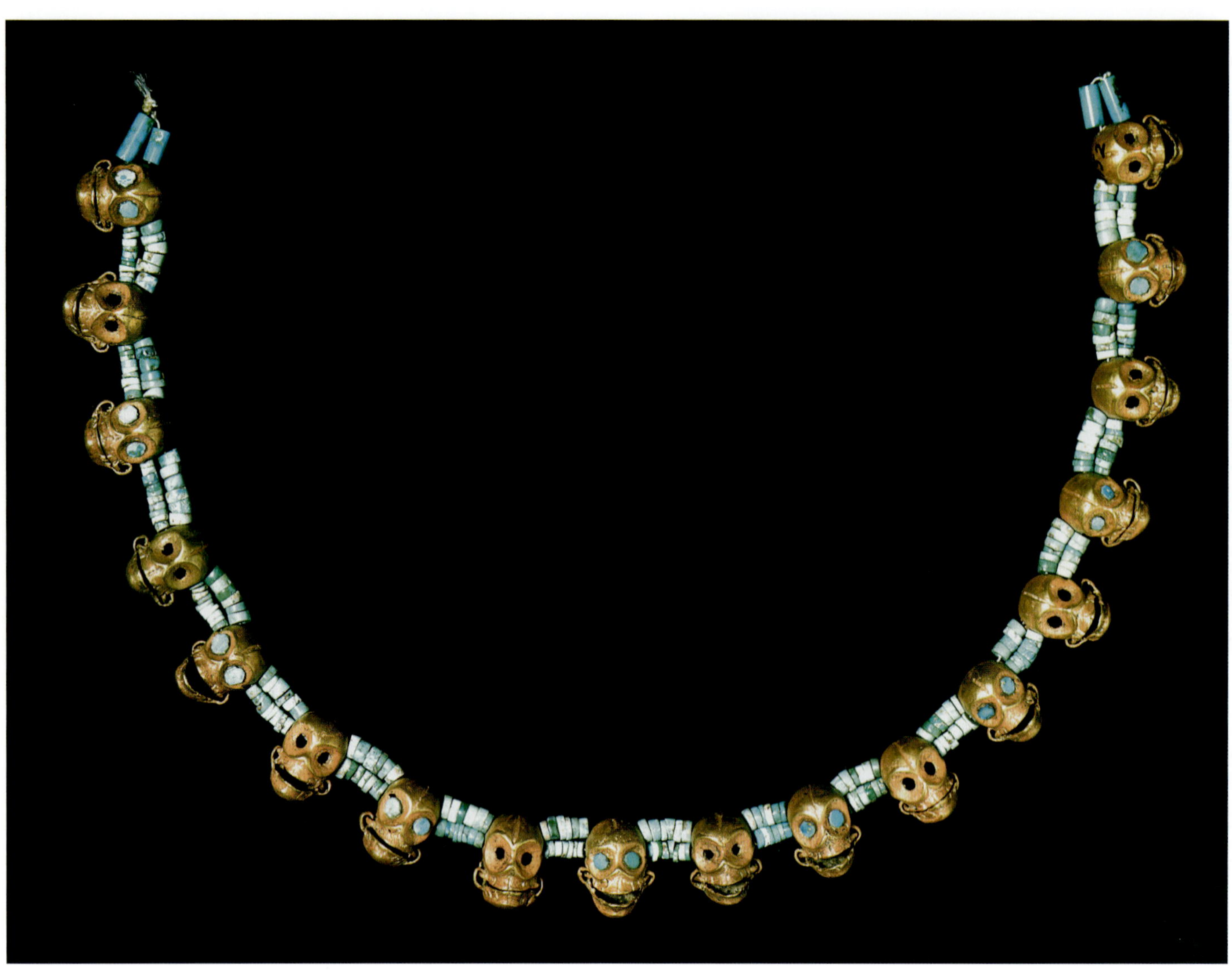

plate 32

NECKLACE WITH ORNAMENTS IN THE SHAPE OF HUMAN SKULLS OR MONKEY HEADS

PLATE 32
Mixteca-Puebla
Postclassic period, AD 900–1520
Cast gold and turquoise
Necklace length: 34.5 cm (13½")
Skull beads: H. 0.15 cm (⅝"); W. 0.12 cm (½");
D. 0.09 cm (⅜")
PC.B.108

ACQUISITION HISTORY:
Purchased from Earl Stendahl, 1962; reportedly from a tomb in southwest Chiapas

EXHIBITION HISTORY:
Art of Aztec Mexico: Treasures of Tenochtitlan, National Gallery of Art, Washington, D.C., September 1983–April 1984

BIBLIOGRAPHY:
Dumbarton Oaks 1963: 27, cat. no. 134; Nicholson with Quiñones Keber 1983: 161, cat. no. 75; Stuart 2003: 142; Izeki 2008: 146, cat. no. 2.1.58

The 18 cast gold beads are similar in iconography to the shell skull necklace also in the collection (PC.B.083, Plate 43). Here, however, the treatment seems to be playful, as careful and skilled artisanry produced these heads with jaws that move up and down. They may represent the heads of spider monkeys, or human skulls. A detail such as moveable jaws suggests that his necklace was probably made for close-up observation and enjoyment in intimate social settings.

This detail also shows the great artisanship of Late Postclassic gold workers. Motolinía (1950 [1541]: 241) noted that "in casting a piece and making it in a mold they surpass the Spanish silversmiths, for they can cast a bird whose tongue, head, and wings move, and they can mold a monkey or other monster which moves its head." Double rows of turquoise beads alternate with the cast gold skulls and echo the inlays of the eyes. Turquoise is mostly found in northwestern Mexico and the southwestern United States. It was brought to Central Mexico by long-distance trade. The use of turquoise, like gold working, is a Postclassic innovation, and among the Aztecs it was especially associated with rulers. By extension, the royal headdress (*xiuhuitzolli*), a blue peaked frontlet, was worn especially by deities with the lord (*tecuhtli*) elements in their names, such as Ilamatecuhtli, Mictlantecuhtli, and Tonacatecuhtli (Nicholson 1973: 87).

JQ AND STE

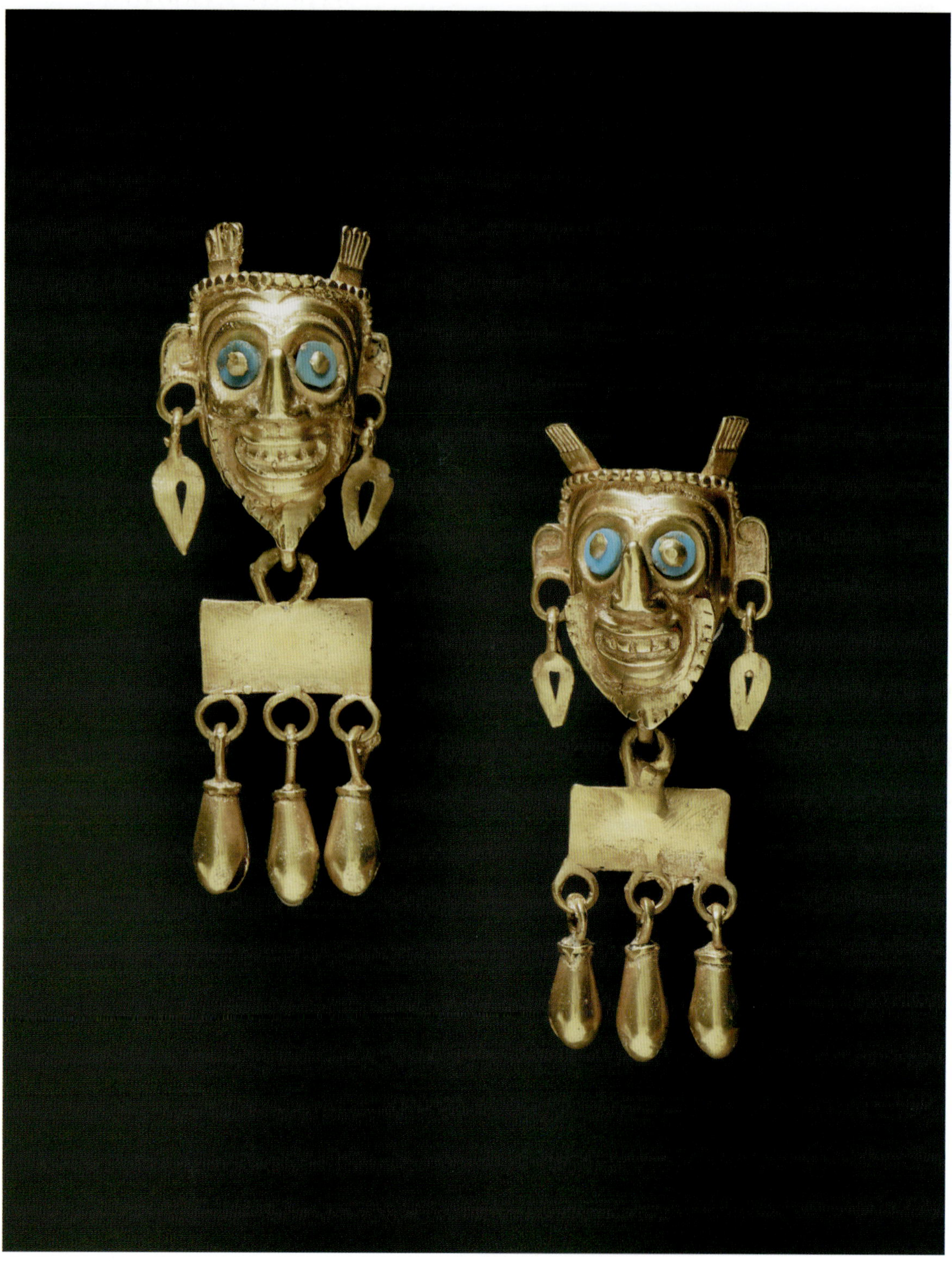

plate 33

PAIR OF EARRINGS

PLATE 33
Mixtec
Postclassic period, AD 900–1520
Cast gold and turquoise
H. 6.03 cm (2⅜"); W. 2.22 cm (⅞"); D. 1.91 cm (¾")
PC.B.109a, PC.B.109b

ACQUISITION HISTORY:
Purchased from Earl Stendahl, 1962

BIBLIOGRAPHY:
Dumbarton Oaks 1963: 27–28, cat. no. 135; Heiniger and Heiniger 1974: pl. 134

This pair of earrings combines mask-like faces with a suspended flat bar from which dangle elongated bells. The faces are typical of Mixtec-style ornaments, and important examples of this type of mask-like face have been found on gold objects from several locations. Most famous are those from the Mixtec Tomb 7 at Monte Albán, which include plaques and pectorals (Caso 1969: 83–97). On several, deities are depicted whose attenuated bodies are arrayed as kneeling against rectangular plaques, and the mask-like heads are surmounted by elaborate square headdresses worked in cast gold false filigree (Caso 1969: 93–95, lám. 7; González Licón 1994: 186, figs. 147, 148). Such ornaments have been identified as pectorals. Another example of this type is an object said to have been found in Papantla, Veracruz, depicting the fire god Xiuhtecuhtli, with details worked in false filigree (Tinoco 2004a: 38, cat. no. 159).

Although these examples take the form of pectorals, heads of this style were also used in composite ornaments, such as PC.B.107. An example from Monte Albán's Tomb 7 is far more elaborate, with the face covered by an eagle mask, from which is suspended an abstracted butterfly and two rows of four bells (Caso 1969: 105, lám. IIC). This ornament measures 3¼ inches, so that the heads on the Dumbarton Oaks objects are similar in size to that of the Tomb 7 piece.

The grinning faces of the PC.B.109 objects have eyes in the shape of concentric circles, typical of the way that eyes are depicted on monkeys in Central Highlands art. The plaques are suspended from the ends of pointed goatees. The ears have very large holes from which dangle earrings in the pointed oval shape associated with the cut section of the conch shell—one diagnostic trait of Quetzalcoatl. In fact, the monkey is related to Quetzalcoatl in his guise as Ehecatl (Miller and Taube 1993: 118).

STE

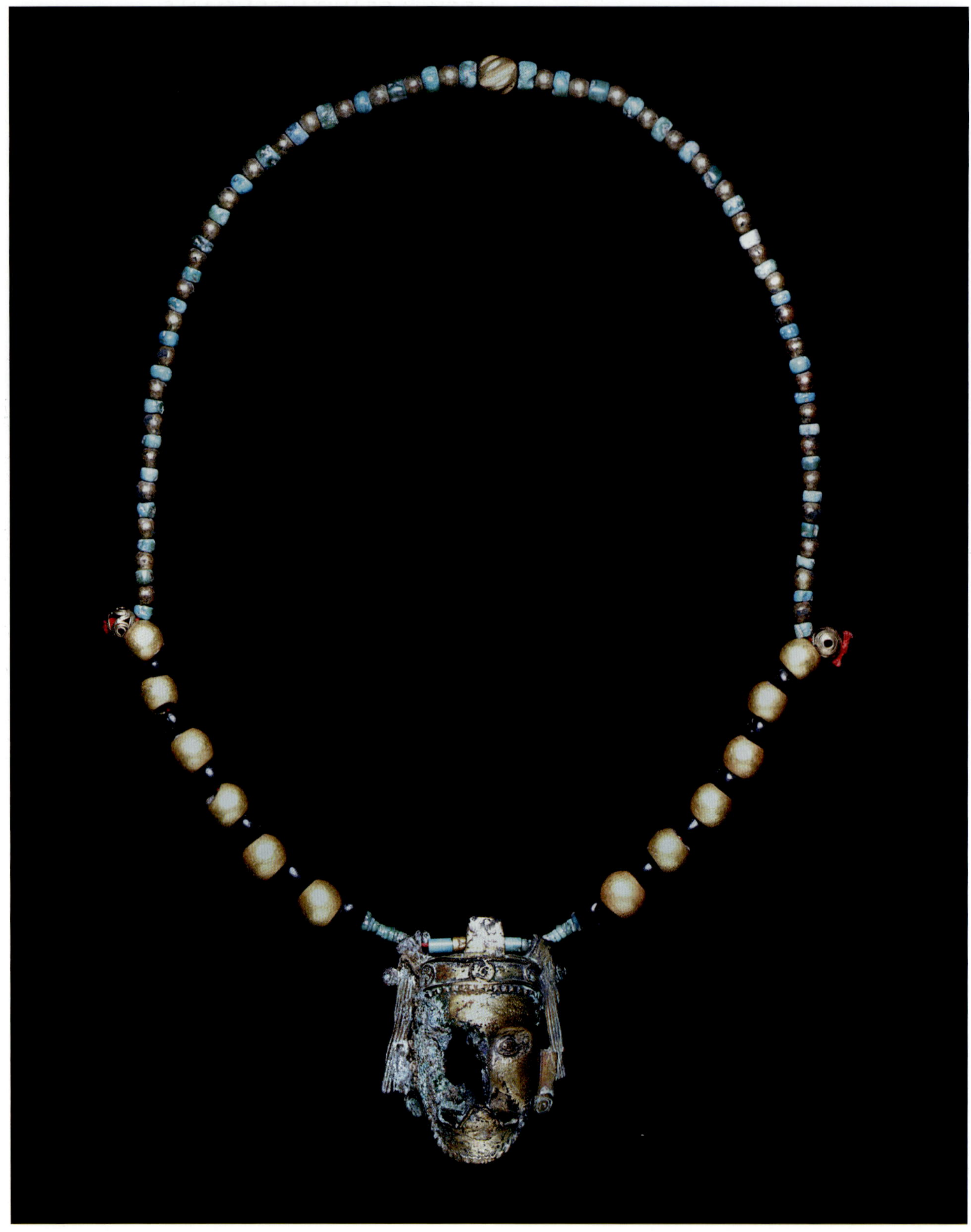

plate 34

NECKLACE WITH PENDANT

PLATE 34
Mixtec-Aztec
Postclassic period, AD 900–1520
Gilded copper
Necklace: L. 63.5 cm (25")
Pendant: H. 5.5 cm (2⅛"); W. 4.76 cm (1⅞");
D. 3.18 cm (1¼")
PC.B.107

ACQUISITION HISTORY:
Purchased from Earl Stendahl, 1960

EXHIBITION HISTORY:
Indigenous Art of the Americas, National Gallery of Art, Washington, D.C., July 1960–April 1962 (NGA 756)

BIBLIOGRAPHY:
Dumbarton Oaks 1963: 27, cat. no. 133

This composite ornament is fashioned as a necklace of beads of various materials, including some that are covered with gold foil (Dorothy Hosler, personal communication, November 1997), and a pendant in the shape of a head. As was discussed in the essay on PC.B.109 (Plate 33), such pendants are well known, and there are examples from Tomb 7 at Monte Albán and from a tomb in Coixtlahuaca in the Mixteca Alta (Tinoco 2004c), as well as the unprovenienced Xiuhtecuhtli pendant from Mexico City (Tinoco 2004b).

Those faces are all interpreted as the fire god Xiuhtecuhtli on the basis of their fanged mouths and beards. The face of PC.B.107 also has a beard, but this characteristic is sometimes also associated with Quetzalcoatl. The face is surmounted by a headband decorated with a disk motif. Such headbands are found on some of these mask-like faces, such as the mask of Xipe Totec found in Tomb 7 (Caso 1969: 97–99, lám. 10). Stylized elements in false filigree, perhaps representing hair, decorate the sides of the face.

The material of the head has been described as copper covered with gold. The face has sustained considerable damage, and where the surface has been destroyed, the piece has corroded. Possibly the object was cast of a gold and copper alloy (tumbaga), and then the surface was treated so as to remove the copper, leaving the gold—a treatment termed "mise-en-couleur." It is unclear whether the pendant and bead necklace (or some part of it) formed a coherent composition in antiquity.

STE

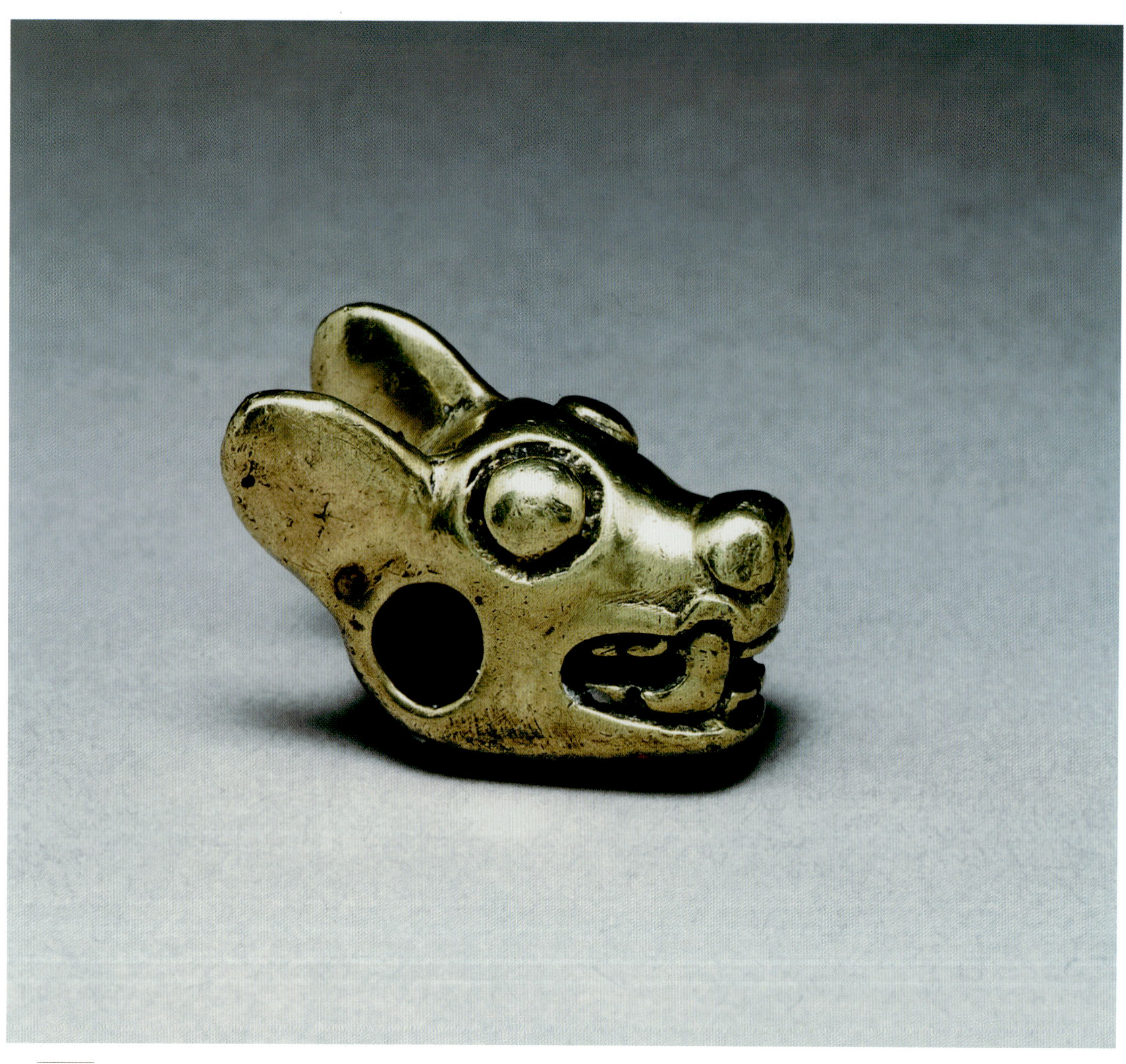

plate 35

GOLD BEAD IN THE FORM OF AN ANIMAL HEAD

PLATE 35
Mixtec
Postclassic period, AD 900–1520
Cast gold
H. 1.91 cm (¾"); W. 1.27 cm (½"); D. 2.86 cm (1⅛")
PC.B.110

ACQUISITION HISTORY:
Purchased at Sotheby's on 9 June 1937; formerly in the collection of Jean Holland

EXHIBITION HISTORY:
Special Exhibit of Latin American Silver, Pan American Union, Washington, D.C., October–November 1941; *Ancient American Art,* Santa Barbara Museum of Art, Santa Barbara, Calif., April–June 1942; M. H. de Young Memorial Museum, San Francisco, July–August 1942; Museum of Art, Portland, Ore., September–October 1942; *Indigenous Art of the Americas,* National Gallery of Art, Washington, D.C., April 1947–July 1949 (NGA 28)

BIBLIOGRAPHY:
Sotheby's 1937: no. 167, pl. III; Greenwood 1942: cat. no. 24; Santa Barbara Museum of Art 1942: cat. no. 99; Bliss 1947: 16, 90, cat. no. 66; Bliss 1957: 266, cat. no. 233, pl. CII, middle right; Dumbarton Oaks 1963: 28, cat. no. 138

This simple, charmingly rendered animal head was cast as one piece (Dorothy Hosler, personal communication, November 1997). It has a perforation, indicating that it may have functioned as a bead or a pendant. The animal appears to be a canid, judging from the shape of the head, the snout, the fangs, and the ears. Both coyotes and dogs were well known to the Aztecs and were commonly depicted in art.

The dog was held in special regard by the Aztecs, because it was a major source of protein in a culture with few domesticated animals. Dog breeders and sellers were thought to have lucrative jobs, and even birth under the day sign of the dog was considered lucky: "all came to be capes [for him]" (Sahagún 1979a [1569]: 19–20), the woven cape or mantle being a form of money in Aztec society. But beyond that basic importance, the dog was appreciated as "a constant companion . . . happy, amusing" (Sahagún 1963 [1569]: 16), even accompanying its master into the afterlife, where it was valued for its qualities of sensitivity to "sounds and smells that are imperceptible to humans" (Benson 1997: 24).

The coyote also had a dual identity in the Aztec mind, one with rather more sinister implications. It was respected for being "cunning, astute . . . [in hunting it is] quite as astute as a man" (Sahagún 1963 [1569]: 6–7). But "it is in every way diabolic," exacting revenge for being thwarted in its pursuits, but also fair-minded, and could be "grateful and appreciative" by repaying an act of kindness with its own sort of generosity (Sahagún 1963 [1569]: 7). It seems fitting that the greatest of all Aztec kings was named Fasting Coyote (*Nezahualcoyotl* in Nahuatl; ruled Texcoco ca. AD 1433–72). As his name implies, this king was astute and cunning, and a survivor as a long-term ally of his cousins, the rulers of Tenochtitlan. This small ornament may represent a coyote, and would call to mind the great fifteenth-century ruler.

STE

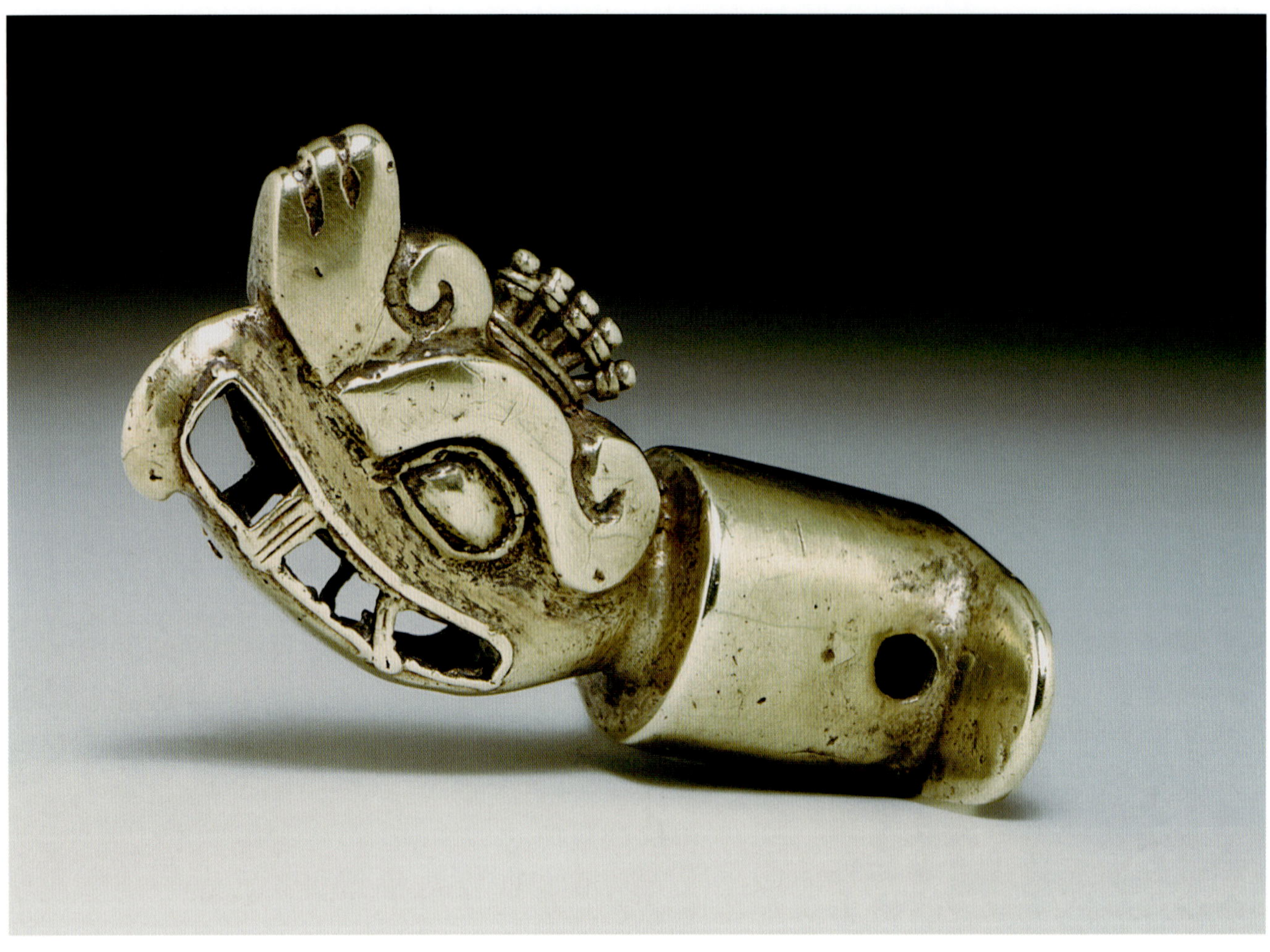

plate 36

GOLD LABRET IN THE FORM OF AN ANIMAL HEAD

PLATE 36
Mixteca-Puebla
Late Postclassic period, ca. AD 1500
Cast gold
H. 1.91 cm (¾"); W. 2.54 cm (1"); D. 4.13 cm (1⅝")
PC.B.091

ACQUISITION HISTORY:
Purchased from C. L. Morley, 1947

EXHIBITION HISTORY:
Indigenous Art of the Americas, National Gallery of Art, Washington, D.C., April 1947–July 1949, November 1952–July 1962 (NGA 336); *Art of Aztec Mexico: Treasures of Tenochtitlan,* National Gallery of Art, Washington, D.C., September 1983–April 1984

BIBLIOGRAPHY:
Bliss 1947: 19, 90, cat. no. 89; Bliss 1957: 244, cat. no. 67, pl. L, second row, right; Dumbarton Oaks 1963: 28, cat. no. 136; Nicholson with Quiñones Keber 1983: 154, cat. no. 68; Solís and Carmona 1995: cat. no. 156

Labrets or lip plugs (*bezotes* in Spanish) were decorations worn through a hole pierced in the lower lip. They have an uneven distribution in the ancient Americas and appear sporadically in such places as coastal Alaska, the Northwest Coast, and at various other points along the Pacific Coast. They also appeared in Central Mexico, where they became one of the defining culture traits of Mesoamerica (Kirchhoff 1981 [1943]).

Lip plugs were popular among the elites of the Central Highlands in the Postclassic period, and they were among the most basic pieces of jewelry. They are mentioned in Sahagún's encyclopedic 12-volume *General History of the Things of New Spain* as part of a set of essential types of adornment. Sahagún's informants emphasized the primary place of gold by placing it first among the minerals in the *General History*'s eleventh book, "Earthly Things," which began with animals and plants and then moved to minerals. Sahagún seems to have based the organization of his work on the Aristotelian "great chain of being," beginning with the gods and descending down the cosmic scale; thus we know that the order of any set of items has significance. In the eleventh book, after indicating how gold was found, Sahagún's informants say "they melted it, cast it; they . . . formed necklaces, bracelets, ear pendants, lip plugs, etc." (Sahagún 1963 [1569]: 233).

Many known lip plugs include an animal in their design (Nicholson with Quinones Keber 1983: 154–155). The Dumbarton Oaks example is similar to another lip plug made of cast gold in the form of a crested bird's head (Solís 2004: 293, top, 364, no. 160). The Dumbarton Oaks lip plug has been identified as an eagle (Lothrop in Bliss 1957: 244, cat. no. 67; Dumbarton Oaks 1963: 28), but Nicholson (1983: 154) notes that the knobbed crest on the top of the head is also found on other birds, whereas the supraorbital ridge is characteristic of reptiles, as are the depictions of the fangs and the treatment of the mouth. We may also note that teeth, as shown, are not found in birds. Nicholson suggests that the head is of a composite creature.

Lip plugs were given as awards. Sahagún's informants note that when "vanguard merchants" who opened up new territories to Aztec exploitation did their job well, the emperor "paid special honors; he inserted in their lips golden lip plugs" (Sahagún 1959 [1569]: 6–7). But the merchants, who were commoners, were careful not to inspire jealousy among the nobles. Merchants wore these signs of favor "only on feast days" (Sahagún 1959 [1569]: 24). The rulers, however, wore them whenever the occasion required. Figure 16 shows the Texcocan ruler Nezahualcoyotl (ruled ca. AD 1433–72) arrayed for battle, lip plug in place.

STE

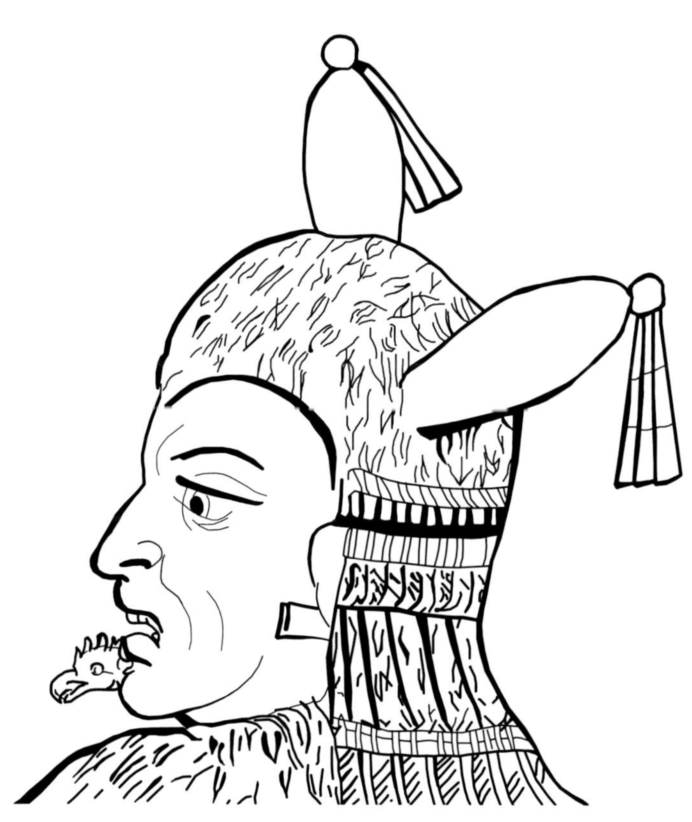

fig. 16
The great Aztec king Nezahualcoyotl, who ruled the Aztec capital Texcoco from 1433 to 1472, is shown here in a drawing after the early colonial Codex Ixtlilxochitl wearing a gold labret similar to PC.B.091. Drawing by Susan Toby Evans (after Codex Ixtlilxochitl 1996: fol. 106).

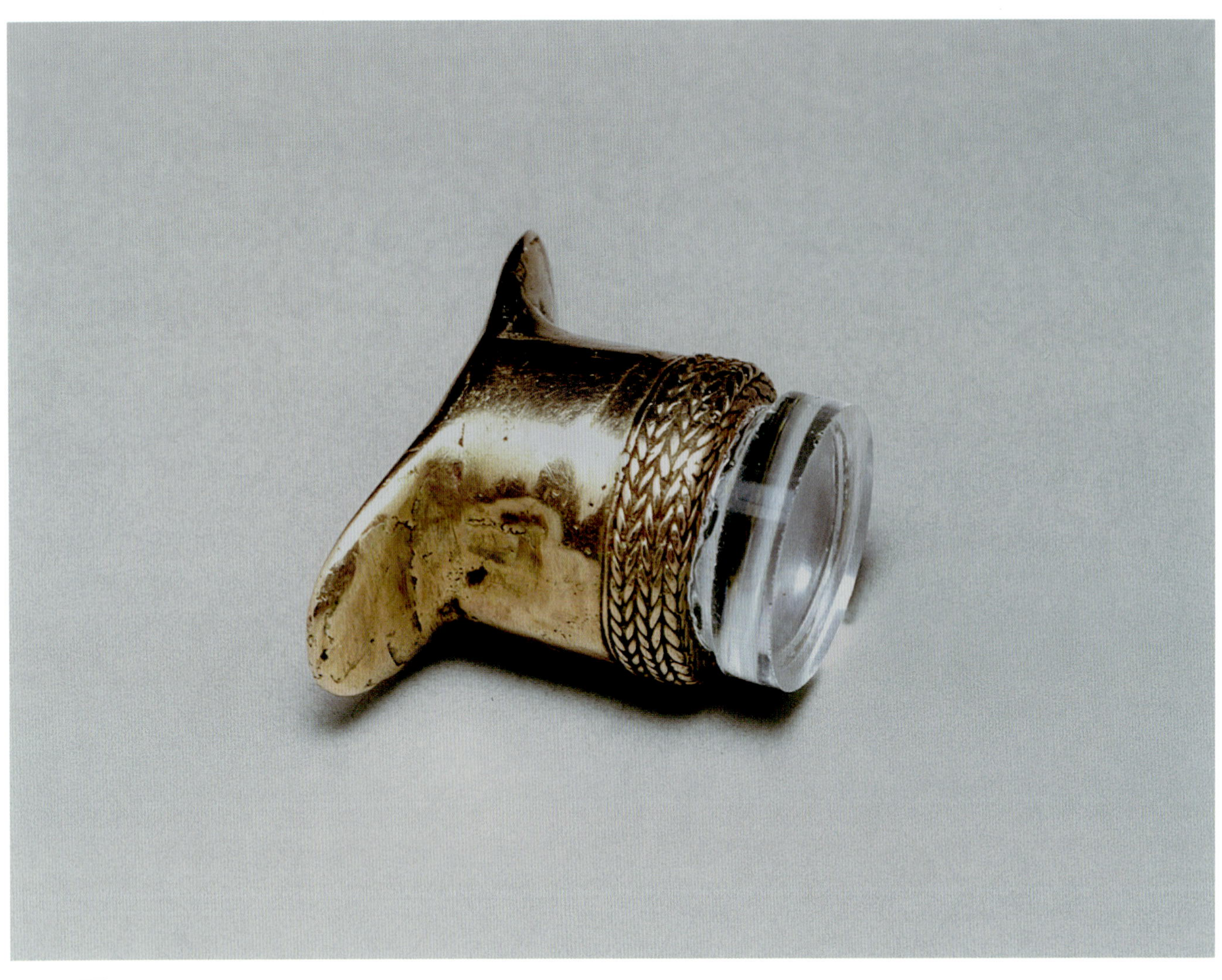

plate 37

GOLD LABRET

PLATE 37
Mixteca-Puebla
Postclassic period, AD 900–1520
Cast gold
W. 3.0 cm (1⅕"); D. 2.1 cm (13⁄16")
PC.B.092

ACQUISITION HISTORY:
Purchased from Earl Stendahl, 1942

BIBLIOGRAPHY:
Bliss 1947: 19, 95, cat. no. 88; Bliss 1957: 244, cat. no. 66, pl. L, second row, left; Dumbarton Oaks 1963: 28, cat. no. 137

This lip plug was part of a composition whose original nature is unknown. When the object was purchased, it consisted of a gold base, a crystal shaft, and a silver bird head at the distal end. Two authorities who examined the object when it included the bird head stated: "This piece is at best made up. I suspect the shaft is modern. The gold base may be old. The bird head may be a forgery or an adaptation of some other object, possibly Peruvian, to the labret. The workmanship is very inferior and . . . [probably not] Mexican" (Sawyer and Wise n.d.).

The date of this observation is not noted in extant records. In 1989, however, it was determined that the object was a composite, partly based on the observation that the crystal was "too long." The total length of the labret is documented as 2⅞ inches in 1957 (Lothrop in Bliss 1957: 244, cat. no. 66). In addition, the bird head was thought to be copper. The object was sent to the Conservation Department of the Fogg Art Museum, Harvard University, where the pieces were separated. The Record of Treatment by the Fogg technicians notes that the parts of the object had been put together "with a plasteline (sic) which softened in acetone" (Center for Conservation and Technical Studies n.d.). The materials were identified as gold, silver, and glass. The shaft was cut to its present short length at the request of Dumbarton Oaks personnel for "aesthetic purposes."

In 1992, the bird head was studied by a conservator from the Freer and Sackler Galleries of the Smithsonian Institution, Washington, D.C. The conservator noted that it showed traces of gold, and that pitted depressions on the surface suggested that the piece was cast. The thinness of the metal, however, suggested that it was hammered sheet metal. The conservator thought that the areas of gold indicated that the object may have been gilded at one time, with subsequent losses (unpublished report on file at Dumbarton Oaks). Superficial gilding of this sort was not common in ancient American metallurgy, however.

The extensive examination of and interventions on this piece are noteworthy and seem to have been prompted by the less-than-perfect joining of the three elements of the original object. The length of the glass rod alone, however, should not have been a criterion for shortening it, as many examples of *bezotes* with long rods are known from ancient Mexico. The shortening for aesthetic purposes seems to have been based on models of stone lip plugs, which tend to be short. Perhaps the length of a lip plug was determined by a combination of status or occasion, with shorter varieties used by lower ranking persons or for everyday use and longer ones reserved for elites or special occasions.

JQ

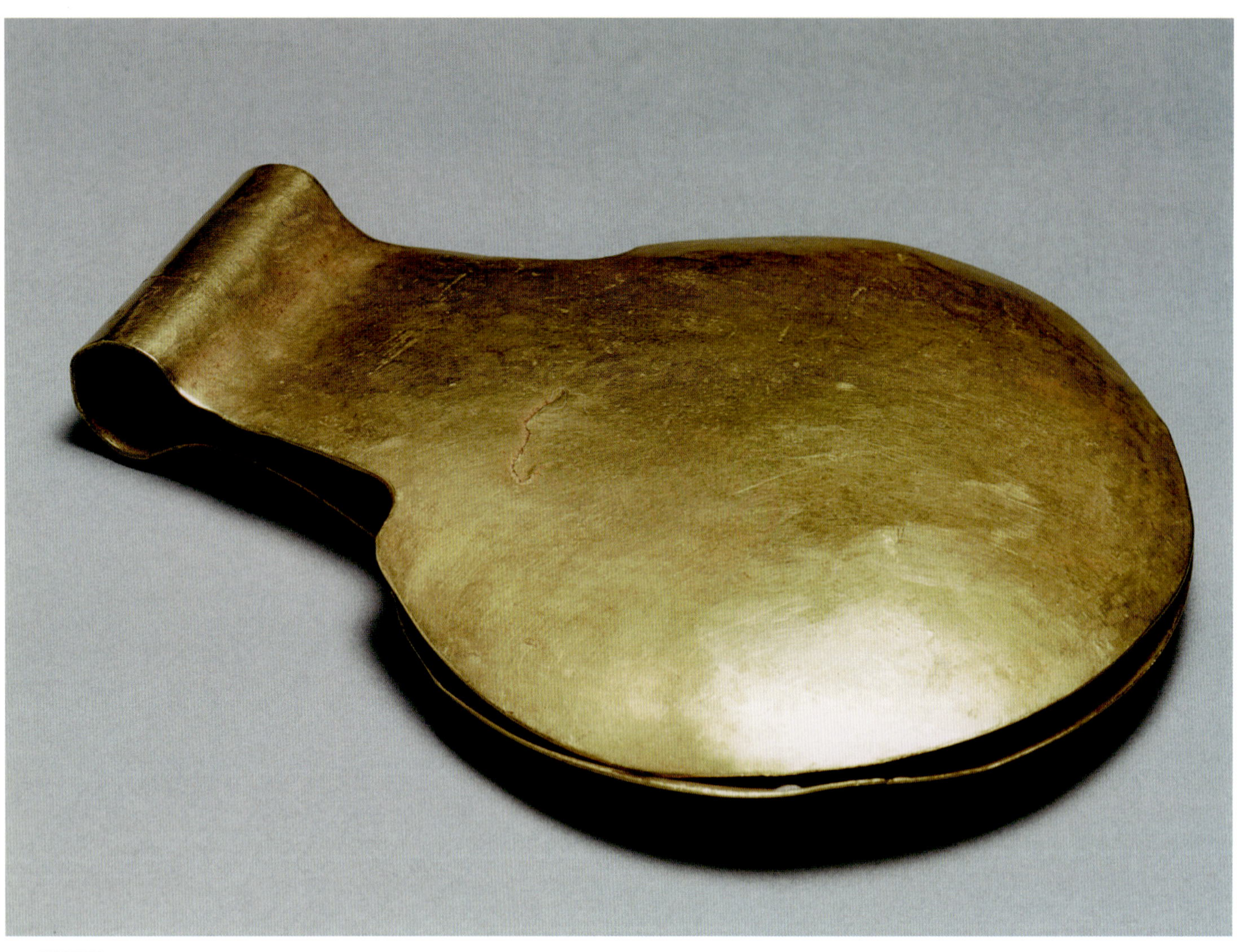

plate 38

PLATE 38
Mixtec
Postclassic period, AD 900–1520
Hammered gold
H. 7.4 cm (2⅞"); W. 5.6 cm (2¼"); D. 1.1 cm (⅜")
PC.B.106

ACQUISITION HISTORY:
Purchased from Earl Stendahl, 1958; reportedly found in Chiapas

EXHIBITION HISTORY:
Präkolumbische Kunst aus Mexico und Mittelamerika, Haus der Kunst, Munich, October–December 1958; *Kunst der Mexikaner,* Kunsthaus, Zürich, January–March 1959; *Kunst aus Mexico und Mittelamerika,* Akademie der Künste, Berlin, October–November 1959; *Präkolumbische Kunst aus Mexico und Mittelamerika,* Künstlerhaus, Vienna, December 1959–February 1960; Historisches Museum, Frankfurt am Main, May–September 1960; *Arte Precolumbiana del Messico e dell'America Centrale,* Palazzo delle Esposizioni, Rome, November–December 1960

BIBLIOGRAPHY:
Haus der Kunst München 1958: cat. no. 243, ill. opp. p. 80; Akademie der Künste 1959: cat. no. 850, ill. opp. p. 96; Kunsthaus Zürich 1959: cat. no. 654, pl. VII; Künstlerhaus Wien 1959: cat. no. 766, ill. opp. p. 80; Centro di Azione Latina 1960: cat. no. 137; Historisches Museum Frankfurt am Main 1960: cat. no. 132, pl. 10; Dumbarton Oaks 1963: 27, cat. no. 132

Tweezers from ancient Mesoamerica bear little resemblance to their modern counterparts: they are large and relatively flat, seeming to lack the focused functional capacity of the present-day implement. Examples of ancient tweezers varied in size, but they typically had a clamshell-like shape, bringing together two identical convex ovals, the hinge produced by folding the metal.[80]

Unlike the elaborate gold objects made by the lost wax casting technique, tweezers were made by pouring the molten metal into shallow open molds, creating flat blanks—sheets of metal that were then cold-hammered into shape. This relatively simple metalworking technique was used in western Mexico in the initial period of production of metal objects.

Tweezers were among the objects worn by the elites of the Postclassic Tarascan Empire of western Mexico. They were worn pendant style, suspended from a necklace, and apparently insofar as they had a practical role, it was as a depilatory device. Yet they clearly also functioned as status markers, given their luxurious material.

The Dumbarton Oaks tweezers are elegant in their design. In size, they fall between the two examples from Monte Albán's Tomb 7 that Caso (1969: 123–125, lám. 21) discusses and illustrates. They are also intermediate in shape, Caso's examples being circular and axe-shaped, whereas PC.B.106's circle is slightly shouldered. This range in size and shape nicely frames the variety found in this curious but stylish type of ornament.

STE AND JQ

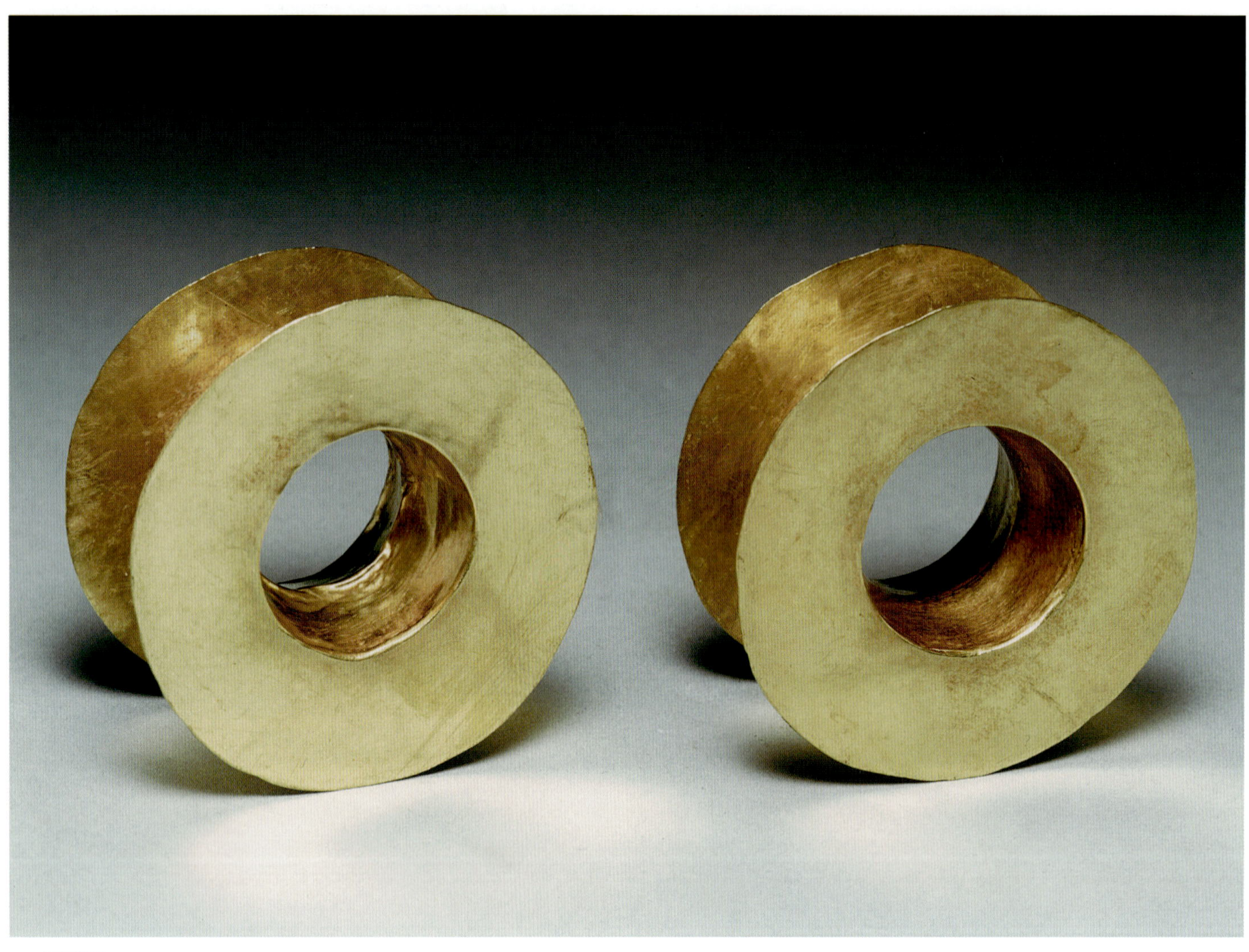

plate 39

GOLD EAR ORNAMENTS

PLATE 39
Mixtec-Aztec
Postclassic period, AD 900–1520
Hammered gold
H. 2.6 cm (1"); Diam. 5.4 cm (2⅛")
PC.B.105

ACQUISITION HISTORY:
Purchased from Earl Stendahl, 1958; reportedly found in Chiapas

EXHIBITION HISTORY:
Präkolumbische Kunst aus Mexico und Mittelamerika, Haus der Kunst, Munich, October–December 1958; *Kunst der Mexikaner*, Kunsthaus, Zürich, January–March 1959; *Kunst aus Mexico und Mittelamerika*, Akademie der Künste, Berlin, October–November 1959; *Präkolumbische Kunst aus Mexico und Mittelamerika*, Künstlerhaus, Vienna, December 1959–February 1960, Historisches Museum, Frankfurt am Main, May–September 1960; Arte Precolumbiana del Messico e dell'America Centrale, Palazzo delle Esposizioni, Rome, November–December 1960

BIBLIOGRAPHY:
Haus der Kunst München 1958: cat. no. 242, ill. opp. p. 80; Akademie der Künste 1959: cat. no. 849, ill. opp. p. 96; Kunsthaus Zürich 1959: cat. no. 653, pl. VII; Künstlerhaus Wien 1959: cat. no. 765, ill. opp. p. 80; Centro di Azione Latina 1960: cat. no. 136; Historisches Museum Frankfurt am Main 1960: cat. no. 131, pl. 10; Dumbarton Oaks 1963: 27, cat. no. 131

Ear piercing was among the most common of body modifications in ancient Mesoamerica, attested to by depictions in art and the great variety of ear ornaments. Materials ranged from paper and reeds to gold and jade. Shapes and sizes varied also, but most incorporated a cylindrical shaft, which might serve as the armature for more elaborate ear adornments or might itself be the adornment, sometimes called an "ear spool" after its shape (an alternate term, "ear plug," invites confusion with the modern meaning of this expression). Ear spool cylinders were generally hollow and flanged at both ends.

Gold ear spools were reserved for the elite. An Aztec king, dressing for a dance, "adorned and arrayed himself" with a labret and gold ear spools and "with [these] costly goods he went in procession and danced" (Sahagún 1979b [1569]: 56). The ruler also wagered them in games of chance, such as the ball game: the ruler's teams were summoned, the equipment was laid out, and also "all which the ruler was to wager in the game . . . capes . . . lip plugs, the golden ear plugs, . . . the golden necklaces . . . the majordomos brought out and placed in the ball court" (Sahagún 1979b [1569]: 58). The king also wagered such goods on the board game, *patolli*. The Otomí, another ethnic group of the Central Highlands, also reserved gold ear spools for the elite: "the ear plugs of the . . . brave warriors, were gold" (Sahagún 1961 [1569]: 178).

The Bliss Collection pair of gold ear spools is simple and elegant. This simplicity makes it difficult to hypothesize about provenience, because the basic form was widely distributed geographically, though limited socially to those who were of high birth or had achieved high rank. Each ear spool may have been hammered from a single piece of metal or from several pieces and then joined.[81]

STE AND JQ

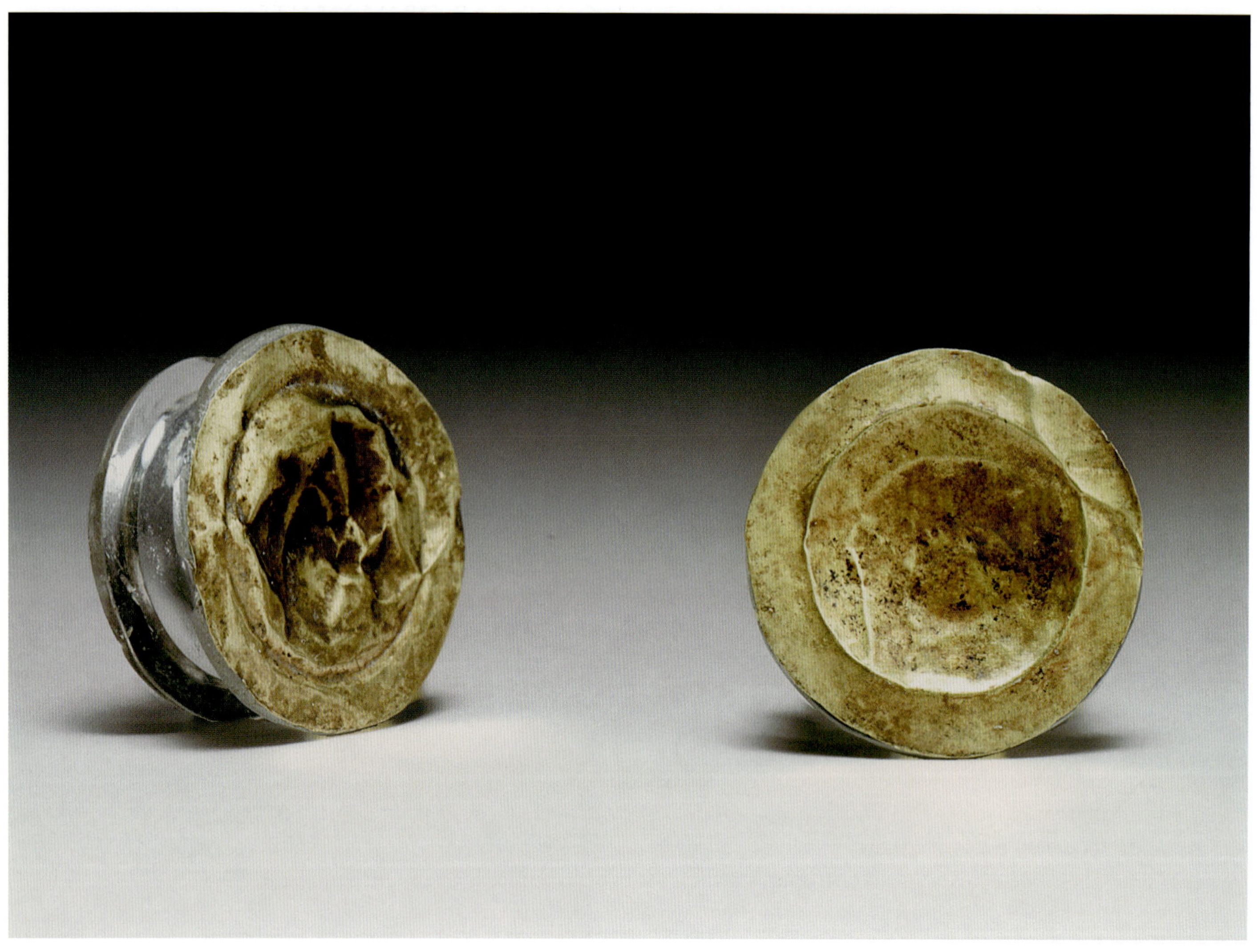

plate 40

ROCK CRYSTAL AND GOLD EAR ORNAMENTS

PLATE 40
Mixtec-Aztec
Late Postclassic period, AD 1200–1520
Crystal and hammered gold
H. 1.1 cm (⅜"); Diam. 2.5 cm (1")
PC.B.090

ACQUISITION HISTORY:
Purchased from C. L. Morley, 1947

EXHIBITION HISTORY:
Indigenous Art of the Americas, National Gallery of Art, Washington, D.C., April 1947–July 1949; January 1956–July 1962 (NGA 335)

BIBLIOGRAPHY:
Bliss 1947: 19, 95, cat. no. 87; Bliss 1957: 244, cat. no. 69, pl. L; Dumbarton Oaks 1963: 25, cat. no. 117

Rock crystal is a form of quartz. The Aztecs received it in tribute from the Huaxtepec province in the Valley of Morelos (Berdan 1996: 130–131). Working it into objects, particularly those as precisely matched as the Bliss Collection's ear spools, would have been challenging, because rock crystal is even harder than obsidian. In this regard it is similar to jade, both rating a 6.5–7.0 on the Mohs scale, but rock crystal lacks the structural toughness of jade, making it more difficult to work. Thus these rock crystal ear ornaments represent a high degree of artisanship and many hours of work.

Technical examination of this pair of ear ornaments revealed that a modern adhesive was used to attach the gold disks (Jett n.d.). This observation could indicate that either the ancient composite form underwent modern restoration or it is a modern composition.

We do know, however, that ear ornaments of rock crystal and gold were popular in Postclassic times. The Aztec Empire was in the process of expanding when the Spaniards arrived in the New World. In typical fashion, the Aztec vanguard merchants would establish gift exchange relations between the Aztec king and the local elites, and these relations would then, through diplomatic or military actions, become political ties as the target province was brought into tributary status. By ca. AD 1500, this process was beginning in the region of Acalan, along the southwestern coast of the Yucatan peninsula, and Emperor Ahuitzotl's traders brought gifts that were worthy of royal families—fine textiles of palace quality and "what the princesses required: golden bowls for spindles, and ear plugs of gold and of rock crystal" (Sahagún 1959 [1569]: 18).

STE AND JQ

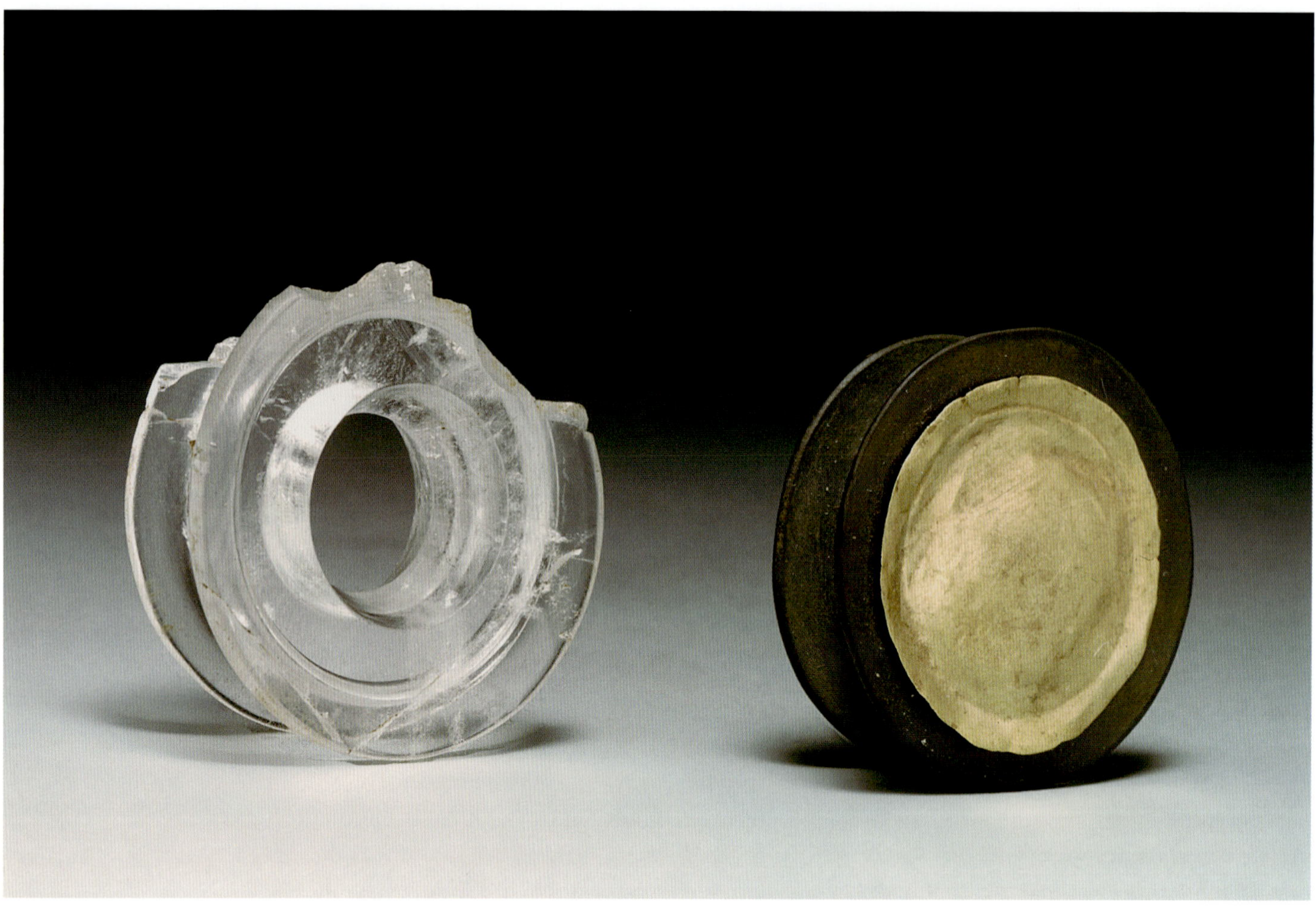

plate 41

CRYSTAL, OBSIDIAN, AND GOLD EAR ORNAMENTS

PLATE 41
(left: PC.B.084, right: PC.B.088)
Mixtec-Aztec
Postclassic period, AD 900–1520
Crystal
D. 1.25 cm (½"); Diam. 3.4 cm (1¼")
PC.B.084
Mixtec-Aztec
Postclassic period, AD 900–1520
Obsidian and gold
Diam. 3.7 cm (1⅜")
PC.B.088

ACQUISITION HISTORY:
PC.B.084: Purchased from Earl Stendahl, 1942
PC.B.088: Purchased from Earl Stendahl, 1941

EXHIBITION HISTORY:
PC.B.084: *Indigenous Art of the Americas*, National Gallery of Art, Washington, D.C., April 1947–May 1948, January 1956–July 1962 (NGA 71); *Aztecs*, Royal Academy of Arts, London, November 2002–April 2003
PC.B.088: *Indigenous Art of the Americas*, National Gallery of Art, Washington, D.C., April 1947–May 1948, January 1956–July 1962 (NGA 115); *Die Azteken und ihre Vorläufer: Glanz und Untergang des Alten Mexico*,

EXHIBITION HISTORY: *(continued)*
Roemer- und Pelizaeus-Museum, Hildesheim, Germany, June–November 1986; Haus der Kunst, Munich, December 1986–March 1987; Oberösterreichisches Landesmuseum, Linz, Austria, April–August 1987; Louisiana Museum of Modern Art, Humlebæk, Denmark, August–November 1987; Musées royaux d'Art et d'Histoire, Brussels, December 1987–March 1988; National Archaeological Museum, Athens, May–July 1988; Société du Palais de la Civilisation, Montreal, July–October 1988; *Aztecs*, Royal Academy of Arts, London, September 2002–April 2003; Ethnologisches Museum, Berlin, May–August 2003; Art and Exhibition Hall of the Federal Republic of Germany, Bonn, September 2003–January 2004

BIBLIOGRAPHY:
PC.B.084: Bliss 1947: 19, 95, cat. no. 86; Bliss 1957: 244, cat. no. 70, pl. L, top left; Solís and Carmona 1995: cat. no. 161; Matos and Solís 2002: 255, color pl., cat. no. 195; Saunders 2003: 20, fig. 2
PC.B.088: Bliss 1947: 24, cat. no. 118; Bliss 1957: 244, cat. no. 68, pl. L, top right; Dumbarton Oaks 1963: 25, 118; Boone 1986e: cat. no. 261; Louisiana Museum 1987: 82, cat. no. 276; Matos and Solís 2002: 255, color pl., cat. no. 195; Traxler 2002a: 448, cat. no. 195

These two ear ornaments together represent a range of materials that were worked into a form popular as ear ornaments in ancient Mesoamerica. PC.B.084 was carved from rock crystal, and its transparent beauty is matched by the high level of artisanship necessary to produce something so delicate from such a hard material that is also relatively brittle.

Ear spool PC.B.088 is made of light-gray obsidian. Obsidian was one of the most important commodities circulating in the Postclassic economy (Smith 2003: 117), so essential that it was one of the limited set of resources that crossed political borders (Berdan 2003: 93). It was critical as a raw material for cutting tools and thus for the manufacture of most other tools, as well as for the manufacture of goods. Its use as the material for ear spools renders this beautiful but utilitarian volcanic glass into a form of adornment for the working classes: merchants carried many expensive elite goods; they also carried obsidian ear plugs to be "used by the common folk" (Sahagún 1959 [1569]: 8).

The gold disk that covers the aperture of PC.B.088 was recently attached, having been removed from another ear ornament. Although our knowledge of Postclassic sumptuary laws and types of rewards for achievement in various lines of endeavor is incomplete, this composite piece seems anomalous, because it combines the material of commoner ear spools—obsidian—with gold, which was reserved for the elites.

JQ AND STE

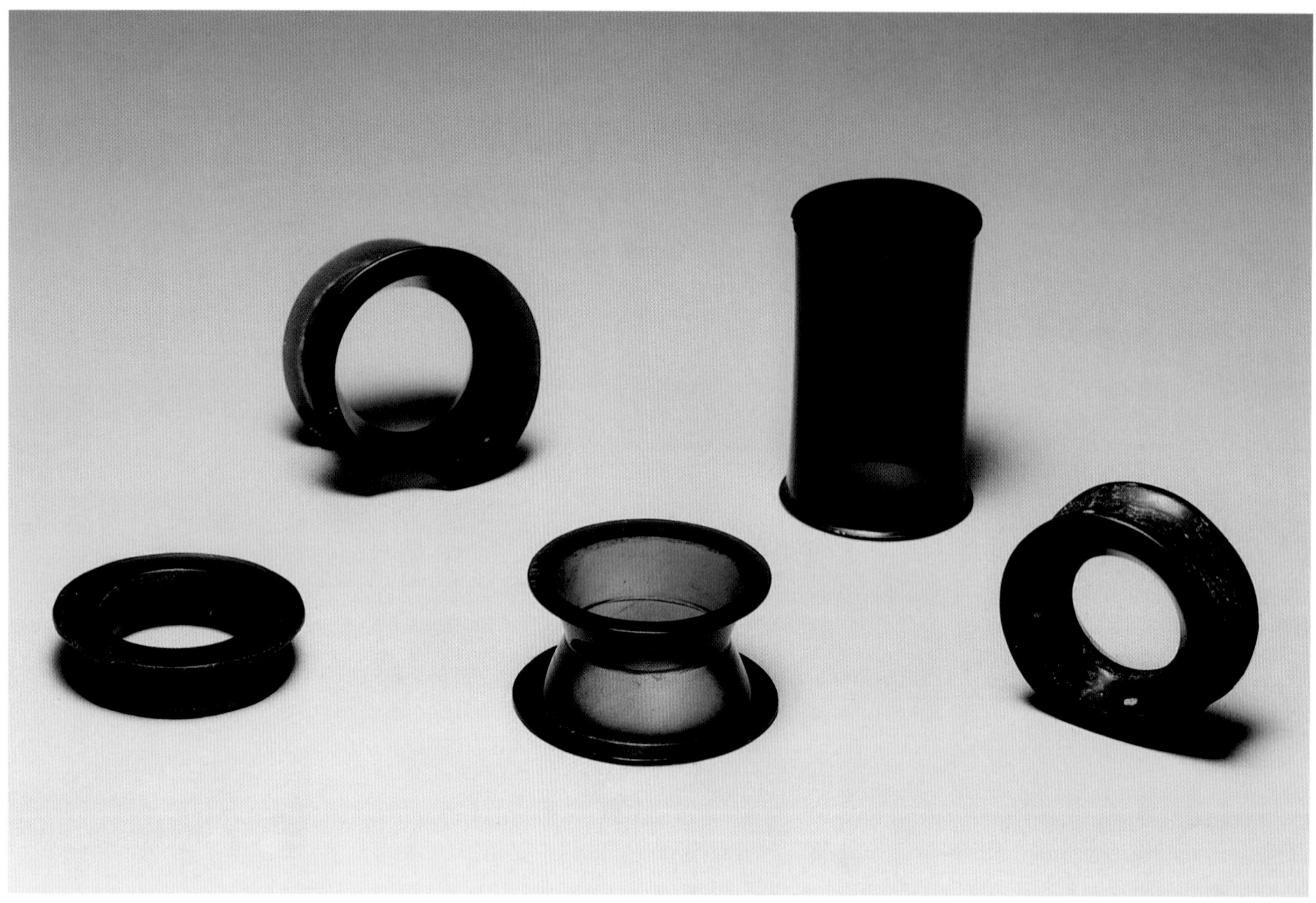

plate 42

OBSIDIAN EAR ORNAMENTS

PLATE 42
(left to right: PC.B.086, PC.B.089a, PC.B.089b, PC.B.085, PC.B.087)
Mixtec-Aztec
Late Postclassic period, AD 1200–1520
Obsidian
H. 4.9 cm (1⅞"); Diam. 3.0 cm (1¼")
PC.B.085
Mixtec-Aztec
Late Postclassic period, AD 1200–1520
Obsidian
H. 0.95 cm (⅜"); Diam. 3.75 cm (1½")
PC.B.086
Mixtec-Aztec
Late Postclassic period, AD 1200–1520
Obsidian
H. 1.25 cm (½"); Diam. 3.75 cm (1½")
PC.B.087
Mixtec-Aztec
Late Postclassic period, AD 1200–1520
Obsidian
H. 2.0 cm (¾"); Diam. 4.1 cm (1⅝")
PC.B.089a, PC.B.089b

ACQUISITION HISTORY:

PC.B.085, PC.B.089a, and PC.B.089b: Purchased from John Wise, 1947; reportedly from the vicinity of Texcoco (Basin of Mexico). PC.B.086 and PC.B.087: Purchased from Earl Stendahl, 1941

EXHIBITION HISTORY:

PC.B.085 and PC.B.089a: *Indigenous Art of the Americas*, National Gallery of Art, Washington, D.C., April 1947–July 1949, February–July 1954, January 1956–July 1962 (NGA 347 and NGA 346)

PC.B.086 and PC.B.087: Indigenous Art of the Americas, National Gallery of Art, Washington, D.C., April 1947–July 1949, January 1956–July 1962 (NGA 48 and NGA 358)

PC.B.086: *Ancient American Art*, Santa Barbara Museum of Art, Santa Barbara, Calif., April–June 1942; M. H. de Young Memorial Museum, San Francisco, July–August 1942; Museum of Art, Portland, Ore., September–October 1942

BIBLIOGRAPHY:

PC.B.085: Bliss 1947: 24, cat. no. 115; Bliss 1957: 246, cat. no. 73, pl. L, bottom center; Dumbarton Oaks 1963: 24, cat. no. 116

PC.B.086: Santa Barbara Museum of Art 1942: cat. no. 121; Bliss 1947: 24, cat. no. 117; Bliss 1957: 244, cat. no. 71, pl. L, third row; Dumbarton Oaks 1963: 25, cat. no. 118

PC.B.087: Bliss 1947: 24, cat. no. 119; Bliss 1957: 244, cat. no. 71, pl. L, third row; Dumbarton Oaks 1963: 25, cat. no. 118

PC.B.089a and b: Bliss 1947: 24, cat. no. 114; Bliss 1957: 246, cat. no. 72, pl. L, bottom left and right; Dumbarton Oaks 1963: 24, cat. no. 116

These obsidian ear ornaments are masterpieces of Pre-Columbian craftsmanship. Obsidian is volcanic glass and has the glass-like qualities of being both hard (5.0–5.5 Mohs scale) and highly brittle, making it extremely difficult to work. Obsidian is best known as Mesoamerica's premier raw material for cutting tools, such as knives and blades, made by using such techniques as chipping, pressure flaking, and blade-core manufacturing. To craft hollow cylindrical pieces such as these ear spools would require great skill in the use of extremely laborious ground stone techniques, perhaps even employing simple rotary tools, not commonly associated with Pre Columbian technology (for further discussion of the possible use of rotary drills in Pre-Columbian Mesoamerica, see "Stone Vessels," this volume).

Because stone working is a technology of material reduction, we assume that the blank rough form for the hollow obsidian ear spool would be a cylinder of obsidian with a cylindrical hollow. The final steps would have required careful and laborious grinding and polishing to produce smooth surfaces.

Obsidian was associated with the "dark light" of Tezcatlipoca, the "Lord of the Smoking Mirror," one of the most powerful Mesoamerican deities. The long tube of PC.B.085 is particularly striking as an example of virtuosity in lithic technology. The pair of hourglass-shaped ear spools (PC.B.089a and PC.B.089b) is unusual in form. producing a precise uniform angle at the narrowest point required extraordinary skill on the part of the artisan.

JQ

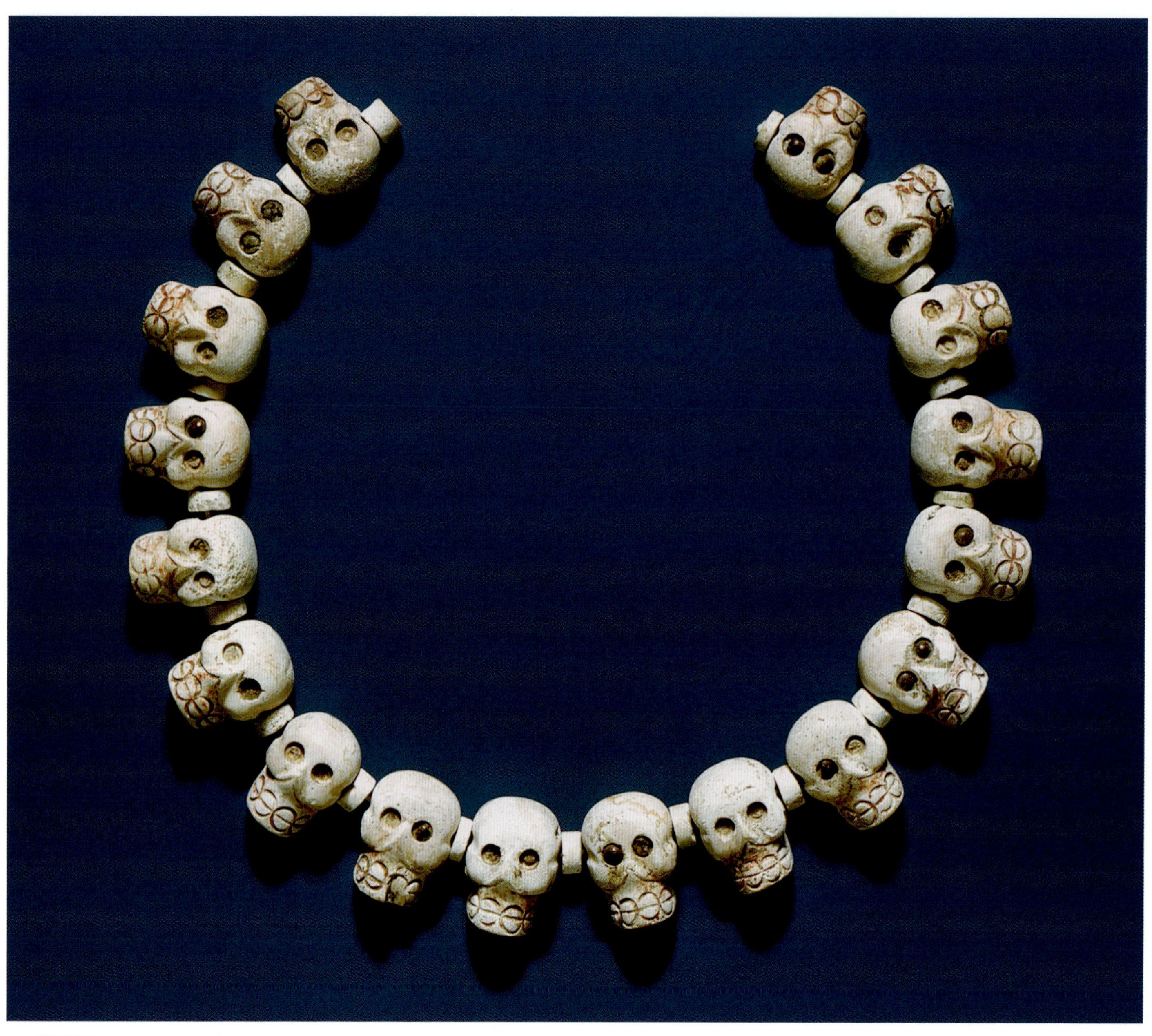

plate 43

NECKLACE WITH BEADS IN THE SHAPE OF HUMAN SKULLS

PLATE 43
Mixtec-Aztec
Late Postclassic period, AD 1200–1520
Carved shell
Necklace: L. 39.4 cm (15½")
Each skull bead: H. 2.5 cm (1")
PC.B.083

ACQUISITION HISTORY:
Purchased from John Wise, 1947; reportedly from the vicinity of Texcoco

EXHIBITION HISTORY:
Indigenous Art of the Americas, National Gallery of Art, Washington, D.C., April 1947–March 1952 (NGA 353)

BIBLIOGRAPHY:
Bliss 1947: 24, 119, cat. no. 116; *Artes de México* 1957: pl. 5; Bliss 1957: 243, cat. no. 60, pl. XLVI; Dumbarton Oaks 1963: 24, cat. no. 115; Alcina Franch et al. 1992: 160, pl. XXXVIII

The impressive motif of this necklace is presented by 18 nearly identical carved shell beads in the shape of skulls, separated from one another by simple disk spacer beads. All were carved from thick shell that has been identified as *Spondylus*, possibly *Spondylus princeps*. Traces of red pigment, perhaps cinnabar, are present in a few crevices of some skulls; other skulls still bear eye inlays of hematite. Some of the eyes are partly broken, revealing that they were formed in the shape of a round-headed pin.

The symbolism of this necklace plays with two concepts: the fertile waters of the home of the shell and the fertility ensured by human sacrifice. The carved beads suggest the dry, bleached crania of sacrificial victims as they were displayed in the temple complex on the public skull rack (*tzompantli* in Nahuatl). The cord passing through the skulls mimics the way in which skulls were arrayed on wooden poles on the rack. Life and death are thus interlinked and dependent on each other.

The use of the skull motif in a necklace also occurs in sculptures of Aztec deities. Female deities, such as Coatlicue and the Tzitzimime, commonly wear skulls as part of the ornaments of their necklaces. Such deities brought together death imagery and the concept of fertility.

If the assemblage is complete as originally created, the 18 skulls conform to Mesoamerican numerological concepts. The solar year was organized into 18 periods of 20 days each, each of the 18 units with its own name. Thus each skull may symbolize a period in which cycles of life and death continually revolve, and the high-ranking person who wore the necklace would have been a fierce, walking *tzompantli*.

JQ

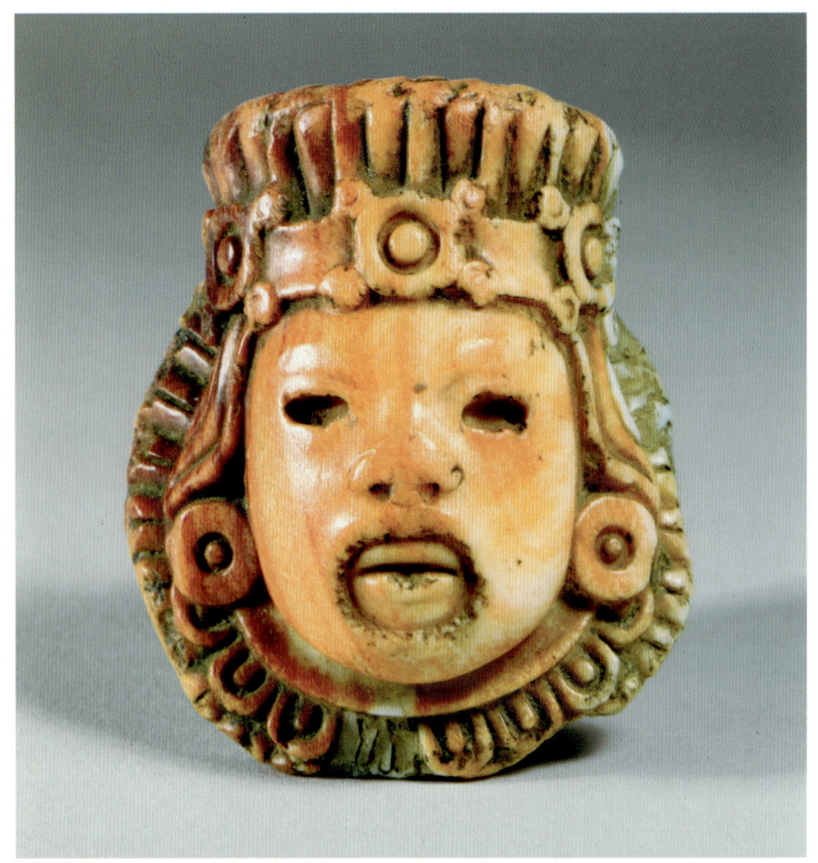

plate 44a

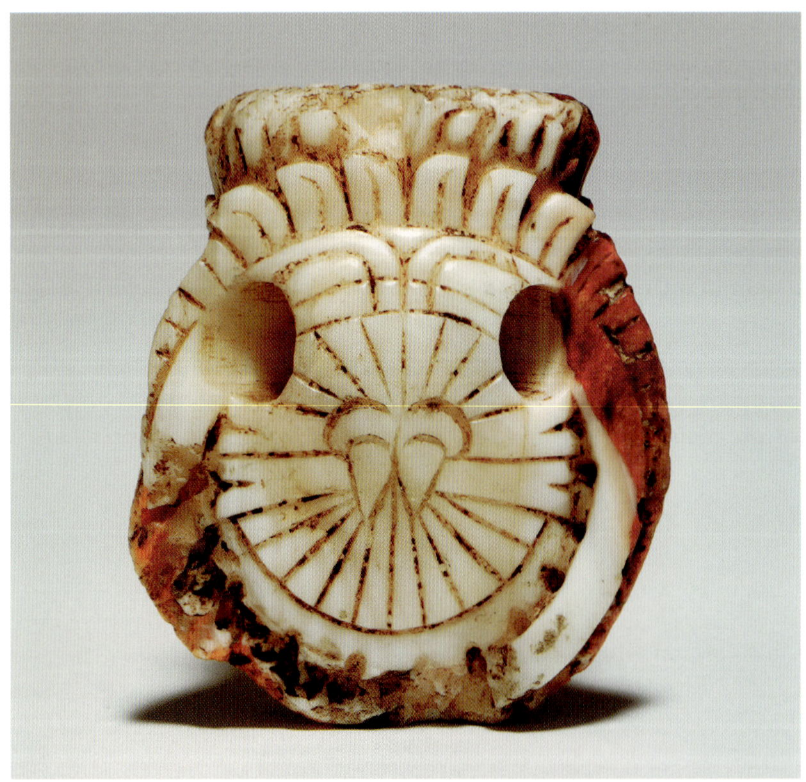

plate 44b,
back view

PLATE 44
Aztec
Late Postclassic period, ca. AD 1500
Carved *Spondylus* shell
H. 5.5 cm (2⅛"); W. 4.6 cm (1¾")
PC.B.082

ACQUISITION HISTORY:
Purchased from Ernest Brummer, 1947; formerly in the collection of Joseph Brummer

EXHIBITION HISTORY:
Indigenous Art of the Americas, National Gallery of Art, Washington, D.C., November 1952–July 1962 (NGA 372); *Art of Aztec Mexico: Treasures of Tenochtitlan*, National Gallery of Art, Washington, D.C., September 1983–April 1984; *Aztecs*, Royal Academy of Arts, London, September 2002–April 2003; Ethnologisches Museum, Berlin, May–August 2003; Art and Exhibition Hall of the Federal Republic of Germany, Bonn, September 2003–January 2004; *The Aztec Empire*, Guggenheim Museum, New York, October 2004–February 2005; Guggenheim Museum, Bilbao, Spain, March–September 2005

BIBLIOGRAPHY:
Kelemen 1943: 346–347, pl. 282b; Bliss 1957: 243, cat. no. 59, pl. XLXI; Dumbarton Oaks 1963: 24, cat. no. 112; Bray 1968: 135, fig. 58; Nicholson with Quiñones Keber 1983: 109, cat. no. 37; Traxler 2002c: 478, cat. no. 314; Traxler 2004c: 51, cat. no. 224; Vila Llonch 2008d: 194–195

This carving depicts the head of the god Xipe Totec, "Our Lord the Flayed One," an important Postclassic deity in the Central Highlands of Mexico as well as in the Gulf Lowlands. To mimic the cycles of life and death—and thus ensure that new life would break forth from dying husks—Xipe Totec's priests wore the flayed skins of victims sacrificed in the rites of the god. This practice is represented in art by the depiction of a living face underneath the taut skin of a flayed sacrificial victim, most distinct in the mouth and chin protruding through the stretched orifice of the flayed skin.

In PC.B.082, the figure is depicted wearing a headdress of short, compacted, and trimmed feathers bound below by a wide band. The band is decorated with three circular symbols for preciousness, possibly referring to jade. It may also suggest Xipe Totec's role as the patron deity of goldsmiths, who regarded the flayed skin of sacrificial victims as analogous to "a golden sheathing" (Miller and Taube 1993: 188). Impersonators of the deity, wearing the victim's flayed skin, often decorated themselves with feathers and gold jewelry (Traxler 2004c: 51).

Each preciousness symbol is surrounded by four additional exterior jewels to create a quincunx, symbolic of the five directions. Below tufts of hair protruding from the headdress, large ear ornaments flank the lower face, and a ruff of feathers extends from behind the headdress around the head.

The reverse of the object is relatively flat and pierced with large holes to thread a suspension cord horizontally (Plate 44b). This suggests that the head was part of a larger necklace ensemble, although it could have been worn alone. Carved into the back is a design that Nicholson with Quiñones Keber (1983: 109) identifies as a pleated paper rosette. In the center of the rosette are two cone-shaped elements set in circular bases and from which two bifurcated paper strips extend horizontally. Such rosettes often decorate the rattle-staff (*chicahuaztli*), the ritual instrument that is most closely associated with fertility, because its rattling noise mimicked the sound of rain. This fertility theme is consistent with Xipe Totec's most important association—that with agricultural fertility, the flayed skin representing the rotting hull of a germinating seed.

This object was carved from a *Spondylus* shell. *Spondylus*, the spiny oyster or thorny oyster, was a valued material for elite artisanship in both Mesoamerica and South America (Pillsbury 1996). Cortés wrote to the king of Spain that as he met Motecuzoma II on the causeway to Tenochtitlan, "a servant of his came with two necklaces . . . made from red snails' shells . . . and from each necklace hung eight shrimps of refined gold almost a span in length" (Cortés 1986 [1519–26]: 85). The red-shelled *Spondylus princeps* was relatively soft and easy to carve, but the source of the mollusk was the deep waters of the Pacific, and they required specialized divers to retrieve them. Given the size of the Xipe Totec head, the original shell must have been quite large, and the sculpture thus represented an investment of raw material that was rare, expensive, and difficult to procure.

JQ AND STE

VALUED POSSESSIONS: MATERIALITY AND AESTHETICS IN WESTERN AND SOUTHERN MESOAMERICA

JAVIER URCID

The objects discussed in this section are thought to have originated from a broad area encompassing the modern western states of Jalisco and Colima, through Guerrero, Oaxaca, and perhaps even Chiapas and the Central Highlands, all in Mexico. Temporally, they probably span more than a millennium. When confronted with interpreting objects with attributed provenience and for which chronological control is lacking, scholars have traditionally relied on the notion of style—understood here as culturally constructed choices that guide or dictate the production of materiality—to bring some semblance of temporal and spatial dimensions to the objects.

Yet, while researching the objects in this section, it became imperative for me to assume that style as a phenomenon does not necessarily covary with language or ethnicity, or for that matter that the concept of style cannot be viewed as a nonrecursive process between human action and cultural structure with clearly marked and easily definable temporal boundaries. Quite the opposite, because by postulating a dialectical relation between stylistic constraints and innovation, as well as multiple outcomes ensuing in the context of interregional interaction (such as exchange, imposition, and emulation) or historical development (disjunction, selective appropriation, conservatism, and revivals), the usefulness of the concept of style for addressing issues of provenience and temporal context for objects becomes limited. Therefore, I avoided assigning stylistic attributions.

The aim of the catalogue entries in this section is to highlight certain cultural (mostly technological, functional, and ideological) commonalities that pervaded Mesoamerica both spatially and temporally. Given such an aim, the present introductory synthesis is partly structural and partly contextual. Both approaches presuppose that the perception of the objects under discussion as being charged with aesthetic value is not exclusive to the modern collector or viewer but applies as well to the native commissioner and the artisan who brought the raw material into shape.

We know little about the meanings embedded in the processes of searching and collecting raw and exotic materials for crafting them into objects. The same applies to the meanings linking the underlying manufacturing technologies with the uses of the finished products. But even a cursory perusal of the linguistic legacy of Mesoamerica makes clear the existence of a rich lexical repertoire that highlights the aesthetic value placed on the visual, auditory, and tactile responses to certain raw materials and on objects made out of them. Such lexemes as iridescence, resplendence, smoothness, coldness, and sharpness are but token testimonies of native categories concerning the aesthetic apperception and value attributed to materiality.

The structural approach referred to above allows us to link seemingly unrelated objects as part of a set of sacred propositions. For instance, what could be a common dimension between a deer effigy vessel (PC.B.137, Plate 46), presumably manufactured in western Mesoamerica no later than AD 200, and a carved wooden dart thrower (PC.B.144, Plate 71), possibly crafted in southwestern Mesoamerica more than a millennium later? The link between these disparate objects, made of different media and bearing diverse imagery, is the symbolic value of deer in Mesoamerican thought. Closely related to the sun, in turn recognized for its life-giving properties, deer played an important role in vernal rituals designed to petition for rain and against drought, and to ensure agricultural fertility and hence human fecundity and societal prosperity. But the hunting and offering of deer was also part of a symbolic substitution whereby hunting was to ritual warfare as the deer was to the captive. Thus the deer effigy vessel could provide a visual metaphor for capturing a prisoner destined for a vernal sacrificial ritual.

The elaborately carved dart thrower, however, must have been the weapon of a ruler charged with the office of sacrificer. It would have been used in rituals where captives were profusely bled by inflicting dart wounds prior to the offering of their hearts to the sun. Although the imagery carved on the dart thrower in the Bliss Collection does not make an explicit allusion to deer, other late, carved dart throwers used for the same purpose make overt visual statements to impersonators of Mixcoatl-Camaxtli, the god of hunting in the Tetla-Mixteca and Nahua traditions, who instituted ritual warfare by delivering a deer (captive) from the sky to be properly kept prior to its immolation.

The contextual approach is another profitable way to deal with seemingly disparate objects in this section. The known archaeological record from the later part of the pre-Hispanic sequence allows us to link 13 of the 32 objects presented here. Although each item may have come from a different locality, this subset "replicates" part of the mortuary assemblages found in tombs from Monte Albán and Zaachila, in the central valleys of Oaxaca. Thus, human remains (skulls PC.B.097, PC.B.098, and PC.B.099; Plates 63, 64, and 65, respectively); tesserae of diverse materials (also PC.B.097, PC.B.098, and PC.B.099); mosaic-decorated wooden disks (PC.B.566, Plate 62); travertine vessels (PC.B.113, PC.B.114, and PC.B.115; Plates 67, 68, and 69, respectively); green stone fan handles in the shape of serpents (PC.B.094 and PC.B.136; Plates 60 and 59, respectively); the rectangular bar pendant (PC.B.126, Plate 54); and obsidian blades (PC.B.143b and PC.B.143c; Plate 61), one of them with its gilded sheath (PC.B.143a; Plate 61), are known to have been part of the valued possessions that accompanied high-ranking burials over large portions of southwestern Mesoamerica and the Central Highlands during the last two centuries before the Spanish conquest.

Analysis of this subset of objects yielded substantial evidence to postulate that although the components of certain composite objects are of pre-Hispanic origin, their combination and assembly are not. That is specifically the case of the mosaic-decorated skulls and wooden disk. Despite the questionable assembly of some of the objects, the subset poses important questions regarding the value assigned to materiality in the process of mediating social relations. Many of these crafted objects were crucial to marking high social rank, and their circulation as part of gift-giving and dowry exchanges was a key component in the process of building up prestige, wealth, and political clout.

For example, according to European cultural conceptions, in general, removing such valued materials from circulation by using them as mortuary offerings appears contradictory, given their economic and political functions. Yet their integration into the realm of the ancestors provides us with insights about Mesoamerican eschatology, about notions of endings and beginnings. The arbitrary distinction between the world of the living and that of the dead is a Western construct that contrasts with Mesoamerican thought. Funerary rituals in Mesoamerica undoubtedly marked a termination but were also meant to signal continuity. In a larger contextual framework, the notion of continuity—particularly with regard to the landscape in both its physical and social dimensions—is best exemplified by the practice of multiple embeddings of funerary memorials at specific locales, leading to superimposed and increasingly monumental constructions that constantly reformulated a social memory linking the prestige of corporate groups and their differential access to landed estates.

Several other objects in this section also have close counterparts with funerary offerings dating between AD 300 and 1500, although not necessarily as sets. These include travertine vessels (PC.B.111, PC.B.113, PC.B.114, PC.B.115, PC.B.116, and PC.B.117; Plates 66, 67, 68, 69, and 70, respectively), stone beads (PC.B.123, Plate 53), jadeite ear disks (PC.B.122a and PC.B.122b, Plate 49), a spirally grooved tubular bead (PC.B.135, Plate 58), and an inlaid shell piece (PC.B.540, Plate 45). Two in particular (travertine vessels PC.B.116 and PC.B.117) are characterized by miniaturization, a common symbolic strategy in Mesoamerica to mark materiality associated with the ancestral realm. Besides the funerary context, few items are known to have been part of other ritual contexts. Two green stone plaques carved with the idealized, nonindividualized rendering of a ruler (PC.B.129 and PC.B.130, Plates 50 and 51, respectively) are known to occur in the pan-Mesoamerican archaeological record of the eighth to tenth centuries AD as part of dedicatory caches deposited, probably, to consecrate special buildings. And two types of objects, including the small green stone figurine (PC.B.095, Plate 57) and obsidian blades (PC.B.143a, PC.B.143b, and PC.B.143c), figure prominently in the accounts of early colonial inquisitions as being part of the contents of sacred bundles that memorialized ancestors. Their deployment in petitioning rituals activated their role in the concerns of the living, assisting them in obtaining needed favors from the divine for societal well-being.

The reader will note that the individual entries pay special attention to technologies and manufacturing steps. Given that the majority of objects in this section are made out of lithic materials (green stones, jade, jadeite, turquoise, travertine, and obsidian), lapidary technologies figure prominently, but these should be taken simply as an example of how processes of manufacture can assist in accounting for the recycling of raw materials, the reuse of debitage, the unfolding process of charging an object with aesthetic value through its manufacture, and how certain crafts mediated social relations at both local and interregional levels. Despite the potential of experimental archaeology to measure the energetics of ancient lapidary methods, little has been done to replicate drilling techniques. Such techniques required a masterful ability to employ certain tools while reducing raw material to a designed shape, balancing the physical constraints of the materials with the desired form. These processes of crafting are best exemplified by the production of travertine vessels (see "Stone Vessels," this volume).

Given the nature and features of some of the objects, their study enabled a phenomenological approach aimed at elucidating their probable use or function. Different methods of suspension were evaluated on the stone maskette (PC.B.121, Plate 47), one of the carved plaques (PC.B.131, Plate 52), the bar pendant (PC.B.126), the eagle heads (PC.B.060 and PC.B.061, Plates 55 and 56, respectively), the seated stone figure (PC.B.095), and the spirally grooved bead (PC.B.135). This approach allowed me to test ways these objects might have been suspended, sewn to supports of various kinds, hafted, or used as composite objects. I also examined containers, such as the ceramic effigy vessel of a man carrying a deer (PC.B.137) and the ceramic effigy vessel of a head with open mouth (PC.B.139, Plate 48) to determine the types of substances they may have contained (liquids, hard solids, or powdered materials). Special attention was given in the analysis to the presence or absence of wear to determine use or, in the case of presumed composite objects, their contact with adjacent elements. The mostly negative results of this line of inquiry, however, are probably due to treatments that the objects may have undergone in modern times to bring in or highlight their pristine condition and appeal.

Although many questions remain regarding the way the objects described and interpreted in this section were imbued with value, the technical, functional, structural, contextual, phenomenological, and comparative approaches followed in their analyses revealed both singularities and commonalities that bespeak pan Mesoamerican symbolic codes.

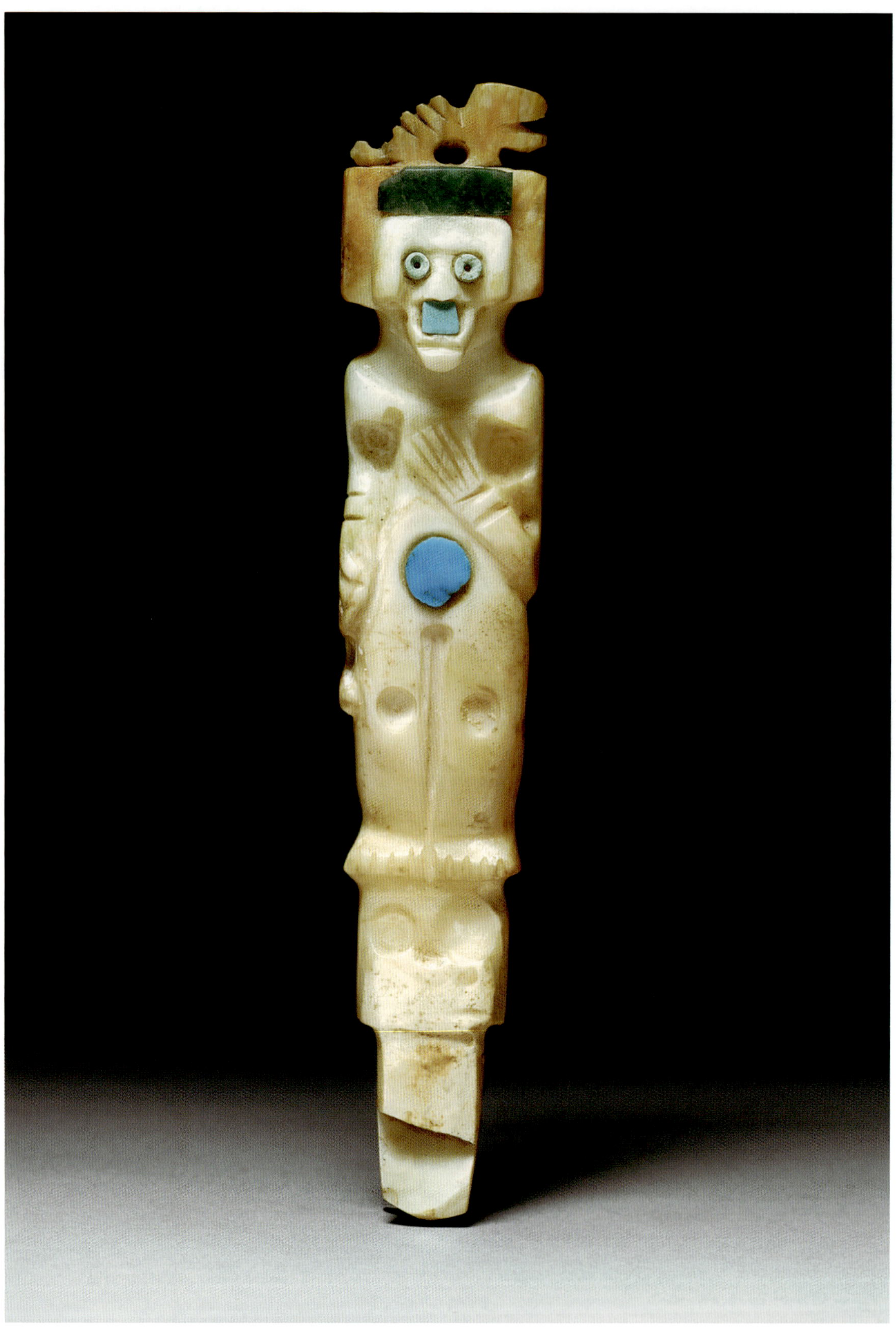

plate 45

PLATE 45
Western Mexico
Probably Early Preclassic period, 1500–800 BC
Carved shell, inlaid with turquoise and jadeite
H. 12.0 cm (4¾"); W. 2.2 cm (⅞"); D. 1.5 cm (⅝")
PC.B.540

ACQUISITION HISTORY:
Gift of John A. Stokes, Jr., 1964, in memory of Robert Woods Bliss

BIBLIOGRAPHY:
Dumbarton Oaks 1969: cat. no. 451

This object depicts a human being standing on a pedestal with its left hand placed on the chest and the right one—seemingly holding a curved scepter—to the side. Although the raw material was thoroughly worked to generate the human figure, its dimensions, flatness, and profile curvature suggest that the shell is *Strombus*. At its base, the object has a flattened rounded peg, implying that it was probably a hafted piece originally inserted at the top end of a scepter or baton. A small portion of the hafting tenon on the front has chipped away, and a crack is present on its posterior surface (Figure 17). The personage is depicted as if wearing a top garment. This is evidenced on the front by an undulating line just below the left shoulder and by another, lengthier one that crosses diagonally on the right side of the chest. This line appears to mark the border of a shawl-like cover. Both forearms exhibit wristbands. However, these undulating incisions do not wrap around the piece. Furthermore, the outlines of the arms on the back of the figure are also rendered by means of curved lines. Although the representation is of unmarked gender, the fingers and toes are indicated with fine short incisions. Deeper linear depressions demarcate the boundary between the legs on both sides of the piece. The main features of the human face are also clearly marked by incisions, including circular eyes, a broad nose, and a U-shaped lower lip.

The figure is topped by a headdress with the image of an animal seen from the front in profile view. In addition, two flaps hang down laterally. A space between the interior outline of the headdress and the face of the figure may stand for the personage's hair, although this section was left plain. The animal appears to stand on a pedestal marked above the presumed figure's hair. The animal faces to the left of the figure and shows the outline of the mouth, the depression of the neck, parallel incisions along its back, a seemingly long tail, the belly, and the extremities. These anatomical features suggest that the rendered creature is an alligator, an iguana, or a lizard. Although most of the object is solid, the outline of the animal's belly and extremities required open work on the piece, constituting the only part of the object with a small perforated area. The removal of this portion was accomplished by drilling two adjacent small holes. Because both perforations exhibit conical profiles, their tapering direction indicates that they were done from front to back.

Inlays further enhanced the piece. Shallow depressions were made in several parts of the figure's body and on the pedestal to facilitate their adherence. Originally, the piece had a total of 21 inlays, but only five remain in place. These include a thin rectangular plaque of jadeite to highlight the pedestal on which the animal in the headdress is standing, small circular turquoise inlays on the eyes, a tiny squared plaque of turquoise affixed between the nose and the lower lip (signaling a nose plug), and a relatively large circular roundel of bright blue turquoise in the figure's navel. Additional circular inlays

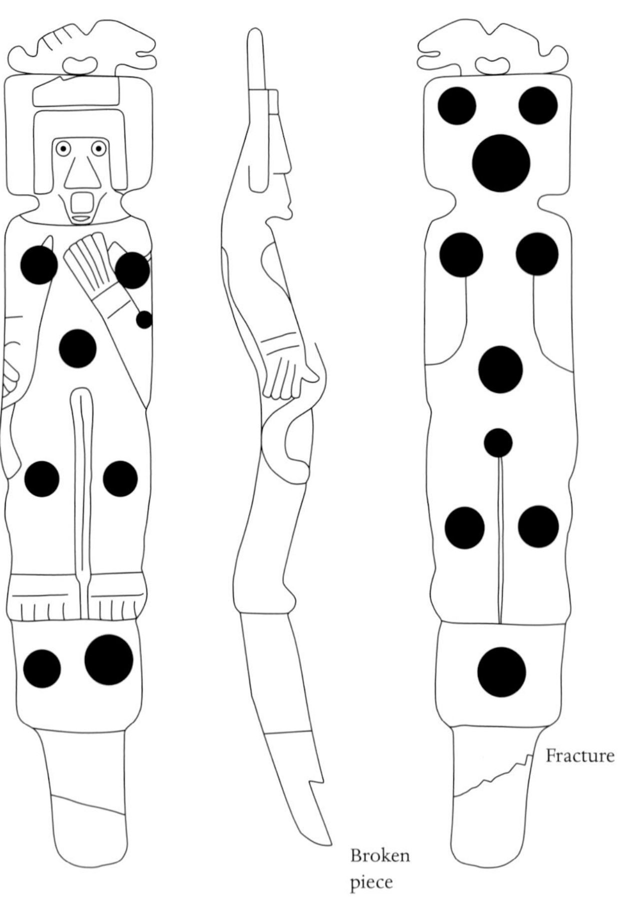

fig. 17
Front, side, and back of carved shell figure PC.B.540. Drawing by Elbis Domínguez.

of variable sizes on the front of the object, now lost and of unknown material, were fixed on the shoulders (2), the knees (2), and the pedestal (2). The circular inlays that decorated the back of the piece, also of variable sizes, were fixed to the head (3), on the shoulders (2), at the base of the back (1), at the juncture between the legs (1), behind the knees (2), and on the pedestal (1).

The empty depressions for the missing inlays are concave and smooth, and no macroscopic traces of the natural adhesive that was once used to keep the inlays in place are evident. The concave nature of the depressions seemingly eliminates the possibility that they were produced by drilling. Rather, grinding the shell, with the aid of a fine abrasive medium and a stick with a thick and blunt end, may have produced them. There is also a small circular depression at the point where the left arm of the figure bends upward. This depression was probably produced with a drill and may have been intended to enhance the shape of the folded arm. The same applies to a pronounced depression marking the anterior twisting of the curved scepter carried in the figure's right hand.

The overall distribution of the inlays on the front of the figure's body appears to render an ordered scheme of the world, that is, four directions marked by the inlays on the shoulders and knees, and a fifth, central point in the navel. The same applies to the distribution of inlays on the back of the body. Here, the quadripartite structure around an axis mundi is seemingly masked by the inlays in the back of the head, at the junction of the legs, and in the pedestal. Yet the presence of such a scheme is unmistakable if one considers the uniformity in the size of the five depressions that signal it. Several lines of evidence, including the purported function of the piece as the hafted end for a scepter, the representation of a figure on top of a pedestal, the inlays to mark a nose plug and the eyes, and the quadripartite distribution of larger inlays on both the front and back of the figure, indicate the representation of a high-ranking individual. The object of which this piece was originally part would have been the material symbol of such a rank. The scepter held by the figure, which is curved like the shell piece, may be the representation of the object itself. Although lacking details, the overall shape of the scepter may be an iconic Mesoamerican rendition of a serpent. If so, the object and its representation may be visual metaphors for lightning. Such pan-Mesoamerican symbolism often denotes the role of rainmaker, a prerogative closely linked with rulership. The significance of the animal figured on top of the shell piece remains elusive, but it may signal membership in a particular hereditary social group.

The manufacture of shell pieces decorated with inlays of exotic materials has a wide spatial and temporal distribution in Mesoamerica,[82] yet the choice of representing an ideal of the human body characterized by a thin, slender appearance, with relatively squared outlines, and with upper and lower extremities integrated to the body, seemingly points to West Mexico[83] as the region where the piece was manufactured and used. The crafting of shell ornaments is well attested in western Mesoamerica throughout pre-Hispanic times.[84] Yet their production between 500 BC and AD 300 appears to have favored the use of *Spondylus* shells, to emphasize open work, and to render human figures with extremities slightly separated from the body. Subsequent production of shell pieces, dating between AD 300 and 600, continued these stylistic choices. The closest parallel in terms of representing the human figure, although rendered in ceramics, is with materials from the "Opeño" archaeological culture that developed in Michoacán between 1500 and 800 BC (see Mountjoy 1998: 250). Those societies are known to have had both gathering and agricultural economies, and the differential material wealth in their burials already evidences social ranking, a societal feature that is congruent with the interpreted meaning of the shell piece in the Bliss Collection.

JU

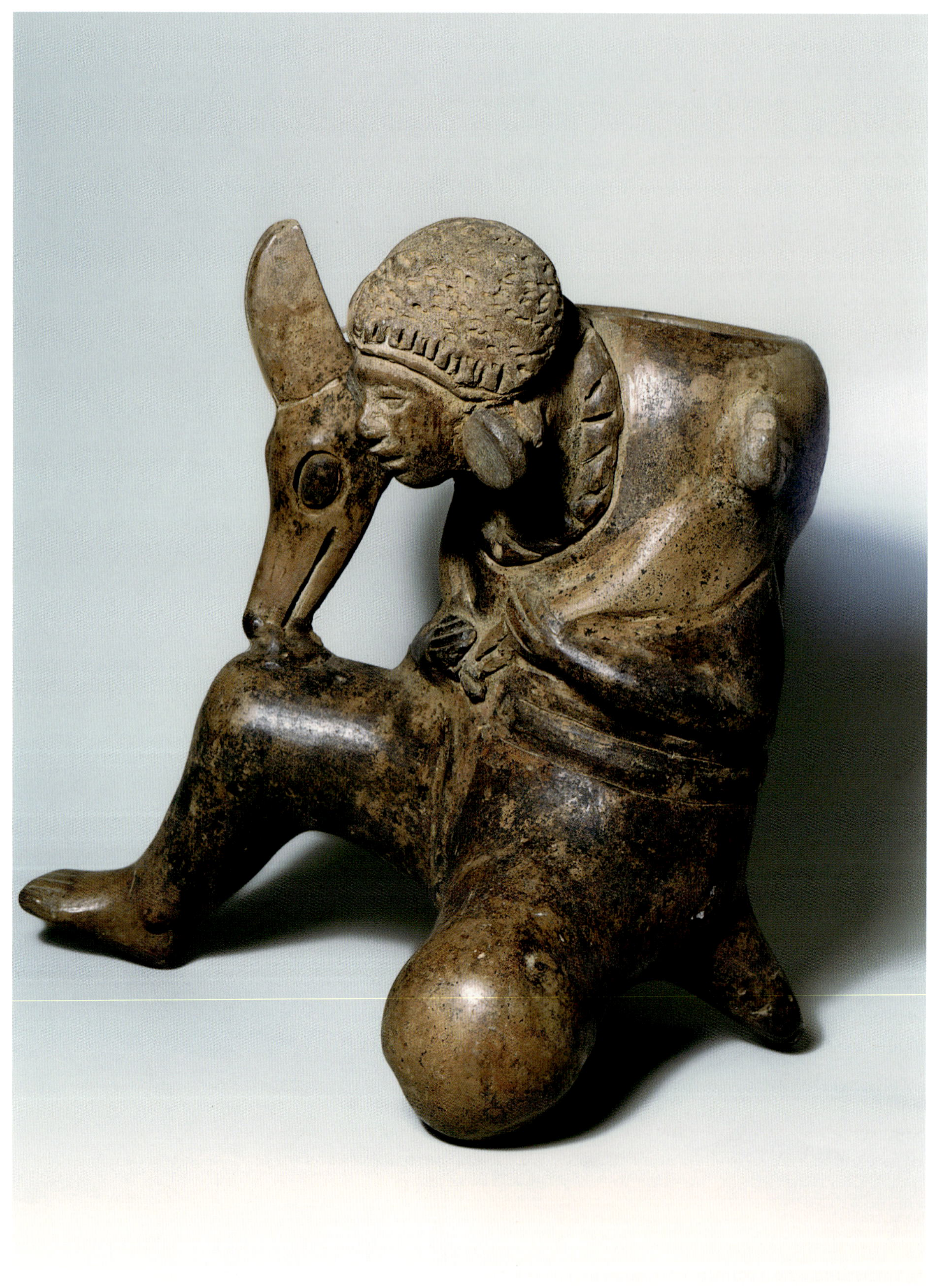

plate 46

CERAMIC EFFIGY VESSEL WITH MAN AND DEER

PLATE 46
Western Mexico
Possibly Late to Terminal Preclassic period,
200 BC–AD 350
Ceramic
H. 17.8 cm (7"); W. 17.0 cm (6⅝"); D. 15.1 cm (6")
PC.B.137

ACQUISITION HISTORY:
Purchased from Earl Stendahl, 1944

EXHIBITION HISTORY:
Indigenous Art of the Americas, National Gallery of Art, Washington, D.C., April 1947–July 1949, February 1954–July 1962 (NGA 238)

BIBLIOGRAPHY:
Instituto Nacional de Antropología e Historia 1946: fig. 263; Bliss 1947: 28, 135, cat. no. 136; Christensen 1955: 170; *Artes de México* 1957: pl. 25; Bliss 1957: 248, cat. no. 101, pl. LXI, bottom; Dumbarton Oaks 1963: 31, cat. no. 158; Soustelle 1967a: 20, illus. no. 18; National Geographic Society 1983: 381, center; Association of American Colleges 1987: 3

This effigy vessel assumes the shape of a semi-kneeling personage about to lift a deer on his back. The animal is held by the hoofs while its torso forms the upper backside of the vessel. The head of the deer projects forward from the right side of the human figure, its snout resting against the bent right leg of the personage. The long ears of the stag are joined, and the short tail appears incised with parallel lines on the back of the vessel. The arms of the personage, his left foot, two of the extremities of the deer, and its tail are appliqués to the vessel. The proportion of the human head to the rest of the features in the vessel is rather small.

The personage is male, as indicated by a loincloth slightly modeled over the surface and then emphasized by incised lines. The toes of both feet are shown by means of incised lines, as are the fingers of the hands and the hoofs of the deer. The extended foot of the figure also indicates the malleolus of the tibia by a slight projection on the surface. The personage wears a rope around his neck, disk-shaped ear spools seemingly fastened in the back by a thick band, and a coiffure divided in half by a band. One side of the headdress is lower than the other, but both have the same texture, indicated by punctures on the clay.

The chamber of the vessel opens into the hollow head and legs of the human figure (Figure 18). The head of the stag is also hollow and connects to the vessel. Thus the container was probably not used to store liquid but rather some solid material. The height of the container and its approximate circumference measured at the mouth, which is slightly expanded compared to the rest of the vessel because of the modeled position of the deer's body, does not generate enough interior space for large items. An adult hand does not fit into the mouth of the vessel; fingers can reach barely halfway into the container.

The exterior surface of the effigy vessel appears to have been burnished and polished with a stick, as striations are evident in some parts. The left knee, the right heel, and the left toes provide a tripod support for the vessel. The head shows evidence of a repair.

The figure has been interpreted as a hunter carrying a deer (Bliss 1957: plate 61), but an analogy

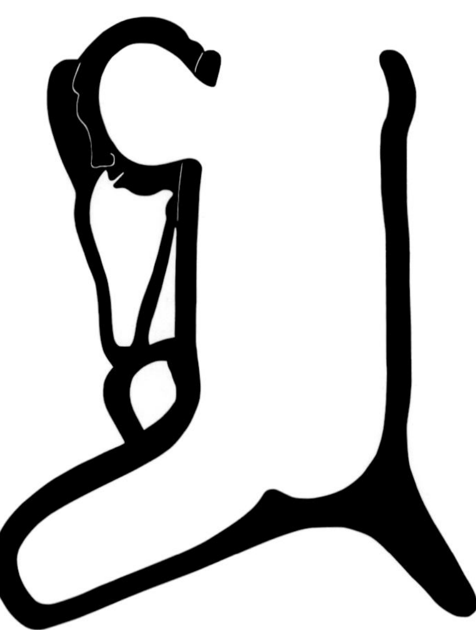

fig. 18
Cross section of ceramic effigy vessel PC.B.137 indicating solid and hollow parts. Drawing by Elbis Domínguez.

can be established between the three-dimensional rendering in the effigy vessel and two-dimensional scenes painted on Late Classic polychrome vessels from the Yucatan peninsula (Figure 19).[85]

The scene on the effigy vessel in the Bliss Collection does not indicate that the deer is dead, because no extended tongue, closed eyes, or limp body is indicated. Thus the rope around the neck of the personage could allude to the use of a noose snare, one of the ways in which deer were captured alive in ancient Mesoamerica. Central Mexican as well as Maya almanacs (Figure 20) and stone monuments (see Voss and Kremer 1998: 74) depict this mode of hunting. The capture of live deer and their sacrifice were part of vernal agricultural rituals (Montolíu 1977; Pohl 1981).

In the Dumbarton Oaks effigy vessel the rope around the neck of the personage, his fancy ear spools, and the elaborate coiffure may suggest as well the pan-Mesoamerican metaphor of a warrior taking a prisoner and the symbolic substitution of the captive for a stag (Figure 21). The joined ears of the stag would be equivalent to the pulled hair of the captive, a visual metaphor also rendered in a Classic Maya polychrome vessel in the Bliss Collection that alludes to a form of sacrifice whereby captives acting as deer were tied to a scaffold, partially burned, and then immolated by shooting them with darts (Figure 22).[86] Aside from its agricultural connotations, the enactment of scaffold sacrifice in which the victim was

fig. 19
Flattened rendering of Late Classic polychrome tripod plate from Yucatan with deer-capturing scenes (Museo Nacional de Antropología e Historia, Mexico City, cat. no. 10-079006). Drawing by Elbis Domínguez (based on Schmidt et al. 1998: 561, no. 169).

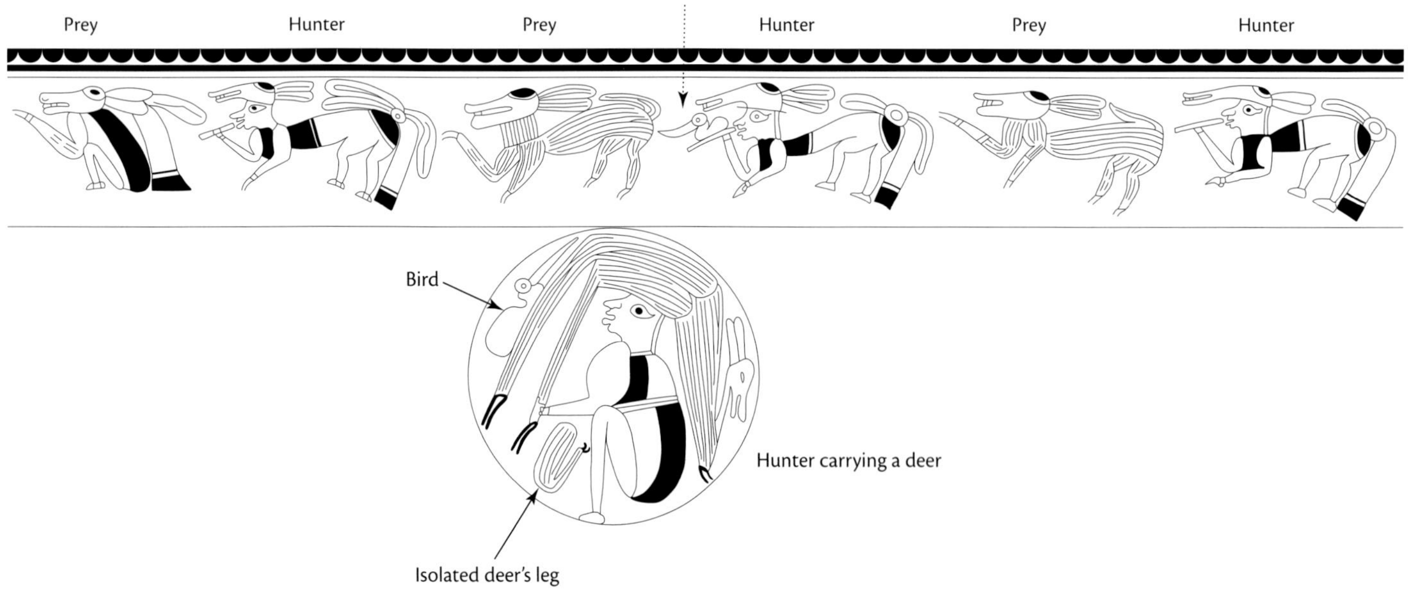

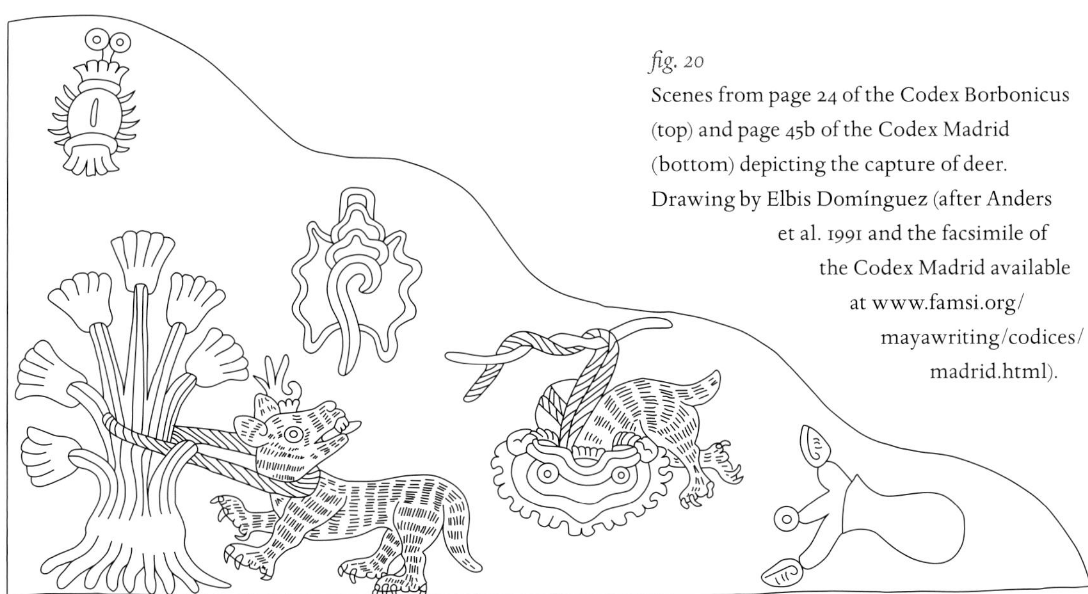

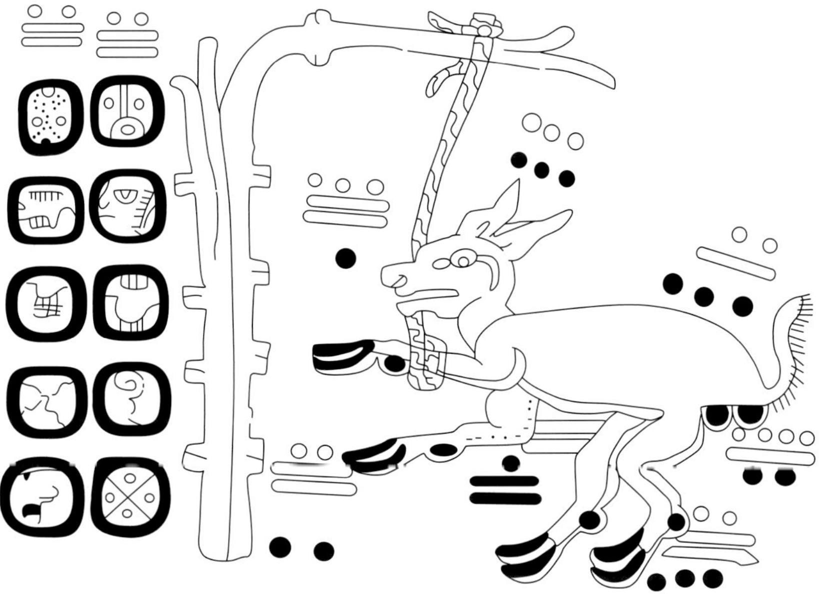

fig. 20
Scenes from page 24 of the Codex Borbonicus (top) and page 45b of the Codex Madrid (bottom) depicting the capture of deer. Drawing by Elbis Domínguez (after Anders et al. 1991 and the facsimile of the Codex Madrid available at www.famsi.org/mayawriting/codices/madrid.html).

symbolically substituted for a deer seemingly formed part of accession ceremonies (Pohl 1981; Taube 1988).

Another link between deer symbolism and warfare becomes apparent in a passage from a story of creation recounted in *Historia de los mexicanos por sus pinturas*.[87] After the creation of the sun and the moon, the story tells us that:

> In the fourth year of the fourth [set] of thirteen [years], after the great flood, there was a loud noise in the sky, and a double-headed deer fell from it, and Camaxtli [the God of War] ordered it to be picked up and told the men living then in Cuitlahuac, three leagues from Mexico [Tenochtitlan], to take the deer as their god, and so they did, and they fed him during four years with rabbits and snakes and butterflies. And in the eighth year of the fourth [set] of thirteen [years] (that is, four years after), there was war between Camaxtli and neighboring peoples, and to defeat them he took the deer, and carrying him on his back, he vanquished them. And in the second year of the fifth [set]

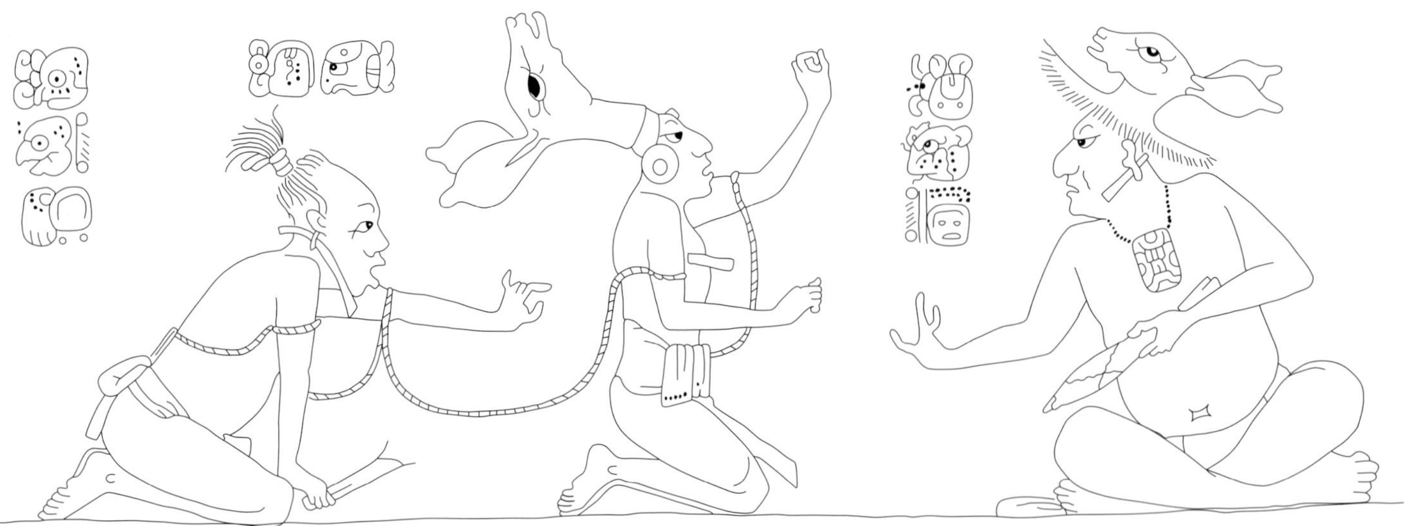

fig. 21
Scene from an incised alabaster vessel showing the hunting of deer as a metaphor for the capture of prisoners for sacrifice, ca. AD 700. Drawing by Elbis Domínguez (based on Kerr n.d.a: no. 1606).

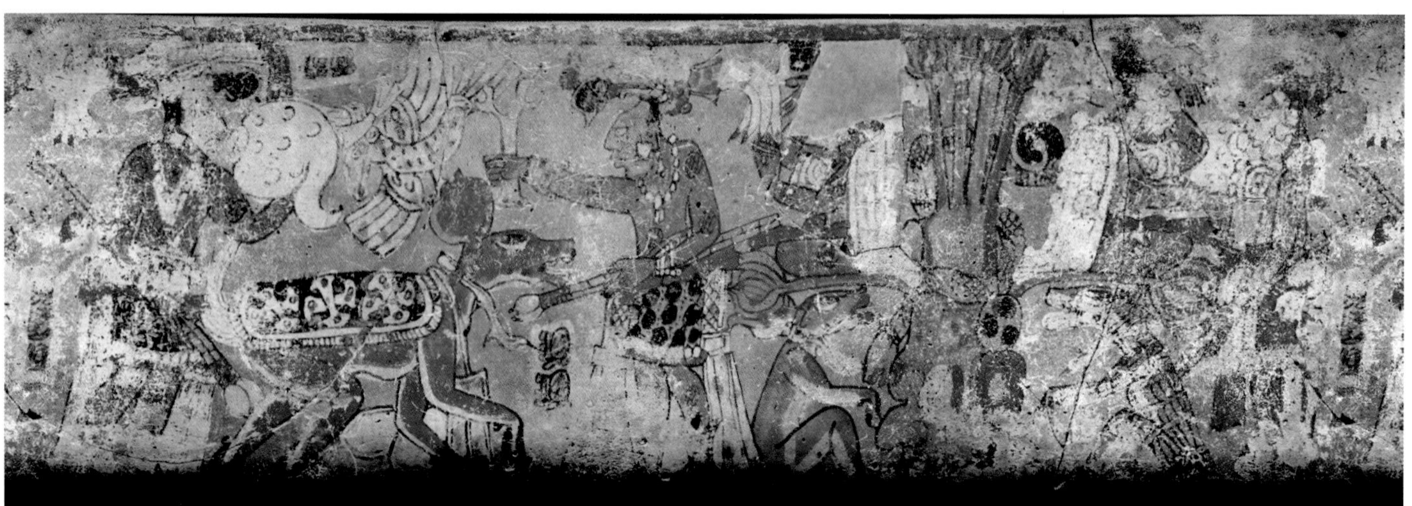

fig. 22
Rollout view of Dumbarton Oaks Maya vase PC.B.203 depicting the metaphorical substitution of the hunting of deer for the capture and sacrifice of a prisoner of war. Photograph K2785 © Justin Kerr.

> of thirteen [years] (that is, two years after the end of a Calendar Round), the god Camaxtli offered a celebration to the sky, kindling many fires and sponsoring feasts, and until the end of the fifth [set] of thirteen [years] after the great flood Camaxtli made war, and with it he fed the sun. (Garibay 1996: 37; translation by the author, clarifying words and emphasis added)

Although the lack of contextual information for the effigy vessel in the Bliss Collection precludes elucidating its intended ritual use, the ideational link between warfare, agricultural success, and rulership may denote a third layer of meaning in the object. By carrying the stag on his back, a leader bears the burden and the responsibility for success in agricultural production and social reproduction (Pohl 1981).

An earlier catalogue description (Lothrop in Bliss 1957: 248, cat. no. 101) assigned the object to the Tarascan style and assumed that it may have originated in the area of the modern state of Colima in West Mexico. Such a stylistic attribution implies that the vessel was manufactured during the later part of the pre-Hispanic sequence. Alternatively, and based on a comparison with Late Preclassic materials, the vessel bears resemblances to ceramic objects from the Comala style of Colima and southern Jalisco (200 BC–AD 350) (see Townsend 1998: cat. nos. 26, 28). The similarities are both thematic and formal, especially with regard to surface treatment. The vessel shares a more distant resemblance with a ceramic figurine attributed to Xochipala, Guerrero, and presumably dating to the Early Preclassic.[88] In this case the resemblance in both objects is striking in terms of the lower body's posture. However, the effigy vessel exhibits conspicuous differences with the Colima and Guerrero materials. For one thing, the Princeton piece is not a vessel but a solid figurine whose head to body size ratio approximates a naturalistic relation. Although some of the ceramic effigies adhering to the Comala style have smaller heads relative to body size (see Townsend 1998: 31, figs. 25–26; 42, fig. 11) or are receptacles, such as the vessel under consideration, the extremities are separated from the human body. In contrast, the vessel in the Bliss Collection does not exhibit such a stylistic feature except for the neck and head of the deer.

Although the effigy vessel PC.B.137 is not typical of the Comala style, it is worth noting that the symbolic substitution of the hunting of the deer and the capture of prisoners for their sacrifice seems to be visually expressed in a remarkable effigy vessel from Late Preclassic western Mesoamerica (Townsend 1998: 31). Whether the effigy vessel at Dumbarton Oaks is earlier or from a different region, these examples attest to the deep historical roots in native conceptions about deer, warfare, fertility, and political office.

JU

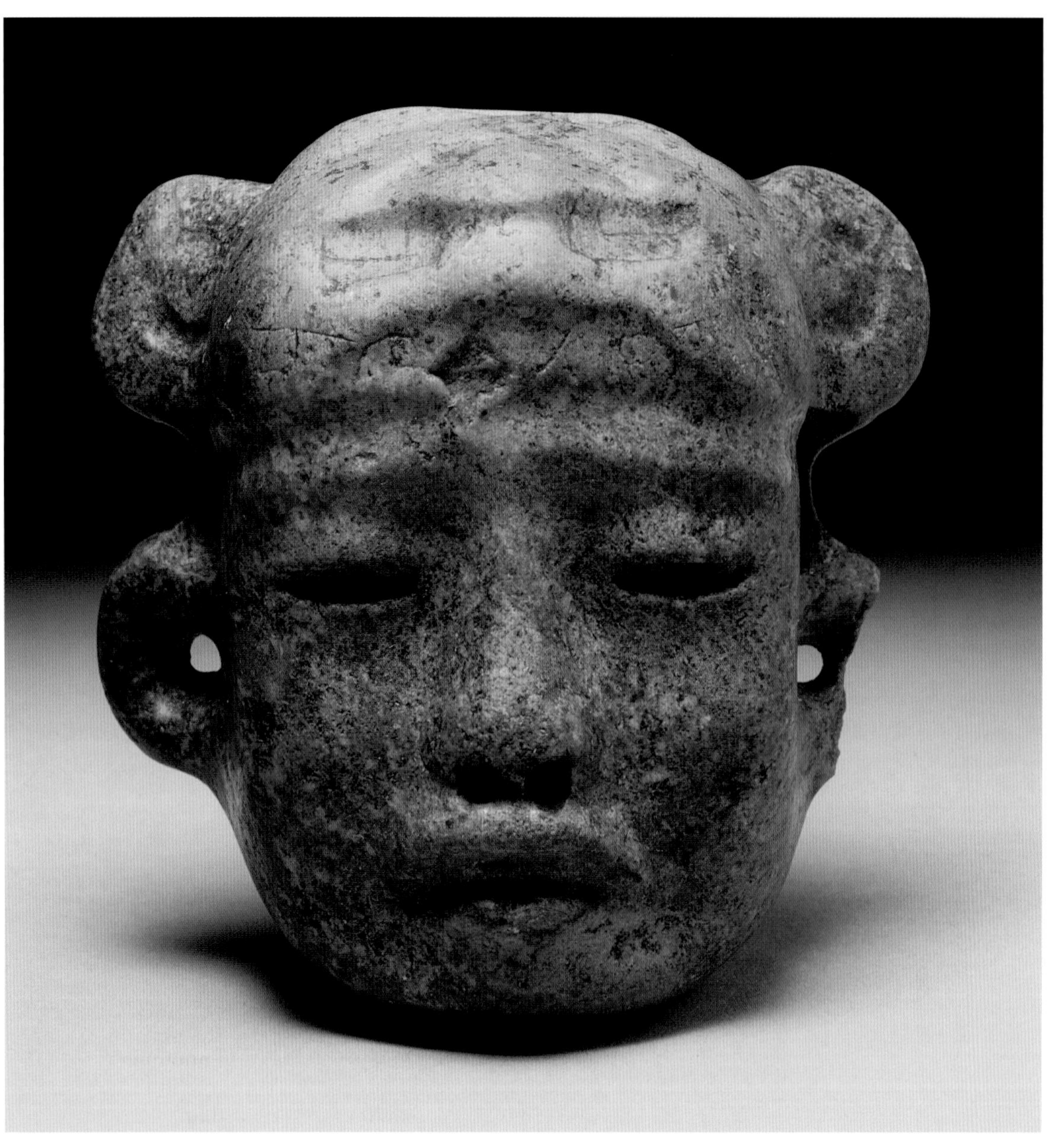

plate 47

MINIATURE MASKETTE

PLATE 47
Southern Mexico
Late to Terminal Preclassic period, 200 BC–AD 200
Serpentine
H. 10.0 cm (3⅞"); W. 9.75 cm (3⅞"); D. 5.4 cm (2⅛")
PC.B.121

ACQUISITION HISTORY:
Purchased from Ernest Brummer, 1947; formerly in the collection of Joseph Brummer

EXHIBITION HISTORY:
Indigenous Art of the Americas, National Gallery of Art, Washington, D.C., 1952–62 (NGA 370)

BIBLIOGRAPHY:
Bliss 1957: 247, cat. no. 85, pl. LIV; Dumbarton Oaks 1963: 5, cat. no. 16

This maskette depicts the head of a personage wearing a jaguar helmet. The piece is heavy for its size, and given its presumed use for suspension or attachment, a section was carved from the back, most likely to lighten its weight and facilitate the perforation of several holes (Figure 23). The piece was hollowed by drilling two large holes to a depth of 2 cm, using drill bits of slightly larger than 4 cm in diameter. Two large holes traverse the maskette laterally, probably to provide means of suspending or fastening it.

The ears were also bored with biconical holes, each done in two stages, from front and back. The left ear is chipped off, but the hole is intact. These perforations may have been for attaching miniature ear ornaments. Two smaller bores that indicate the nostrils are connected at their deepest end, suggesting that a movable nose plug was appended.

The maskette has two more conical holes, initiated from the exterior, piercing its inferior border. These perforations probably facilitated the

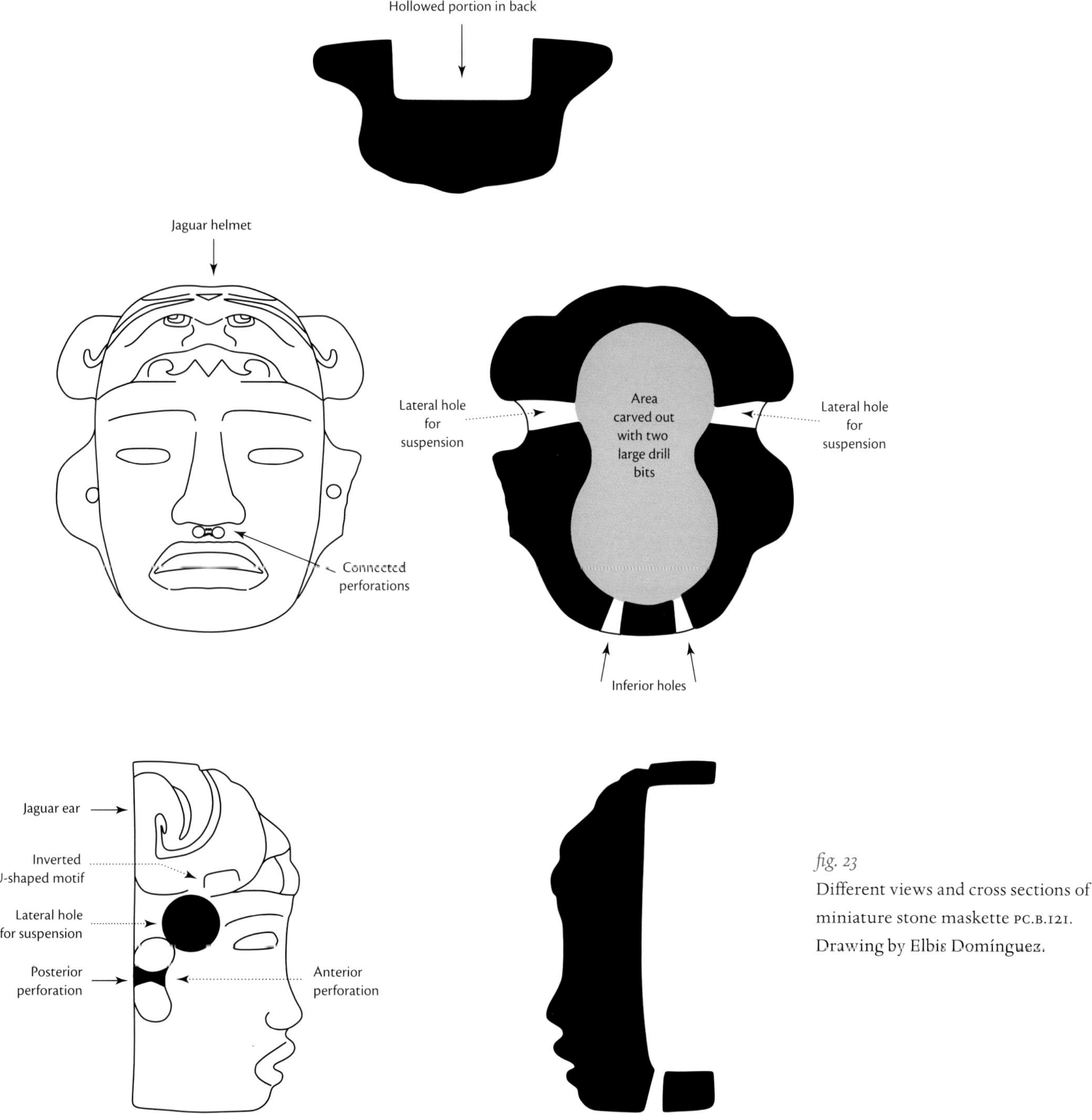

fig. 23
Different views and cross sections of miniature stone maskette PC.B.121. Drawing by Elbis Domínguez.

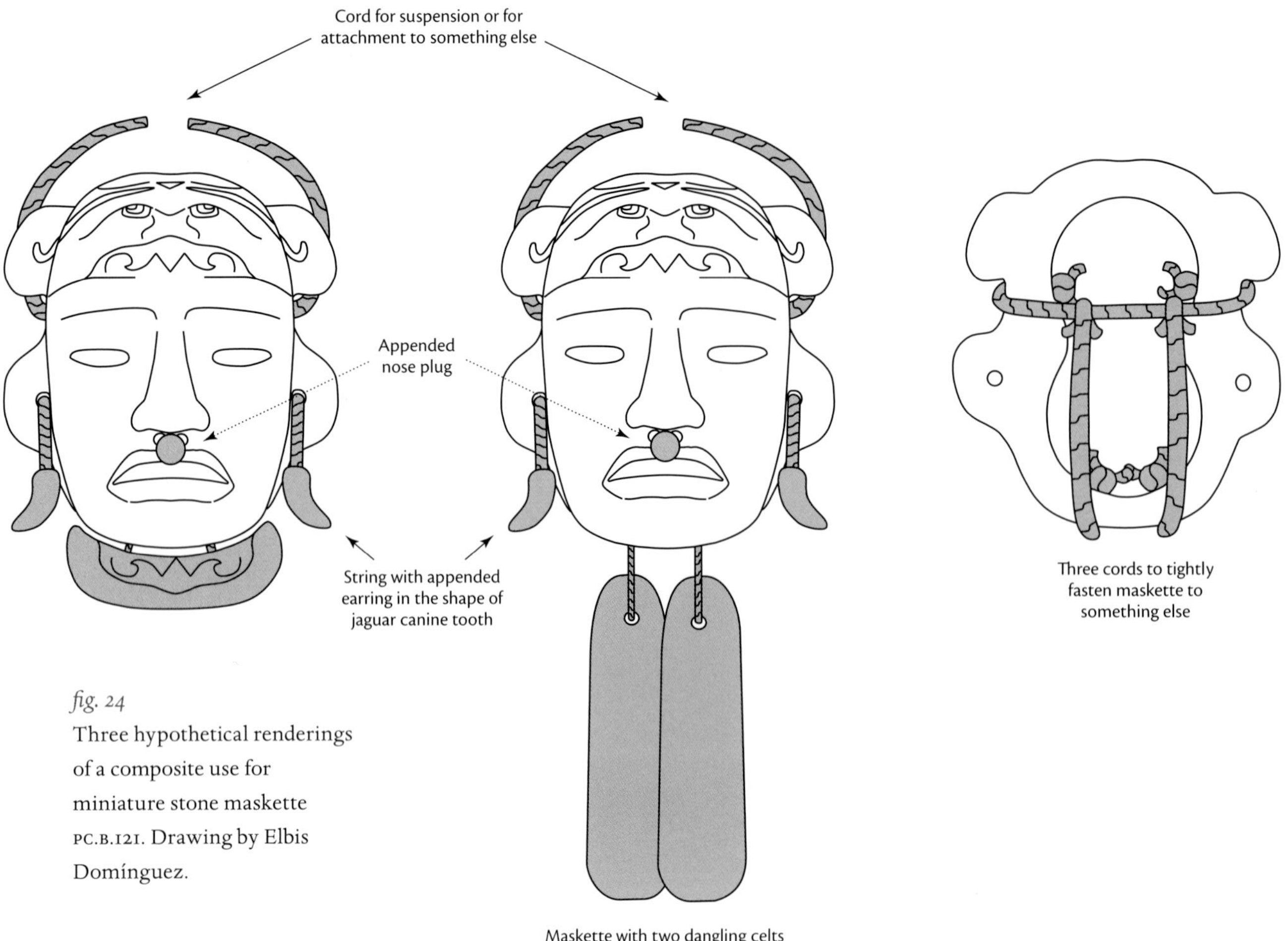

fig. 24
Three hypothetical renderings of a composite use for miniature stone maskette PC.B.121. Drawing by Elbis Domínguez.

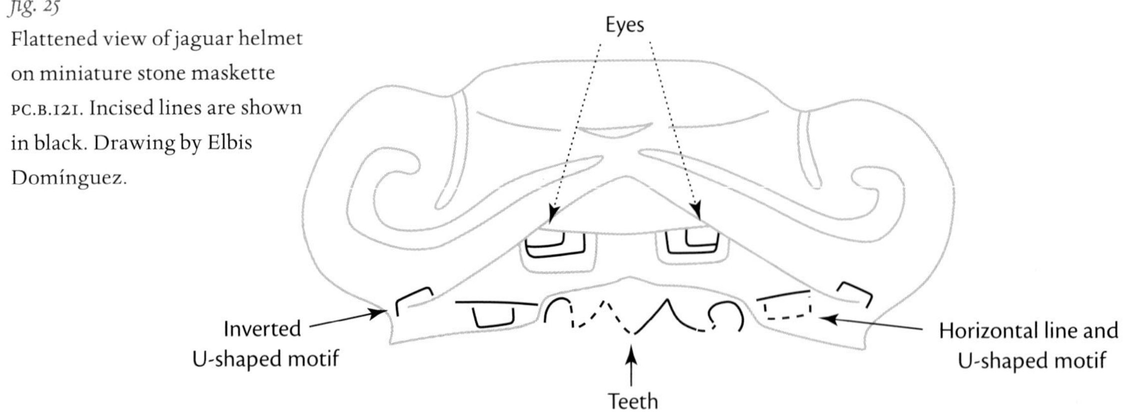

fig. 25
Flattened view of jaguar helmet on miniature stone maskette PC.B.121. Incised lines are shown in black. Drawing by Elbis Domínguez.

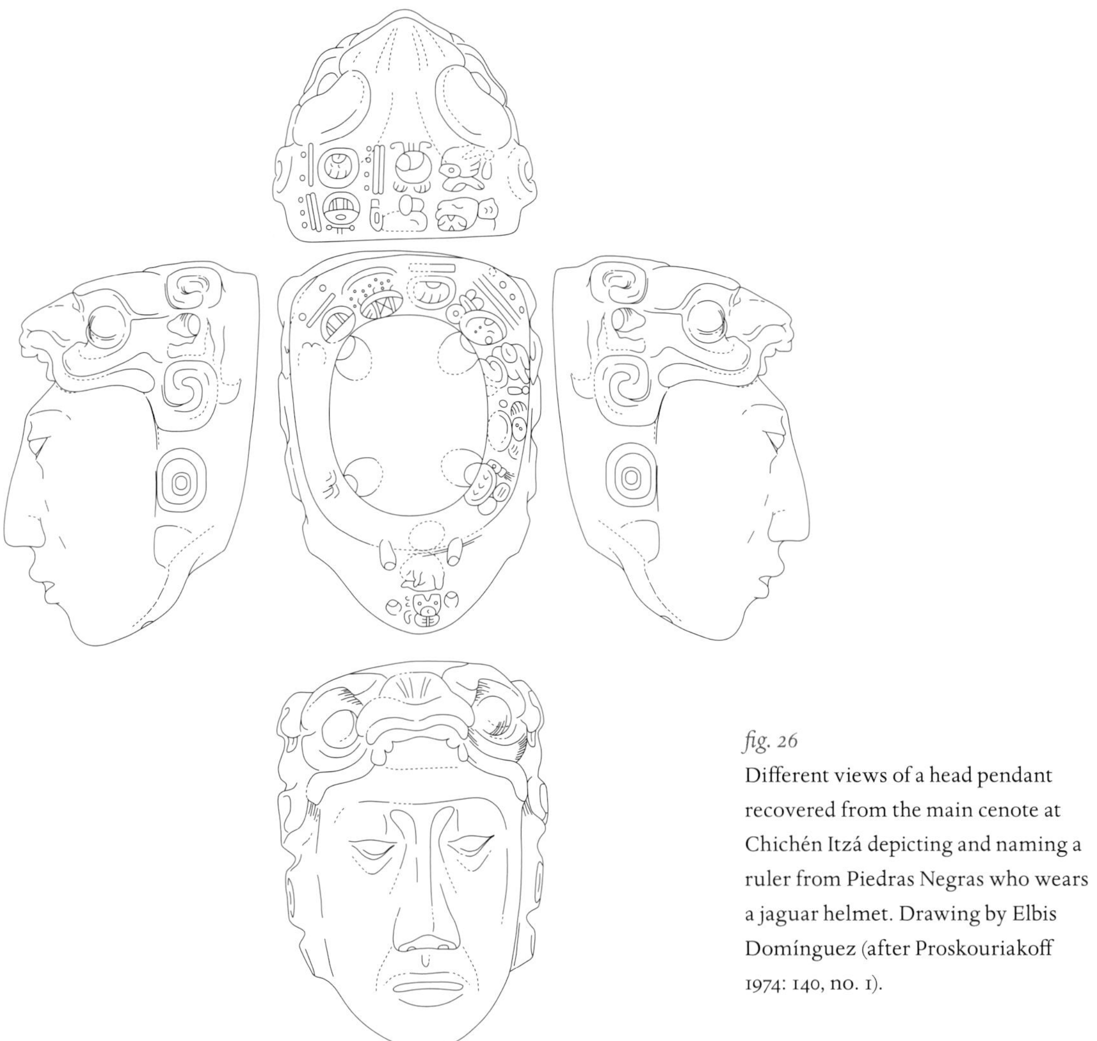

fig. 26
Different views of a head pendant recovered from the main cenote at Chichén Itzá depicting and naming a ruler from Piedras Negras who wears a jaguar helmet. Drawing by Elbis Domínguez (after Proskouriakoff 1974: 140, no. 1).

suspension of additional ornaments—perhaps to articulate an appended and movable lower jaw of the jaguar's helmet, or simply to lace two additional cords to the transversal one and tie the maskette firmly and securely to something else (Figure 24). Thus the maskette may have been intended as a pendant or as a buckle.

Incised lines mark the eyes and the teeth in the jaguar's helmet. A small area in the dentition is chipped off. U-shaped motifs are incised on either side below the jaguar's ears. Two additional motifs between the teeth and the inverted U-shaped motif consist of a straight line above and a U-shaped bracket below (Figure 25).

The physiognomy of the maskette resembles other known Late Preclassic revivals of the Olmec style from southwestern Mesoamerica, combining sculpting with incised lines (see Pahl 1977: fig. 1; Urcid 2002). The lapidary technique of deep hollowing in the back of maskettes, masks, and head pendants spans much of the pre-Hispanic sequence, as is evident in examples from Early Preclassic Gulf Lowlands to later works from Teotihuacan, the Maya area, and Mexico-Tenochtitlan (see Medellín Zenil 1971: pls. 64–65; Walsh 2003: 64). A Late Classic head pendant recovered from the main cenote at Chichén Itzá is conceptually similar to the Bliss Collection maskette: it depicts a human head wearing a jaguar helmet with the upper jaw only, with similar hollowing on the back and similar paired perforations on the inferior aspect of the piece (Figure 26). The pendant from Chichén Itzá includes on the posterior surface a Maya inscription that identifies it as an image of Yo'nal Ahk II, who began ruling Piedras Negras in AD 687 (Martin and Grube 2000: 145).

Wearing jaguar helmets was a social practice signaling high social rank, confined to royal and noble individuals. However, the theme of the maskette could also allude to the pan-Mesoamerican conception of a "companion spirit," a being—usually an animal—with whom people shared their essences (Houston and Stuart 1989).

JU

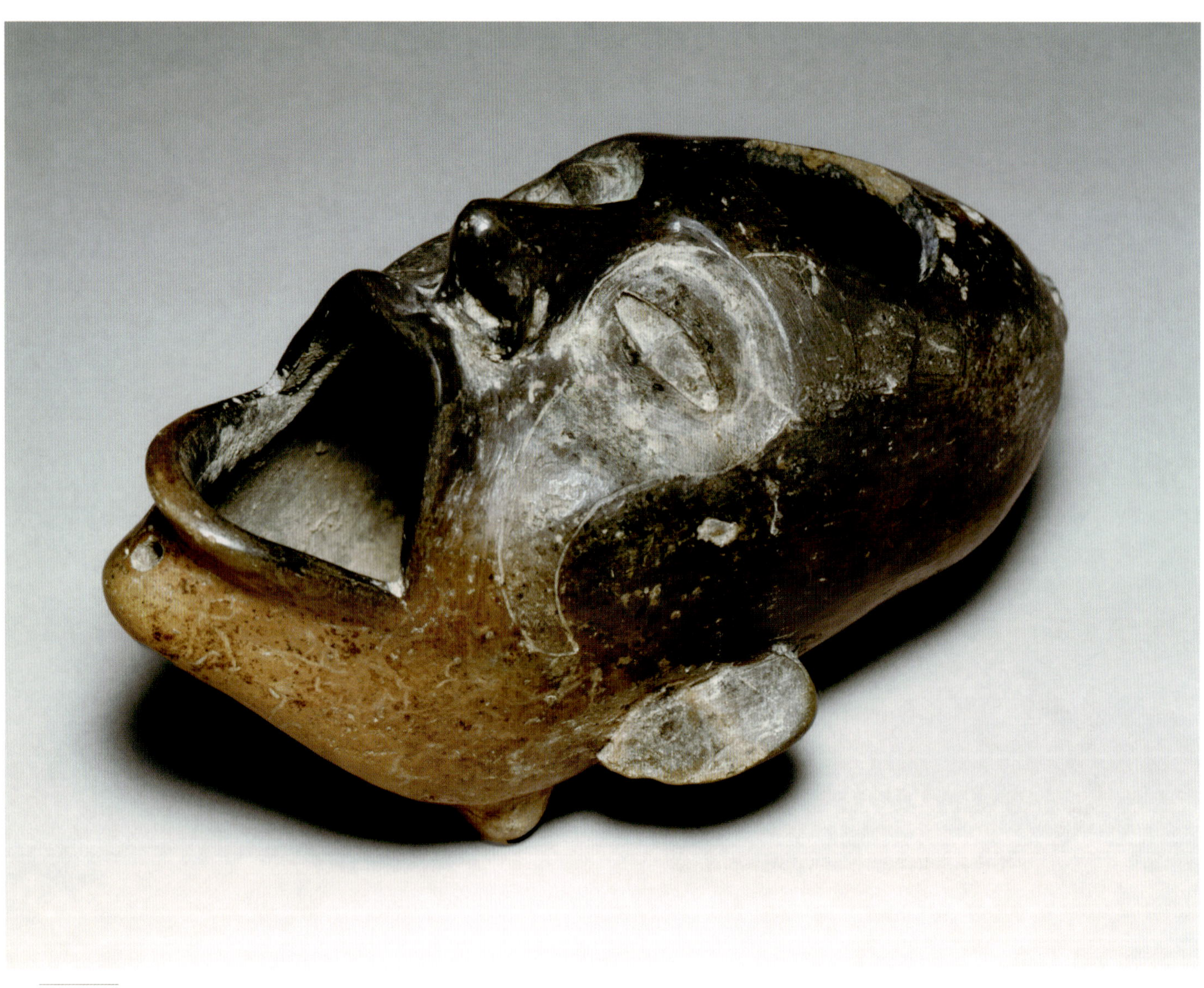

plate 48

CERAMIC EFFIGY VESSEL OF FACE WITH OPEN MOUTH

PLATE 48
Late to Terminal Preclassic period, 200 BC–AD 200
Ceramic
H. 7.9 cm (3⅛"); W. 7.8 cm (3¹⁄₁₆"); D. 13.7 cm (5⅜")
PC.B.139

ACQUISITION HISTORY:
Purchased from John Stokes, 1960

BIBLIOGRAPHY:
Dumbarton Oaks 1963: 9, cat. no. 42

Resting on conical supports on the back of the head, this small tripod vessel has two large openings, one in the forehead and the other simulating a wide-open mouth (Figure 27 and Figure 28, left). The vessel is dark gray, with a lighter brown or tan on the lower left side of the face, under the chin, and on the underside of the head, resulting from uneven firing. The external surface of the head, with the exception of the ears, is highly burnished. A small bonnet-like headdress element with punctuate marks was added as an appliqué.

Two incised motifs encircle the eyes; the interior areas were left unburnished. Both motifs terminate in pointed curved scrolls on the cheeks. An additional three bands of decreasing size are above the left eye. The nostrils are indicated by thick conical punctures that penetrate 3–5 mm into the clay. Two small perforations, one above the opening in the forehead and the other below the open mouth, are 3.2 mm in diameter, apparently made by leaving in place thin wooden sticks that burned away during firing. The border of the opening in the forehead was smoothed; the edge of the mouth was burnished. The differences in finish and the position of the openings suggest that the mouth was the main aperture of the vessel.

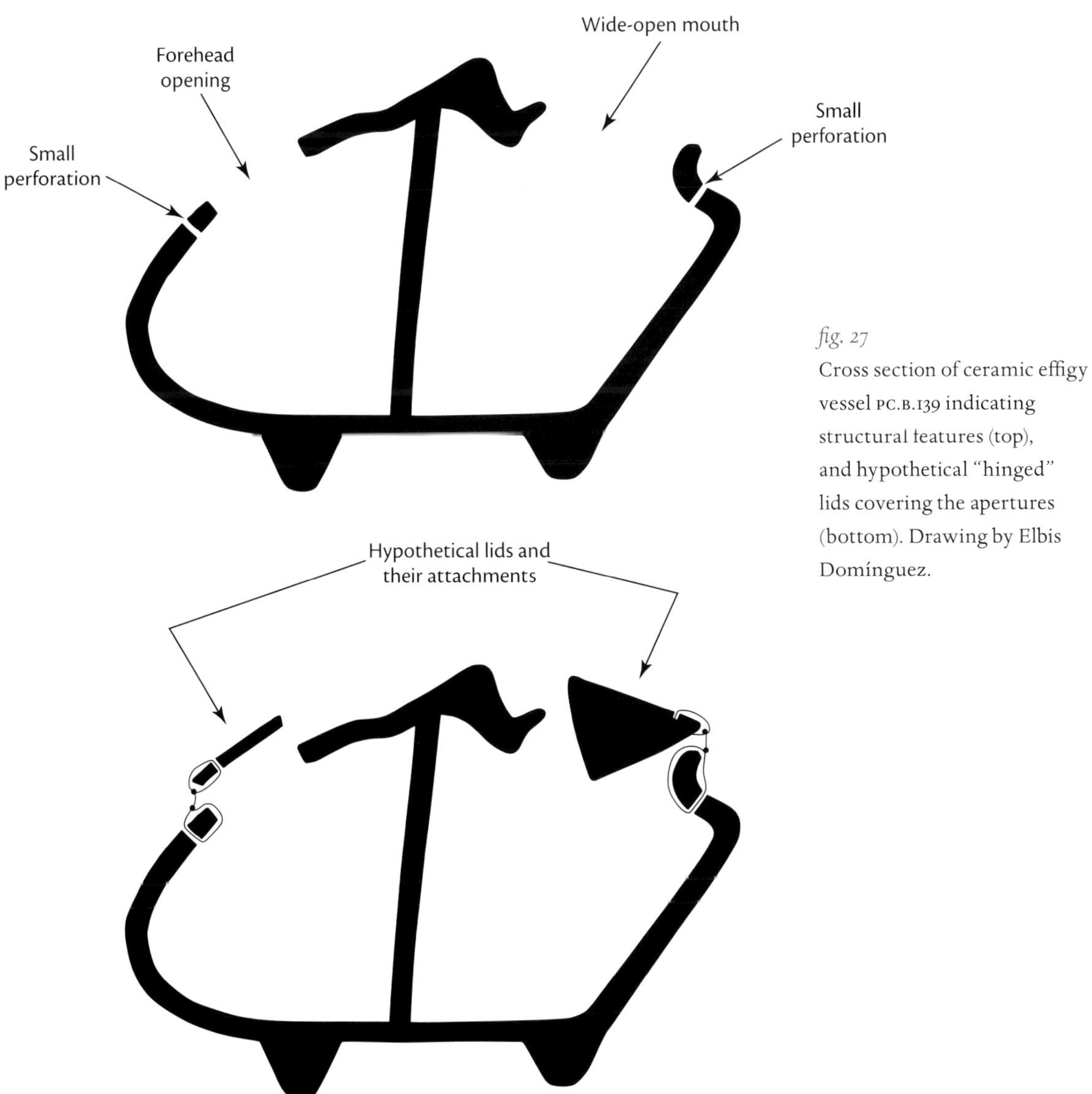

fig. 27
Cross section of ceramic effigy vessel PC.B.139 indicating structural features (top), and hypothetical "hinged" lids covering the apertures (bottom). Drawing by Elbis Domínguez.

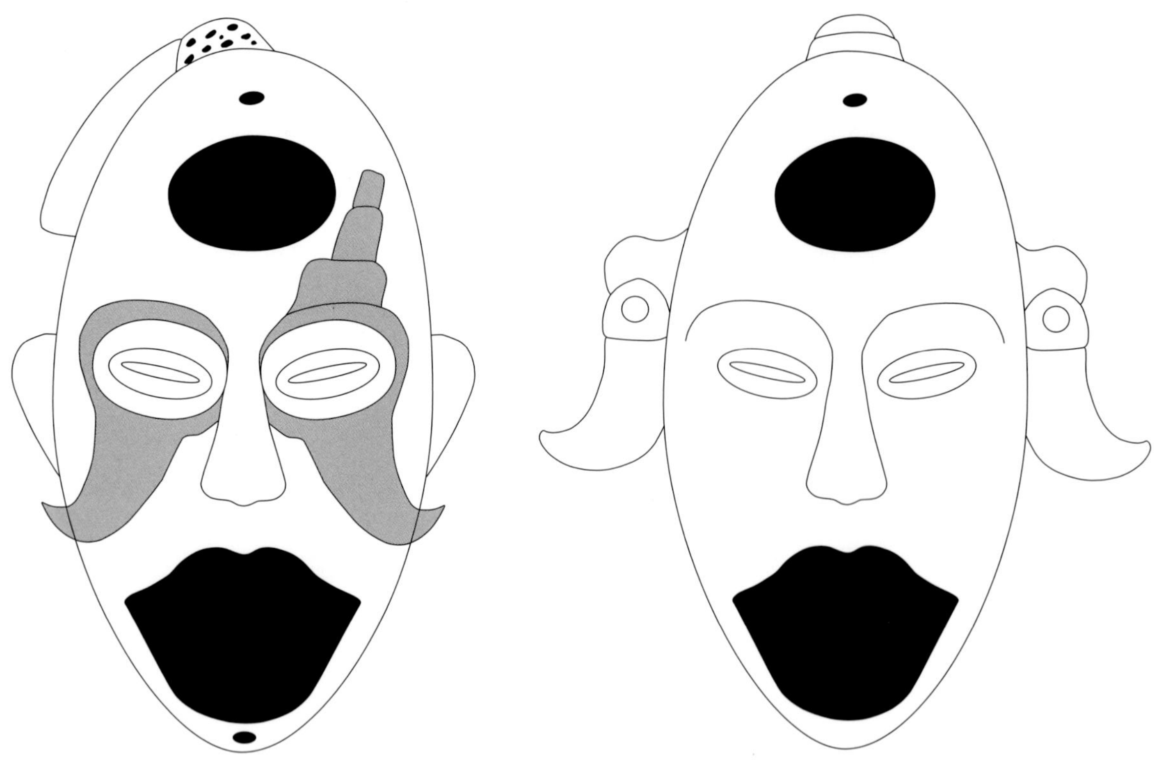

fig. 28
Flattened view of faces on ceramic effigy vessel PC.B.139 (left) and on a ceramic effigy vessel attributed to the Totonacs in the Anahuacalli Museum in Mexico City (right). Drawing by Elbis Domínguez (right image after López Portillo et al. 1982: 114).

The interior of the vessel is partitioned by a flat clay plaque. It is not known what this bipartite receptacle once contained. Small holes near the mouth and forehead openings could have served as hinges for securing small lids with strings. The internal clay wall was not fused before firing, and possible resulting cracks would have permitted liquids to pass from one chamber to another. Presumably the vessel was meant to contain a substance in solid state (powdered?) and that such content, sealed with covers, was easily retrieved by some kind of spoon.

Similar effigy vessels are known from various collections, but none has a secure provenience or date.[89] They range between 12 and 22 cm in length, but it is uncertain whether they have supports and internal partitions that define separate chambers. The effigy vessel in the Anahuacalli Museum (Figure 28, right) is similar to the one in the Bliss Collection, differing in the incorporation of curved pointed scrolls on the face of the latter example into the shape of the ear ornaments in the former.[90]

The possible function of this type of object has been posited as a libation cup (Johnson 1992) or a scribal paint repository (Parsons et al. 1988: 80).[91] The open-mouthed gesture, together with the incised marks under the eyes in the example from the Bliss Collection, and the closed eyes and tied hairdo indexing a warrior's rank in the vessel from the Castillo Collection (Valenzuela 1945: fig. 65) seemingly relate these examples to the Xipe Totec complex. Perhaps the conception for the much later vessels in the shape of a flayed head (see Beyer 1965c, 1965d) was derived from the earlier examples considered here, and although their function may have been quite different (serving a liquid versus keeping powdered pigments), both types could have been related to rituals centered on human immolation and flaying of the body. The seemingly wide spatial and temporal distribution of small open-mouthed effigy vessels suggests the possibility of a diversity of contextual uses. Some, like this effigy vessel in the Bliss Collection, may have been part of the tool kit for artists from several Mesoamerican scribal traditions, that is, receptacles in which powdered pigments were kept prior to them being diluted; others may have stored powdered pigments applied to the human body before raids or immolation. Yet others could have been used as drinking vessels in rituals centered on Xipe Totec.

JU

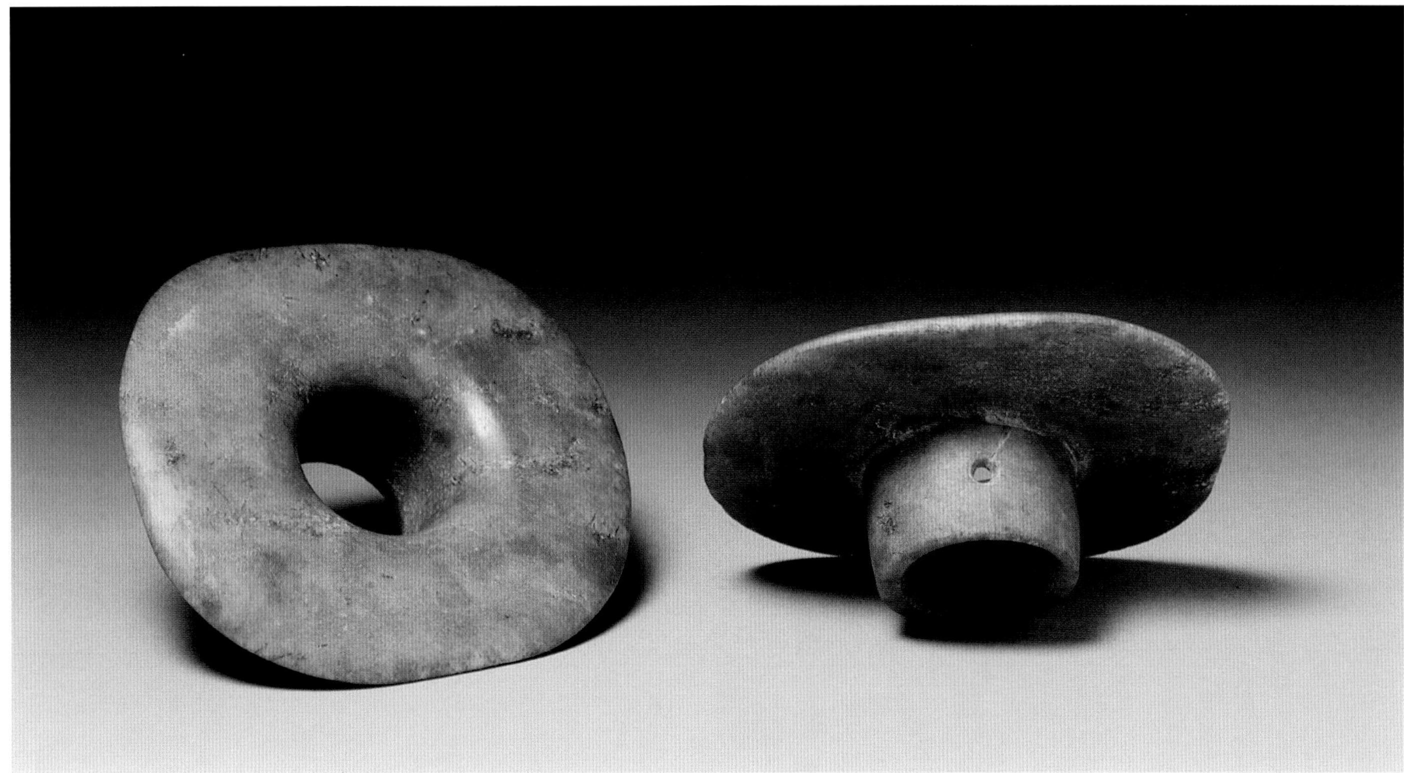

plate 49

PAIR OF EAR FLARES

PLATE 49
Classic period, AD 300–800
Quartzite
PC.B.122a: H. 2.7 cm (1⅟16"); W. 7.3 cm (2⅞");
D. 8.1 cm (3³⁄16")
PC.B.122b: H. 2.5 cm (1"); W. 7.3 cm (2⅞"); D. 7.9 cm (3⅛")
PC.B.122a, PC.B.122b

ACQUISITION HISTORY:
Purchased from Earl Stendahl, 1942

EXHIBITION HISTORY:
Indigenous Art of the Americas, National Gallery of Art, Washington, D.C., April 1947–May 1948, November 1952–July 1954, January 1956–July 1962 (NGA 67)

BIBLIOGRAPHY:
Bliss 1947: 14, 79, top, cat. no. 48; Bliss 1957: 246, cat. no. 82, pl. LVI, bottom; Dumbarton Oaks 1963: 30, cat. no. 149

Ear flares like these were common personal adornments of elite individuals, both male and female. To be worn, the flares were assembled with elements that included the flares, their backings, and the throat disks that sealed, on the front, the central opening in the flares (Figure 29). More complex assemblages included a stem—whose function was to enlarge the neck and receive the backing—and beads of different shapes and sizes, mounted in front or behind the flares. The most elaborate ear ornaments were heavy enough to require a counterweight affixed to the posterior end of the assemblage to secure the ornaments. Parts, such as the backing or the stem, are sometimes lacking in archaeological contexts, implying that they were perishable, probably wood (Kidder et al. 1977 [1946]: 106).

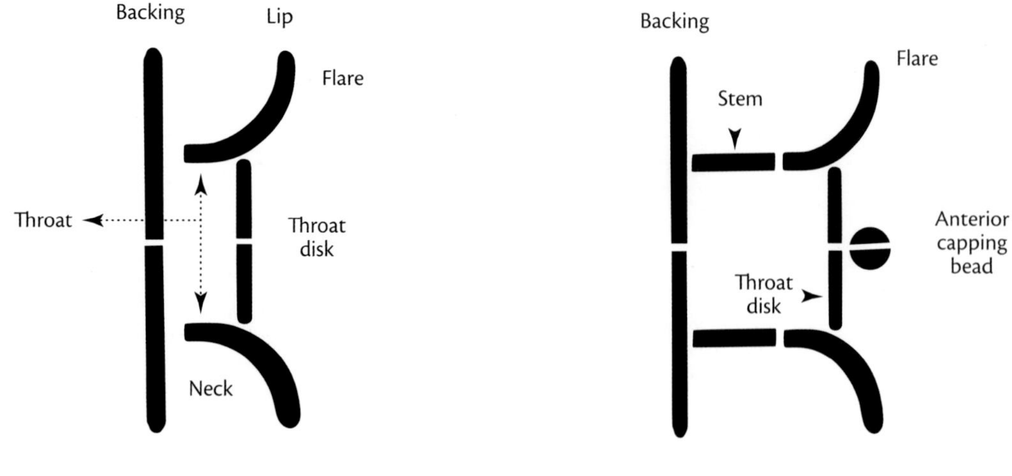

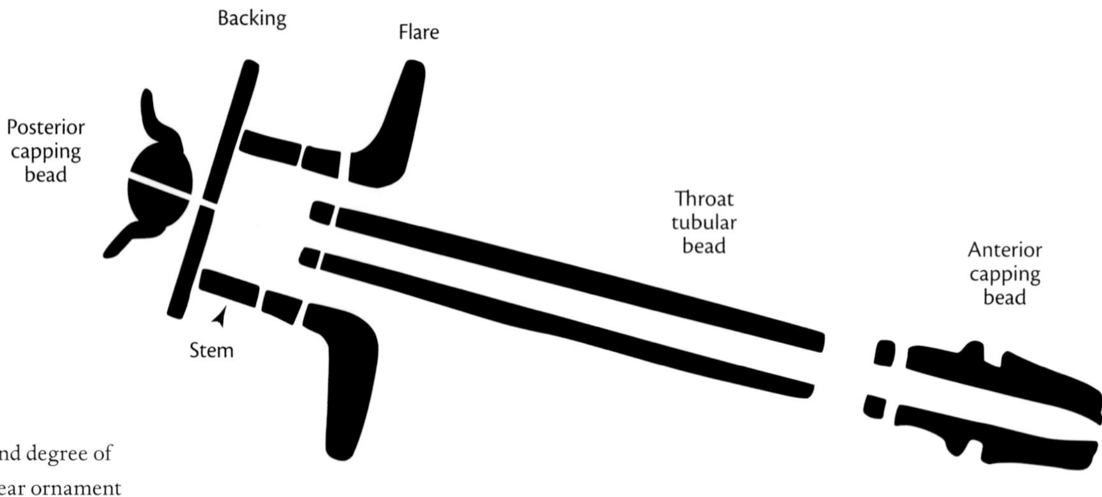

fig. 29
Components and degree of elaboration in ear ornament assemblages. Drawing by Elbis Domínguez (based on Kidder et al. 1977 [1946]: figs. 43, 45).

Flares PC.B.122 are approximately 5.3 mm thick, rectangular with a rounded lip, and protruding from the back is a neck 2 cm long, ending in a clean straight cut. They are identical in color and shading, having been derived from the same piece of raw material. The lack of polish on their posterior surfaces allows reconstruction of manufacturing technique (Figure 30). First, a natural piece of quartzite was worked into a pre-form in the shape of a parallelepiped, which was drilled in the center, then sawn to produce two halves. Each half was drilled again to define the neck of the piece, stopping a few millimeters before the back of the flare, leaving a hollow drill core to define the throat.

Then the pieces were sawed with a string from the exterior toward the neck in the center. Sawing was done in small bursts, probably to allow reapplication of water and additional abrasive medium between bursts, as indicated by multiple scars running parallel to the four sides on the posterior surface. The corners, with multiple linear scars at a 45° angle, served as guides to ensure cutting the flare to the same thickness and to eliminate unevenness. Preliminary finishing removed roughness around the neck, corners, and throat,

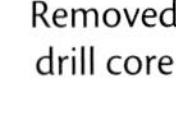

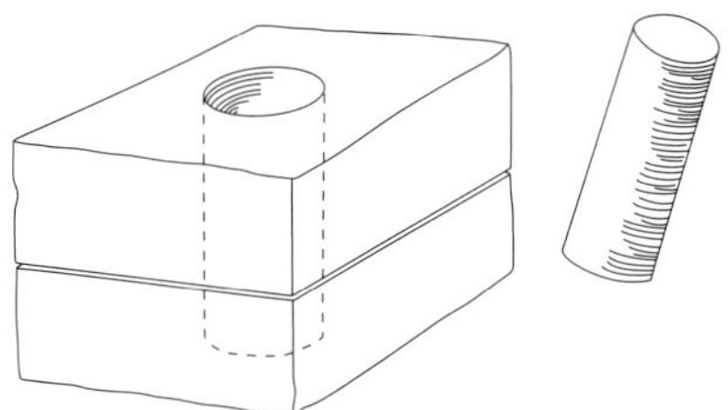

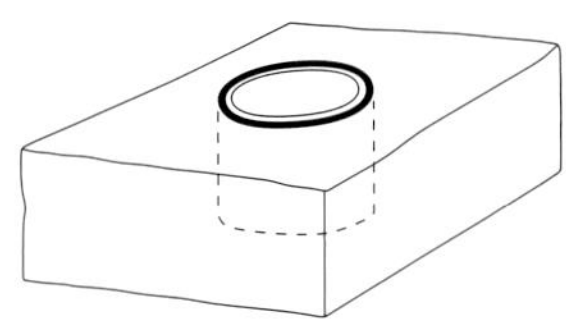

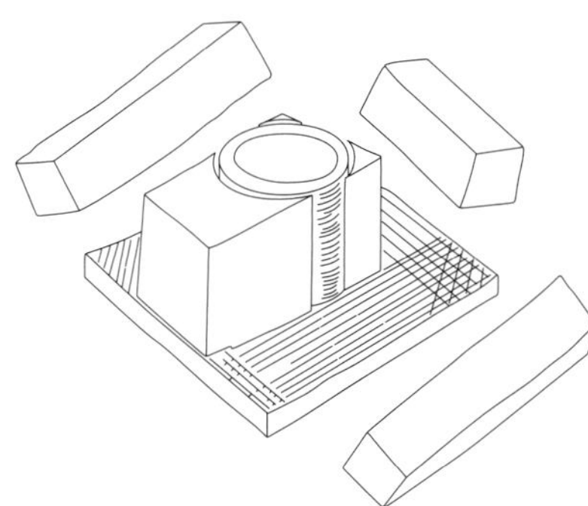

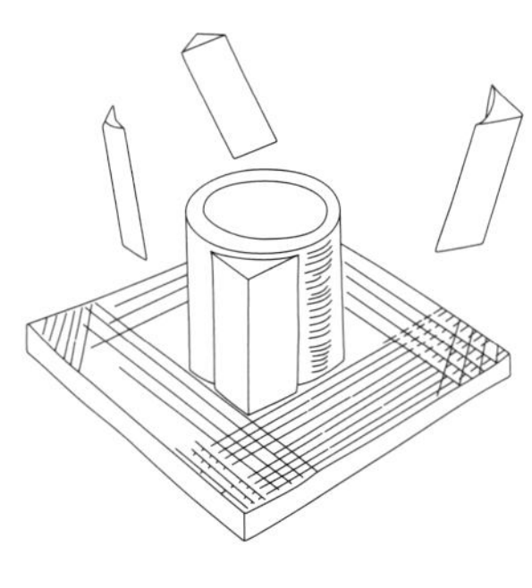

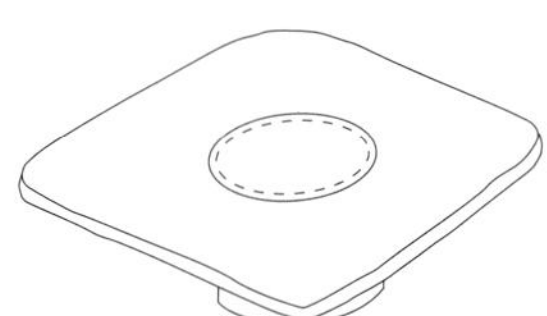

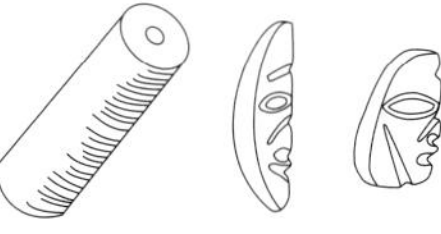

fig. 30
Steps in the manufacture of flares. Drawing by Elbis Domínguez (after Digby 1972: fig. 4).

and also thinned the lip of the flares. The pieces were then polished on their fronts only.

The finishing on flares PC.B.122 suggests minimal effort to produce a fine appearance, contrasting sharply with examples that are thoroughly polished and have inscriptions incised on the exterior surface of the neck, which, when worn, were covered by the earlobe. Yet there are reported cases of flares whose workmanship has been characterized as careless (Kidder et al. 1977 [1946]: 107).[92]

The thickness of the necks in flares like those in the Bliss Collection suggests that they were intended for adults, once a hole in the earlobe had been enlarged through the progressive use of increasingly thicker ear ornaments as a person grew from childhood to adulthood. Although there are no data on the weight of flares or of entire ear ornament assemblages, the impressionistic sense while handling the pieces in the Bliss Collection is that the items must have exerted a considerable tension and downward pull on the earlobes. Repeated use of these sumptuary goods through the life of a person must have led to a substantial enlargement of the lobes, an anatomical detail that is seldom evident in representations of individuals wearing them.[93]

JU

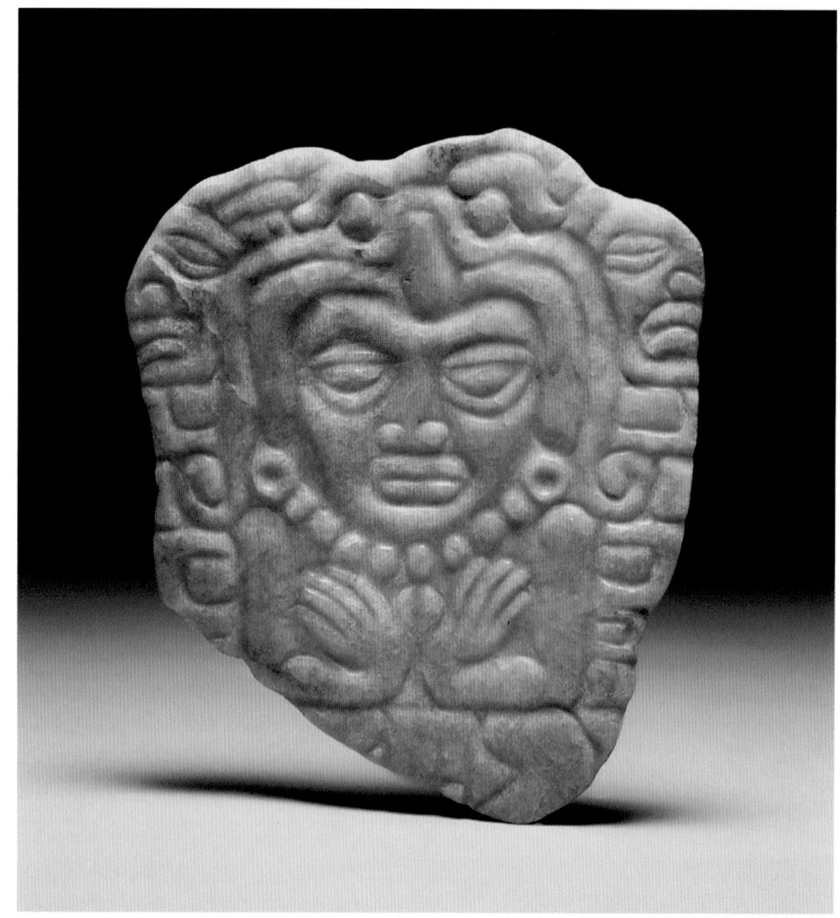

plate 50

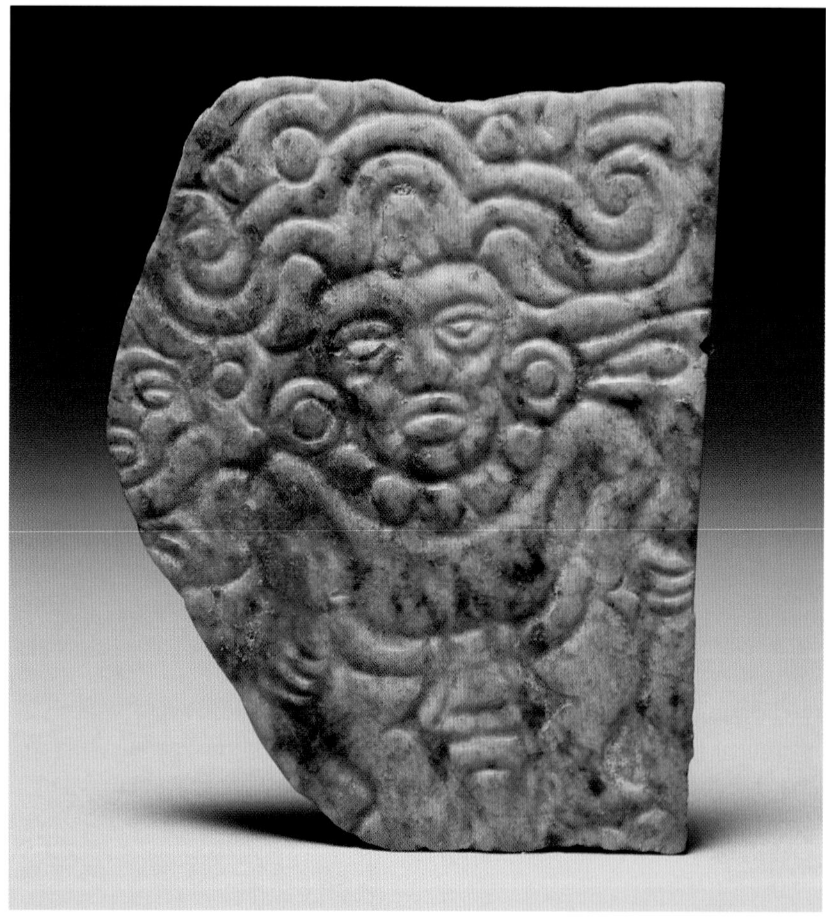

plate 51

PLATE 50
Late Classic period, AD 700–900
Jadeite
H. 11.4 cm (4 ½"); W. 9.9 cm (3 7/8"); D. 1.0 cm (3/8")
PC.B.129

PLATE 51
Late Classic period, AD 700–900
Diopside jadeite and feldspar
H. 8.8 cm (3½"); W. 7.3 cm (2⅞"); D. 0.8 cm (¼")
PC.B.130

ACQUISITION HISTORY:
PC.B.129: Purchased from C. L. Morley, 1947; formerly in the collection of John Wise.
PC.B.130: Purchased from C. L. Morley, 1947

EXHIBITION HISTORY:
Indigenous Art of the Americas, National Gallery of Art, Washington, D.C., April 1947–July 1962 (PC.B.129: NGA 338; PC.B.130: NGA 339)

BIBLIOGRAPHY:
PC.B.129: Kelemen 1943: 293, pl. 239a; Bliss 1947: 12, cat. no. 33; Bliss 1957: 247, cat. no. 95, pl. LVIII, top right; Gump 1962: 20; Dumbarton Oaks 1963: 29, cat. no. 145; Sáenz 1964: photo 8
PC.B.130: Bliss 1947: 12, 73, cat. no. 34; Bliss 1957: 247, cat. no. 93, pl. LVIII, top left; Dumbarton Oaks 1963: 29, cat. no. 146

These plaques were probably pendants. PC.B.129 was manufactured by sawing a block of raw material from opposite directions, using a string, water, and an abrasive medium, meeting close to the vertical axis of the piece (Figure 31). The perpendicular planes of both cuts were slightly uneven; after sawing, the plaque (PC.B.129) was snapped from its matrix, leaving a rib on both surfaces that was then smoothed and polished. The plaque's borders were ground and polished, leaving a distinctive beveled edge. Dual angled perforations with diameters of 3.4 and 2.7 mm were worked from two directions on the upper third of the plaque. After engraving, the plaque was polished.

PC.B.129 depicts a standing male, hands joined against the chest, palms out, a difficult posture considering the right-angle bend of the arms. He wears a loincloth, his head is decked with an owl helmet and human heads in profile on either side, and he is adorned with ear spools and a beaded collar. The figure lacks its right leg, yet the object's edge on this side is beveled and smooth.

The pendant PC.B.130 depicts a standing male, his overall posture differing from that of the PC.B.129 figure; the arms and hands hang to the sides of the body. The hands do not display symmetry; the left one shows its palm, an anatomically infeasible posture. The figure wears a loincloth, ear spools, a beaded collar, and a helmet in the shape of a serpent, with only one human head in profile view (on the right side of the figure). This subsidiary figure also wears a serpent helmet, and the engraver seems to have dealt with space limitations by merging parts of the imagery. Thus a single, ophidian curving snout on the left is shared by both the profile and split versions of the helmets. To the left of the main figure are straight and curved engraved lines, possibly suggesting the undulating body of a serpent. A rectangular design between the man's legs may represent a stool.

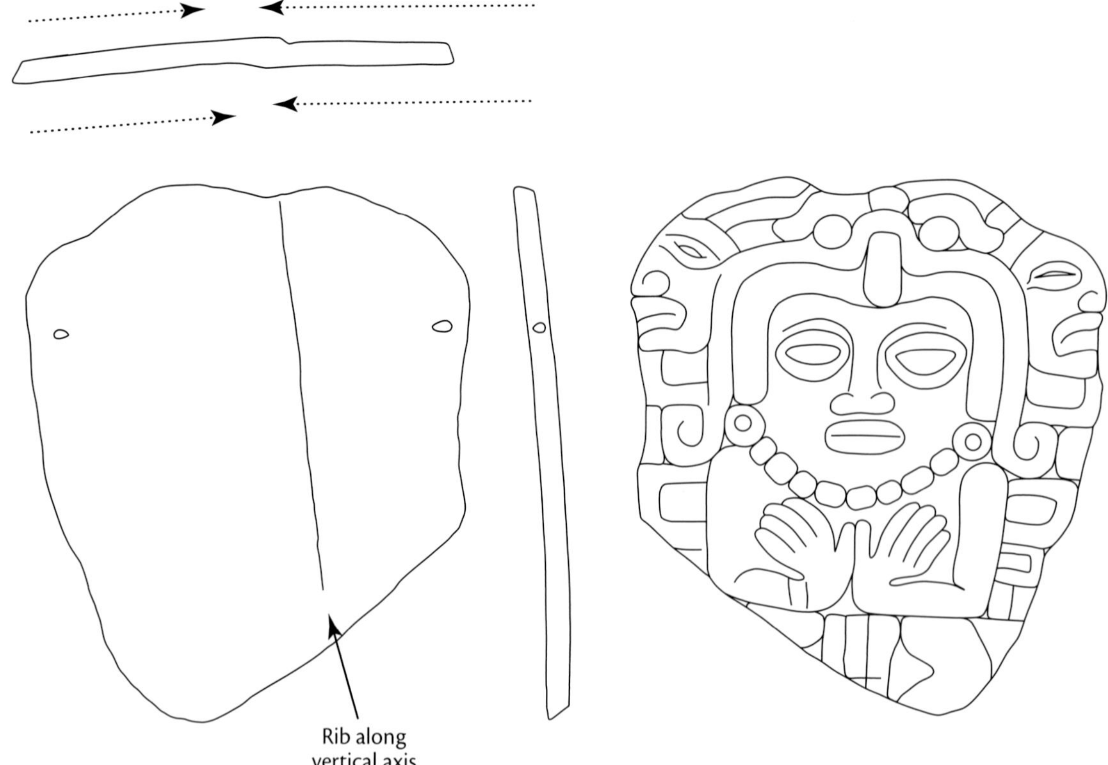

fig. 31
Manufacturing features on carved jadeite plaque PC.B.129. Dotted arrows indicate the directions of sawing. Drawing by Elbis Domínguez.

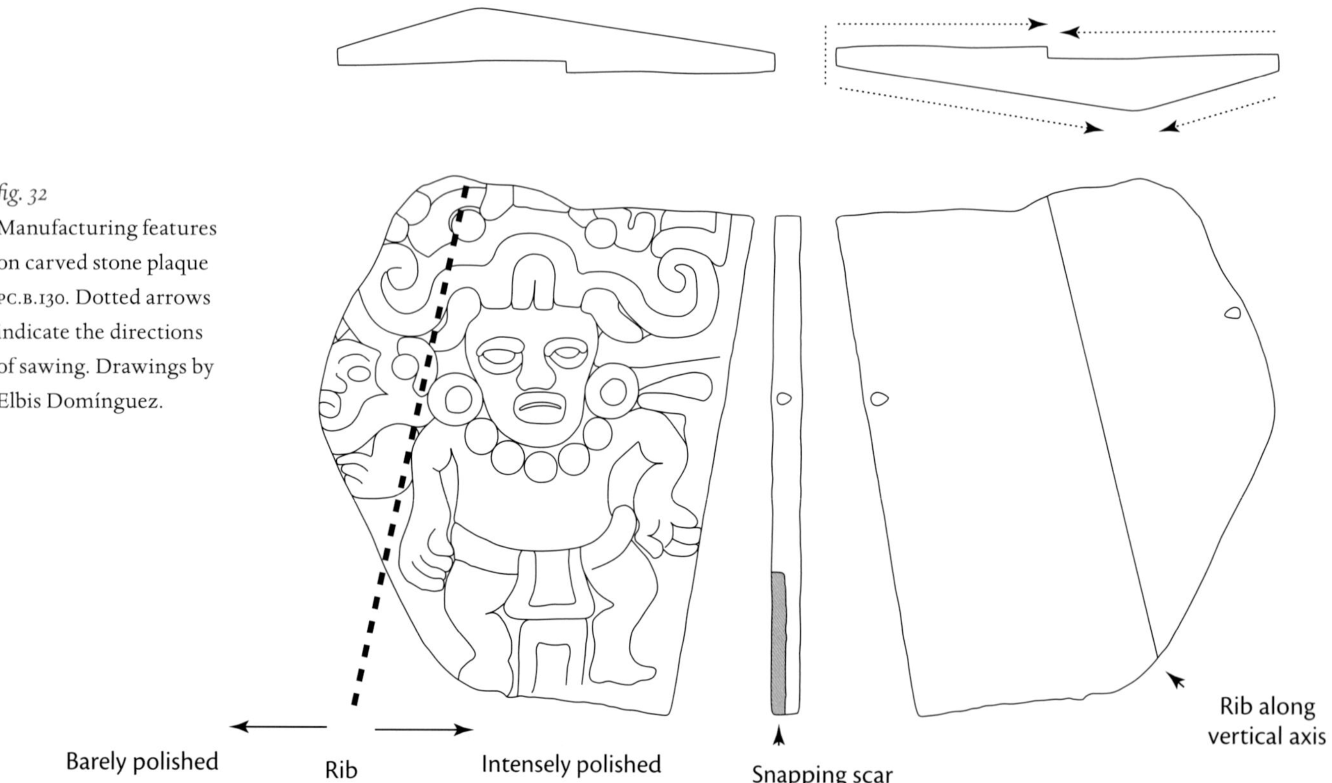

fig. 32
Manufacturing features on carved stone plaque PC.B.130. Dotted arrows indicate the directions of sawing. Drawings by Elbis Domínguez.

Plaque PC.B.130 was manufactured using the same procedures as for PC.B.129, except that the nature of the raw material required less effort to generate a uniformly thin plaque (Figure 32). As a result, the engraved area has two planes with pronounced inclinations, with the plaque's greatest thickness at the point where the two planes meet. Traces of a second rib, where sawing reached its deepest course, occur along the vertical axis of the posterior surface. The surface was smoothed, but the rib was left coarse. The plaque's lateral surfaces were sawed as well; most are slightly beveled. Upper and left surfaces are rough, suggesting grinding but not polishing. The right lateral surface, perpendicular to the posterior plane, bears traces of a thin snapping scar.

Two dual perforations on the upper third of PC.B.130 were drilled from both directions; they are about 2.6 mm in diameter, biconical in cross section and with oval openings. After engraving, the piece was almost entirely polished, but irregularities left by the manufacturing process made consistent finishing difficult. As a consequence, the carved figure received more polishing.

Pendants like PC.B.129 and PC.B.130 became common as elite goods between AD 700 and 900. Similar examples have been found in many regions (Figure 33),[94] most often as parts of caches consecrated to buildings or as accoutrements in high-ranking primary and secondary human burials. Differences occur in material, engraving technique, presence of perforations for suspension, and the figure's posture and paraphernalia (Caso 1965: 910–911; Proskouriakoff 1974: 162–174; Rands 1965: 570–573), but the overall theme is an ideal of rulership, portraying the ruler as warrior and/or diviner. This ideal is usually engendered as male and is shown with open or closed eyes, distinct states of being indexed by oval or lunate-shaped eyes. These figures' difficult or impossible anatomical positions may constitute a representational strategy of depicting the human body simultaneously from different points of view, and/or marking an elite body language that signaled a specific code. Some have interpreted the figures as dwarfs (Kelemen 1943: 1: 239), but emphasis on head, torso, and hands at the expense of the lower extremities is simply the dictated convention used by the lapidaries who crafted these objects, explaining the lack of certain details, like part of a leg or a toe.

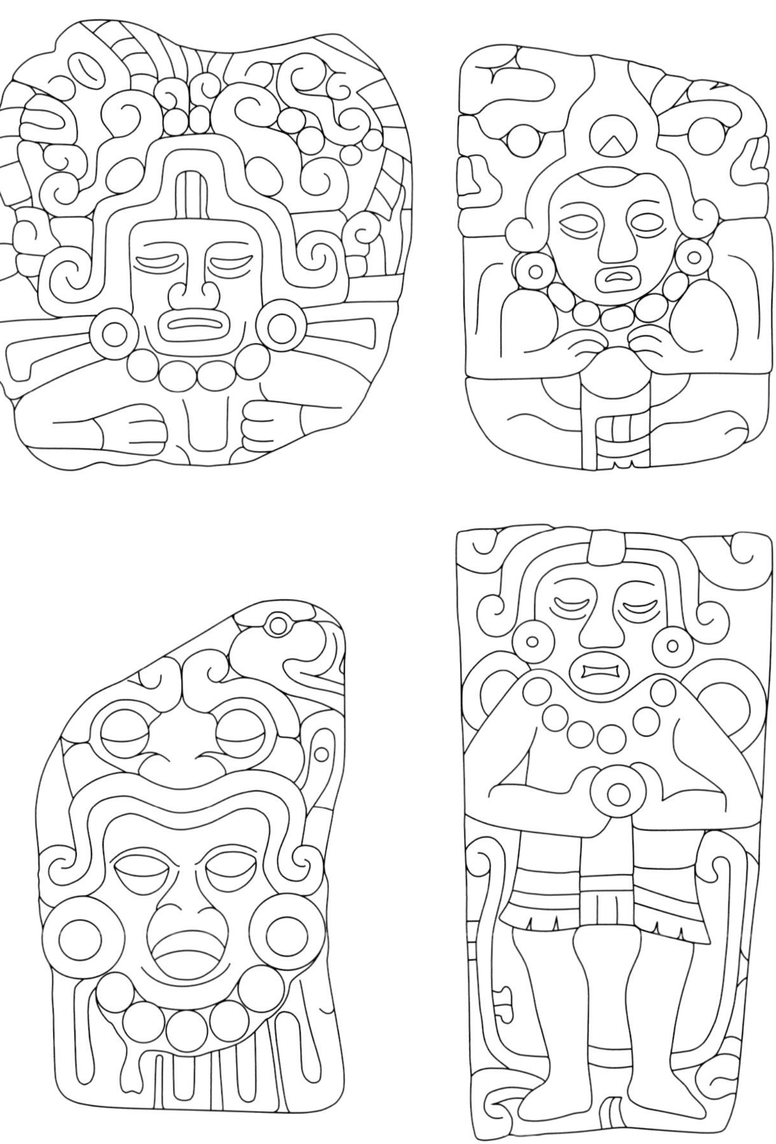

fig. 33
Late Classic stone plaques from Xochicalco, Morelos (upper left); Palenque, Chiapas (upper right); Cerro Xochitecatl, Tlaxcala (lower left); and Tula, Hidalgo (lower right). Drawing by Elbis Domínguez (after López Luján 1995: 62; Sáenz 1963: 22; Palavicini and Reyes 2005: 74; and Acosta 1957: plate 28-1).

The material's shape guided the design of the representation of the body, emphasizing key elements by resorting to visual synecdoche and dispensing with elements understood as redundant.

Although these figures are rarely lavishly clad, their serpent and owl helmets are indirect allusions to warfare. Paucity of garments suggests the ritual act of fasting. Closed eyes on some plaques may allude to memorializing a dead ruler or may be related to the act of divination, a ritual performance clearly evinced by examples where the human figure holds a mirror against the chest (Acosta 1957: 167).[95] Human heads carved in profile could signal trophy heads or deceased ancestors, interpretative alternatives congruent with the inferred semantic values of warfare and divination. The latter two were of course linked, as it was necessary to prognosticate success in raids aimed at securing sacrificial victims. As caretakers of communities and their followers, rulers had the perceived obligation of procuring goods, including humans for immolation, necessary to reciprocate the gods and fulfill the primordial covenant: to please the divine and thus ensure agricultural production and human reproduction.

It appears that pectorals like these did not always serve as actual personal adornments, though this function is evident in their placement as sumptuary belongings with certain deceased individuals, such as in Tomb 2 in Temple XVIII at Palenque (Sáenz 1963: 22), or accompanying secondary interments, like Burial 1 from the Building of the Feathered Serpents at Xochicalco (see Sáenz 1963: pls. III, IV). However, their presence in votive caches implies the production or reuse of items intended to substitute for the body of the ruler by placing in offertory caches the most distinctive markers of the paramount political and religious office. Thus this type of object may have embodied the persona of the ruler, and its fusion with the perceived qualities of the material may have enhanced the sacrality of the plaques. Their placement prior to the construction of specific buildings was probably intended to propitiate or augment the ritual efficacy of the built space.

JU

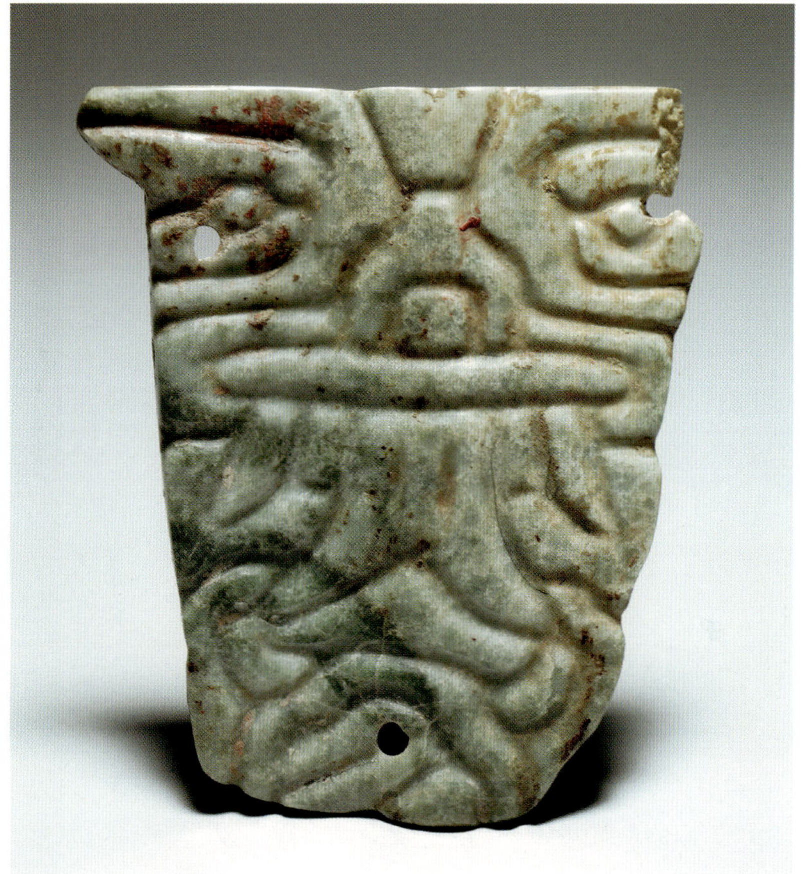

plate 52

CARVED STONE PLAQUE

PLATE 52
Zapotec
Late Classic period, AD 700–900
Jadeite
H. 9.0 cm (3½"); W. 8.0 cm (3⅛"); D. 8.0 mm (¼")
PC.B.131

ACQUISITION HISTORY:
Purchased from Julius Carlebach, 1952

EXHIBITION HISTORY:
Indigenous Art of the Americas, National Gallery of Art, Washington, D.C., November 1952–July 1962 (NGA 499)

BIBLIOGRAPHY:
Bliss 1957: 247: cat. no. 90, pl. LVIII, top left; Dumbarton Oaks 1963: 30, cat. no. 152

Sporting recognizable signs of Zapotec writing, this plaque has several marks that allow retracing the steps of its manufacture and subsequent reuse (Figure 34). Raw material was perforated twice from opposite directions to cut a thin plaque from it.[96] The cutting process was initiated from two opposite directions, and at the end of the slicing process the plaque was snapped off, leaving a rib on both surfaces. Both sides were smoothed and polished, as were all borders of the plaque, with beveling on the lower and right borders.

The plaque's front side shows an anthropomorphic representation of Cociyo, the Zapotec god of lightning and rain, poised over a hill glyph

fig. 34
Manufacturing features on the back of carved plaque PC.B.131. Dotted arrows indicate the directions of sawing; solid arrows indicate the directions of drilling. Drawing by Elbis Domínguez.

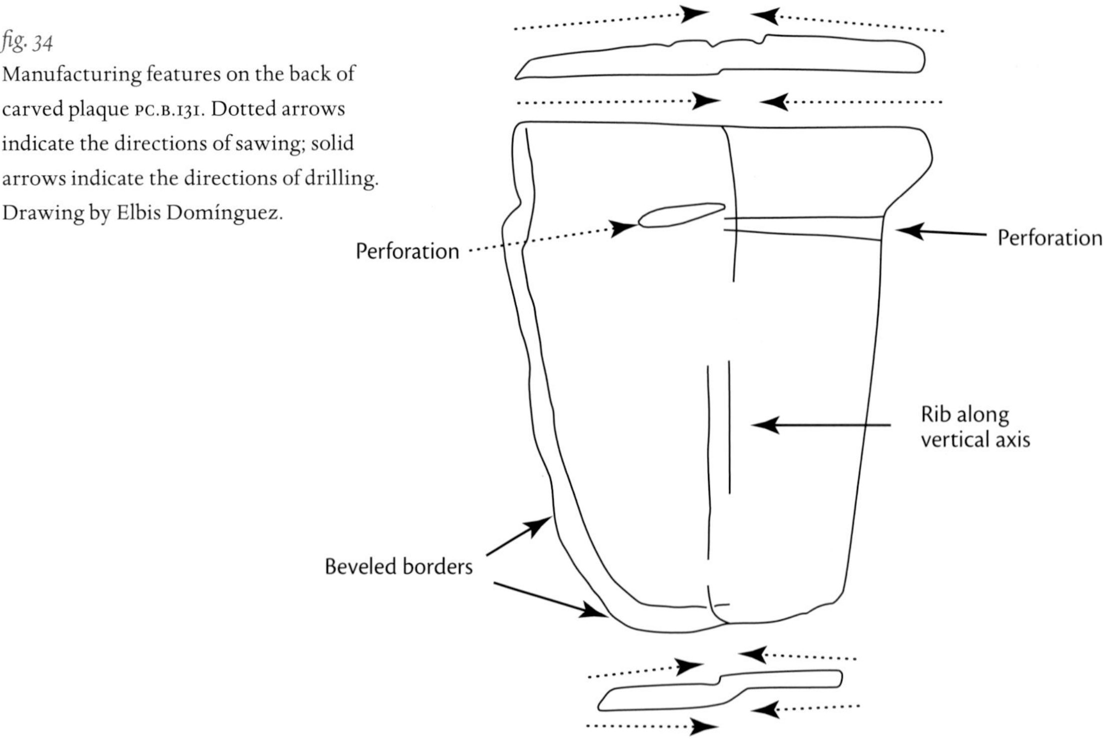

fig. 35
Carved imagery on the front of carved plaque PC.B.131 and comparison with glyphs from Monte Albán. Drawing by Elbis Domínguez.

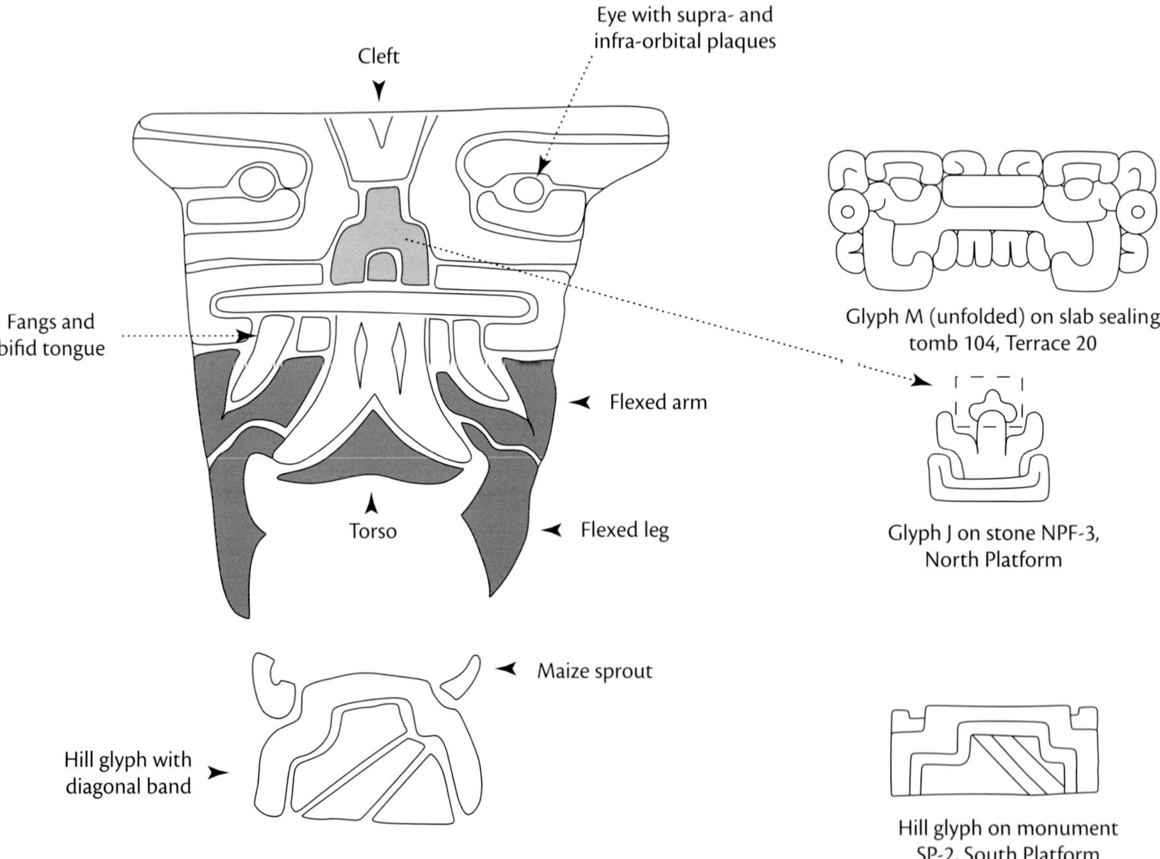

(Figure 35), with iconic allusions to maize. The inwardly split image of the impersonator's face shows the eyes framed by supra- and infraorbital plaques, a cleft in the forehead, the corncob glyph (J) as substitute for the nose, teeth, and a prominent bifid tongue. Slightly folded arms and legs make up the sides of the body, and the frontal depiction of the torso is marked by a triangular space below the bifid tongue. There are slight differences in the paired rendering of the eyes, the extremities, and the maize motifs of the hill glyph; otherwise the composition displays bilateral symmetry. Once finished, the piece may have formed part of a mosaic composition on an unknown object.

Subsequent reuse of the plaque is evidenced by several holes drilled perpendicularly from back to front (Figure 36). The completed lower hole has minute spicules along its circumference, indicating that the perforation was executed with a hollow drill bit and that the core was snapped before the drill passed through the plaque. The same is evident for the perforation near the figure's left eye. On the back surface the hole is complete, but on the front only half of the perforation left an opening. It appears that a third hole passing through the right eye of the Cociyo image led to a crack at the base of the plaque's upper right extension. To avoid complete breakage, this perforation was abandoned.[97] Another hole was begun in approximately the same place but from the front surface, probably causing the upper right extension of the plaque to break off; the fractured edge was not smoothed or polished. A fifth perforation only penetrated 1 or 2 mm, leaving a hollow drill scar 5.3 mm in diameter. This hole obliterated the terminus of one of the initial perforations that were executed prior to cutting the plaque. Given their relative positions, the three complete perforations were not meant to suspend the object but perhaps to fasten it to something else.

Both surfaces have traces of red pigment, and a thin, unevenly dispersed layer of another, yellowish material; it is unknown when these were applied. The plaque's imagery follows graphic canons common to southwestern Mesoamerica in Classic times (AD 300–800), but its provenience is uncertain; it could have been manufactured in one place and transported to another, or it could be the work of a craftsman distant from Zapotec Oaxaca who emulated those graphic conventions.

JU

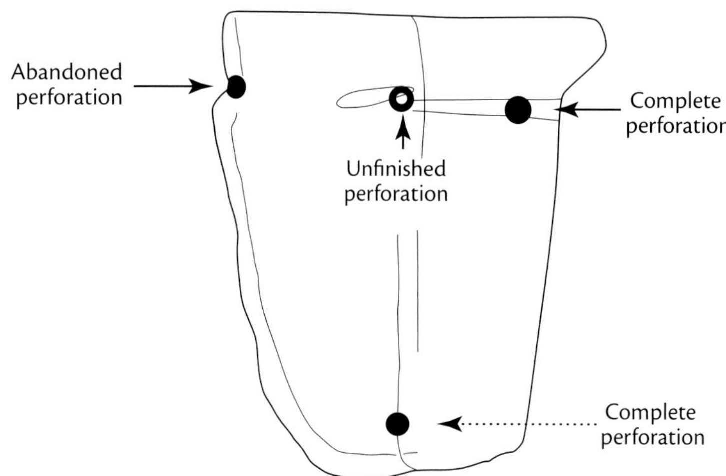

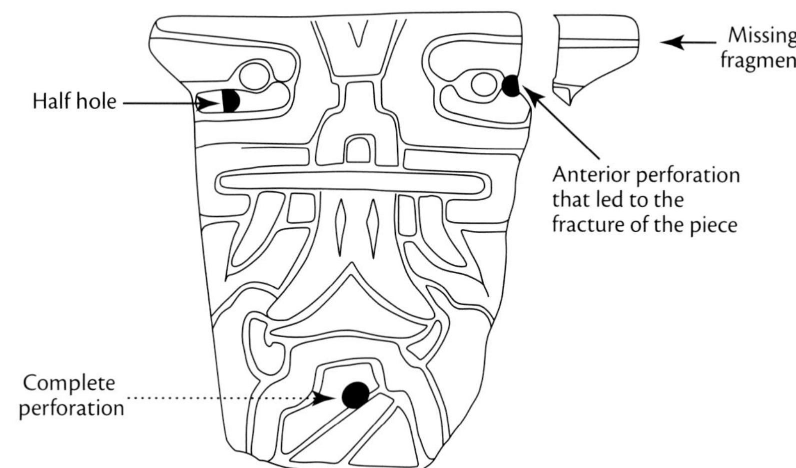

fig. 36
Features of reuse on the back (top) and front (bottom) of carved plaque PC.B.131. Drawing by Elbis Domínguez.

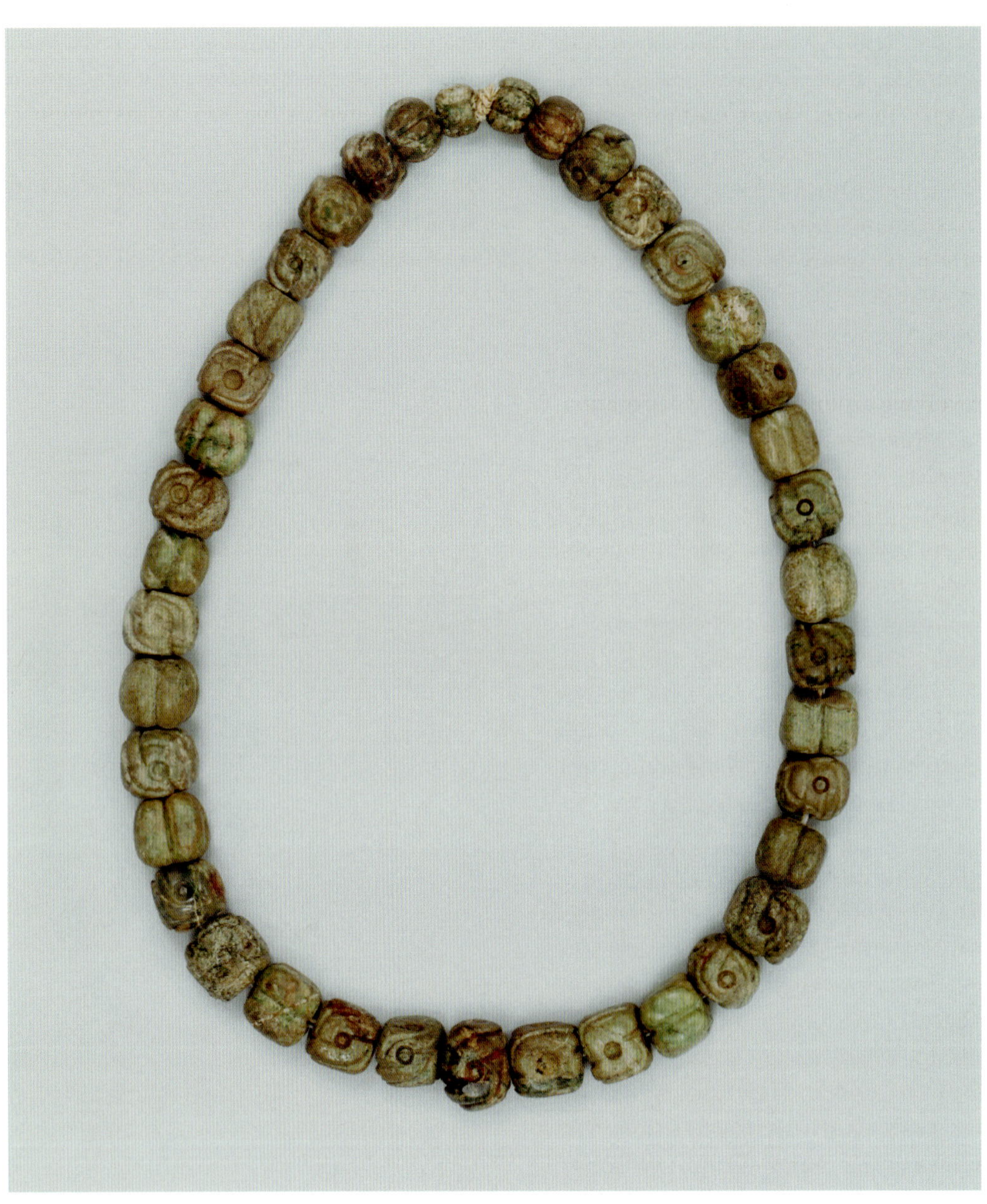

plate 53

NECKLACE

PLATE 53
Probably Late Classic period, AD 600–900
Jadeite and serpentine
Necklace: L. 71.0 cm (29")
Beads: Diam. 1.3 cm (½") to 2.5 cm (1")
PC.B.123

ACQUISITION HISTORY:
Purchased from Earl Stendahl, 1950; reportedly from the vicinity of San Gerónimo, Guerrero

EXHIBITION HISTORY:
Indigenous Art of the Americas, National Gallery of Art, Washington, D.C., November 1952–July 1962 (NGA 491); *The Aztec Empire*, Guggenheim Museum, New York, October 2004–February 2005; Guggenheim Museum, Bilbao, Spain, March–September 2005; *The Aztec World*, The Field Museum, Chicago, October 2008–April 2009

BIBLIOGRAPHY:
Bliss 1957: 246: cat. no. 78, pl. XLVIII, bottom right; Charlot 1958: 42–43; Dumbarton Oaks 1963: 29, cat. no. 144; Murro 2004a: 42, cat. no. 181

This necklace includes 39 stone beads of cuboid shape, resulting in six surfaces for each piece. The beads vary in size: larger examples measure 2.55 cm by 2.07 cm by 2.42 cm, and smaller pieces are 1.39 cm by 1.39 cm by 1.5 cm. Most of the beads have an olive green color. Aside from variation in size, the beads also differ in their configuration and/or decoration; with five distinctly recognizable types (Figure 37). Type 1 is represented by 18 beads that have an interlacing pattern of scrolls revolving around a shallow perforation done with a hollow tubular drill bit. The two surfaces that touch neighboring beads have a squared shape with a bore traversing the pieces. Two beads of this type bear traces of red pigment. Type 1 may be a three-dimensional rendering of the glyph for "knot" used in some Mesoamerican scribal traditions.

Type 2, of which there is only one bead, has an elevated circular ring with an interior concentric groove accomplished by a shallow perforation that was made using a hollow tubular drill bit. The two surfaces that touch neighboring beads are similar to the other sides, except that no concentric groove is present. This bead may be a three-dimensional rendering of the glyph for "earth" (center and four corners) common to several Mesoamerican scripts.

Type 3 includes 14 beads, 12 large and 2 small versions. The cubic pieces display four lobes in each surface. Only those that touch neighboring beads have a bore in the center. Type 4 beads, represented by two exemplars, display in each surface nine lobes. The surfaces that touch neighboring beads sport the transverse perforation. Types 3 and 4 may include representation of flowers.

Type 5, with only four beads, resembles type 1 except that the objects are flatter, so that the borders of the scrolls reach the edge of the cuboid pieces. Another difference is that the shallow holes were executed with a solid tubular drill bit. One of these beads has minute traces of red pigment.

Despite the bulkiness of the beads, the entire ensemble is not particularly heavy. Similarly sized lobed globular beads, some dating as early as AD 300, have been found in southeastern Mesoamerica, at ancient settlements such as Kaminaljuyu and Zacaleu (Rands 1965: 562, figs. 1, 2). Later examples, probably representing squashes, come from the main cenote at Chichén Itzá (Proskouriakoff 1974: 58, pl. 19). A set of eight hollow carved beads with representations of mirrors (with actual pyrite inlays), attributed to the Río Balsas region of Guerrero and dated between AD 300 and 900 (Von Winning 1968b: 27), bears some resemblance to the set of beads in the Bliss Collection. Not only do they include raised surfaces and carved motifs, but they also have traces of red pigment.

JU

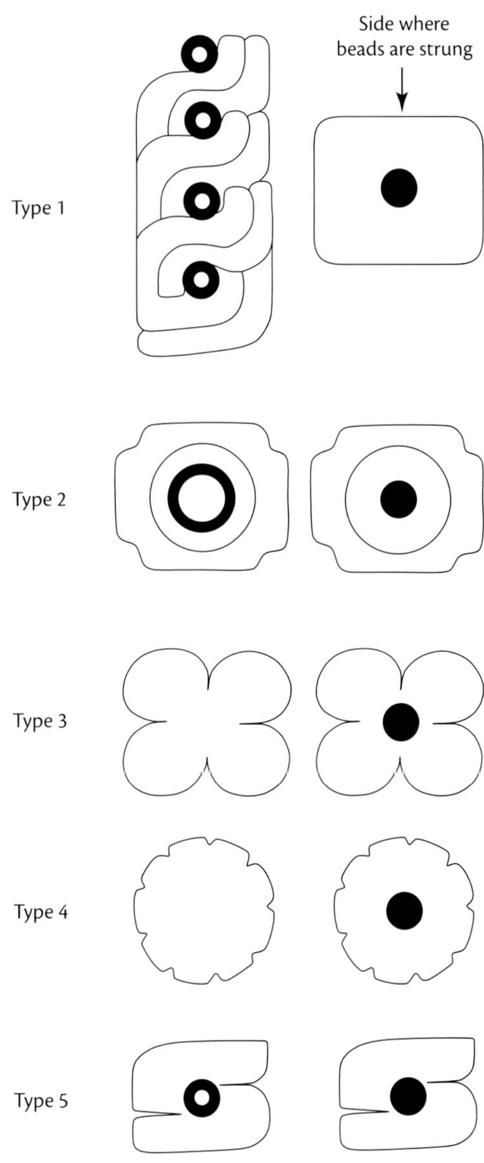

fig. 37
Main categories of beads from necklace PC.B.123. Drawing by Elbis Domínguez.

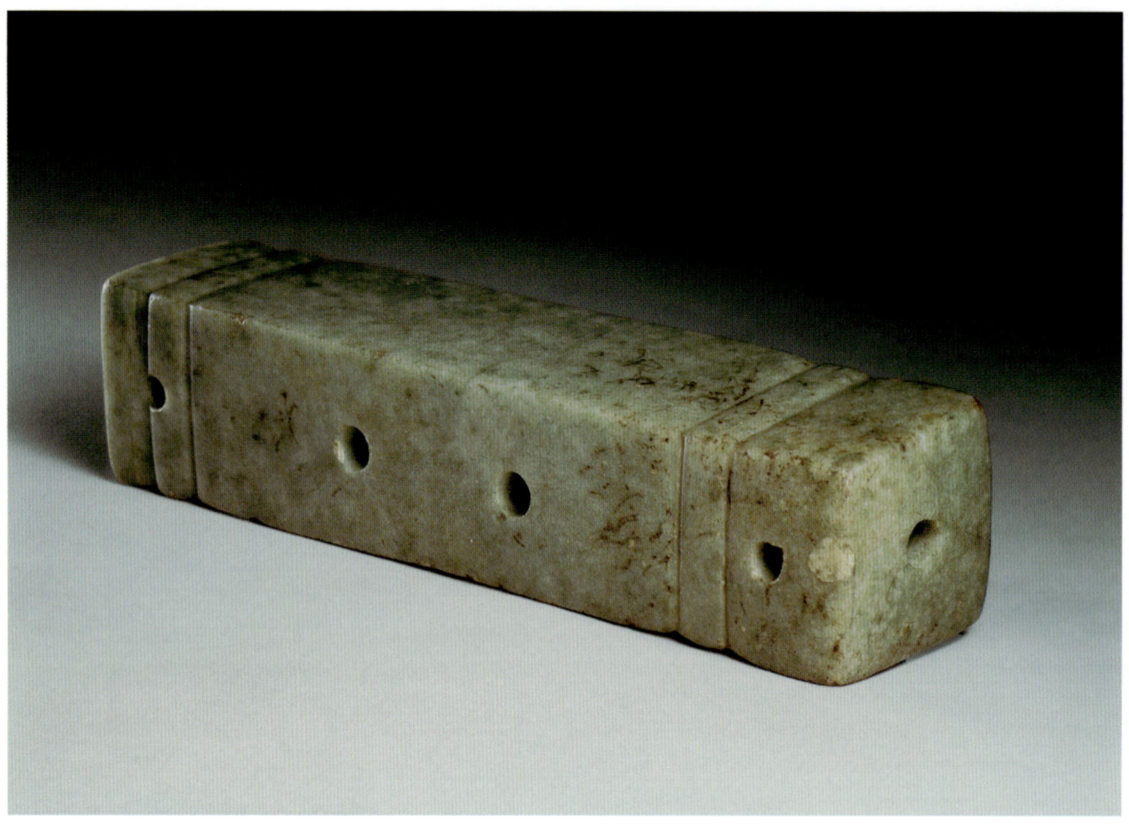

plate 54

BAR PENDANT

PLATE 54
Probably Classic or Postclassic period, AD 400–1500
Jadeite
H. 15.0 cm (5⅞"); W. 3.5 cm (1⅜"); D. 3.3 cm (1¼")
PC.B.126

ACQUISITION HISTORY:
Purchased from Earl Stendahl, 1954; reportedly from the Río Balsas drainage, Guerrero

EXHIBITION HISTORY:
Indigenous Art of the Americas, National Gallery of Art, Washington, D.C., January 1956–July 1962 (NGA 602)

BIBLIOGRAPHY:
Bliss 1957: 246, cat. no. 80, pl. LXVIII, lower right;
Dumbarton Oaks 1963: 25, cat. no. 123

This jadeite bar has a muted olive color. Compared to PC.B.134 (see Taube 2004b: 140–141), the piece is relatively heavy. The bar's tapering and slanted surfaces resulted from slight deviations in the process of cutting the block. Both ends flare out slightly and were decorated in low relief with a thin transversal band, indicating that the object is a stone representation of a bundle of soft material tied at both ends (Figure 38).

The bore traversing the length of the bar has an uneven course and thickness, which was produced by several hollow tubular drill bits with slightly different diameters, ranging between 6.0 and 6.5 mm. Drilling proceeded from two directions, the perforation allowing for suspension. There is no evidence of wear at either end of the bar, but the bar was a pendant forming part of a composite necklace. Four additional perforations drilled from the inferior surface of the object are perpendicular to the main bore in order to suspend dangling elements; their location indicates the proper way the pendant was worn.[98]

When the bar pendant was originally manufactured, the four secondary holes went through the initial longitudinal borings, stopping as soon as the upper portion of their course was reached.[99] The secondary perforations are not symmetrically placed in relation to one another or in relation to the "tying" bands on the ends of the bar. Yet, even if one takes into account their altered diameters, it is evident that they were made with drill bits similar to those used for making the longitudinal bore. Their slight differences can be accounted for in terms of the continuous reduction of the bits as the perforations were made.

This type of pendant has a wide distribution in Mesoamerica, with examples from Piedras Negras (Rands 1965: 562, fig. 6), and Monte Albán Tomb 7 (Caso 1969: pl. LVII). At Xochicalco, several have been found with high-ranking primary or secondary burials (see Sáenz 1963: pl. V). Representations of some paramount rulers also depict this type of pendant, like that of Copán's sixteenth and last ruler Yax Pasah on Altar Q (see Martin 2001: fig. 169). Thus even though the meaning of the tied bundle, which these banded prismatic stones replicate, remains unknown, they formed part of the sumptuary goods of nobles and royal figures.

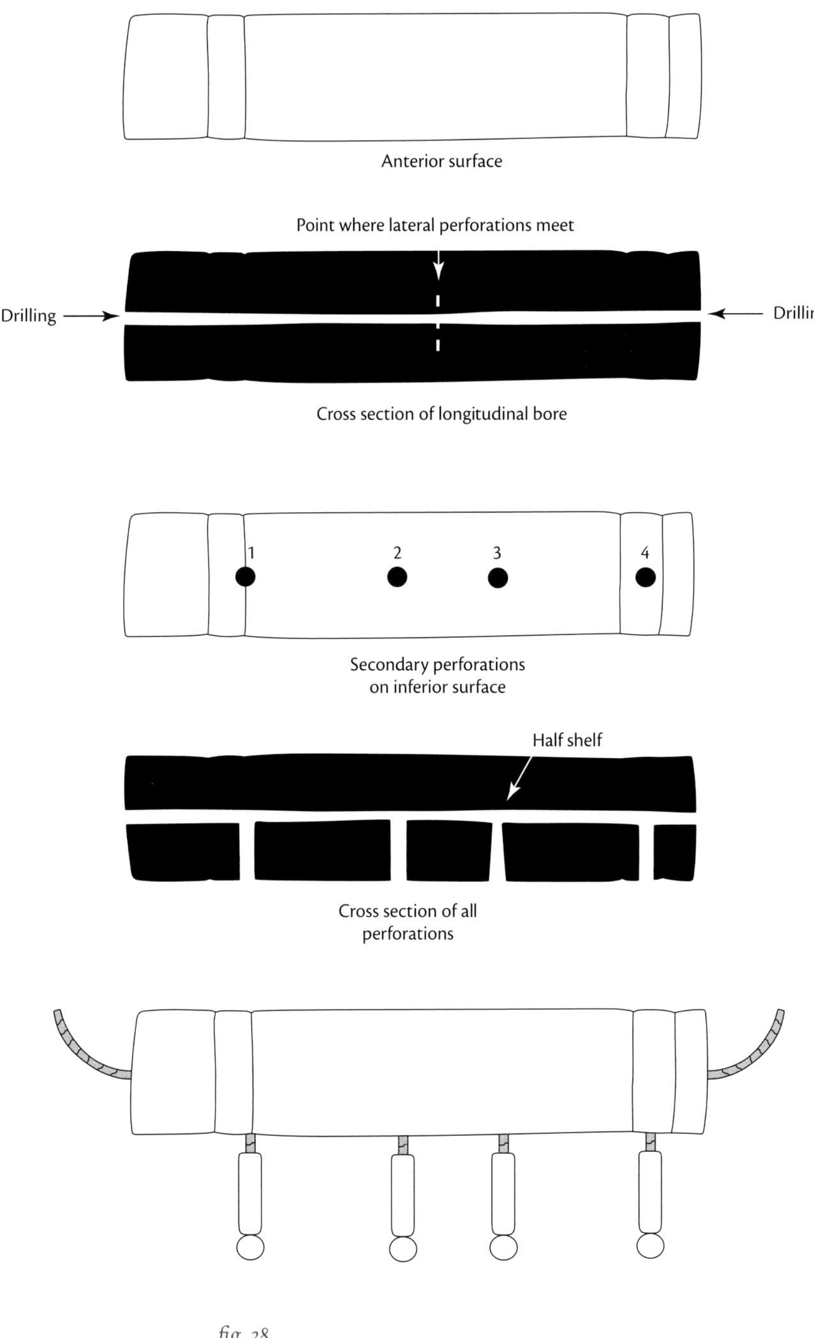

fig. 38
Sides and cross sections of bar pendant PC.B.126 and a hypothetical rendering of the original composite object. Drawing by Elbis Domínguez.

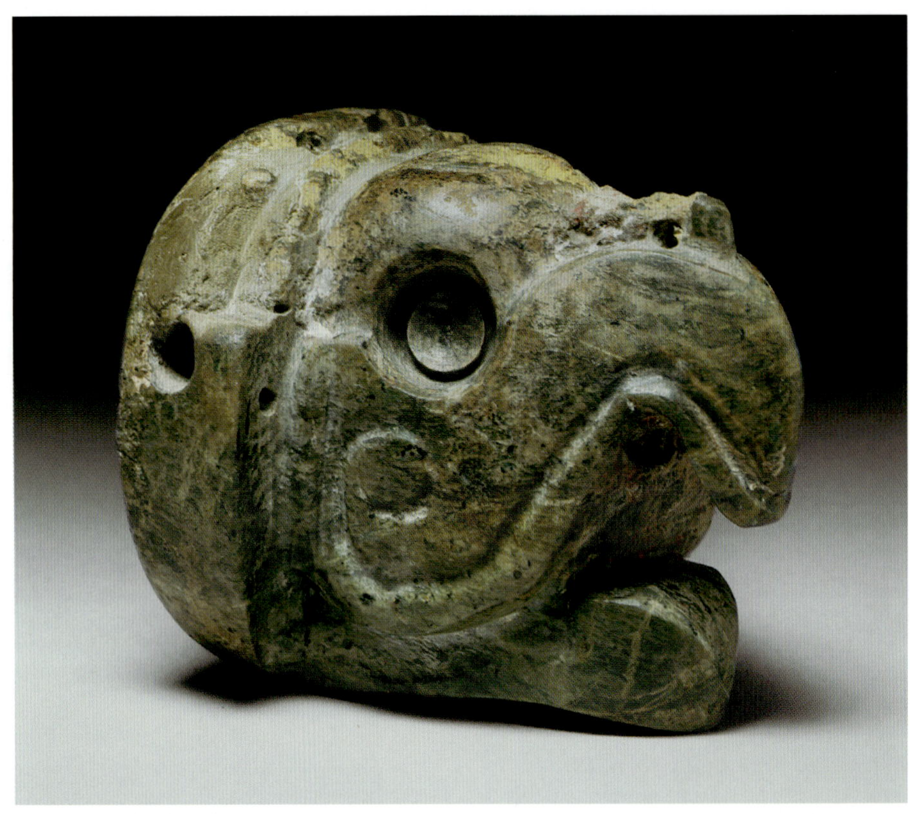

plate 55

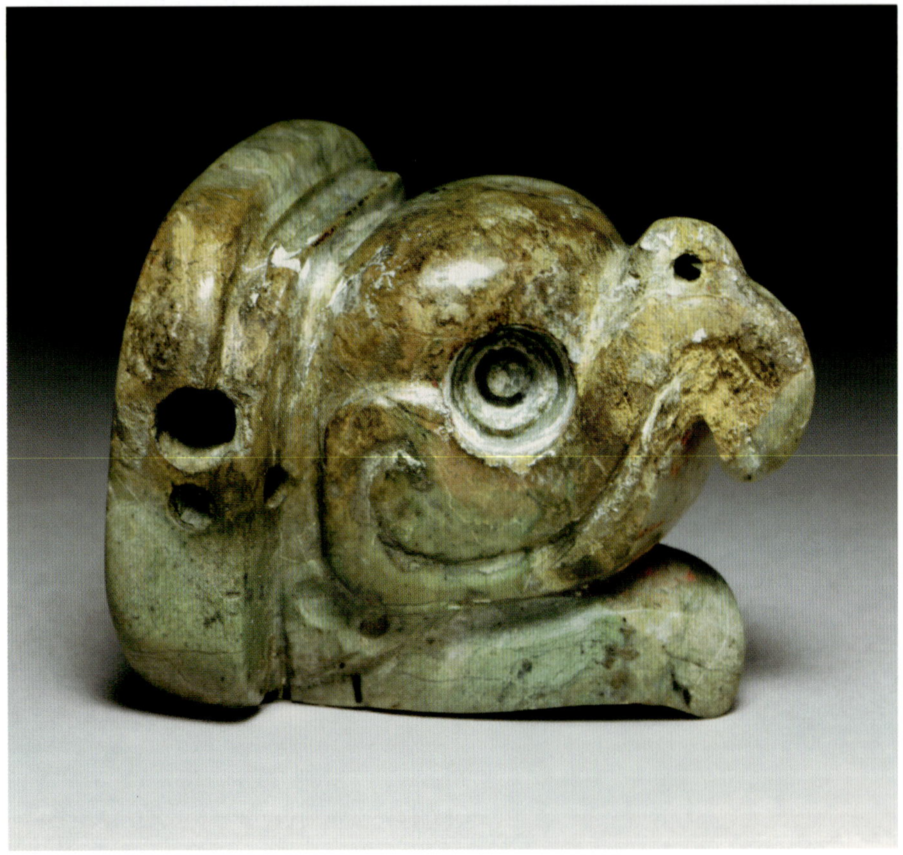

plate 56

PLATE 55
Late Postclassic period, AD 1200–1520
Diopside jadeite or omphazite
H. 5.2 cm (2"); W. 5.7 cm (2¼"); D. 6.0 cm (2⅜")
PC.B.060

PLATE 56
Late Postclassic period, AD 1200–1520
Diopside jadeite or omphazite
H. 4.7 cm (1⅞"); W. 5.4 cm (2⅛"); D. 5.8 cm (2½")
PC.B.061

ACQUISITION HISTORY:
Purchased from Earl Stendahl, 1943; reportedly from the vicinity of San Gerónimo, Guerrero

EXHIBITION HISTORY:
PC.B.060: *Indigenous Art of the Americas,* National Gallery of Art, Washington, D.C., April 1947–July 1949, November 1952–July 1962 (NGA 61)
PC.B.061: *Indigenous Art of the Americas,* National Gallery of Art, Washington, D.C., April 1947–July 1949, November 1952–July 1962 (NGA 62); Dumbarton Oaks, December 1963; *Die Azteken und ihre Vorläufer: Glanz und Untergang des Alten Mexico,* Roemer- und Pelizaeus-Museum, Hildesheim, Germany, June–November 1986, Haus der Kunst, Munich, December 1986–March 1987, Oberösterreichisches Landesmuseum, Linz, Austria, April–August 1987, Louisiana Museum of Modern Art, Humlebæk, Denmark, August–November 1987, Musées royaux d'Art et d'Histoire, Brussels, December 1987–March 1988, National Archaeological Museum, Athens, May–July 1988, Société du Palais de la Civilisation, Montreal, July–October 1988; *Aztecs,* Royal Academy of Arts, London, September 2002–April 2003; Ethnologisches Museum, Berlin, May–August 2003; Art and Exhibition Hall of the Federal Republic of Germany, Bonn, December 2003–January 2004

BIBLIOGRAPHY:
PC.B.060: Bliss 1947: 13, cat. no. 42; Bliss 1957: 239, cat. no. 43, pl. XXX; Dumbarton Oaks 1963: 29, cat. no. 147
PC.B.061: Bliss 1947: 13, 75, cat. no. 41; Bliss 1957: 239, cat. no. 42, pl. XXX; Dumbarton Oaks 1963: 29, cat. no. 147; Boone 1986a: cat. no. 257; Louisiana Museum 1987: 82, cat. no. 274; Traxler 2002b: 447, cat. no. 192

There is no direct evidence of the initial steps in the manufacture of PC.B.060. A block of raw material was probably cut and ground, yielding a pre-form that outlined its main elements, including the beak, the top of the head, a protrusion atop the beak to hold a small perforation, and a disk-like core behind the head. For finer definition of volumes, the craftsman probably used cutting, incising, and drilling, the latter evidenced by shallow marks left by thin hollow drill bits of approximately 4.3 mm in diameter visible on the junction between the disk-like core on the back of the head and the lower and upper beaks.

Large holes were bored to define the eyes in a two-step process. The right eye has a concave, polished bottom, suggesting the use of a conical or spherical solid drill bit approximately 1.45 cm in diameter. A second drill using a hollow bit, 1.14 cm in diameter, cut the bottom of the earlier perforation. The perforation for the left eye was first executed with a conical or spherical solid bit 1.4 cm in diameter, followed by a superficial perforation by a hollow drill 3.4 mm in diameter. The second drilling in each eye created uneven surfaces that would have enhanced the adherence of a bonding material used to keep inlays in place. These inlays, together with any adhesive residue, eventually fell off.

The hole in the protuberance above the beak of PC.B.060, 2.7 mm in diameter, has a straight course, suggesting that a single perforation proceeded from either the right or the left side. The piece was also bored from side to side, proceeding

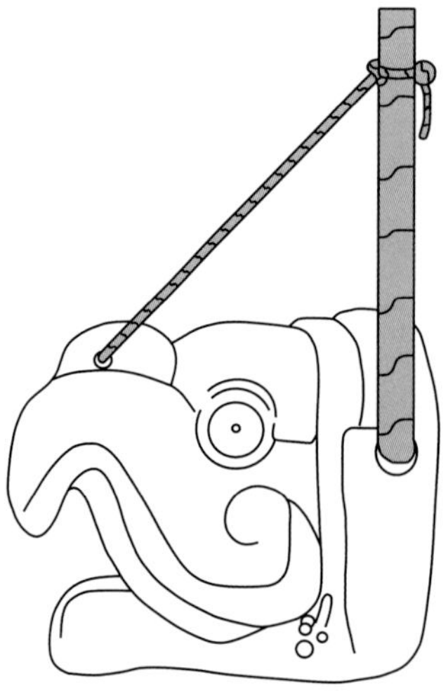

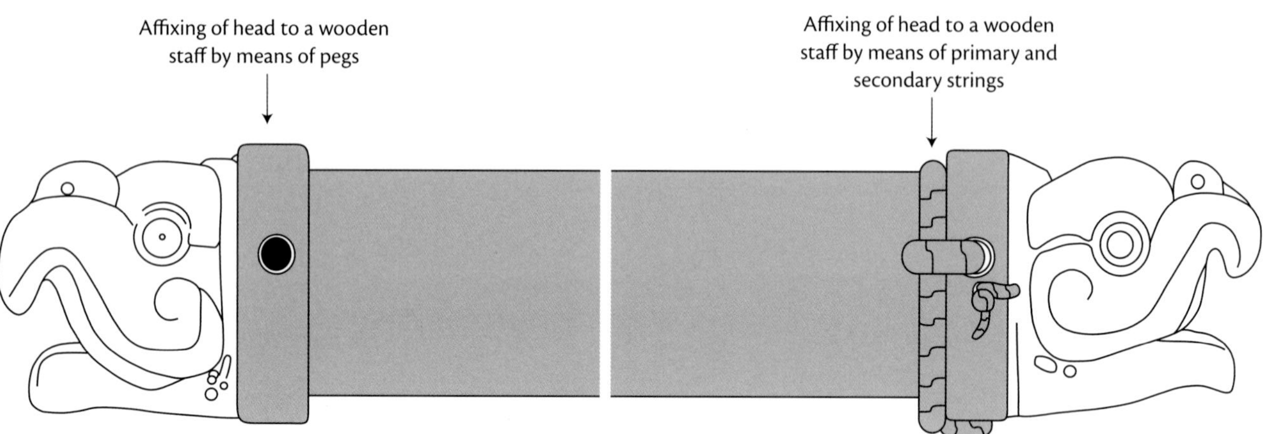

fig. 39
Alternatives for suspending (top) or affixing (bottom) the eagle heads PC.B.060 and PC.B.061. Drawing by Elbis Domínguez.

from both ends, in the middle of the disk-like core. Perforations that traverse the core do not seem to taper and were done at slightly inclined angles. The superior border of the core is stepped, and the outer band on the anterior surface of the disk has traces of at least three shallow marks left by hollow tubular drill bits. Portions of this band, however, appear to have eroded and then were mended with some kind of paste. Shallow drill bit marks suggest that, before the mending, the outer band may have had originally six shallow perforations. One of these is clean and exhibits clear evidence of the use of a thin tubular hollow drill bit 4 mm in diameter. These perforations must have held inlays, now missing. Slightly affected by erosion, the back surface of the core was originally ground and polished, as was the inferior surface of the eagle head. Scanty traces of a red pigment cover some surfaces, including portions that had been repaired.

The bores that traverse the piece do not seem to be related to suspension. Suspended from a string passed through the main bore, the weight of the piece makes it tilt forward. Although the tilting can be counteracted by fixing a string to the hole in the protuberance above the beak and tying it to the other string, suspension would have required several points of anchorage (Figure 39).

Eagle head PC.B.061 is almost identical to PC.B.060 but with important differences. The manufacturing procedure must have been the same, yet PC.B.061 has a bore perforated in the disk-like core that traverses vertically from the inferior surface to the juncture between the two lateral perforations. In addition, the anterior surface of the core has two holes, slightly below the main lateral bores, perforated at an angle to connect with corresponding holes on the sides of the core. On the left side of the piece are traces of a shallow mark left by a thick hollow tubular drill bit slightly above and behind the main bore, probably an initial, failed attempt to perforate the core, abandoned because eventually the hole would have been too close to the posterior surface of the head. On the same side are traces of three marks left by a thin hollow tubular drill bit. Their linear arrangement along the groove delineating the boundary between the upper and lower beaks attests to a drilling technique that created deeper contours and enhanced differential volumes in the heads.

Other conspicuous differences are the marks left by the drill bits used to make the holes for the eye inlays. The concentric circles at the bottom of these perforations indicate that the two-step process involved the use of hollow tubular drill bits of different diameters, the first hole done with a thicker bit.

The presence of a vertical bore in the lower half of the disk-like core supports the previous observation that the heads were not meant to be suspended. The configuration and location of perforations in PC.B.061 point, rather, to their having been affixed to a composite object. There was apparently no attempt to smooth the abandoned perforation on the left side of the core in PC.B.061, suggesting that this part of the head was not meant to be seen. Despite their slightly different dimensions, the eagle heads were probably intended to decorate a staff, baton, or ceremonial bar, with the two heads partially inserted at the ends of a wooden shaft. Main bores in the heads could have been aligned to holes on the ends the shaft and used to secure the three parts with string and possibly pegs. In PC.B.061, the two paired perforations that traverse at an angle the anterior and lateral surfaces of its core may have acted as reinforcement to affix the head to the shaft (see Figure 39, bottom).

Although conceptually this arrangement would generate a two-headed eagle, PC.B.060's possible inlays in the circling band behind the eagle's head may have distinguished the "head" of the object from its "tail," but red pigment covered both ends. If the eagle heads were part of a staff, the small perforations in the protrusions above the beaks could have held dangling miniature ornaments.

No actual counterpart for such a double-headed object is known, either in representations or in material culture. Yet the concept of double-headed eagles as alter egos to powerful individuals is seemingly portrayed several times in the Codex Nuttall (Figure 40; see also Anders et al. 1992a, facsimile pages 16, 21). Imagery of double-headed eagles endures in native textile traditions, as in bags and *huipiles* (blouses) woven by Huichol and Mixtec women (Beyer 1965a: fig. 1). Present-day accounts of the meaning of double-headed serpents in *huipiles* from the Pacific littoral of Oaxaca state that:

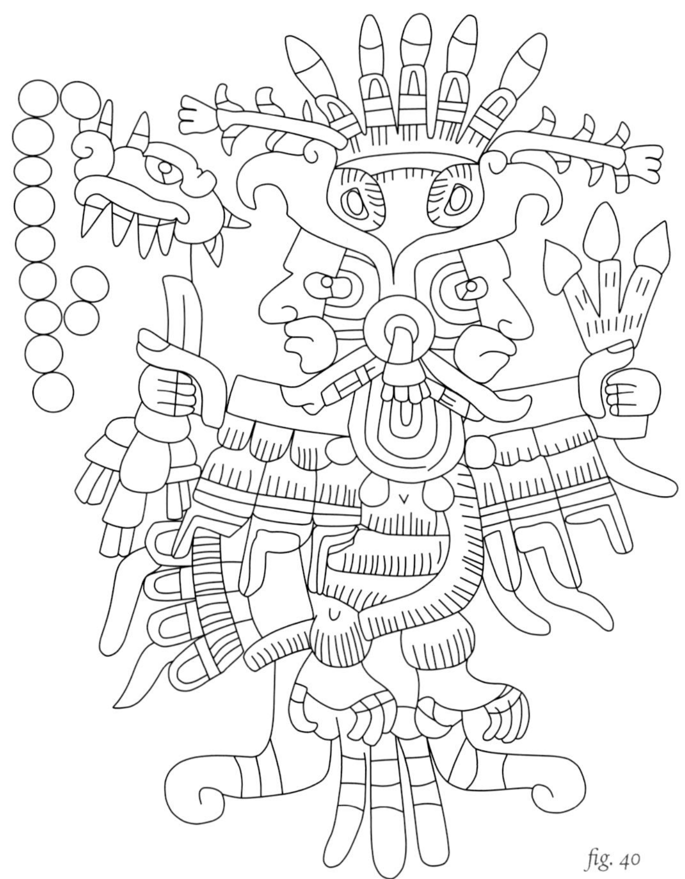

fig. 40
Double-headed eagle alter ego of 12 Alligator from the Codex Nuttall (page 19). Drawing by Elbis Domínguez (after Anders et al. 1992a).

> This bird existed many years ago; it resembled an eagle named Tasu Koo. The double-headed bird represents the power, the union of two souls, that become but one being. It does not mean that the eagle has two heads, but that two lives become one. This [type of] *uipil* is like a seal or a symbol carried by a Mixtec woman, and it signals that she is married. The bird with two heads appears on the back, the front, and in each shoulder of the *uipil*. (Cruz Ortíz 1994: 142; translation by the author)

JU

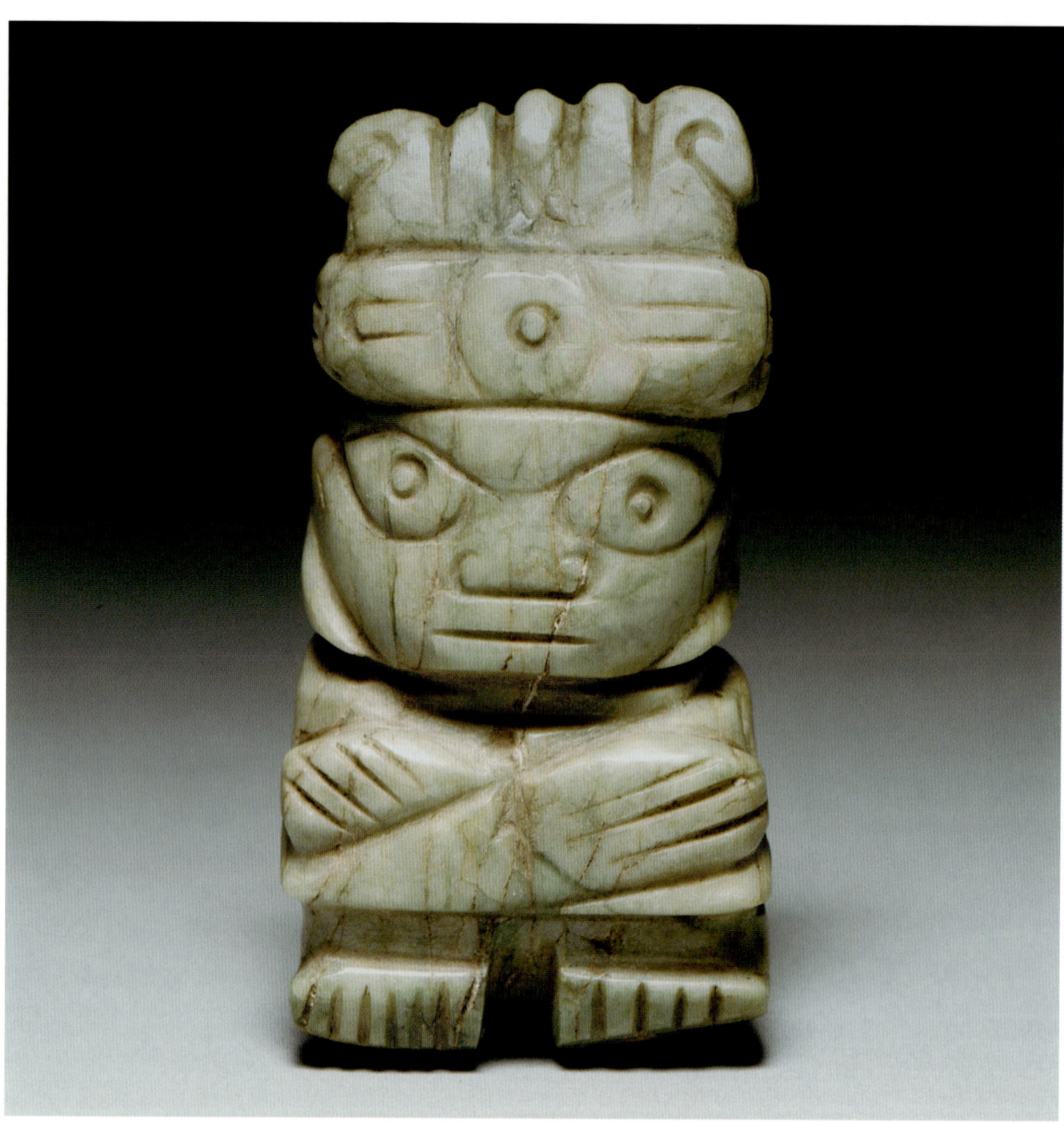

plate 57

SEATED FIGURE

PLATE 57
Mixteca-Puebla
Late Postclassic period, AD 1300–1520
Diopside jadeite
H. 7.1 cm (2¾"); W. 3.7 cm (1½"); D. 2.3 cm (⅞")
PC.B.095

ACQUISITION HISTORY:
Purchased from C. L. Morley, 1947

EXHIBITION HISTORY:
Indigenous Art of the Americas, National Gallery of Art, Washington, D.C., April 1947–July 1949, November 1952–July 1962 (NGA 331)

BIBLIOGRAPHY:
Bliss 1947: 12, 72, left, cat. no. 30; Bliss 1957: 247, cat. no. 96, pl. LVIII, bottom right; Dumbarton Oaks 1963: 25, cat. no. 122

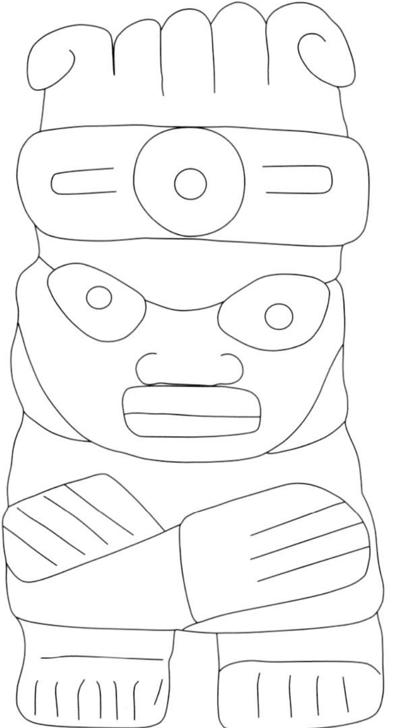
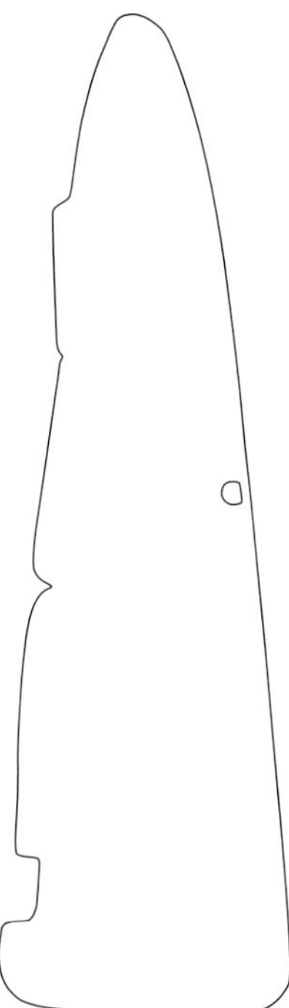
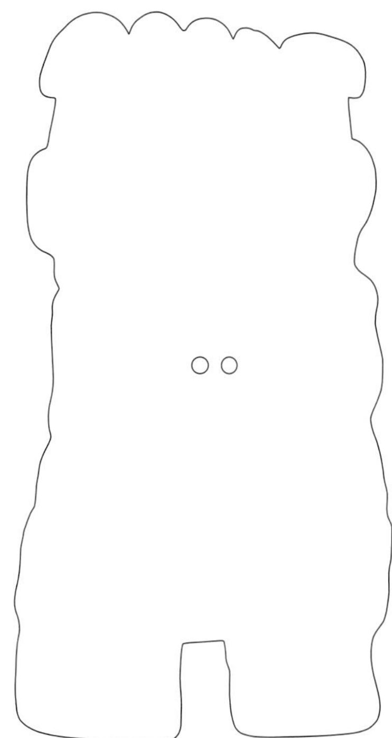

fig. 41
Front, side, and back of seated figure PC.B.095. Drawing by Elbis Domínguez.

This small, blocky figurine depicts a seated personage with its legs flexed against the torso, arms crossed, and hands placed in front of the knees. The anatomical details and posture were marked only on the anterior surface of the object. On the back and sides, the piece is flat and smooth, except for a pair of small perforations located in the center of the posterior surface (Figure 41). Relatively broad at the base and tapering at the top, the piece has a triangular shape. Facial features, including the eyes, nose, and mouth, are emphasized, creating a slight volume for the eyebrows, lips, and—faintly—the cheeks. The figure's right arm passes in front of the left one; a line indicating the wrist distinguishes the hand from the forearm. Fingers on both hands are marked by fine lines; the right one has four digits, and the left hand has five. A wide groove underneath the figurine clearly differentiates the legs. Short lines depict toes on bare feet; the right foot has seven toes, and the left foot has five. The figure wears no sumptuary goods or garments except for a headband topped by three vertical stripes (probably feathers) that are framed by two lateral stripes that end in scrolls. The headband has a small disk in the forehead.

The horizontally aligned perforations on the back of the figurine are next to each other and penetrate the surface at slight angles. Both holes, 3 mm in diameter, meet a few millimeters below the surface. These tiny holes must have served to suspend the object, but their location and relative positions make it unlikely that the object served as a pendant. Rather, the figurine may have been strung to a garment or affixed to a supporting device of some kind.

The object belongs to a category of stone figurines commonly referred to as *penates*, a Spanish word taken directly from Latin meaning "domestic deities worshipped by pagans." Archaeologists in the 1940s began using this term from Roman archaeology to designate ubiquitous blocky figurines with a prismatic or cuboid form dating to Late Postclassic times that were made of a variety of materials and appeared in varied contexts—mostly nonprimary—and had a wide distribution in southwestern Mesoamerica (Figure 42). *Penates* vary considerably, mostly in size (they range from 5 to 40 cm), posture, and degree to which anatomical features and garments are represented. Most depict humans or humans wearing masks, the face of the Rain God being recurrent. Only a few have been found in primary contexts, including 55 examples offered in dedicatory caches associated with the Templo Mayor at Mexico-Tenochtitlan (see Matos 1990: 86), but these differ from other

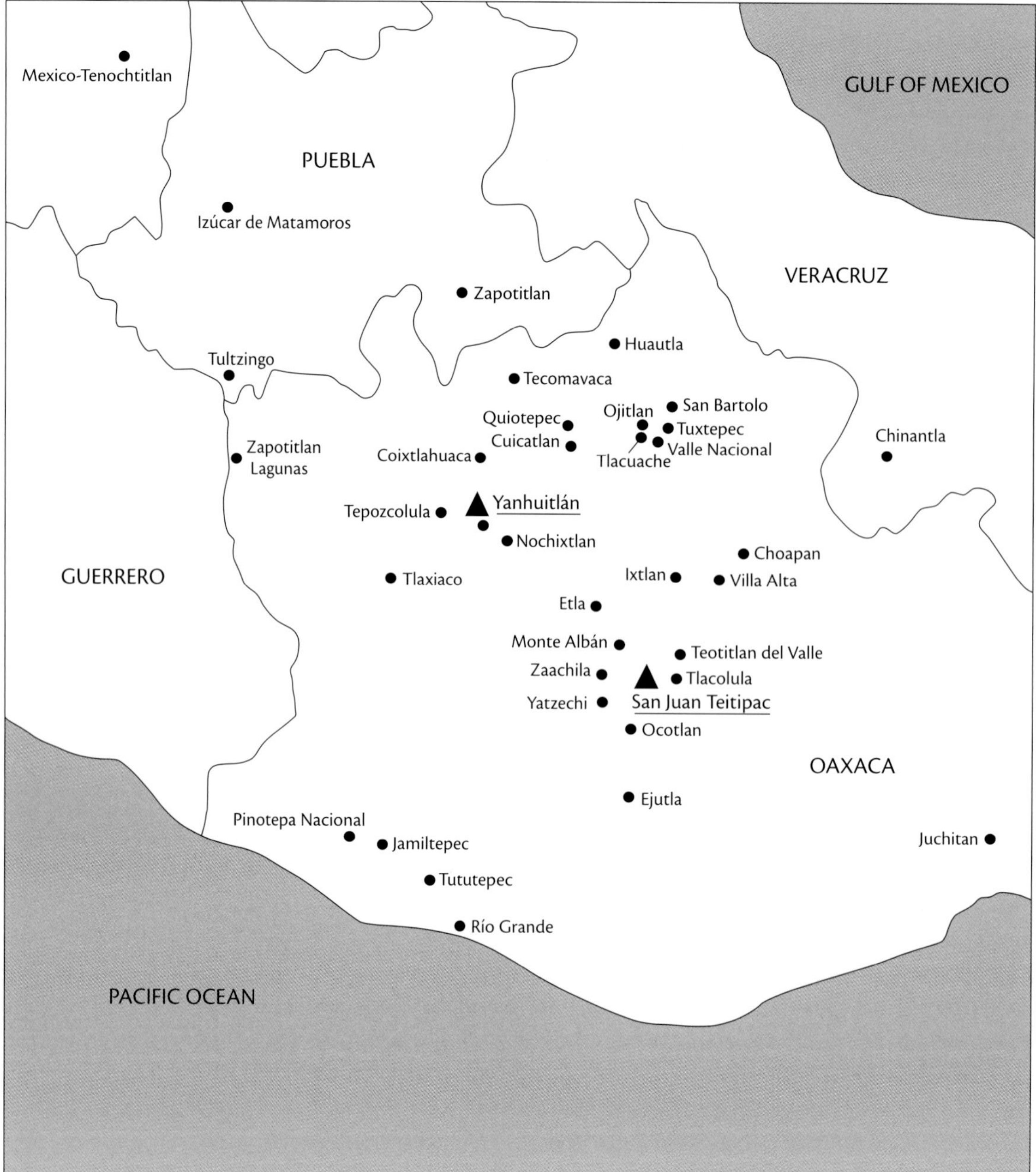

fig. 42
Map of known distribution of Late Postclassic stone figures (dots) and provenience of inquisitorial trial records that mention stone "idols" as part of propitiatory rituals (triangles). Map drawn by Elbis Domínguez (after Urueta Flores n.d. [1990]: 138 bis).

penates in their high level of craftsmanship and larger size.

Penates are frequently sculpted as seated with crossed arms, seeming to mimic the way dead individuals were arranged before being wrapped as mortuary bundles, publicly displayed during funerals, and eventually placed in tombs or caves (Caso 1942: 62). Hence they may be miniature representations of ancestors. Records of inquisitorial idolatry trials conducted by Spanish missionaries against native peoples substantiate that small stone figures, referred to as "idols," formed an integral component of domestic and public rituals aimed at invoking dead ancestors in the face of life crises. One of those records from the central valleys of Oaxaca, dated 1574, contains the trial against Diego Vásquez, a noble from San Juan Teitipac, and the declaration of a witness named Diego Hernández, from neighboring San Pablo Güila, who said that approximately 3½ years earlier, while visiting the abode of Diego Vásquez, at the time convalescent, he saw in his house a box containing a small stone, the length of a finger, carved with the figure of an idol of a yellowish color, and he also saw inside the box another green rounded stone without figure ("Informaciones . . . subjeta al pueblo de Titiquipaque . . . sobre pertinencia, posesión y culto de ídolos de los Indios" ([fol. 1r]; Meer n.d.: 37; translation by the author).

The records of an earlier inquisitorial trial (1544–46) against the ruler and governors of Yanhuitlán contain the declarations of several witnesses (Jiménez Moreno and Mateos Higuera 1940; Sepúlveda 1999). From these statements it transpired that the main accused, Don Domingo, kept custody of 20 sacred bundles—described as "boxes"— each one identified by its own calendrical name and thus representing a deceased ancestor. The boxes are said to have contained, among other things, green stone anthropomorphic figurines, balls of rubber, copal, bundles of feathers, and the paraphernalia for self-sacrifice. Because of the missionaries' surveillance and the surreptitious nature of these activities, the native nobles transferred the sacred bundles from one place to another, assisted by nobles from subject communities who performed in accordance with the ancient priestly organization. On many occasions, the accused deployed the sacred bundles in domestic or other sacred loci, like hills and caves, and performed rituals to invoke the ancestors and petition them for rain, abundant maize, health, and general welfare. Some of these rituals, enacted on behalf of the community, involved human sacrifice or the immolation of animals, including dogs and birds of several kinds.

Ancestors and the living could personify deities or take the attributes of gods, which could account for additional variability in stone figurines. The miniature representation of ancestors in stone had deeper historical roots in southwestern Mesoamerica, but earlier versions were manufactured in very different styles.

JU

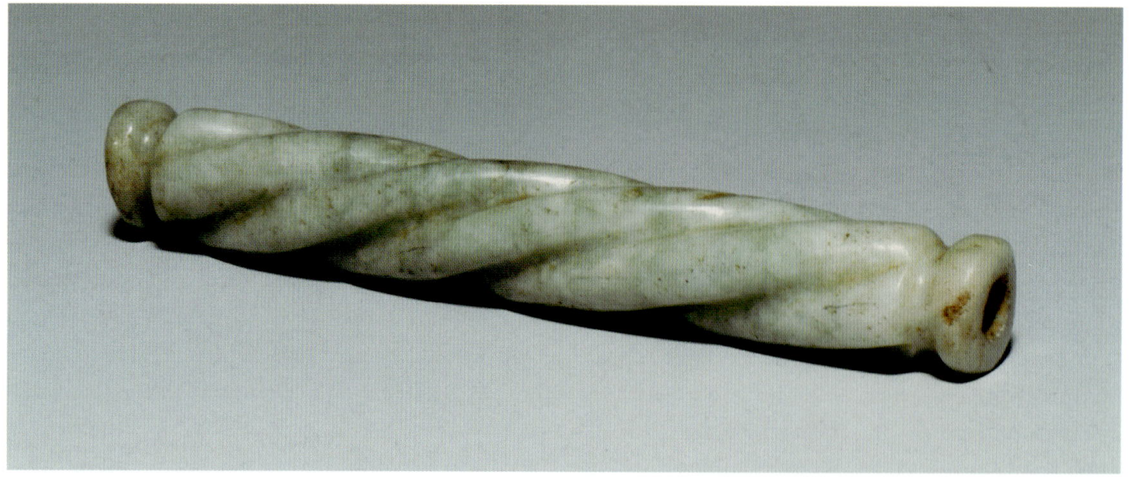

plate 58

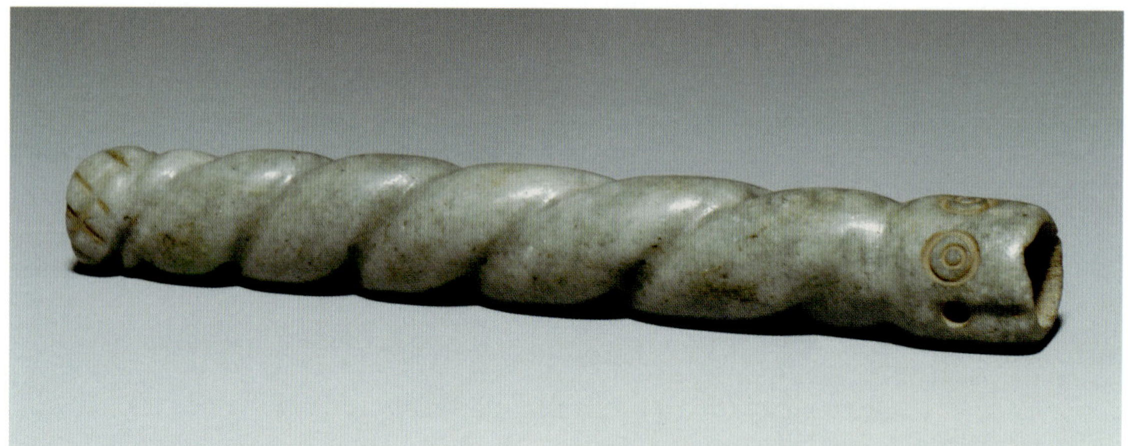

plate 59

STONE TUBES WITH SPIRAL GROOVES

PLATE 58
Late Postclassic period, AD 1200–1520
Diopside jadeite
L. 9.8 cm (3⅞"); Diam. 1.4 cm (½")
PC.B.135

PLATE 59
Late Postclassic period, AD 1200–1520
Diopside jadeite
L. 12.8 cm (5⅜"); Diam. 1.7 cm (⅝")
PC.B.136

ACQUISITION HISTORY:
Purchased from Earl Stendahl, 1942

EXHIBITION HISTORY:
Indigenous Art of the Americas, National Gallery of Art, Washington, D.C., April 1947–July 1949, November 1952–July 1962 (PC.B.135: NGA 75; PC.B.136: NGA 73); *The Aztec Empire*, Guggenheim Museum, New York, October 2004–February 2005; Guggenheim Museum, Bilbao, Spain, March–September 2005; *The Aztec World*, The Field Museum, Chicago, October 2008–April 2009

BIBLIOGRAPHY:
Bliss 1947: 14, 79, cat. nos. 51, 52; Bliss 1957: 247: cat. no. 92, pl. LVIII, bottom center; Dumbarton Oaks 1963: 25, cat. no. 119; Younger 2004: 43, cat. no. 184

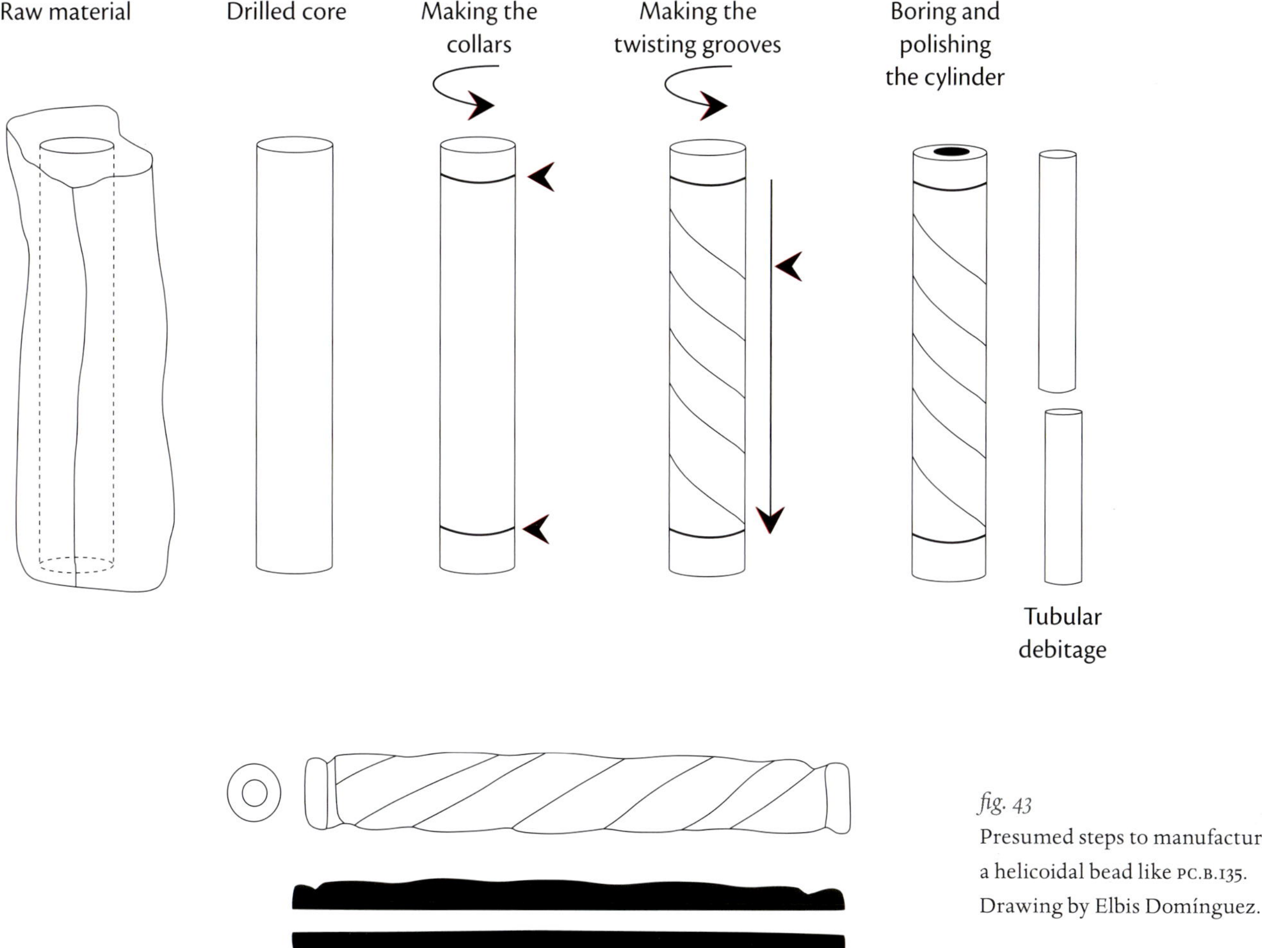

fig. 43
Presumed steps to manufacture a helicoidal bead like PC.B.135. Drawing by Elbis Domínguez.

PC.B.135 is a spirally grooved tubular bead, collared at both ends and circular in cross section without flattened sides. The internal perforation traversing the bead resulted from boring from both sides, each hole exhibiting longitudinally a conical shape and having different outer diameters.[100] Drilling the cylinder proceeded in stages as the drill bits wore down, and there was a slight deviation in the two opposite courses.

On the exterior surface, the even width of the bands that twirl lengthwise across the shaft of the bead suggests the deployment of a device that enabled both the fixing and the rotation of a solid tube of jadeite while a steady tracking movement with a sharp instrument generated the twisted guide lines (Figure 43). This strongly suggests the synchronized work of two artisans, one rotating the cylinder while the other marked the guide lines. The initial grooves, probably incised after defining the collared ends, were deepened by either repeating the same movement with the rotating device or by etching them manually. The spiral grooves could have been finished first before the cylinder was bored, but their polishing must have been the final manufacturing step.

In Mesoamerica, helical jade beads appear as early as the fourth century AD and in burial contexts (Kidder et al. 1977 [1946]: fig. 150a; Woodbury and Trik 1953: II: fig. 280f). Spirally grooved beads seem to be more common after the tenth century, when they were manufactured from other green stones and obsidian.[101] Most, if not all, spirally grooved beads may have served as personal accoutrements in funerary offerings. Although the examples recovered from the main cenote at Chichén Itzá may be an exception, those found in offerings associated with the Templo Mayor of Mexico-Tenochtitlan occur exclusively in caches containing cremated human remains (López Luján 1993: 220–237).

The main cenote at Chichén Itzá yielded a relatively large quantity of helicoidal beads that may date to between the tenth and the thirteenth centuries, but only four were jade[102] (Proskouriakoff 1974: pl. 24b, no. 13, pl. 25a); most of the spirally grooved beads were obsidian. Macroscopic inspection based on color differences and neutron activation analysis of these beads suggests diverse obsidian sources, including highland Guatemala, Pachuca (Hidalgo, Mexico), and Ucareo (Michoacán, Mexico). The five complete examples are approximately the same size as PC.B.135,[103] but they differ by their beveled ends or their faceted shafts. The predominance of fragments (53) indicates that, before being thrown into the cenote, most obsidian beads became shattered and crackled, most likely by intentionally exposing them to fire (Moholy-Nagy and Ladd 1992: 106). In general, obsidian beads from the cenote form two classes: spirally grooved and collared end (the one in the Bliss Collection combines both attributes).

Lothrop interpreted PC.B.135 and PC.B.136 as "spirally grooved tubular beads . . . [that] may have been handles of fans used for the ceremonial lighting of fire" (Lothrop in Bliss 1957: 247, cat. no. 92). This interpretation may have assumed that the spiral grooves mimicked the rotation of sticks to spark fires. Yet native depictions of fire making do not show the use of fans. Furthermore, PC.B.135's small bore strongly suggests that the object served as a pendant rather than as a handle for a composite item; a thin perforation would have allowed the passing of a suspending cord but not hafting or attaching an added element.

Beads from the main cenote at Chichén Itzá, however, are thought to be parts of larger ornamental ensembles. To account for their double- or single-beveled ends, Moholy-Nagy and Ladd (1992: 106) proposed that the beads may have formed composite collars with several concentric rows of tubular beads, based on a depiction of such adornment on a warrior decorating a gold disk from the cenote. However, the representation depicts plain tubular beads.

The recovery of four obsidian beads, almost identical to those from Chichén Itzá, in two burials from a single cist at Zacaleu (Woodbury and Trik 1953: 95–96) does not lend support to the idea that they formed elaborate pectorals, unless the parts were separated and placed in burials of different individuals. The general paucity of helical beads in burials at Kaminaljuyu, Zacaleu, Texmilincan, and Tenochtitlan suggests that those from Chichén Itzá's cenote were from multiple offering episodes of one or two beads, perhaps with human remains, rather than from offerings of complete, assembled pectorals.

Helical beads may be iconic renderings of ropes or coiled serpents. Their exclusive presence in funerary offerings at the Templo Mayor at Mexico-Tenochtitlan and their occurrence there in pairs or sets of five suggest that they were symbolically related to the path of the soul through the layered cosmos (López Luján 1993: 229–237). In Mesoamerican cosmovision, ontological transformations of the body and movements between layers of the cosmos were thought to follow helical paths, as illustrated in the *danza del volador,* a ritual in which eagle impersonators descend from the top of a tall pole, acting as avatars of the sun in their path to the earthly layer to take offerings of sacrificial victims.

PC.B.136 is a spirally grooved tube, collared at both ends, with two flattened sides. On one of the collars, wider than the other, each nonflattened side of the tube has a pair of circles, shallow perforations made with a thin tubular hollow drill bit. The object's other collared end has crosshatch markings. These features and the twisting bands that run lengthwise along the exterior surface of the tube clearly indicate that the object has the shape of two entwined serpents whose heads appear opposite to each other on one end and whose scaled bellies are exposed on the other end (Figure 44).

The cylinder was bored from both ends using drill bits of different size.[104] The ample bore traversing the tube was evidently not meant to provide a means of suspending the object as a pendant but to allow sufficient room for hafting. Thus the object was the handle for a composite object, most likely a feathered fan. Different in form, the object is functionally and conceptually similar to PC.B.094 (Plate 60).

In addition to the main bore, the end with the heads of the entwined serpents has two perforations, 3.1 mm in diameter, below the rim. A groove runs from each hole to the border of the object, marking the division of the ophidian heads,

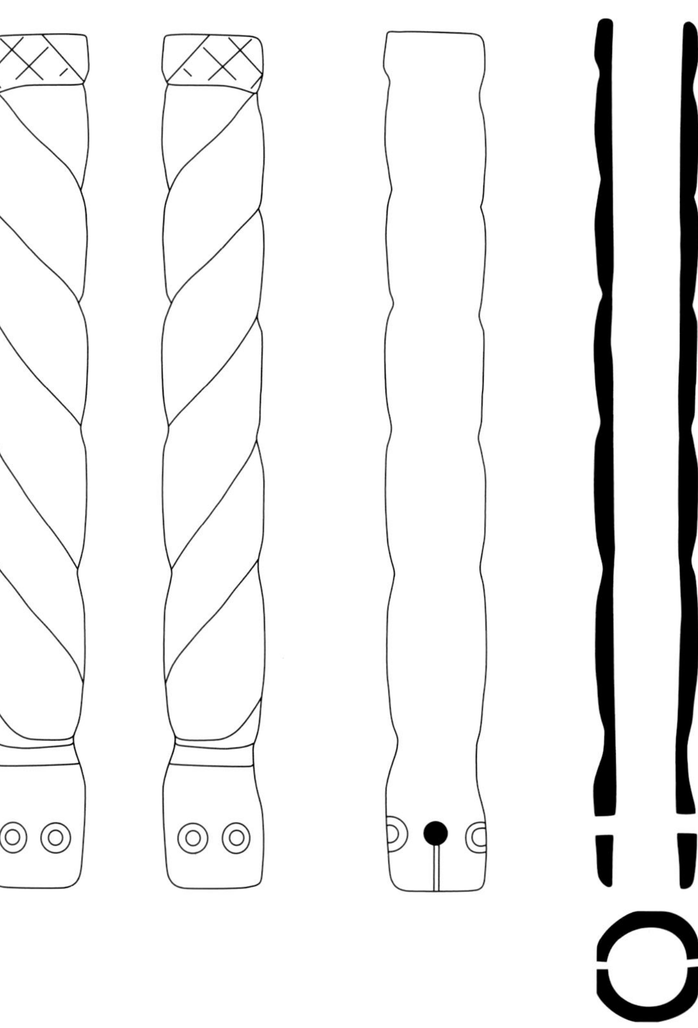

fig. 44
Features of the grooved hollow tube PC.B.136. Drawing by Elbis Domínguez.

but possibly with an additional function, such as guides for thin cords that, with the aid of the transversal perforations, fastened a hafting ring like PC.B.118 (Plate 70) inside that end of the handle. If so, the presumed fan differs from PC.B.094: the serpent heads were at the distal rather than the proximal end of the object. Alternatively, transversal holes and lateral grooves between the serpent heads could have guided a cord that allowed suspending the handle from the wrist. This alternative would place the serpent heads at the fan's proximal end, just as for PC.B.094.

There are no traces of wear that would have been caused by inserting a hafting ring into either end of the cylinder, but perhaps the added piece was made of wood or bone. Despite its different function, the manufacturing procedure of PC.B.136 must have been the same as that for the spirally grooved bead PC.B.135. One of the flattened sides of the tube has coarse areas with a distinct brownish coloration, suggesting that before its discovery the object rested on this flat end. Today both borders of the object are slightly chipped.

JU

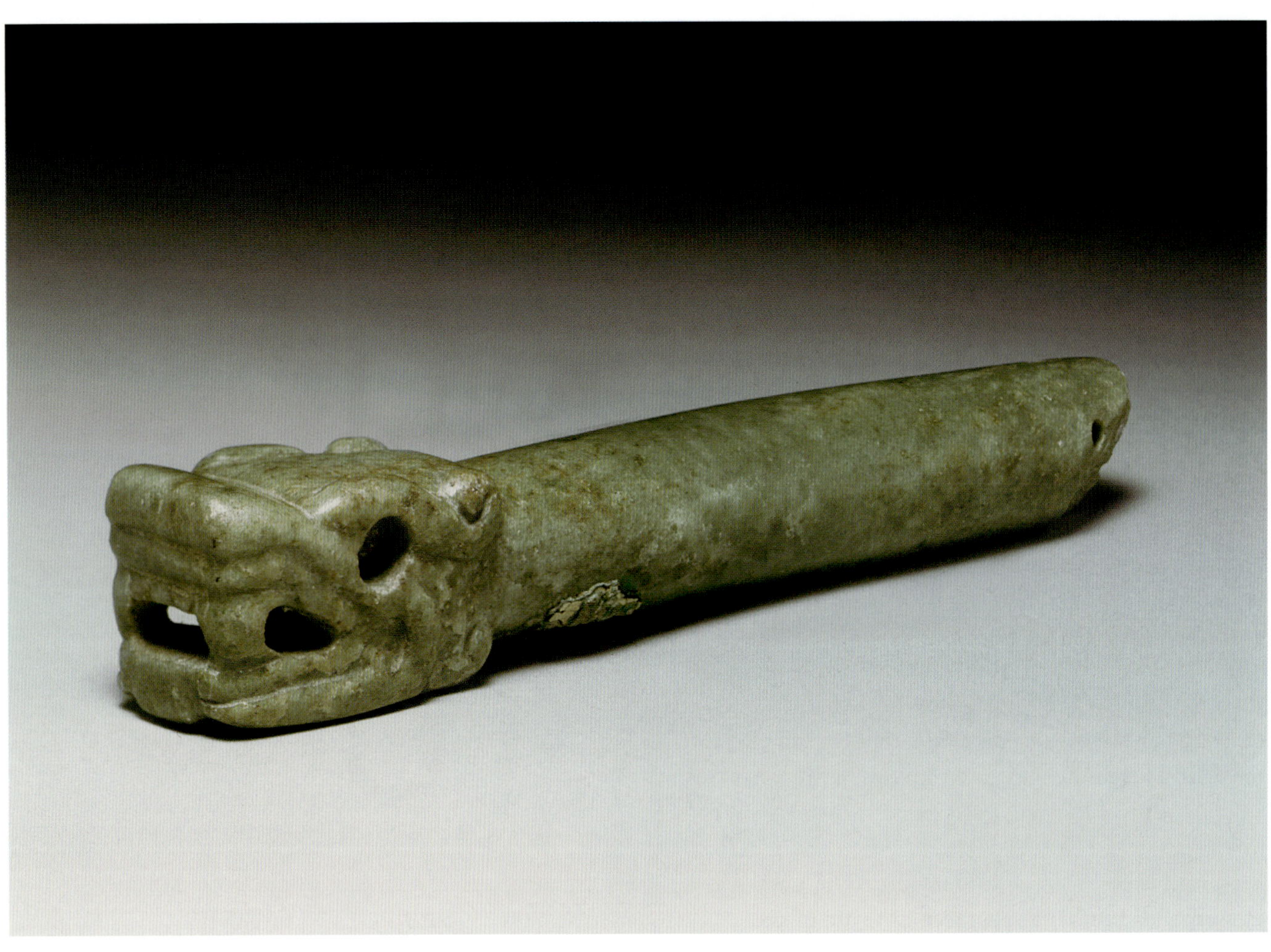

plate 60

FAN HANDLE

PLATE 60
Southwestern Mesoamerica or Central Highlands
Late Postclassic period, AD 1300–1520
Jadeite
L. 14.6 cm (5¾"); H. 2.7 cm (1 1⁄16"); W. 2.2 cm (⅞")
PC.B.094

ACQUISITION HISTORY:
Purchased from Earl Stendahl, 1961

BIBLIOGRAPHY:
Dumbarton Oaks 1963: 25, cat. no. 121

The head of a serpent is rendered on the proximal end of this handle for a composite object; the distal portion is hollow to allow the hafting of a now-lost attachment (Figure 45). The handle is tubular, but the serpent's head is quadrilateral. Its eyes are marked by perforations 5 mm deep, probably for inlays, but no traces of the bonding material remain. The snake's maw is hollowed, rendering its jaws open and menacing. No manufacturing marks are visible, but the hollowing of the mouth must have been accomplished by drilling. The frontal view of the serpent reveals three teeth, and a protruding bifid tongue, slightly embossed, wraps over the posterior surface of the object.

The handle's distal end is hollow, accomplished by a perforation 1.22 cm deep into the object's longitudinal axis. In the interior of this perforation are marks typical of a hollow drill bit, including a clearly defined ring at the bottom and striations perpendicular to the longitudinal axis, caused by an abrasive medium and the rotation of the drill. There is no wear indicative of hafting. A small portion of the distal end, on the left side, is now broken and missing.[105]

Adhered to one side of the handle, just behind the serpent's head, is a tiny piece of a thin gilded sheet, a fragment that must be part of the material that made up the missing part once hafted into the handle. The representation of a long-distance trader on page 18 of Codex Laud (Figure 46; Anders and Jansen 1994) clarifies the probable configuration of the composite object, showing distinctly the serpent handle topped by a circular and presumably flattened canopy characterized by a red frame and a cross-hachured interior painted yellow or gilded. The jade serpent-headed handle found in Monte Albán Tomb 7 also had fragments of "a sheet of gold," as inferred by Caso (1969: 142), based on remnants of a cement-like substance and the microscopic traces of that metal.[106]

The manner in which the gilded upper part of the object was hafted to the handle remains unknown, but small holes on the distal end must have facilitated its fastening. This type of composite object may be similar to one called the

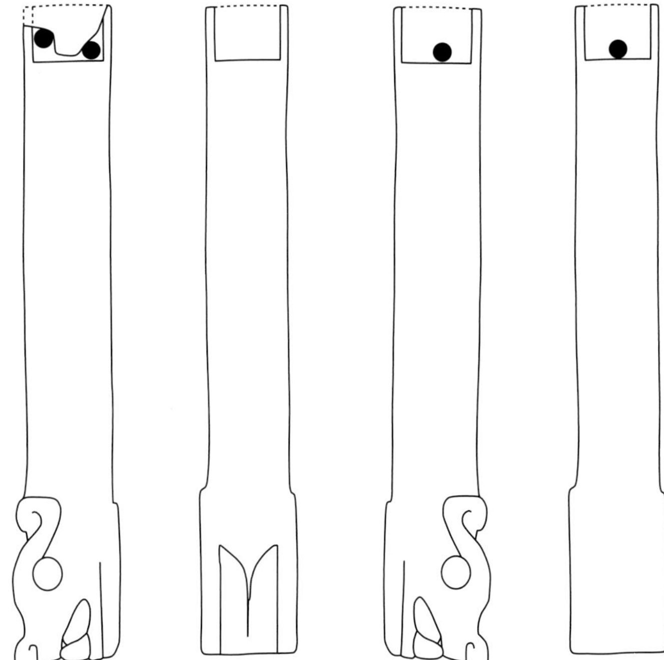

fig. 45
Features of the fan handle PC.B.094. Drawing by Elbis Domínguez.

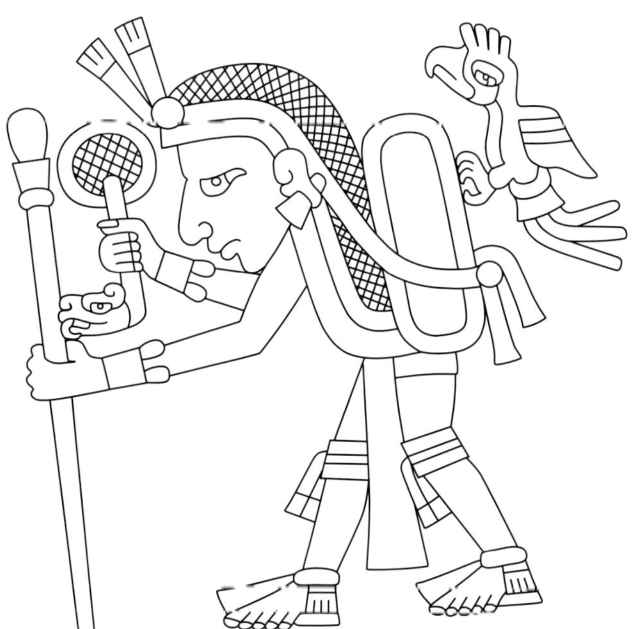

fig. 46
Long-distance merchant holding a fan with serpent-shaped handle from the Codex Laud (page 18). Drawing by Elbis Domínguez (after Anders and Jansen 1994).

coxoliecaceoaztli (crested guan feather fan covered with troupial feathers at the bottom), one of the most prestigious insignia bestowed on professional Aztec merchants who were successful in military campaigns while trading (Sahagún 1959 [1569]: 4, 22). Among Mixtec-speaking peoples, feathered fans marking high rank were referred to as *huichi* (Caso 1969: 117).

An early twentieth-century description of an heirloom fan or whisk suggests that the hafted piece consisted of a wooden arched plaque on which up to five rows of feathers of increasing size were inserted. Each row contained 18 feathers and was a different color, including—from the handle to the tip of the object—red, blue, red, green, and yellow feathers (Caso 1969: 116–117). Following Sahagún's informants' description of the *coxoliecaceoaztli*, Caso (1969: 142) also suggested that the opening in the serpent's jaw in some of the known examples was used to suspend additional feathers.

Fans and whisks were important insignia in Mesoamerica since very ancient times, although not necessarily or exclusively related to long-distance merchants. Despite the differential preservation of the two main parts of this type of object, at least 10 examples of serpent-headed handles in jade, jadeite, and cast gold with false filigree are known.[107] Hollow tubular objects without serpent heads on one end but with small perforations on the other may have also been handles of fans or whisks that signaled high social rank. Examples manufactured in various materials are known. Some are stone, either plain or spirally grooved (see PC.B.136, Plate 59); others are elaborately incised or carved animal bone. The majority of known handles—with or without serpent heads—date to the later part of the pre-Hispanic sequence (AD 1300–1520).

The use of serpent-headed handles as parts of fans or whisks hinted at in the Codex Laud finds archaeological confirmation. The example in jade from Monte Albán Tomb 7 was found inserted in a bracelet placed around an almost pulverized human radius (Caso 1969: 117), and one of the two jadeite handles from Zaachila Tomb 2 lay adjacent to the bones of a left forearm (Gallegos 1978: 110, fig. 71).

JU

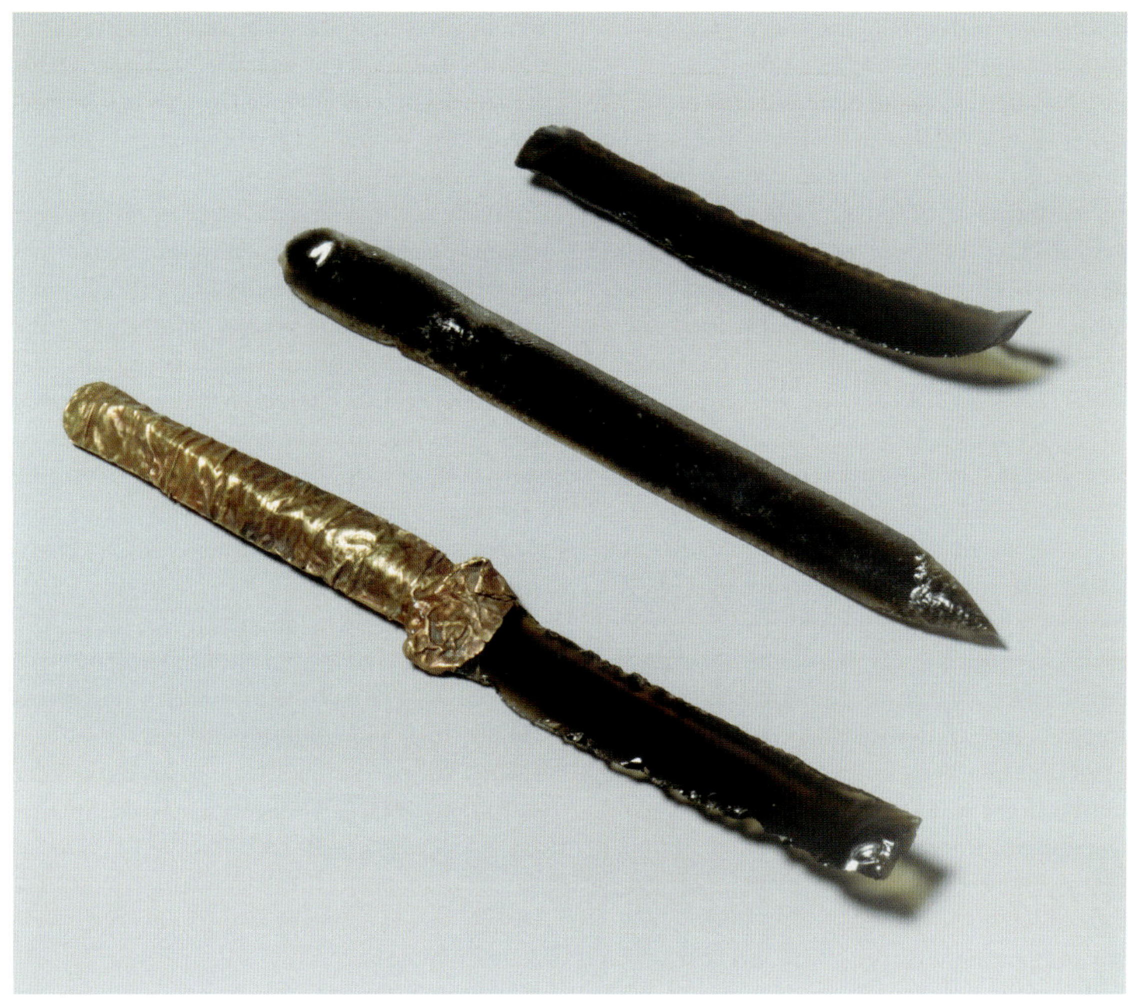

plate 61

OBSIDIAN BLADES WITH GOLD SHEATH

PLATE 61
Probably Late Postclassic period, AD 1300–1600
Obsidian and hammered gold
PC.B.143a: L. 16.2 cm (6⅜"); W. 2.02 cm (¾");
D. 1.02 cm (⅜")
PC.B.143b: L. 9.5 cm (3¾"); W. 1.48 cm (⅝");
D. 0.3 cm (1/8")
PC.B.143c: L. 14.3 cm (5⅝"); W. 1.3 cm (½");
D. 0.3 cm (⅛")
PC.B.143a, PC.B.143b, PC.B.143c

ACQUISITION HISTORY:
Purchased from John Stokes

Blade PC.B.143a (bottom blade in Plate 61) is a slightly curved blade of green obsidian, probably from the Pachuca source. A thin and elongated sheet of a metal alloy wraps around the tip of the blade. The blade's striking platform and bulb of percussion—production scars left at the point where the blade was detached from a core—are readily evident on the object's exposed end. Pressure-flaked retouching along both sides of the blade and on both surfaces varies: along one side it is much smaller and more careful, yielding a straighter edge, whereas the other side has crude pressure flaking, yielding pronounced notches and an uneven edge.

The location of the piece of metal at the tip rather than at the base of the blade indicates that the metal is not a handle; rather it is a sheath to encase the blade. Although evidently hollowed, the sheath had been crushed and is now flattened, straight, corrugated, and firmly pressed around the tip of the blade, which is now broken into several small fragments. In profile view, the distal end of the sheath is elliptical and is therefore the least flattened part. This condition hints at what must have been an ample enough cover to accommodate the curved blade.[108]

The sheath must have been manufactured from a hammered sheet of a metal alloy that includes gold. The sheet would have been folded longitudinally, but any traces of the seam are obscured by the sheath's present condition. Its original opening, now firmly pressed around the tip of the blade, flares out slightly, suggesting that it was reinforced by a narrow strip of hammered metal affixed around the sheath's border. Although here the surface is also corrugated, the corners of the reinforcing strip seem evident, showing folding in opposite directions. The manufacturing details of the sheath at its upper end are obscured by a hardened transparent substance, probably modern glue to bind together the two pieces just below the sheath's presumed reinforced border.

Blade PC.B.143b (top blade in Plate 61) is an incomplete, slightly curved green obsidian blade that also has an evident striking platform and bulb of percussion. The tip probably broke in antiquity, as the broken edge appears to have been smoothed. Scars of fine pressure flaking are visible on both edges and both surfaces, as is a feather-like pattern of fine striations along the spine on the outer surface of the blade.

Blade PC.B.143c (middle blade in Plate 61) is a complete blade manufactured from green obsidian. It is quite straight. One end has a thin striking platform and a bulb of percussion, whereas at the other a pointed tip 1.5 cm long has been retouched with fine pressure flaking on its interior surface only. No other retouching is present on the side edges of the blade. There is also a feather-like pattern of fine striations along the spine on the outer surface of the implement. Traces of soil adhere to both surfaces.

Golden sheaths for obsidian blades seem novel in the known inventory of ancient Mesoamerican material culture, but the manufacturing process and the ritual and nonceremonial uses of cutting blades are well known. The lengths of the three blades in the Bliss Collection, their almost pristine condition despite their fragility, and the association of one of them with a metal casing suggest ritual purposes, specifically as instruments to draw blood from the body.

Self-mortification of fleshy parts rich in blood vessels, such as the earlobes, tongue, male genitalia, and calves, was a penitential act to maintain reciprocity in a moral and spiritual covenant between humans and the sacred. Self-sacrifice was a pan-Mesoamerican practice with deep historical roots. The earliest cutting or perforating implements date to ca. 1000 BC or earlier. Some were

fig. 47
Three men and a woman drawing blood from their earlobes with obsidian blades from the Codex Madrid (page 95a). Drawing by Elbis Domínguez (after the facsimile of the Codex Madrid available at http://www.famsi.org/mayawriting/codices/madrid.html).

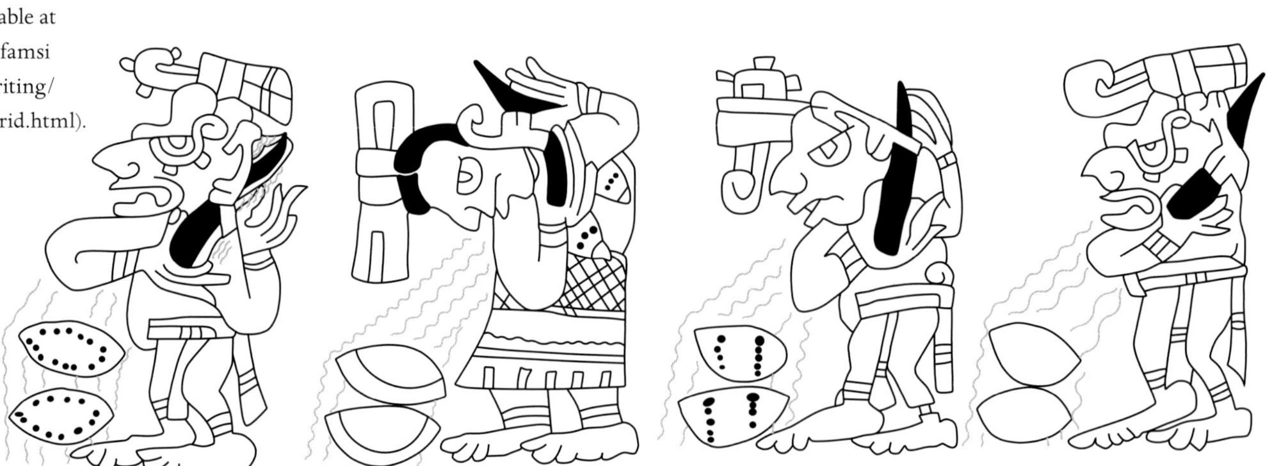

of natural origin, such as stingray spines; others were such artifacts as stone perforators (for example, Taube 2004b: 122–126), obsidian imitations of stingray spines, sharpened wooden sticks, ropes with thorns, and obsidian blades.

The ethos of some Mesoamerican peoples, like the Maya or the Mexica, placed heavy emphasis on the graphic representation of self-sacrifice in elite and state-sponsored art (Figure 47). In other regions, such as Oaxaca or the Gulf Lowlands, scenes of bloodletting are less common or were intentionally veiled. Yet archaeological evidence and sixteenth-century documentation from many parts of Mesoamerica attest to its widespread geographic range.

Contrary to what sponsored art seems to project, self-sacrifice was by no means restricted to the nobility and the ruling elite or staged exclusively in temples and royal courts, although its practice by members of these social strata acquired special significance not only because of the perceived obligation of rulers as benefactors of their communities but also because of the economic and political interests that high-ranking corporate groups had in perpetuating their rights and privileges. Common people also practiced self-sacrifice, both in the domestic realm and in cultivated fields. Prior to raiding, warriors engaged their ancestors and consulted oracles to prognosticate the outcome of war and determine whether the time for combat was propitious. And individuals with particular specializations and knowledge petitioned for divine favors by offering their blood in spiritually charged places, such as caves, springs, and atop mountains and hills.

JU

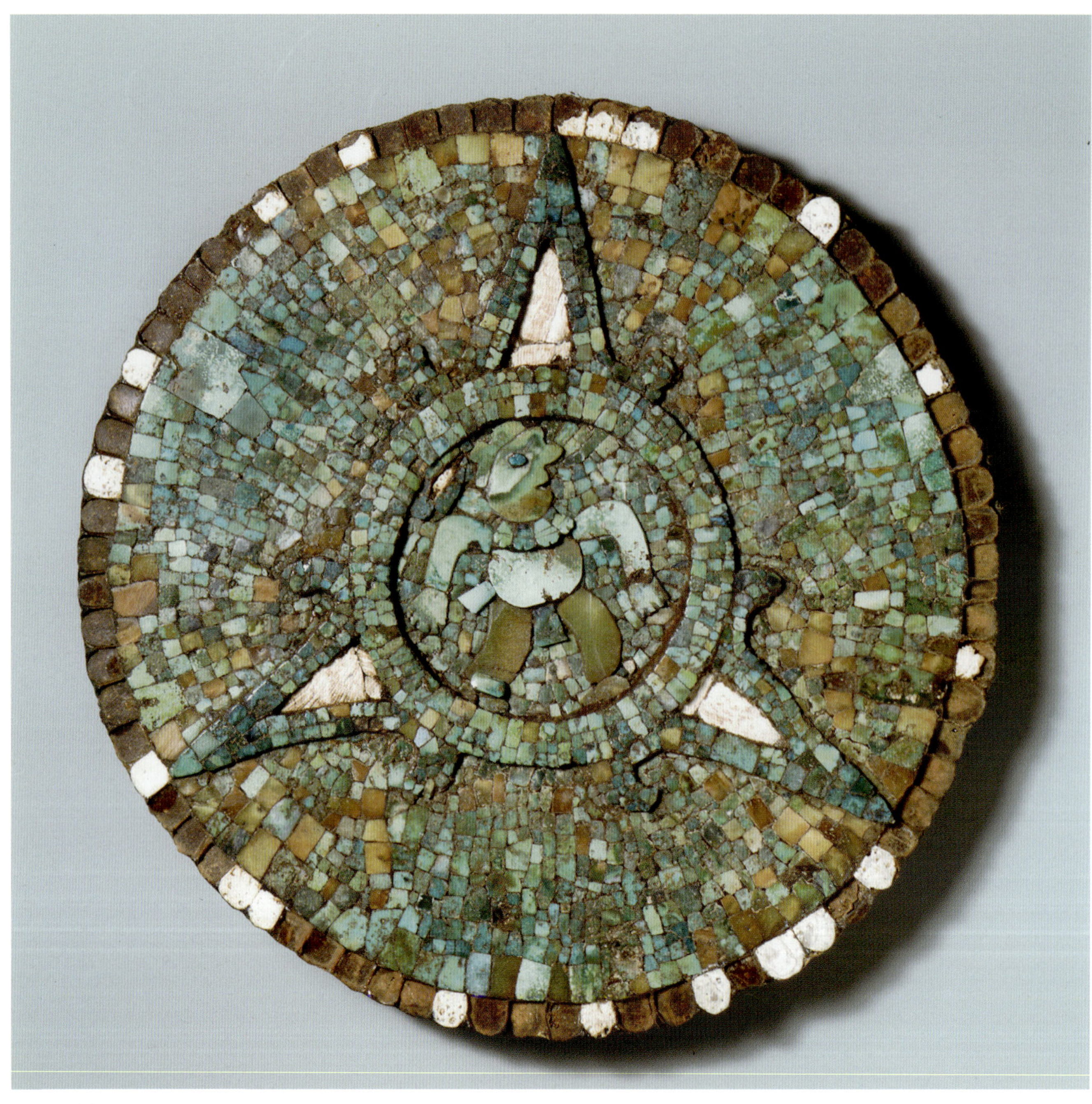

plate 62

DISK WITH MOSAIC INLAYS

PLATE 62
Mixtec-Aztec style
Late Postclassic period, AD 1300–1520, reassembled in modern times
Wood with shell, coral, turquoise, and jade tesserae
D. 1.6 cm (⅝"); Diam. 12.0 cm (4¾")
PC.B.566

ACQUISITION HISTORY:
Purchased from Everett Rassiga, 1969

BIBLIOGRAPHY:
Dumbarton Oaks 1969: cat. no. 453; Izeki 2008: 142, cat. no. 1.8.4

This circular wooden disk is convex on the back and flat on the front, where it is inlaid with tesserae of different materials arranged to form an image of a sun disk with a human figure inside it. The inner ring, forming the sun and its three solar rays, and the interior figure are in higher relief; the interior surface of the roundel is slightly sunken in relation to the surface of the outer ring. Between the wooden frame and the inlay's dark brown layer are probably the remnants of the adherent for the tesserae.[109] The outer ring, composed of nail-shaped plaques of shell, is incomplete, with obvious marks left by the many missing plaques. The rest of the mosaic decoration is intact. The individual pieces, of various sizes and materials, are highly polished. The larger tesserae inside the sun's rays are white and characterized by conspicuous striations, suggesting the eroded outer surface of a specific kind of shell.

The human figure is rendered mostly in jade and turquoise mosaics and combines profile and frontal views. Two plaques mark the loincloth, indicating that the figure is male. Other accoutrements include a headdress and a necklace, and plaques forming these elements are the only ones detailed with fine incised lines. Those forming the necklace seem to represent shells. Those making up the hands have small notches along the inferior edge, indicating fingers. The figure has three small bits of worked stone on top of the underlying mosaic, and these highlight the eye, right ankle, and a bracelet on the left wrist. Although the latter is missing, the resin used to affix it to the disk still remains (Figure 48).

The wood supporting the mosaic decoration is very light and exhibits both the natural veins as well as striations in different directions, probably cutting marks from shaping the piece. Small shallow perforations characteristic of insect damage are visible in the wood, features that seem to have been present prior to the object's assembly. A large curved crack on the back surface may be of more recent origin. On one side of the wooden disk, two sets of small perforations traverse the posterior and lateral surfaces. These perforations are biconical and were evidently done separately; they provided suspension for the disk and are symmetrically placed to allow viewing the human figure in vertical position. The sun disk's upper ray does not coincide with this vertical axis.

The form and posture of the human figure fall within known regional variations of representation for late pre-Hispanic times. Incised details in some of the plaques and the overlaying of small pieces to highlight details are present in other pieces with mosaic decoration. Also, the theme of a human figure inside a sun disk is prevalent in many objects, inlaid or not, that are securely dated to after the thirteenth century AD. The disk

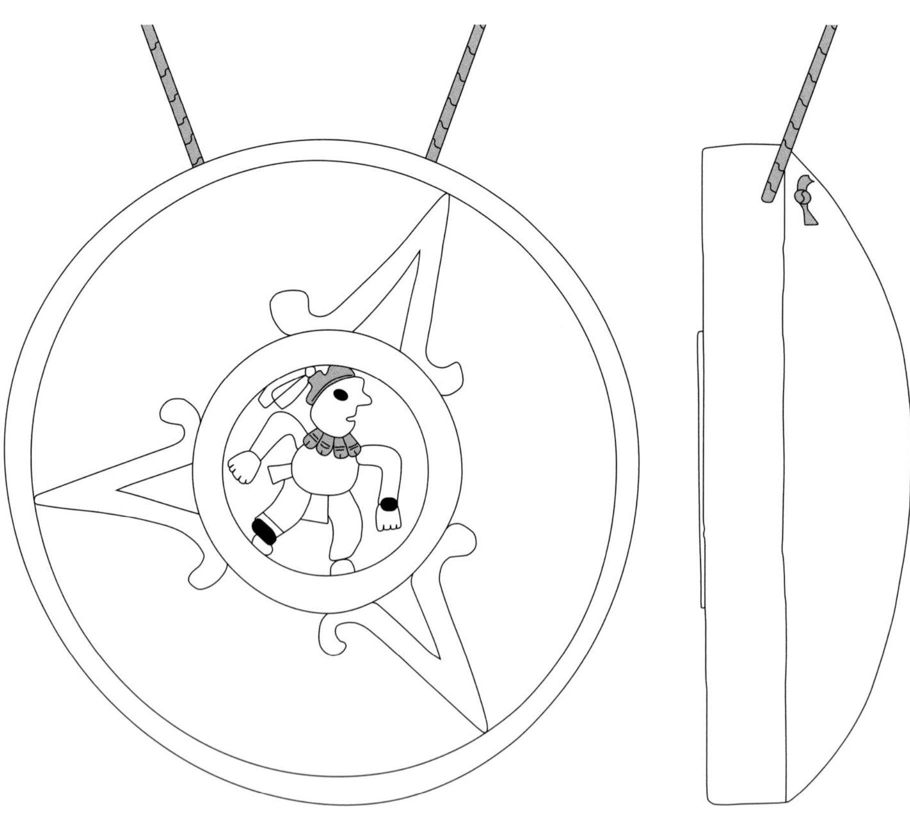

fig. 48
Front and side of inlaid wooden disk PC.B.566. The tesserae in gray are incised. Those in black were laid on top of underlying ones. Drawing by Elbis Domínguez.

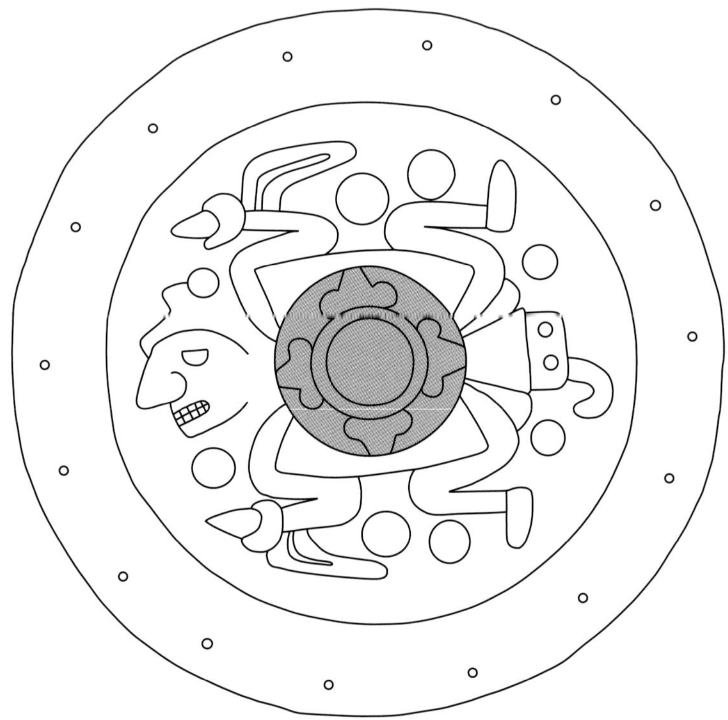

fig. 49
Carved wooden base of a shield probably once inlaid with tesserae, found in La Picuda Los Lirios, near Acapulco, Guerrero. The inner gray area highlights a sun disk with four rays. Drawing by Elbis Domínguez (after Bernal 1967: 55, photo 1).

PC.B.566, however, remains unique in form, size, and presumed function.

At least four different types of wooden disks inlaid with mosaic decoration are known from Mesoamerica. The smallest, averaging 5 cm in diameter, appear to be ear flares. One example reputedly from Zaachila, Oaxaca, is also convex, but in contrast to PC.B.566, this is the inlaid surface (Sánchez Scott 2001: 40). A second type of inlaid disk is a pectoral; these range between 27 and 34 cm in diameter. Two of them, with turquoise and turtle carapace mosaic decoration, were found placed on the chests of immolated children buried at the foot of the Tlaloc shrine (offering 48) in the Templo Mayor at Tenochtitlan (López Luján 1993: 199, fig. 79). A third type is the shield used by high-ranking warriors; these range between 30 and 40 cm in diameter (see McEwan 1994: 76; Seler 1996 [1904]: 126, 128). Aside from their size, these objects are invariably characterized by having small perforations in the perimeter (Figure 49), probably for fastening different kinds of additional items (feathers, hair, strips of fur, dangling trinkets) or as marks left by pegs used to hold in place sheets of hammered gold. Mosaic decoration on the shields varies and most often makes reference to solar imagery. A fourth type of wooden disk is smaller than shields and ranges between 20 and 30 cm in diameter. These objects lack peripheral perforations and are often scalloped around the edge (see Caso 1938: 65; Sánchez Scott 2001: 53). They have a central mosaic pyrite mirror with two perforations near the reflecting inner core, a feature that implies their use as the posterior mirrored clasps or brooches worn by high-ranking warriors and by the impersonators of certain deities (see Acosta 1961: figs. 8, 21).

Compared to these four types of disks, PC.B.566 is unique in the convexity of the posterior surface. Furthermore, irrespective of function, the four types of inlaid disks noted above display a quadripartite layout in the mosaic decoration, a structural feature that is also recurrent in actual depictions of the sun. The overall form of the inlaid disk in the Bliss Collection, the traces of a thick adhesive base to the tesserae, and the representation of a sun disk with three rays only reveal its spurious nature. The authenticity of the tiny plaques, including incised pieces, suggests that (as in the case of the human skulls PC.B.097, PC.B.098, and PC.B.099; Plates 63, 64, and 65, respectively) tesserae manufactured in pre-Hispanic times were reconfigured in the recent past by someone who failed to grasp, among other things, the fourfold conception of time and space in ancient Mesoamerican worldview.

JU

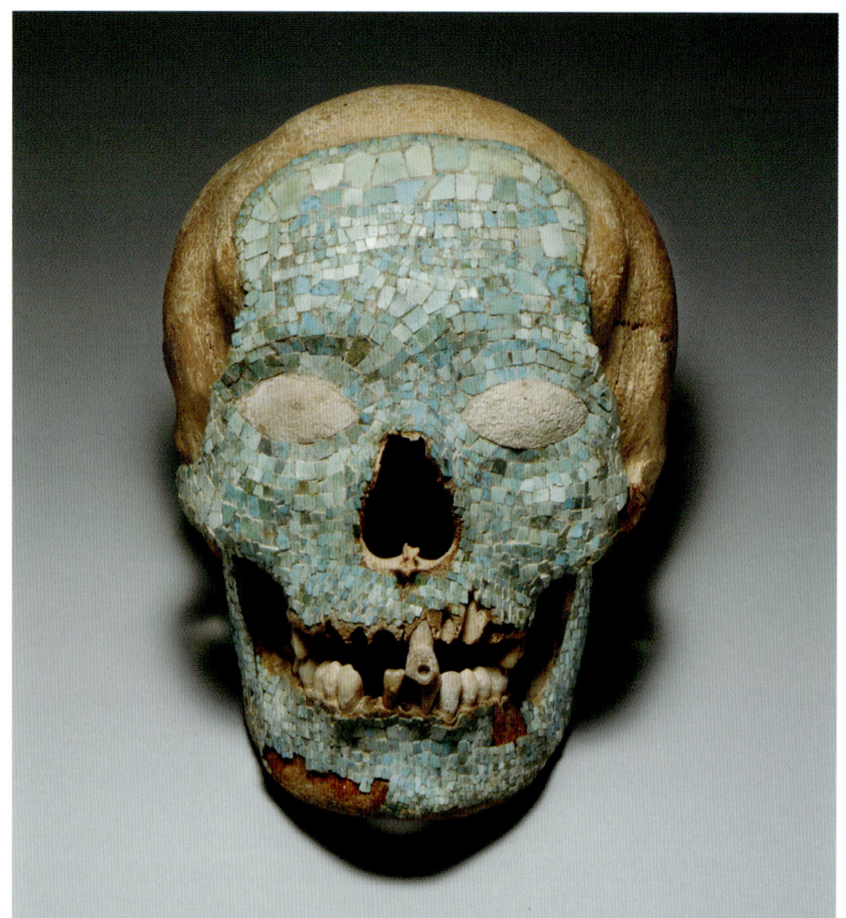

plate 63

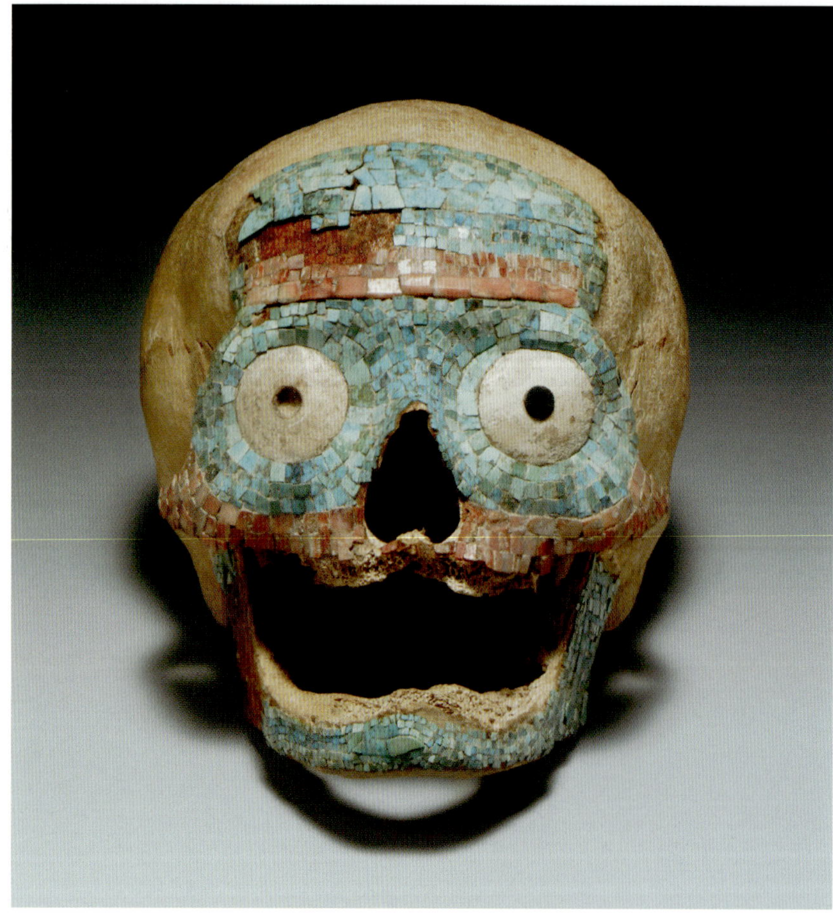

plate 64

PLATE 63
Mixteca-Puebla style
Late Postclassic period, AD 1300–1520, reassembled in modern times
Bone, stone, and shell
H. 21.2 cm (8⅜"); W. 15.0 cm (5⅞"); D. 16.4 cm (6½")
PC.B.097

PLATE 64
Mixteca-Puebla style
Late Postclassic period, AD 1300–1520, reassembled in modern times
Bone, stone, and shell
Cranium: H. 14.9 cm (5⅞"); W. 16.2 cm (6⅜");
D. 17.5 cm (6⅞")
Mandible: H. 6.9 cm (2¾"); W. 12.6 cm (5");
D. 9.9 cm (3⅞")
PC.B.098

PLATE 65
Mixteca-Puebla style
Late Postclassic period, AD 1300–1520, reassembled in modern times
Bone, stone, and shell
Cranium: H. 14.4 cm (5⅝"); W. 13.85 cm (5½");
D. 18.35 cm (7¼")
Mandible: H. 7.1 cm (2¾"); W. 12.4 cm (4⅞"); D. 10.1 cm (4")
PC.B.099

ACQUISITION HISTORY:
PC.B.097 and PC.B.098: Purchased from Helmut de Terra, 1960; reportedly from eastern Guerrero. PC.B.099: Purchased from Earl Stendahl, 1959; reportedly from the vicinity of Tilantongo, Oaxaca

BIBLIOGRAPHY:
PC.B.097: Dumbarton Oaks 1963: 26, cat. no. 125
PC.B.098: Dumbarton Oaks 1963: 26, cat. no. 126

Skull PC.B.099 was from a middle-aged adult, possibly male, perhaps 30–40 years old.[110] The skull was not intentionally reshaped when the individual was an infant, nor are there cut marks indicating defleshing prior to inlaying. Root marks are present in the mandible, but roots and dirt are not present in the skull's interior, probably because of thorough cleaning during its most recent treatment. Mandibular condyles are missing, but the mandible probably pertains to the cranium, based on the similar condition of upper and lower alveoli and matching curvature of the dental arch. The skull's interior is reinforced with a thick layer of epoxy resin. Breakage around the foramen magnum includes destruction of the left side of the occipital. The cranial vault has been largely reconstructed, and other portions of the skull are also reinforced.

The skull was acquired at an unknown date by Earl Stendahl, who said that it had been found near Tilantongo, Oaxaca. Stendahl subsequently obtained a small box with loose teeth and tesserae (see below), said to be part of the skull. In 1959 he sold the skull, teeth, and mosaic pieces to Robert Woods Bliss. Norman Wiener, hired to restore it, reported that the skull was damaged and that mosaics still present appeared to have been badly glued with clay to make it more salable (Wiener n.d.a). After removing the tesserae and reconstructing the skull, Wiener reassembled a mosaic decoration using the plaques that were originally associated with the skull as well as loose pieces that were mixed with those from the skulls PC.B.098 and PC.B.097 (Wiener n.d.a). The sorting of three different sets of tesserae (each for one of the skulls) appears to have been done on the basis of manufacturing details, color similarities, and differential degree of polishing. Comparing photographs of skull PC.B.099 before (Figure 50) and after (Plate 65) Wiener's restoration shows a significant difference in the overall pattern of inlays.

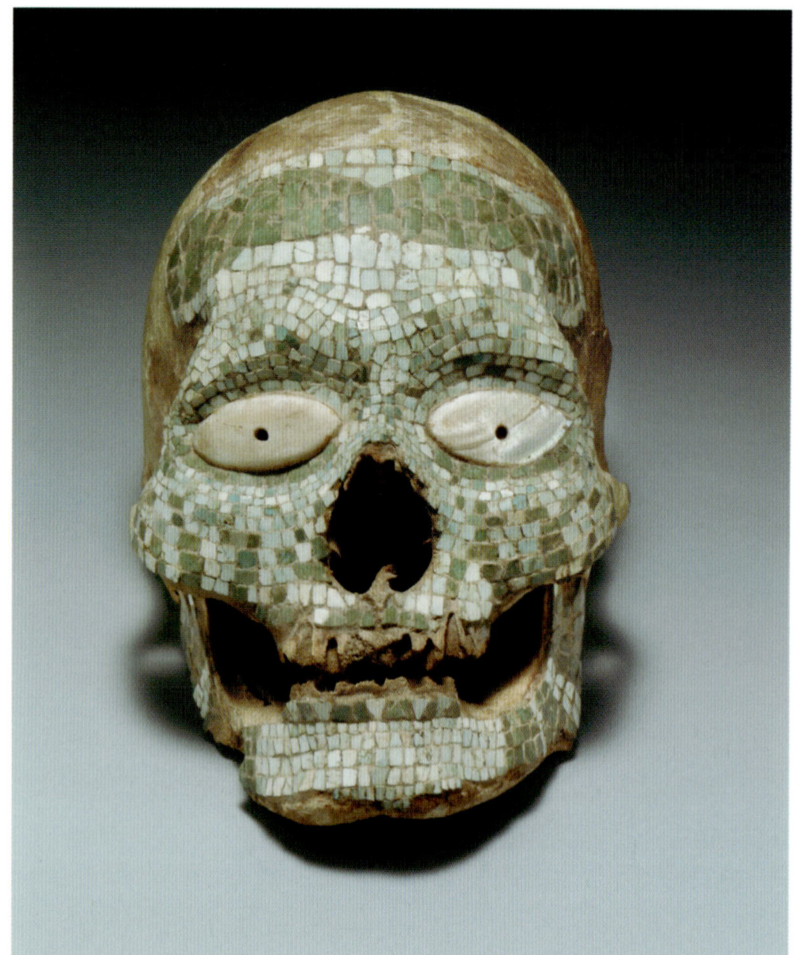

plate 65

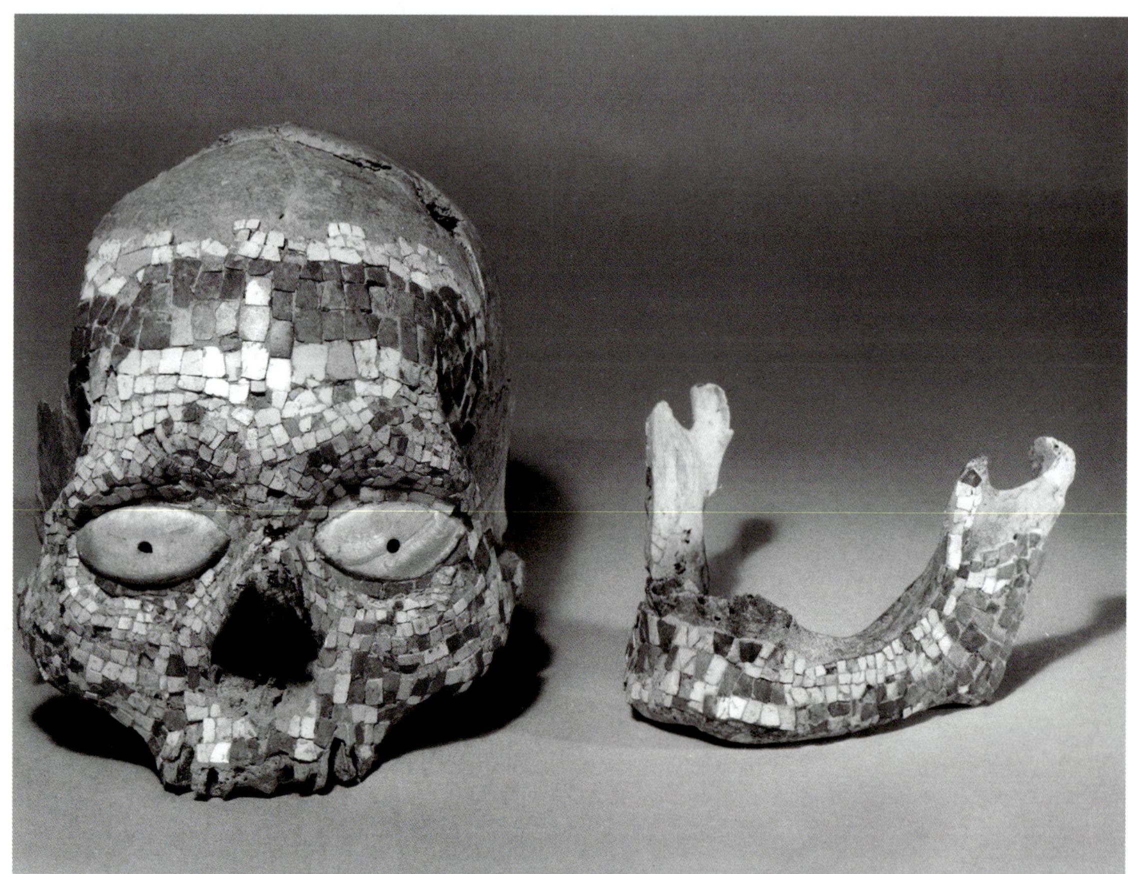

fig. 50
Skull PC.B.099
before Wiener's
1962 restoration.

Before Wiener's intervention the mosaic decoration on the skull covered the face and the mandible only, the latter being inlaid exclusively on the anterior surface. The right side of the mandibular body is now mended from breakage, and no inlays cover the repaired sections. The borders of the nasal aperture bear no evidence of internal decoration. Despite the lack of teeth, the undisturbed thin borders of the alveoli suggest that extant teeth were not covered with inlays.

Plaques of turquoise and pink shell were glued to the skull when purchased by Robert Woods Bliss. The mother-of-pearl eye inlays, unpolished, have small disk fillings to simulate the pupils—probably made of obsidian and 3.6 mm in diameter. The turquoise tesserae are polished polygons, varying in size and shape. Dark and light green colors predominate, with small pieces of turquoise blue. None of the plaques from the skull have become loose, precluding further observations as to the technique of manufacture, but some edges of affixed tesserae have straight cuts. Others appear chipped, a condition suggesting pressure snapping in the process of manufacture. Affixing the plaques, Wiener left narrow spaces between them that were filled with the supporting substance, and the placement of the plaques over the bone surface is uneven. These characteristics are not evident in the workmanship seen in other known inlaid skulls.[111] It is unclear how Wiener came to conclude that the skull's decoration in the forehead included a motif of a twisted double strand.

Robert Woods Bliss purchased skulls PC.B.098 and PC.B.097 in 1960 from Helmut de Terra. Skull PC.B.098 apparently belonged to a middle-aged adult, possibly a woman, between 30 and 40 years old at the time of death.[112] The skull is broad and seems to have been subjected to intentional reshaping, but irregular flattening is perceptible only on the occipital bone. Reshaping caused the formation of a noticeable bun at the bregma (Figure 51). The lack of visible cut marks implies that no defleshing preceded its decoration.

Except for some evidence of soil inside the right mental foramen, the skull is now thoroughly clean, but rodent damage is perceptible at the opening on the left side of the foramen magnum. Root marks are present on the cranium's external surface and on the mandible. There is no

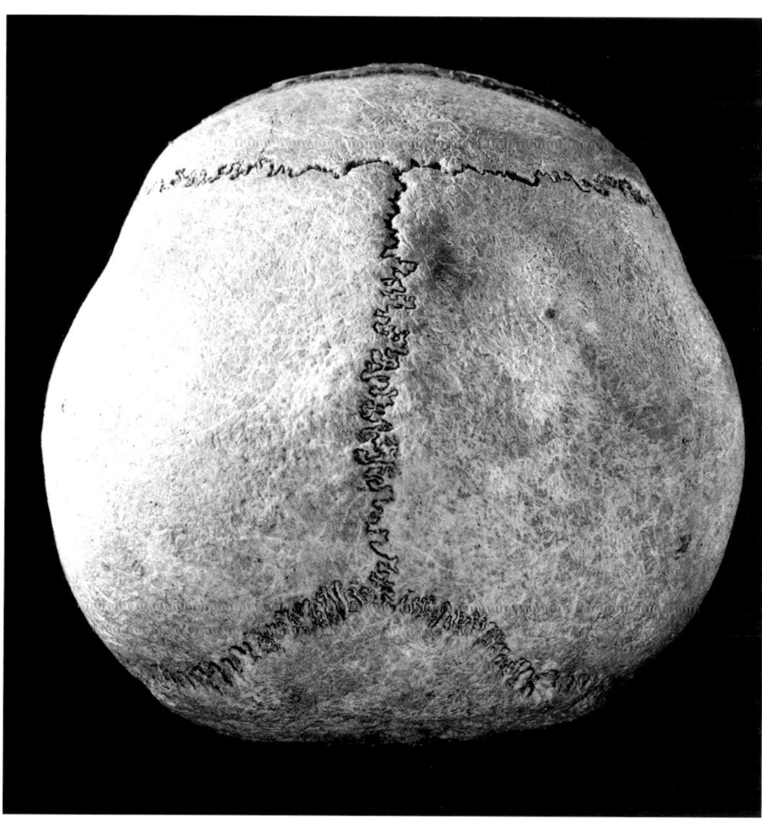

fig. 51
Detail of skull PC.B.098 showing flattening of the occipital bone and bun at the skull's bregma.

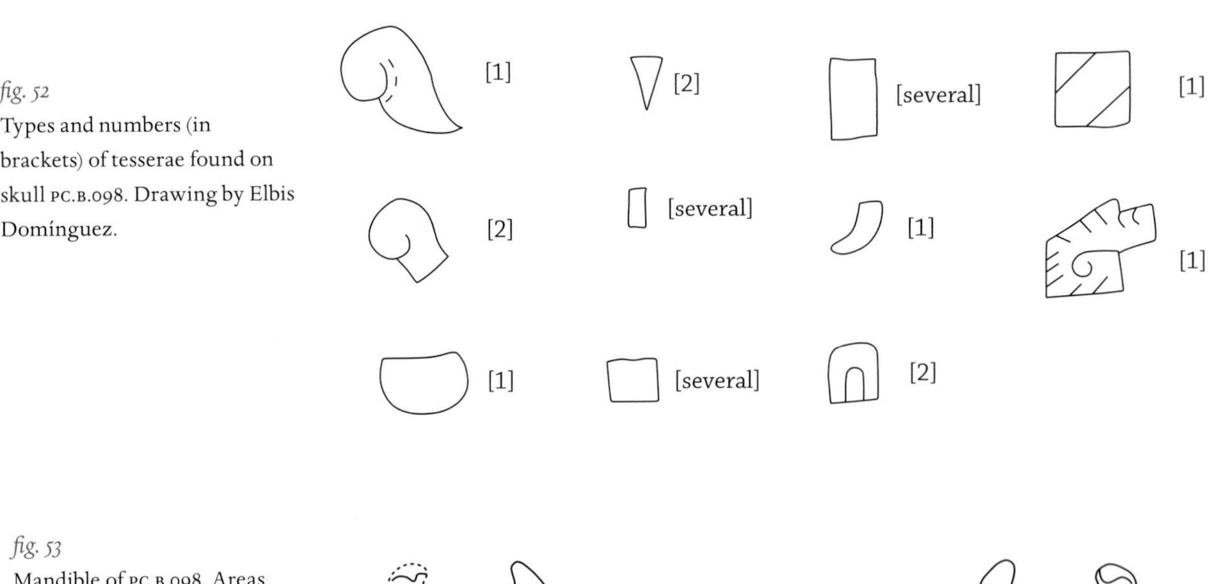

fig. 52
Types and numbers (in brackets) of tesserae found on skull PC.B.098. Drawing by Elbis Domínguez.

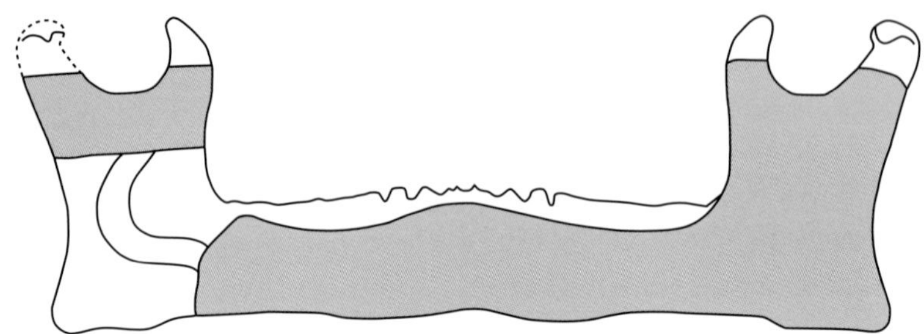

fig. 53
Mandible of PC.B.098. Areas with extant mosaic decoration are shown in gray; two painted parallel curved lines on the exterior surface of the right ascending ramus are visible where the mosaic decoration fell off. Drawing by Elbis Domínguez.

evidence that the nasal cavity's interior was decorated. Glued tesserae were polished and vary in size and color. Dark and light blue and green colors are present, but turquoise-blue predominates. Several large plaques on the mandible have special, irregular forms and/or incisions (Figure 52). These tesserae are undoubtedly of Pre-Columbian origin, but evidently not enough of the original pieces were present for Wiener to create a meaningful pattern. Where the restored mosaic has fallen away from the right side of the jaw, the bone surface bears two parallel black lines in a curvilinear pattern, and the ventral surface has a band of darker color (Figure 53). Because of the mandible's present condition, these markings cannot be fully assessed, but they probably originated from Wiener's restoration.

On the skull's forehead Wiener assembled a rectangular pattern of contrasting turquoise plaques with tesserae of pink shell. The first row above the eyebrow, of shell, is made from thicker plaques. The adhesive under the mosaic varies in color and texture, probably from differences in gluing material used by the restorer, because they coincide with the rows of differently sized plaques. The round eye inlays differ in color and texture: the right one appears to be from a thin animal bone, whereas the left one may be shell. The pupil on the latter is a circular plaque of black color, possibly smoked quartz rather than obsidian. The eye inlay without pupil filling has a straight perforation measuring 7.6 mm in diameter. In contrast, the pupil on the left eye is only 3.9 mm in diameter.

Skull PC.B.097 appears to have been from a young adult, possibly female, probably between 24 and 28 years old at the time of death.[113] Cranial remodeling, similar to the less-pronounced remodeling of skull PC.B.098, is of the tabular erect type and led to a broadening of the skull. The skull is fairly complete except for a broken portion around the foramen magnum as well as the posterior portion of the right parietal bone. The cranium's external surface has many root marks, more than on skulls PC.B.098 and PC.B.099; they are close to the mosaic-covered area and probably continue beneath it. The scalloped and pointed shape of the tooth (Figure 54), attained by the process of filing the edges of the crown (type C7), has been widely documented in other Mesoamerican burials that span from ca. 300 BC to the early colonial period (Romero 1986: table 5). In the center of its labial surface, the tooth had a now-missing inlay, but the perforation (about 3 mm in diameter) has traces of a residue, perhaps remnants of adhesive. The combination of the C7 type of filing and the incrustation (type G15) is known only from burials from the island of Jaina, off the coast of Campeche, dating to between AD 400 and 900 (Romero 1986: table 15). Dental embellishment frequently involved other teeth, but this pattern of modification has not been documented for PC.B.097, and the decorated tooth's size suggests that it does not belong to this skull.[114]

Two boxes of loose teeth (both labeled PC.B.813C) are part of the collection. One contains 18 incisors from at least six children, 16 incisors from at least four adults, nine canines from at least six adults, eight lower premolars from at least six individuals, seven upper premolars from at least five individuals, and four molars from at least three individuals (one is peg shaped), and an incisor from a small mammal, larger than a mouse or a rat. The second box contains five adult central incisors from at least four individuals. Four, from at least three individuals, had small circular incrustations embedded on the labial surfaces. The three inlays include two of green stone and one of pyrite. Six other adult teeth were very worn.

Skull PC.B.098 was stored with a bag containing several small laminated fragments of a black material, gilded on both sides, possibly part of the item that was hafted to the distal end of the jadeite handle PC.B.094 (Plate 60). The presence of these mosaic pieces suggests that the skulls and the teeth, tesserae, and serpent handle hafted with a perishable gilded material came from the same archaeological deposit. These pieces were also associated with a thin prismatic turquoise tessera with several polished planes on one side and a rugged, untreated texture on the other (Figure 55). Another mosaic fragment has a small stony pearl attached to it. Some of the loose pieces had slightly beveled edges, which coincides with observations made by Caso (1969: 64) on the tesserae that decorate the skull from Tomb 7 at Monte Albán.

The available evidence indicates that, considered separately, the three skulls and the associated mosaic pieces are of Pre-Columbian origin. However, their integration as decorated items is questionable. Compared to two known decorated skulls with known proveniences (from the main cenote at Chichén Itzá [Moholy-Nagy and Ladd 1992: 132–140] and from Tomb 7 at Monte Albán [Caso 1969: 62–69]), the Dumbarton Oaks examples show important differences.

First, the Chichén Itzá and Monte Albán skulls were cut away at the top of the cranial vault.[115] Then the base and other openings of both skulls were sealed. Mandibles in both skulls were kept articulated, although that in the skull of Tomb 7 belongs to a different individual.

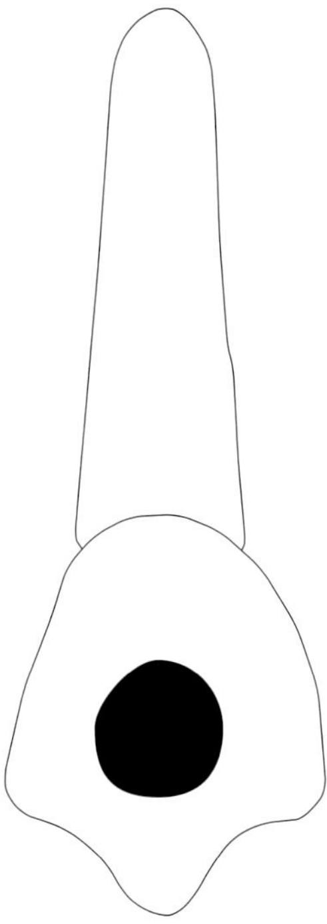

fig. 54
Filled and formerly inlaid central incisor glued to skull PC.B.097. Drawing by Elbis Domínguez.

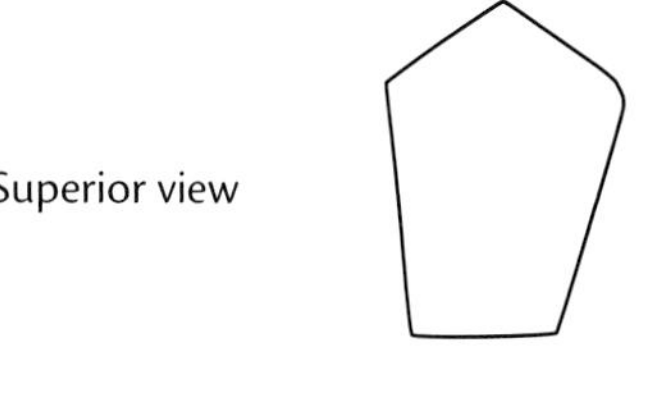

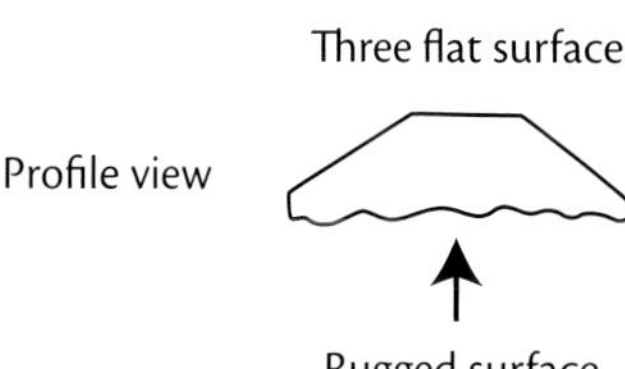

fig. 55
Prismatic tessera found in a bag accompanying skull PC.B.098. Drawing by Elbis Domínguez.

Possible cut marks on the Chichén Itzá skull may indicate defleshing prior to decoration. There are no conclusive data as to whether the two skulls were defleshed prior to decoration. In contrast, the root marks on the three Bliss Collection skulls imply decoration once the bones were dry. The Monte Albán and Chichén Itzá skulls have circular eye inlays, whereas the eye inlays in skulls PC.B.099 and PC.B.097 are elliptical, more common in wooden faces with mosaics, which have been recovered archaeologically.[116] Other observations that support an argument against the authenticity of the decoration on the skulls at Dumbarton Oaks pertain to the area covered by decoration,[117] to inconsistencies in material and size for eye inlays in skull PC.B.098, and PC.B.097's decorated tooth that belonged to another individual.

To account for all the incongruities exhibited by skulls PC.B.097, PC.B.098, and PC.B.099 requires drawing on our present knowledge of the formation processes and taphonomy of funerary deposits in southwestern Mesoamerica. A possible scenario would involve the accidental discovery of at least one rich funerary deposit in a cave or a masonry tomb somewhere in Oaxaca, Puebla, or Guerrero that contained the remains of several individuals. This deposit would have also included an offering with at least four inlaid wooden faces (two sets with elliptical eye inlays and two sets with circular eye inlays) and a disk with a mosaic composition similar to those found in Tomb 1 at Zaachila (Gallegos 1978) and in Cueva Cheve (González Licón and Márquez Morfín 1994; Steele and Snavely 1997). This scenario would account for the fine roots growing into the deposit and the state of decay of the inlaid objects, with loose tesserae and inlays. Materials retrieved included the skulls of at least four individuals, the teeth of many more (assuming all the loose teeth have the same origin), and partially collected scattered tesserae from inlaid objects.

These materials were assembled into mosaic-covered skulls, appearing on the antiquities market at the same time. Earl Stendahl acquired one, Helmut de Terra purchased two, and both sold the skulls to Robert Woods Bliss in 1959 and 1960. A fourth skull was offered to Bliss at the same time, but he declined it. Norman Wiener, the restorer of the three skulls in the Bliss Collection, told Bliss that the fourth skull's authenticity was questionable, because the mosaic work had been applied with Duco cement (Wiener n.d.b). With regard to skull PC.B.099, Wiener also had commented that it "had been badly damaged either before or at the time of excavation. The skull had been badly glued together and many mosaics reset with clay apparently to make it more salable" (Wiener n.d.a).[118]

Diego de Landa provides a tantalizing account that may hint at the origin and function of some decorated skulls in Mesoamerica:

> In antiquity, they cut the heads of the Cocom lords when they died, and once boiled, they defleshed them, sawing half of the skull at the top and leaving intact the face with the mandible and teeth. To these half "skulls" they supplied what was missing in flesh with a certain resin, and they sculpted it very faithfully as the original face, and they kept [the decorated skulls] with the wooden statues [containing the cremated remains of ancestors], all of which they displayed in the domestic altars, together with their idols, in great reverence and subservience; and on every festive occasion they offer them food so that they will not be in need of anything. (Landa 1959 [1566]: 59–60; translation by the author)

Mosaic-decorated skulls like the one found in Tomb 7 at Monte Albán (which, except for the lack of resin mimicking the physiognomy of a dead person, has modifications similar to those described by Landa) were most likely used as resonance chambers. Together with grooved human and deer bones, they were used as percussion instruments to produce a distinctive sound during the funerals of warriors, much like the exemplar painted on page 24 of the Codex Vindobonensis (Anders et al. 1992b; Beyer 1969b).

Other decorated skulls, seemingly decorated along the top of the vault, may have been used as ancestral symbols to validate the transgenerational transfer of rights and privileges. One Zapotec genealogical record from ca. AD 900 depicts the handling of one such heirloom skull during an important ritual centered on a child who is later enthroned in the same monument (see Urcid 1999: 242, fig. 8).

JU

STONE VESSELS

Stone vessels are the legacy of an old and enduring lapidary tradition in Mesoamerica. These containers were undoubtedly commissioned and used by elites, but their functions remain unknown. Those with known contexts served as accoutrements for the afterlife or were offerings in building dedications (Sáenz 1963: 13; Valenzuela 1945: fig. 40). Yet stone vessels probably had other uses before final deposition in those contexts. Manufacture of vessels from relatively soft stony materials of diverse geological origins and chemical compositions, such as alabaster, marble, onyx, and travertine, took place in several parts of Mesoamerica by the first century BC if not earlier (Easby and Scott 1970: no. 51; Luke et al. 2003; Woodbury 1965: 168). This lapidary tradition continued through the Spanish conquest and into the present. Its wide geographic and temporal dimensions in pre-Hispanic times can be outlined by considering the sources of raw materials, the presence of containers, manufacturing debitage, and the occurrence of tools that must have been used to produce the vessels (Figure 56).[119]

Considering the diverse geological origins of alabaster (salt deposits), marble (metamorphic rock), onyx (igneous rock), and travertine (calcite deposits) in the tectonic plates underlying Mesoamerica, one would expect a fair number of sources of raw material. Three sources of marble are known from the Ulúa Valley (Luke 2003). Travertine, a form of massive calcium carbonate ($CaCO_3$) has many sources resulting from deposition by springs or rivers, yet only a few are reported, including those near Tula (Castillo 1970: 49), Tecali (Jiménez Salas et al. 2000), and Miahuatepec in southern Puebla; Xicotlan and Chila in northwestern Oaxaca (Cook de Leonard 1971: 210); and Zinacantan, Chiapas (Berlin 1946: 27).

Examples of unfinished stone vessels provide insights into manufacturing procedures (Castillo 1970; Saville 1900; Von Winning 1986b). Raw material was extracted from its matrix by cutting a block with strings (Figure 57). The next step involved finishing the exterior features, regardless of whether the vessels were plain or decorated.[120] This step required techniques such as cutting, drilling, grinding, chiseling, pecking, and

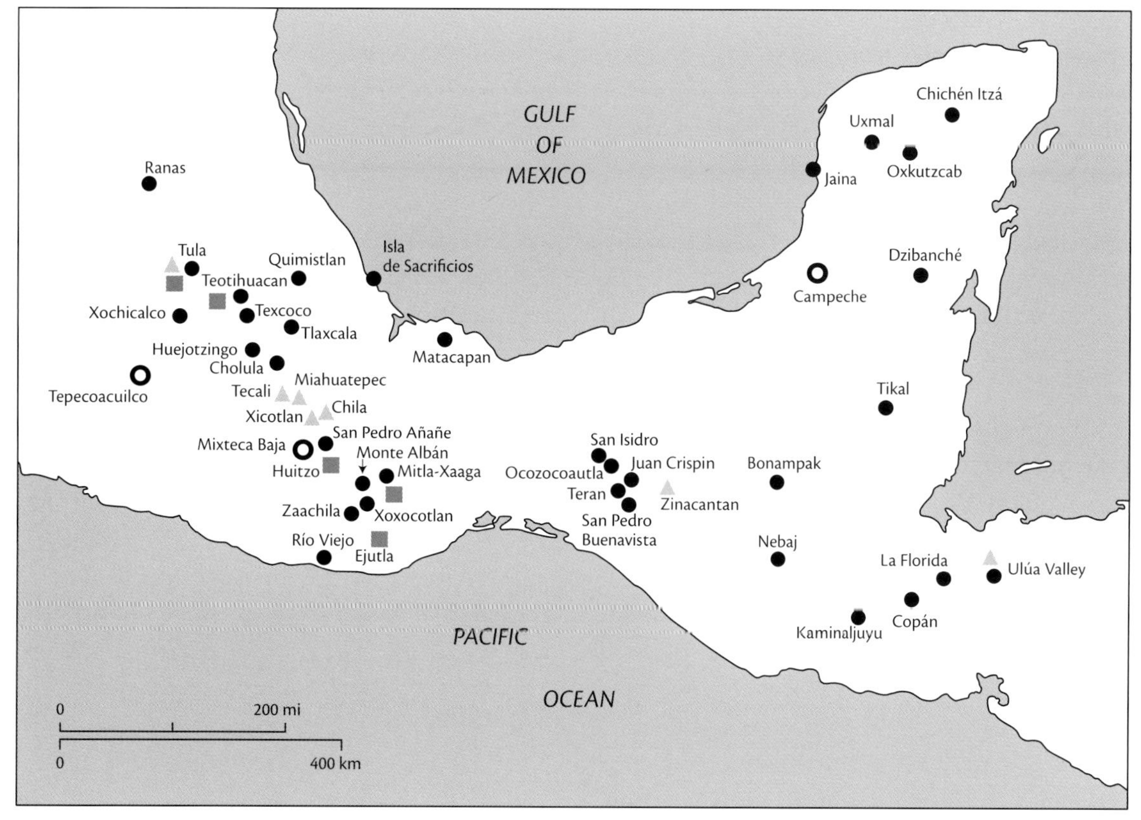

fig. 56
Map of Mesoamerica showing locations where travertine and marble sources (light gray triangles), vessels from specific sites (solid dots), vessels with regional provenience only (hollow circles), and tubular debitage (dark gray squares) have been found. Drawing by Elbis Domínguez.

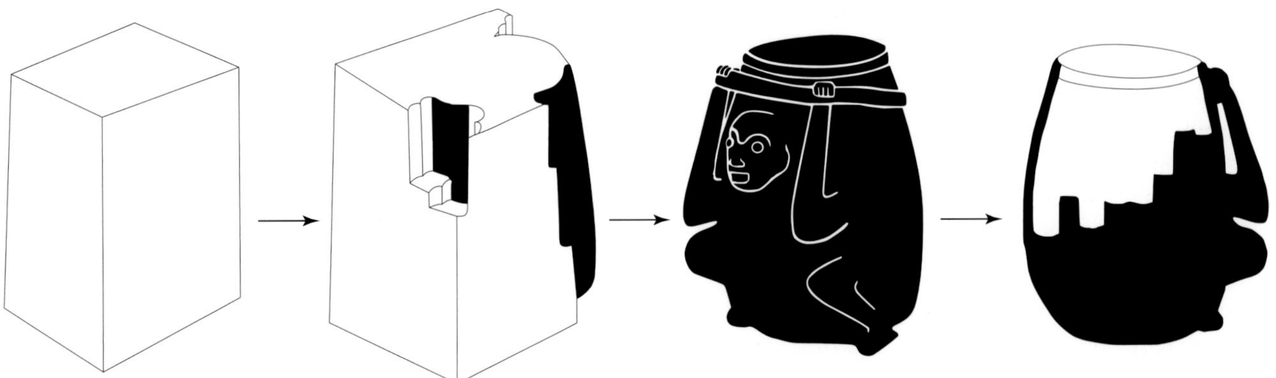

fig. 57
Main steps in the manufacture of a travertine effigy vessel. Drawing by Elbis Domínguez.

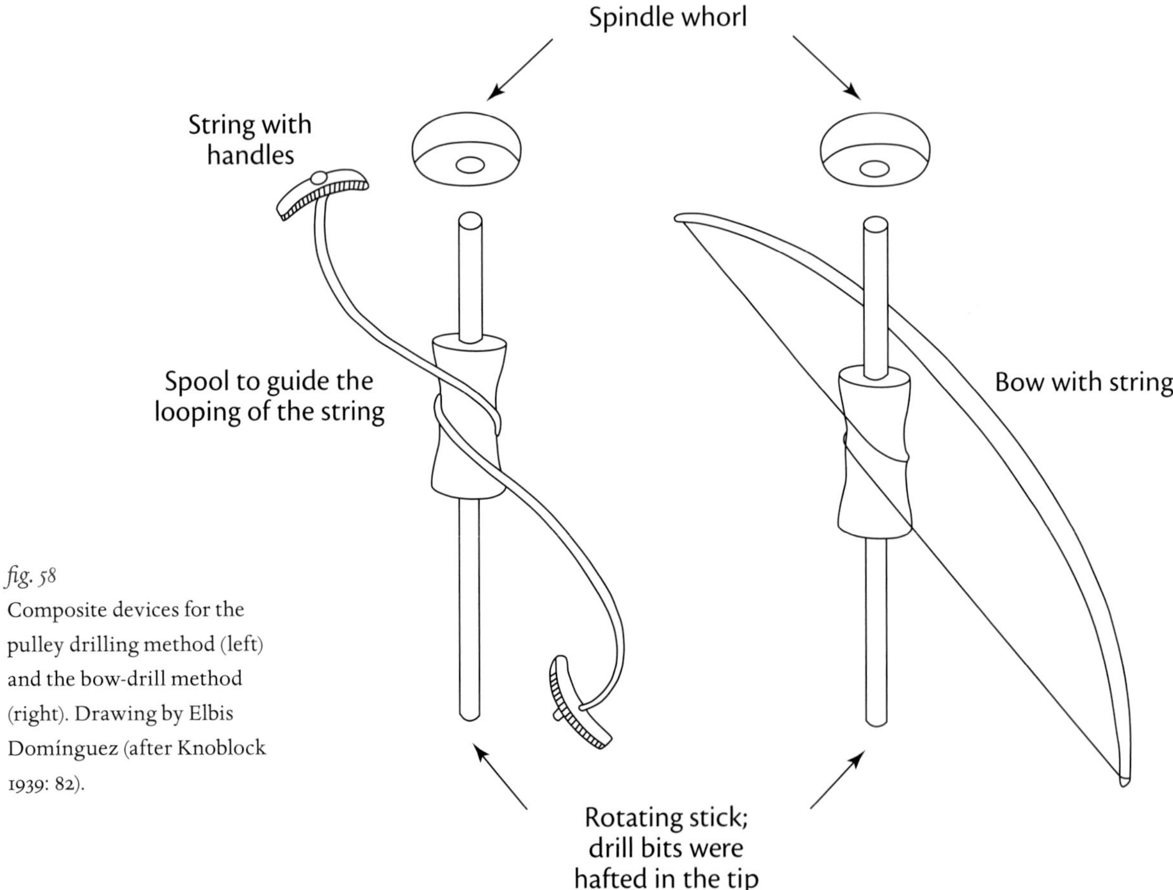

fig. 58
Composite devices for the pulley drilling method (left) and the bow-drill method (right). Drawing by Elbis Domínguez (after Knoblock 1939: 82).

polishing. Once the exterior was completed, the artisans carved out the vessels with tubular hollow drill bits made from animal long bones and reeds (Holmes 1897: 304–309; Saville 1900: 106), or perhaps with solid bits made of hard wood.

Although no tool kit has ever been found or reported, ethnographic accounts of drilling technologies among other native peoples of the Americas, such as the Inuit (see Fitzhugh and Kaplan 1982: 169, 254), suggest that the pulley and the bow-drill methods may have been used to manufacture these vessels. The bow-drill permits an artisan to work alone, as it frees one hand from the task of powering the rotation of the drill to control the point of contact between the drill bit and the object being manufactured. The pulley method requires a mouthpiece to gain such control indirectly (Figure 58).

These drilling technologies, used skillfully and assisted by abrasives, permitted relatively fast progress in the extraction of raw material to form the vessel's interior. Water was probably not added to the abrasive medium, as it softens reed drill bits (Knoblock 1939: 99). Finishing involved chiseling, pecking, grinding, smoothing, and polishing the scars left by the drilling. Another form of evidence of this process is drilling debitage from hollowing the receptacles or from sculpting exterior features. Short cylindrical cores generated by tubular hollow bits have been found at Teotihuacan (Turner 1992: 100, 102, fig. 9), Mitla (Flannery and Marcus 1983: 300), Xaaga, Huitzo, Ejutla (proveniences of cores in the ex-Museo Frissell in Mitla), and Tula (Diehl and Stroh 1978).[121] Their dimensions approximate those of the shallow marks in the unfinished vessels.

The actual hollow tubular drill bits of bone are less-direct evidence for the manufacture of stone vessels. Brawbehl, the Late Preclassic (200 BC–AD 200) component of Yegüi, near Tlacolula, Oaxaca, yielded one that measured 3.57 cm long and 1.64 cm in diameter. Although not in a primary context, two bone objects that appear to be parts of a drilling kit were recovered in excavations there. These were a flat thin disk of bone with a perforation in the center and a tubular hollow portion of a long bone from a medium to large mammal. The former could have been the spindle whorl; the latter bears all the marks expected of a drill bit. One end has a clean cut and walls of uniform thickness; the other has an uneven rim with walls of varied thickness. Around its external surface are circular striations perpendicular to the long axis of the bone, suggesting rotation and the use of an abrasive (Figure 59). The length and diameter of this bone drill bit falls within the range of the drilling scars left in unfinished vessels.[122]

Stone vessels are decorated in diverse regional and local styles (Figure 60). Because sourcing methods are only available for marble (Luke 2003), and assessments of the chemical signature of travertine or alabaster for sourcing purposes remain to be developed or applied, production locales may be discernable only by matching

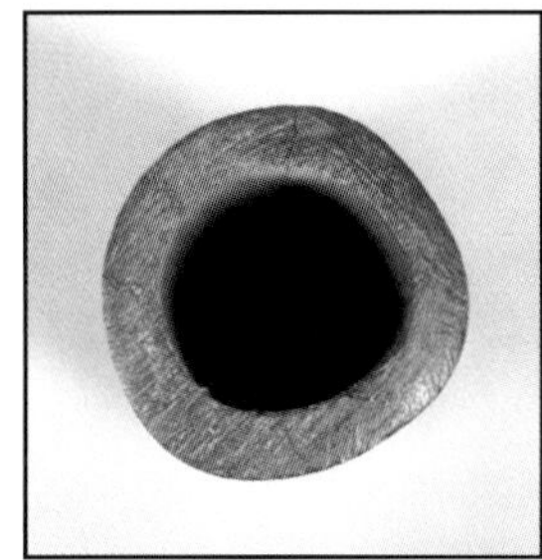

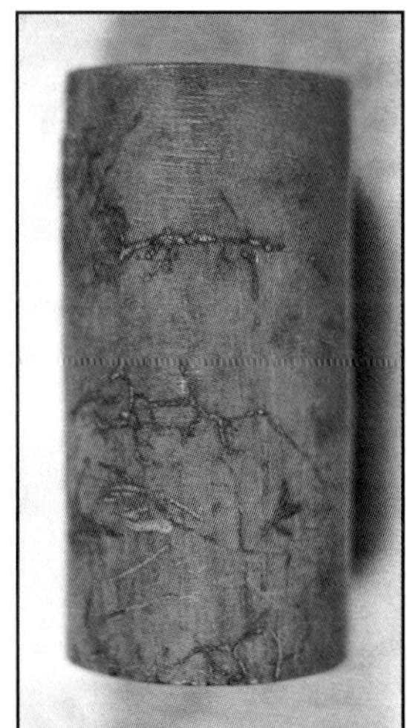

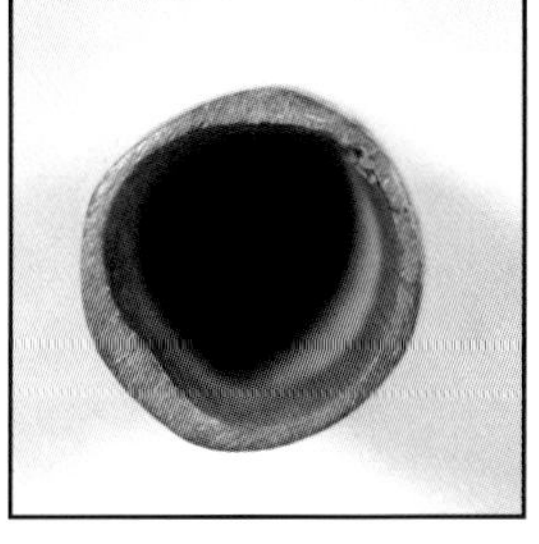

fig. 59
Bone drill bit from Brawbehl, Oaxaca. Photographs by Javier Urcid.

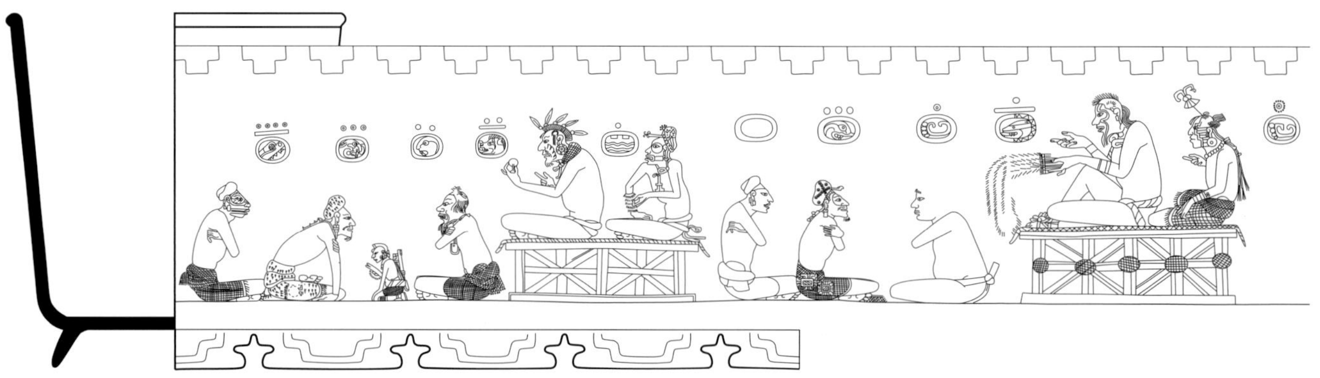

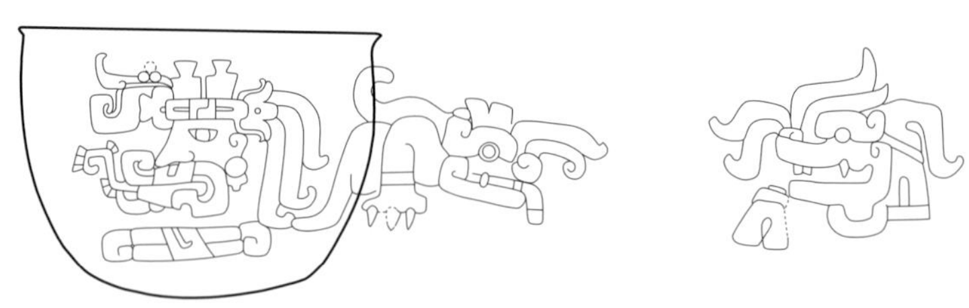

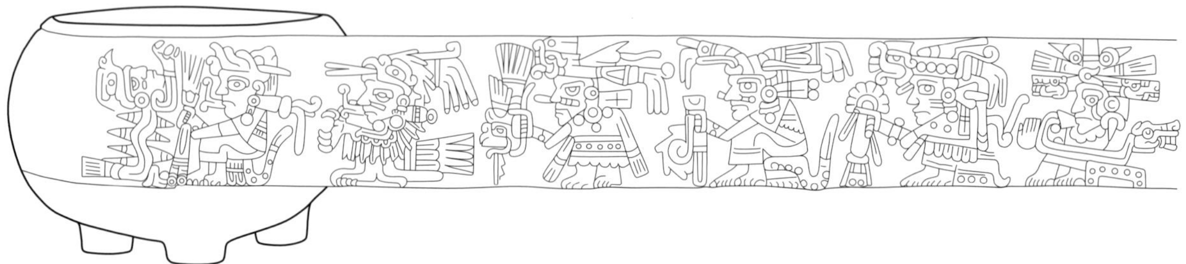

fig. 60

Decorations on incised travertine vessels. Top: vase with slab supports incised in a style of the Maya Lowlands and glyphs in the Central Mexican scribal tradition, unknown provenience, ca. AD 700. Center: semi-hemispherical bowl with Ñuiñe-style inscriptions, unknown provenience, now in the ex-Museo Frissell, Mitla (cat. no. 4046). Bottom: tripod hemispherical bowl incised in the Late Postclassic interregional style, unknown provenience, now in the Musée du quai Branly, Paris (cat. no. 71.1924.13.2062). Drawing by Elbis Domínguez (after Kerr n.d.a: no. K-319; Paddock 1966: 143, fig. 136; and Lehmann 1938: 291).

stone and ceramic vessel forms. For example, an unfinished barrel-shaped tripod vessel carved with Zapotec-style glyphs has counterparts in the ceramic vessel assemblage of the Pitao (AD 350–550), Peche (AD 550–650), and Xoo phases (AD 650–850) (Figure 61). This method of determining provenience has limited applicability when similar vessel forms are widespread. Approximate locales where vessels manufactured somewhere else were enhanced by incising, carving, or painting imagery in local systems of visual communication can also be discerned on the basis of iconographic and epigraphic analysis.[123]

A complex network connecting production loci, modifying localities, and interregional distribution can be modeled by the finite and differential distribution of the raw material and the variability in vessel shapes and decorations (Figure 62). By this network, a vessel found at Chichén Itzá (locality A) could have been carried from a place

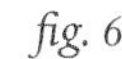

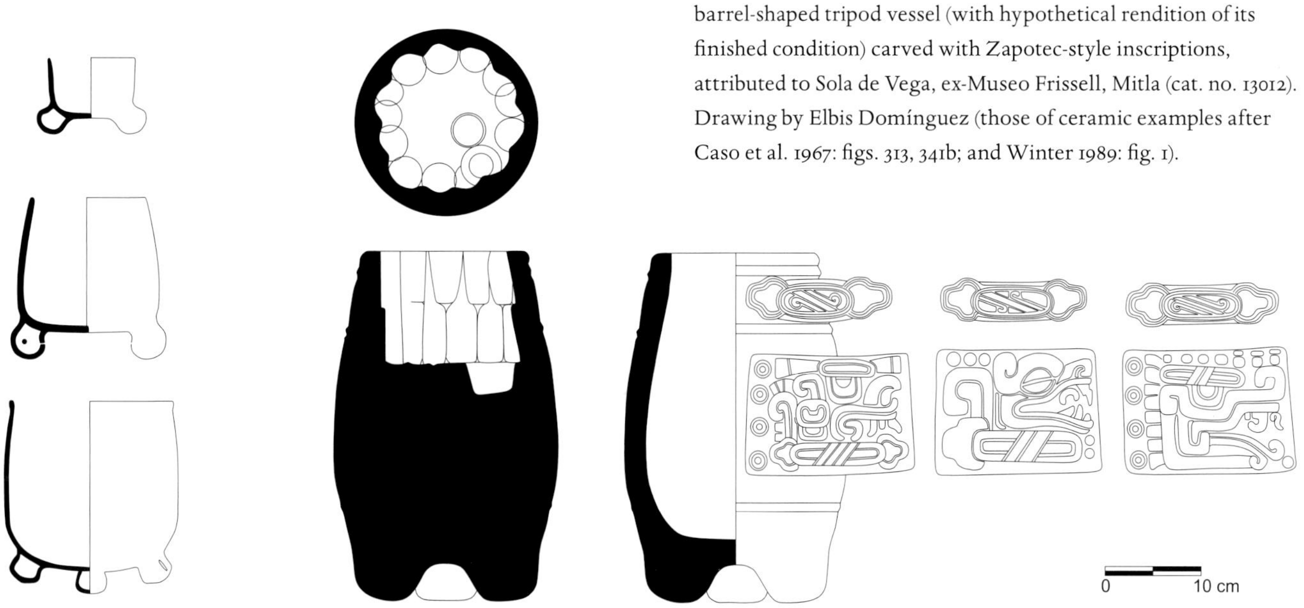

fig. 61
Similarities in shape between ceramic and travertine vessels. Left: barrel-shaped tripod vessels in the pottery assemblage of Monte Albán (AD 350–800). Center and right: unfinished travertine barrel-shaped tripod vessel (with hypothetical rendition of its finished condition) carved with Zapotec-style inscriptions, attributed to Sola de Vega, ex-Museo Frissell, Mitla (cat. no. 13012). Drawing by Elbis Domínguez (those of ceramic examples after Caso et al. 1967: figs. 313, 341b; and Winter 1989: fig. 1).

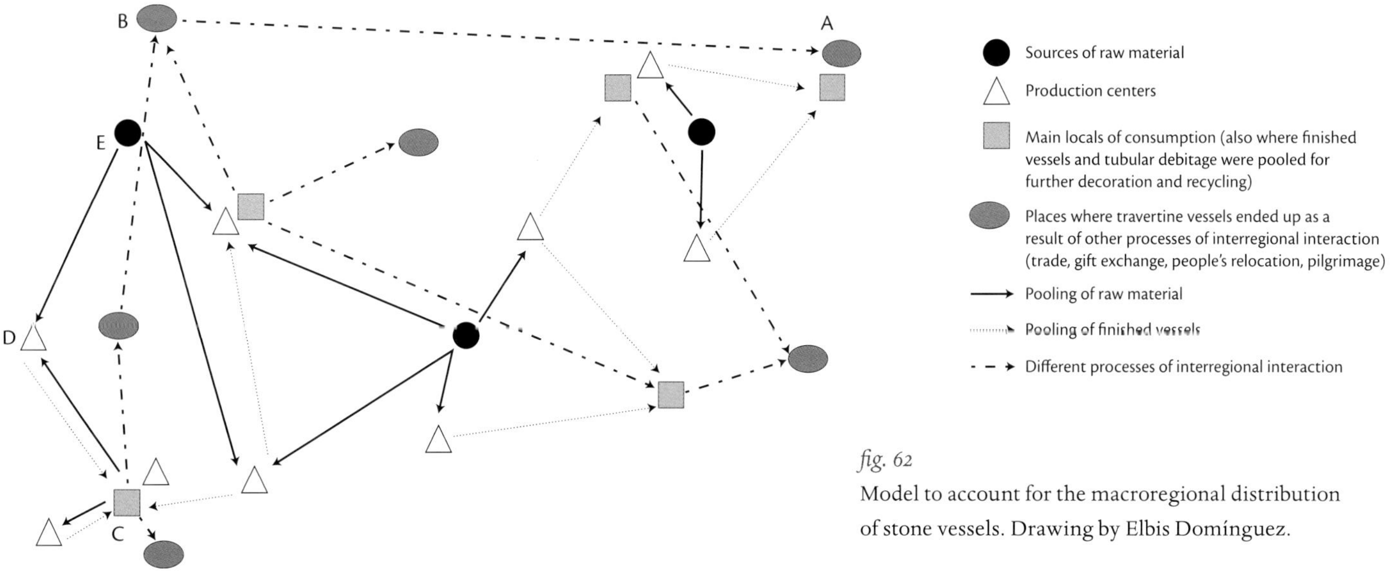

fig. 62
Model to account for the macroregional distribution of stone vessels. Drawing by Elbis Domínguez.

in central Veracruz (locality B) by pilgrims who commissioned its incising after purchasing it (or exchanging it) in northwestern Oaxaca (locality C). The vessel would have been made at a nearby place (locality D), which procured the raw material from southern Puebla (locality E).

The labor-intensive production of stone vessels and the high value of the raw material ensured the care of these items even after accidental breakage. Several examples had been restored by the crack-lacing method, which involved the perforation of small holes near broken edges to tie fragments together by means of thin strings. Such restorations may have also involved the use of resins as adhesives to fix fragments in place and to seal the interior surface. Such curation highlights the value of heirlooms in ancient Mesoamerica and the role they played for ancient peoples in imagining their own past.

JU

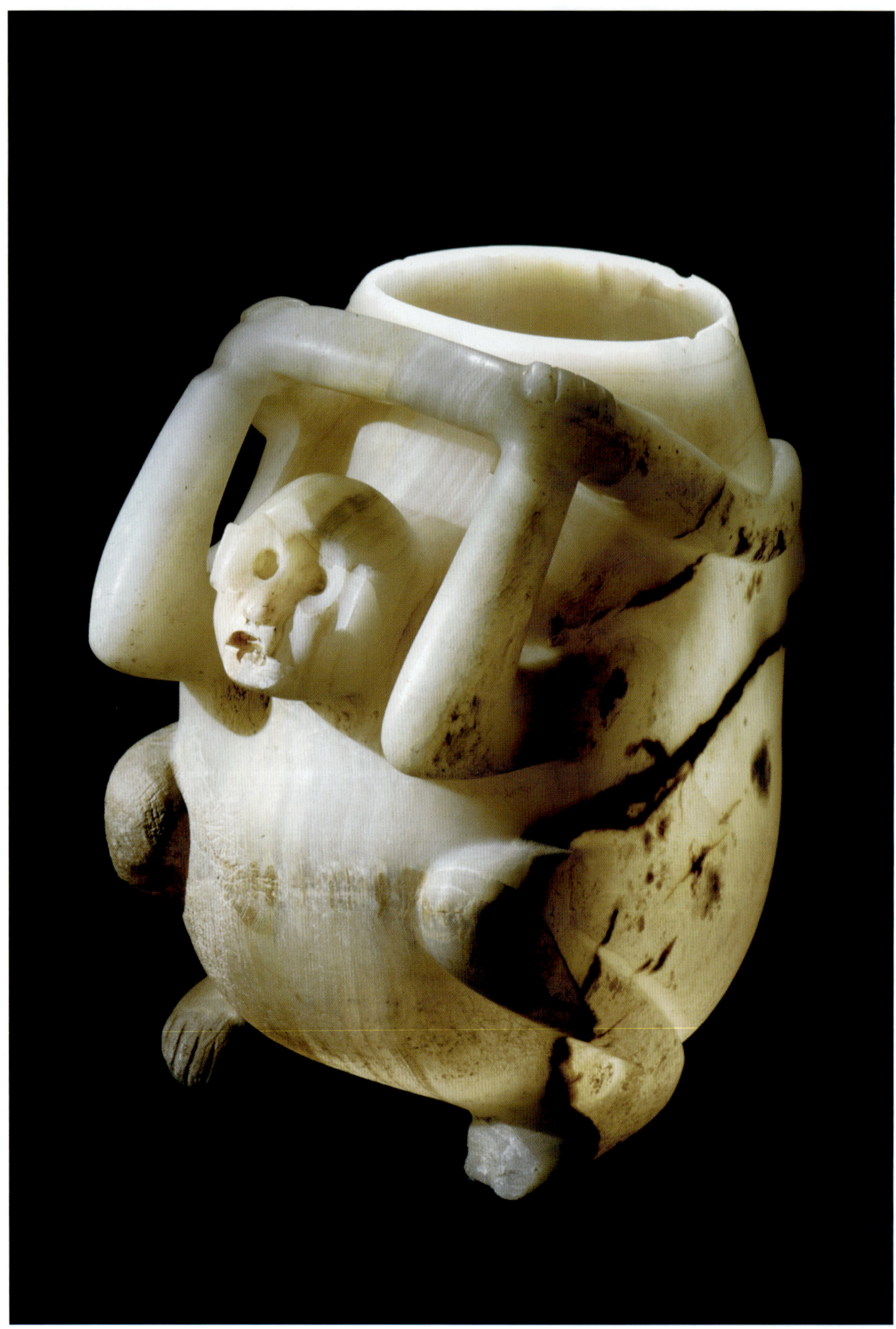

plate 66

STONE JAR IN THE SHAPE OF A MONKEY

PLATE 66
Late Postclassic period, AD 1300–1520
Travertine
H. 31.5 cm (12⅜"); W. 19.7 cm (7¾"); D. 30.4 cm (12")
PC.B.111

ACQUISITION HISTORY:
Purchased from Earl Stendahl, June 1941

EXHIBITION HISTORY:
Ancient American Art, Santa Barbara Museum of Art, Santa Barbara, Calif., April–June 1942; M. H. de Young Memorial Museum, San Francisco, July–August 1942; Museum of Art, Portland, Ore., September–October 1942; *Indigenous Art of the Americas*, National Gallery of Art, Washington, D.C., April 1947–July 1962 (NGA 54)

BIBLIOGRAPHY:
Santa Barbara Museum of Art 1942: cat. no. 29; Bliss 1947: 21, 100–101, cat. no. 96; Christensen 1955: 209, 244, fig. 200; Artes de Mexico 1957: pls. 9, 10; Bliss 1957: 246, cat. no. 74, pl. LI; Dumbarton Oaks 1963: 28, cat. no. 139; Davies 1983: fig. 36; Alcina Franch et al. 1992: 84, pl. XIII

This slightly oblong, barrel-shaped vessel has the form of a monkey in a squatting position with its arms above and behind the head, grasping its own tail that encircles the vessel (Figure 63). Only the portion of the tail on the anterior portion of the vessel is freestanding, having its points of origin placed laterally. The course of the tail around the superior portion of the vessel is carved in low relief. The length of the tail and its coiled end—a detail that reveals its prehensile nature—suggest that the animal represented in the vessel is a spider monkey. The posture of its hands is not clear. The fingers taper toward the posterior surface of the freestanding portion of the tail but are also rendered on the anterior surface, giving the impression that the visible portion of the hands is the palmar and not the dorsal side.

The head of the monkey sticks out from the wall of the vessel by a thick peg that mimics the neck. The hairless area surrounding the eyes of spider monkeys was reproduced with a beveled depression done with a thick solid drill bit. The eyes were then marked by means of two consecutive drilling episodes using solid bits of decreasing diameter. Such double perforation created a deep and uneven surface to enhance the sticking properties of an adhesive that must have held in place inlays simulating the eyes. Smaller perforations, 2.3 mm in diameter, produced the nostrils. Five others, ranging between 3.4 and 5.6 mm, probably facilitated the adherence of three upper and two lower inlaid teeth. Other facial features, like the ears and the forehead, appear to have been finished by grinding flat surfaces. The missing lower lip, however, must have broken some time after the vessel was finished, perhaps relatively recently.

Flexed knees and the feet protrude substantially from the body of the vessel. The left foot has been broken off. The right foot's four grooves define five toes. The plantar surfaces of the feet and of the tail provide a very shallow tripod support to the vessel. Except for some other chipping on the lip of the vessel, it is in good condition; its interior is quite smooth and does not exhibit any traces of the hollowing drill marks, having been thoroughly polished inside.

On the outer surface are several marks left by hollow tubular drill bits, particularly at

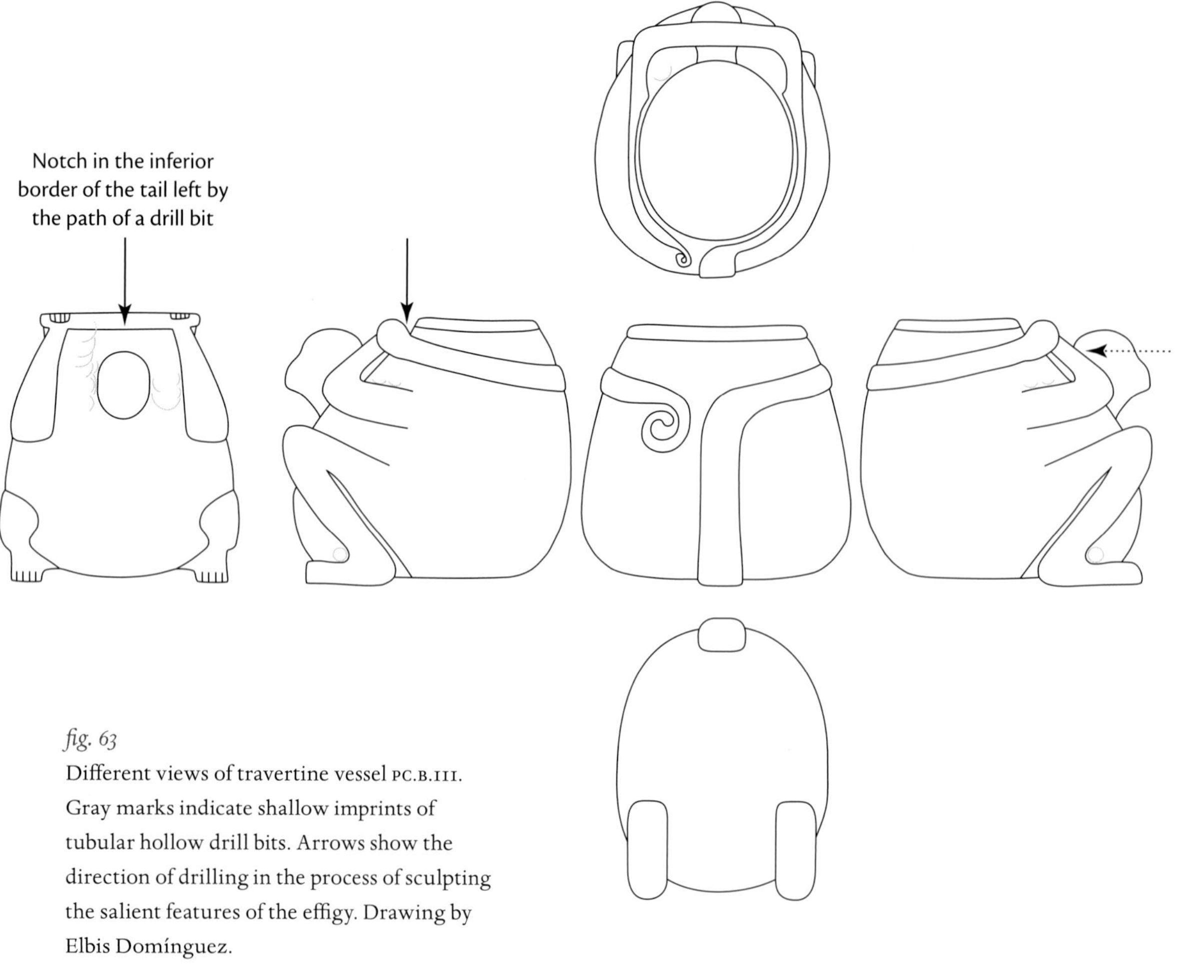

fig. 63
Different views of travertine vessel PC.B.111. Gray marks indicate shallow imprints of tubular hollow drill bits. Arrows show the direction of drilling in the process of sculpting the salient features of the effigy. Drawing by Elbis Domínguez.

certain interstices in the protruding portions of the monkey's effigy. Most of the marks are where the protruding head and rising arms with the tail-grasping hands were sculpted; others occur at the anterior juncture between the legs and the feet. The sides of the primate's face have depressions generated by the path of the drills as they perforated the effigy from the front. Along the inferior border of the protruding tail is another slight curved notch indicative of a drill bit's path as it aimed at extracting raw material from above the monkey's head. Drill bit marks also evidence an approach from above to hollow the head and the freestanding portion of the tail. The drilling marks that could be measured exhibit exterior diameters ranging between 1.51 and 1.90 cm. Such a thickness is fairly standardized, and the range probably reflects the process of thinning as the drill bits wore down. The few measurable interior diameters indicate that the wall thickness of the tubular drill bits varied between 1.8 and 6.0 mm. The maximum thickness suggests that the drills, if made of bone, probably originated from the femora of small mammals, as this anatomical element has the thickest layer of cortical bone in its shaft.

A fair number of monkey effigy vessels are known,[124] and these display interesting patterns and two major types: one of monkeys with their hands resting on their heads and knees, the other of primates that hold their own tails, as does PC.B.111. Both types were inlaid with obsidian, pyrite, or mother-of-pearl eyes. Some retain the adhesive substance for the inlays, and some

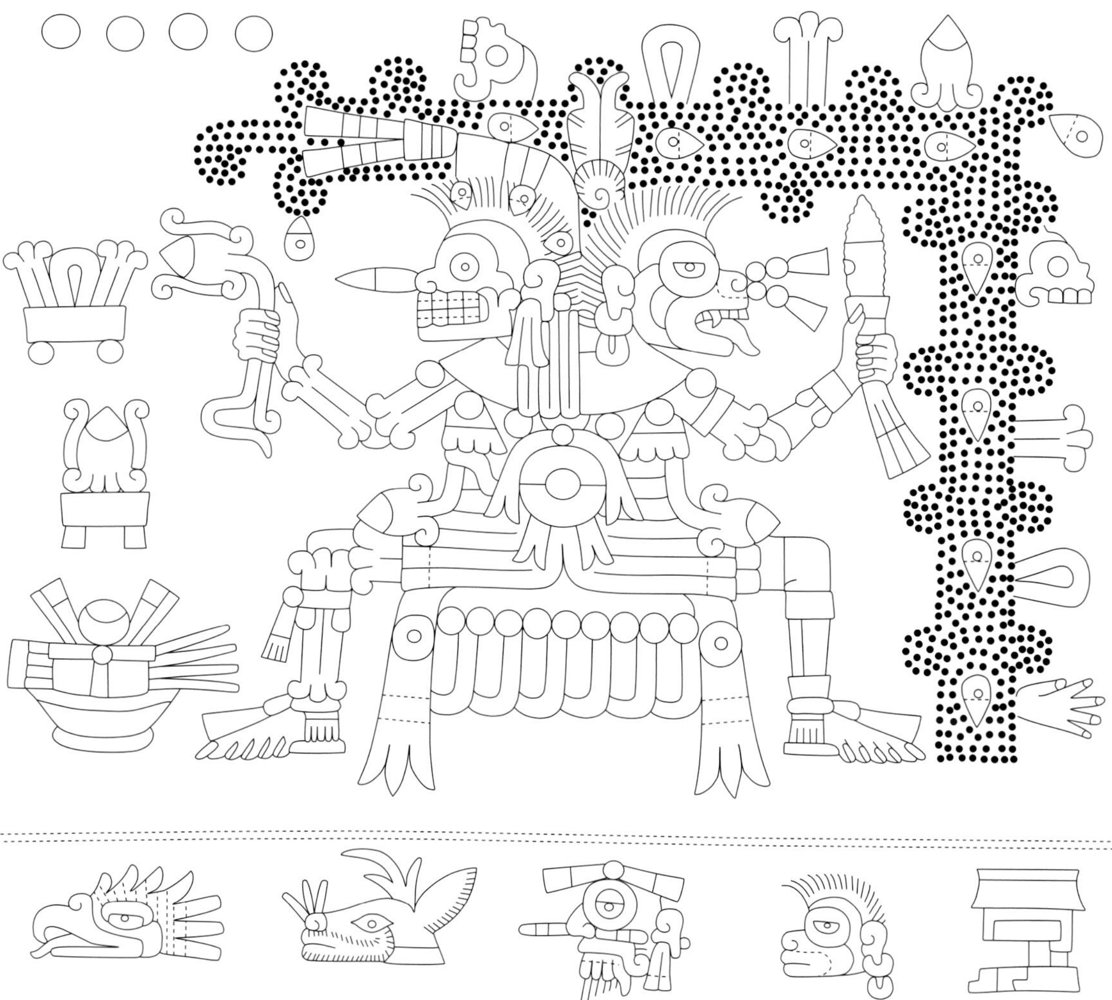

fig. 64
Possible eschatological implications of monkey imagery in the Codex Laud (page 14). Drawing by Elbis Domínguez (after Anders and Jansen 1994).

have shell inlay teeth. Cross-cutting both types based on the posture of the monkey is the representation of male genitalia. At least one has wrist bracelets indicated in low relief, and another has traces of red pigment. The other vessels range in height from 13 to 20 cm, making PC.B.111 the tallest and presumably the heaviest. Only one of these vessels has a reported funerary context, although it was unearthed without controlled excavations (Beyer 1969a).

The spider monkey's popularity as a subject on stone vessels may relate to the saga of a failed creation, in which monkeys featured importantly, before the advent of true humans, or perhaps it alludes to the playful character of the patron deities of artisans. The association with a human burial of the only vessel with reliable archaeological context, however, strengthens a still-unresolved symbolic relationship between death and the monkey. Such a link has been noted in codical studies: in the Maya Dresden Codex, the monkey is "invariably represented with death symbols" (Thompson 1939: 145), something equally applicable to such non-Maya books as the Codex Vienna or Codex Laud (Figure 64; Beyer 1965b).[125] The manufacture of vessels in the shape of a monkey using travertine may have had its source of inspiration in the much older production of similar forms in ceramics. The earliest well-dated ceramic examples were manufactured between 200 BC and AD 100 (Winter and Marcial 2004).

JU

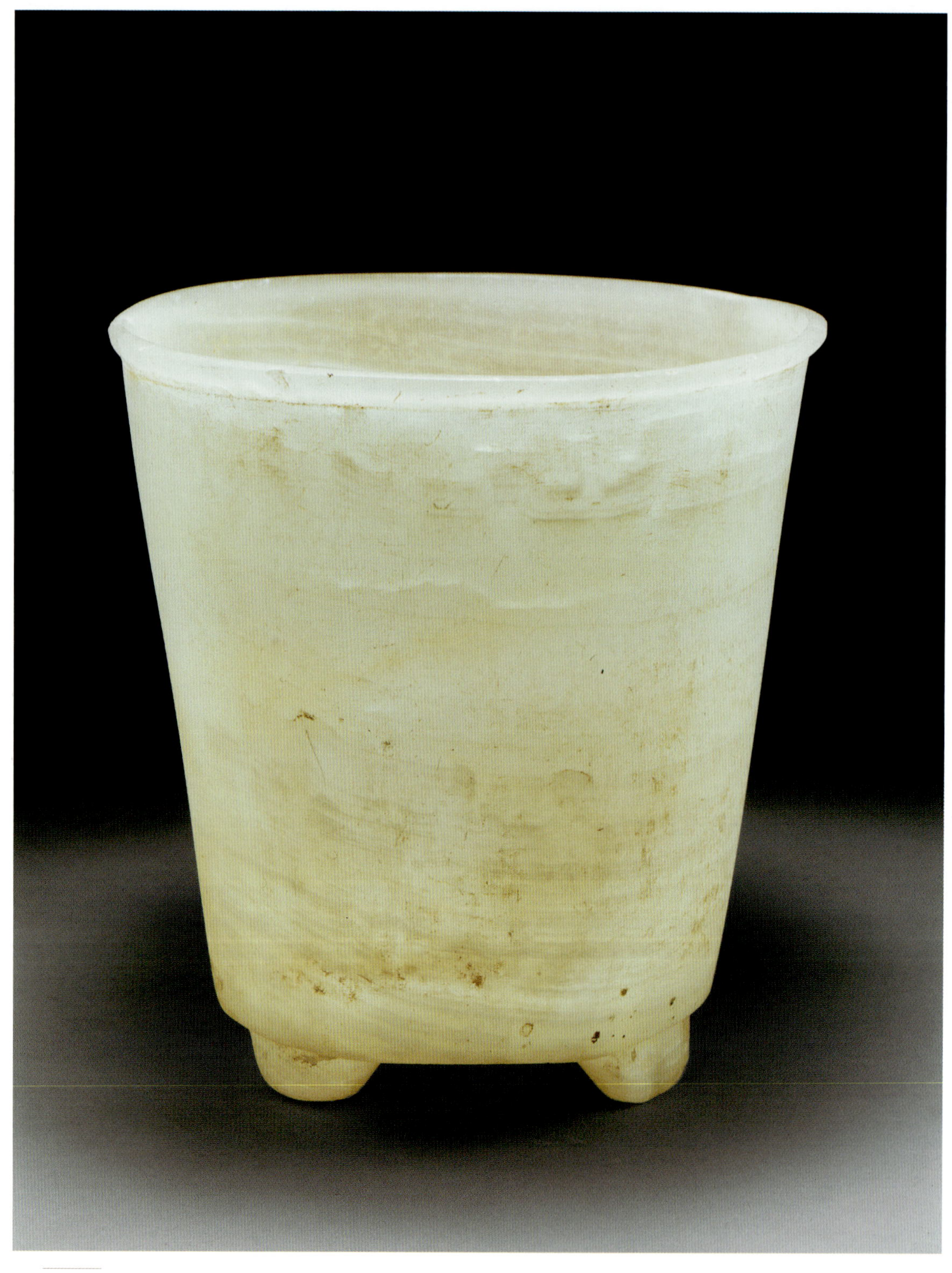

plate 67

PLATE 67
Late Classic or Early Postclassic period, AD 700–1000
Travertine
Vase: H. 23.2 cm (9⅛"); Max. Diam. 22.1 cm (8¾");
Min. Diam. 15.4 cm (6⅛")
Supports: H. 1.9 cm (¾")
PC.B.113

ACQUISITION HISTORY:
Purchased from Earl Stendahl

EXHIBITION HISTORY:
Indigenous Art of the Americas, National Gallery of Art, Washington, D.C., April 1947–May 1948; February 1954–July 1962 (NGA 234)

BIBLIOGRAPHY:
Bliss 1947: 21, 102, cat. no. 97; Bliss 1957: 246, cat. no. 75, pl. LII, top; Dumbarton Oaks 1963: 28, cat. no. 141

This travertine tripod vessel has straight, flaring walls and a thicker, slightly undulating rim. The tripod supports are short (less than 2 cm); one is circular, whereas the other two have a straight surface facing the lower edge of the container. This peculiarity most likely resulted from correcting the position of the supports; otherwise, part of their circumference would have been flush with the walls of the vessel (Figure 65, bottom). The correction allowed the supports to remain underneath the container. The walls of the vessel are thin, which gives the jar considerable translucency. Such a property demonstrates both the natural horizontal layering of travertine as well as the human-made vertical streaks generated by the hollowing out of the interior through the use of tubular hollow drill bits. The vessel was thoroughly ground, smoothed, and finished.

Although the container is attributed to Veracruz, a similar tripod vessel with straight flaring walls comes from the Late Classic Tomb 2 in Mound 1 at San Isidro, Chiapas (Lowe 1998: 40, 212). A close resemblance can also be established with a travertine vessel found at Xochicalco (see Sáenz 1963: pl. III), and to another one attributed to San Gerónimo, Guerrero (Cleveland Museum of Art n.d.: cat. no. 1990.252), except that these examples have stepped slab supports characteristic of the Classic period.

JU

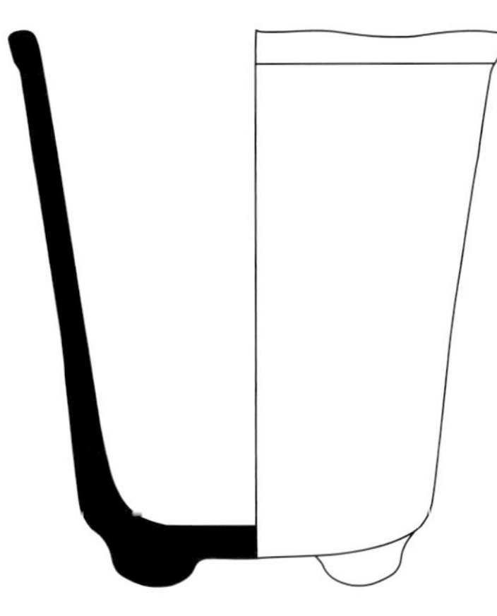

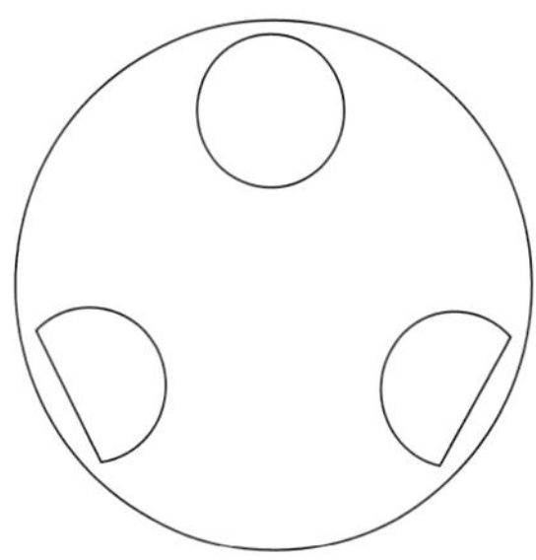

fig. 65
Features of travertine vase PC.B.113.
Drawing by Elbis Domínguez.

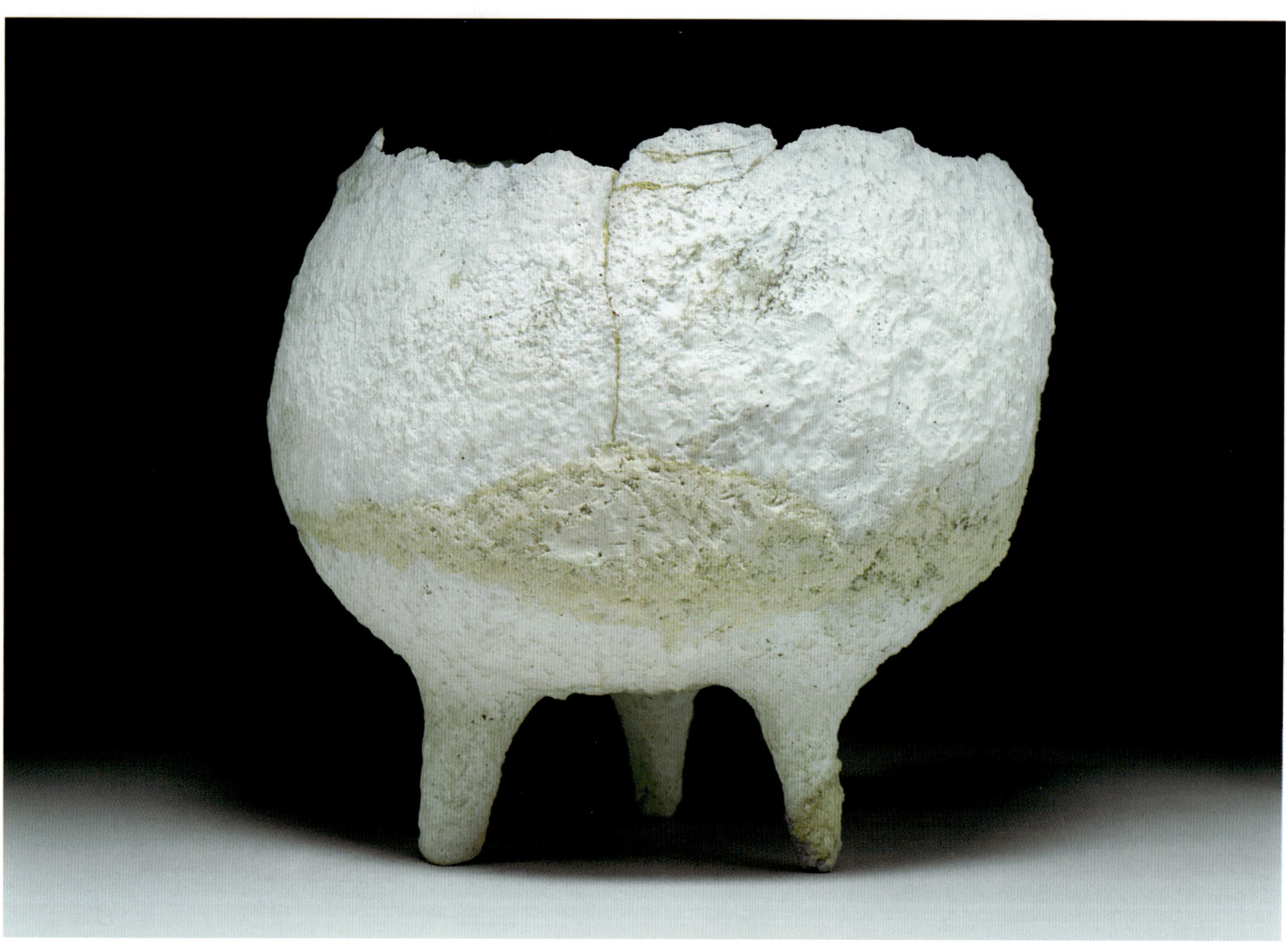

plate 68

JAR

PLATE 68
Southwestern Mexico
Late Postclassic period, AD 1300–1520
Travertine
Jar: H. 14.6 cm (5¾"); Max. Diam. 16.5 cm (6½")
Supports: H. 3.71 cm (1⅜")
PC.B.114

ACQUISITION HISTORY:
Purchased from Earl Stendahl, 1944

EXHIBITION HISTORY:
Indigenous Art of the Americas, National Gallery of Art, Washington, D.C., April 1947–July 1949; January 1956–July 1962 (NGA 232)

BIBLIOGRAPHY:
Bliss 1947: 21, 103, cat. no. 98; Bliss 1957: 246, cat. no. 77, pl. LIII, top; Dumbarton Oaks 1963: 28, cat. no. 142

This globular vessel has three long conical supports placed underneath the bowl, rather than to the sides, and thus they define a small base. In its recent history, the object underwent considerable reconstruction: the surviving portion of the walls had broken off from the base, and many pieces were unavailable. A conservator rebuilt the lower portion of the vessel's body by applying a thick layer of epoxy resin. The container is heavily eroded as well, so that all of its superior part is missing. Erosion affected both the interior and exterior surfaces, thinning the walls and leading to the structural failure of the bowl. Although there is one section of the walls that is entirely missing, the inside surface is less uneven than the exterior.

The vessel's material is probably travertine, judging by its white color and apparent hardness. The better condition of the interior suggests that the vessel lay inverted in the context that led to its erosion. Given travertine's properties, including its sedimentary origin and hardness, water action might have been conducive to such deterioration. Because of its condition, there are no marks that may have been left by the manufacturing procedures. Although incomplete, the lower shape of the vessel is very similar to some ceramic forms that were much in vogue in the regions of northwestern Oaxaca and southern Puebla between AD 1300 and 1520 (Lind 1994: 86–88; Sánchez Scott 2001: 89), a similarity that allows for its hypothetical reconstruction (Figure 66).

JU

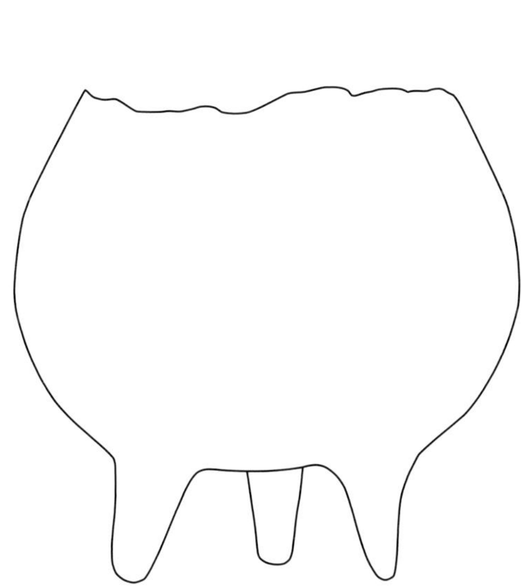

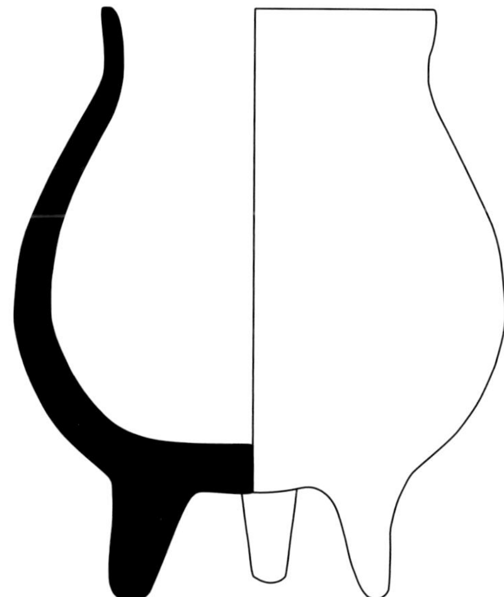

fig. 66
Travertine jar PC.B.114 (left) and its hypothetical original shape (right). Drawing by Elbis Domínguez.

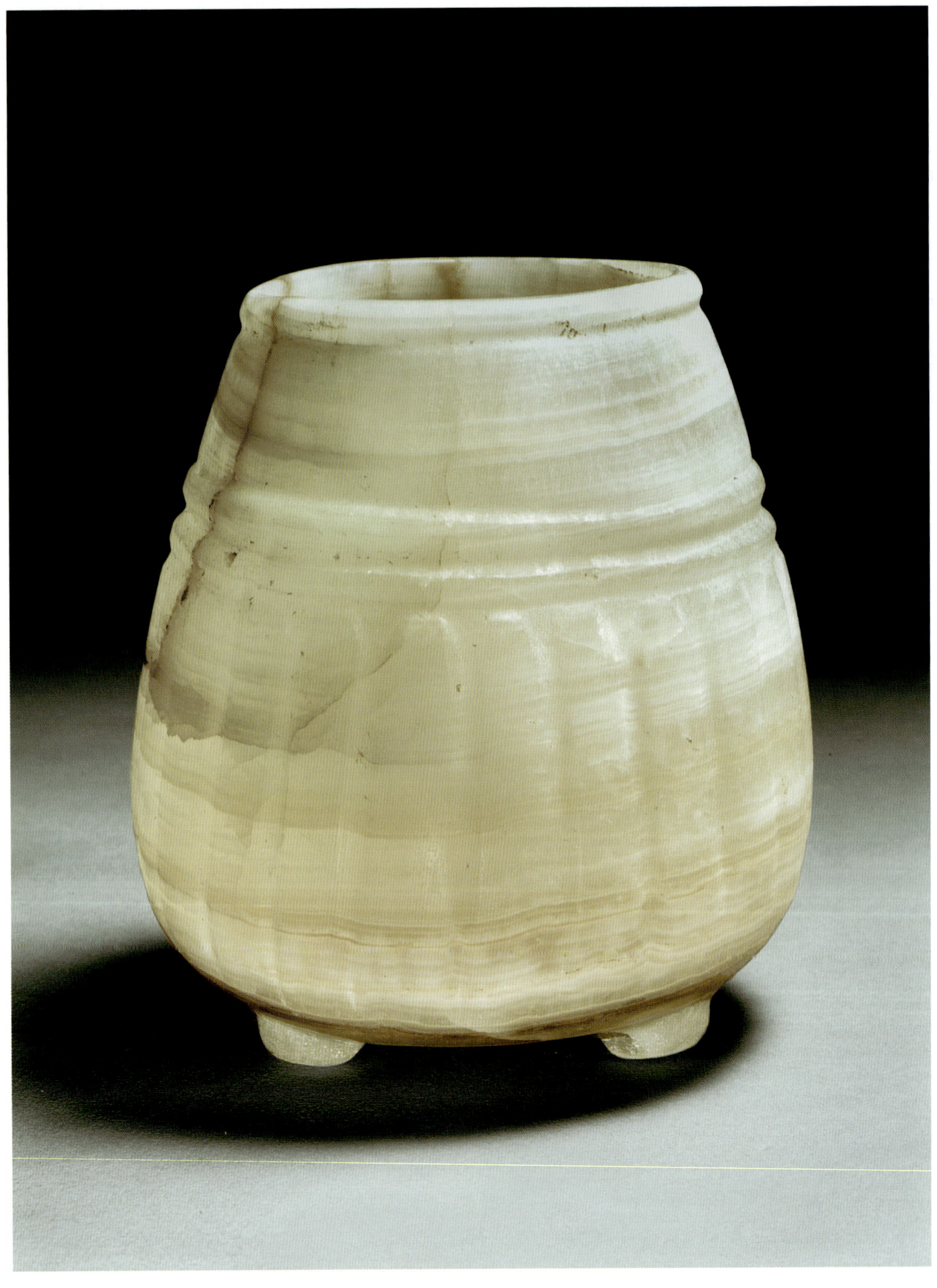

plate 69

PLATE 69
Late Postclassic period, AD 1300–1520
Travertine
H. 15.8 cm (6¼"); Diam 14.3 cm (5⅝")
PC.B.115

ACQUISITION HISTORY:
Purchased from Earl Stendahl, 1957; reportedly from Juan Crispin, north of Tuxtla, Chiapas

EXHIBITION HISTORY:
Indigenous Art of the Americas, National Gallery of Art, Washington, D.C., December 1958–July 1962 (NGA 719)

BIBLIOGRAPHY:
Dumbarton Oaks 1963: 29, cat. no. 143

This tripod barrel-shaped vessel was manufactured from a stone striated in white and brown, changing to purple-brown toward the base. On the exterior the vessel has a conspicuous lip defined by a deep groove 6 mm below the border; this groove is also the upper limit of a broad plain band in the upper part of the vessel. Defined by a second horizontal groove, this plain band is followed by the fluted upper border of a panel that covers most of the vessel's body with vertical grooves. The supporting legs are small knobs placed under the container.

The interior walls have a smooth surface, but at the bottom, one can see 23 shallow marks of the tubular hollow drill bits that were used to carve out the container (Figure 67). The reduced size of the vessel's mouth prevents measuring the diameter of the tubular marks. Except for one, all are incomplete and appear in the periphery of the bottom surface, at the juncture with the walls of the vessel. Toward the center the surface is slightly concave and smooth, but it shows some chiseling marks. The exterior surface, including the underside and the tripod knobs, was thoroughly ground and smoothed. There is, however, no polishing. The vessel is broken and repaired in recent times, having three glued fragments on one side that form part of the vessel's rim.

Although the vessel presumably comes from a locality in northern Chiapas, its form and decoration are strikingly similar to a vessel found in Isla de Sacrificios in central Veracruz (Nuttall 1910: 284, pl. VIII, nos. 1–3). A similar decoration, but on a different vessel shape, appears in a Postclassic travertine jar found at Nebaj, Guatemala (Smith and Kidder 1951: fig. 83b).

JU

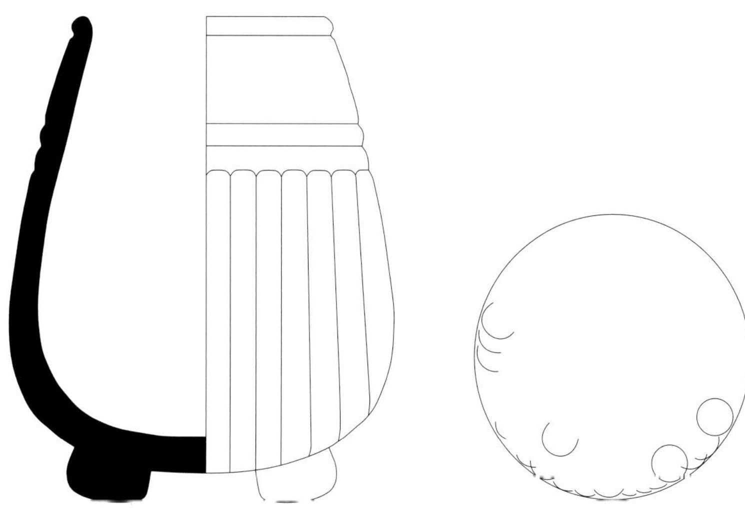

fig. 67
Different views of travertine jar PC.B.115 showing traces of its hollowing in the interior bottom. Drawing by Elbis Domínguez.

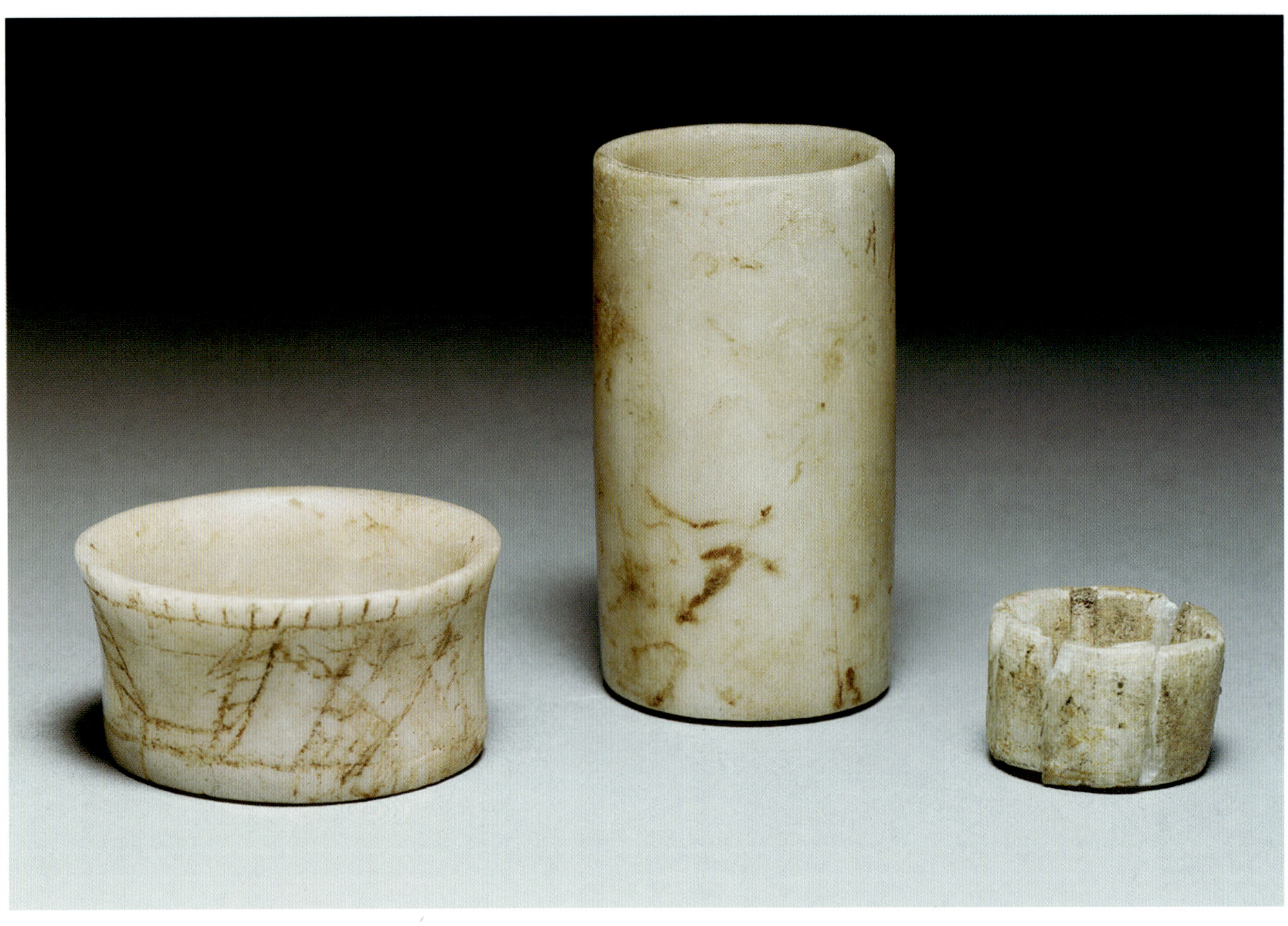

plate 70

SET OF MINIATURE STONE VESSELS AND STONE RING

PLATE 70
Probably Late Classic period, AD 600–900
Calcite
PC.B.116: H. 4.6 cm (1¾"); Diam. 2.6 cm (1")
PC.B.117: H. 1.8 cm (¾"); Diam. 3.6 cm (1½")
PC.B.118: H. 1.25 cm (½"); Diam. 1.9 cm (¾")

The type of alabaster from which miniature vessels PC.B.116 and PC.B.117 were manufactured is so consistent as to suggest that the vessels formed part of a set. Sets of miniature objects are common in mortuary offerings throughout Mesoamerica. The production of minute objects and their deposition in such contexts suggest the metaphorical preoccupation of leaving tokens of sustenance to the dead to feed their souls in the afterlife.

PC.B.116 is a perfectly tubular vase made of calcite, not translucent but ivory in color with some brown speckles. The vase was probably manufactured by boring a solid tube that in turn may have been derived from drilling a block of calcite using a hollow tubular bit (Figure 68). After hollowing the cylinder, the interior and exterior surfaces were abraded and smoothed but not polished. The interior walls were smoothed in the upper third of the vessel; deeper into the container are several concentric grooves around the wall left by the rotation of the drill. Concentric striations can be seen at the bottom of the vessel's interior, suggesting that this part of the object was also abraded and smoothed.

PC.B.117 is a flat-bottomed conical bowl with slightly flaring walls. Being more open and broader, the object was thoroughly smoothed and polished but without leaving a shiny appearance. Macroscopically one cannot see the striations of the drill bit that must have been used to hollow the vessel. The exterior surface of the object is decorated with incised motifs in geometric configurations, including trapezoidal and triangular forms (Figure 69). Some parts of the design were hachured, and others were finely

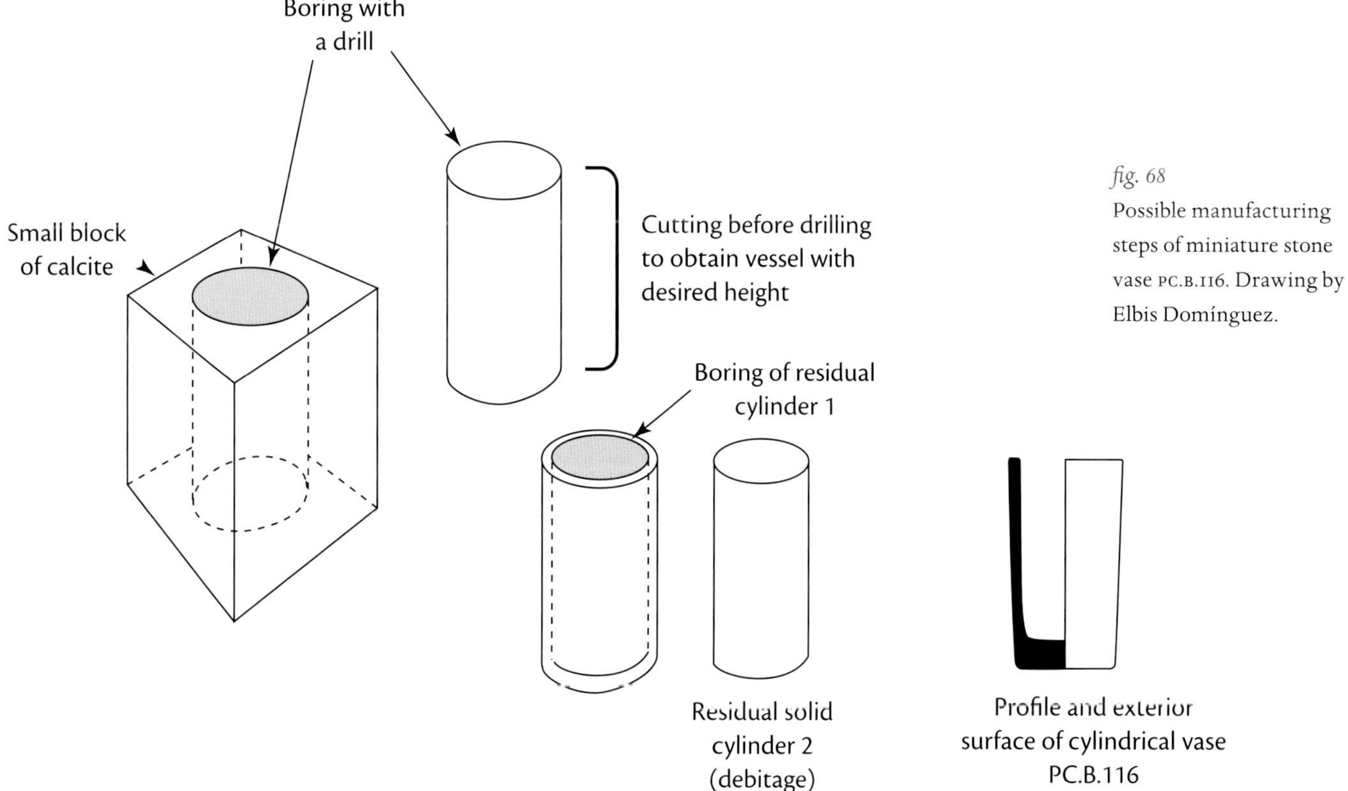

fig. 68
Possible manufacturing steps of miniature stone vase PC.B.116. Drawing by Elbis Domínguez.

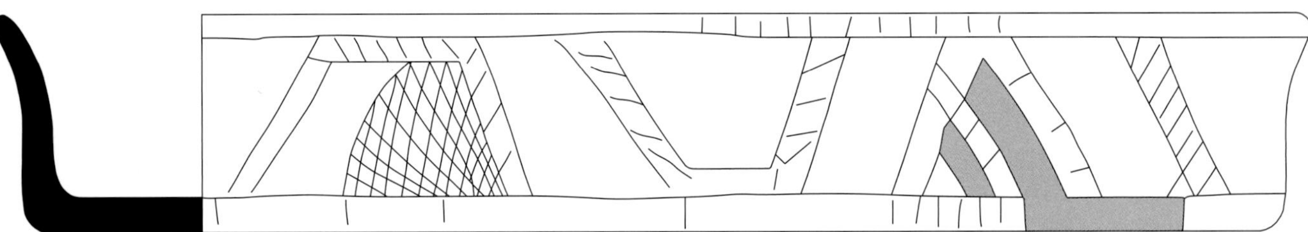

fig. 69
Profile of miniature stone bowl PC.B.117 and rollout drawing of motifs incised on its exterior surface. Drawing by Elbis Domínguez.

Superior view

Lateral view

Profile view

Inferior view

fig. 70
Different views of stone ring PC.B.118. Drawing by Elbis Domínguez.

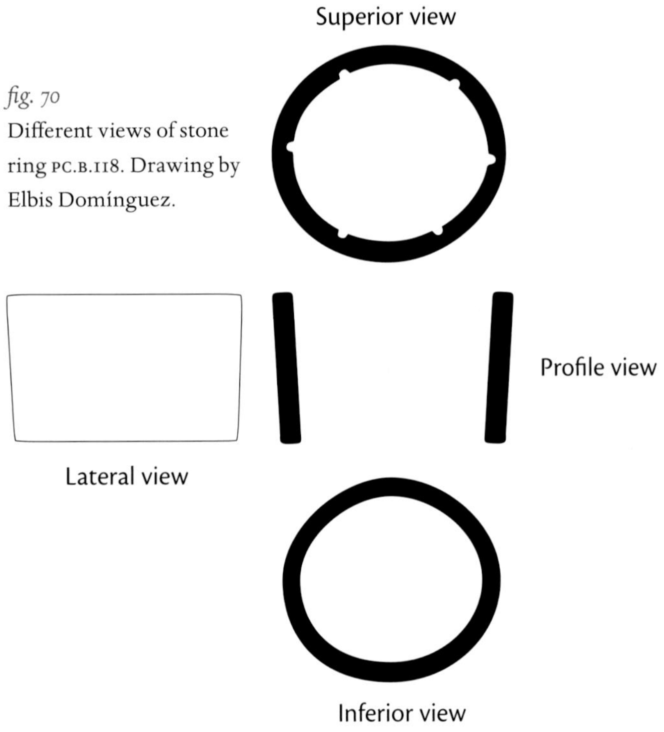

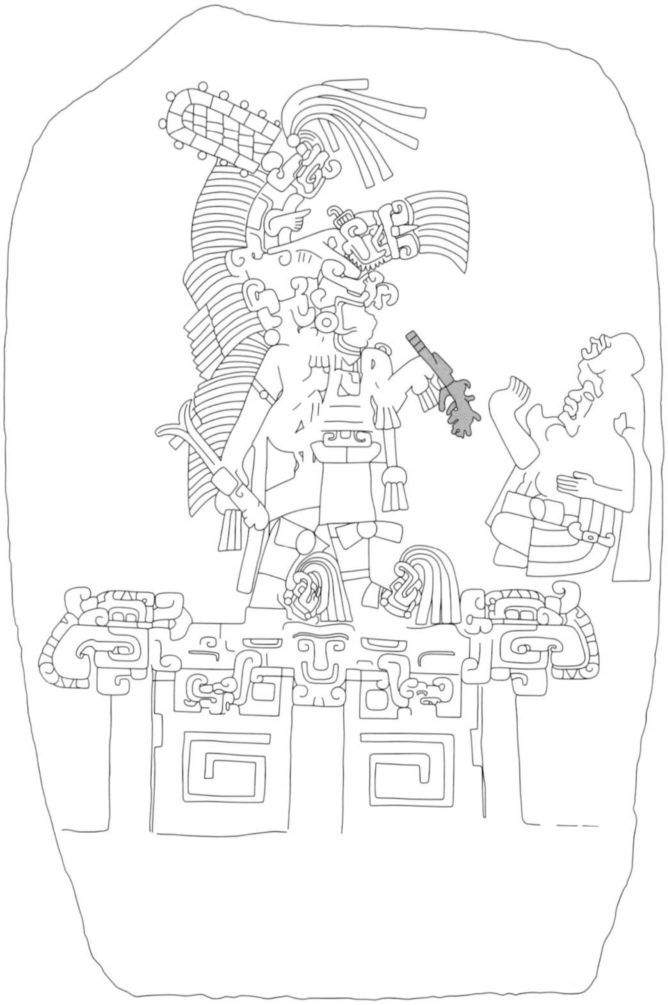

fig. 71
Possible depiction of a fly whisk (indicated in gray) in the portrayal of a ruler on Monument 1 from El Mesón (now Ángel R. Cabada), southern Gulf Coast Lowlands (200 BC–AD 200). Drawing by Elbis Domínguez.

ground with emery, leaving a slightly roughened yet even surface.

The stone ring (PC.B.118) is small, slightly oblong, and conical (Figure 70); it would have formed part of a composite object. The calcite is not translucent, although the exterior surface of the object was abraded and smoothed. The appearance is dull rather than polished. No striations that may have been left in the process of reducing its surface are visible. The concentric lines evident on the interior surface of the ring may be original linear bands typical of calcite deposits. Also on the interior are six grooves that run from the middle of the walls to the broader end of the ring. The ring is broken from vertical fractures into five pieces. It has been unevenly mended stemming from warping and distortion of the material. The fractures that caused the breakage of the object do not correspond in alignment to the grooves. The latter are not evenly spaced around the circumference of the ring.

Similar objects, although made out of jadeite, were recovered from the main cenote at Chichén Itzá (see Proskouriakoff 1974: 70, pl. 31-d). The shape of the object and the interior vertical grooves suggest that the ring was probably a holder for feathers, flowers, or other types of fibers. Such a holder, in turn, could have been hafted to one end of a wooden or bone handle. Perhaps the composite object of which this ring was part was a fly whisk or a fan made with feathers, an object indispensable in outdoor appearances and courtly life. Although depictions of fans in Mesoamerican art are more common, the few known renderings of fly whisks suggest that in certain contexts they served as important status markers (Figure 71).

JU

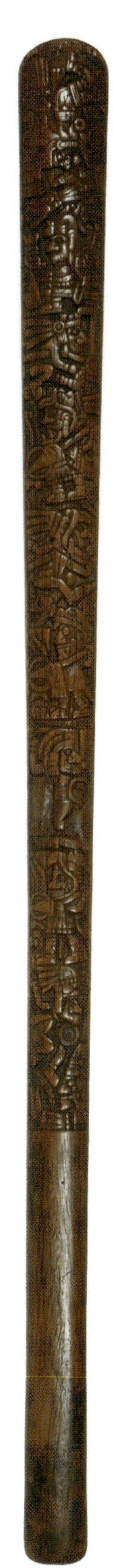

plate 71a, back view

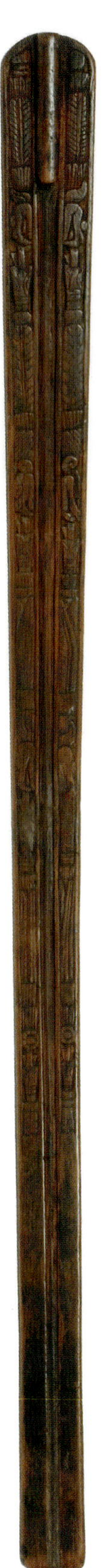

plate 71b, front view

DART THROWER

PLATE 71
Probably Mixteca Alta
Late Postclassic period, AD 1200–1520
Wood
L. 60.3 cm (23¾"); W. 3.8 cm (1½"); D. 1.6 cm (⅝")
PC.B.144

ACQUISITION HISTORY:
Purchased from Ernest Brummer, 1947; from the collection of Joseph Brummer

EXHIBITION HISTORY:
Indigenous Art of the Americas, National Gallery of Art, Washington, D.C., February 1954–July 1962 (NGA 375); *Die Azteken und ihre Vorläufer: Glanz und Untergang des Alten Mexico,* Roemer- und Pelizaeus-Museum, Hildesheim, Germany, June–November 1986; Haus der Kunst, Munich, December 1986–March 1987; Oberösterreichisches Landesmuseum, Linz, Austria, April–August 1987; Louisiana Museum of Modern Art, Humlebæk, Denmark, August–November 1987; Musées royaux d'Art et d'Histoire, Brussels, December 1987–March 1988; National Archaeological Museum, Athens, May–July 1988; Société du Palais de la Civilisation, Montreal, July–October 1988

BIBLIOGRAPHY:
Sydow 1923: 414; Bliss 1957: 244, cat. no. 65, 245, fig. 15, pl. XLIX; Palencia 1959: 407, fig. 20; Robertson 1959: 106; Dumbarton Oaks 1963: 24, cat. no. 113; Nicholson 1967: 17; Burland 1973: 110; Boone 1986g: cat. no. 274; Louisiana Museum 1987: 69, cat. no. 71; Alcina Franch et al. 1992: 248–249, fig. LX; Vila Llonch 2008e: 196–197

This dart thrower was manufactured from a single, straight, and slender strip of a hard wood with a dark reddish-brown color. The distal end, where the implement ends in the hook where darts were engaged, is 1.62 cm thick. Along the transverse plane, the thrower is wider at the distal end (3.81 cm) and tapers to 2.7 cm at the proximal end. The groove for the darts on the upper surface is approximately 6 mm wide and 3–4 mm deep. The implement is now restored from a fracture—approximately two-thirds its length from the distal end—that broke it into two pieces. There are no striations or wear indicative of the finger loops that must have been laced toward the proximal end of the shaft, nor is there evidence of wear indicative of use in the grip area, along the groove for the dart, or in the peg of the propelling hook. Yet the lack of such evidence may be due to the restoration and the cleaning of the object.[126] The dart thrower now includes two modern nails added as structural reinforcement.

The shaft's upper and lower surfaces are carved; both sets of carvings are read by placing the object vertically with the distal end up and reading the imagery from top to bottom. The upper surface of the thrower has, on either side of the groove on which the actual projectiles were placed, an incised linear sequence of four paired darts (Figure 72). When using the thrower, the carved darts would have been aligned with the actual ones. These representations include the projectile points, a carved shaft close to the hafting of the points, feathers, and a blunt butt that was probably hollow so as to engage them in the hook of the thrower. The points have broad, flaring stems, a shape seemingly intended to facilitate their hafting to the shafts and to achieve the effect of barbed projectiles. As veritable harpoons, such darts could not have been retrieved from the target without inflicting further damage. Although the representations of darts are shown as mirror images so as to display bilateral symmetry, each

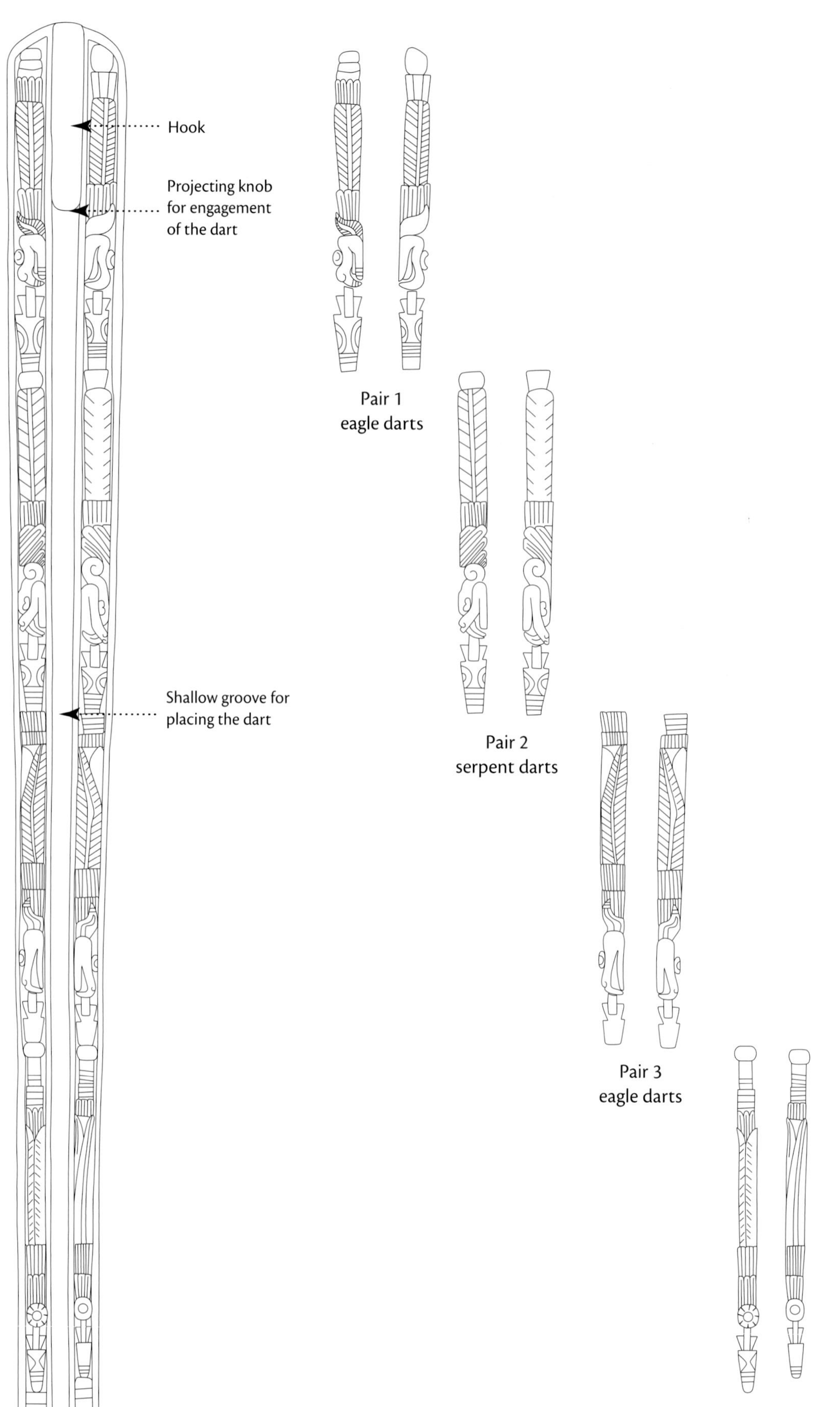

fig. 72
Darts carved on the superior surface of dart thrower PC.B.144. Drawing by Elbis Domínguez.

pair exhibits asymmetrical details. The first pair, from back to front, has shafts decorated near the projectiles with eagle heads; the second pair sports shafts with serpent heads. The third displays eagle heads. The dart shafts in the last pair, longer than the others, are decorated with rosettes. The feathers on the posterior ends differ between pairs and exhibit variations within pairs.

Ten figures, one over the other, are depicted on the inferior side of the dart thrower. The top nine are full-body images; the last is only a face in profile. Differences in headgear, garments, and other ornaments individualize each representation. The first personage, in descending position (Figure 73), is the most important individual in the scene; his rank is highlighted by such features as an eagle headdress with a feathered crest and a ready-to-use dart thrower. The solar band behind him identifies him as an impersonator of the Sun God. His face is adorned with a nose plug; his belt and leg bracelets have dangling bells. A speech scroll next to his mouth is flanked by two bundles of feathers and followed by a skeletonized mask and a serpent head with feathers in the back; this composition could signal a phonetic utterance in a specific language or a graphic message indexing meaning without encoding speech. The serpent head with feathers recalls objects like PC.B.094 (Plate 60) and PC.B.136 (Plate 59): handles of feathered and/or gilded insignia marking military

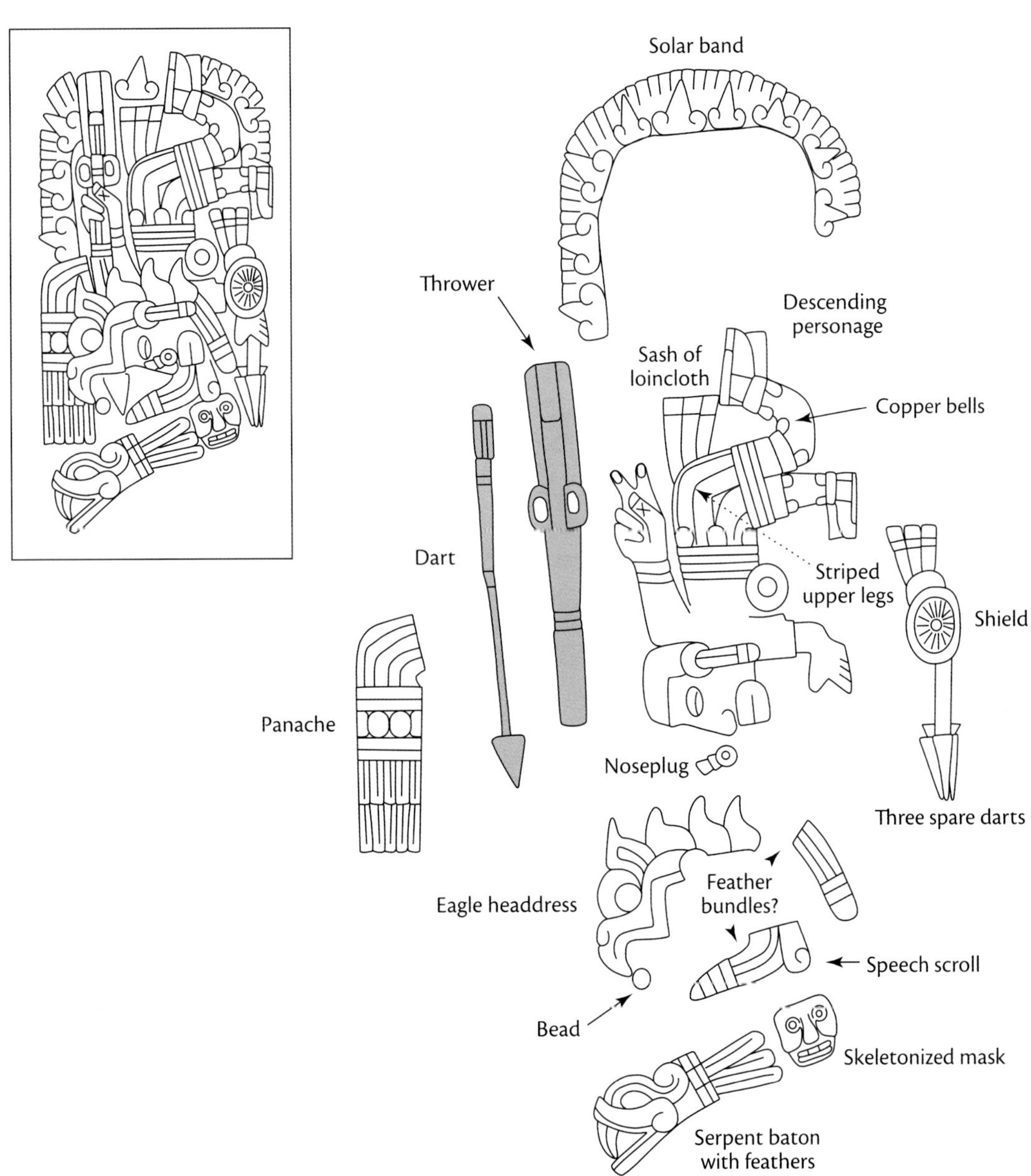

fig. 73
Descending personage carved on the inferior distal end of dart thrower PC.B.144 (inset) and exploded view of same. Drawing by Elbis Domínguez.

fig. 74
Examples of finger grips (left) and how they were laced to dart throwers like one of unknown provenience now in the British Museum (right). Drawing by Elbis Domínguez (right image after Beyer 1965e; and Pasztory 1983: colorplate 53).

Marine shell finger grip carved as two entwined serpents. Main cenote at Chichén Itzá. Length 3.9 cm

Shell finger grip with raised buttons. Said to be from Nochixtlan, Oaxaca. Length 4.6 cm (Harvard Peabody Museum, cat. no. 04-24-20/C3745)

Shell finger grips associated with a decayed dart thrower found in Structure 5D at Tikal, Guatemala. Length 8 cm

Small perforation to suspend ornaments (piece of jaguar skin and feathers)

Shell finger grip laced to handle section

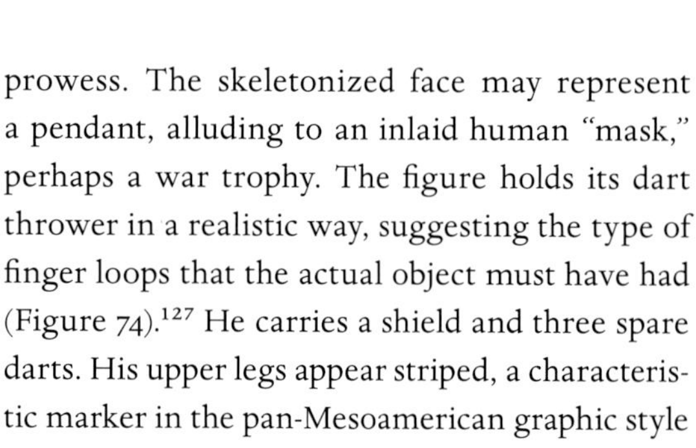

prowess. The skeletonized face may represent a pendant, alluding to an inlaid human "mask," perhaps a war trophy. The figure holds its dart thrower in a realistic way, suggesting the type of finger loops that the actual object must have had (Figure 74).[127] He carries a shield and three spare darts. His upper legs appear striped, a characteristic marker in the pan-Mesoamerican graphic style of Postclassic times to represent warriors as both successful fighters and potential sacrificial victims (Olivier 2004: 320).

The eight figures below the descending personage are dressed as warriors and arranged in two ranks, facing left and facing right (Figure 75). Details of posture and accoutrements suggest that the warriors facing left are depicted as victorious

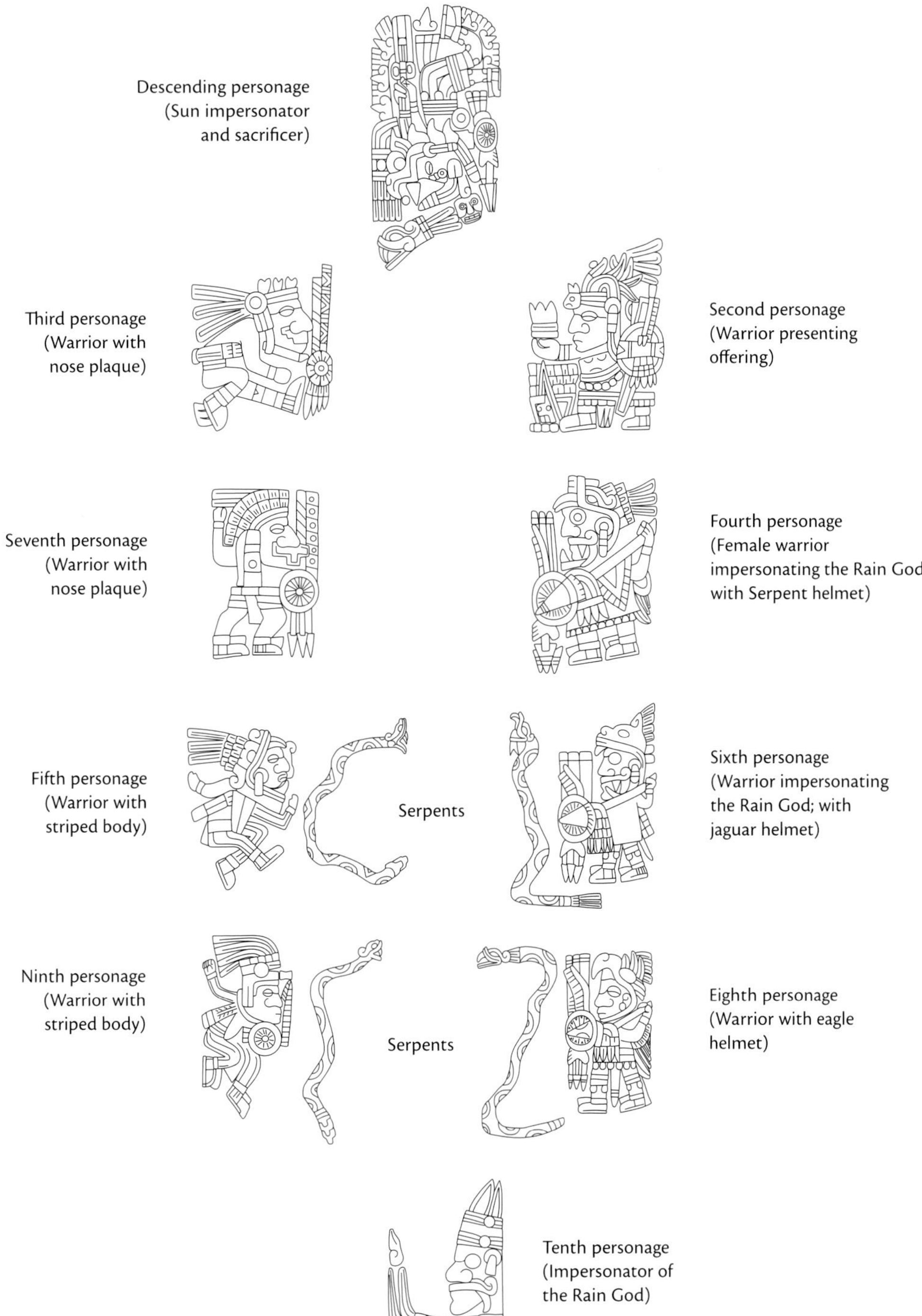

fig. 75
Structural patterns in the personages carved on the inferior surface of dart thrower PC.B.144. Drawing by Elbis Domínguez.

while those facing right are vanquished. Those facing left (personages 2, 4, 6, and 8) appear to advance in procession, and all except personage 2 (below the descending warrior) are depicted in menacing, threatening gestures, holding shields, throwers, and darts and thrusting long lances. The second personage carries a thrower, darts, and the most decorated shield, and he seems to present an offering of a small bundle with a trefoil element on top. In front of his legs appears the annual date 3 or 4 Rabbit. Warriors 4 and 6 wear the mask of the Rain God. Quite significantly, the fourth figure wears a female pointed overdress.

The warriors facing to the right (personages 3, 5, 7, and 9) assume more dynamic poses, but only the third and seventh figures carry darts and/or

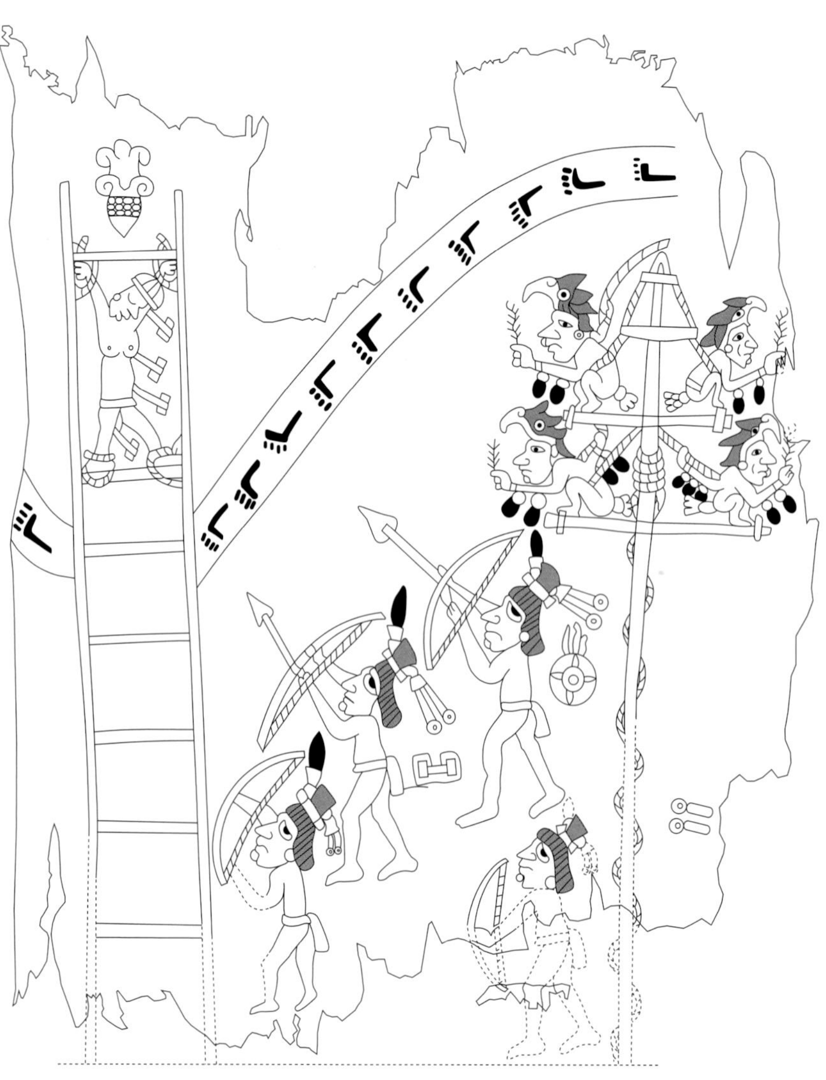

fig. 76
Enactment of the Voladores ritual and scaffold sacrifice depicted in the Tutepetongo roll (page 10), Cuicatlan Cañada, Oaxaca, ca. AD 1540. Drawing by Elbis Domínguez (after Doesburg 2001).

shields, and they appear to be relinquishing their weapons. They also wear "butterfly-shaped" nose plaques. Although warriors 5 and 9 are shown with striped bodies and as if brandishing weapons, none were rendered (but the ninth warrior seems to hold a shield and possibly a dummy weapon, perhaps a feather substituting for a club). The fifth warrior has a speech scroll. Overall, the garb of this second set of warriors is less elaborate than those facing left. Another structural pattern begins after the fourth figure. Individuals 5 and 6 appear, respectively, amid right- and left-facing serpents, as do personages 8 and 9, except that the direction of each serpent is the reverse of that of the upper warriors. Warrior 7, lacking an ophidian, is the center of this unfolding pattern.

The carving on the dart thrower's lower surface ends with the profile head of a Rain God impersonator, with buccal mask and protruding fang. The figure's double-banded headdress is topped by a two-prong element representing eagle feathers (*cuauhpilolli* in Nahuatl), an attribute of Mixcoatl-Camaxtli. A feather ornament below the face may signal a flow of water; it is topped by a scroll.

Interpreting the dart thrower's narrative scene begins with the descending posture of the first figure. Other known scenes of descending personages relate to scaffold sacrifices wherein war captives, tied to wooden racks, were wounded with darts or arrows prior to immolation by heart extraction. The Tutepetongo roll clarifies the dart thrower figure's eagle outfit: next to a scene of scaffold sacrifice is a tall pole with platforms where four individuals outfitted as eagles sit (Figure 76).[128] This scene undoubtedly represents an immolation ritual in which enactors symbolically representing the four corners of the world mimicked the descending flight of eagles who, on their descent from the pole, received the sacrificial offering.

A similar ritual of descending in flight from a tall pole, the Voladores ("flyers") ceremony, is still practiced today, without its human sacrificial component.[129] The main protagonists are five men who dance on a platform atop the pole: one at the apex plays a flute and drum; the others dance before flying down head first while tied by ropes to their ankles. Whether or not the leader is dressed as an eagle, he is considered "an eagle because, with his flute, he speaks the language of birds" (Ichon 1973: 389). Usually the Voladores wear a conical cap whose decoration symbolizes the sun and its rays (Ichon 1973: 380).

Analysis of scaffold sacrifice scenes and the continuities pervading contemporary Voladores performances provides the basis for a polysemous decipherment of the carvings on both surfaces of the dart thrower in the Bliss Collection. The narrative refers to several temporally overlapping events that are linearly arranged along the weapon. The descending eagle impersonator signals, by synecdoche, the performance of a flying ritual, and his dart-hurling posture alludes to a scaffold sacrifice. The subsequent eight warriors, when rearranged according to their facing direction, represent a warfare event and capture of those shown facing right. Several visual puns reinforce the depiction of a raid. Shield-and-darts was a metaphor for "war" in Nahuatl (*mitl chimalli*), and darts embodied warriors: a captor would utter "it is really my dart" (Olivier 2004: 319). Serpents associated with the last two pairs of confronting warriors also allude to ritual warfare, and the last two right-facing warriors are fully marked as sacrificial victims by their striped bodies. The annual date 3 or 4 Rabbit carved below the second personage situates in historical chronology the warfare event and/or the scaffold sacrifice. The four pairs of darts carved on the superior surface of the thrower reinforce the allusion to the sacrifice of four captives, each representing one of the four quarters of the world. The solar band behind the descending eagle-man indexes these sacrifices as consecrated to the sun.

The descending figure's primacy is made evident by elaborate accoutrements and by his position at the apex of the flying ritual. Structurally, the Voladores ritual is implied by a quadripartite pattern that synthesizes the fourfold conception of the cosmos, including time.[130] Thus the descending figure is the dancer at the top of the pole, and the four victorious warriors capturing and/or sacrificing the prisoners are the four flyers that accompany him (Figure 77). Two additional details support this interpretation. One of the captors/sacrificers wears a female pointed tunic (*quechquemitl* in Nahuatl), like the transvestism of one of the four flyers in some contemporary Voladores rituals. Additionally, the descending figure's identity as a Rain God impersonator (with the ornament of eagle feathers related to Mixcoatl-Camaxtli carved on the opposite end of the narrative) implies that the ritual's purpose was to honor the sun with a war sacrifice while petitioning for rain and a good crop. Atop the pole, the descending figure is in the axis mundi, an intermediary between the celestial (the realm of the sun and its avatar, the eagle) and the terrestrial (the realm of the Rain God and hence of human and social needs). The ritual's fertility overtones are emphasized by three allusions to the Rain God (fourth, sixth, and tenth personages) and reinforced by the only "female" (human fecundity), who wears a mask of the Rain God (fourth personage).

Possibly the wood for the thrower was derived from a tree that became the pole for a Voladores ritual. When not in use the weapon may have been positioned vertically to mimic the pole, signaling in turn the endowed capacity of its owner to center the world through highly specialized ritual enactments: dancing at the top of the pole, descending as an eagle, darting his captive(s), performing divination to prognosticate social welfare (good rain, agricultural surplus, health, fecundity, and success in future raids to acquire captives and perpetually sustain the primordial covenant), and executing the final immolation to offer the victim's heart to the sun in return for divine favors. Such ritual performances were calendrically prescribed and enacted following the highly integrated cultural constructions of quadripartite time and space that formed the core of indigenous epistemologies. In addition, it is known that on the enthronement of a new ruler the incumbent shot darts or arrows to the four directions to prove

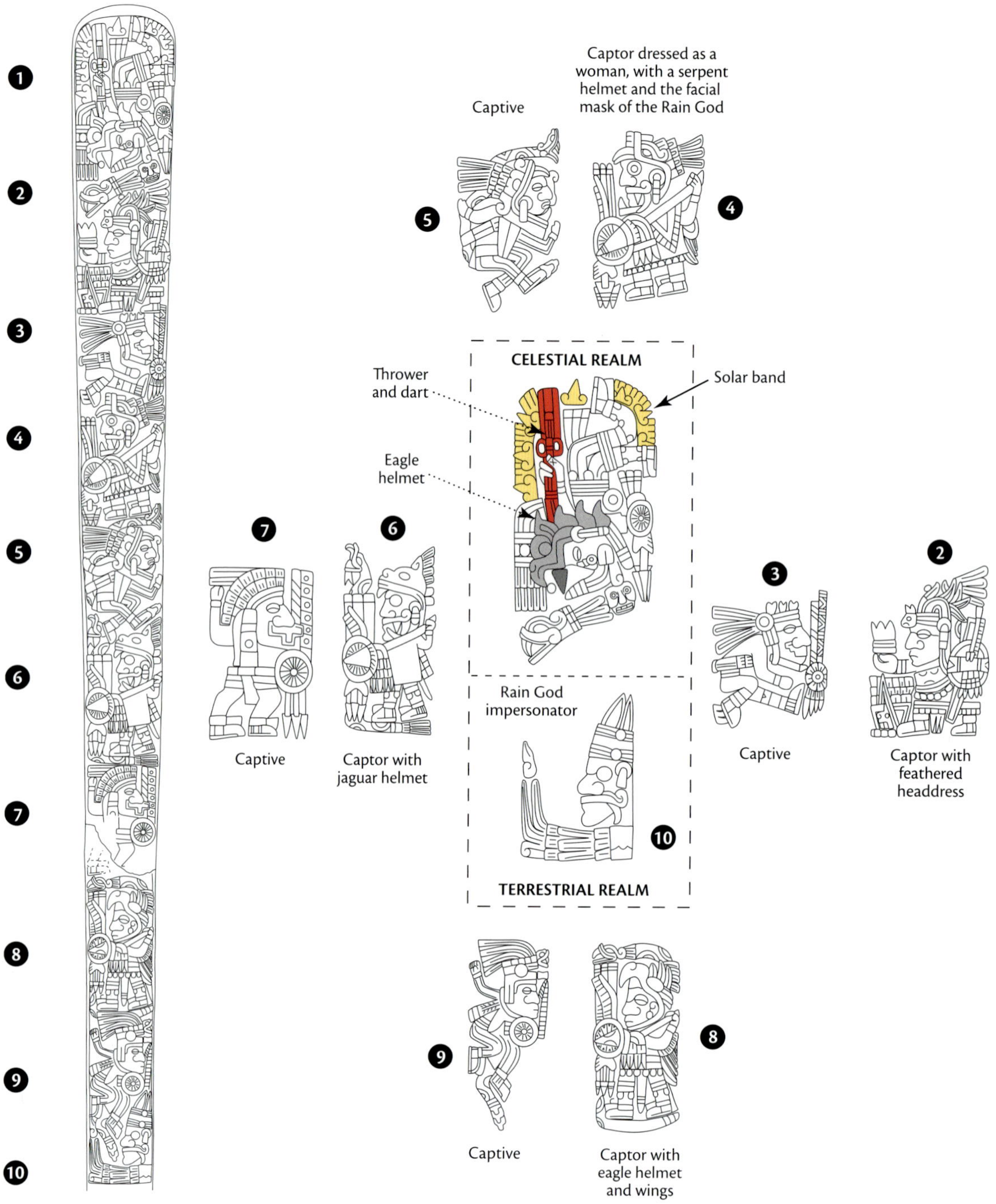

fig. 77
Linear narrative carved on the inferior surface of dart thrower PC.B.144 rearranged to mimic the quadripartite structure of the Voladores ritual. Drawing by Elbis Domínguez.

his success as warrior, diviner, interlocutor with the sacred, and societal provider, and to symbolically reify or redefine the territory of his polity (Oudijk 2002). Thus it is possible that the thrower was commissioned for a ritual of accession, and the annual date in the narrative could pertain to an enthronement celebration.

Other carved dart throwers have narratives with thematic parallels to that of PC.B.144. Figures in descending posture dressed as eagles, framed by a sun disk, and brandishing a dart thrower are also rendered on throwers now in the Museo di Storia Naturale dell'Università di Firenze, Florence (cat. no. 8040), in the Museo Nazionale Preistorico ed Etnografico Luigi Pigorini, Rome (cat. nos. 4212a, 4212b), and in the National Museum of the American Indian (cat. no. 10/8724). Although the authenticity of one of the Pigorini Museum dart throwers (cat. no. 4212b) has been questioned (Beyer 1934), this weapon and the one

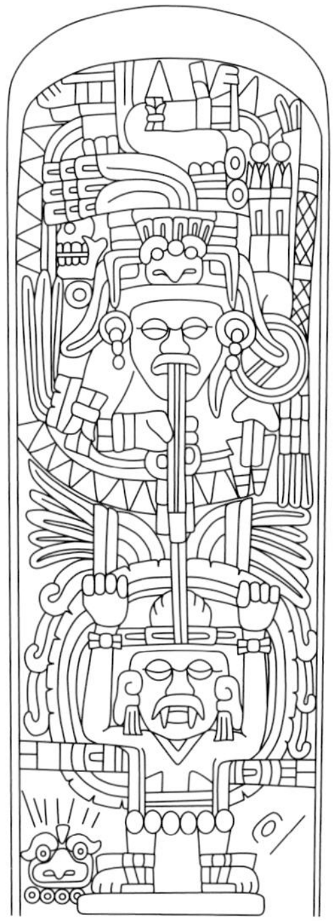

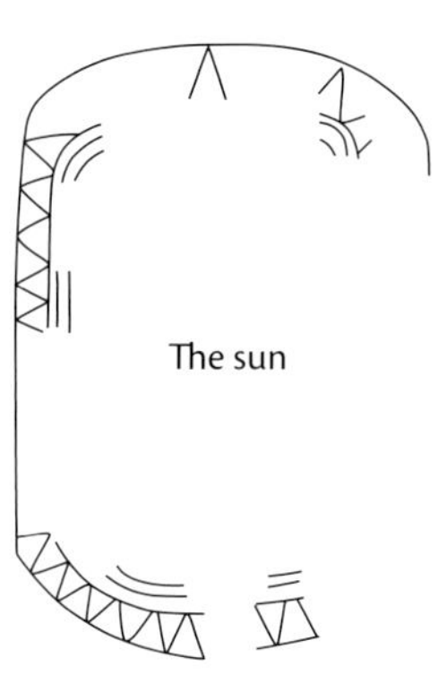

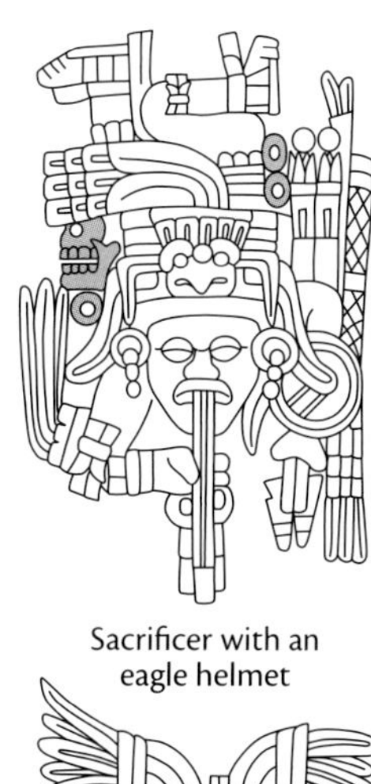

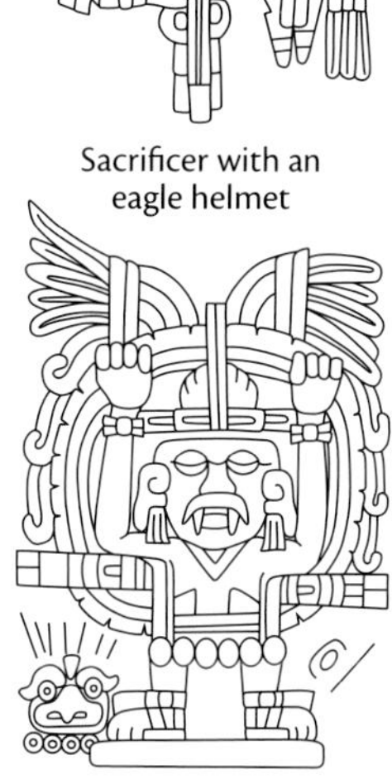

fig. 78
Carving on the lower distal end of dart thrower 8040 in the Museo di Storia Naturale dell'Università di Firenze, Florence. A sacrificer named 3 Skull (in gray) descends from the sun with an eagle headdress and a dart thrower, followed by a darted victim tied to a scaffold. A divination mirror is carved in the background. Drawing by Elbis Domínguez (after Bushnell 1905: plate XXI).

in Florence make explicit visual reference to sacrifice by darting, depicting the sacrificial victim tied to a wooden frame with a large divinatory mirror in the background (Figure 78). The imagery carved on the inferior surface in the dart thrower now in the British Museum (cat. no. AM 5226) depicts a descending impersonator of Mixcoatl-Camaxtli (Beyer 1965e) accompanied by a Cloud-Serpent that indexes "Rain." The impersonator brandishes a dart and wears as an earring the hoof of a deer (referencing the symbolic substitution of the deer hunt for the capture of sacrificial victims to be offered to the sun). Although a second carved thrower now in the National Museum of the American Indian (cat. no. 10/8723) does not allude to the Voladores ritual or to scaffold sacrifice, its imagery refers to human immolation (the figure on the inferior surface in the posterior end has a flint knife in his chest) and narrates a founding event when a fire was drilled.

References to sacrifice and fertility are made in a second dart thrower in Florence (cat. no. 8039) by depicting a sacrificer's alter ego (a human-turtle with a flint knife in his hand) and by several representations of Rain God impersonators. The narrative scene carved in a dart thrower from Tlaxiaco, in the Mixteca Alta (now in the Museo Nacional de Antropología in Mexico City) includes a Rain God impersonator holding a divinatory mirror. Three other carved throwers, two in the Ethnologisches Museum in Berlin (purchased in Tlaxiaco) and the other in the Museo Nacional de Antropología in Mexico City, depict Cloud Serpents. Those on the Berlin objects are marked with linear sequences of hummingbirds nibbling on flowers, the birds being the insignia of the god of war (Huitzilopochtli) in the northern Nahua tradition. Two more carved throwers from Tlaxiaco (one in the Museo Nacional de Antropología in Mexico City [cat. no. 11-3022] and the other in the Staatliches Museum für Völkerkunde in Munich [cat. no. 27-12-1]) are actually shaped as Cloud Serpents. The narratives on almost all these carved throwers end with references to the Rain God or to the Earth God, the latter symbolically depicted as the jaws of an alligator wide open as if devouring sacrificial victims.

The function of these dart throwers remains to be clarified; PC.B.144 and 13 other surviving examples are elaborately carved and, at times, even gilded (Bushnell 1905; Callegari 1934; Laurencich Minelli 1993; Mazzetti 1993; Meeks n.d.). The dart thrower was part of the insignia of several deities, including Quetzalcoatl, Xiuhtecuhtli, Tonatiuh, Tezcatlipoca, Tlahuizcalpantecutli, Mixcoatl-Camaxtli, and Huitzilopochtli (Seler 1991 [1904]).[131] Based apparently on the graphic representation of dart throwers with many deities, some authors have assumed that decorated throwers were ceremonial rather than utilitarian (Easby and Scott 1970: no. 293; Heflin 1963; Kellar 1955; Nuttall 1891; Umberger n.d.), which implies that they were only ritually used as symbolic tokens. Follett (1932: 384), for instance, thought that elaboration on throwers rendered their "primary use almost an impossibility," and Saville (1925: 37) argued that elaborate dart throwers were "ceremonially used in certain religious festivals and processions." Often the evidence used to support such arguments is the depiction of figures holding throwers but no darts, a position readily dismissed if one assumes that painters resorted to synecdoche. Furthermore, the known data on the sizes and weights of carved throwers fall within the range of similar fully functional weapons (Whittaker n.d.a, n.d.b).[132]

Dart throwers decorated on their posterior ends with animal heads (serpents or birds) were indeed used in warfare and served as markers of high military rank: a battle scene in the codex of Yanhuitlán (Jiménez Moreno and Mateos Higuera 1940: 56–57) depicts a Mexica high-ranking warrior hurling darts at two Spanish soldiers who lead allied native fighters attacking with bows and arrows. This thrower has a serpent head in the posterior end, similar to the Tlaxiaco examples or those dredged from Chichén Itzá's main cenote.[133] The codex illustration also seems to show dangling feathers, a detail known from the 1519 description of throwers obtained as booty by the Spaniards along the Gulf Coast and sent by Hernán Cortés to Charles V (Saville 1925: 43). Such a detail is also supported by the existence of a small perforation at the tip of the posterior end in several extant throwers.

Other known decorated throwers from Mesoamerica may have been deployed in scaffold sacrifices. Even though there is no evidence of wear in the dart thrower in the Bliss Collection, this instrument most likely belonged to a paramount ruler, was used in warfare, and inflicted wounds on captured warriors during darting sacrifices as a prelude to their immolation by heart extraction. Although charged with high aesthetic value, the dart thrower in the Bliss Collection and other highly decorated examples were deadly weapons aimed at humans whose offering fulfilled a primordial pact between mortals and the divine.

JU

ART OF THE GULF LOWLANDS: THE CLASSIC VERACRUZ FLORESCENCE AND POSTCLASSIC HUASTEC APOGEE

S. JEFFREY K. WILKERSON

The coastal lowlands of the Gulf of Mexico was one of the more socially complex and artistically expressive regions in the greater ancient Mesoamerican sphere of high culture (Figure 79). Encompassing the coastal plains and adjoining uplands along the western rim of the Gulf of Mexico in what is today eastern Mexico, this environmentally diverse and fertile zone focuses geographically on the modern state of Veracruz. In the Pre-Columbian era it was situated between the well-populated urbanized polities of the Central Highlands to the west and the numerous kingdoms of the Maya Lowlands to the southeast. This strategic location made the zone an obligatory terrestrial and maritime pathway for commerce, migration, and warfare. In spite of energetic neighbors, the area developed its own dynamic cultures, vigorous societies, and dramatic art styles, influencing surrounding and even very distant peoples.

The Gulf Lowlands achieved a remarkable artistic florescence in the Early Classic period (ca. AD 300–900). During this time, especially in the central portion of this vast district, there emerged the regional manifestations of art, architecture, and culture that are today referred to as "Classic Veracruz."[134] An astonishing amount of artwork and a plethora of ornate structures have been encountered here. From intricate ceramic figurines to monumental sculptures in clay, from small portable stone sculptures to large carved panels in temple sanctuaries, and from lavishly decorated ballcourts to enormous ornate buildings, the area was visibly saturated in art and ritualism. To this stimulating setting in time and space the majority of the splendidly representative Gulf Lowlands objects in the Dumbarton Oaks Bliss Collection belong.

In spite of being a contiguous coastal band with largely humid tropical lowlands, this region has a highly diverse landscape encompassing extraordinarily varied climates, exploitable natural resources, and rainfall patterns, as well as an enormous range of flora and fauna. Except for certain larger river basins, the terrain rapidly ascends in elevation from sea level into the often snow-capped Sierra Madre Oriental, with peaks as high as 5,900 m. Beyond the mountains are the arid margins of the Central Mexican plateau at 2,500 m altitude. The northern boundary of the Gulf Lowlands culture area is the same as that of the larger Mesoamerican culture area, with its seaward extensions of the often dry Sierra de Tamaulipas. To the south and east, the Gulf Lowlands encompass the muggy swampland of extreme western Tabasco.

Although the internal cultural boundaries were labile over time, at its greatest extent this

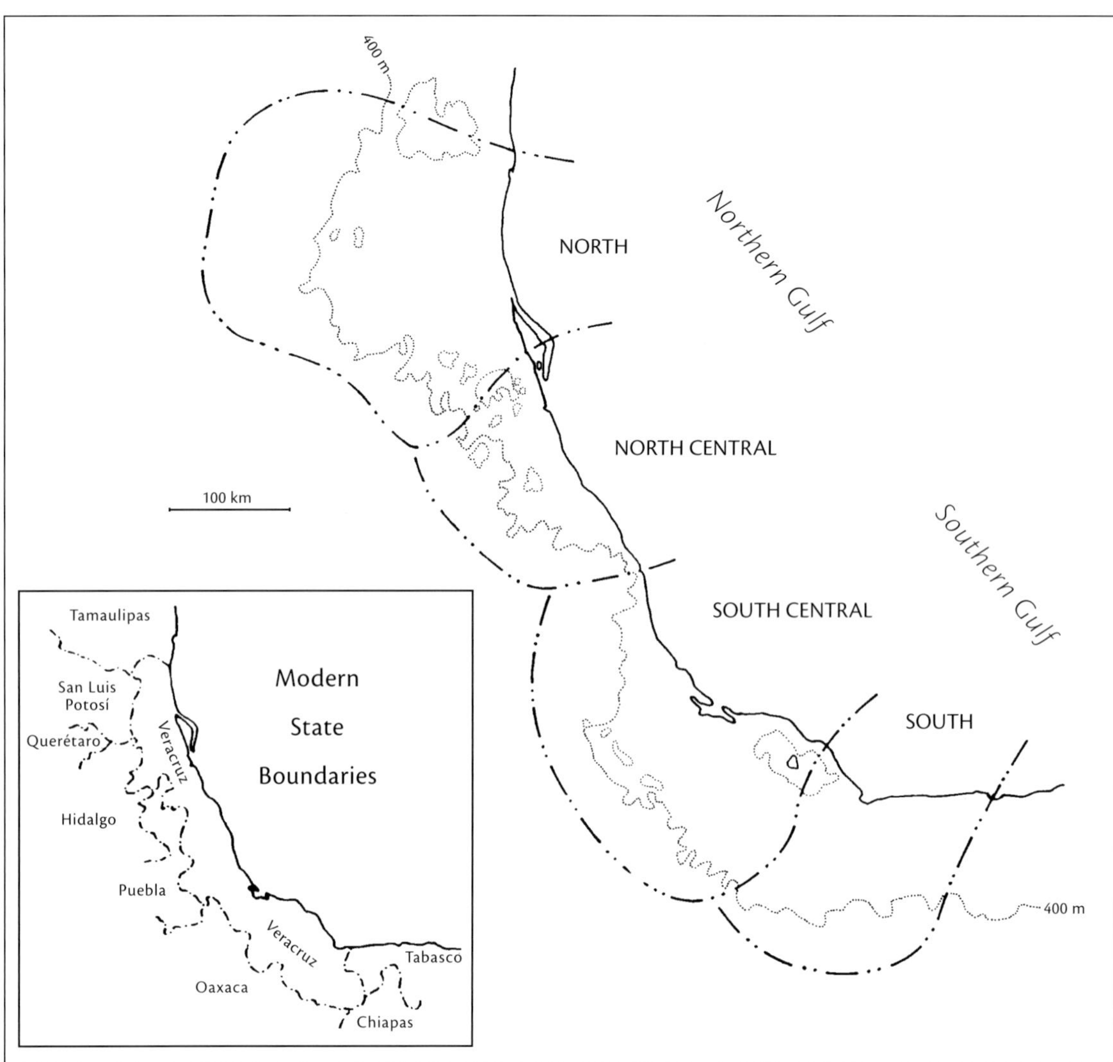

fig. 79
Natural and cultural regions of the Mexican Gulf Coast in Pre-Columbian times. Map by the Institute for Cultural Ecology of the Tropics/S. Jeffrey K. Wilkerson.

vast territory covered almost a thousand kilometers of coastline and penetrated inland for distances up to 200 km. It included the area covered by many modern states of Mexico: all of Veracruz, large portions of Tamaulipas and Tabasco, the eastern reaches of San Luis Potosí, Querétaro, and Hidalgo, and adjacent edges of Puebla and Oaxaca. The internal cultural divisions of this extensive area were both temporally profound and geographically variable. In large part corresponding to natural regions separated by higher elevations, the cultural units continually subdivided and grew in number during a very long culture history stretching back at least 8,000 years.[135]

By the beginning of the Late Preclassic period (ca. 300 BC–AD 300) there were four Gulf regions: north, north-central, south-central, and south. Together the first two can be called the northern Gulf and the latter two the southern Gulf. Although these regions shared certain traditions, each manifested its own vigorous variants of culture and art at distinctive moments. The southern Gulf was the focus of the Olmec expansion during the later part of the Early and Middle Preclassic periods (ca. 2400–1000 BC and 1000–300 BC, respectively).

The non-Olmec objects of the Dumbarton Oaks Collection from the Gulf Lowlands, the focus of the articles in this section of the catalogue, date to the Classic period (AD 250/300–900) and the Postclassic period (AD 900–1520) and come from at least three—and perhaps all four—of the regional units. Many of the sculptures in this remarkable collection are thought to epitomize Classic Veracruz art.

Two salient aspects of the Classic Veracruz expression are its distinctive architecture and its inimitable art. These two modes of cultural symbolism are intrinsically related in the Gulf Lowlands. Much of the monumental art is situated or embedded in architectural contexts, and architectural features are frequently represented on both monumental and portable sculptures. Both architecture and art, in turn, reflect the complex tenets of elite religion and the manifold prerogatives of rulership (Wilkerson 1999, 2001d, 2001e). Nowhere is this more evident than at El Tajín, the greatest Classic Veracruz metropolitan center and the largest Gulf Lowlands city of its day.

In about the third century AD, El Tajín was a valley community of only local prominence in the north-central region. Throughout the later Late Preclassic period and the local Protoclassic period (together, ca. AD 100–300) the predominant population center was some 65 km to the southeast, at the much larger city of El Pital, probably a multiethnic city-state with a broad geographic supremacy (Wilkerson 1993, 1994a, 1994b, 1997b). With the demise of El Pital during the Early Classic period (ca. AD 300–600), El Tajín rapidly evolved into an aggressive provincial kingdom. During the Late Classic (ca. AD 600–900) it was probably a tribute state, perhaps even a regional empire, before its eventual tumultuous demise ca. AD 1100, at the end of the local Epiclassic period. El Tajín attained the greatest social centralization among its contemporaries in the Gulf Lowlands, fully representative of mature Classic Veracruz culture and art.

At El Tajín, Classic Veracruz architecture achieved its zenith.[136] Varied cut stone buildings were erected, often employing recessed niches and greatly extended "flying" cornices. Constructions were covered with thick cement and painted, often with murals. Grand terraces were formed to segregate the elite zones and temples of the city. Some structures were capped with truly massive flat cement roofs that were nearly modern in scope. There were also walled ritual compounds, and at least 15 formal stone ballcourts. The preponderance of such courts in the urban setting—unusual in Mesoamerica, where most cities had but one or two—was not by chance.

The principal rituals of the expanding metropolis focused on the ball game, consumption of vision-inducing pulque,[137] commemoration of rulership, elite veneration of the bellicose deity associated with the planet Venus, and human sacrifice. Once largely distinct, these cults merged over time into a macro-cult; its portals of access to the divine were diverse rites related to ballcourts. Construction of new courts or renovation of favored ones seems related to ruler accession and lineage affirmation, as well as to victory celebrations. Artwork set in these courts and associated structures, and that expressed in related portable sculptures, reflects the intensely syncretic nature of Classic Veracruz religion, demonstrating deliberate and formal merging of rulers with the divine and expressing temporal power on the ritual template of the ball game.

Classic Veracruz art has overlapping regional expressions, many highly localized. Human and animal forms are frequently rendered in double-outline format or with a raised border, particularly at El Tajín and throughout the north-central region and surrounding zones (see PC.B.050, Plate 75). Scrolls, commonly interlocking, and routinely enfolding anthropomorphic or zoomorphic faces or limbs, are widespread. Often, like luxuriant clouds, scrolls with varied formats, multiple meanings, and contextual significance engulf or frame the core elements of carvings. Many sculptures, especially monumental ones, are narratives, presenting one scene from a sequence of linked ritual acts. These scenes may represent rulers—sometimes as deity impersonators, occasionally as mortal protagonists—in reenactments of mythological events with the gods themselves (Figure 80).[138]

The depictions are frequently baroque in design, filling practically all available space around the image of the principal personage. Accoutrements of rank and divine symbols or beings swirl about the central figure or figures. Abundant detail, split images, elaborate headdresses, name glyphs, and diverse sizing of figures often obfuscate the central action or individual being portrayed in such sculptures. It is highly probable that many Gulf Lowlands stone sculptures were polychromed with paint. Occasionally some were dusted with red ochre. Many objects, particularly portable items, had inlays of diverse materials, such as bone, shell, obsidian, teeth, pyrite, and asphalt.

Most monumental sculpture is in low relief on sandstone, limestone, or basalt. Sculptures in the round are carved from basalt columns or boulders. Many of the better-known examples come from the north-central region, within a hundred kilometers or so of El Tajín. Portable sculptures, many of them ball game accoutrements rendered

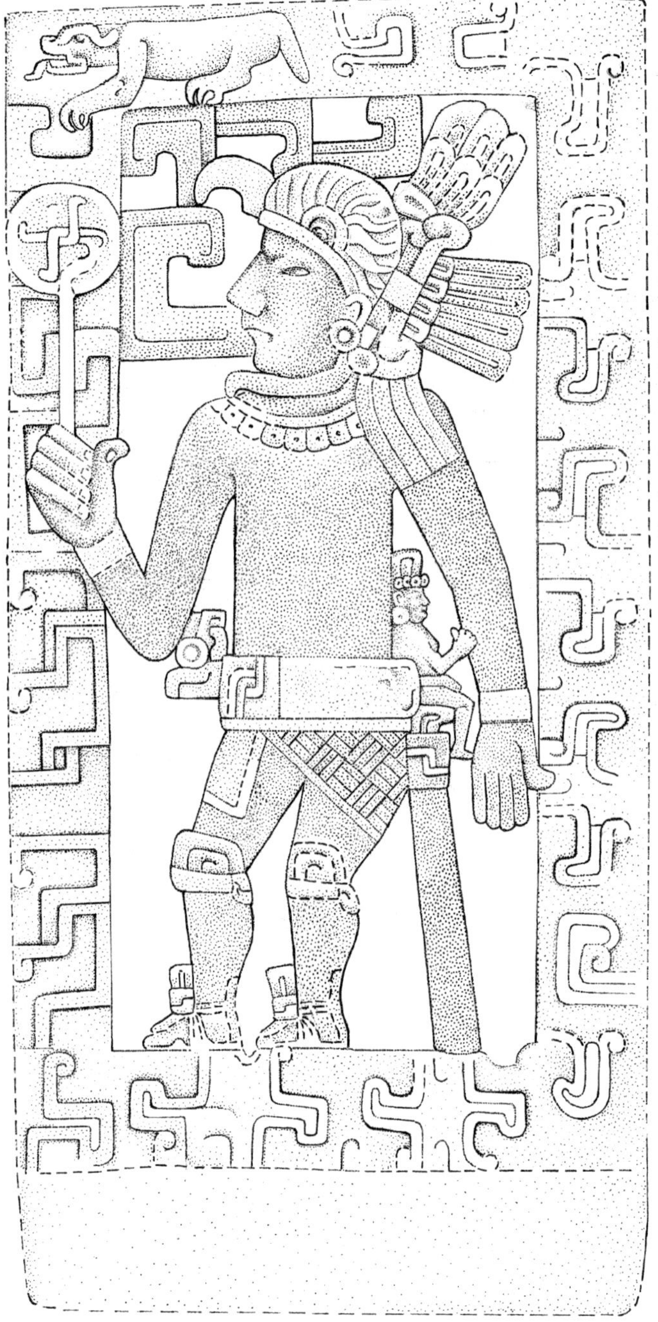

fig. 80
Monumental carving in Classic Veracruz style found on Building 5 at El Tajín. This carving is probably one of a sequence of temple tablets depicting ball game rites of a specific ruler. He performs a song, chant, or recitation, and possibly a dance, costumed in a zoomorphic headdress and ritual ball game attire with sculptural paraphernalia at his waist and hand. The figure emerges from a divine setting in a cloud-like scroll frame embracing a sacrificed feline. Drawing by the Institute for Cultural Ecology of the Tropics, Miguelangel Garcia/S. Jeffrey K. Wilkerson.

in stone, are much more widespread throughout the Gulf Lowlands. These objects are dispersed broadly, found at sites of all sizes, most often as grave goods, but are particularly abundant in the two central regions. They are also found in the south and north Gulf regions. Such sculptures were frequently carved from relatively soft basalt, but in some locales they were also made from harder stone, as well as soft green serpentine.

Monumental art at the metropolitan centers commemorated and enhanced the rulers, their lineages, their preferred cults, and the hegemony of their cities, but portable ball game art appears to have reinforced in parallel fashion similar values for individuals of the regional elites over a very extensive area. Such carvings were declarations of rank and station, as well as potent symbols of the right to participate in elite forms of the ritual ball game. These sculptures affirmed status and prerogatives;

they were not only exhibited in public ball game rites but also ultimately became treasured mortuary offerings, presumably for continued use in the hereafter (Wilkerson 1971, 1984, 1990, 1997d). In this respect, these sculptures were made for eternity.

Artisans in these cultures used other media besides stone. Clay was important in the southern Gulf Lowlands where sculptural stone was scarce and political factionalism may have complicated the movement of valued raw materials. Many Classic cults, especially in the south-central region, expressed identity through diverse terracotta images ranging from miniature figurines up to monumental life-sized statuary (see PC.B.051, Plate 73). The latter include massive fired likenesses as well as the elaborate unfired representations of deities in temple sanctuaries. Among the most collected categories of these earthen sculptures are the so-called Sonriente—"Smiling Face"—figurines, which were widely distributed and are abundant at sites large and small.[139]

In the northern Gulf Lowlands during the Postclassic period, an artistic florescence associated with aggressive multiethnic kingdoms transformed the region's ritualism and art. Sweeping westward into the highlands and well south along the coast, these labile societies clashed with one another and with existing centers that had flourished in the Classic period. The bellicose expansion of these mostly Huastec Mayan- and Nahua-speaking realms truncated the long evolution of the Classic Veracruz style in its northern reaches and fostered the spread of a distinct, severe style of slab stone sculpture (Fuente 1980; Wilkerson 2000).

Rendered predominantly in sandstone flag stones, the carvings range greatly in size, generally from a short and portable 50 cm up to stationary images more than 2 m in height. Representations of males predominate in this corpus and seem primarily to depict rulers celebrating conquests and ascension to rulership; at times the carvings may have commemorated the ruler's death. Renditions of women are also abundant. Some are rulers, dressed in the accoutrements of both rulership and war. But many are in the guise of various goddesses, and some may portray death in childbirth, an event that in the belief structure of the day conferred warrior status on the deceased.

Facial features, expressions, and postures of both male and female sculptures are largely stereotypic and rigid, although some clearly pertain to specific individuals. Such statuary varies greatly in the quality of execution, the finest achieving an exceptional control of detail and proportion. It is noteworthy that even in times of great social turmoil and internecine strife, artisans were still encouraged and achieved remarkable likenesses. The small Dumbarton Oaks statue of a woman (PC.B.533, Plate 72) is one of the finer examples of the genre.

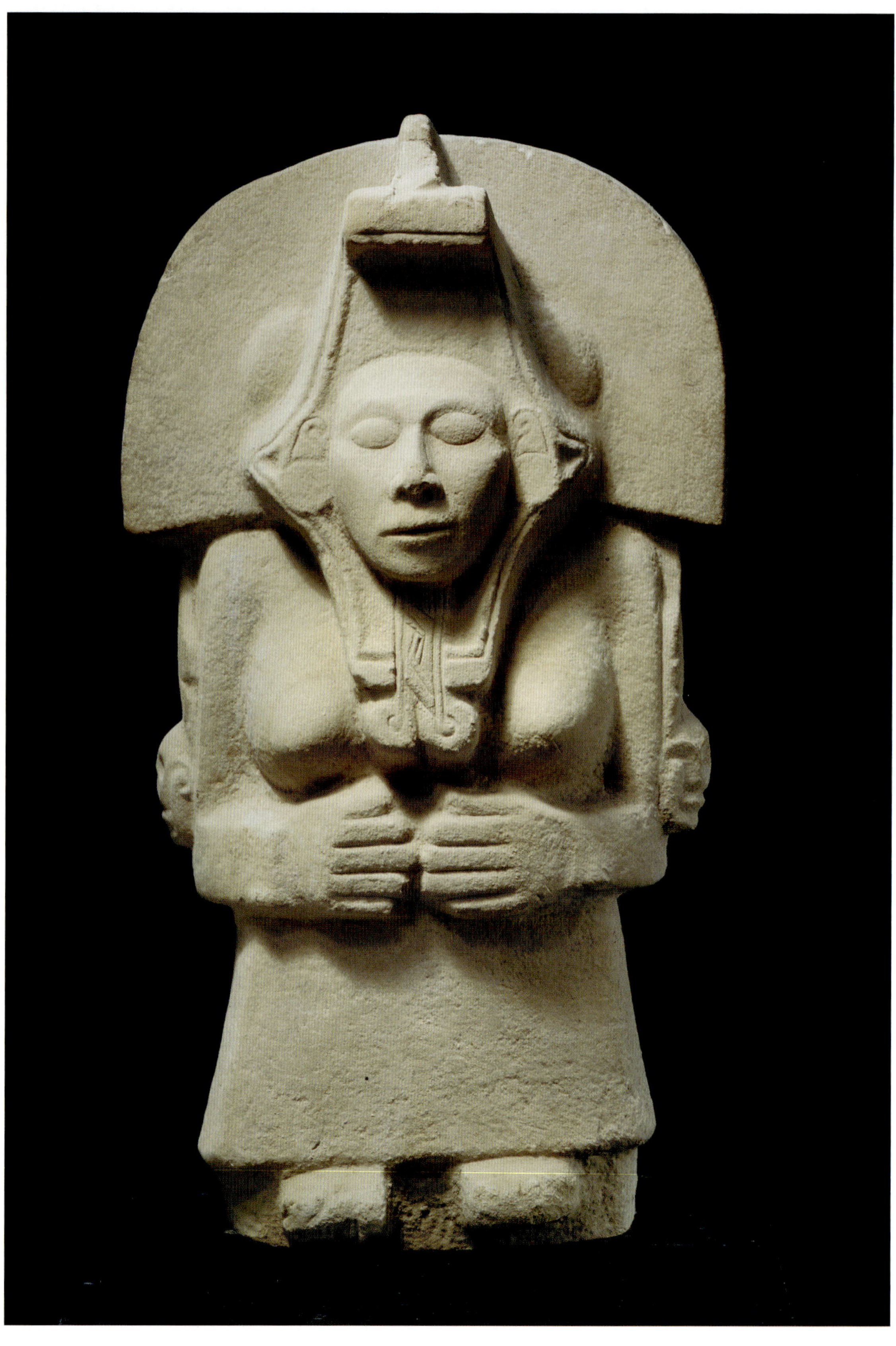

plate 72

FEMALE DEATH FIGURE

PLATE 72
Huastec; Northern Gulf Lowlands
Postclassic period, AD 900–1520
Sandstone
H. (excluding base) 73.0 cm (28¾"); W. 40.5 cm (16")
PC.B.533

ACQUISITION HISTORY:
Purchased from John Stokes, 1963

BIBLIOGRAPHY:
Dumbarton Oaks 1969: cat. no. 452; Fuente 1975: 30; Fuente 1985: fig. 6

During the great Huastec-Nahua expansion of the Postclassic period in the upper Gulf Lowlands, a notable artistic florescence was manifest in stone sculptures by the working of slabs, mainly sandstone flags. The bellicose explosion of the district's multiethnic kingdoms, often with Nahua elites but including various displaced ethnic groups, took this new sculptural form to the borders of the northern Gulf Lowlands and beyond.

With the violent conquests of these mostly ephemeral realms, earlier sculptural formats and styles largely disappeared, generally replaced with severe stone figures in a style traditionally called Huastec, after the principal inhabitants of this district, which was commonly known as the Huasteca. Although the corpus of large-scale Huastec statuary mostly depicts males, usually rulers, there are many female representations in an array of formats in which goddess impersonators with their symbolic attire predominate (Wilkerson 2000).

Before exploring the nature of such divine associations, however, it is important to examine the Dumbarton Oaks sculpture, one of the finest of its kind, and the only Bliss Collection object of the period from the northern Gulf Lowlands. More three-dimensional than most carvings from the area, it embodies many attributes of Huastec stone carving at its zenith and is shaped from good quality sandstone.

The sculpture's surface is pitted, primarily along the sides, because of the irregularly compacted nature of the stone as well as its original shaping. When fresh, this type of rock tends to have a bright yellow color but fades to beige, or even off-white, over time. Portions of the surface, principally in front, are flaking, as the relatively soft stone ages and is exposed to humidity. Nonetheless, the sculpture is in better overall condition than most known examples.

Most Huastec anthropomorphic statuary is one-fourth to one-third life size, although a few, primarily depicting males, are life size. Female figures, including headdresses, vary from 40 to 170 cm in height. This figure is in the lower portion of that range. On its own, the size of the figure would approach portable size, but the ample, unadorned pedestal base beneath the figure's feet indicates that the sculpture was meant to be erected at least in a semi-permanent manner. Most such statues in the Huastec style come from temple sanctuaries, which sometimes included more than one sculpture.

Here the face, perhaps a mask, emerges from a relatively large monster-maw helmet. The jaws are ornately rendered with a scroll-like projection for the snout. The monster's decorated bifurcate tongue extends down between the breasts to just above the waist. The beast's bulbous eyes bulge out from the figure's semicircular headdress. This spreading, fan-like adornment, used as the effigy headgear's backdrop, is the quintessential Huastec ceremonial accoutrement, visual affirmation of high status, rulership, or divinity.

The nude upper torso has widely separated breasts; formally posed hands nearly touch on the abdomen. A long skirt hangs down to the feet, best described as blocked out rather than carved. Typical of Huastec carving, less attention is paid to detail in the lower figure, especially the legs. The arms are adorned with pendant skulls attached to a cloth or leather flap in the form of a "holly leaf" design that also occurs in Huastec warrior tattoos.

The human mask, especially when viewed from the side, is unusually individualistic. Although such visages are most often stereotypic in these sculptures, this particular likeness has personal features. The large flared nose is accentuated by the sharply receding forehead characteristic of intentional cranial remodeling. The strong jaw recedes, its slackness leaving the slightly lopsided lips parted as in repose. The large eyes are blank and expressionless. The complete countenance gives the deliberate impression of a specific death mask.

The statue's squat appearance and stocky proportions belie its importance. In the northern Gulf Lowlands, particularly in the southern reaches at the time of this style, female sculptures were often small, even when depicting rulers, and the woman commemorated here was of very high status. Dangling craniums on the arms, uncommon in both male and female statuary from the core coastal Huastec area, are associated with warfare, rulership, and perhaps lineage (Wilkerson 2000). The monster motif, more common and geographically widespread, strongly indicates elevated female rank and divine impersonation.

But what gods are being imitated? Conventionally, in modern accounts, Huastec deities have Nahuatl names assigned in Aztec times, implying that these earlier gods of the Gulf Lowlands have connotations similar to those in the Central Highlands of Mexico at the time of contact. There is thematic overlap, but Huastec deities have their own significance. In this case, regional and temporal distinctions are essential to understanding the symbolic context of the sculpture.

Many of these female images from the northern Gulf are indiscriminately called Tlazolteotl figures (for example, Beverido Duhalt 2006; Fuente 1992; Medellín Zenil 1983). To Late Postclassic Nahuatl speakers of the highlands, this goddess was the patron of carnal vices, curing, and purification. Sometimes thought to be one of the powerful underworld and night lords, she was appeased by bloodletting. However, the earlier Huastec counterpart was Ixcuina, an ancient deity of the lowlands with broader earth goddess implications than the attributes mentioned above, including water abundance, fertility, warfare, flaying rituals, and lunar associations, and by extension a descending goddess who enters the underworld.

The earth goddess in hybrid reptilian monster form was thought to swallow the setting sun and the accompanying souls of both women who died in childbirth and deceased warriors. Thus the deity's mouth was the living entrance to the underworld, and this faculty of the goddess is depicted here. There are parallels to the Aztec earth deity Tlaltecuhtli, but the Huastec goddess was more encompassing and multifaceted. Enduring traditions in the Gulf Lowlands today reflect these once-common interlocking Pre-Columbian beliefs.

Surviving vestiges of these divine permutations from antiquity are at times evoked among indigenous groups in the former Huastec area of dominance. In one folk practice, women offer strands of hair to the waning sun, a deception to cheat the earth goddess from swallowing their souls.[140] Similar deception and concealment may be a motivation for identity-hiding masks common to such statues. Misleading the often capricious and malevolent gods, especially those of the night or underworld, is a Mesoamerican tradition of great time depth.

Metaphorical descent and ascent to and from the underworld were probably royal Huastec coronation rituals (Wilkerson 2000). The statue PC.B.533 may portray an important woman in the accoutrements of Ixcuina, wearing a stone death mask in a dynastic ritual invoking divine sanction for rulership renewal or change. Seemingly, such female statues were frequently paired in temples with larger renderings of males, often in warrior attire, that are probably ascension markers for rulers.[141]

Such statuary could be from practically any portion of the northern Gulf Lowlands' large core coastal area. However, the stone's grain and the rendering of detail in PC.B.533 suggest an origin in a zone of proficient sculptors with high artistic standards. This object is most probably from the slopes of the Sierra Otontepec. On the southern side in the upper north-central Gulf Lowlands, at such sites as Piedra Labrada and Zacamixtle, similar stone and styling were used in some of the most dynamic and expressive sculptures of the period.

SJKW

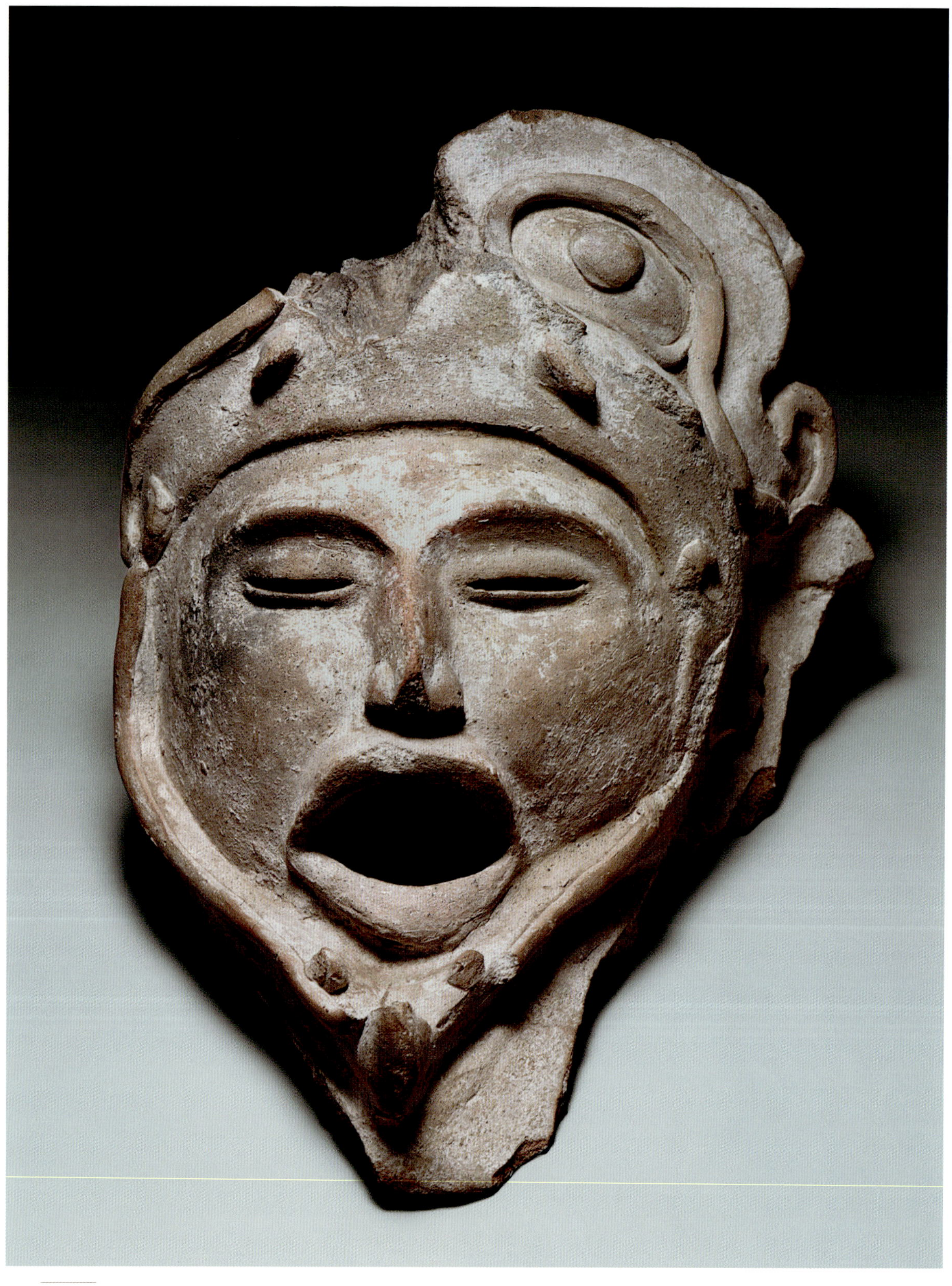

plate 73

CERAMIC HEAD

PLATE 73
Regional Monumental style; south-central Gulf Lowlands
Late Classic period, AD 600–900
Ceramic
H. 29.1 cm (11½"); W. 22.5 cm (8⅞"); D. 13.1 cm (5⅛")
PC.B.051

ACQUISITION HISTORY:
Purchased from Helmut de Terra in 1952; formerly in the collection of William Spratling

EXHIBITION HISTORY:
Indigenous Art of the Americas, National Gallery of Art, Washington, D.C., February 1954–July 1962 (NGA 554)

BIBLIOGRAPHY:
Christensen 1955: 244, fig. 198; Bliss 1957: 238, cat. no. 32, pl. XXIV; *Natural History* 1958: 129; Dumbarton Oaks 1963: 21, cat. no. 103

This fragment is from a large, probably monumental fired clay figure, which, if complete, would have been a meter or more high. It is a head with a death expression, its eyes closed to slits and the mouth rigidly open in a broad oval. The eye ridges and nose are sharply defined. The paste is well mixed with sand temper and fully fired. Around the head is a zoomorphic helmet, its upper portion broken off. This headgear seemingly represents a curious mythological creature with a large button eye framed by a scroll that is defined with a fillet of clay.

The human face is placed in a maw that has features of both a bird beak and reptilian jaws. Rounded teeth are shown, suggesting that this may be a form of monster with avian-crocodilian attributes. Such hybrid beasts occur in Gulf Lowlands statuary at the end of the Late Classic period and throughout the Postclassic. As earth monsters they were thought to devour the dead at the entrance to the underworld.

This item has been ascribed to the Remojadas style of south-central Veracruz, which dates to the Terminal Preclassic and Early Classic periods (ca. AD 1–600). Among other divergences from the norm for this style, however, there is no asphalt decoration on this figure, one of the style's salient features. The modeled features, size, paste, and decorations suggest that it is not of that localized styling, nor is it likely to have been from that vicinity. Monumental statuary of these proportions and with these attributes is not currently known from Remojadas or the immediate district.

When this ceramic head was first described in the late 1940s to 1960s, it was fashionable to label practically all large ceramic figures from south-central Veracruz, regardless of origin, as being from Remojadas or executed in its style. It was not until the 1970s that the truly monumental ceramic sculptures of El Zapotal became widely known (Gutiérrez Solana and Hamilton 1977). That key site is situated about 70 km to the south. This item is much more closely related to the ceramic statuary from that district, both stylistically and structurally.

Although such figures can be found in various parts of the southern Gulf Lowlands, most of the sites with ceramic sculptures of this size and thematic context are on the northern side of the Río Papaloapan, and especially along the Río Blanco tributary. This low region, with few appropriate stones for carving, is crammed with sites of all sizes that often yield large numbers of ceramic figures. Part of this zone, known as the Mixtequilla, has an especially high density of sites and artifacts.

Many such exquisite sculptures were intentionally broken in antiquity when they were buried as offerings. Often large numbers of figures were interred at the same time. It is probable that ascension ceremonies of rulers, construction dedications, cyclical Venus celebrations, or victories of conquest motivated such multiple offerings.

This item is from an important monumental figure depicting a male with a monster helmet. It probably dates to the Terminal Classic. Many helmeted figures, often warriors, are known from the lower elevations of the south-central area of Veracruz. Deity impersonators, one of which is probably represented in PC.B.051, are also depicted. Sometimes the Maize God is shown sacrificed in the ballcourt with such an avian-monster helmet. The quality of the workmanship in this clay sculpture is above average, and the complete figure would have been striking indeed.

SJKW

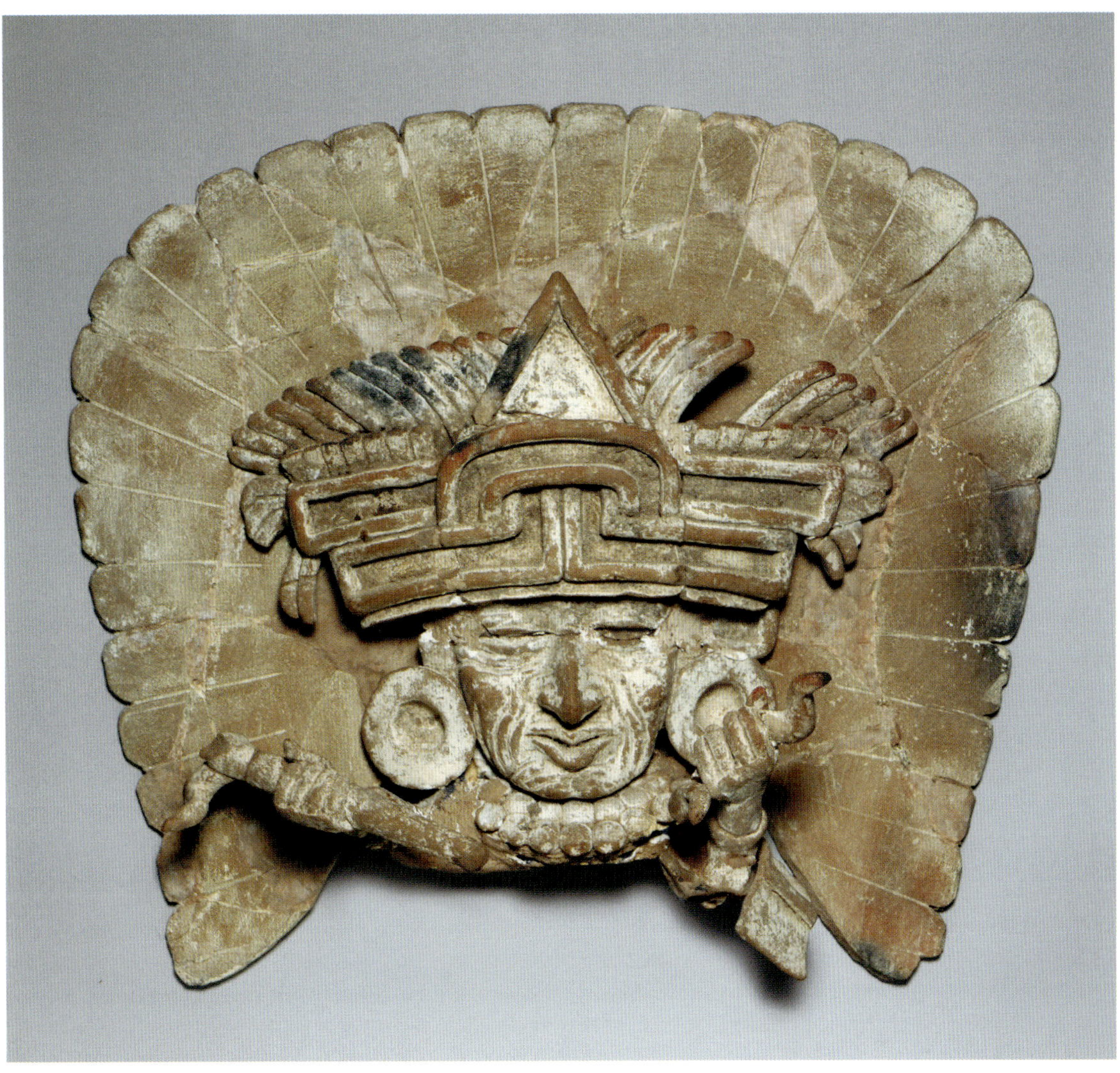

plate 74

FRAGMENT OF AN INCENSE BURNER

PLATE 74
Lirios; south-central Gulf Lowlands
Early Classic period, AD 300–600
Ceramic
Face and headdress: H. 27.2 cm (10¾"); W. 34.3 cm (13½")
Backing: H. 19.5 cm (7¾"); W. 22.3 cm (8¾")
PC.B.052

ACQUISITION HISTORY:
Acquired ca. 1963

Once part of an incense burner, this artifact consists of several pieces: a face with a headdress, a backdrop, and hands and arms. It has been part of the Bliss Collection since about 1963 (Elizabeth Benson, personal communication, 22 August 2002).

The face has a prominent nose and wrinkled skin, and wears an imposing headdress featuring an inverted "V" or ray form over a complex trapezoid, suggesting a stylized A-O year symbol. This is surmounted by a short panache. Although the face is carefully modeled, the headdress and panache are composed of fillets of clay appliquéd to the background. The figure wears large clay ear spools and a double strand of clay beads. His hands and arms are modeled of clay fillets, and each hand grasps a snake or a snake-shaped scepter. The arms have been crudely and recently attached to either side of the base of the face. The background form seems to represent an abstract feather panache.

The figure is in fragile condition and has numerous breaks. In spite of the figure's poor condition and haphazard reconstruction, the pieces seem to have once been part of a whole composition, because the clay is consistent in color, quality of grain, type of temper, and white slip.

The wrinkled visage is typical of a Mesoamerican deity known as the Old God or the Old Fire God, found throughout the Central Highlands as well as in West Mexico, Oaxaca (González Licón and Márquez Morfín 1990), the south-central Gulf Lowlands (Stark 2001: 204), and the Guatemala Highlands (Lothrop 1933, 1936)—in fact, the Old Fire God's territory corresponds well to Mesoamerica's zone of active volcanoes. In representational form, he is often depicted as a seated figure in stone or ceramics as part of an incense burner; such incense burners seem to have been part of household rather than temple rituals. The Old Fire God was known as Huehueteotl to the Aztecs, and was thought to represent an elderly avatar of Xiuhtecuhtli, the Central Mexican fire god, who was associated "with youthful warriors and rulership" (Miller and Taube 1993: 189). He is thought to have been the principal deity at Cuicuilco, the Late Preclassic city in the Basin of Mexico that was abandoned after volcanic activity in the southern basin subjected it to ash falls and lava flows. Its population may have contributed to the growth of Teotihuacan at this time: Old Fire God incense burners have been found in domestic contexts in the city, which is itself a safe distance from active volcanoes.

The Bliss Collection incense burner, however, is not similar to Central Mexican specimens. Rather, it more closely resembles Old Fire God incense burners found in southern Veracruz. Images of the Old Fire God are common in this region and seem to express localized ceramic figure traditions. The most famous of these was excavated at Cerro de las Mesas (Drucker 1943b: 11–14). Discussing this find, Coe (1965: 702) wrote that "there is no doubt that huge clay sculptures of this type (Drucker's 'Monumental Ware') as well as the extremely similar modeled figurines called 'Lirios' are of the Early Classic period, both here and at other sites in the area" (see also Miller 1991: 30).

Coe (1965: 704) further discussed this general type of artifact as characteristic of Tres Zapotes III ceramics: "As noted for Cerro de las Mesas, this probably also marks the beginning, perhaps the apogee, of the large, modeled grotesque clay figurines of the Lirios type: wrinkled old men like that at Cerro de las Mesas (the spider-webby appearance of the wrinkles is identical at both sites), men with open mouths, bag-eyed and bearded men. All are hollow, usually with large, hollow irises" (see also Weiant 1943: pl. 39). Figurines in this style were found in the Mixtequilla area (Stark 2001: 204–205, 210–211).

The Lirios type was defined from figurines found at the Lirios site, a few miles from Tres Zapotes (Drucker 1943a: 83). Lirios pieces are unusual in the delicacy of their expression and modeling. The Lirios type of Old Fire God examples included figurines, such as the one that Stirling (1940) reported, as well as incense burners. In describing Lirios figures, Drucker (1943a: 83–84) lists a number of characteristics that correspond to those of the Dumbarton Oaks figure: they are made of reddish brown paste, sometimes "markedly sandy" in texture; they are hand-modeled (rather than mold-made) figures with appliquéd pieces; there is an emphasis on naturalism in the faces, suggesting portraiture and including a variety of facial expressions; "aged individuals, with seamed and sunken cheeks, are fairly common"; hands consist of "gracefully curving but apparently boneless long fingers and a thumb"; headdresses are formed by strips of clay; and clay ears and ear spools are attached to the sides of the head.

In addition to an affinity with south-central Veracruz based on stylistic traits, the origin of this piece in that region has been substantiated to some degree by instrumental neutron activation analysis, which determined that the clay is probably from the area of the Río Blanco drainage of the Río Papaloapan basin. A sample from the figure was tested with a large set of samples from utilitarian and service vessels from that area (Stark et al. n.d.).

The sample from PC.B.052 was assigned to the overall western lower Papaloapan basin compositional group, but it could not be placed in any of the three subgroups of sherds from this region, "possibly because the clay and temper selected for a special ritual item were not the same exactly as those used for the pots in household use" (B. Stark, personal communication, 10 August 2005). The western lower Papaloapan basin has Río Blanco as its principal channel, and the Mixtequilla region and Cerro de las Mesas are along the lower Río Blanco drainage, whereas Tres Zapotes is in the eastern part of the lower Río Papaloapan drainage.

Thus, although the Bliss Collection Old Fire God incense burner is incomplete, the masterful depiction of its portrait face earns it well-deserved respect for its quality. Based on its style and material, it seems likely that it can be classified as Lirios ware, and that its provenience was south-central Veracruz, dating to the Early Classic period. This probable location and period of use, together with its design and iconography, indicate that it was a type of object fairly common in its culture, being used for rituals honoring fire and the hearth.

STE

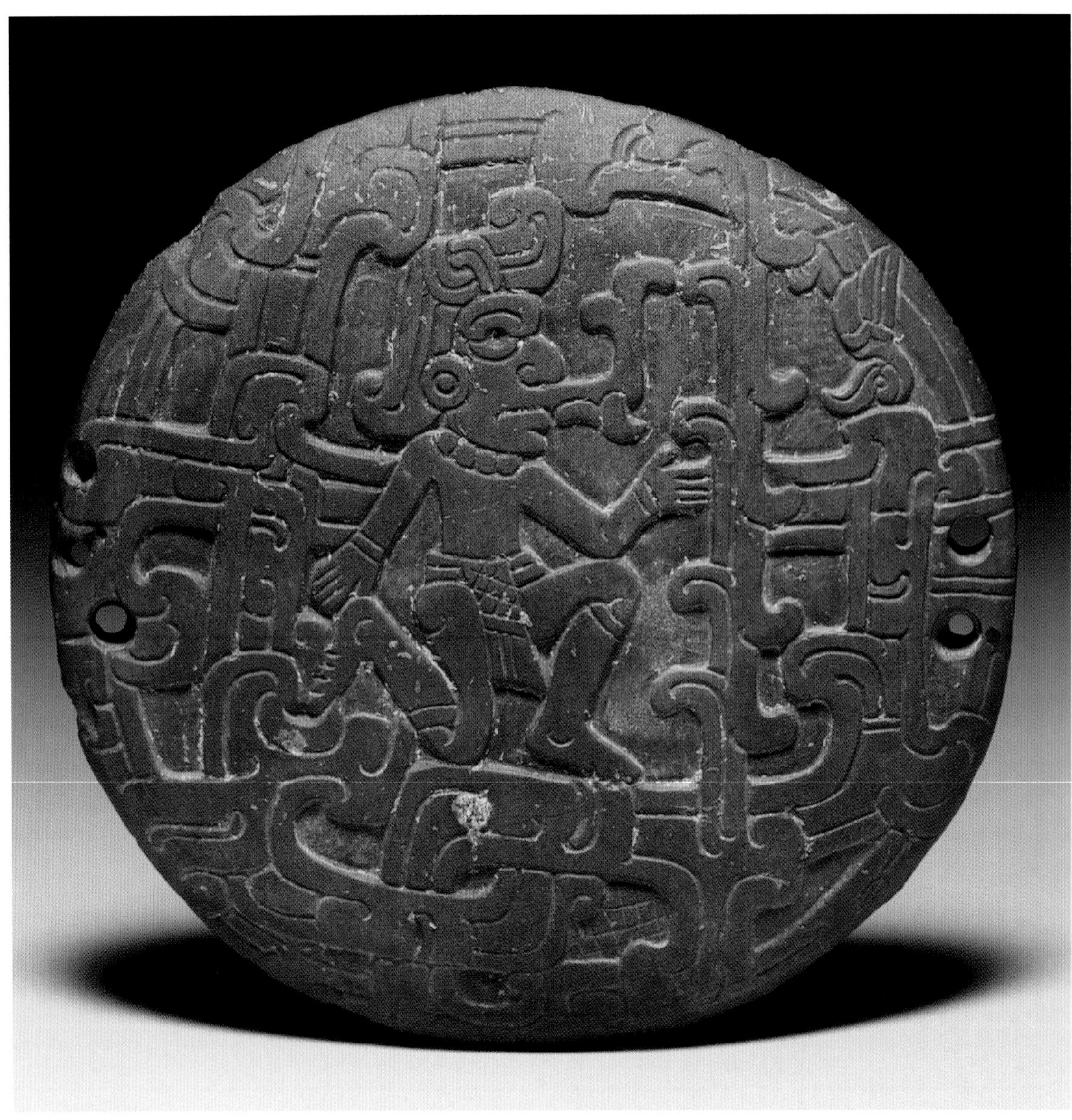

plate 75

CARVED PLAQUE

PLATE 75
Classic Veracruz; north-central Gulf Lowlands
Early Classic period, AD 300–600
Slate
H. 12.0 cm (4¾"); W. 12.35 cm (4 ⅞"); D. 1.0 cm (⅜")
PC.B.050

ACQUISITION HISTORY:
Purchased from Earl Stendahl, 1955

EXHIBITION HISTORY:
Indigenous Art of the Americas, National Gallery of Art, Washington, D.C., April 1956–July 1962 (NGA 676)

BIBLIOGRAPHY:
Bliss 1957: 232, 235–236, cat. no. 20A, pl. XI; Covarrubias 1957: 185–187, pl. XLIV; *Arts* 1958: 16; Cook de Leonard 1959: 554, cat. no. 35; Disselhoff and Linné 1960: 61, fig. 32; Dumbarton Oaks 1963: 21, cat. no. 102; Willey 1966: I: 142; Young-Sanchez 1990: 340, fig. 24

This small, rare, and delicately carved plaque is one of the Pre-Columbian world's more esoteric objects. It is also one of the finest Gulf Lowlands items in the Pre-Columbian Collection at Dumbarton Oaks. The depicted scene is incised with certain background portions scraped away or crosshatched. The scrollwork is ornate and likely of Early Classic date. Made of dark slate, such sculptures have traditionally been considered to be the backing for pyrite mirrors.

As with most of the known examples, this one has a single figure incised at its center. A long-haired man is on one knee with his arms extended. The wrists are wrapped. His body attire, the knee wrappings and shortened breechcloth, strongly suggest a ball game player. The posture is reminiscent of the position used to return a low ball in the ritual game, or a pose of veneration from an associated rite. A stone bead necklace around his throat indicates high status, as does his composite ear spool, often shown on rulers and gods. The eye has a supraorbital plate or scroll, common in Classic Veracruz art.

The head has two identifying attributes: the first is long hair tied in a knot, which is frequently worn by the Rain God. In front of the face is not a speech symbol, as sometimes has been indicated. Rather, the upper lip is extended with an additional tooth and a fang protruding downward, before the lip moves upward in a bifurcate scroll. This compound second attribute is also associated with the Rain God or his impersonators.

A plant-like staff is in front of the figure, and he may be reaching for it. The Rain God is often shown holding vegetative, scrolled, serpentine, or twisted insignia as if they were scepters. The bird perched on the upper leaf and peering at the figure is possibly a keel-billed toucan (*Ramphastos sulfuratus*), but could be a stocky parrot (*Amazona* sp.) or, less likely, one of the nightjars (*Caprimulgidae*) rendered with an elongated beak. Sometimes the Rain God is shown with a bird scepter. The staff here may be embellished with corn leaves, which are present in some Classic Veracruz scenes of ball game sacrifice.

Accompanying scrollwork further clarifies the ball game context. Two elaborate scroll sequences extend upward from beneath the figure's feet, very probably representing twin ballcourt serpents. They intertwine below and perhaps above the figure. Looping lines of scrolls that extend over the double bands surrounding the plaque as a border provide a dynamic perspective.

At El Tajín, narrative scenes of later date than this plaque show what are almost certainly pulque-induced visions. In these large sculptures, from the circular coils of such snakes emerge images of the underworld gods or past rulers. Some of these depictions are placed in a ballcourt. Such apparitions appear to be related to ascension ceremonies in which the sanctions of certain predecessors and gods are sought from their abode in the afterlife.

So few plaques have been encountered that it is difficult to understand their thematic variation and purpose. Nevertheless, it is likely that mirror backs reproduced an aspect of such vision scenes. In the case of this plaque, the figure may be an ancestral ruler in the guise of the Rain God, or perhaps it is the evoked deity himself on an underworld ballcourt. Probably it was carved as part of rites associated with ruler ascension, confirmation of lineage, or right of governance. Perhaps, too, pyrite or hematite mirrors were considered windows on the underworld or its denizens. Inevitably such treasured accoutrements of status would be buried with the honored individual for his trip to the hereafter.

It should be noted that the diameter of this plaque, as well as that of the other known examples, is very close to the width of the hole in standard ball game markers (*tlaxmalacatl* in Nahuatl) shown in the El Tajín sculptures as well as in actual stone rings from central and eastern Mexico. Additionally, these plaques directly approximate the diameter of the ball used in two surviving forms of the game, one using the forearm, the other a mallet. Such sculptures may have symbolized the mystical powers of prophecy and vision, derived from the gods and divine ancestral rulers, by means of the central element of the ritual itself: the ball.

The object's back has drilled indentations, possibly to anchor an adhesive for still another surface, presumably pyrite or other reflective material. Thus the object's ritual use may have required access to both its sides. Yet the use of these plaques as mirror backs has not been clearly demonstrated. However, a sculptural depiction from El Tajín shows a ball game figure holding in front of him, like a scepter on the end of a short staff, a scroll-ornamented object of similar proportions (Figure 81), suggesting a symbol of prerogative.

Other possible uses are implied by multiple perforations on opposite edges of this and other plaques, generally along the horizontal center axis of the depiction. These suggest that it was tied to something, perhaps a frame or even a garment. Sculptural scenes at El Tajín suggest still other possibilities. Some Rain God and bird impersonators wear belts that always run from the left shoulder to the right side and bear an ovoid mirror or plaque, clearly a divine accoutrement of rank and station. Regardless of how initially employed, like so many of the ritual objects of the ball game cult, these items ultimately became funerary offerings.

The plaque was reportedly from the Misantla region in the central mountains of Veracruz, but it is almost certainly from a part of the Gulf Lowlands that was traditionally reached through Misantla. Covarrubias (1957) indicated that two plaques were found close to the town of Vega de Alatorre. His illustration of one of them shows a carving in very similar style, though slightly stiffer, with many comparable elements. Plaque PC.B.050 is likely to be the other plaque; together they may well illustrate distinct moments in a single mythological sequence. Quite near Vega de Alatorre are notable sites, such as Las Higueras, Aparicio, Tacahuite, and El Diamante. The last two have Early Classic occupation. Nearby Aparicio, from which has come large-scale Classic Veracruz sculpture, is seemingly largely of Late Classic date but may have an earlier component. This superb and eccentric sculpture is likely to have come from this area, most likely Tacahuite.

Purportedly there are slate sources in the mountains between the Gulf beaches and Misantla, and this general region is a possible source for the handful of other known plaques in this medium and format. Although few in number, they were spread widely and have been found at Kaminaljuyu in Guatemala (Kidder et al. 1977 [1946]: fig. 156) and in Highland Central Mexico. They must have been much valued in commerce or, more likely, for specific ritual purposes.

The Dumbarton Oaks plaque depicts a symbol-laden scene that may be from a particular vision sequence charged with mythological import. A deity or its impersonator, with Rain God attributes, is shown in a reverential act in or near a ballcourt. The baroque rendering is carefully crafted and fully within the fluorescent Classic Veracruz style. Although its purpose is unknown, this exquisite sculpture is one of the rarest stone carvings from ancient Veracruz and one of the most exceptional objects in the Bliss Collection.

SJKW

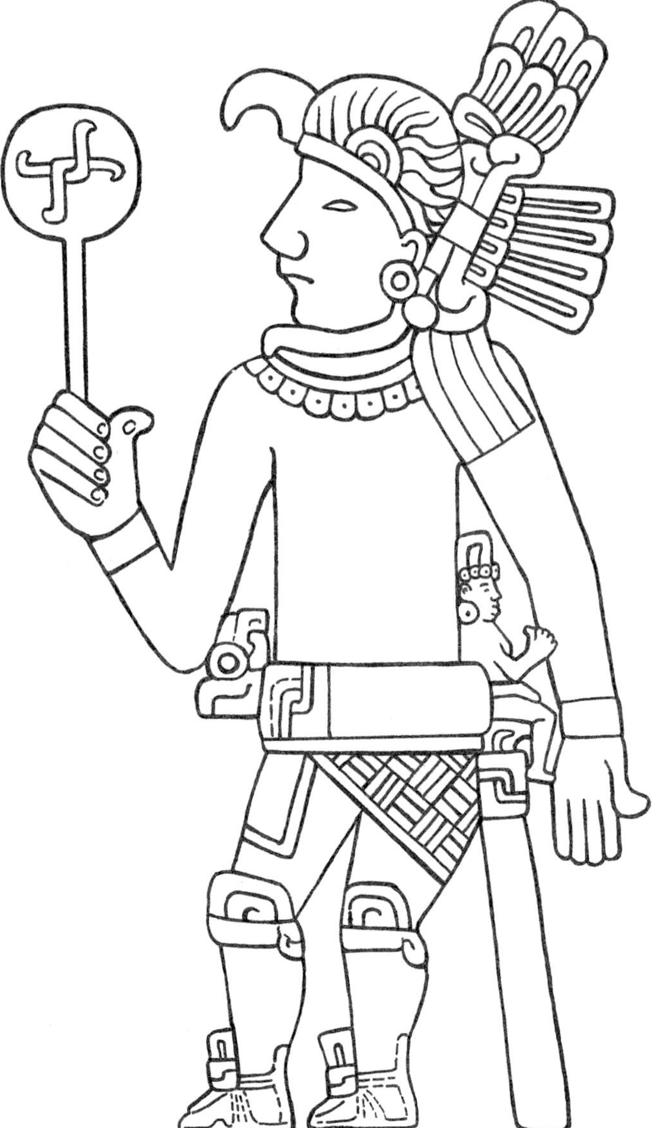

fig. 81

Detail of the high-ranking protagonist in the Building 5 tablet at El Tajín. Dressed in a bird helmet and ball game knee protectors, he wears what is almost certainly a form of yoke around his waist. On one edge of this accoutrement is a bird hacha and on the opposite is an anthropomorphic palma. In the figure's hand is the shaft of an object that resembles a hafted carved mirror. Drawing by the Institute for Cultural Ecology of the Tropics, Miguelangel Garcia/S. Jeffrey K. Wilkerson.

PORTABLE BALL GAME SCULPTURES

The ancient Mesoamerican ball game cult had its apogee in Classic Veracruz culture. In the Gulf Lowlands, and especially in the aggressive centralized polities of the north-central region, the ball game was elevated to an all-encompassing core ritual and true collective obsession rarely seen in the ancient societies of the Americas. It was thought to be a rite of chance and divine inspiration performed by the principal deities in the underworld and imitated by mortals. When performed in the formats of the ruling elite, it could lead, as it did in the mythological lore, to sacrificial death by decapitation or other means.

Institutionalized, the ball game macro-cult in the Gulf Lowlands became a matrix for many elite rituals that encompassed ruler ascension rites, Venus calendar events, lineage homage, vision-inducing ritual drinking, human sacrifice, status affirmation, and deity impersonation, as well as public celebrations of cyclic warfare and state conquest. As a prerogative of nobility in certain formats, the cult linked the most popular rites of the time and justified rulership. As a widespread social phenomenon, it internally unified the predominantly multiethnic and highly stratified societies of the Gulf Lowlands. It was also at the heart of a shared belief system that shaped the world-view of Classic Veracruz culture and art.[142]

Although ritually codified, the game had multiple manifestations and varying import at distinct levels of regional societies and across diverse ethnic groups. In ancient and modern times, the ball game has evolved in its format, configuration, and significance, which has led it in disparate directions. In northwestern Mexico today the game's formats vary at the village level, employing the hip, forearm, and mallet for propelling the rubber ball. These forms appear to derive from once-common game varieties of considerable antiquity that existed throughout the Mesoamerican heartland, including Veracruz.

Other variants of the ritual game used sticks, hand stones, heavy gloves, and field markers or goals. Some of these playing accoutrements are still found today, mostly in Central Mexico. The use of circular stone goals, although common in the highlands at least by the Postclassic period, appears to have only arrived in the Gulf Lowlands just before European contact. Almost certainly even more forms of the ball game were once played. These ancient configurations appear to have evolved as the ritual game was adapted to the varying social contexts of the Mesoamerican societies. There certainly was an accelerated change in the ball game rituals of the Gulf Lowlands during the Classic period.

Some ball game variations were graded along class lines, from the elaborate, choreographed, and rigid elite patterns enacted in stone-sided courts with stands for spectators through labile popular forms played in dusty open spaces amid enthusiastic bettors and bustling crowds. In fact, "Dusty Court" is the designation of the playing area of the underworld gods in the *Popul Vuh,* a colonial-period compilation of very ancient myths. In such sagas death literally came to both powerful gods and noblemen in the dust of the ballcourts.

In spite of the variant modes of play through time, space, or social rank, scoring methods were generally consistent, computed in set-like phases and based primarily on body faults as well as failed and out-of-bounds returns. Somewhat like modern tennis, one side's advantage of several points could suddenly be equalized. However, there were no regulation periods, often making for exhausting games of very long duration. Colonial and modern meets have been postponed because of darkness and resumed the next day. Endurance and the "will of the gods" were major factors in the ritual game. Betting was, and still is, common—it was not just associated sacrifices that drew spectator interest.[143]

With the remarkable popularity of the ball game, the associated ritual paraphernalia, primarily the accoutrements of players, became the ultimate symbols of the prerogative of participation in the more elite formats. Although only stone examples have survived, it is likely that they imitate earlier forms worked in wood and skin. Regardless of origin, these forms clearly attained a sacred status in the Gulf Lowlands and eventually became heavily ornamented emblems of ritual involvement. The three most common forms are known today by fanciful misnomers: yokes (*yugos*), palmas (palmate stones), and hachas (axes). On these portable sculptures Gulf Lowlands artisans elaborated some of ancient America's most intricate and extraordinary decoration, and many of these often-small objects represent the zenith of Classic Veracruz art.

With the collapse of Classic Veracruz civilization, the longlived and pervasive ball game focus of the Gulf Lowlands abruptly ended, along with the carving of portable ball game sculptures. The demise followed a bellicose Epiclassic florescence in the north-central region and a dynamic Terminal Classic manifestation in the south-central region. The ball game rite continued, but with a highland flavor in many areas and without the earlier macro-cult status that had made it the very center of Classic Veracruz ritualism. Gone, too, were the stunning, if enigmatic, portable sculptures that—beginning with stone yokes, then hachas, and finally palmas—were carved for at least a millennium and a half.

SJKW

YOKES

These U-shaped sculptures were whimsically named in the nineteenth century as a result of a perceived similarity of shape to that of a yoke for oxen. They constitute an ancient and enduring Gulf Lowlands sculptural tradition that in some regions is likely to have been elevated to cult status. The actual function of this sculpture's prototype was probably to protect the ball game player's waist. By the late Middle Preclassic period, waist protectors made of wood and probably leather, used in the ball game itself, were reproduced in stone throughout central Veracruz. At that time the preferred medium was gray, often dense, volcanic rock. The "yokes" themselves appear to have been originally undecorated, although in later times many were recarved with diverse motifs.

Throughout the many subsequent centuries of elaboration these objects, and even their fragments, were clearly considered very sacred. Their ultimate use, as with all sculpted ball game paraphernalia, would be as cherished and prestigious mortuary offerings (Wilkerson 1971), accompanying the deceased to an afterlife where the gods of the underworld presided over the same ball game. Ritual scenes from Late Classic El Tajín and Chichén Itzá show some types of yokes worn primarily in post-game rites, often involving human sacrifice. Although the earliest yokes may have approximated the form of the game protectors actually worn in the ritual encounters, later ones in the Gulf Lowlands appear to be primarily stylized waist bands that served as platforms for the attachment of other sculptures—hachas and palmas, discussed below.

The possession of any of the major sculptural paraphernalia of the ball game, but especially a yoke, signaled the elite prerogative to play elaborate ritual forms of the game. Much as medieval European jousting helmets were symbols of station and privilege, these Mesoamerican items had strong connotations of social rank. Their public exhibition in game rites or related ceremonies would enhance their owners' status. The yoke tradition has the greatest time depth and duration of the various ball game subcults, except for veneration of the rubber ball itself—the one indispensable item in all forms of the ritual.

By the end of the Early Preclassic period, rubber balls were ritually submerged in springs in southern Veracruz, perhaps as gifts to the powerful gods at these perceived aquatic entrances to the underworld (Ortiz et al. 1997; Rodríguez and Ortiz 1994). Throughout the pre-Hispanic era they continued as votive offerings as well as sacred symbols of the ritual ball game. At El Tajín they are depicted resting in special rounded containers, apparently set in temple sanctuaries, between episodes of use in the courts. Sculptures and murals in the Gulf Lowlands show that larger game balls at times contained a human skull, consistent with the game's emphasis on decapitation. Sometimes the victim is shown initially seated upright on such a ball. Probably these rubber-encased skulls were from high-status player-prisoners, such as captured rulers, who were sacrificed in the playing courts. Even in death these individuals had a prominent role in the ball game.

Many balls were much smaller: many Late Postclassic stone goal rings have diameters as small as 10 or 11 cm, and some balls used in modern versions of the game are fist-sized. But Classic depictions show balls that are knee high and occasionally even larger. Such spheres of solid rubber, even without a skull, could weigh upward of 20 kg, and their impact could cause injury or even death: protectors were necessary.

The earliest stone yokes, often the heaviest and largest, tend to have an exterior lateral convex protrusion that, if used in game play, would repel the solid rubber ball, although probably uncontrollably. However, no known yokes have chip marks or fractures from such use. Yokes have narrow interiors with little variation to suggest individual sizing: slim and youthful players could wear such sculptures, but not necessarily the veteran participants or aging rulers who used the courts. Yokes were probably worn in rites associated with the ball game and were standardized sculptures imitating customized and composite game protectors made of such materials as wood, leather, and even compacted cotton. Many of the early stone yokes have closed ends, suggesting a padded wooden rod curved in a closing "U" and bound by a flat tablet latch.

On yokes that do not have closed ends, one of the earliest decorative motifs is commonly called "monster of the earth." This design, with numerous variants, appears to have been most popular in the Late Preclassic period and, especially in the south-central Gulf region, continued well into the Classic period. It has a wide mouth and face with supraorbital plates in reptilian fashion, suggesting that wearing a yoke, or the actual ball game protector, symbolically placed the player within the jaws of death. The maw was thought to be that of the mythical female monster of the underworld, who was located in the west and who swallowed the sun. The death connotation of the ball game is very old in the Gulf Lowlands, and it is a persistent theme in ball game sculptures (Wilkerson 1984). Its presence at such an early date implies that much of the mythical and sacrificial framework of the ball game, so heavily emphasized in later sculptures, was already in place well before the Classic period.

In ancient times earlier yokes are likely to have been encountered when older burials were disturbed in the process of refurnishing temple sanctuaries and undertaking new construction. Some of these salvaged objects were then saved and resculpted. The practice of decorative reuse of yokes is very common in the Gulf Lowlands during the Classic period. In fact, it is probable that even new yokes were produced in two stages: first the roughhewn U-shaped form was created and then the surfaces were polished and/or carved. These stages were not necessarily immediately sequential or undertaken by the same artisans. By the time of the Classic apogee of yoke carving, each step may have reflected different grades, or ritual stations, attained by the owner-participant in the ball game cult. Narrative scenes in sculptures at El Tajín suggest that plain yokes were covered with elaborate perishable decoration or precious stones in some rites; thus sophisticated carving would have been just one way a yoke was ritually ornamented.

Sometimes the design runs off the stone, generally on the bottom edge, as in the elaborately carved Dumbarton Oaks yoke PC.B.035 (Plate 76). The patterns thus may have preexisted, perhaps for larger sized sculptures, or more likely, they were first drawn by a talented artist with mastery of the peculiar yoke iconography who was perhaps consulted at a major metropolitan center. In rendering the often complicated image on the multifaceted surfaces of the increasingly angular Classic yokes, local sculptors may have had difficulties reducing it to the available space. Additionally, the final smoothing and sometimes polishing of the surfaces prior to carving would further reduce the overall size.

It is also clear that in some regions yokes were initially divided into segments by sculptors, such as appear on two of the Dumbarton Oaks "plain" yokes (PC.B.036 and PC.B.037; Plates 77 and 78). The final design was then also subdivided and carved. Generally the carving of yokes appeared to proceed from the upper interior edge to the external lower perimeter, where the designs were often truncated for lack of space. In addition to some sizing distinctions with regional implications, carved yokes also appear to have design components or configurations that probably corresponded to localized cult emphasis and preferences, especially throughout the Classic period in both north-central and south-central Veracruz. By that time many different stone media—particularly green stone—were popular, and some (such as the carved Dumbarton yoke PC.B.035) were quite hard.

Yokes were carried well beyond the confines of the Gulf Lowlands in the Classic period. They appeared in western Mexico, Central America, and near the northeastern frontier of Mesoamerica. In all probability, these widespread examples reflect the movement of Gulf peoples, or groups heavily influenced by them, who carried this sculptural symbol of the ball game cult with them in their migrations or travels.

SJKW

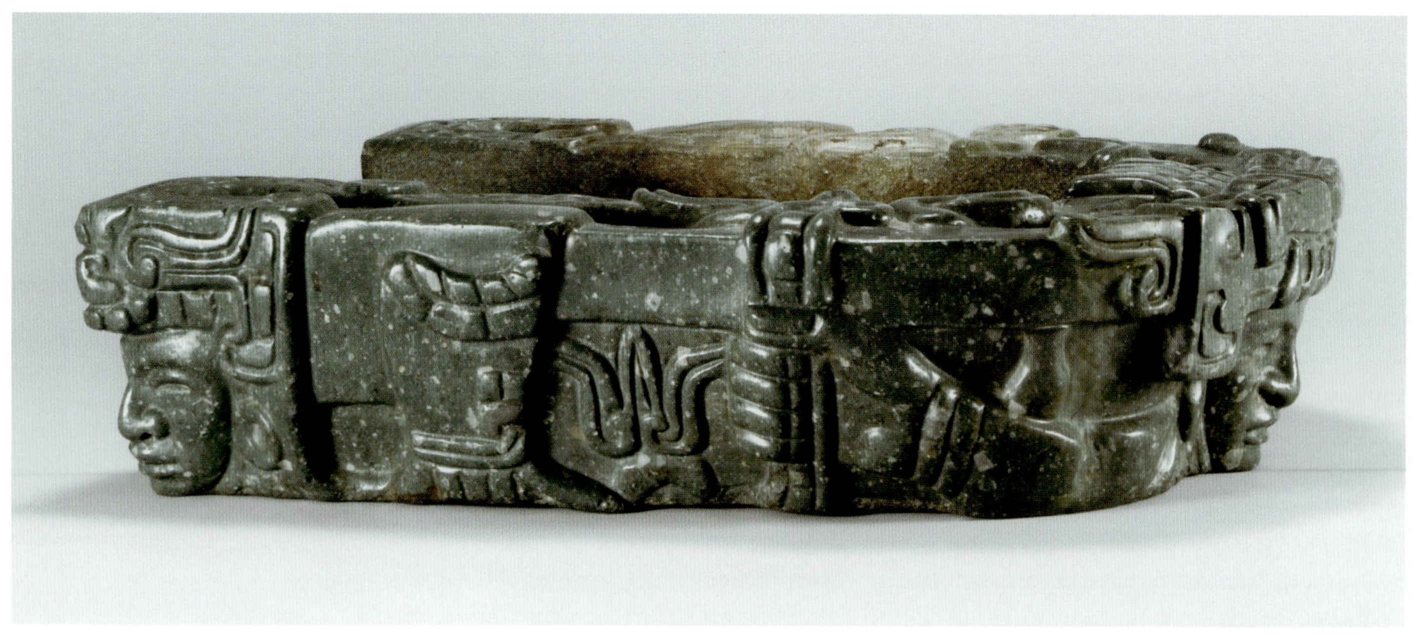

plate 76a

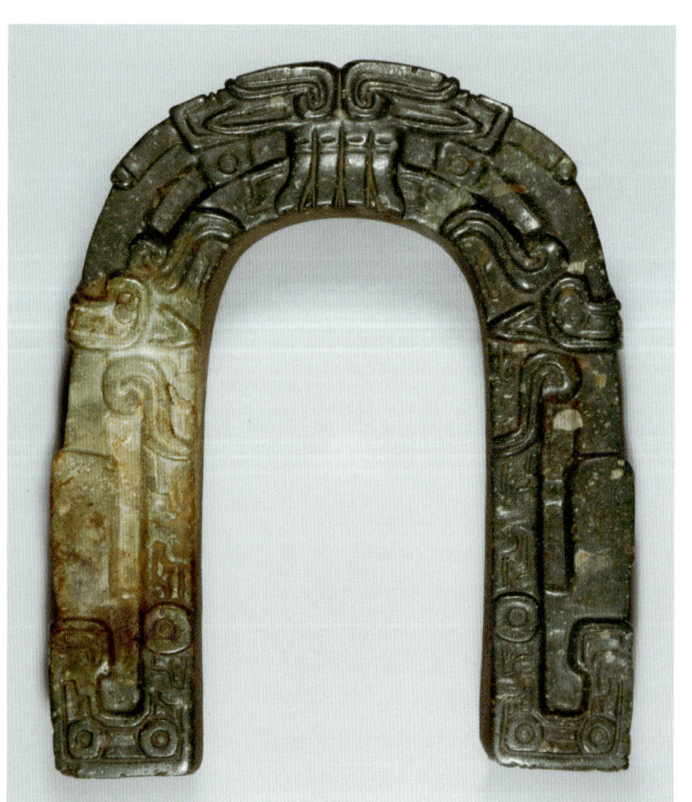

plate 76b, top view

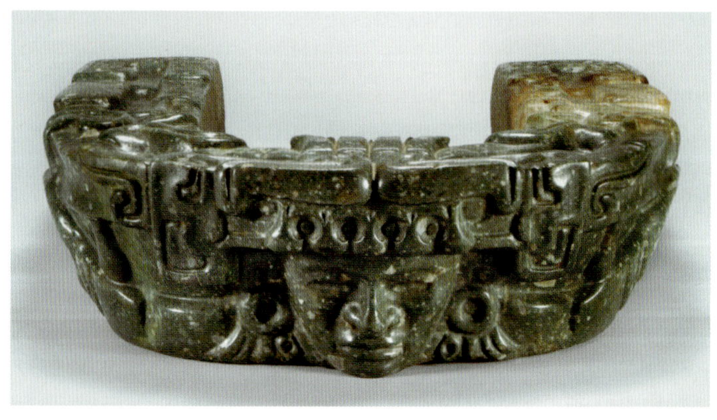

plate 76c, front view

PLATE 76
Classic Veracruz; north-central Gulf Lowlands
Late Classic period, AD 600–900
Diorite porphyry
H. 11.1 cm (4⅜"); W. 38.1 cm (15"); D. 43.2 cm (17")
PC.B.035

ACQUISITION HISTORY:
Purchased from Ernest Brummer in 1947; formerly in the collections of Alfredo Chavero (1900), Mexico, and Joseph Brummer

EXHIBITION HISTORY:
An Exhibition of Pre-Columbian Art, Fogg Art Museum, Cambridge, January–March 1940; *Indigenous Art of the Americas,* National Gallery of Art, Washington, D.C., May 1948–July 1962 (NGA 381); *Art Méxicain du Précolombien à nos jours,* Musée national d'Art moderne, Paris, May–July 1952; *Mexikansk Konst från Forntid till Nutid,* Liljevalches Konsthall, Stockholm, 1952

BIBLIOGRAPHY:
Lino Fábrega 1900: 344–349, unnumbered pl.; Peabody Museum of Archaeology and Ethnology and Fogg Art Museum 1940: cat. no. 39; Pleasants 1940: 88; Liljevalchs Konsthall 1952: cat. no. 665c; Musée national d'Art moderne 1952: I: cat. no. 323; Christensen 1955: 203, 237, fig. 182; Bliss 1957: 236, cat. no. 21, fig. 11, pl. XXVIII; Dumbarton Oaks 1963: 12, cat. no. 87; Willey 1966: I: 143

Stone yokes are the archetypal Classic Veracruz art objects. Highly varied in their decorative motifs, they are among the most eccentric portable sculptures of ancient Mesoamerica. Yoke PC.B.035 has both a long collection history and many uncommon attributes. It is an exceptional example of the genre. It is made of diorite porphyry, a much harder material than the green stone commonly used for polished Classic yokes. Once the general U-form had been fashioned by chiseling and pecking with a still harder rock or bone, the elaborate depiction on the exterior surface was achieved by various techniques, such as drilling. Reed drill holes are still visible on the object's front and in some of the ornamental spools on top. Sawing was used around the feather headdress, leaving some residual crests of stone. Interior and bottom, both undecorated, are pecked only. Decorated surfaces are highly polished.

The left branch of the yoke shows discoloration and fracture from fire. Such pyrogenic alteration is compatible with the sculpture being exposed in an active slash-and-burn cornfield (milpa) or in the burnt debris from cleared rainforest. The right branch is broken and mended near the principal figure's headdress. This is a common fracture point for yokes when dropped or when excessive pressure has been applied to an end. There are some instances where yokes may have been purposely broken—"ritually killed"—in this manner prior to interment as offerings (see Figure 87). Minor chipping occurs along the exterior bottom, but in spite of breakage and battering over a millennium or more, the overall condition of the sculpture is very good.

With their curving and receding sides, U-shaped yokes have few flat surfaces and thus when they are densely carved there is no single perspective from which the sculpted image can be seen in its entirety. A rollout drawing facilitates understanding the theme on the sculpted yoke (Figure 82); differing surfaces and angles make some distortion inevitable, but proportions are respected in the drawing without altering the aggregate image. The carved representation

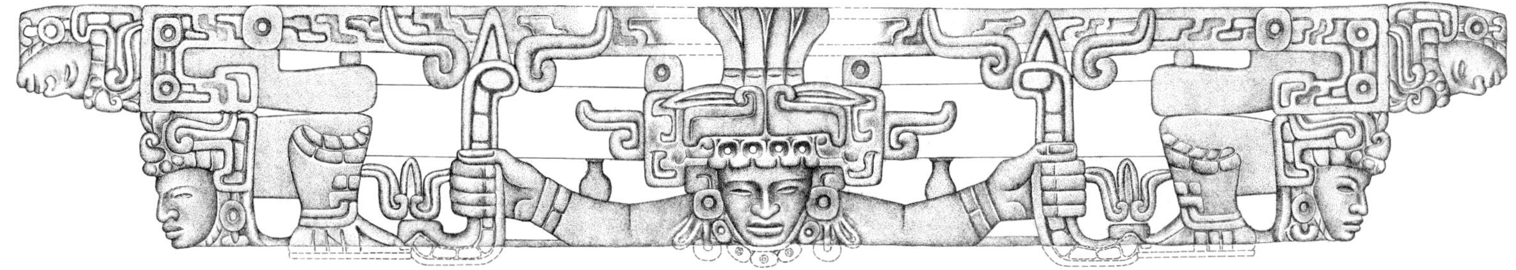

fig. 82
Rollout and flattened view of the iconography on carved yoke PC.B.035. Drawing by the Institute for Cultural Ecology of the Tropics, Miguelangel Garcia/S. Jeffrey K. Wilkerson.

follows an anatomical portrayal and layout common to many yokes and demonstrates conventions frequently found in the sculptures of the El Tajín region in the north-central Gulf Lowlands.

When the disparate surfaces are joined, the image is of a personage dressed in a plumed animal helmet anchored with a chinstrap. The muzzle of the zoomorph spreads above the teeth and is backed by a mounting frame, which supports bunched feathers at its top. Behind the snout are two horizontal lance-shaped spaces, centrally incised, perhaps eyes or ears. They lack the defined supraorbital arch or swirl that customarily characterizes eyes in Classic Veracruz art. Ears, considered diagnostic features in the depiction of some mythological animals, such as bats, are sometimes shown in this pointed shape.

The beast is not a feline or a coyote, which normally displays prominent fangs. However, curved elements just within the lips may be small canines, and between them are what appear to be teeth, noticeably larger in size and broader at their crowns. Some bats, including the hairy-legged vampire (*Diphylla ecaudata* Spix), have upper incisors that are larger than their canines, and they have fan-shaped teeth in front. Some bats have five incisors, as may be shown here. Regardless of the mammal being represented, it appears as a pelt stretched on an elaborate tablet-like head covering. Skin-helmets became especially popular in depictions of rulers in the upper Gulf Lowlands during the subsequent Postclassic period.

The circular drill holes may represent dental incrustations, or possibly these elements are not part of the dentition, but rather a band of stone disks across the forehead, a common accoutrement of rain deities and rulers in the greater El Tajín region. Attached to each side of the frame is a scroll that may represent an ear or a plume. The headdress is large and has diverse elements.

The human head wears composite ear spools; spangles may be distended slit lobes. Semicircular disks may also have been suspended directly beneath the spools. A perforated disk necklace is incomplete; apparently the original design did not fit in the space allotted to it. This truncation suggests that, as in other forms of ball game sculptures, the original design was developed for the initial size of the unadorned object, without anticipating stone loss as carving progressed.

This phenomenon is known from some other yokes, but is far more common on palmas. In fact, almost all of the exterior portrayal on this yoke—except perhaps the end-heads, which seem adapted to the available space—lacks the bottom centimeter or so. Unless the entire yoke was trimmed because of disfiguring fractures, it is likely that the lower portion of the sculpture was carved after the top was completed.

The central human face, with full lips and blank eyes, is mask-like. The visage may be the superimposed countenance of a deity, a not uncommon practice in statuary of the northern Gulf, especially in the Huasteca north of El Tajín. The outstretched arms are adorned with composite wristlets. The hands clasp curved bands with floral-like attachments at either terminus. Although resembling scepters, these are similar to flowered staffs (*oztopilli*) or snake-like lightning bolts (*coatopilli*) grasped by rain gods as fertility symbols, particularly in codices from the end of the Pre-Columbian era. Numerous yokes in the El Tajín region show these objects, sometimes simply portrayed as snakes (Figure 83). At El Tajín, rain, wind, and moon deities clutch similar rods with a single floral decoration, as do royal impersonators of gods participating in pulque rites.

The upraised-arm posture is associated with elite sacrificial rites and deity imitators in sculptures depicting rulers from the Pyramid of the

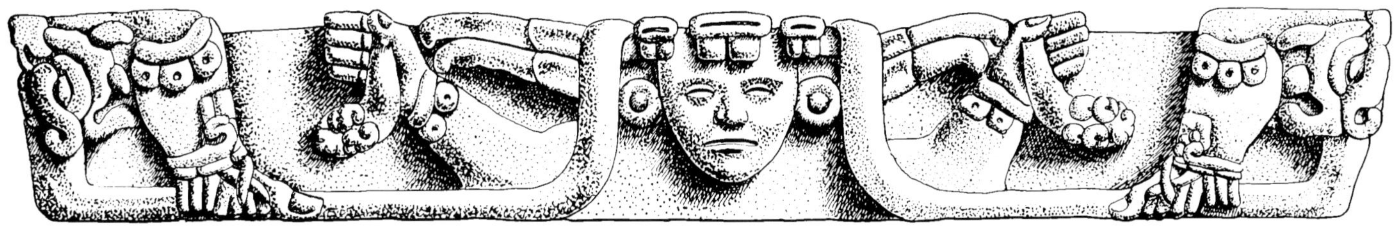

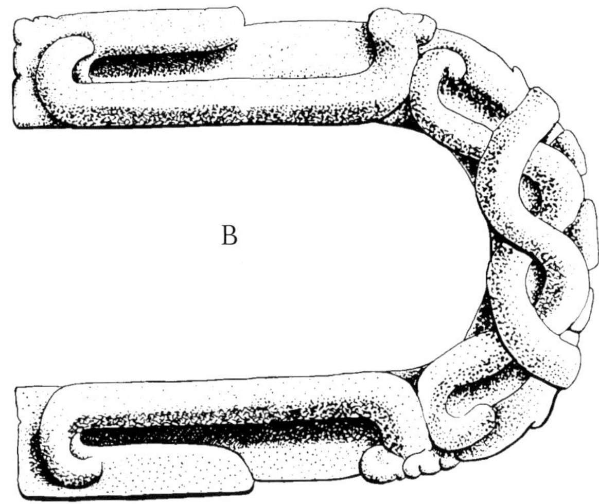

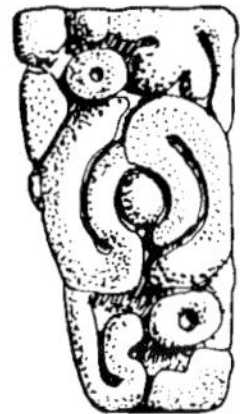

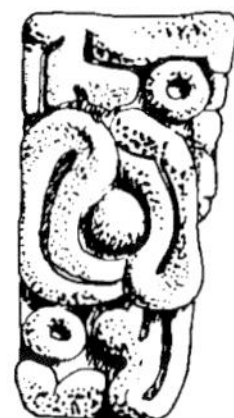

fig. 83
Carved yoke excavated by the author in 1970 at Santa Luisa, in the immediate region of El Tajín. The posture of the human figure, sculptural proportions, and motifs are typical of north-central Veracruz. A: Rollout of the exterior showing snakes being held in the hands of the central figure. B: Top of yoke with interlocked snakes. C: Ends of yoke with reptilian eyes. Drawing by the Institute for Cultural Ecology of the Tropics, Elizabeth Gordon/S. Jeffrey K. Wilkerson.

Niches and the South Ballcourt at El Tajín. It is also a standard stance in the popular Gulf Lowlands pulque cult. Above and slightly behind the PC.B.035 figure's forearms are small globular objects; they appear to be tiny symbolic jars (*ollas*). A similar vessel, albeit more in proportion to human scale, is depicted repeatedly in the panels of the South Ballcourt (Figure 84), with scenes emphasizing the ball game, sacrifice, and pulque rites. In the climactic north-central panel, the gods or their impersonators are grouped around a pulque vat in an underworld temple; the protagonist who dramatically requests pulque holds the jar by the forearm.

On PC.B.035, the rest of the human figure appears toward the ends of the yoke in a squatting posture, not unlike an opening face-off position in sumo wrestling or lacrosse. The upper legs are massive, with huge thighs at right angles to lower legs, adorned with decorative knotted protectors that cover the knee and upper calf. These protectors are part of the gear used by ball game players. Elaborate sandals on the feet are secured by an upturned knot with twin ribbons, also common at El Tajín. The ridge descending from the top of the thigh behind the attached end-heads is probably the edge of the dual sash of the breechcloth (*maxlatl*).

At the ends of the yoke, representing the waist of the figure, are two trophy heads. Both have composite ear spools with suspended semicircular pendants. Their headgear is apparently held in place by a braided rope running beneath the chin. They wear zoomorphic headdresses, perhaps again depicting bats. In this case each zoomorph has a stubby snout and possibly a nose projection, called a "leaf," seen on some fruit-, nectar-, and insect-eating bats.

The heads appear to be attached to an embellished bar that runs the length of the inside edge of

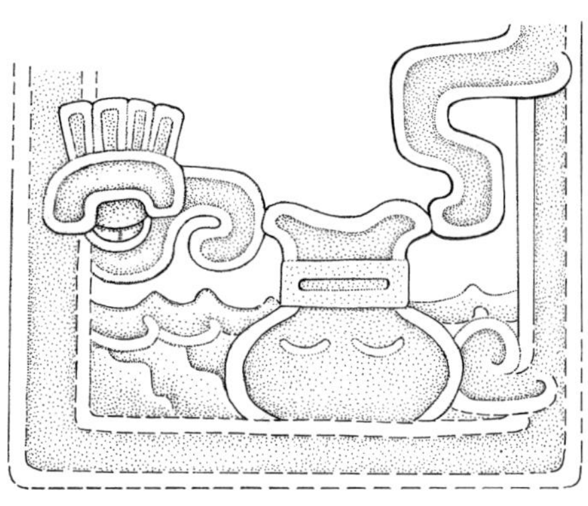

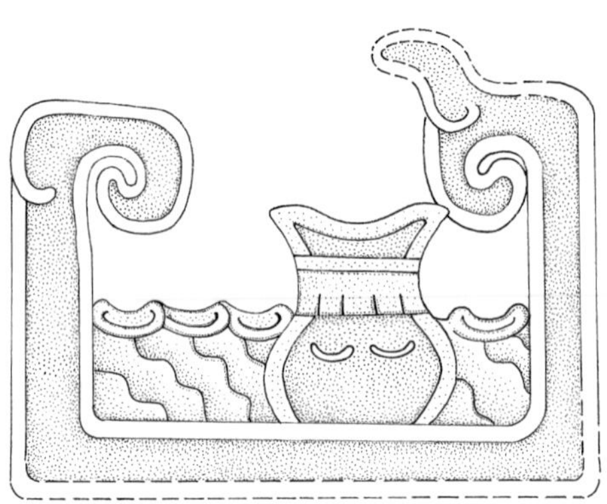

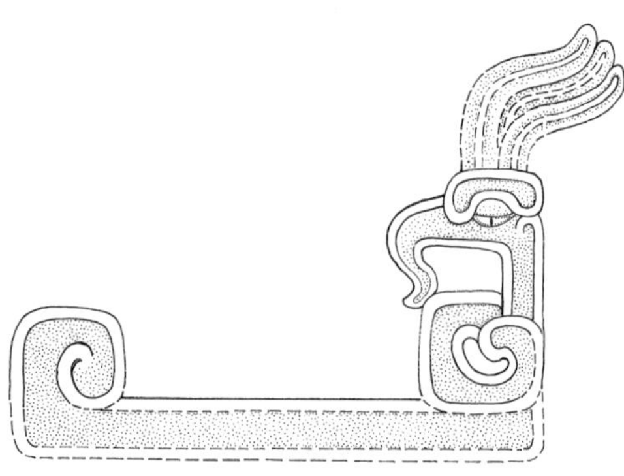

fig. 84
Pulque vats with *ollas* from the southeast and northeast panels of the South Ballcourt at El Tajín (top and center). A vat without a jar from the sanctuary of the Pyramid of the Niches (bottom). Drawing by the Institute for Cultural Ecology of the Tropics, Miguelangel Garcia/ S. Jeffrey K. Wilkerson.

the yoke. This double-headed bar, decorated with bent diagonal scrolls and an occasional spool with squared corners, is a symbol of a liquid-filled vat and consistent with pulque ritualism (Figure 85). A similar vat is shown in a tablet from the sanctuary of the Pyramid of the Niches at El Tajín. The band running from the upper legs and waist along the length of the yoke behind the figure's headdress may represent the hide band that was used to bind the buttocks in the ball game or a stronger—perhaps wood-based—protector.

Several attributes of this yoke are consistent with the beginning of the Late Classic period. The squared spools of the decoration, pendant disks, and upraised hands with symbolic rods are all found in the sanctuary sculptures of the Pyramid of the Niches at El Tajín, where an ancestral ruler is shown performing a series of distinct rituals, including pulque rites. Construction of the building probably began ca. AD 600–700. Deities bearing rods and pulque symbolism are also found in the South Ballcourt, built in the Late Classic.

Bats are depicted in the sanctuary corpus of the Pyramid of the Niches and are explicitly placed in a pulque vat shown in a panel of the North Ballcourt, an important structure perhaps close to the Pyramid of the Niches in date. The bat (*tzinacantli* in Nahuatl) is associated with night, darkness, thunderstorms, the evening star (Venus), and decapitation. All are themes of the ball game ritual and the underworld, including the origin point of pulque in the realm of the Rain God. Bats are associated with the five-part Venus cycle and the mythological confrontation of the ball-playing hero twins with the gods of the underworld in the legends recounted in the *Popul Vuh* (Edmonson 1971). They are also motifs on palmas.

The closest examples of related sculptures with known provenience are from the Tecolutla River Valley, at the edge of which El Tajín is situated, and the Nautla River Valley just to the south. A yoke carved in somewhat similar hard green stone, from a satellite community of the large Santa Luisa site, is in the Museo de Antropología in Xalapa (Veracruz, Mexico). Not as elaborately decorated, it has a number of similar attributes and dress. The probable region of origin of the Dumbarton Oaks yoke is in the catchment of the Tecolutla or the nearby Nautla and Cazones Rivers, all in the heart of the north-central Gulf Lowlands and the core of the climax area for the mature Classic Veracruz style.

This yoke's unusual elements include the highly polished hard stone, drilling scars, figure proportions, uncommon iconographic attributes, and the major design truncation. These features, in conjunction with concerns about the acumen of its original collector in the late nineteenth century, have elicited doubts about its authenticity. By 1900, it was in Mexico City in the Chavero Collection, which is thought to have contained a number of subtly executed fakes.

It should be pointed out, however, that the closest association for the thematic material contained in the carving is to be found in specific sculptures at El Tajín, most of which were not unearthed until at least 30–50 years after the initial collection date of PC.B.035. Furthermore, at the end of the nineteenth century there were few highly embellished yokes that could inspire such a striking portrayal. Most of the upper Gulf Lowlands were still covered in rainforest, and the corpus of yokes in collections did not greatly expand until clearing operations, part of the emerging road network and expanding oil industry of the mid-twentieth century. Unless PC.B.035 is a carefully crafted and iconographically faithful copy of a now-lost and presumably damaged original or a composite of various originals still unknown a century later, it is probable that the challenges of carving the complicated theme in uncommonly hard stone led to some of the curious aspects of this yoke.

The esoteric symbolism of the Classic Veracruz portable sculptures was a product of the complex ritualism and multifaceted mythology associated with the evolution of the ball game cult over many centuries. The image on the yoke probably depicts a specific moment in a post–ball game sacrificial ritual when a ruler evokes the abundance of pulque from the powerful underworld deities—especially the Rain God. Such rites, most likely scheduled in accordance with the Venus calendar, are narrated in great detail in the ballcourts and sculptures at El Tajín. The headdresses of both the central figure and the trophy heads on the yoke ends are suggestive of bat forms, implying the impersonation of one of the significant zoomorphic participants in the underworld ballcourt rites.

SJKW

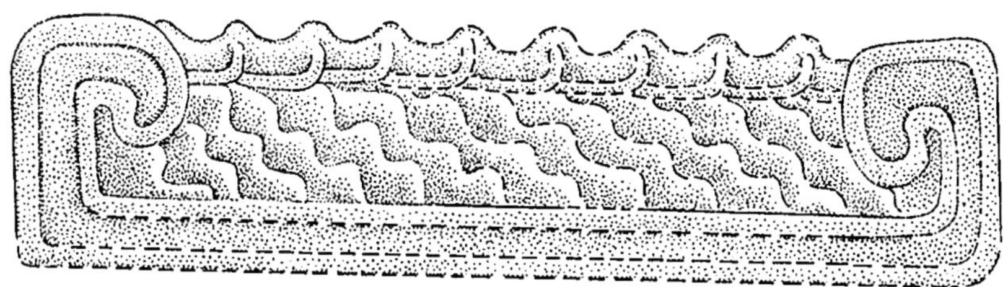

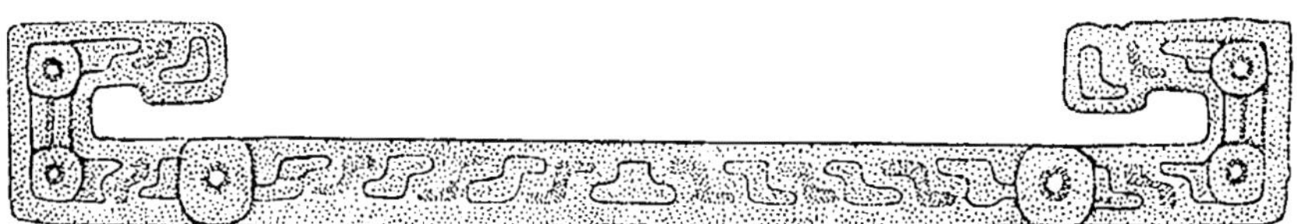

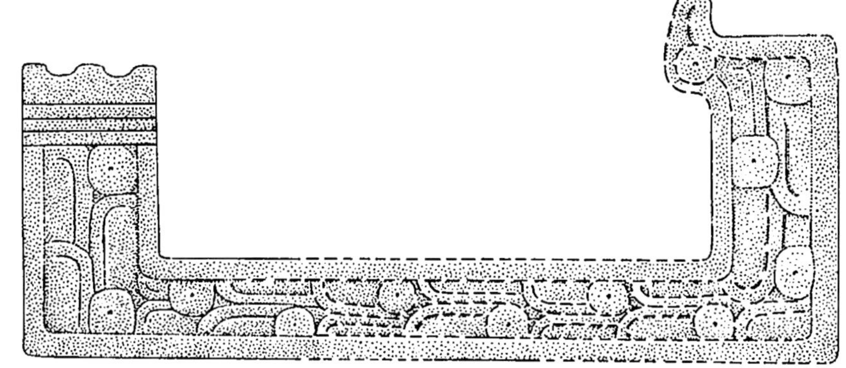

fig. 85
Rollout drawing of the bar from carved yoke PC.B.035 (center), representations of pulque vats from the southwest panel of El Tajín's North Ballcourt (top), and a tablet from the El Tajín's Pyramid of the Niches (bottom). Drawing by the Institute for Cultural Ecology of the Tropics, Miguelangel Garcia/S. Jeffrey K. Wilkerson.

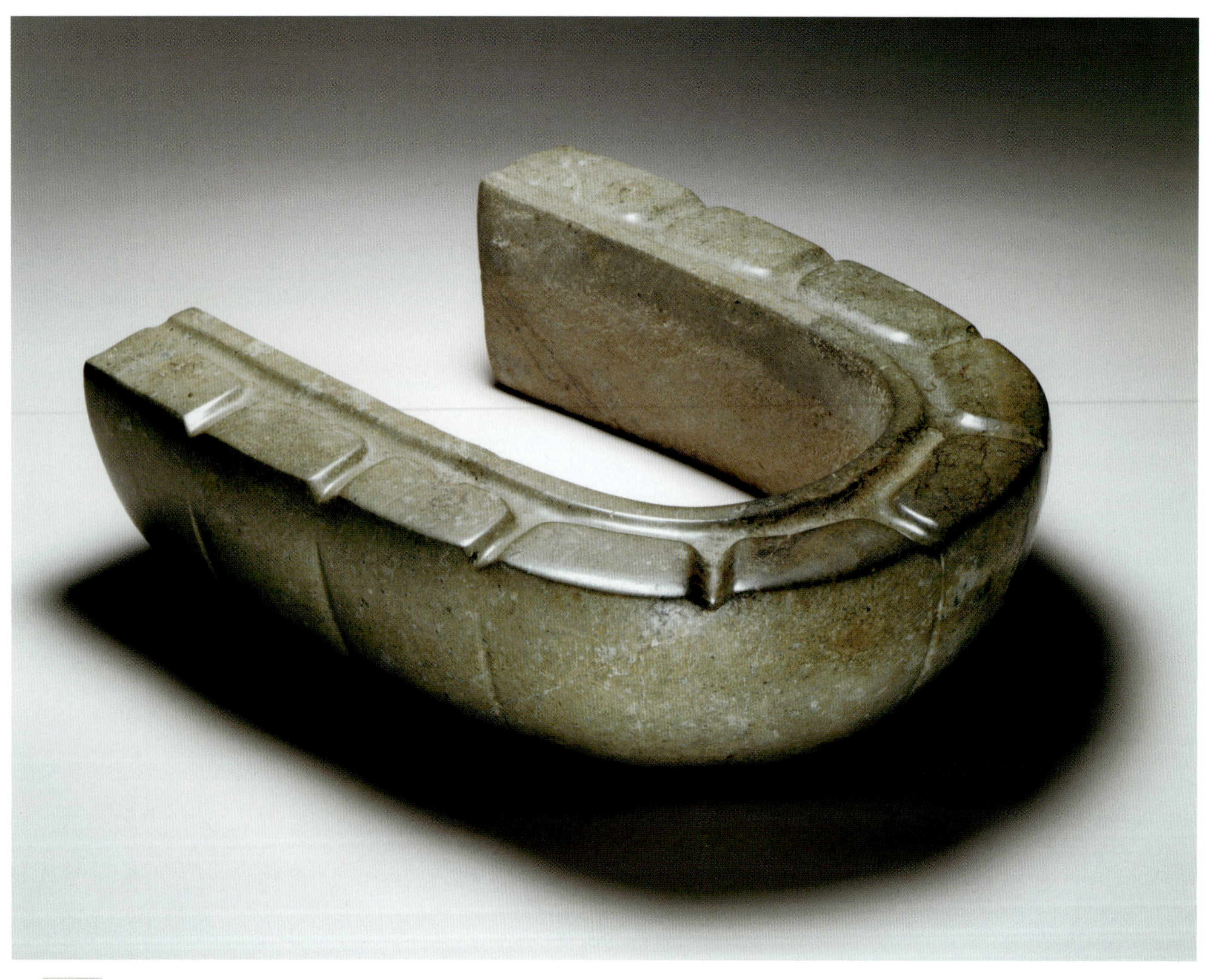

plate 77

PLATE 77
Regional variant of Classic Veracruz; south-central Gulf Lowlands
Late Classic period, AD 600–900
Metadiorite
H. 11.6 cm (4½"); W. 34.0 cm (13⅜"); D. 38.8 cm (15¼")
PC.B.036

ACQUISITION HISTORY:
Purchased from Earl Stendahl, 1948; reportedly from the vicinity of the port of Veracruz

EXHIBITION HISTORY:
Indigenous Art of the Americas, National Gallery of Art, Washington, D.C., August 1949–July 1962 (NGA 406)

BIBLIOGRAPHY:
Bliss 1957: 236, cat. no. 22, pl. XIII; Dumbarton Oaks 1963: 19, cat. no. 88

This yoke and the next (PC.B.037, Plate 78) are of standard proportions and are both probably recarved from earlier plain-surfaced versions. This practice of reuse was common throughout the Classic period in the central regions of the Gulf Lowlands, but it was especially popular in the Late Classic period and in the south-central Gulf Lowlands. In some cases, such reworking led to ornate designs or the filling in of blank spaces between already existing features. Many yokes, and some palmas, were initially unadorned; usually of hard stone, the yokes were polished on the principal exterior surfaces. The blank palmas, often of softer and grittier basalt, were not. Frequently motifs were added, perhaps by a different sculptor. Occasionally it appears that a much older yoke, plain or embellished, would be encountered by chance and altered to fit the current tastes of style or motif.

The mottled green color of the segmented yoke PC.B.036 is within the palette range favored for such sculptures, especially in the south-central Gulf Lowlands. Ten segments on the exterior surfaces formalize or embellish the sculptor's division marks. Carving a motif on the curved and slanting sides of a yoke apparently required establishing a control grid. This technique is shown on a polished plain yoke in the Arensberg Collection (Kubler 1954: no. 160): the upper edges are notched and the carving of the end segments in a monster torso had begun. An analogous polished yoke with notches and carvings, reportedly from underwater offerings at Arroyo Pesquero in the Southern Gulf Lowlands, is at the Princeton University Art Museum (Whittington 2001: 148).

Yoke PC.B.036 takes the division principle further by deepening and extending partition marks to produce a gadrooning effect extending outward from an interior ridge. A similarly marked yoke, but with poor surface preservation, was encountered at El Zapotal in the south-central Gulf Lowlands. Nevertheless, the yoke from the Bliss Collection has a decidedly unfinished quality about it, as if the commissioner had died and the sculptor hurriedly polished the existing surfaces before it was interred as an offering. Such divisions also suggest that there were formulas for the spatial elaboration of even the most common motifs.

SJKW

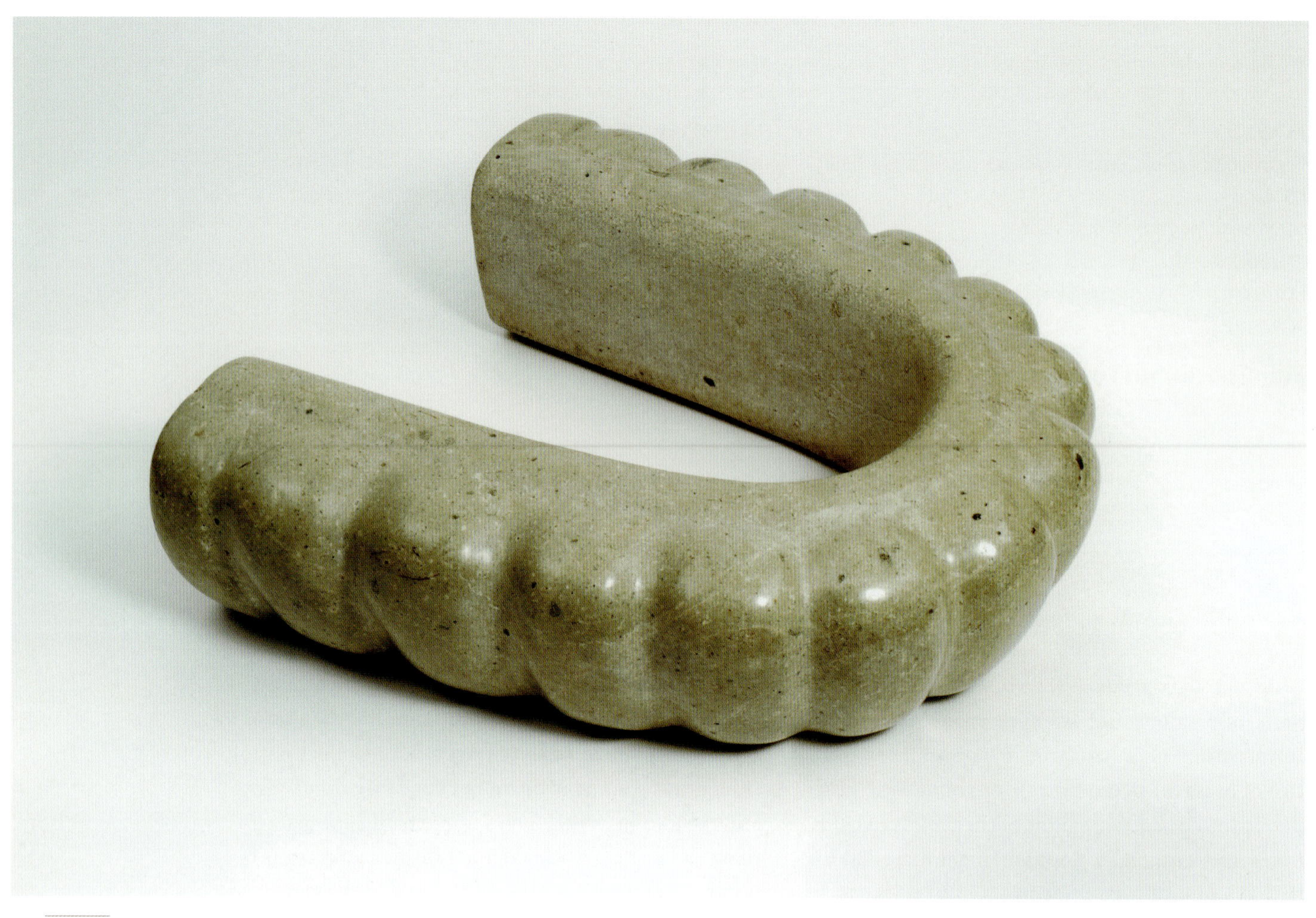

plate 78

YOKE

PLATE 78
Regional variant of Classic Veracruz; north-central Gulf Lowlands
Late Classic period, AD 600–900
Tuff
H. 12.6 cm (5"); W. 40.0 cm (15¾"); D. 40.3 cm (15⅞")
PC.B.037

ACQUISITION HISTORY:
Purchased from John Stokes, 1960

EXHIBITION HISTORY:
Indigenous Art of the Americas, National Gallery of Art, Washington, D.C., September 1960–April 1962 (NGA 738)

BIBLIOGRAPHY:
Dumbarton Oaks 1963: cat. no. 89; Vila Llonch 2008i: 204–205

The off-white or gray yoke PC.B.037 probably has a different history from that of PC.B.036 (Plate 77). It is carved in tuff, not normally favored by Gulf Lowlands sculptors, but not unknown in ball game carvings; a yoke excavated by the author (Wilkerson 1971) at Santa Luisa in the north-central Gulf Lowlands originally had similar color and consistency and was made of a nonlocal stone type brought from a considerable distance (see Figure 83). On PC.B.037, 13 bulbous projections set against a horseshoe-like interior ridge suggest the recarving of an older form of yoke. In cross section, the arms of this yoke reproduce a profile common to much earlier plain unpolished examples that may, in some instances, date back to the Late Preclassic period or even before. This yoke, however, is not made of basalt, commonly used in earlier specimens, and it is polished.

Squash-like forms occur in other sculptural formats along the upper Veracruz coast, expressed in stone and stucco media in the Late Classic period and in ceramics in the Postclassic period. The design, however, is not ordinarily associated with yokes. Although this occurrence may be unique, it likely reflects a localized motif preference, and more examples may eventually be found.

There is some possibility that the yoke's design may intentionally imitate a specific type of padded waist protector. Especially with the use of large balls in some forms of the ball game, similarly padded waist protectors may have been used in the game rite. Cotton wadding wound in cloth over a composite wood protector might ultimately, after use, have had such an undulating surface.

The exteriors of yokes were sacred surfaces requiring careful elaboration, accurate iconography, and correct form so that the sculptures could eventually accompany their owners to the ball game rites of the afterlife. Although some themes are more common than others, there were tremendous regional variations in preferred motifs and materials. However whimsical, baffling, or abstruse these carvings may appear to us today, to their makers and users they once implied precise meanings within a complex mythological and religious framework. They also reflected, even in imitation, the physical requirements of game performance that could vary enormously over time and space.

Such ball game sculptures were highly portable icons of the multifaceted but intermeshed worlds of play, ritual, status, and death. Carved over more than a millennium for local use in many districts of the Gulf Lowlands, some were carried great distances throughout Mesoamerica. The Dumbarton Oaks yokes are fine representatives of not only ancient cult values but also of the quality artisanship that produced these once highly revered objects.

SJKW

HACHAS

Hachas, the Spanish word for "axes," were originally named for their general shape: the lateral flattening to a narrow frontal edge on many examples was thought to approximate a large axe head. They have also sometimes been called "thin" or "ceremonial heads," "votive axes," and "tenoned" or "crested heads." The predominant motifs of all varieties are severed heads. In Classic Veracruz times detached heads were important trophies that were carried or displayed in ball game–associated ceremonies. They were also sometimes defleshed and placed in rubber balls, as well as occasionally used as important burial offerings. Apparently the sacrificed participant's status was commensurate with the significance attached to preserving or using his head or skull. The more elaborate stone hachas seem to memorialize specific individuals, sometimes dressed in the guise of a particular mythical personage from a choreographed sacrificial rite.

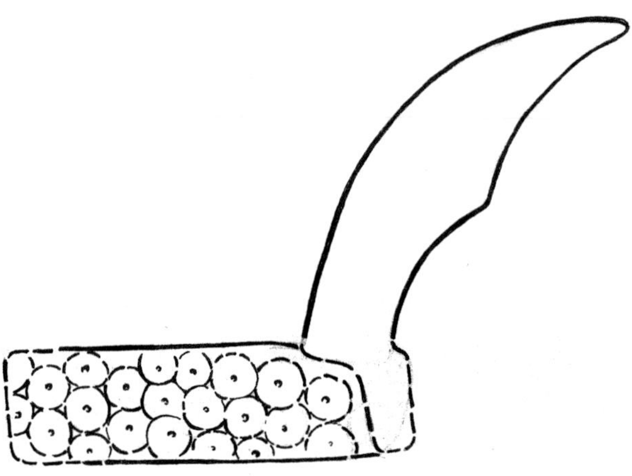

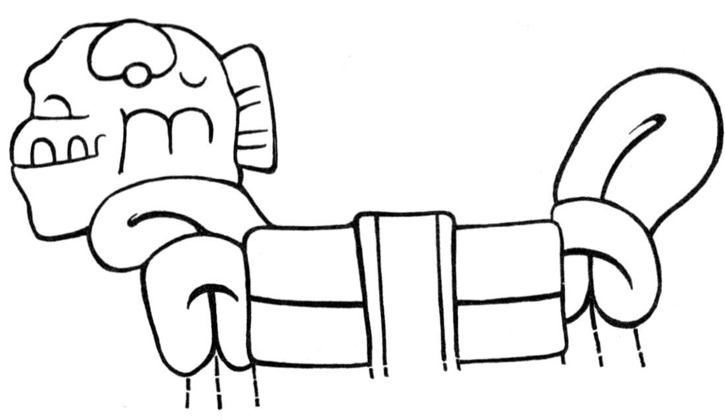

fig. 86
Details from the sculptural fragments of the Building of the Columns at El Tajín. Top: palma attached to a waist protector or yoke that is decorated with beads or disks. Bottom: skull hacha attached to a cloth-bound waist protector. Drawing by the Institute for Cultural Ecology of the Tropics, Miguelangel Garcia/S. Jeffrey K. Wilkerson.

Severed heads predominate among motifs, with considerable variation in depiction and a diverse corpus of ancillary themes. Many heads have bulging or closed eyes, with the open-mouthed countenances of the recently sacrificed. The tongues may protrude in death (PC.B.041, Plate 82). Some hachas are skull-like with the eye sockets void (PC.B.555, Plate 86). Some have skin wrinkled from age, but others may depict skin stretched over a frame or a fleshless skull. Occasionally a head will have zoomorphic ornamentation, insignia (PC.B.046, Plate 85), or even a helmet (PC.B.039, Plate 80). Still others are birds or nocturnal mammals associated with the rituals in the myths and lore of the ball game (PC.B.038 and PC.B.043, Plates 79 and 84). Occasionally, in later hachas, the head itself is suppressed and the space utilized for a scene from a sacrificial ritual (PC.B.040, Plate 81).

Any of these forms may have headdresses or crests along the top of the head. Headdresses are sometimes elaborate and contain secondary themes, scenes, or scrolls and sacrificial motifs. Often there is no clear distinction between the cap-like headdresses and crests (PC.B.042, Plate 83), suggesting a common origin in ritual gear once used in ball game rites. Some examples seem to have had inlays in the eyes and mouths. Although shell and obsidian were frequently used as materials for such decoration, human teeth are known to have been used in some instances.

Even though most hachas are narrow with laterally compressed features, size varies greatly. They range from slightly greater than a clenched fist, through the approximate size of a human skull, to a much larger and slender format with a high headdress, cap (PC.B.549, Plate 87), or crest (PC.B.038). There are some regional variations in dimensions. The largest format appears most prevalent at the higher elevations back from the coast in the northwestern portion of the south-central region, whereas the simple crested forms appear to be most common on the southern Gulf coastal plain. The north-central region has examples of various shapes, but these sculptures appear to be far less numerous than palmas, which achieved a greater popularity there.

Most hachas have a prominent notch incised into the lower back corner of the sculpture; the notch usually describes a right angle and varies from a small percentage of the total sculpture to a very large one. Originally these indentations may have been functional, a means of linking the sculpture with another ritual object during a rite associated with the ball game. Although in certain instances the outline does approximate the profiles of some stone yokes, it is far more likely that the hacha was placed on a wooden yoke, on the upper border of a stone ballcourt, or on some other object altogether (Figure 86). Even then, they would be unstable unless bound with some material.

Other hachas, popular in the southern Gulf region, have a sizable tenon on the back, clearly showing that they were inserted into something solid enough to support their weight. Regardless of the specific mode of adherence or attachment represented by the notch or tenon, it is clear that hachas were conspicuously displayed, and probably venerated, before finally being used as mortuary offerings.

There is a wide array of media for hachas. Many are of basalt with porous surfaces, roughly smoothed, at best. These sculptures are often found in the central mountains of Veracruz and adjoining zones. Other hachas are of serpentine and diverse fine-grained stones that support a carefully polished surface (PC.B.046). These may be found anywhere in central Veracruz but are most prevalent in the south-central area. Many were coated with red ochre when interred as burial offerings. Although the current evidence does not yet positively support this interpretation, it would not be unexpected if it was eventually found that many hachas were once polychromed.

Hachas are occasionally found with stone yokes (Figure 87) but—in spite of some narrative depictions at El Tajín—apparently not with palmas. The suggestion is that hachas grow out of the yoke tradition, which essentially celebrates the game itself, as a way of commemorating decapitation in the post–ball game rites. In contrast, palmas, although partially overlapping thematically with hachas, appear to memorialize participation in various forms of post-game sacrificial rites.

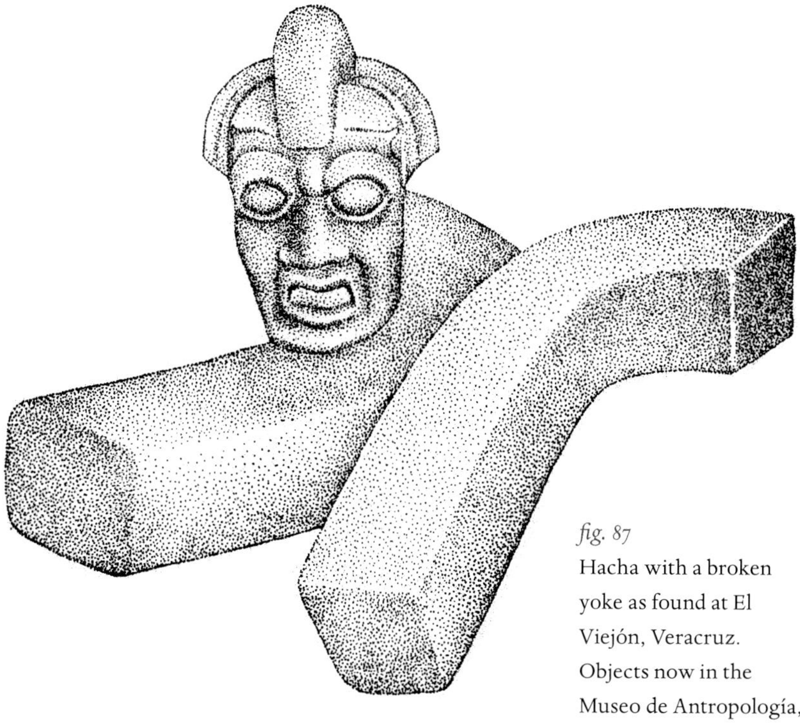

Due to a general lack of archaeological or contextual data, it is difficult to establish the complete time line for hachas. The presently known corpus for the Gulf Lowlands almost certainly dates at least from throughout the Classic period and given the close relationship with yokes, may possibly extend back into the Late Preclassic. Hachas do not seem to date to the Epiclassic period, at least in the northern Gulf region, where palmas seem to have replaced them in popularity during the Late Classic period.

Most hachas, and all in the Dumbarton Oaks Collection, are from the two central regions of Veracruz. Hachas, like yokes, were sometimes carried far from the Gulf Lowlands at various moments in Pre-Columbian history. Major variants of these sculptures are found in southern Guatemala. There is also a gradient, in both motif and shape, between some hachas and various palmas. This convergence may have been most common in the north-central region and the immediate adjoining zones of the south-central region at the height of the popularity of palmas in the Late Classic period.

SJKW

fig. 87
Hacha with a broken yoke as found at El Viejón, Veracruz. Objects now in the Museo de Antropología, Xalapa. Drawing by the Institute for Cultural Ecology of the Tropics, Miguelangel Garcia/ S. Jeffrey K. Wilkerson (after Medellín Zenil 1962: lám. 110).

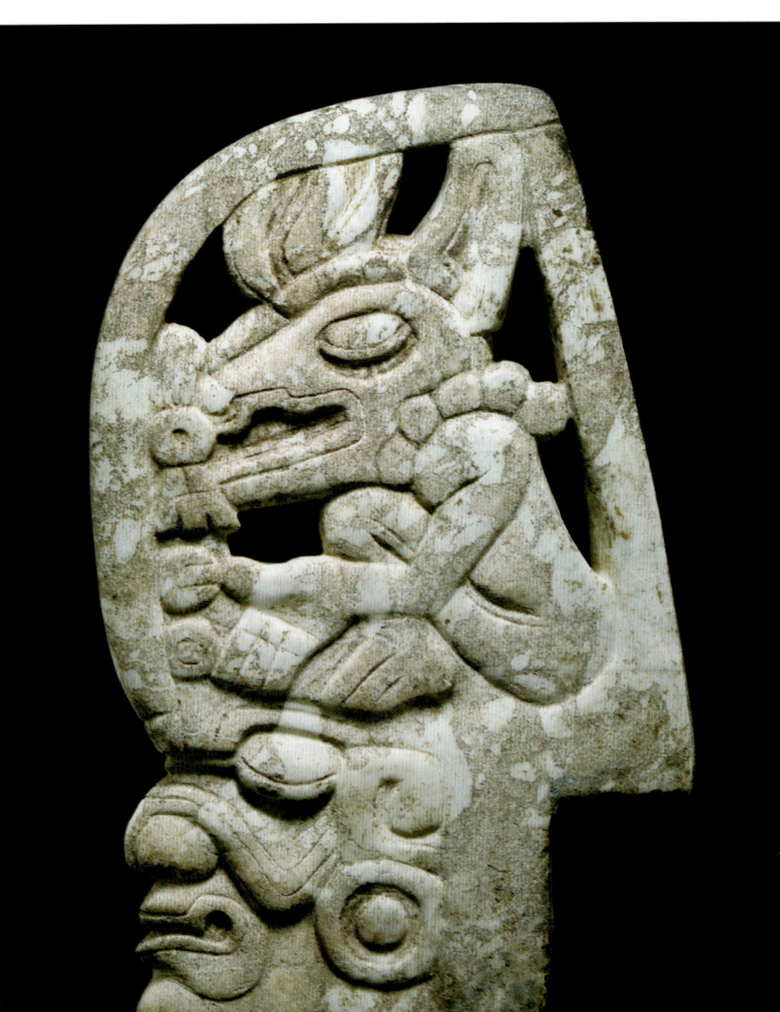

plate 79

PLATE 79
Classic Veracruz; south-central Gulf region
Terminal Classic or Epiclassic period, AD 900–1100
Marble
H. 35.1 cm (13¾"); W. 22.3 cm (8¾"); D. 4.6 cm (1¾")
PC.B.038

ACQUISITION HISTORY:
Purchased from Earl Stendahl, 1956; reportedly from west of Orizaba on the slopes of the Sierra Madre Oriental; formerly in the collection of Amparo Medizobal de Fernandez of Orizaba (Veracruz, Mexico)

EXHIBITION HISTORY:
Indigenous Art of the Americas, National Gallery of Art, Washington, D.C., April 1956–July 1962 (NGA 678)

BIBLIOGRAPHY:
Bliss 1957: 236–237, cat. no. 23A, pl. XIV; Dumbarton Oaks 1963: 19, cat. no. 90; Willey 1966: I: 144; Nicholson 1967: 12

HACHA

In terms of time, space, medium, and format, this white marble sculpture is a companion to the hacha with the sacrificed prisoner motif (PC.B.040, Plate 81). Both are hachas of the large thin type, though PC.B.038 is larger, more complex, and enigmatic in nature, with two superimposed figures that can be examined separately but must be taken together for a meaningful interpretation of the whole. Hacha PC.B.038 dates to near the end of the Classic Veracruz tradition; its stone seems harder than that of PC.B.040, but it has impurities and was once polished.

The base figure, certainly a trophy head, appears to be an elderly male with wrinkles on his face, above his eyes, and on the bridge of his nose. His ears bear large composite ear spools, and his chin has shanks of a probable false beard. The lips meet in front, but the toothless mouth is contorted in a forceful grimace. The large eyes appear to be slits, closed as in death. A prominent bar-like attachment extends from the eye over the upper bridge of the nose; above it are the upper part of the eye socket and forehead abutting a circle under the larger upper image.

This distorted head may well be a Veracruz variant of an aged underworld deity, such as Gods L and N in Maya art. Regardless of the specific image, this sculpture was probably carved to mark the sacrifice of a high-status personage or ruler of note rather than solely to honor a fearsome god. The decapitated man depicted here may have impersonated just such a deity in a sacrificial ball game rite. In the Maya epic *Popul Vuh*, the Hero Twins competed with the underworld gods in the ballcourt. Ultimately, the gods were defeated and beheaded. The head depicted in this hacha may be wearing a skin mask; it also may be named in the scene above.

The upper 60 percent of the sculpture, ostensibly a type of crested headdress or helmet for the lower face, is dominated by a seated zoomorphic figure with a human body. As in PC.B.040, the form is highlighted and the depth of relief is augmented by removal of background stone. Three swept-back feathers rise from the head; the eyes are slits. A necklace with beads of unusual thickness rests upon the shoulders, denoting both sacredness and rank. The legs are drawn up under the chin. The extended hand of the figure appears to be encased in a heavy glove, as might be used in one of the hand formats of the ritual ball game.

The hand opens toward a circle, perhaps representing a ball or a symbol for the number one. The thumb touches an elongated loop symbol, possibly related to the object above it, which covers the end of the animal's snout, studded with triangular teeth. With a loop handle on top, a circle at its center, and three hanging tassels, the device may be a pouch, symbol of preciousness and sacredness. The animal, or more properly the animal impersonator, is probably representing an opossum or deer: both have mythological import.

The first animal was particularly important because the young Hero Twins of the *Popul Vuh* were thought to have returned from death at the hands of the underworld lords as dancing magicians or actors with animal attributes and names, including that of the opossum (Edmonson 1971; López Austin 1993, 1996). Demonstrating their powers of illusion, they decisively defeated the gods, sacrificing some of them. This animal is also called the "old man" and in that capacity is associated with the dawn as well as with the solar and Venus cycles, which were important in the ball game cults of ancient Veracruz (Wilkerson 1984, 1991).

Deer, often with extended ear-like ornaments not shown here, were also supportive participants in the legends of the ball game. In El Tajín's ballcourt sculptures they were rendered with a human body and helmet. Regardless of the correct zoological designation, the impersonator's identity is of a divine animal thought to participate in one of the mythological ball games.

The thick glove may denote a highland ball game variant distinct from the hip and mallet or stick forms that seem to have predominated in the Gulf Lowlands in the Classic period. The hand probably opens toward a numeral—instead of a ball—because the game ball is normally not shown in movement in Classic Veracruz sculpture. Hands often point to name glyphs in the late sculptures at El Tajín. Unless it improbably refers to the stacked items directly above it, the reference here is most likely to the grotesque head immediately below.

Possibly this numeral is part of the name of the mythological animal being portrayed, but far more likely it refers to the name of the individual whose severed head is depicted next to it, perhaps reading One Death, the name of the most powerful underworld overlord who was sacrificed by the Hero Twins. The demise of this aged deity, commonly identified as God L, was the high point of the quest to destroy the malicious power of the fickle rulers of the underworld.

Like some other hachas and many palmas, this sculpture has two registers of information. Palmas frequently have a ritual scene or contextual depiction, often on the back, and a celebrated symbol or protagonist, usually on the front. In this case the upper figure is suggestive of the context, a ball game player with a zoomorphic helmet alluding to a specific mythological event. The base of the hacha has the principal image, the severed head of a sacrificed participant, a trophy rendered in the guise of a major deity from legend.

These merging themes evoke compelling mythology and prerogative. This powerfully rendered, well-crafted hacha probably commemorates the sacrificial death of a high-status individual. This personage could well have been a regional ruler of sufficient standing, and perhaps capriciousness, to die in a ritual reenactment of one of the central events of ball game mythology—the downfall of the underworld's paramount deity.

SJKW

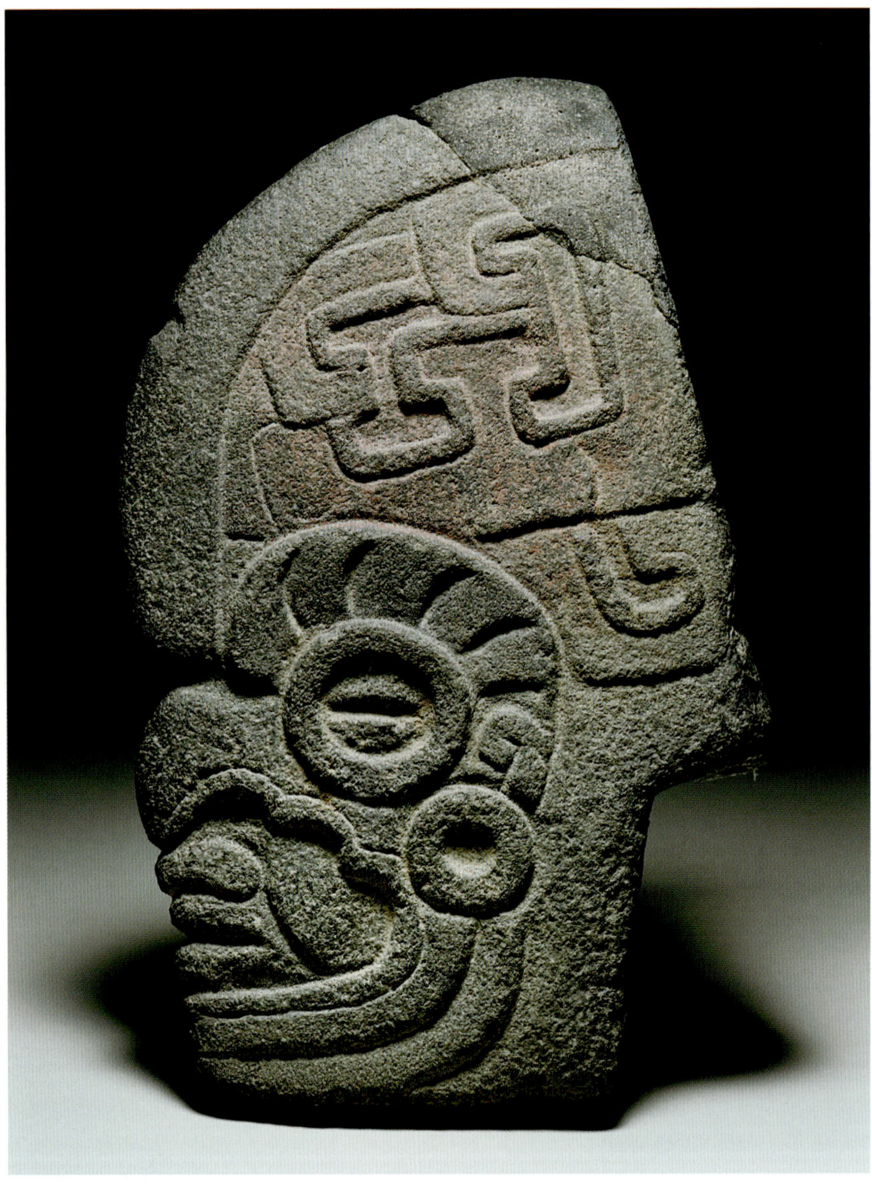

plate 80

HACHA

PLATE 80

Classic Veracruz; central Gulf region
Terminal Classic or Epiclassic period, AD 900–1100
Basalt
H. 35.0 cm (13¾"); W. 5.4 cm (2⅛"); D. 22.0 cm (8⅝")
PC.B.039

ACQUISITION HISTORY:

Purchased from Earl Stendahl

EXHIBITION HISTORY:

Indigenous Art of the Americas, National Gallery of Art, Washington, D.C., April 1947–March 1952, February 1954–July 1962 (NGA 209); *Art Méxicain du Précolombien à nos jours,* Musée national d'Art moderne, Paris, May–July 1952; *Mexikansk Konst från Forntid till Nutid,* Liljevalches Konsthall, Stockholm, 1952

BIBLIOGRAPHY:

Bliss 1947: 22, 107, cat. no. 102; Seymour 1949: 85; Liljevalchs Konsthall 1952: cat. no. 665d; Musée national d'Art moderne 1952: I: cat. no. 333; Proskouriakoff 1954: 79, fig. 3, hacha 3; Rivet 1954: pl. 24; Bliss 1957: 237, cat. no. 24, pl. XVI; *Natural History* 1958: 128; Dumbarton Oaks 1963: 19, cat. no. 91; Alcina Franch 1979: fig. 338; Vila Llonch 2008j: 206–207

This tall, thin hacha is an exceptionally fine example of a major bird motif associated with ball game rites. The nonporous basalt was never polished. This type of stone, widely traded, was preferred for hachas throughout the central Gulf Lowlands. Hacha PC.B.039 depicts a trophy head dressed in a bird helmet capped with a scroll-encrusted crest. The bird shown is not an eagle, as has often been assumed, but rather a macaw (*Ara macao*).

The hood-like covering is secured to the head by a double chin strap. Beneath the beak are the human nose, mouth, and cheek. From the eye circle of the macaw peers the slit eye of the severed head. The human ear with a decorative spool protrudes above the straps. The nostril of the bird may be implied by a crescent indentation on the beak. The distinctive shape of the bird's head and feathers are outlined around the eye. The side of the high crest above the depiction is decorated with scrolls in both deep and shallow rectangular formats. Blood may be represented here.

The sculpture portrays a severed head dressed in a specific macaw helmet as used in a sacrificial ball game ritual inspired by legend. Macaws were directly associated with the remote mythological origins of the ball game. In Mesoamerica representations of the bird were deployed as ballcourt markers at widely separated sites, such as Copán in Honduras and Xochicalco in West-Central Mexico. In the ancient mythical cycles recounted in the Maya *Popul Vuh*—an extraordinary sixteenth-century compendium—a type of avian deity imposter called "Seven Macaw" prominently appears. The malevolent charlatan declares himself to be both the sun and the moon. He and his equally malicious sons are ultimately killed by the young Hero Twins, divine protagonists of the cycles. This action precedes their successful quest to play and defeat the wicked underworld gods in the ball game. Scarlet macaws are thought to be descendents of the divine bird pretender. In Classic Veracruz ball game sculptures, many depictions appear to represent symbolic reenactments of such legendary events.

Hachas depicting macaws may have a wide distribution in the Gulf Lowlands. Generally they focus on the bird itself—as in the excellent example in the Philadelphia Museum of Art's Arensberg Collection (Kubler 1954: no. 148)—and do not combine the bird with the head of the sacrificed impersonator, as in PC.B.039. However, at El Tajín there is a superbly instructive rendition of the greater ritual context for the use of this paraphernalia (see Figure 80). It comes from a large tablet found on a building adjacent to a major ballcourt.

Carved in a stiff transitional style, it is half of an incomplete scene that shows a man speaking, or more likely singing. He is dressed in this type of double-strap macaw helmet and wears a ball game knee protector, a yoke at his waist, a bird—almost certainly a macaw—hacha, and a palma-like effigy. In his hand is a shafted object, quite possibly a slate-pyrite mirror. Above the figure is a reclining feline, very probably sacrificed, with protruding tongue. Also along two sides of the borders are scrolls of the same form as those found on PC.B.039.

The context of this monumental depiction is a ball game ritual in which these accoutrements are worn by mythic impersonators prior to sacrifice. It again suggests that this type of rite with a macaw helmet was widespread. Hachas with such attributes reflect an important dimension of the ritual recreation of what was, to ancient viewers, easily recognizable and significant mythological history. The macaw hacha at Dumbarton Oaks is one of the best examples known of this important avian motif.

SJKW

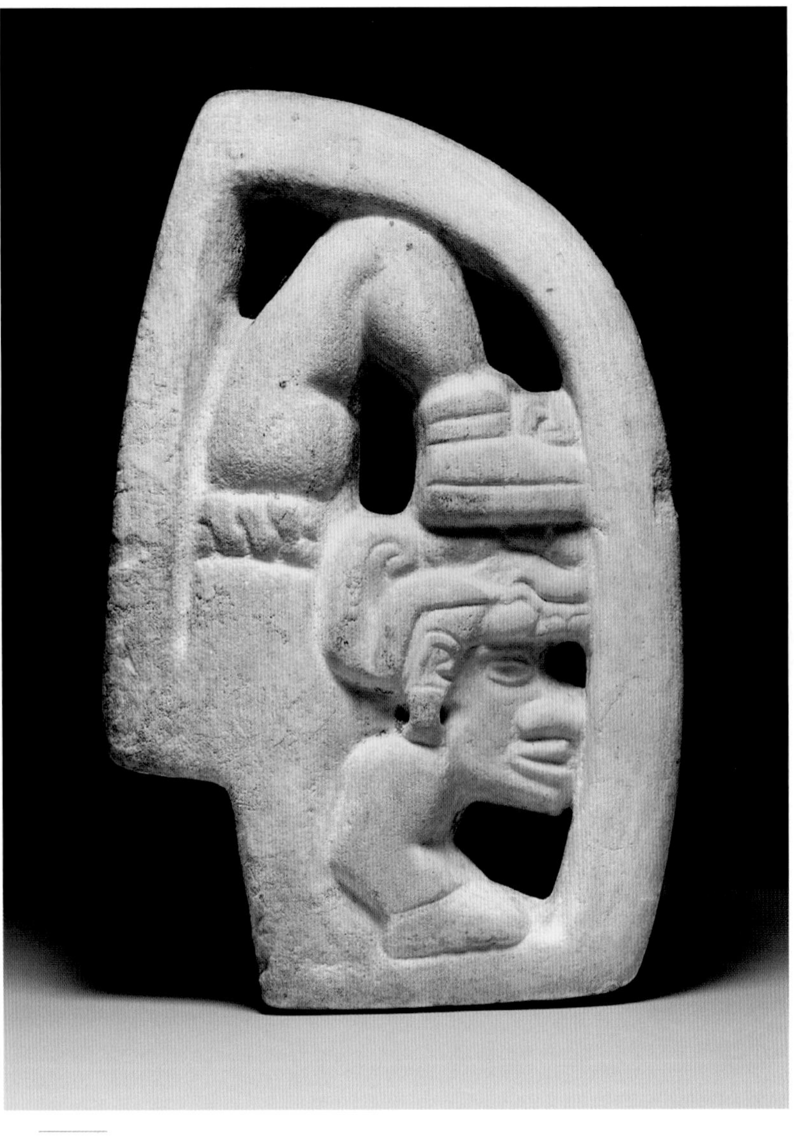

plate 81

PLATE 81
Classic Veracruz; south-central Gulf region
Terminal Classic or Epiclassic period, AD 900–1100
Marble
H. 30.0 cm (11¾"); W. 5.2 cm (2"); D. 19.0 cm (7½")
PC.B.040

ACQUISITION HISTORY:
Purchased from Earl Stendahl, 1940s; reportedly from Tecamalucan, west of Orizaba, on the high slopes of the Sierra Madre Oriental

EXHIBITION HISTORY:
Indigenous Art of the Americas, National Gallery of Art, Washington, D.C., April 1947–July 1962 (NGA 204)

BIBLIOGRAPHY:
Bliss 1947: 22, 109, cat. no. 105; Christensen 1955: 202, fig. 178; *Artes de México* 1957: pl. 12; Bliss 1957: 236, cat. no. 23, pl. XV; Dumbarton Oaks 1963: 19, cat. no. 92

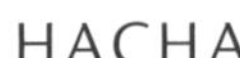

HACHA

This fine, thin hacha is carved from white marble, a medium rarely used in this genre. Its outer surfaces do not seem to have been carefully polished, but its slightly pocked appearance may have resulted from deposition in acidic soils. The piece is also unusual in its probable origin at the southern edge of the range for this particular hacha format. Its style is plainer and perhaps later than that of other hachas in the Bliss Collection. The narrow space inside the border is nearly filled with a three-dimensional figure, accentuated by perforation of the background. This male has been described as an acrobat, but this interpretation is highly unlikely if the work's broader context is considered. As occurs on some hachas and many palmas, the scene is a dramatic moment. Shown is a post-warfare, post–ball game ritual sacrifice.

The figure's torso is unclothed except for a knotted cord about his waist. This restricting accoutrement signifies a prisoner, particularly one who is sacrificed in a form of gladiatorial combat or in rites following a ball game. He wears the elaborate, knotted sandals of the elite and a helmet probably symbolizing a feline. Suspended from his ears are ornaments of curved shell that have the *epcololli* (Nahuatl) hook shape often associated with Venus ceremonialism, which in turn is closely linked with warfare and rulers. The object beneath his hand is possibly a glove, tablet, or shield. Small rectangular shields are sometimes depicted on the wrists or forearms of Gulf Lowlands warriors armed with a spear thrower, the preferred weapon of the elite.

Toward the end of the artistic florescence at El Tajín, analogous figures are depicted as war captives of high status being sacrificed by the great ruler 13 Rabbit. Some are apparently being dispatched—disemboweled and decapitated—on a bench in a ballcourt, whereas others (Figure 88), some more elaborately attired, are slated for gladiatorial death. Such scenes correspond with a very

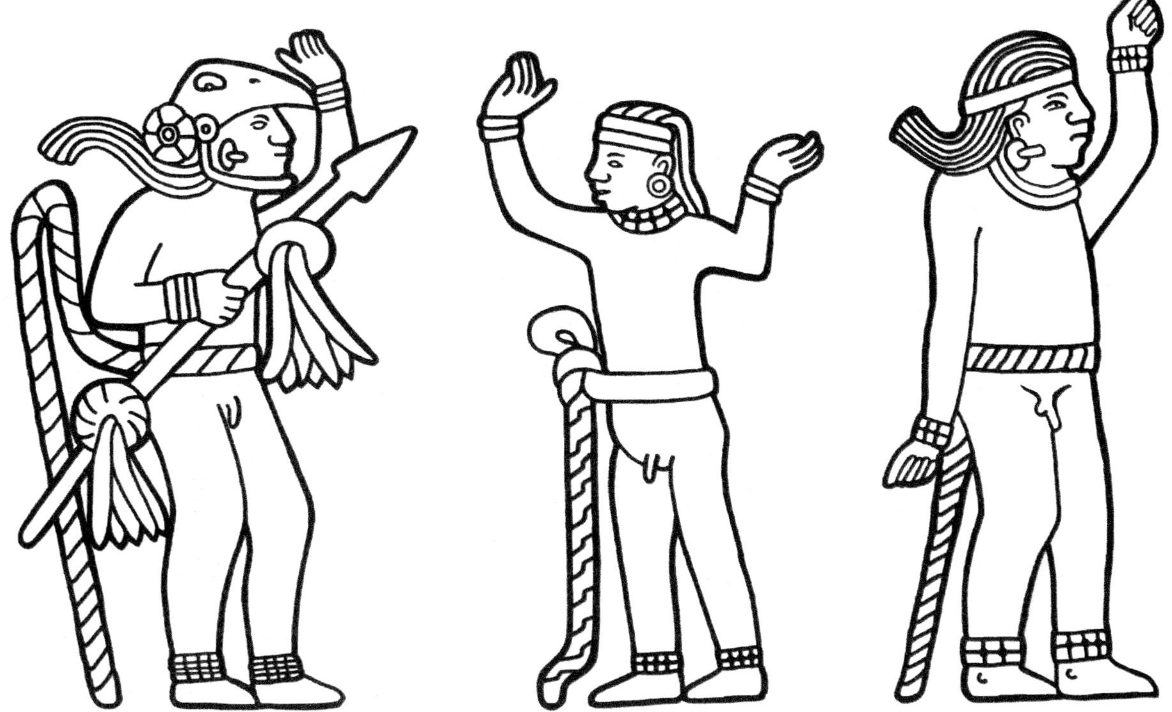

fig. 88
Prisoners with waist cords in sacrificial rites, from the Building of the Columns at El Tajín. Drawing by the Institute for Cultural Ecology of the Tropics, Miguelangel Garcia/ S. Jeffrey K. Wilkerson.

late permutation of elite Gulf Lowlands rituals that foreshadow the widely known Late Postclassic rites in Highland Central Mexico.

Precisely at the apex of the hacha notch the figure bends above the waist, abruptly and unnaturally, as if the abdomen has been opened. This is probably the moment that the captive, restrained by the rope around his middle, falls in ritual combat or when evisceration occurs. The crumpled body is made to fit the available space on the sculpture. As occurs frequently at El Tajín, in the absence of a glyph the name or title may be implied by the feline or jaguar helmet.

A hacha in the Staatliches Museum für Völkerkunde in Munich (Proskouriakoff 1954: fig. 11f) has a similar but more ornate motif. The border, however, is rendered as an encompassing serpent that may symbolize disembowelment. Also, the upper body of the fallen captive appears to have a series of cut marks on the abdomen.

The contorted theme of the Munich and the Dumbarton Oaks hachas has inspired modern monumental sculpture. At Papantla, not far from El Tajín in Veracruz, is an imaginative 1989 rendition of the motif in a large-scale cement artwork. The massive work looms some 10 m over a public sports center and is one of the city's proudest monuments; however, the figure expresses a benign athletic theme rather than an unsettling depiction of ritual human sacrifice.

The reported location where PC.B.040 was collected, Tecamalucan, is not far from Maltrata, where carvings on a large boulder depict, among other images, a temple with niches (Batres 1905; Medellín Zenil 1962). Such buildings are primarily associated with the north-central Gulf Lowlands around El Tajín. This steep-sloped region at 1,700–1,800 m elevation, however, may have been occupied by right of conquest or by a migration southwestward following the destruction of El Tajín toward the end of the first millennium AD.

This hacha may be one of the southernmost examples known in the high-thin format. It certainly demonstrates the continuation of the war-based ball game ritualism of the coastal elites in a very poorly defined frontier region that was situated in the higher elevations of the south-central Gulf district. Its manufacture, as with many hachas and palmas, was probably commissioned to celebrate a sacrifice following an important military victory or conquest. It is likely to be among the last sculptures in the Classic Veracruz style.

SJKW

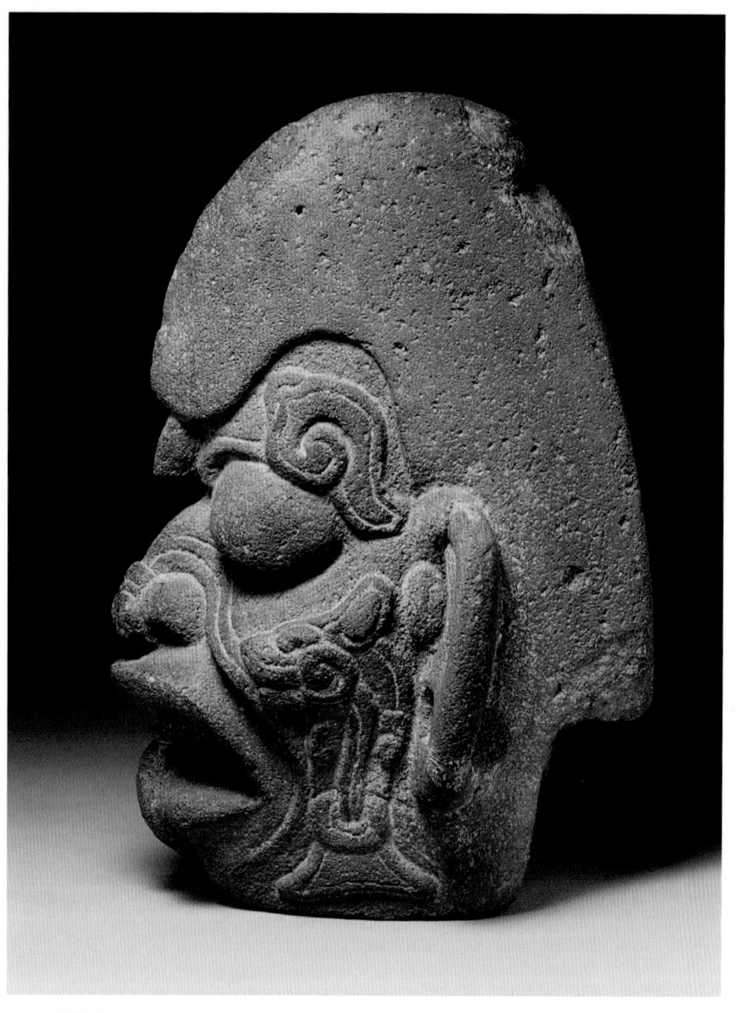

plate 82a

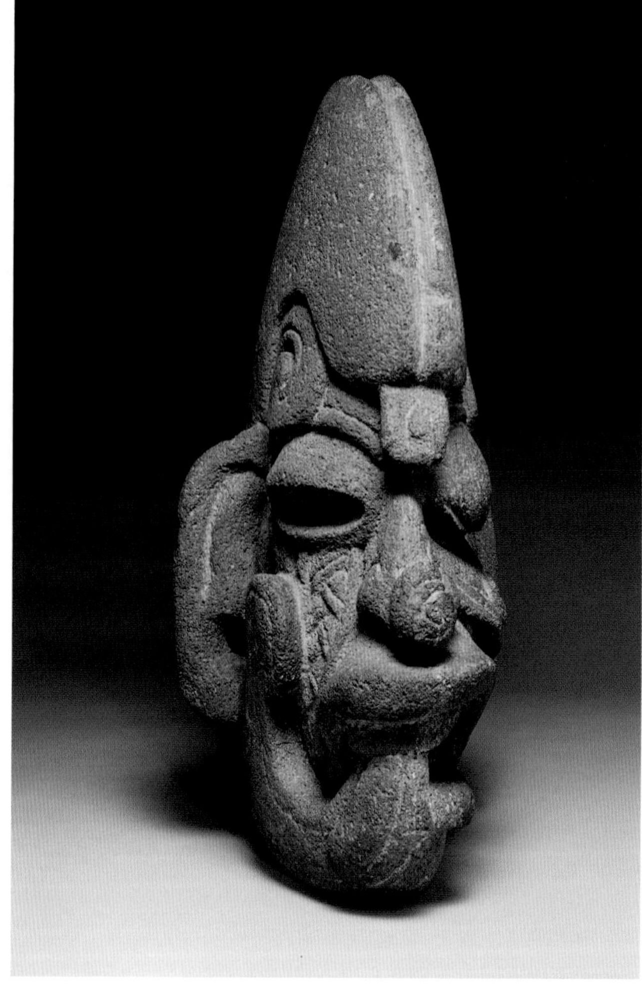

plate 82b, front view

HACHA

PLATE 82
Classic Veracruz; southern Gulf Lowlands
Late Classic period, AD 600–900
Andesite
H. 30.0 cm (11¾"); W. 13.3 cm (5¼"); D. 20.5 cm (8")
PC.B.041

ACQUISITION HISTORY:
Purchased from Earl Stendahl, 1960

EXHIBITION HISTORY:
Indigenous Art of the Americas, National Gallery of Art, Washington, D.C., September 1960–April 1962 (NGA 739)

BIBLIOGRAPHY:
Von Winning 1968b: 215, pls. 299, 300; Dumbarton Oaks 1963: 19, cat. no. 93; Arnold and Pool 2008: dust jacket

Definitely not a standard hacha, this grotesque sculpture is unusual in several respects. The central motif is a distorted face conventionally identified as *dios tuerto* (the "one-eyed god"). Of great antiquity, this theme occurs on very few Gulf Lowlands yokes (ball game apparatus) and on the much smaller miniatures called *yuguitos* ("little yokes"), as well as on numerous ceramic figurines of central and eastern Mexico. This example, however, takes the customary features of such a misshapen head to extremes and even embellishes them.

A tuerto depiction is dualistic: half of the face is normal, half is contorted or deformed, often with one missing eye and a protruding tongue. The "normal" side of this sculpture has a vacant squinting eye, unless it once had an inlay. From the eye descends an odd curving tear line. Out of the mouth, with exposed upper teeth, a large incised scroll emerges from beneath a life-like tongue. Above the eye a tight scroll curl, often a sign of blood, springs from a flap of thick skin.

The contorted side has a huge bulbous eye, as if horribly bloated from blows or literally squeezed out of the skull. The eye and nose are covered with partially wrinkled or scarred skin adorned, perhaps tattooed, with two designs: a curious fish with his head at a right angle to his body, and a conch shell.

The atypically depicted ears on both sides are realistic, protruding, unadorned, and perforated for attaching accoutrements. The upper lip is not bipartite, as often occurs in many dualistic portrayals, but flairs out with greater thickness and a slight down slant on the normal side of the face. The upper portion of the hacha has a groove down its centerline and a strap-like projection onto the forehead that appears to anchor it to the skin flap. This portion of the sculpture, normally flattened, sits atop the face like a Jacobin cap.

The head appears to represent a sacrificed individual wearing the skin mask of an old man over one side of his face and the forehead. The shell sign, as well as the possible age, may indicate an impersonator of God N, one of the underworld and earth gods with relevance to the ball game ritual. What may be fish symbols with a turned head are also shown on the cheeks of an old-man yuguito of possible Late Preclassic date at the University of Notre Dame's Snite Museum of Art (Whittington 2001: 146).

Although certainly bizarre, with many atypical attributes, this hacha may reflect the decapitation of players who impersonate the mythological personages of the underworld ballcourt. The battered, tortured nature of the countenance is in keeping with the torment inflicted on prisoners and legendary underworld deities of the ball game. One of the latter was probably considered a tuerto.

Stylistically, the figure does not conform to norms of known Classic Veracruz sculptures for the north Gulf area, where andesite and basalt are the typical media for hachas. Perhaps it was inspired by a marginal style in the central mountains of Veracruz or the upper zone of the south Gulf area. With the exception of one ear, few of the sculpture's delicate appendages or exposed surfaces have been chipped. Most nicks are along the top of the carving.

In spite of the features that fit the tuerto theme, the known hacha variation, and the medium itself, the preponderance of exaggerated features in the presentation suggests that this peculiar sculpture should only be accepted as authentic with reservations. Future analysis, as well as new finds, may resolve the discrepancies and fully validate the rendering.

SJKW

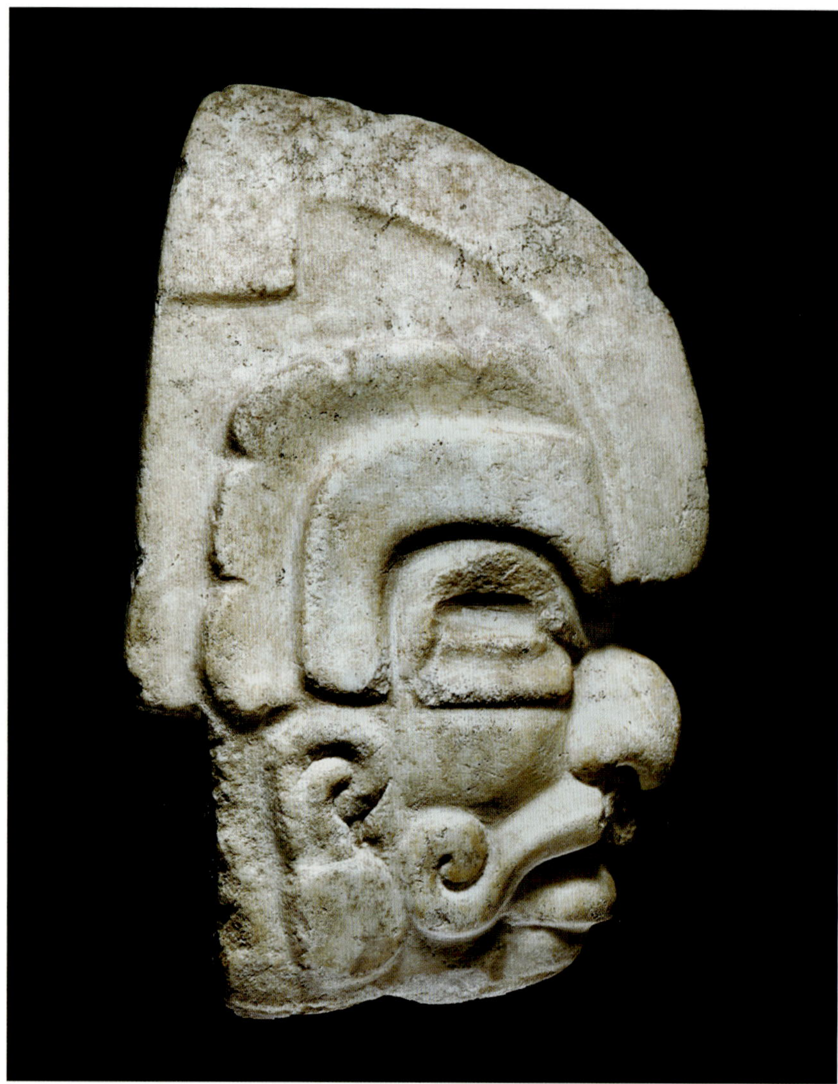

plate 83

HACHA

PLATE 83
Classic Veracruz; south-central Gulf region
Late Classic period, AD 600–900
Marble
H. 25.1 cm (9⅞"); W. 7.6 cm (3"); D. 16.1 cm (6⅜")
PC.B.042

ACQUISITION HISTORY:
Purchased from Joseph Brummer, 1913

EXHIBITION HISTORY:
An Exhibition of Pre-Columbian Art, Fogg Art Museum, Cambridge, January–March 1940; *Ancient American Art*, Santa Barbara Museum of Art, Santa Barbara, Calif., April–June 1942; M. H. de Young Memorial Museum, San Francisco, July–August 1942; Museum of Art, Portland, Ore., September–October 1942; *Indigenous Art of the Americas*, National Gallery of Art, Washington, D.C., April 1947–July 1962 (NGA 55)

BIBLIOGRAPHY:
Peabody Museum of Archaeology and Ethnology and Fogg Art Museum 1940: cat. no. 48; Santa Barbara Museum of Art 1942: cat. no. 39; Kelemen 1943: 114–115, pl. 66b; Bliss 1947: 22, 108, cat. no. 104; Proskouriakoff 1954: 79, fig. 11d; *Artes de México* 1957: pl. 17; Bliss 1957: 237, cat. no. 26, pl. XVII, bottom; Dumbarton Oaks 1963: 20, cat. no. 94

This small hacha, the first Pre-Columbian object collected by Robert Bliss, in 1913, is most probably from the south-central Gulf Lowlands and perhaps from the slopes of the Sierra Madre Oriental. The face has a distinctive, sharply bent, pug nose. The hollowed-out eyes, giving the impression of squinting, are surrounded by a two-piece plaque without scrolls. The upper lip curls backward, extending over the lower cheeks, and a ring-like ornament covers the center of the lip beneath the nostrils. The ears, without spools, terminate in a suspended curved pendant. On the head sits a helmet-like covering with serrated edges, topped by a peaked crest with a raised border.

The extended upper lip is associated with various forms of the Rain God in the Gulf Lowlands. The loop at the midpoint of the lip, probably a jade bead in profile, is a symbol of preciousness and life frequently placed with the dead. The ear pendants are a variant of the hooked *epcololli* form often worn by the sacrificed and also associated with the gods of the planet Venus and wind. The helmet is adorned with short blunt feathers, similar to the macaw motif.

The figure is consistent with portrayals of sacrificed ball game players who are dressed to impersonate various gods on the ballcourt. Although once probably polished, especially the face and helmet, the sculpture now exhibits much battering and numerous scrapes. Much of this alteration appears to be from antiquity.

The notch at the back is smaller than seen on most hachas. The medium, marble, was not commonly used in ancient Veracruz, but is found with somewhat greater frequency in sculptures in the northwestern portions of the south-central Gulf Lowlands. Sculpture PC.B.042 is a good example of a southern variation of one of the main themes of hachas in the Gulf Lowlands.

SJKW

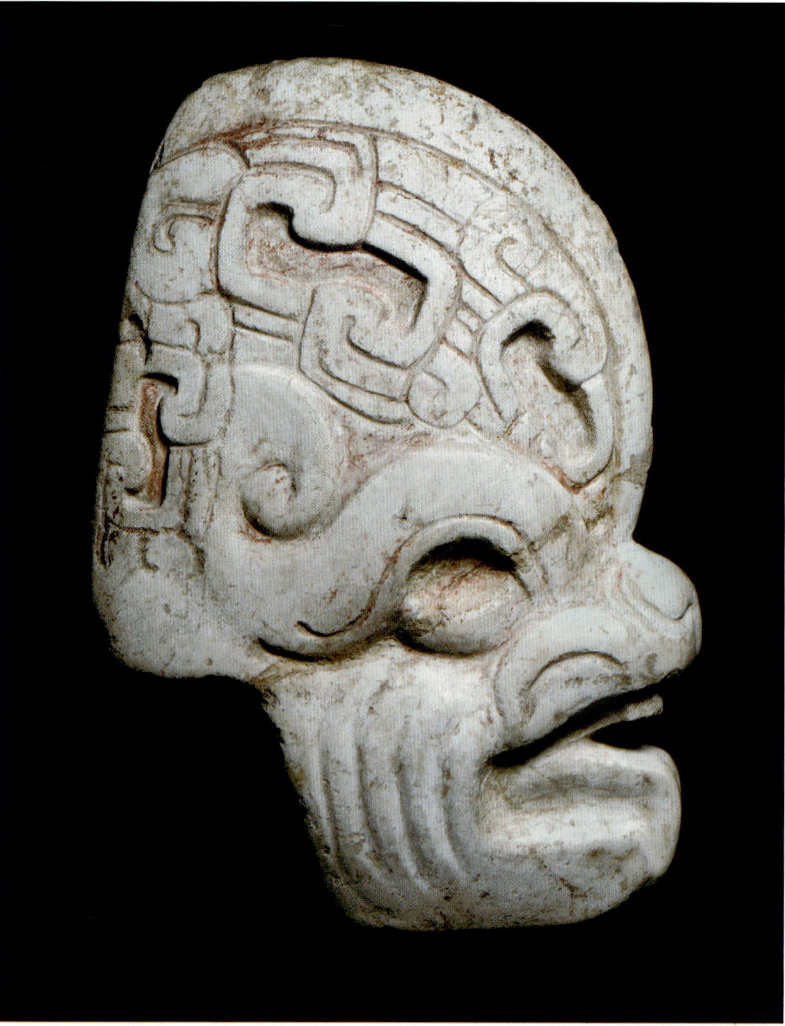

plate 84

PLATE 84
Classic Veracruz; north-central Gulf region or adjacent fringe of south-central region
Early Classic period, AD 300–600
Marble
H. 21.9 cm (8⅝"); W. 7.0 cm (2¾"); D. 15.7 cm (6⅛")
PC.B.043

ACQUISITION HISTORY:
Purchased from Earl Stendahl, 1940s

EXHIBITION HISTORY:
Indigenous Art of the Americas, National Gallery of Art, Washington, D.C., April 1947–July 1962 (NGA 205)

BIBLIOGRAPHY:
Bliss 1947: 22, 106, cat. no. 103; Proskouriakoff 1954: 79, fig. 1, hacha 1; Christensen 1955: 202; *Artes de México* 1957: pl. 14; Bliss 1957: 237, cat. no. 25, pl. XVII, top; Kubler 1962: 76, pl. 39b; Dumbarton Oaks 1963: 20, cat. no. 95; Arnold and Pool 2008: dust jacket

HACHA

This fine marble hacha with a notched form and scroll motif is most likely from the north-central Gulf Lowlands, or the adjacent upper south-central Gulf Lowlands, where marble sculptures are slightly more common and more stone sources are situated. In the former area, however, and particularly at lower elevations, this particular scroll pattern is more widespread.

The sculpture's two sections consist of a zoomorphic head and a hat-like crest covered with scrolls. The figure has a markedly wrinkled face, eyes highlighted by a supraorbital scroll with partial double outline, and possibly there once were inlays in the sockets. The short snout is furrowed; the upper lip furls inward and upward, as when there is a gap between front and back teeth. The open mouth lacks clearly marked teeth or notches for inserting encrusted fangs, common on animal hachas.

A palate-like projection on the maxilla substitutes for delineated teeth. The slightly grooved, languid tongue extends down over the jaw, sometimes a sign of death, but it is not swollen, and the expression gives a sense of panting. Slack and lined cheeks might be specific attributes of the species of animal portrayed, but the indications suggest toothless old age or extreme emaciation.

The subject is probably not a bat, because it lacks common attributes of this animal in the Classic Veracruz style: elongated pointed ears, slit eyes, and an upturned nose. It also lacks the rabbit's signature buckteeth and elongated pointed ears. Other possibilities include the *tepezcuintle* or paca (*Agouti paca*), *tejon* or coatimundi (*Nasua* sp.), and *viejo del monte* or badger (*Taxidea* sp.). In Mesoamerican myth, as in the *Popul Vuh*, tropical nocturnal animals aided the divine heroes in their life-or-death ball games with the malevolent lords of the night.

The appearance of such small sculptures can be changed substantially by incrustations of shell, obsidian, bone, asphalt, or pyrite, which were frequently used for this purpose. These insets could bestow a ferocious aspect on the countenance of a figure that otherwise would be unremarkable and nondescript. A zoomorphic head in Mexico's Museo Nacional de Antropología, with a tongue and nostrils similar to those of PC.B.043, has large bulging eyes, fangs, and incisors of shell and obsidian, giving it a fierce and commanding glare (Rickenbach 1997: item 64).

It is hard to conclusively identify the animal represented here. It may be a hybrid with zoological and mythological attributes. Or it may be a specific deity. A canine form of one of the planet Venus deities is sometimes depicted as emaciated and aged. In later times this dog, occasionally depicted with a protruding tongue, was one of the avatars of Xolotl. This capricious and violent god was also connected with the ball game and the cult of Venus. The veneration of Venus with its cyclical celestial appearances and disappearances was important in the ball game cosmology of ancient Veracruz (Wilkerson 1984, 1991, 1997c).

The extensive collection of hachas at the Museo de Antropología in Xalapa, Veracruz, contains two somewhat similar base figures with distinct upper crests. Both are crafted in porous basalt, less ornate, and not as finely carved as PC.B.043. Of the pair, the complete hacha has a longer, simpler snout with hanging tongue and erect incurving ears (Acosta Lagunes et al. 1992: 131, center). It is probably a canine and lacks wrinkles, scrolls, and provenience.

The broken hacha's face has a short snout, open mouth, and hanging tongue, but with slit death-like eyes and no wrinkles (Acosta Lagunes et al. 1992: 131, left; Medellín Zenil 1960: lám. 64). The broken upper portion, a triangular crest, depicts a headdress and severed hands, possibly with lines of flowing blood. Both are symbols of sacrifice and conquest. The sculpture is from El Viejón, on the coastal plain on the border between the south-central and north-central Gulf Lowlands.

Hacha PC.B.043's crest has scrolls of a variety typically found in the Early Classic period, but which may persist into the Middle Classic. The scrolls are also reasonably similar to those on the Bliss Collection mirror back (PC.B.050, Plate 75). Interestingly, the mirror back may be from the Vega de Alatorre region, just 50 km north of El Viejón, where the broken Xalapa hacha was excavated. Both locations are on the narrow coastal plain of mountainous central Veracruz.

There is also some possibility that the scrolls that swirl back from the forehead of the Dumbarton Oaks figure, along the top of the crest, represent blood. These crest scrolls may have been applied to the sculpture at a later date. Spacing and layout of the crest decoration suggest that this portion of the hacha was originally plain and was subsequently recarved. In fact, the lowermost portion of the scrolls on both sides, just in back of the eye swirls, are crudely pecked and unfinished. Redecoration of ball game statuary is not uncommon, particularly toward the middle of the Classic. It is more commonly observed on yokes and palmas, but the procedure is likely to have been applied to hachas as well.

Although there is a high degree of symmetry on the both sides of the crest, the figure's right surface is more finely carved and finished. The left appears to have received less attention, or perhaps to have been undertaken by an apprentice. The back panel, demonstrating great stylistic affinity with the mirror-back scrolls, is seemingly unconnected to those on the sides and stands as a motif by itself.

This elaborate zoomorphic hacha, like so many of the genre, represents the severed head of a real or mythological participant in the ritual ball game. In ball game rites, players may have worn masks imitating the deity participants who sometimes took animal forms. This ornate sculpture may be associated with a form of the descending god of Venus, also a patron of warfare, sacrifice, and the elite forms of the ball game.

SJKW

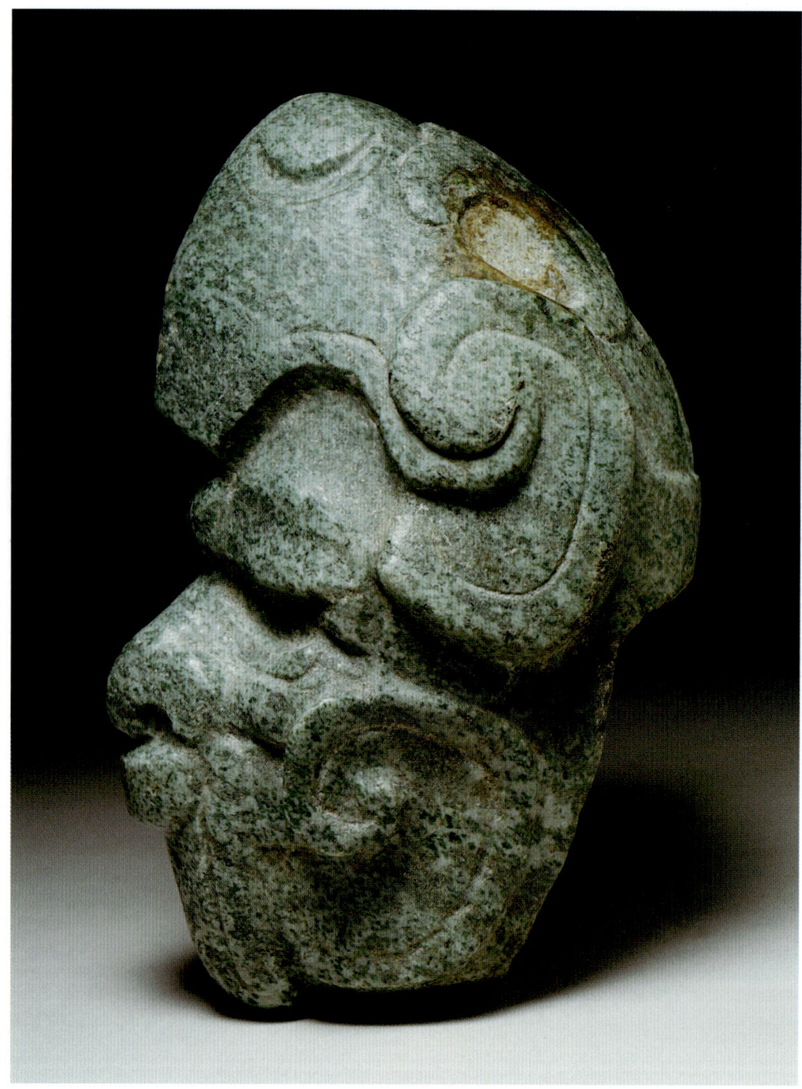

plate 85

HACHA

PLATE 85
Classic Veracruz; south-central Gulf region
Classic period, AD 500–800
Metadiorite
H. 16.3 cm (6⅜"); W. 8.7 cm (3⅜"); D. 10.6 cm (4⅛")
PC.B.046

ACQUISITION HISTORY:
Purchased from Earl Stendahl, 1956; reportedly from the vicinity of Orizaba on the slopes of the Sierra Madre Oriental

BIBLIOGRAPHY:
Bliss 1957: 237, cat. no. 27-A, pl. XIX, views from front, top, and side; Dumbarton Oaks 1963: 20, cat. no. 97

This unusual sculpture is an excellent example of the small polished hachas in hard stone that are most frequently encountered in the south-central Gulf region. It is made of metadiorite, whose green color was preferred for jewelry, small carvings, and yokes. The hacha may date from the end of the Early Classic period or the initial Late Classic. It is part of a small but significant corpus of fine sculptures that are centered on the upper Origaba Valley and result from a direct transplant of lowland ball game rituals to higher elevations (1,700 m and above).[144]

Precise dating for hachas in this area is very difficult. There is a paucity of reliable chronological contexts for the motifs. Additionally, the variants of the Classic Veracruz style are not generally consistent throughout the south-central region. Moreover, artistic attributes in this district were distinctively applied. For example, this item's scroll type is, in the north-central Gulf Lowlands, normally found on certain palmas but not on hachas. Nor is this sculpture a standard hacha with respect to shape. There is no pronounced notch on the lower back, but only a hint of an indentation by the occipital extension of the upper portion of the form. The carving sits on a small base and inclines backward in a dynamic pose.

The figure depicted is a severed human head with distorted features and wearing a zoomorphic helmet. The face has a brooding brow and deep, half-open eyes that almost certainly once held inlays, such as shell or bone. Beneath the eyes a deep incised line may mark the sagging lower eyelid or the edge of a buccal mask.

Directly below the pudgy nose with flaring nostrils is a horizontal ring that appears to be set into the skull at the level where the upper lip should be. The lower jaw is absent, and the tongue hangs straight down with incised lines along its edges. From the area of the missing mandible, two pronounced scrolls in double outline sweep back onto the cheeks; they probably represent blood.

Covering the forehead with its upper beak is a stylized macaw-head helmet. Its eyes were probably once inlaid; surface discoloration there is consistent with a stain from pyrite. Behind the eyes, outlined on their upper sides with a double arc, are three feathers. Scrolls at the lower back of the helmet at the point of articulation of the absent lower beak resemble scrolls on the face.

This hacha appears to represent a form of ritual disfigurement and decapitation analogous to those in the north-central Gulf Lowlands but with some regional peculiarities. The helmet bears, with stylistic variance, the same macaw motif found on other hachas, as well as that worn by figures in ball game rites at El Tajín. However, the ring, missing mandible, and hanging tongue are suggestive of a grisly ritual perhaps more specific to the southern reaches of the Gulf Lowlands.[145]

Dismemberment of the face is likely to have been a presacrificial act, as was evisceration at El Tajín. Such gruesome actions, particularly in the case of captured warriors or rulers, were probably far more common than was previously thought. Sacrifice in ancient Veracruz was not necessarily meant to be a swift trip to the afterlife.

The polished surface, elaborate scrollwork, and probable inlays suggest great care and effort was lavished on this object by the commissioned artisan(s). This diminutive but extremely fine stone sculpture is likely to have commemorated not only an explicit rite but also the protracted ritual death of a specific individual.

SJKW

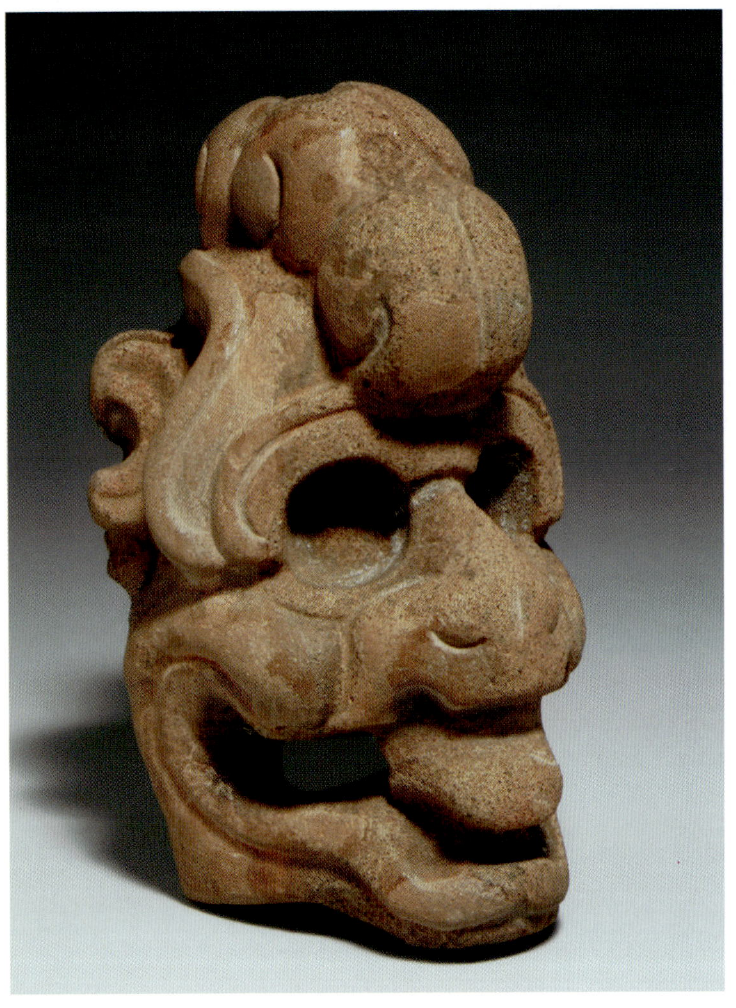

plate 86a

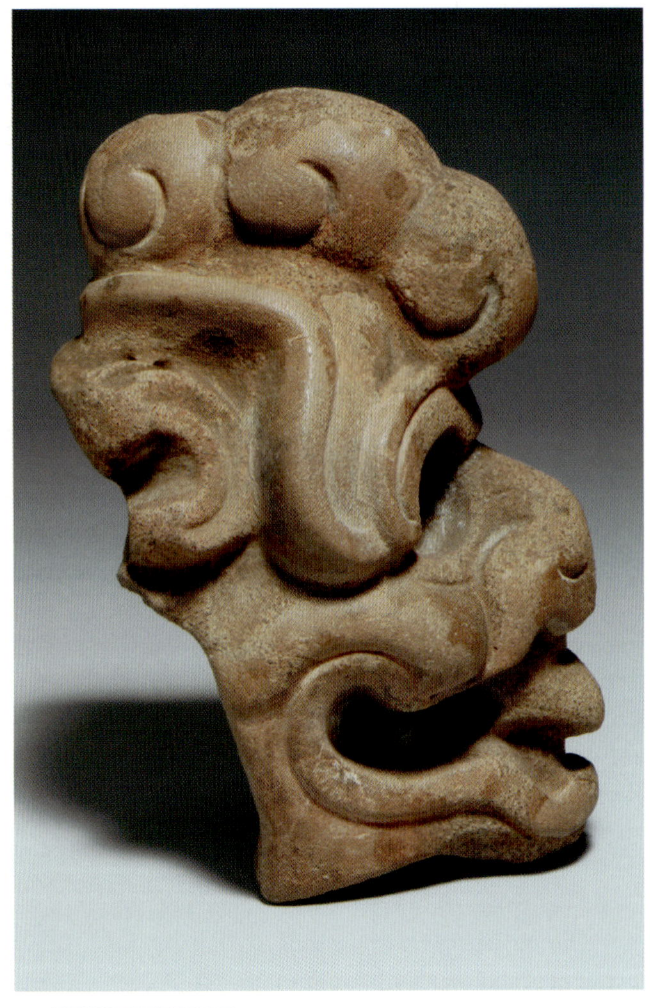

plate 86b, side view

HACHA OR CRESTED HEAD

PLATE 86

Classic Veracruz; south-central Gulf region

Late Classic period, AD 600–900

Basalt

H. 18.5 cm (7¼"); W. 10.7 cm (4¼"); D. 13.5 cm (5¼")

PC.B.555

ACQUISITION HISTORY:

Acquired from Alfred Stendahl by exchange, 1966

BIBLIOGRAPHY:

Von Winning 1968b: 213, pl. 295; Dumbarton Oaks 1969: cat. no. 450; Arnold and Pool 2008: dust jacket

This exceptional sculpture may be a hacha or a form of crested head. It depicts a largely desiccated trophy head, nearly a skull. The piece was once lightly polished and perhaps painted. It probably dates to the Late Classic period.

The currently toothless mouth is open, with a sliver of tongue stuck in the maw. Indentations in the front of both jaws suggest the possibility of settings for fangs. If, as is probable, there were originally such incrustations, they would help explain the faintly canine or feline nose just above. The figure then could be interpreted as wearing a zoomorphic mask.

The sunken eyes may have once held inlays. The sockets are capped by a supraorbital ridge plaque in Classic Veracruz style. The forehead sweeps backward with a similar border to serve as a base for the central crest. The top of the head is adorned with three scrolls, divided by a centerline, that billow up and swirl backward. To the side is half a scroll that may represent a hair knot. This may have been partially recarved, probably in antiquity, when the back of the sculpture was broken. The location suggests a hair arrangement common on the southern coastal plain.

The object portrays a decapitated ball game player probably wearing a canine mask. Gulf Lowlands sculptures sometimes had real teeth, human or animal, set in their features. In this case, it may indicate a Gulf Lowlands variation of the deity Xolotl, sometimes symbolizing the planet Venus as the evening star. The Venus cult, along with its various associated deities, was paramount to warriors and the elite of the Gulf Lowlands during the Classic period. Xolotl, often portrayed with canine features and a skeletal upper body, was thought to be a major participant in the ball game. Players would impersonate him and other significant deities in sacrificial rites held in and around the ballcourts.

This sculpture is, in some respects, intermediate between the notched hachas and the mostly notchless crested heads. The central motif of both is a severed head, although the former has a much greater range of embellishment. They overlap in distribution in Veracruz, with the former predominating in the north and the latter in the south. Although the probable origin for PC.B.555 is in the northern portion of the south-central Gulf Lowlands, these heads have a distribution stretching well down the Veracruz coast into the south Gulf region.[146]

When first carved, incrusted, and likely painted, this sculpture would have been spectacular and fierce in aspect. It is a fine example of how the masterful artists of the Gulf Lowlands could simultaneously embody metaphor, symbolism, and the concept of a trophy head in a small object.

SJKW

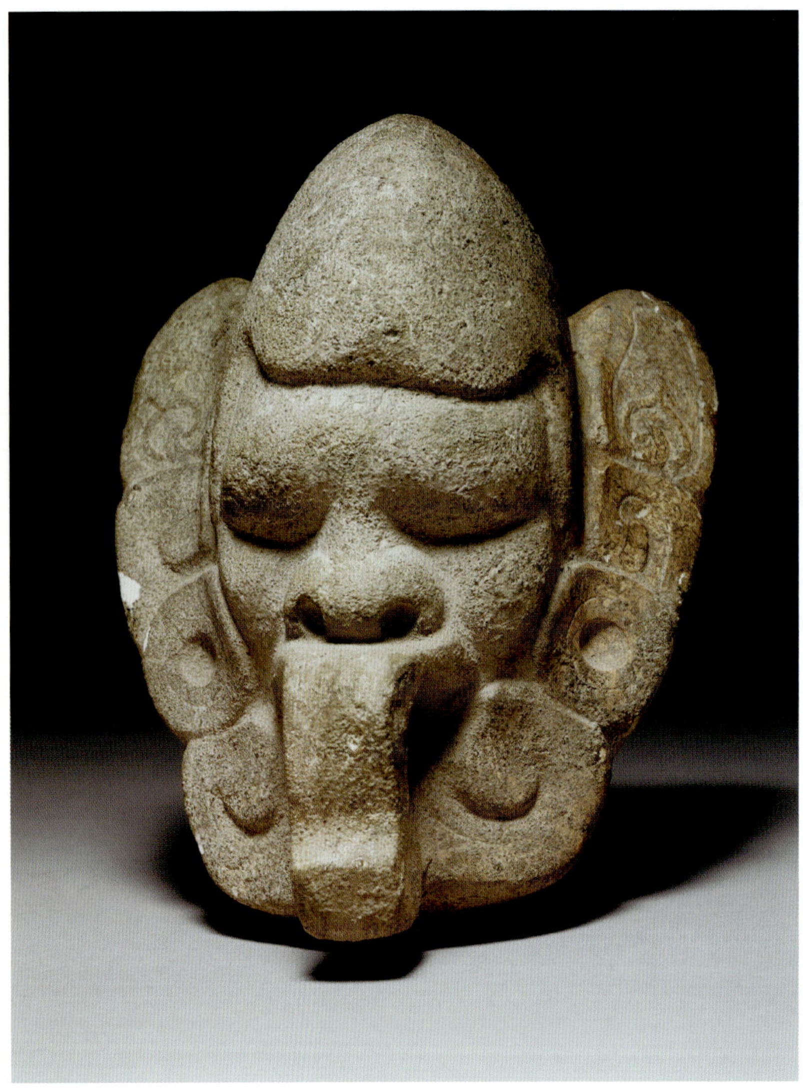

plate 87

HEAD

PLATE 87

Regional Gulf style; possibly from south Gulf Lowlands
Late Preclassic or Protoclassic period, 400 BC–AD 300
Limestone
H. 16.2 cm (6⅜"); W. 12.9 cm (5"); D. 11.9 cm (4⅝")
PC.B.549

ACQUISITION HISTORY:

Purchased from Aaron Furman, 1965

BIBLIOGRAPHY:

Dumbarton Oaks 1969: cat. no. 430

This head has many unusual traits. It is made of relatively soft limestone, probably from a nodule. This medium is not a preferred material for ball game or portable sculptures in the Gulf Lowlands. The sculpture is not a notched hacha, a tenoned head, or a sculpted upright cranium. Rather, it seems to be in a unique category with some attributes from each of these three sculptural forms.

Its flat bottom would have it sit facing upward at an angle, a most uncommon posture. The entire figure has a nearly evenly eroded surface without major nicks. The countenance's puffy face has a flaring nose placed in what appears to be a bullet-shaped cap that sometimes occurs in Late Preclassic representations. The elongated upper lip, often an attribute of the Rain God, ends in a strange block-like bulge. The lower jaw appears to be missing, its location marked by two large scrolls that emerge onto the cheeks perhaps as blood swirls.

The face is flanked by two prominent ridges that begin from the top of the cheek scrolls and flare back along the head. They start with ear spools that have a double outline on their interior and bend up oddly against the figure's cheek. On one side the ear scroll is mostly square and on the other more curved in format. The ears themselves are depicted by hooked scrolls immediately above these features.

There follows on both sides a possible upside-down rendition, via excision, of *epcololli* hooked shell pendants. These accoutrements are common in the upper Gulf Lowlands from the Classic onward and, by the end of the Pre-Columbian era, are associated with wind deities. Here they are decorated with a fine scroll adorned by a pointed protuberance. Under normal circumstances these ornaments, if indeed this is what they are, would be suspended beneath the ear spools or most frequently in lieu of them.

The composition of the head bears diagnostic traits related to disparate periods and regions. The scroll types have a wide and basically Late Classic distribution, primarily on palmas and monumental sculptures in the north-central Gulf Lowlands. The swollen aspect of the face, usually an indicator of death, occurs on some Late Classic heads from the south-central Gulf Lowlands. Such features also occur on some Late Preclassic and Protoclassic sculptures from the same area. None, however, resembles PC.B.549.

The jawless rendition of the lower face, where blood scrolls replace the mandible, is a motif that may have been common particularly in the south-central Gulf Lowlands during the Classic period. Like more than a few ball game sculptures, this head may have undergone some successive recarving, rendering it atypical.

There is a chance that PC.B.549 is from the extreme southern Gulf Lowlands and represents a regional imitation of the hachas and heads with more standard features found in the lower reaches of the adjacent south-central Gulf Lowlands. Little is known of the sculptural corpus from post-Olmec times in the districts at the base of the Gulf of Mexico in southern Veracruz and western Tabasco. Although the piece has several attributes consistent with the southern Gulf regions and the Late Classic period, until more is known of the corpus this anomalous limestone head is best considered to be of questionable authenticity.

SJKW

PALMAS

These awkwardly named carvings, commonly called "palmas" or "palmate stones," constitute one of the most eccentric categories of sculpture in ancient Mesoamerica. The name was coined by Eduard Seler, based on a resemblance of design to palm fronds in a few elongated examples he observed at the close of the nineteenth century. Nevertheless, these diverse ball game sculptures have nothing to do with their botanical appellation. Instead, they appear to be another article of ball game paraphernalia wrought in stone, associated with sacrificial rituals, and elevated to significant veneration. With a beginning in the Early Classic period, their apogee was during the Late Classic, and in some regions in the subsequent Epiclassic period (Wilkerson 1997d).

Palmas were highly popular in, but not restricted to, the north-central Gulf region and environs. Like yokes and hachas, they were sometimes carried afar by migrating groups or elites influenced by Classic Veracruz ritualism. In the Gulf Lowlands they were used in pre- and post-game rites, exhibited as a sign of elite prerogative, and eventually buried as valuable mortuary offerings for the afterlife. Great care was taken in the elaboration of their surface designs. Varied motifs are often forcefully rendered and sometimes full of delicate detail. Scenes from post–ball game ceremonies, rulership rituals, and mythological events are portrayed on these sculptures. Additionally, many are decorated with ball game–associated symbols and divine fauna, often enfolded in the baroque scroll patterns that characterize the zenith of the Classic Veracruz art style.

The preferred medium for palmas was basalt and other varieties of volcanic rock. This stone could be large-grained and porous, making meticulous carving difficult. Other, finer-grained, stones were sometimes used, particularly in the higher elevations toward the Sierra Madre Oriental. Inlays of bone, obsidian, human teeth, and probably shell highlighted the eyes of some figures on palmas, probably occurring commonly in some regions. Like yokes, some palmas were initially shaped without fine smoothing; later the surfaces were carved, probably by different artisans. Also like yokes, some palmas have designs that seem to have been larger than the available surface areas, suggesting problems in adapting existing patterns to the surfaces of these objects.

Palmas are a highly diverse genre of sculptures, varying from the small and squat to the tall, narrow, and elegant, and varying in height from less than 15 cm to 1 m, with regional preferences. The base of these sculptures is usually convex, the back, generally flat or slightly bulging, sweeping up and forward in a gentle arc. The front may have a projecting zoomorphic or human figure in the round, or occasionally a groove-like depression. The top is often spatulate, thinning to a narrow edge. Some have a narrow triangular indentation extending downward, bifurcating the top. A major alternative form suppresses the spreading top in favor of a narrow back, laterally flattened sides, and compressed crest-like ridge at the top, like some hachas. In fact, there is clearly some merging of these two forms of ball game sculptures.

The precise association of the general palma form with the ball game is not as straightforward as for the other game sculptures modeled on ball game protectors and severed heads. The palma's most common shape probably derived from the mallet used in a new form of the game that may have become popular in some regions in about the middle of the Classic period. Wooden mallets of generally similar form and size range exist today in northwestern Mexico in one of the surviving modes of the ball game (Figure 89). As with yokes and hachas, it is unlikely that the sculptures themselves were used in this manner; rather, they symbolically imitate the functional form and represent the prerogative of the elite to participate in this probably special format of the ritual ball game.

Regardless of the specific origin of the shape, in post-game rites palmas were sometimes placed over yoke-like waistbands and exhibited ritually, as were hachas. In early narrative sculptures at El Tajín, both accoutrements are sometimes shown together on opposite sides of a single waist ring (Figure 90), although later depictions in the same city tend to show only palmas. Throughout the El Tajín region itself and the north-central lowlands in general, where all three ball game sculptures were abundant, palmas and hachas seem not to be found together as burial offerings. One palma, quite similar to one of the Dumbarton Oaks

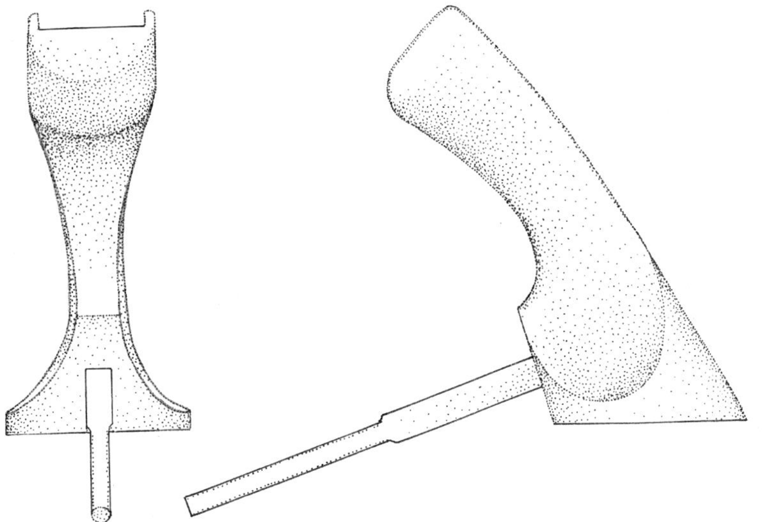
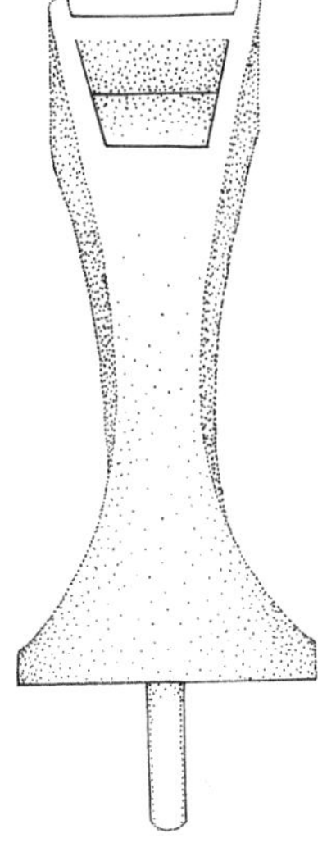

fig. 89
Three views of a wooden mallet (height 36.5 cm) from Sinaloa, Mexico, used in a modern form of the ball game. Institute for Cultural Ecology of the Tropics Ethnographic Collection. Drawing by the Institute for Cultural Ecology of the Tropics, Miguelangel Garcia/ S. Jeffrey K. Wilkerson.

examples and excavated by the author at Santa Luisa (Wilkerson 1984), was unaccompanied by a hacha or stone yoke, but it was inclined forward as if placed in the burial on a perishable yoke-like object. Limited archaeological data and anecdotal descriptions of finds, as well as the narrative sculptures at El Tajín, suggest that palmas came to serve similar ritual purposes as hachas and eventually eclipsed them in use throughout the district.

In fact, the evidence from El Tajín strongly implies that there may have been a growing diversification of sacrificial rituals held in or about the ballcourts as varied forms of gladiatorial combat, evisceration, clubbing, and execution by darts or spears gained prominence. Beheading clearly continued its direct association with the ball game. However, other forms of ritual death, including perhaps heart removal at the very end of the Classic Veracruz expression, came to have a significant place in the ritualism of human sacrifice that centered on the ball game. In other regions—especially to the south, where hachas predominated—there may have been a continued emphasis on the older decapitation rites. Palmas may never have been as popular in those regions dominated by smaller polities as they were at El Tajín, the great metropolitan center of Classic Veracruz civilization, with its rapidly evolving elite ritualism during the Late Classic and Epiclassic periods.

Some of the more elaborate palmas have a personage prominently depicted on the front, often in lavish ritual garb and sometimes sculpted in the round, as well as a scene from an associated rite on the back. The emphasis in such composite depictions goes beyond the celebration of a single symbol, such as the severed head of the typical hacha. Here all surfaces are used to demonstrate the larger ritual context of one of the ball game ceremonies. Thematically, these scenes resemble the ornate narrative sculptures of the Building of the Columns at El Tajín, probably mostly of very late Classic as well as very early Epiclassic date, where rulers celebrate conquests, ballcourt sacrifices, and mythological reenactments. Such palmas are closely associated with elite religion and rulership and may also represent the merging of new rituals with the ball game macro-cult of the Gulf Lowlands. Some complex, multifigure depictions appear to be reenactment scenes from the ball game mythology of the Hero Twins expressed in the myths recounted in the *Popol Vuh*.

Other palmas have only scroll patterns, at times with human heads or deity faces peering out. Severed hands are important motifs. Mammals and reptiles are common, including deer, coyotes, rabbits, coatimundis, bats, alligators, and iguanas. Many sculptures have divided tops, much like raised bird wings. Birds are major themes in palmas, especially in the smaller sculptures, and are represented at Dumbarton Oaks by PC.B.044 (Plate 88) and PC.B.045 (Plate 89). Birds are important symbols in the Gulf Lowlands, associated with diverse deities, rites, and specific ritual gear. Water birds, a popular motif in ceramic sculpture and

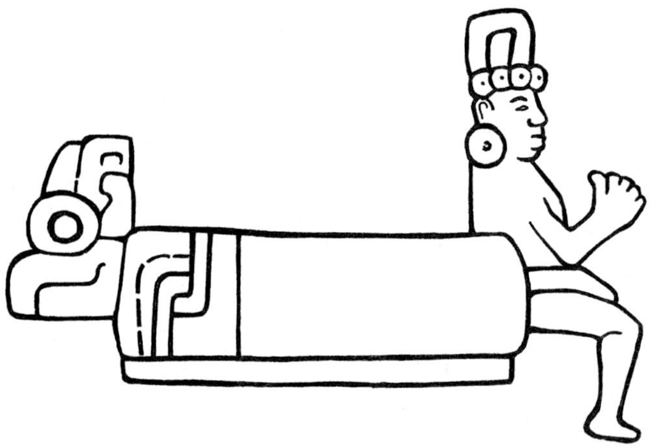

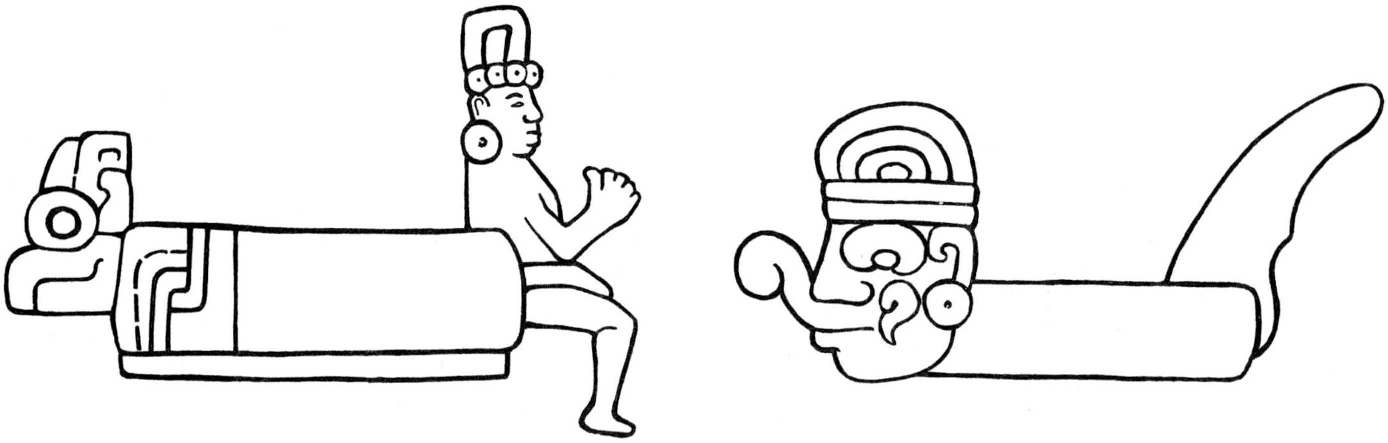

fig. 90
Hachas (left) and palmas (right) attached to waist protectors or yokes in the sculptures of El Tajín. Top: from the waist of the protagonist on the Building 5 tablet. Bottom: from the dress of a ball game player in the northwest panel of the South Ballcourt. Drawing by the Institute for Cultural Ecology of the Tropics, Miguelangel Garcia/S. Jeffrey K. Wilkerson.

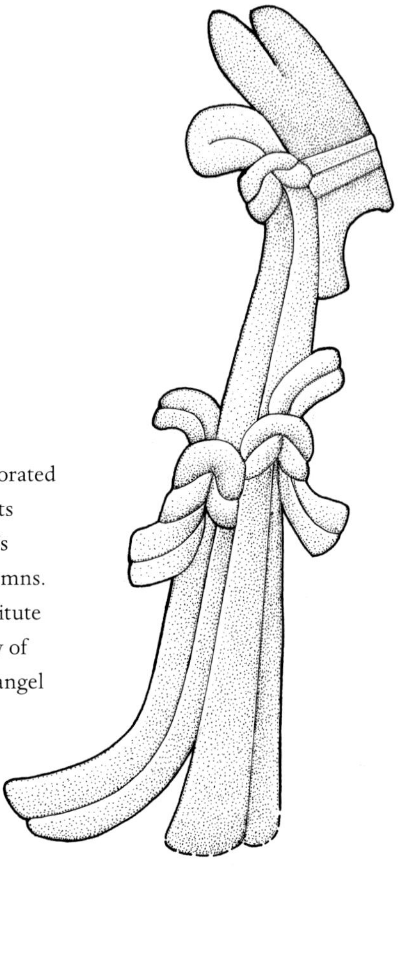

fig. 91
Bifurcate palma decorated with sashes and knots in the art of El Tajín's Building of the Columns. Drawing by the Institute for Cultural Ecology of the Tropics, Miguelangel Garcia/S. Jeffrey K. Wilkerson.

some Classic Veracruz art, appear to be associated with the underworld and rain deities. Carnivorous and carrion birds are particularly associated with sacrificial rituals. They appear on palmas as parts of scenes and as individual carvings. These themes probably have regional significance, being more numerous in the north-central area, and almost are certainly of very long duration in the palma tradition.

Palmas in the form of realistic avian figures were especially popular in the greater El Tajín area in the Late Classic period. In the city's narrative sculptures the same birds are generally shown in similar positions in scenes of mythological reenactments by rulers. Interestingly, these birds often are depicted mounted on leather bags made for the ritual drink pulque. The avian palmas may well be depictions in stone of the birds used—and perhaps sacrificed—in specific ball game pulque rites, as well as symbolic representations of the original bird protagonists in the ball game myths. These sculptures constitute an important subset of the palma corpus.

Quite a few of the smaller palmas have parallel rows of front-to-back perforations that would permit attachment of other decoration or perhaps affixing of the sculpture itself to a heavy cloth. It is clear from the narrative sculptures at El Tajín that palmas were ritually decorated. One depiction shows long cloth sashes with elaborate bows that were attached to exhibited palmas in certain rituals (Figure 91). Such embellishment on the art of the Gulf Lowlands is often associated with sacrifice.

SJKW

PALMA

PLATE 88
Classic Veracruz; probably from the greater El Tajín region
Late Classic period, AD 600–900
Basalt
H. 33.5 cm (13⅛"); W. 17.3 cm (6¾"); D. 21.5 cm (8½")
PC.B.044

ACQUISITION HISTORY:
Purchased from Earl Stendahl, 1941

EXHIBITION HISTORY:
Ancient American Art, Santa Barbara Museum of Art, Santa Barbara, Calif., April–June 1942; M. H. de Young Memorial Museum, San Francisco, July–August 1942; Museum of Art, Portland, Ore., September–October 1942; *Indigenous Art of the Americas*, National Gallery of Art, Washington, D.C., April 1947–July 1962

BIBLIOGRAPHY:
Bliss 1947: 21, 104–105, cat. no. 99; Proskouriakoff 1954: 68, fig. 10b; *Artes de México* 1957: pl. 13; Bliss 1957: 237, cat. no. 27, pl. XVIII; Dumbarton Oaks 1963: 20, cat. no. 96; Davies 1983: fig. 12

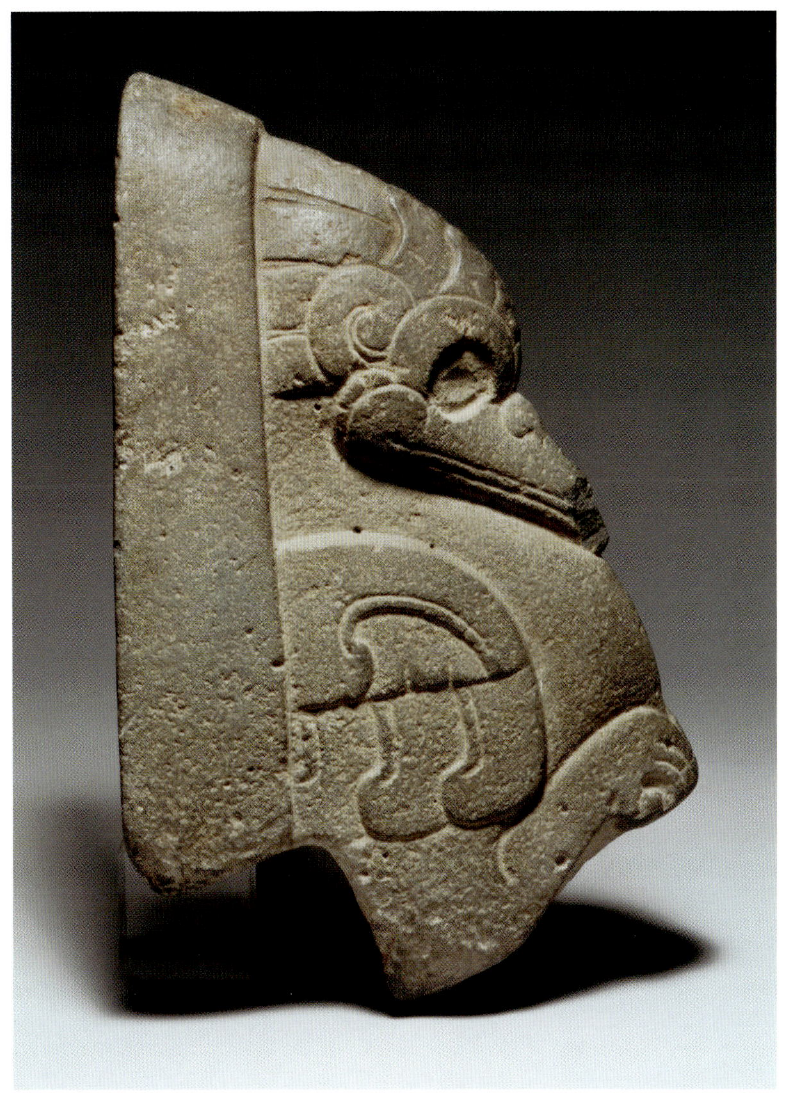

plate 88

This sculpture is an excellent example of a distinctive type of bird palma, found predominantly in the north-central Gulf area and especially in the Tecolutla and Nautla River Valleys. Most known examples are less three-dimensional than this one; many do not have the "backboard" that is present here. Practically all do share a similar posture and a comparable treatment of the wings and talons.

Analogous examples, if slightly less robust in features, are found in the Arensberg Collection (Kubler 1954: nos. 155, 157) and the American Museum of Natural History (303.3/2355). The palma most similar to PC.B.044, with an even more three-dimensional presentation of the theme, was excavated by the author at the site of Santa Luisa and is now at the Museo de Antropología in Xalapa, Veracruz (Figure 92).

Bird motifs are common in Classic Veracruz art and are associated with ball game ritualism, particularly with visions and sacrifices. One of the most explicit portrayals of a vision is from El Tajín's South Ballcourt, where a large dancing avian figure participates in a major pre-game rite. Also at El Tajín's Building of the Columns, where numerous sacrificial rites are depicted, birds, or bird skins, are shown in palma-like postures appended to skin containers carried as accoutrements in ball game–associated rituals. This category of palma may be stone renditions of these trophy birds.

It is also possible that composite mythological creatures are being depicted in such art, but in this class of palmas a specific bird is shown. Generally these birds are depicted with upraised talons and full extended fronts as if they have just

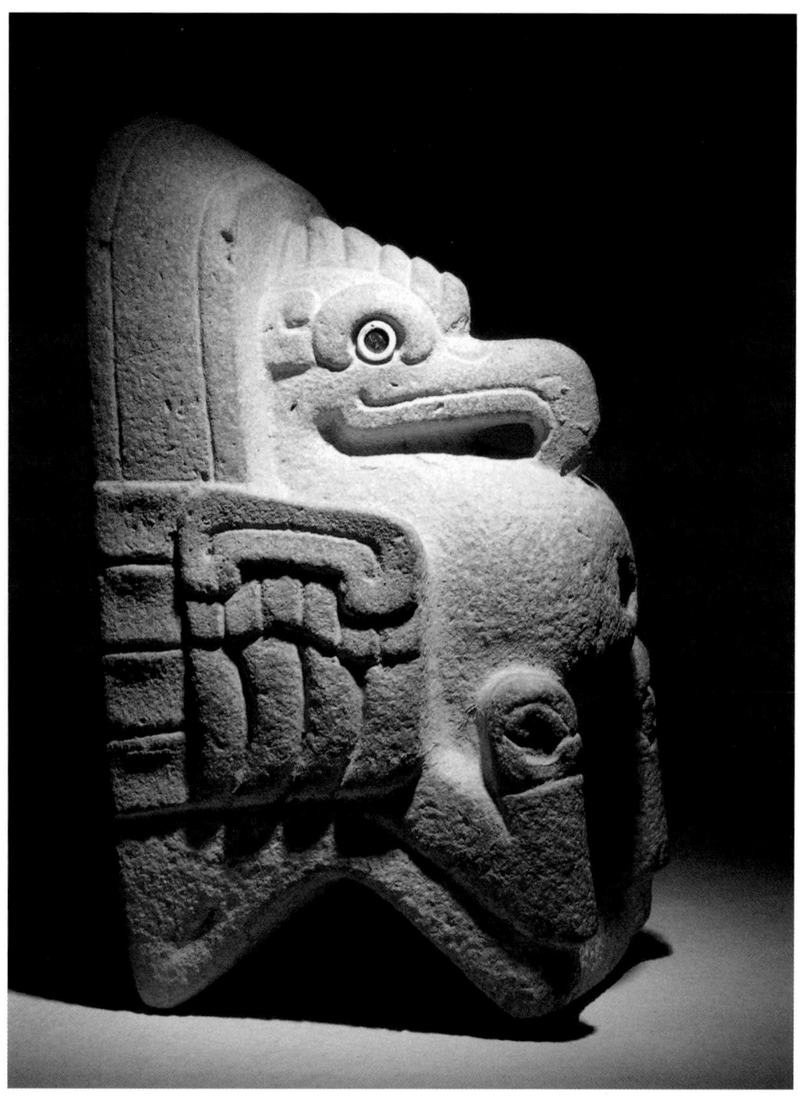

fig. 92
Bird palma with inlaid eyes of obsidian and bone excavated by the author in 1974 at Santa Luisa, now at the Museo de Antropología in Xalapa, Veracruz. Photograph by S. Jeffrey K. Wilkerson.

gorged themselves, and some—like PC.B.044—appear to have been gluttonous indeed, with long beaks curved downward for tearing flesh. The wings tend to be divided into primary and secondary feathers. The short crest on the head often has backward-curving front feathers with longer feathers sweeping directly back.

These birds have been called vultures or eagles, but the common king vulture, also a day sign in the ritual calendar, has a mostly bald head totally lacking a crest. There are several candidates among eagles, hawks, kites, and falcons. However, the head of the crested caracara (*Polyborus plancus*), commonly called *quebrantahuesos* ("bone breaker") in the tropics, is most similar to that shown in these palmas. It has a black crest, a red face, and a white and black body. It is both a bird of prey and an avid eater of carrion.

Although not as numerous as vultures, these large, strong birds aggressively feed with them on carrion. They also hunt live prey, including snakes. Several will congregate about a kill or carcass and gorge themselves, apparently in order of dominance. This is a far more striking, assertive, and colorful bird than the vulture and so is more likely to have played a role in ball game ritual. Apart from its probable link in antiquity with both death and the consumption of the sacrificed, this large bird of prey may have been thought to have powers of prophecy. In the countryside of Veracruz today this surly bird is credited with being able to announce weather changes—including droughts, storms, and floods—with its long, rancorous calls. This belief may be a carry-over from the Pre-Columbian myth that certain birds were messengers of the underworld gods, which included the rain deity.

Many palmas originally had inlaid eyes made from diverse materials. The Santa Luisa example had green obsidian eyes set in a sawed long bone, remarkably duplicating the harsh stare of a bird of prey. The inlay appears to have been held in place by a daub of asphalt. Palma PC.B.044 has indentations in the eye sockets that are likely to have held inlays. Also, a few palmas with this and other motifs apparently were stucco-coated and painted. No evidence of such surface treatment remains on this item.

The backboard behind the bird is found on a number of palmas, and although it might represent part of a ball game mallot, its precise purpose here is unknown. It is usually plain, although on the Santa Luisa example it has decorative lines on its sides. At times, the birds almost appear to be pinned to the board. Many palmas have carved backs, and it is fully possible that the surface once sported a painted scene. It is also possible that mythologically these birds were sometimes thought to carry something on their backs.

Although these sculptures may have been transported considerable distances, even into Central America, they appear to originate in the El Tajín region in north-central Veracruz. The battering on the present example is likely to be ancient and is not atypical for such carvings, suggesting both use and transport mishaps. The Dumbarton Oaks carrion-bird palma embodies many of the salient qualities of this important class of sculptures.

SJKW

PALMA

PLATE 89
Classic Veracruz ; north-central Gulf region
Late Classic period, AD 600–900
Diorite
H. 17.9 cm (7"); W. 13.5 cm (5¼"); D. 12.0 cm (4¾")
PC.B.045

ACQUISITION HISTORY:
Purchased at Sotheby's on 9 June 1937; formerly in the collection of Jean Holland

EXHIBITION HISTORY:
An Exhibition of Pre-Columbian Art, Fogg Art Museum, Cambridge, January–March 1940; *Ancient American Art*, Santa Barbara Museum of Art, Santa Barbara, Calif., April–June 1942; M. H. de Young Memorial Museum, San Francisco, July–August 1942; Museum of Art, Portland, Ore., September–October 1942; *Indigenous Art of the Americas*, National Gallery of Art, Washington, D.C., April 1947–July 1954, January 1956–July 1962

BIBLIOGRAPHY:
Sotheby's 1937: no. 182, pl. IV; Peabody Museum of Archaeology and Ethnology and Fogg Art Museum 1940: cat. no. 43; Santa Barbara Museum of Art 1942: cat. no. 221; Bliss 1947: 22, cat. no. 100; Bliss 1957: 238, cat. no. 31, pl. XXIII; Dumbarton Oaks 1963: 20, cat. no. 98

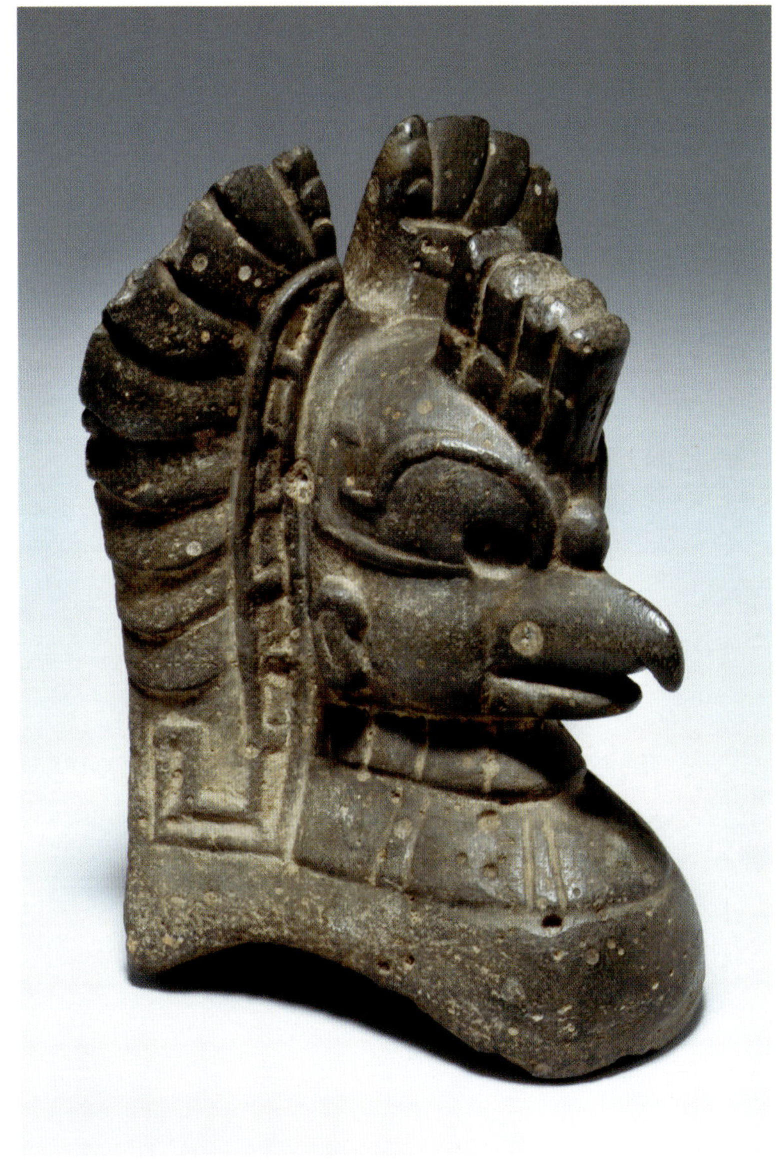

plate 89

This diminutive bird sculpture belongs to an unusual variety of palma of unconfirmed geographic distribution that is likely to have originated in or about the north-central Gulf Lowlands in the Late Classic period. Very small palmas were of a handy size for transport and occur on the Gulf coastal plain in limited numbers. Several in similar format, but with distinct motifs, have been found in the adjacent northern part of the state of Puebla. This particular specimen is executed in hard dark stone, an unusual medium for palmas. It is reportedly from near the city of Puebla in the Central Highlands of Mexico, some 200 km inland from the Gulf Coast.[147]

Of miniature size and squat appearance, the sculpture is executed in a variant of the Classic Veracruz style that abbreviates and compresses many elements. The head of a crested carnivorous bird rests on a standard palma base. The open beak, with a nostril bulb at its base, is largely straight with a pronounced elongation and hook on its upper half. The smallish eyes are round indentations, possibly for inlays, at the corner of stylized scrolls. The ridge between the scroll-brows is wrinkled or feathered. Ears are depicted well back of puffy cheeks in an anthropomorphic mode.

Around the neck is a square stone necklace atop what may be pendants or a cape-like garment.

The whole abuts what is probably a representation of a backboard with a segmented, almost niche-like design that ends in squared scrolls. This element is, in turn, fringed with two opposing groups of feathers that approximate raised wings. The posterior surface is arched forward and plain. The bottom is gently curved. Most of the hard stone is polished and pockmarked from natural impurities. There is some battering, apparently ancient.

The figure appears to be that of a bird impersonator in one of the pre–ball game rituals. But this is not the same bird depicted in palma PC.B.044 (probably a caracara) or in hacha PC.B.039 (a macaw). This avian figure has a crest of four stubby feathers that rise upward and slightly to the front. Short flanking feathers surround the crest plumes. The bird is probably an eagle and quite possibly the black hawk-eagle (*Spizaetus tyrannus*), a large, impressive bird of prey with a distinctive erect crest of short black and white feathers. It resides in both lowlands forests and lower elevation cloud forests. It was probably associated with a specific deity thought to participate in ball game rituals and most probably with pre-game vision sessions. This rite, with musical accompaniment and a dancing eagle, is shown at El Tajín's South Ballcourt.

There too, the impersonator raises his wings. This bird posture, as when landing, appears to be the inspiration for the notched form of the palma back. The bifurcate format is common in palmas, and not just those with bird motifs. At times the back is sufficiently split that the wings appear as totally separate. Such rendering may be a tradition of considerable time depth in the genre.

The same type of bird, but with a more complete body, is found in the Arensberg Collection (Kubler 1954: no. 156). Another example was recorded in a Mexican collection in 1931. This bird is sometimes also found on larger palmas in the north-central Gulf area, and particularly in the greater El Tajín region. An example, now in Mexico City, from Tuzapan (west of El Tajín) shows a man dressed in a huge helmet with this motif, leaning against the bifurcate background (Proskouriakoff 1954: fig.12i).

Tropical birds and their impersonators are integral parts of ancient Gulf Lowlands ritualism. This unusual small sculpture is an excellent example of how major palma themes can be compressed and reduced to their essential elements. It also demonstrates one of the extreme variations of the Classic Veracruz artistic expression.

SJKW

ABBREVIATIONS

cat. no.	catalogue number
cm	centimeters
D.	depth
Diam.	diameter
fig.	figure
g	grams
H.	height
JQ	Jeffrey Quilter
JU	Javier Urcid
km	kilometers
L.	length
lám.	lámina
mm	millimeters
NJS	Nicholas J. Saunders
STE	Susan Toby Evans
SJKW	S. Jeffrey K. Wilkerson
W.	width

NOTES

1 This famous passage, written in 1520, is quoted by Esther Pasztory (2005: 7), who noted Dürer's emphasis on ingenuity, not artistic merit.

2 Olmec objects in the Bliss Collection at Dumbarton Oaks are described in Taube (2004b).

3 These patterns are extrapolated from the findings of Tlatilco's Temporada 4 excavations (García Moll 1999: 21; García Moll et al. 1991: 30), in which approximately 216 separate individuals were recovered from mortuary contexts, and 45 were buried with figurines.

4 This typology was devised by Clarence Hay and refined and extensively published by George Vaillant (discussion in Vaillant and Vaillant 1934: 24).

5 George Vaillant was apparently the first to publish the term, already in common use: "it is known vulgarly as the 'pretty lady' type" (1930: 34). The term has been critiqued as "the product of a narrow point of view that perceives women . . . as created primarily for the entertainment of an audience. Such an attitude is the result of serious neglect of the study of women's roles in the Preclassic period as they pertain directly to the iconographic meaning of female figurines" (Bernal-García n.d. [1988]: 17). But perhaps, in the cultural context of the time, referring to a naked woman as a "pretty lady" would have been an act of gallantry, not derision.

6 The depiction of two faces might accurately depict the result of a congenital condition, diprosopy, in which case this type of figurine could be the world's oldest scientifically correct depiction of a medical condition (Bendersky 2000). However, diprosopy is extremely rare, with only about 85 cases reported in the past 350 years, and, furthermore, such individuals are always stillborn (Honan 2000). Thus it would seem unlikely that a scientifically accurate depiction would be of an adult, as the Tlatilco figurines of this type portray.

7 It most closely resembles a rare Chupícuaro type labeled "large hollow figurine" by Porter (1956: 556) and "polychrome" in Frierman's (1969: xi) description of the Chupícuaro figurines in the Natalie Wood Collection. Similar examples shown in the catalogue of the St. Louis Museum are much larger (24 and 26.5 cm high) and are hollow (Parsons 1980: 58–59, fig. 68).

8 Our present knowledge about the city's material culture is considerable compared with what was known prior to the publication of the Teotihuacan map (R. Millon 1973). Before the map revealed that the city's pyramids were surrounded by 2,000 residential compounds extending over an area of 20 km (8 sq. mi.), some influential scholars still regarded the site as a vacant ceremonial center, consisting of the massive monuments and little else.

9 These mouth masks are often referred to as butterfly-shaped; they also mimic the *talud* and *tablero*, decorative architectural styles with a vertical panel (tablero) above a sloping apron (talud). They are also found on mural images of the Teotihuacan Goddess, a mysteriously masked being (Pasztory 1993e: 50).

10 At Teotihuacan, textiles were found with burials, mostly dating from the third and fourth centuries AD (Sempowski 1994: 144, 146), and from other excavations (Sánchez Sánchez 1982b: 252).

11 The timing of use of woven fabrics in the Basin of Mexico remains puzzling. Vaillant's (1930: 38) report that "[t]extiles were probably extensively used" at Formative period Zacatenco was based on degraded evidence, possibly basketry. Similarly, early "spindle whorls" are problematical. To spin thread of consistent quality requires a well-balanced fly wheel on the spindle. As Stark (2001: 218–219) has noted, such objects as perforated worked sherds may have served other purposes, but many would have needed compensatory balance to function as spindle whorls.

12 Spindle whorls could have been made of perishable material, but, given Teotihuacan's strong ties with the Gulf Lowlands, knowledge of ceramic whorls would have led to their adoption, because they are more durable and function better than do wooden ones, and are much easier to manufacture as well.

13 Problems included malnutrition (Widmer and Storey 1993), climate change (Gill 2000: 293; Keys 1999), and severe soil erosion from the Teotihuacan Valley's deforested slopes.

14 In fact, Taube (1983: 127) reconstructs the Teotihuacan version of the creation of the earth as involving an "earth disk [that] is a great pyrite mirror surrounded by an ocean rim of feathers and precious stones."

15 These paintings indicate Teotihuacan trade relations with the Maya, and even "the physical presence of the Maya, . . . faces with Maya profiles, of high-ranking persons . . . the association between human figures and glyphic symbols" (Foncerrada 1980: 189–190). Tetitla possibly housed Maya traders (Kolb 1987: 124), but despite foreign influences and themes, Tetitla "was by no means a Maya 'barrio'"—with its Teotihuacan architecture, it may have been the residence of Teotihuacan traders or diplomats (Taube 2003: 311). The jade chalchihuitl disks and quetzal plumes in the Net-Jaguar Murals "could come only from the Maya region. . . . The Net Jaguars . . . are ethnically mixed and bear costume elements and regalia from the Maya region, Oaxaca, and the Gulf Coast. . . . [such as] the short jaguar-pelt skirt worn by Classic Maya gods and kings" (Taube 2003: 299, 301). The Net-Jaguar Murals "display a true synthesis of Teotihuacan and foreign styles" (Taube 2003: 312), and provide insights into the Teotihuacan view of the Maya area: "a place of great wealth: the source of cacao, jade, and quetzal plumes" (Taube 2003: 313).

16 The placement of jaguar imagery at porticos may refer to astronomical events (Ruíz Gallut et al. 1996: 357), an association known from the contact era.

17 Noting the motif's similarity to expression of the interlace scroll designs of the Gulf Lowlands, Taube identified another foreign design influence in these murals, one that Winning saw, characterizing the net jaguar as "a Teotihuacan conception that originated . . . through the absorption of influences from the Veracruz region, manifested in the elaboration of the interlaced motif. . . . Its cult evolved only in Teotihuacan and in its satellite, Azcapotzalco, and disappeared with the fall of the metropolis" (Von Winning 1987: I: 102).

18 Pasztory (1993e: 59) has also remarked on the nature of Teotihuacan net jaguar: "Only a culture such as this could have come up with as strange a beast as the net-jaguar, a creature made up of nothing, but wrapped so to speak, in a net. . . . In a tradition in which representation is generally flat, the over- and underweaving of the net is rendered with the illusion of three dimensions; we do not miss the fact that it is a net and that there is nothing behind it except background color."

19 The kneeling posture is rare in Teotihuacan art, but "extremely common in Classic Gulf Coast art and can readily be traced to the Middle Preclassic Olmec style" (Taube 2003: 301). In Classic Veracruz and Maya art, kneeling on one leg may signify respect, such as while presenting offerings, and Tetitla's net jaguars may be "making supplicatory offerings in the form of music and ritual hand scatterings to the free-standing structure. . . . the Net Jaguar murals may pertain to rituals performed in the immediate vicinity of Room 11, the principal structure of the main patio at Tetitla" (Taube 2003: 301, 303). The profile posture may identify the figures as supplicants rather than celebrants, according to Kubler (1967: 7), who distinguished the latter by their frontal rather than profile posture.

20 This "bar pectinated" functioned as a "'zone separator' in the borders of mural paintings" (Langley 1986: 324). Sawfish rostra were among sacred offerings at Tenochtitlan's Templo Mayor; the sawfish is associated with "Cipactli, the original feminine and aquatic monster that symbolized earth and its abundant production" (López Luján 2005: 191).

21 Only one cylinder tripod was present in the 70 burials found at Tlajinga 33, the poorest of the city's excavated apartment compounds. At affluent compounds, such as Tetitla, Xolalpan, and Zacuala Palace, the proportions were much higher.

22 Elsewhere at Teotihuacan, this form appears in a relief mural excavated from the Street of the Dead Complex (Morelos García 1982).

23 Berlo's interpretation is in part based on similarities to the "Winged goddess descending from the vines. Mural 3, Room 12, Zone 5a" (1992: 141, fig. 13). Her analysis of PC.B.064 is as follows:

> The frontal anthropomorphic icon has a red face and butterfly proboscis headgear. The figure's arms are extended, and the hands grasp scepters from which cascades of water flow. Within the water are glyphic symbols familiar from many of her other manifestations. Large wing-like elements form her body. This image alternates with a short-hand emblematic version in which wings, butterfly eyes, antennae, and proboscis are carefully rendered. Above the emblem, a variant of the 7 Reptile Eye glyph appears. This glyph is often found in association with the goddess; indeed, Winning (1987: 155–160) believes that 7 RE is one goddess variant. (Berlo 1992: 141–142)

24 On a similar tripod vessel at the Fine Arts Museum of San Francisco (Berrin and Pasztory 1993: cat. no. 138, illustrated on p. 83) "two individuals performing rituals related to the bird/butterfly cult are shown in full regalia" (Conides 1993: 253).

25 The motif of wavy diagonals against a field is another familiar Teotihuacan theme with a meaning more complicated than we can appreciate. Murals show shells and sea creatures arrayed against the field, which may be red (as in La Ventilla, Sector 4, North Room, or in Tetitla's Portico 26). Other murals (e.g., Tetitla's Mural 8) seem to show the field as agricultural. This intriguing and recurring design deserves comprehensive study.

26 The adornos are identical to those on a cylinder tripod vessel at the Los Angeles County Museum of Art (Berrin and Pasztory 1993: 261, no. 154).

27 Walsh (2003: 63–64) cites 12 masks from archaeological contexts; of these, 3 were excavated at Teotihuacan within the past 50 years, found in Teotihuacan administrative contexts along the Street of the Dead (Cabrera et al. 1982). The project reports reveal that there may have been four, but the information is difficult to interpret (Jarquín and Martínez 1982: 103, 110 [Elemento no. 193], and 106, lám. 3 [fragment]; Sánchez Sánchez 1982a: 243 [Elemento no. 107]; Sánchez Sánchez 1982b: 270 [Elemento no. 163]).

28 The twentieth-century sculptor Henry Moore drew inspiration from such pieces; referring to mask PC.B.054, Braun noted that "This mask exemplifies . . . the Mexican highland style Moore admired" (Braun 1993: 109).

29 Author's translation of "En contraste con la absoluta abstracción de muchas máscaras, en las que los caracteres de un rostro parecen quedar reducidos a simples motivos geométricos, este ejemplar de la Colección Wood-Bliss [sic] tiene casi la intensidad patética de un retrato; los labios sufrientes, semiabiertos como en el instante que precede a la muerte, le otorgan una realidad humana."

30 Umberger (1987: 89, fig. 29) provides an example of an Aztec sculpture with Teotihuacan general form, the "Mexica Tlaloc in the form of Teotihuacan Old Fire God brazier" found in Tenochtitlan's Templo Mayor precinct. The Aztecs valued Teotihuacan masks; several were cached in the Templo Mayor (López Luján 2005: 105, fig. 50). One, cached in Offering 82, is in Teotihuacan style but is "of Aztec manufacture" (Matos 1994: 112–113, fig. 99). None of the Templo Mayor masks, however, departs strongly from neutral facial expressions, even those pieces depicting injury and death.

31 Coatlicue, "Serpent Skirt," the mother of Tenochtitlan's patron deity, Huitzilopochtli, was killed by her other sons and by her daughter Coyolxauhqui. Huitzilopochtli avenged this death using the Fire Serpent as his weapon. Coatlicue's statue, several meters tall, is in the Museo Nacional de Antropología in Mexico City.

32 "The Aztecs were . . . known for their beautifully simplified plants, animal and shell sculptures . . . otherwise unusual in Mesoamerica, as well as for their images in stone of functional objects (such as drums) originally made in other materials" (Umberger 1996: 224).

33 "The serpent was the incarnation of water, earth, the underworld, blood, female and male fertility, life, death, and immortality due to its unique change of skin . . . a symbol of the life and death energies that ruled the cosmos. It was thus associated with the most important gods, who were sometimes manifest as fantastic beings formed by the combination of features of several animals, like the feathered serpent" (Garza 2004: 73).

34 A tall coiled serpent carved in a coarse volcanic rock was found at Teotihuacan in excavations southwest of the Street of the Dead Complex (Sánchez Sánchez 1982b: photo 7). The object and its possible age are not discussed in the text, but the scale in the photograph indicates that it was about 16.5 cm (6.5") high and its base was roughly 12.5 cm (5") across.

35 The Field Museum of Natural History (Chicago) rattlesnake (accession number 48126; Mexican Fine Arts Center Museum 1992: 78, cat. no. 14, fig. 70) is 61 cm (24") across, nearly identical in diameter to PC.B.070; it also winds counterclockwise from the head.

36 A "coiled serpent . . . [with] a sculptured body consisting of simply rendered cylindrical segments that suggest life in their convex forms. Clearly defined identifying details such as the rattles, tongue, and teeth are the only ornament; no trivial design or iconographic symbol hides the beauty of the simple shapes. Like some of the colossal sculptures, the bottom of these serpent sculptures is also carved, . . . an abstract design is created by the serpent's overlapping scales" (Pasztory 1983: 214, pls. 173, 174).

37 "The number of rattle segments cannot be used to accurately gauge a snake's age. Each time a snake sheds its skin, it adds another segment to the base of the rattle. . . . some shed as many as four times in a season. As a snake moves about in its habitat, its rattle keeps getting broken or scraped off" (Fergus 2000: 421).

38 The sculpture in the Hamburgisches Museum has accession number B 3639 and is illustrated in Eggebrecht (1986: 2: cat. no. 160).

39 In fact, "the Teotihuacan War Serpent probably constitutes an ancestral form of the Xiuhcoatl; in Classic period iconography, the War Serpent appears with flames, the grass motif, and the trapeze-and-ray year sign" (Miller and Taube 1993: 189).

40 An example of a clear depiction of the Fire Serpent's skin is on a stone box, on which the body of Xiuhcoatl rings the exterior (Gutiérrez Solana 1983: 66).

41 Almost all Fire Serpents have "two or more horizontal paper strips, each with a knot in the middle, arranged in a vertical stack and placed between the body and the 'year-sign' tail. This device . . . has long puzzled Aztec specialists, but is now well known to Maya iconographers . . . as the preeminent sign of blood and blood sacrifice . . . It may well have been that the stack of knots was transmitted to the Aztecs from the Maya through the Toltecs, for it is also very common at . . . Tula" (Coe 1991c: 564).

42 Alcina Franch (1992: 198) cites Umberger's (1984: 75) interpretation.

43 "As Pasztory has noted (1983: 252) this is one of the few large stone sculptures for which there are two known examples, practically identical: the one that serves as the basis of our commentary and another example in Mexico's Museo Nacional de Antropología (Heyden 1972)" (translation by STE of Alcina Franch 1992: 198). Heyden's figs. 8 and 9 are photographs of the Museo Nacional example (Cat II-3301). Gutiérrez Solana (1978: 5, figs. 3, 4) mentions three that are similar: the Dumbarton Oaks example and two at the Museo Nacional.

44 See Heyden's (1972) discussion of Xiuhtecuhtli and his relationship to Aztec rulership.

45 "the Aztec facial ideal: a long head, wide mouth, straight nose, and eyebrows set close to the eyes" (Pasztory 1983: 254). In mask PC.B.072, Tezcatlipoca is "the eternally youthful warrior and patron of the telpochcalli, the military academy for young men and boys" (Coe 1991a: 548).

46 "The smoking mirror normally consists of a circular design with a shaft through it and two curling forms, representing smoke, emerging on both sides. . . . The emblems referred both to the ruler and to the deity Tezcatlipoca. The speech of the ruler was compared to a mirror: '*I set before you a light, a torch, a model, a measuring rod, a great mirror.* This phrase was said of a lord who spoke to the people and placed before them excellent words. . . . He told them . . . You shall take it as a *model,* you shall take it as an example so that you may live properly or that you may speak well' (Sullivan, 1963, p. 151). Smoke and mist signified fame and glory: 'This was said about a king not long dead whose *smoke and mist,* meaning his *fame and glory,* had not yet vanished' (Sullivan, 1963, p. 145)." (Pasztory 1983: 83)

47 Late Postclassic rulers practiced divination and sorcery; one famous example was the Texcocan king Nezahualpilli (ruled ca. 1472 to ca. 1514 AD), who frightened Tenochtitlan's ruler Motecuzoma II with his predictions of the downfall of the Aztec Empire. However, Tezcatlipoca, as the omniscient arch-sorcerer, was associated with this important divinatory device, which might even have been the origin of his supernatural personality and cult.

48 Sahagún's informants said that "the day sign Two Reed . . . was a very good day sign; because also at that time they honored Tezcatlipoca. . . . And . . . he who was then born . . . would become rich" (Sahagún 1979c [1569]: 56).

49 The date on the back of mask PC.B.072 "has also been interpreted historically (Bliss 1957: 243; Dumbarton Oaks 1963: 23), equated with the year 2 Acatl, 1507. A multiple reference may have been intended" (Nicholson with Quiñones Keber 1983: 106). In 1959, Robertson (1959: 107) wrote that "the Bliss Collection has two dated Aztec pieces, . . . both dated in the year 2 Acatl/Reed or 1507." Other, similar renditions of the Reed glyph are known: "This [PC.B.072] Acatl sign is stylistically similar to that on the Stone of the Five Suns . . . and, especially, to the one on the Fifty-two-year bundle stone. . . . Like them it depicts a section of jaguar skin on the vessel that is portrayed here in cross-section" (Nicholson with Quiñones Keber 1983: 105–106). Pasztory cites similar glyphs on the "Dedication Stone" and inside the cover of the Ahuitzotl Box (Pasztory 1983: 150, 164).

50 Nicholson (1971a: 118) noted that it is very difficult to make positive attributions of period or provenience based on the relative refinement of Aztec sculpture because of "considerable variation in sculptural quality of objects produced contemporaneously in a single place, not to speak of variation between communities and, perhaps most importantly, provincial lag." Conversely, Basin of Mexico sculptors might adopt refinements first established in other regions.

51 Examples of this style include the "Seated Standard Bearer" (Metropolitan Museum, New York; Pasztory 1983: 214, pl. 170) and "Mask" (American Museum of Natural History, New York; Pasztory 1983: 253, pl. 266).

52 Musée de l'Homme, Palais de Chaillot, Place du Trocadéro, Paris, Accession no. 87101568; the date attribution is by Hamy (1883: 13–14).

53 In Michoacán, on separate visits, the Franciscan fathers Alonso Ponce and Juan de Torquemada remarked admiringly of this skill and commented how this shiny black stone made excellent *aras* and mirrors (Torquemada 1943 [1615]: 3: 210).

54 The chronicler Gonzalo Fernández de Oviedo y Valdés owned four examples and recorded that Viceroy Mendoza had sent two to the Spanish king (Fernández de Oviedo y Valdés 1946: 89, 92).

55 Museum für Völkerkunde, Vienna, Accession no. 10416.

56 The finds of the Templo Mayor of Tenochtitlan/Mexico City have been widely reported; see Bonifaz Nuño (1981), Boone (1987), Broda et al. (1987), Heyden and Villaseñor (1984), Matos (1990, 1994), López Luján (1993, 2005), and López Portillo et al. (1981).

57 Such pieces include polished representations of a squash (Nicholson with Quiñones Keber 1983: 113, no. 40), several fleas (Alcina Franch et al. 1992: no. 9 [MNA 11-4714]; Eggebrecht 1986: no. 194), several grasshoppers (Alcina Franch et al. 1992: no. 10 [MNA 11-4657]; Eggebrecht 1986: no. 196; Nicholson with Quiñones Keber 1983: 117, no. 43), a frog (Eggebrecht 1986: no. 158), an owl (Eggebrecht 1986: no. 195), the head of a dog (Alcina Franch et al. 1992: no. 27), a reclining feline (Nicholson with Quiñones Keber 1983: 119, no. 44), anthropomorphic figures (García Moll et al. 1991: 145, 203; Instituto Nacional de Antropología e Historia 1946: no. 236; Parsons 1980: 123), and deities (Eggebrecht 1986 nos. 146, 149, 151, 162, 188; Pasztory 1983: 245, color pl. 49).

58 In Vienna (Museum für Völkerkunde, Accession no. 12.585), it is "possibly listed in the inventory of the collection of Archduke Karl of Steiermark in 1590 . . . but it cannot be traced with certainty much further back than 1881" (Nicholson with Quiñones Keber 1983: 124, no. 47).

59 Examples are shown in Alcina Franch et al. (1992: no. 39), Bonifaz Nuño (1981: pl. 53 and p. 184, pl. 60 and p. 185, pl. 72 and p. 186, pl. 76 and p. 186, pl. 80 and p. 187, pl. 82 and p. 187), and Matos (1990: 16, 90a, 90b, 92); and deities are shown in Alcina Franch et al. (1992: no. 37), Bonifaz Nuño (1981: pl. 46 and p. 184, pl. 70 and p. 186, pl. 75 and p. 186), and Matos (1990: 134, 136).

60 Dean and Leibsohn (2003: 27) have discussed PC.B.071's star turn in this film, regarding its new gold coat and possible change in proportions as indicating a modern Western sensibility transforming a Pre-Columbian conceptualization. Because this object is pivotal to the opening sequence of the film, these changes might have been made in the interest of visual clarity and cinematic expediency.

61 "Considerada como uno de los mejores ejemplos del arte azteca, esta estatua de Tlazoltéotl, madre de Cintéotle (dios del maíz) y de Xochiquetzal (Flor Emplumada), diosa de las flores y de los oficios, representa a la diosa en el acto del alumbramiento. Imagen de un realismo dramático, en ella mito y realidad, se funden" (Fabbri and Gibelli 1965: 103).

62 Hayden Herrera, Kahlo's biographer, said of one of her paintings that it recalled a famous Aztec childbirth sculpture (Herrera 1979).

63 In his article on fakes, Ekholm (1964: 25) wrote: "The material most prized in ancient times as well as by modern collectors is the green Mexican jade or jadeite. . . . For substitutes, the fakers have employed every kind of green stone they could find. . . . Most of these have a more mottled character than those stones the ancients found most desirable."

64 This pose is another anomaly. García Cisnernos (1970) presented about 80 figurines from Middle America that were "maternity" subjects—most were women holding or carrying small children, and none were women giving birth.

65 The Borbonicus figure wears a body suit of human skin and is a highly stylized and expressionless figure all but hidden by accoutrements.

66 Tlazolteotl is typically portrayed with the area around her mouth blackened, face painting that indicates the filth the goddess eats in receiving last confessions.

67 "Tlaçolteotl . . . her realm, her domain, was that of evil and perverseness . . . lustful and debauched living. . . . One recited before her, all vanities . . . all unclean works—however ugly, however grave; avoiding nothing because of shame. . . . The confession . . . evil and perverseness, debauched living—these Tlaçolteotl offered one, cast upon one, inspired in one. And likewise she forgave, set aside, removed [corruption]. She cleansed one." (Sahagún 1970 [1569]: 23)

68 Klein (1975: 73) notes Tlazolteotl's importance as a goddess of maize, who "properly belongs to a separate category of Post-Classic deities whose special function was to fertilize the crops."

69 See Solís (1982) for an analysis of the range of postures occurring in Aztec sculpture; that of PC.B.071 is not among them.

70 Holes are located on the figure's head (two pairs in front of the upper ears, one on each ear lobe, and one on each side of the jaw below the ears), in the hair (one on each side, just above shoulder level), on the buttocks (two pairs just above the grasping hands), and on the feet (one on the outside of each foot).

71 Breton owned a ceramic replica of the piece (CalmelsCohen 2003: cat. no. 6235).

72 About PC.B.079, Pasztory (1983: 253) writes: "There is no prototype in any other medium for the sculpture of a rabbit with a helmeted man's head emerging from its belly."

73 Discussing how ancient Mesoamericans thought about excrement, Miller and Taube (1993: 86–87) note the consumption of excrement in penitential rites, and show page 10 from the Codex Borgia, which depicts an "excremental stream pouring towards the moon sign," which contains a rabbit.

74 Klein (2000: 12) associates such motifs with Cihuacoatl and the Tzitzimime: "the skull-and-crossbones design connoted the time of the Creation and the powers of regeneration and healing."

75 Bliss Collection objects have not been analyzed to determine the extent to which such techniques as soldering have been used. Further technological analyses, such as x-radiography, will clarify these issues (Dorothy Hosler, personal communication, November 1997).

76 Nicholson with Quiñones Keber (1983: 156) claim that the necklace and ear ornaments PC.B.101 were discovered together.

77 Nicholson with Quiñones Keber (1983: 156) claim that these were found with the necklace ornaments of PC.B.100.

78 On this and similar pieces, the suspension rings may have been soldered to the pendant; x-radiography of one of the artifacts could determine whether this occurred (Dorothy Hosler, personal communication, November 1997).

79 The ornaments resemble members of gastropod families *Ampullariidae, Hydrobiidae,* and *Viviparidae.*

80 "This tweezer shows no evidence of joining and is virtually certain to have been hammered from one piece" (Dorothy Hosler, personal communication, November 1997).

81 This issue can be resolved through x-radiography (Dorothy Hosler, personal communication, November 1997).

82 For some examples, see Berjonneau et al. (1985: no. 324), Beyer (1933), Coe (2005: 151, no. 102), and Dockstader (1964: no. 99).

83 West Mexico includes the modern states of Michoacán, Colima, Jalisco, and Nayarit.

84 For some examples, see Anawalt (1998: 249, fig. 34), Kelly (1947: pl. 17), López Mestas and Ramos (1998: 62, fig. 12), and Von Winning (1971: 21).

85 For other examples, see Coe and Kerr (1982: 100, no. 54), Kerr (1989: 53, vessel K808; see also K808 in the Kerr Maya Vase Database [Kerr n.d.a]), Reents-Budet (1994: 263, no. 6.35), and Schmidt et al. (1998: 561, no. 169).

86 The scene on page 24 in Codex Borbonicus illustrated in Figure 20 may depict the metaphor: deer = captive, hunting = warfare, consumption = sacrifice, showing on the lower left corner the "capture of a war prisoner" and immediately to the right "his sacrifice" (rendered with the visual trope of a tied deer being swallowed by the earth).

87 This document is attributed to Fray Andrés de Olmos and was written in the Basin of Mexico ca. 1533.

88 The figurine is in the Art Museum, Princeton University (cat. no. L1971.306). See Whittington (2001: 157, no. 23).

89 Examples include a vessel possibly from southern Veracruz (Castillo Collection; Valenzuela 1945: fig. 65), one attributed to Monte Albán (Covarrubias Collection; Covarrubias 1957: pl. XXXII), one purportedly from San Salvador (Museo Nacional David J. Guzmán; Dockstader 1964: no. 126), one attributed to Tilantongo (Cleveland Museum of Art, cat. no. 1990.199), an unprovenienced vessel (Zollman Collection; Parsons et al. 1988: 80, no. 57), an unprovenienced vessel (Ranieri Collection; see Kerr n.d.b: Kerr Pre-Columbian Portfolio no. 5596), and an unprovenienced vessel (Art Museum, Princeton University; Johnson 1992: 82-A). In addition, four more unpublished vessels are attributed to Oaxaca and are housed today in the ex-Museo Frissell, Mitla (one vessel), the National Museum of the American Indian (cat. no. 235036; one vessel), and in the Museum of Fine Arts in Houston (cat. nos. 88.56, 89.33; two vessels).

90 Very different is an example from El Salvador (Dockstader 1964: no. 126), characterized by a spout at one end of the vessel, five protruding clay rings, and facial incisions. Although most vessels of similar type depict a human head, those in the Covarrubias Collection (see Covarrubias 1957: pl. XXXII) and in the Cleveland Museum of Art (n.d.: accession no. 1990.199) render the physiognomy of a monkey. The vessels in the Covarrubias Collection and the Anahuacalli Museum resemble PC.B.139 by having more than one opening, but they are the only ones that seem to have had covers attached by means of strings passing through small adjacent perforations.

91 These uses do not seem to apply to the spouted version from El Salvador. It has been suggested that the protruding incisors in the vessel from the Zollman Collection (Parsons et al. 1988: 80, no. 57)—and by extension the example in the Art Museum, Princeton University (Johnson 1992: 82-A)—could have held a brush or been used to facilitate removal of excess paint from a brush.

92 Lacking the complete ear ornament assemblages, it is impossible to determine how the flares in the Bliss Collection were assembled and worn, but based on deductions from excavated materials, several alternatives are possible (see Kidder et al. 1977 [1946]: fig. 45).

93 Depictions of enlarged ear lobes triggered by the use of heavy, composite ornaments may be seen on a ceramic effigy from Mound X at Monte Albán (Caso and Bernal 1952: 339) and on the woman depicted on Lintel 24 from Yaxchilan (Schele and Miller 1986: cover photograph).

94 For similar plaques found in Monte Albán (Oaxaca), Chichén Itzá (Yucatan), and Bilbao (Guatemala), see Solís et al. (1993: 75, no. 16), Coggins and Shane (1984: 77, no. 70), and Parsons (1969), respectively.

95 For discussions of the graphic representation of mirrors in Mesoamerica, see Taube (1992, n.d.). The plaques shown in Figure 33 (upper and lower right) depict personages holding mirrors over their chests.

96 Both drillings entered at an oblique angle or parallel to what eventually became the posterior surface of the object. The residual trail of one of the perforations is an oblong and elongated deep groove 1.73 cm long, with a maximum diameter of 3.3 mm and minimum of 1.5 mm. The trail of the other perforation evidences the drilling of a hole extending for 3.1 cm, with an outer diameter of 4.3 mm and an inner one of 2.2 mm. The conical shape of these holes is consistent with a reduction in the size of drill bits as they perforated the original block of raw material.

97 This hole had penetrated 3.7 mm of 6.1 mm.

98 Three of these perforations exhibit slight chipping in the borders. Three others (holes 1, 2, and 4) have slightly different diameters (5.1, 5.2, and 6.5 mm, respectively), but the perforations maintain the same diameter all the way through despite cutting through 1.35 cm of stone before reaching the longitudinal bore. Hole 3 is conical in shape, as is expected of ancient lapidary technologies, tapering some 0.7 mm until reaching its end (from 6 mm at the opening to 5.3 mm at the end). The slight chipping at the edges of three of the secondary holes and the uniform diameter along the trajectories in three others suggest that the secondary holes were fully (holes 1, 2, 4) or partially (hole 3) retouched in recent times, probably by using an electric drill and a steel bit.

99 Hole 3 even has a thin shelf on one of its halves. Hole 2, placed close to the midline of the bar, exposed the two separate courses for the drilling of the longitudinal bore.

100 One hole is 5 mm in diameter; the other is 6.2 mm. The rotational striations of these perforations near their openings are not macroscopically obvious.

101 Later examples come from localities widely distributed across Mesoamerica, including Chichén Itzá, Yucatan

(Moholy-Nagy and Ladd 1992: 106–109); Texmilincan, Guerrero (García Payón 1941: 350–351), Zacaleu, Guatemala (Woodbury and Trik 1953: 241); and the twin cities of Mexico-Tenochtitlan and Mexico-Tlatelolco, in the Basin of Mexico (García Moll et al. 1990: 149; López Luján 1993; Serra Puche and Solís 1994).

102 These four exhibit some differences from PC.B.135, including their rectangular or oblong shape, overall smaller size, double-banded ends, and less-pronounced obliqueness in the grooves that decorate their shafts.

103 They measure 7.7–9.4 cm in length and 1.0–1.1 cm in diameter, and the inner perforation is 4–5 mm in diameter.

104 The perforation done on the crosshatched end is 8.8 mm in diameter; the one traversing the heads of the serpents is 1.4 cm in diameter. Slight deviations in the course of the perforations indicate that they were done in stages related to the wear of the bits.

105 After the distal portion of the handle was hollowed, four small holes were made at the level of the deepest mark left by the previously drilled cavity. These perforations were drilled from the outside and are perpendicular to the walls of the hollowed end. Their distribution around the circumference of the object is not equidistant or symmetrical. One is on the anterior surface, another is on the right side, and two are placed on the left surface. One of these holes is slightly unaligned in relation to the others, being closer to the distal border of the handle.

106 Identical fragments of gilded thin sheets, sometimes with rusted material over one side, were found in the small paper bag associated with skull PC.B.098. From these loose fragments it became clear that the thin sheets were gilded on both sides. Another possible implication is that the loose mosaics in the bag, the skulls (PC.B.097, PC.B.098, and PC.B.099), and the serpent-headed handle (PC.B.094) may have come from the same tomb.

107 These include four serpent handles from Oaxaca: two recovered from Monte Albán Tomb 7 (Caso 1969: 116, 142, pls. XVIII, XXIX) and two from Zaachila Tomb 2 (Gallegos 1978: 105, figs. 69, 71). Another handle is reported from Ingenio La Gloria, Veracruz. A sixth example was found in Offering 41 from the Templo Mayor at Mexico-Tenochtitlan (Alcina Franch et al. 1992: 76, no. 20). Two handles of unknown provenience are now in the National Museum of the American Indian (one with cat. no. 131599), and another one, also of unknown provenience, is now in the Museo Nacional de Antropología in Mexico City. Another serpent handle, construed as "Maya-Toltec," is in the Metropolitan Museum of Art in New York (http://www.metmuseum.org/toah/ho/07/caa/hod_1979.206.1132.htm).

108 Comparison of the relative sizes of the blade and metal sheet reinforces the idea that what appears to be a single object is actually two related artifacts. Although the maximum length of the exposed portion of the blade is slightly larger (8.68 cm) than the length of the metal section (8.44 cm), the difference of 2.4 mm plus the size of the hidden tip of the blade (no more than 1 cm) can be attributed to the shrinkage of the casing caused by its crushing. The maximum width of the metal end is 2.02 cm, whereas the maximum width of the blade at its base is just 1.2 cm. This leaves enough room to accommodate the curvature of the obsidian implement.

109 This layer is, at least on the edges of the disk, 3.7 mm thick.

110 This assessment is based on the stage of the basilar synchondrosis, degree of closure of the cranial sutures, and lack of degenerative processes commonly associated with advanced age. The extant portions of the skull do not show evidence of pathological conditions, and although no teeth are present, dental problems are suggested by the antemortem loss of most molars and the advanced stage of resorption of the alveolar cavities. Most of the anterior teeth were lost postmortem, but crowding of the lower incisors can be inferred from the extant sockets.

111 Examples include a skull from Monte Albán Tomb 7 (Caso 1969: 64, pl. IV); a skull in the British Museum (McEwan 1994: 75); a skull purported to be from southwest Chiapas (Ludington Collection; Von Winning 1968b: 246, no. 334); a skull attributed to the Mexica (Serra Puche and Solís 1994: 222); a skull in the Indiana University Art Museum (Coe 1986: 31, no. 16); and one purportedly from Teotitlan del Camino, Oaxaca (now in the Rijksmuseum voor Volkerkunde, Leyden; Solís et al. 1993: 107).

112 This assessment is based on the stage of the basilar synchondrosis, degree of closure of the cranial sutures, and lack of degenerative processes commonly associated with advanced age. The extant undecorated portions of the skull do not reveal pathological conditions, except for a slight porosity in the occipital bone and a thin layer of new bone deposition on the ventral left side of the mandibular body. This bony remodeling extends frontally along the lower border and close to the midline of the mandible. Several upper teeth were lost before death, as the sockets show an advanced state of resorption. The alveoli of the maxillae are missing, so no observation can be done on the upper dentition. Two-thirds of the mandibular alveoli in the dental arch have also been destroyed.

113 The age assessment is based on the complete eruption of the lower third molars (the upper ones were lost postmortem) and lack of dental wear on the extant teeth. Based on the pointed chin, small size of the mastoid process, and unpronounced supramastoid crest, the individual may have been female. The superior nuchal line, however, is well marked. Despite her young age, the sagittal suture is completely obliterated, in contrast to both the coronal and lambdoidal sutures. The pronounced intentional reshaping to which the head was subjected may have triggered such a differential and premature closure.

114 Although the match with the socket seems close, there is a thin gap around the anterior rim. In addition, the tooth obtrudes from the superior occlusal plane, and yet the mandibular incisor that enters in contact with it shows no evidence of malocclusion. The right lateral incisor also does not seem to belong to this individual, because it exhibits slight differences in color and in dental wear on the occlusal surface.

115 Another skull with the top portion of the cranium removed, but without traces of having been inlaid, was found in Cacaxtla (Lombardo de Ruíz et al. 1991: pl. 168; Palavicini and Reyes 2005: 74).

116 Examples include two anthropomorphic wooden faces and a zoomorphic wooden face from Zaachila Tomb 1, ca. AD 1450 (Sánchez Scott 2001); an anthropomorphic wooden face from a burial in the Valley of Tehuacan, ca. AD 1450 (Solís and Leyenaar 2002); and most of the Postclassic wooden faces found in the Santa Ana Teloxtoc cave in Southern Puebla (Vargas 1989).

117 Decoration covers their faces only. Although this characteristic is shared with the decorated example without provenience now in the British Museum—which is generally accepted by the scholarly community to have been decorated in antiquity—the latter actually has the posterior portion of the cranium cut away (Holmes 1914: 98), making it similar to the decorated splanchnocrania found in several of the offerings in the Late Postclassic main temples at Mexico-Tenochtitlan and Mexico-Tlatelolco (see, for example, Matos 1990: 79).

118 The fourth skull in this story may be the one now in the Indiana University Art Museum (cat. no. 64.15; see Coe 1986: 31, no. 16) or the one in the Rijksmuseum voor Volkenkunde, Leiden (cat. no. 4007-1; see Solís et al. 1993: 107). Given the close similarities in the decoration of these skulls and those in the Bliss Collection, there is the possibility that Wiener himself was also involved in "restoring" it.

119 In addition to the localities shown on the map, travertine vessels have been reported from three localities in Western Mesoamerica: Tepic, Nayarit (Lumholz 1904); Jiquilpan, Michoacán (Noguera 1944); and Infiernillo, on the border between Michoacán and Guerrero (Castillo 1970: 50).

120 The variety of exterior treatments is exemplified by a spouted vessel with the effigy of a bird of unknown provenience (now in the ex-Museo Frissell, Mitla; Carmona 1999); a barrel-shaped vessel with a human figure wearing a jaguar helmet from Isla de Sacrificios (now in the British Museum; McEwan 1994: 33); a flaring vessel with integrated spout, openwork decoration in the band below the lip, and incised imagery that is attributed to Guerrero (in the Müller Collection, Switzerland; Von Winning 1968b: no. 343); and a fragmentary vessel recovered from Tomb B, Mound 5 at Xoxocotlan, Oaxaca. The fragments of this final exemplar had traces of a stucco coating with painted designs in various colors (Saville 1899: 354).

121 Data from some of the unfinished vessels yield core lengths that vary between 1.0 and 3.4 cm. The diameter of the cores depends on the thickness of the drill bits, but measurements from the same unfinished vessels provide ranges between 1.4 and 2 cm. The dispersed finding of 19 drilling cores in a household unit in Tula and the lack of evidence for other manufacturing steps in the production of stone vessels (Diehl and Stroh 1978) indicate that at least in some cases, cores were distributed to other contexts from workshops that were probably attached to noble houses. The purpose of this allocation of debitage remains unknown.

122 However, no debitage of lapidary work—of travertine or other type of stone—was found in the excavated portions of Brawbehl.

123 For example, the Kerr Maya Vase Database (Kerr n.d.a) includes at least seven stone vessels that were incised or carved in styles from highland or lowland southeastern Mesoamerica (K319, K1606, K1949, K3296, K4340 [vessel at Dumbarton Oaks], K4692, and K7749) and four vessels that originated in the Ulúa Valley (K2593, K6622, K6623, and K8782).

124 Monkey effigy vessels include examples from Isla de Sacrificios (National Museum of the American Indian, cat. no. 16337), of unknown provenience (Museo de Xalapa; Vizcaíno 1988: 60), attributed to Veracruz (private collection; Joyce 1916: pl. C), attributed to central Veracruz (Thomas Gilcrease Institute, Tulsa, Okla.; Von Winning 1968b: no. 317), attributed to the Mixteca-Puebla region (Metropolitan Museum of Art; Pasztory 1983: 250), attributed to Veracruz (Yale University Art Gallery, New Haven, Conn.; Kubler 1986: no. 125), found in a burial at Huexotzingo (Beyer 1969a: 395), and a vessel attributed to highland Oaxaca (St. Louis Art Museum; Parsons 1980: no. 173). Two more examples are known to be in the University Museum, Philadelphia (Palacio de Bellas Artes 1934: nos. 44A, C), and a third one is in the collection of the National Museum of the American Indian (cat. no. 950-1250; Dockstader 1973: 85, no. 97). Another, reported by Von Winning (1986a), is in the National Gallery of Victoria, Melbourne.

125 Although earlier writers took the imagery of the Maya God C as that of a monkey, Taube (1992) does not favor such iconic identification, adding that its imagery appears to embody the concept of godliness rather than standing for a specific deity.

126 The object was treated in the 1980s by applying a 3 percent B72, a plastic solution that made the surface appear glossy. Prior to treatment, the dryness of the wood led a conservator to infer that the thrower had been in a dry cave (Record of Treatment, April 1986, unpublished report on file at Dumbarton Oaks).

127 Finger grips must have been two loops of shell, bone, stone, or a metal alloy. Finger grips of different materials have been reported from many regions of Mesoamerica (Ekholm 1962; Kelly 1947; Kidder 1947; Linné 2003b [1942]; Piña Chán 1960; Séjourné 1959). Data collected by the author on such items in museum collections (*n* = 12) range in weight from 9.7 to 34.2 g. Assuming an average weight of 19.84 g for a single finger loop, the total weight of the dart thrower in the Bliss Collection would have been approximately 175.78 g (6.2 oz). For comparison, the weight of a baseball is between 142 and 149 g (about 5 oz).

128 The Tutepetongo (or Tututepetongo) roll is an early colonial painting (ca. AD 1540) from the southern end of the Cuicatlan Cañada, Oaxaca. Like several of the known scenes of scaffold sacrifice, the one depicted on page 10 of the Tutepetongo roll shows the sacrificers shooting at the victim with bows and arrows. But other scenes of this type of sacrifice, such as the one pictured in a graffiti on a wall in Room 2 of Structure 5D at Tikal (see Trik and Kampen 1983: fig. 38) or the one painted on page 10 in Codex Becker I (see the facsimile in Caso 1996), show the enactment of the ritual with darts and throwers.

129 Such contemporary enactments take place in communities with Totonac, Otomí, Huastec, Nahua, and Tepehuan linguistic affiliations, extending over the modern states of Hidalgo, northern Puebla, and central Veracruz. The series of ceremonies lasts several days (Ichon 1973: 377–392; Stresser-Péan 2005), and some, including the ritual cutting of the tree to be used as the pole, involve the offering of chickens, burning of incense, libations with an alcoholic beverage, and chanted incantations. Certain components of the paraphernalia, the number of dancers, the number of "musical phrases" played in the dances at the base of the pole (at times 13), the constituents of offerings placed near the pole (13 figurines dedicated to the tree and 2 dedicated to the earth), and the commitment of the dancers to perform for 4 consecutive years, link the Voladores ritual to structural features of the ancient calendar. Although ethnographic accounts report a variable number of rotations around the pole while the flyers descend, the emphasis of the ritual on orientation and revolutions has lead to the assumption that in antiquity, the aim was to coordinate the descent of the four flying dancers so that they completed 13 rounds, thus enacting symbolically the completion of a cycle of 52 years (4 times 13) (Ichon 1973: 389). Other features of contemporary rituals, including at times the role of the lead dancer as healer, the dressing as female by one of the male dancers, the prescribed sexual abstinence of the five dancers (to prevent, among other things, fatal falls), the explicit account by elder informants that the flying ritual is a dance "for water," and the part of incantations dedicated to the "thunders" (Ichon 1973: 387–389) make it clear that the traditional versions of the Voladores still retain—aside from their solar connotation—a great deal of fertility and fecundity symbolism.

130 The Calendar Round of 52 solar years is divided into four sets of 13 years; the Divinatory Count of 260 days is divided into four cycles of 65 days.

131 These deities are from later pre-Hispanic documentary sources pertaining mostly to Nahua and Tetla-Mixteca traditions.

132 Although the jade throwers in the Bliss Collection (PC.B.017a, PC.B.017b) were characterized as "ceremonial rather than utilitarian" (Bliss 1957: 235), it remains to be demonstrated whether they were intended for use, particularly by juvenile rulers. A contrast should also be made with some 30 miniature, nonfunctional throwers made of wood, white stone, or ceramics that have been found as votive offerings in several caches associated with the main temples of Mexico-Tenochtitlan and Mexico-Tlatelolco. The length of these examples ranges between 17 and 21 cm (Angulo 1966; Gamio 1921; López Luján 1993, 2006). A thick jade dart thrower 38 cm in length from Douglas, Belize (Follet 1932: 385, fig. 14) may be too heavy to have been functional.

133 For examples of carved throwers with serpent heads, see Coggins and Ladd (1992: 245–252 [C6738, C6739]), Saville (1925: pls. XVII, XVIII), and Seler (1991 [1904]: 216). A carved thrower with a bird head found at Metlapilco, near Cuautla, Morelos, is illustrated in Cook de Leonard (1956: 185).

134 Tatiana Proskouriakoff's (1954) pioneering study of art forms brought the term "Classic Veracruz" into general, and still followed, usage.

135 The evolution over millennia of these cultural and natural units is discussed in detail in Wilkerson (1974, 1988, 1997a, 2001a, 2001b, 2001c, n.d. [1972]).

136 Descriptions of El Tajín date back to 1785 (Ruiz) and include nineteenth-century accounts (for example, Humboldt 1811; Márquez 1804; Nebel 1836), early archaeological reconnaissance (Palacios 1926; Palacios and Meyer 1932), the initiation of formal exploration (García Payón 1943, 1955, 1957; García Vega 1939), and more recent examinations of the art and architecture (for example, Brüggemann et al. 1992; Kampen 1971; Sarro 2006; Wilkerson 1976, 1980, 1987, 1997c, 1999).

137 Pulque is a fermented beverage made from the sap of the agave (century plant or maguey).

138 Discussions of the ritual contents of sculpture, particularly at El Tajín, can be found in García Payón (1973), Kampen (1971), Koontz (n.d. [1994]), Ladrón de Guevara (1999), and Wilkerson (1976, 1984, 1987, 1990, 1991, 1997c, 1997d, 2001d, 2001e).

139 The Sonriente label is a significant misnomer, essentially a projection of Western values of expression in the interpretation of Pre-Columbian facial features. These figures are actually fully consistent with the attributes of a strong regional pulque cult emphasizing drunken visions rather than lighthearted mirth (Wilkerson 1984).

140 This belief is still extant in the north-central area of Veracruz and was recorded by the author in the Papantla district in 2003. Further to the east it was also noted by Gutiérrez Marié (2000). In the latter community the focus of the belief was on avoiding death in childbirth.

141 Included in this corpus is the large, ornate sculpture of a male ruler that is now in the plaza at Amatlan but was originally from Zacamixtle in the 1960s. Local lore about the site suggests that it was paired with a smaller female statue.

142 The social and ritual contexts mentioned here are examined in Wilkerson (1984, 1990, 1997d, 1999, 2001e). Ball game contexts are also considered by multiple authors in Bussel et al. (1991), Scarborough and Wilcox (1991), and Whittington (2001).

143 Ample reviews of the convoluted scoring rules for the three surviving formats of the ball game are found in Leyenaar (1978, 1992, 2001).

144 A basalt hacha was also found at above 2,500 m at Napatecuhtlan, nearly 90 km north of the Origaba Valley.

145 In the lore recorded in the *Popul Vuh,* nightjars (*Caprimulgidae*) were the lackadaisical guardians of the gardens of the Lords of the Underworld. When the birds failed to prevent the Hero Twins from robbing the gardens, their mouths were slit open in punishment. The beak of this avian helmet, however, is consistent with a macaw.

146 They are also sometimes found with plain, usually polished, yokes.

147 Although it is credible that this sculpture came from the vicinity of that city, it is also possible that there was some confusion with the use of the term "Puebla" when the origin was recorded. The term also designates the state. If the state was meant, then the palma is likely to have come from the northern panhandle that runs along the border with Veracruz, where other small palmas have been found.

Acosta, Jorge

1957 Exploraciones arqueológicas en Tula, Hidalgo. *Anales del Instituto Nacional de Antropología e Historia* 9: 119–169.

1961 La indumentaria de las cariátides de Tula. In *Homenaje a Pablo Martínez del Río en el vigésimoquinto aniversario de la primera edición de* Los orígenes americanos (Ignacio Bernal, Jorge Gurria, Santiago Genovés, and Luis Aveleyra, eds.): 221–229. Instituto Nacional de Antropología e Historia, Mexico City.

Acosta Lagunes, Agustín, Michael D. Coe, Felipe Solís, and Beatriz de la Fuente

1992 *Museum of Anthropology of Xalapa.* Government of the State of Veracruz, Xalapa, and Studio Beatrice Trueblood, Mexico City.

Akademie der Künste

1959 *Kunst aus Mexiko und Mittelamerika. [Ausstellung] Hochschule für Bildende Künste, Berlin, vom 3. Okt. bis 22. Nov. 1959.* Berlin-Dahlem, Berlin.

Alcina Franch, José

1979 *Die Kunst des Alten Amerika.* Herder, Freiburg, Germany.

1983 *Pre-Columbian Art.* Harry N. Abrams, New York.

1992 Xiuhcóatl. In *Azteca • Mexica* (José Alcina Franch, Miguel León-Portilla, and Eduardo Matos Moctezuma): 198. Lunwerg Editores, Barcelona.

Alcina Franch, José, Miguel León-Portilla, and Eduardo Matos Moctezuma

1992 *Azteca • Mexica.* Lunwerg Editores, Barcelona.

Anawalt, Patricia Rieff

1993 Rabbits, *Pulque,* and Drunkenness. In *Current Topics in Aztec Studies* (Alana Cordy-Collins and Douglas Sharon, eds.): 17–38. San Diego Museum Papers 30. San Diego Museum of Man, San Diego, Calif.

1996 Aztec Knotted and Netted Capes. *Ancient Mesoamerica* 7: 187–206.

1998 They Came to Trade Exquisite Things. In *Ancient West Mexico: Art and Archaeology of the Unknown Past* (Richard F. Townsend, ed.): 233–249. Art Institute of Chicago, Chicago, and Thames and Hudson, New York.

Anders, Ferdinand, and Maarten Jansen

1994 *La pintura de la muerte y de los destinos: Libro explicativo del llamado Códice Laud.* Akademische Druck- und Verlagsanstalt, Graz, Austria, and Fondo de Cultura Económica, Mexico City.

Anders, Ferdinand, Maarten Jansen, and Luis Reyes García

1991 *El libro del ciuacoatl: Homenaje para el año del Fuego Nuevo; Libro explicativo del llamado Códice Borbónico.* Sociedad Estatal Quinto Centenario, Madrid Akademische Druck- und Verlagsanstalt, Graz, Austria, Fondo de Cultura Económica, Mexico City.

Anders, Ferdinand, Maarten Jansen, and Gabina Aurora Pérez Jiménez

1992a *Crónica mixteca: El rey 8 Venado, Garra de Jaguar, y la dinastía de Teozacualco-Zaachila; Libro explicativo del llamado Códice Zouche-Nuttall.* Sociedad Estatal Quinto Centenario México, Madrid, Fondo de Cultura Económica, Mexico City, and Akademische Druck- und Verlagsanstalt, Graz, Austria.

1992b *Origen e historia de los reyes mixtecos. Libro explicativo del llamado Códice Vindobonensis.* Akademische Druck- und Verlagsanstalt, Graz, Austria, and Fondo de Cultura Económica, Mexico City.

Angulo Villaseñor, Jorge

1966 *Un tlamanalli encontrado en Tlatelolco.* Instituto Nacional de Antropología e Historia, Mexico City.

1987a Nuevas consideraciones sobre los llamados conjuntos departamentales especialmente Tetitla. In *Teotihuacan, nuevos datos, nuevas síntesis, nuevos problemas* (Emily McClung de Tapia and Evelyn Childs Rattray, eds.): 275–315. Universidad Nacional Autónoma de México, Mexico City.

1987b El sistema *otli-apantli* dentro del área urbana. In *Teotihuacan, nuevos datos, nuevas síntesis, nuevos problemas* (Emily McClung de Tapia and Evelyn Childs Rattray, eds.): 399–415. Universidad Nacional Autónoma de México, Mexico City.

1996 Teotihuacán: Aspectos de la cultura a través de su expresión pictórica. In *La pintura mural prehispánica en México*. Vol. 1, *Teotihuacán*, bk. 2: *Estudios* (Beatriz de la Fuente, ed.): 65–186. Universidad Nacional Autónoma de México, Instituto de Investigaciones Estéticas, Mexico City.

Anton, Ferdinand

1973 *Die Frauen der Azteken-, Maya-, Inka-Kultur.* Verlag W. Kohlhammer, Stuttgart.

1977 *Alt-Amerika und seine Kunst.* VEB E. A. Seemann Verlag, Leipzig.

Armillas, Pedro

1950 Teotihuacán, Tula y los toltecas. *Runa, Archivo para las ciencias del hombre* 3 (1–2): 37–70.

Arnold, Philip J., and Christopher A. Pool (eds.)

2008 *Classic Period Cultural Currents in Southern and Central Veracruz.* Dumbarton Oaks Research Library and Collection, Washington, D.C.

Art Conservation Technical Services

n.d.a Report on PC.B.063. Manuscript on file, Dumbarton Oaks Research Library and Collection, Washington, D.C., 21 May 1992.

n.d.b Report on PC.B.066. Manuscript on file, Dumbarton Oaks Research Library and Collection, Washington, D.C., 21 May 1992.

n.d.c Report on PC.B.067. Manuscript on file, Dumbarton Oaks Research Library and Collection, Washington, D.C., 21 May 1992.

n.d.d Report on PC.B.068. Manuscript on file, Dumbarton Oaks Research Library and Collection, Washington, D.C., 21 May 1992.

n.d.e Report on PC.B.064. Manuscript on file, Dumbarton Oaks Research Library and Collection, Washington, D.C., 15 October 1992.

Art Digest

1950 Review of the Taft Exhibition. *Art Digest* 25 (3).

Artes de México

1957 *Artes de México.* Vol. 3, no. 17.

1973 *Artes de México.* Vol. 10, no. 173.

Art International

1959 *Art International* 3 (3/4): 45.

Arts

1958 *Arts* 33 (1): 16.

Association of American Colleges

1987 *Liberal Education* 74 (4): 3.

Batres, Leopoldo

1905 *La lápida arqueológica de Tepatlaxco-Orizaba.* Tipografía de Fidencio Soria, Mexico City.

Becker-Donner, Etta

1962 *Präkolumbische Malerei.* Brüder Rosenbaum, Vienna.

Bendersky, Gordon

2000 Tlatilco Sculptures, Diprosopus, and the Emergence of Medical Illustrations. *Perspectives in Biology and Medicine* 43: 477–501.

Benson, Elizabeth P.

1993 The Robert Woods Bliss Collection of Pre-Columbian Art: A Memoir. In *Collecting the Pre-Columbian Past* (Elizabeth Hill Boone, ed.): 15–34. Dumbarton Oaks Research Library and Collection, Washington, D.C.

1997 *Birds and Beasts of Ancient Latin America.* University Press of Florida, Gainesville.

Berdan, Frances F.

1989 *The Aztecs.* Chelsea House, New York.

1996 The Tributary Provinces. In *Aztec Imperial Strategies* (Frances F. Berdan et al.): 115–135. Dumbarton Oaks Research Library and Collection, Washington, D.C.

2003 The Economy of Postclassic Mesoamerica. In *The Postclassic Mesoamerican World* (Michael E. Smith and Frances F. Berdan, eds.): 93–95. University of Utah Press, Salt Lake City.

Berjonneau, Gerald, Emile Deletaille, and Jean-Louis Sonnery

1985 *Rediscovered Masterpieces of Mesoamerica: Mexico-Guatemala-Honduras.* Editions Arts, Boulogne, France.

Berlin, Heinrich

1946 Archaeological Excavations in Chiapas. *American Antiquity* 12: 19–28.

Berlo, Janet Catherine

1992 Icons and Ideologies at Teotihuacan: The Great Goddess Reconsidered. In *Art, Ideology, and the City of Teotihuacan* (Janet Catherine Berlo, ed.): 129–168. Dumbarton Oaks Research Library and Collection, Washington, D.C.

Bernal, Ignacio

1967 Nuevos descubrimientos en Acapulco, Mexico. In *The Civilizations of Ancient America* (Sol Tax, ed.): 52–56. Cooper Square, New York.

Bernal-García, María Elena

n.d. Images and Labels: The Case of the Tlatilcan Female Figurines. M.A. thesis, Department of Art, University of Arizona, Tucson, 1988.

Berrelleza, Juan Alberto Román

2004 L'uomo e la società Azteca. In *I tesori degli Aztechi* (Felipe R. Solís Olguín, ed.): 28–73. Electa, Milan.

Berrin, Kathleen, and Esther Pasztory (eds.)

1993 *Teotihuacan: Art from the City of the Gods.* Fine Arts Museums of San Francisco, San Francisco, and Thames and Hudson, New York.

Beverido Duhalt, Maliyel

2006 "Tlazoltéotl." Museo de Xalapa. *Arqueología mexicana,* edición especial 22: 74–75.

Beyer, Hermann

1933 *Shell Ornament Sets from the Huasteca, Mexico.* Middle American Research Series 5. Tulane University, New Orleans, La.

1934 The New Atlatl, Found in Italy, a Falsification. *American Anthropologist* 36: 632–633.

1965a La doble águila en el México prehispánico. *El México antiguo* 10: 461–464. Originally published 1921, *Revista de revistas,* 27 November, Mexico City.

1965b El mono mitológico de los mexicanos y los mayas. *El México antiguo* 10: 444–460. Originally published 1913, *International Congress of Americanists, Proceedings of the XVIII Session, London 1912,* Pt. 1, Harrison and Sons, London.

1965c Sobre un antiguo vaso mexicano en forma de cabeza. *El México antiguo* 10: 353–359. Originally published 1920, *Memorias y revista de la Sociedad Científica "Antonio Alzate,"* 35: 81–90.

1965d Otro antiguo vaso mexicano en forma de cabeza. *El México antiguo* 10: 360–364. Originally published 1921, *Memorias y revista de la Sociedad Científica "Antonio Alzate,"* 35: 195–201.

1965e Sobre una representación del dios Mixcoatl en el atlatl mexicano del Museo Británico. *El México antiguo* 10: 326–329. Originally published 1923–1924, *Archiv für Religionswissenschaft* 22.

1969a El tesoro del cacique de Huejotzingo. *El México antiguo* 11: 393–399.

1969b Una representación auténtica del uso del omichicahuaztli. *El México antiguo* 11: 541–545.

Blade, Rafael

2002 Dossier: Aztecas. *Historia y vida* 34 (416): 32–53.

Bliss, Robert Woods

1947 *Indigenous Art of the Americas: Collection of Robert Woods Bliss.* National Gallery of Art, Smithsonian Institution, Washington, D.C.

1957 *Pre-Columbian Art.* Phaidon, London.

Boardman, John

2006 *The World of Ancient Art.* Thames and Hudson, London.

Bone, Lesley

1988 Construction and Condition of the Wagner Mural Fragments. In *Feathered Serpents and Flowering Trees: Reconstructing the Murals of Teotihuacán* (Kathleen Berrin, ed.): 232–233. Fine Arts Museums of San Francisco, San Francisco.

Bonifaz Nuño, Rubén

1981 *The Art in the Great Temple: México-Tenochtitlan.* Instituto Nacional de Antropología e Historia, Mexico City.

Boone, Elizabeth Hill

1982 Towards a More Precise Definition of the Aztec Painting Style. In *Pre-Columbian Art History: Selected Readings* (Alana Cordy-Collins, ed.): 153–168. Peek Publications, Palo Alto, Calif.

1986a Adlerkopf. In *Glanz und Untergang des Alten Mexico,* Vol. 2 (Arne Eggebrecht, ed.): cat. no. 257. Verlag Philipp von Zabern, Mainz am Rhein, Germany.

1986b Anhänger. In *Glanz und Untergang des Alten Mexico,* Vol. 2 (Arne Eggebrecht, ed.): cat. no. 262. Verlag Philipp von Zabern, Mainz am Rhein, Germany.

1986c Halsschmuck. In *Glanz und Untergang des Alten Mexico,* Vol. 2 (Arne Eggebrecht, ed.): cat. no. 263. Verlag Philipp von Zabern, Mainz am Rhein, Germany.

1986d Obsidianspiegel im Holzrahmen. In *Glanz und Untergang des Alten Mexico,* Vol. 2 (Arne Eggebrecht, ed.): cat. no. 354. Verlag Philipp von Zabern, Mainz am Rhein, Germany.

1986e Ohrspule. In *Glanz und Untergang des Alten Mexico,* Vol. 2 (Arne Eggebrecht, ed.): cat. no. 261. Verlag Philipp von Zabern, Mainz am Rhein, Germany.

1986f Schlangenkopf. In *Glanz und Untergang des Alten Mexico,* Vol. 2 (Arne Eggebrecht, ed.): cat. no. 156. Verlag Philipp von Zabern, Mainz am Rhein, Germany.

1986g Speerschleuder. In *Glanz und Untergang des Alten Mexico,* Vol. 2 (Arne Eggebrecht, ed.): cat. no. 274. Verlag Philipp von Zabern, Mainz am Rhein, Germany.

1989 *Incarnations of the Aztec Supernatural: The Image of Huitzilopochtli in Mexico and Europe.* Transactions of the American Philosophical Society 79, pt. 2. American Philosophical Society, Philadelphia, Pa.

1996 Robert Woods Bliss and Pre-Columbian Art. In *Andean Art at Dumbarton Oaks,* Vol. 1 (Elizabeth Hill Boone, ed.): 1–10. Dumbarton Oaks Research Library and Collection, Washington, D.C.

2000 *Stories in Red and Black: Pictorial Histories of the Aztecs and Mixtecs.* University of Texas Press, Austin.

Boone, Elizabeth Hill (ed.)

1987 *The Aztec Templo Mayor.* Dumbarton Oaks Research Library and Collection, Washington, D.C.

Borhegyi, Stephan F. de

1965 Archaeological Synthesis of the Guatemalan Highlands. In *Archaeology of Southern Mesoamerica,* Pt. 1 (Gordon R. Willey, ed.): 3–58. *Handbook of Middle American Indians,* Vol. 2 (Robert Wauchope, ed.). University of Texas Press, Austin.

Bories, Alain, and Michael D. Coe

2002 *Aztèques: L'épopée des peuples du Mexique.* Sélection du Reader's Digest, Paris.

Braniff C., Beatriz

1998 *Morales, Guanajuato y la tradición Chupícuaro.* Colección científica 373. Instituto Nacional de Antropología e Historia, Mexico City.

Braun, Barbara

1993 *Pre-Columbian Art and the Post-Columbian World: Ancient American Sources of Modern Art.* Harry N. Abrams, New York.

Bray, Warwick

1968 *Everyday Life of the Aztecs.* Putnam, New York.

Breslow, Nancy

1980 Frida Kahlo. *Américas* 32 (3): 33–39.

Broda, Johanna, David Carrasco, and Eduardo Matos Moctezuma

1987 *The Great Temple of Tenochtitlan: Center and Periphery in the Aztec World.* University of California Press, Berkeley.

Brüggemann, Jürgen K., Sara Ladrón de Guevara, and Juan Sánchez Bonilla

1992 *Tajín.* El Equilibrista, Mexico City.

Burchwood, Katharine Tyler

1972 *The Origin and Legacy of Mexican Art.* A. S. Barnes, South Brunswick, N.J.

Burkhart, Louise M.

1988 Doctrinal Aspects of Sahagún's Colloquios. In *The Work of Bernardino de Sahagún: Pioneer Ethnographer of Sixteenth-Century Aztec Mexico* (J. Jorge Klor de Alva, H. B. Nicholson, and Eloise Quiñones Keber, eds.): 65–82. Institute for Mesoamerican Studies, State University of New York, Albany.

Burland, Cottie A.

1973 *Montezuma, Lord of the Aztecs.* Weidenfeld and Nicolson, London.

Bushnell, D. I., Jr.

1905 Two Ancient Mexican Atlatls. *American Anthropologist* 7: 218–221.

Bussel, Gerard W. van, Paul L. F. van Dongen, and Ted J. J. Leyenaar (eds.)

1991 *The Mesoamerican Ballgame: Papers Presented at the International Colloquium "The Mesoamerican Ballgame 2000 BC–AD 2000" Leiden, June 30th–July 3rd, 1988.* Rijksmuseum voor Volkenkunde, Leiden.

Cabrera Castro, Rubén

1990 Funerary Bundle Figure. In *Mexico: Splendors of Thirty Centuries:* 98–99. Metropolitan Museum of Art, New York.

1993a Human Sacrifice at the Temple of the Feathered Serpent. In *Teotihuacan: Art from the City of Gods* (Kathleen Berrin and Esther Pasztory, eds.): 100–115. Fine Arts Museums of San Francisco, San Francisco, and Thames and Hudson, New York.

1993b Mask with Shell Teeth. In *Teotihuacan: Art from the City of the Gods* (Kathleen Berrin and Esther Pasztory, eds.): 186. Fine Arts Museums of San Francisco, San Francisco, and Thames and Hudson, New York.

1996 Zona 11: gran conjunto. In *La pintura mural prehispánica en México.* Vol. 1, *Teotihuacán,* bk. 1, *Catálogo* (Beatriz de la Fuente, ed.): 18–25. Universidad Nacional Autónoma de México, Instituto de Investigaciones Estéticas, Mexico City.

Cabrera Castro, Rubén, Ignacio Rodríguez, and Noel Morelos

1982 *Teotihuacán 80–82: Primeros resultados.* Instituto Nacional de Antropología e Historia, Mexico City.

Callegari, Guido V.

1934 Un nuevo precioso atlatl mexicano antiguo recientemente descubierto en Roma. In *Actas y trabajos científicos del XXV Congreso Internacional de Americanistas (La Plata, 1932),* Vol. 2: 7–9. Coni, Buenos Aires.

CalmelsCohen

2003 *André Breton: 42, rue Fontaine.* CalmelsCohen, Paris.

Campbell, Joseph

1974 *The Mythic Image.* Princeton University Press, Princeton, N.J.

Carmona Macías, Martha

1999 Oaxaca: Un arte sacro en arcilla, jade y oro. In *Los hombres de las nubes: Arqueología mexicana, zapoteca, y mixteca.* Secretaría de Relaciones Exteriores, Consejo Nacional para la Cultura y las Artes, Mexico City.

Carpenter, Elizabeth (ed.)

2007 *Frida Kahlo.* Walker Art Center, Minneapolis, Minn.

Caso, Alfonso

1938 *Thirteen Masterpieces of Mexican Archaeology* (Edith Mackie and Jorge R. Acosta, trans.). Editoriales Cultura y Polis, Mexico City.

1942 *Culturas mixteca y zapoteca.* Culturas precortesianas 1, Biblioteca del maestro 23. Ediciones Encuadernables el Nacional, Mexico City.

1959 Nombres calendáricos de los dioses. *El México antiguo* 9: 77–100.

1965 Lapidary Work, Goldwork, Copperwork: Oaxaca. In *Archaeology of Southern Mesoamerica,* Pt. 2 (Gordon R. Willey, ed.): 896–930. *Handbook of Middle American Indians,* Vol. 3 (Robert Wauchope, ed.). University of Texas Press, Austin.

1969 *El tesoro de Monte Albán.* Memorias del Instituto Nacional de Antropología e Historia 3. Instituto Nacional de Antropología e Historia, Mexico City.

1996 Interpretación del Códice Colombino. In *Códice Alfonso Caso: La vida de 8-Venado, Garra de Tigre (Colombino-Becker I).* Patronato Indígena, Mexico City. Originally published 1966, *Codex Colombino,* chap. 1, Sociedad Mexicana de Antropología, Mexico City.

Caso, Alfonso, and Ignacio Bernal

1952 *Urnas de Oaxaca.* Memorias del Instituto Nacional de Antropología e Historia 2. Instituto Nacional de Antropología e Historia, Mexico City.

Caso, Alfonso, Ignacio Bernal, and Jorge R. Acosta

1967 *La cerámica de Monte Albán.* Memorias del Instituto Nacional de Antropología e Historia 13. Instituto Nacional de Antropología e Historia, Mexico City.

Castillo Tejera, Noemí

1970 Tecnología de una vasija en travertino. *Boletín del Instituto Nacional de Antropología e Historia* 41: 48–52.

Center for Conservation and Technical Studies

n.d. Report on PC.B.092. Manuscript on file at Dumbarton Oaks Research Library and Collection, Washington, D.C., 17 March 1989.

Centro di Azione Latina and Palazzo delle Esposizioni

1960 *Arte precolombiana del Messico e dell'America Centrale.* Centro di Azione Latina, Rome.

Charlot, Jean

1958 The Indian beneath the Skin (Review of 1957 Catalogue). *Art News* 57 (3): 49, 55.

Chicago, Judy

1981 *The Birth Project Newsletter.* Through the Flower, Benicia, Calif.

Chicago, Judy, and Edward Lucie-Smith

1999 *Women and Art: Contested Territory.* Watson-Guptill, New York.

Christensen, Erwin O.

1955 *Primitive Art.* Thomas Y. Crowell, New York.

Clendinnen, Inga

1995 *Aztecs: An Interpretation*. Cambridge University Press, Cambridge and New York.

Cleveland Museum of Art

1946 *Art of the Americas*. Cleveland Museum of Art, Cleveland, Ohio.

n.d. Photograph. Electronic document, http://www.clevelandart.org/explore/departmentWork.asp?deptgroup=13&recNo=63&display=, accessed December 2005.

Codex Borbonicus

1899 *Codex Borbonicus: Manuscrit mexicain de la Bibliothèque du Palais Bourbon (livre divinatoire et rituel figuré) publié en facsimilé, avec un commentaire explicatif par M.E.-T. Hamy*. Ernest Leroux, Paris.

Codex Chimalpopoca

1992 *History and Mythology of the Aztecs: The Codex Chimalpopoca* (John Bierhorst, trans.). University of Arizona Press, Tucson.

Codex Ixtlilxochitl

1996 *Códice Ixtlilxochitl*. Akademische Druck- und Verlagsanstalt, Graz, Austria, and Fondo de Cultura Económica, Mexico City.

Codex Mendoza

1992 *The Codex Mendoza* (Frances F. Berdan and Patricia Rieff Anawalt, eds.) University of California Press, Berkeley.

Coe, Michael D.

1965 Archaeology: Veracruz and Tabasco. In *Archaeology of Southern Mesoamerica*, Pt. 2 (Gordon R. Willey, ed.): 679–715. *Handbook of Middle American Indians*, Vol. 3 (Robert Wauchope, ed.). University of Texas Press, Austin.

1986 The Art of Pre-Columbian America. In *African, Pacific, and Pre-Columbian Art in the Indiana University Art Museum* (Roy Sieber, Douglas Newton, and Michael D. Coe): 9–47. Indiana University Press, Bloomington.

1991a Mask of Tezcatlipoca. In *Circa 1492: Art in the Age of Exploration* (Jay A. Levenson, ed.): 548, cat. no. 364. National Gallery of Art, Washington, D.C., and Yale University Press, New Haven, Conn.

1991b Mirror. In *Circa 1492: Art in the Age of Exploration* (Jay A. Levenson, ed.): 548, cat. no. 365. National Gallery of Art, Washington, D.C., and Yale University Press, New Haven, Conn.

1991c Xiuhcoatl. In *Circa 1492: Art in the Age of Exploration* (Jay A. Levenson, ed.): 564, cat. no. 388. National Gallery of Art, Washington, D.C., and Yale University Press, New Haven, Conn.

2005 *The Maya*. 7th ed. Thames and Hudson, New York.

Coe, Michael D., and Justin Kerr

1982 *Old Gods and Young Heroes: The Pearlman Collection of Maya Ceramics*. Israel Museum, Maremont Pavilion of Ethnic Arts, Jerusalem.

Coggins, Clemency Chase, and John M. Ladd

1992 Wooden artifacts. In *Artifacts from the Cenote of Sacrifice, Chichen Itza, Yucatan* (Clemency Chase Coggins, ed.): 235–344. Memoirs of the Peabody Museum of Archaeology and Ethnology, Harvard University, Vol. 10, no. 3. Harvard University Press, Cambridge, Mass.

Coggins, Clemency Chase, and Orrin C. Shane (eds.)

1984 *Cenote of Sacrifice: Maya Treasures from the Sacred Well at Chichén Itzá*. University of Texas Press, Austin.

Coloquio Internacional Sobre Estados Depresivos

1960 Coloquio Internacional Sobre Estados Depresivos, Buenos Aires. 21–23 de Marzo de 1960. Pamphlet on file, Dumbarton Oaks Research Library and Collection, Washington, D.C.

Comisarenco, Dina

1996 Frida Kahlo, Diego Rivera and Tlazolteotl. *Woman's Art Journal* 17(1): 14–21.

Conides, Cynthia

1993 Tripod Vessel. In *Teotihuacan: Art from the City of the Gods* (Kathleen Berrin and Esther Pasztory, eds.): 253. Fine Arts Museums of San Francisco, San Francisco, and Thames and Hudson, New York.

1997 Social Relations among Potters in Teotihuacan, Mexico. *Museum Anthropology* 21: 39–54.

Conides, Cynthia, and Warren Barbour

1999 Tocados dentro del paisaje arquitectónico y social en Teotihuacan. In *Ideología y política a través de materiales, imágenes y símbolos* (María Elena Ruiz Gallut, ed.): 411–430. Universidad Nacional Autónoma de México, Instituto de Investigaciones Antropológicas [e] Instituto de Investigaciones Estéticas, and Instituto Nacional de Antropología e Historia, Mexico City.

Cook de Leonard, Carmen
1956 Dos atlatl de la época teotihuacana. In *Estudios antropológicos publicados en homenaje al doctor Manuel Gamio* (Eusebio Dávalos Hurtado and Ignacio Bernal, eds.): 183–200. Dirección General de Publicaciones, Mexico City.
1959 La escultura. In *Esplendor del México antiguo,* Vol. 2 (Carmen Cook de Leonard, ed.): 519–606. Centro de Investigaciones Antropológicas de México, Mexico City.
1971 Minor Arts of the Classic Period in Central Mexico. In *Archaeology of Northern Mesoamerica* (Gordon Ekholm and Ignacio Bernal, eds.): 206–227. *Handbook of Middle American Indians,* Vol. 10 (Robert Wauchope, ed.). University of Texas Press, Austin.

Cooper Union Museum for the Arts of Decoration
1951 *Alter Ego: Masks, Their Art and Use.* New York.

Cortés, Hernan
1986 [1519–1526] *Letters from Mexico* (Anthony Pagden, trans. and ed.). Yale University Press, New Haven, Conn.

Covarrubias, Miguel
1943 Tlatilco, Archaic Mexican Art and Culture. *DYN: The Review of Modern Art* 4–5: 40–46.
1950 Tlatilco: El arte y la cultura preclásica del valle de México. *Cuadernos americanos* 9 (3): 149–162.
1954 *The Eagle, the Jaguar, and the Serpent: Indian Art of the Americas.* Alfred A. Knopf, New York.
1957 *Indian Art of Mexico and Central America.* Alfred A. Knopf, New York.

Cruz Ortíz, Alejandra
1994 El uipil de novia. In *La pintura de la muerte y de los destinos: Libro explicativo del llamado Códice Laud* (Ferdinand Anders and Maarten Jansen, eds.): 139–147. Akademische Druck- und Verlagsanstalt, Graz, Austria, and Fondo de Cultura Económica, Mexico City.

Davies, Nigel
1983 *The Ancient Kingdoms of Mexico.* Penguin Books, New York.

Dean, Carolyn, and Dana Leibsohn
2003 Hybridity and Its Discontents: Considering Visual Culture in Colonial Spanish America. *Colonial Latin American Review* 12: 5–36.

Diehl, Richard A., and Edward G. Stroh
1978 Tecali Vessel Manufacturing Debris at Tollan, Mexico. *American Antiquity* 43: 73–78.

Digby, Adrian
1972 *Maya Jades.* British Museum, London.

Disselhoff, Hans-Dietrich, and Sigvald Linné
1960 *The Art of Ancient America; Civilizations of Central and South America.* Crown, New York.

Dockstader, Frederick J.
1961 Before and After Columbus. *Art in America* 49 (3): 24–43.
1964 *Indian Art in Middle America: Pre-Columbian and Contemporary Arts and Crafts of Mexico, Central America, and the Caribbean.* New York Graphic Society, Greenwich, Conn.
1973 *Indian Art of the Americas.* Museum of the American Indian, Heye Foundation, New York.

Doesburg, Sebastián van (ed.)
2001 *Códices cuicatecos Porfirio Díaz y Fernández Leal: Edición facsimilar, contexto histórico e interpretación.* Miguel Angel Porrúa, Mexico City.

Drucker, Philip
1943a *Ceramic Sequences at Tres Zapotes, Veracruz, Mexico.* Bulletin 140, Bureau of American Ethnology. Government Printing Office, Washington, D.C.
1943b *Ceramic Stratigraphy at Cerro de las Mesas, Veracruz, Mexico.* Bulletin 141, Bureau of American Ethnology. Government Printing Office, Washington, D.C.
1952 *La Venta, Tabasco: A Study of Olmec Ceramics and Art.* Bulletin 153, Bureau of American Ethnology. Government Printing Office, Washington, D.C.
1955 *The Cerro de las Mesas Offering of Jade and Other Materials.* Anthropological Papers 44, Bulletin 157, Bureau of American Ethnology. Government Printing Office, Washington, D.C.

Dumbarton Oaks
1963 *Handbook of the Robert Woods Bliss Collection of Pre-Columbian Art.* Dumbarton Oaks, Trustees for Harvard University, Washington, D.C.
1969 *Supplement to the Handbook of the Robert Woods Bliss Collection of Pre-Columbian Art.* Dumbarton Oaks, Trustees for Harvard University, Washington, D.C.

Durán, Diego

1971 [1574–1579] *Book of the Gods and Rites and The Ancient Calendar* (Fernando Horcasitas and Doris Heyden, trans. and eds.). University of Oklahoma Press, Norman.

1994 [1581] *The History of the Indies of New Spain* (Doris Heyden, trans.). University of Oklahoma Press, Norman.

Easby, Elizabeth K., and John F. Scott

1970 *Before Cortés: Sculpture of Middle America.* Metropolitan Museum of Art, New York.

Edmonson, Munro S.

1971 *The Book of Counsel: The Popul Vuh of the Quiche Maya of Guatemala.* Middle American Research Institute 35. Tulane University, New Orleans, La.

Eggebrecht, Arne (ed.)

1986 *Glanz und Untergang des Alten Mexico: Die Azteken und ihre Vorläufer.* 2 vols. Verlag Philipp von Zabern, Mainz am Rhein, Germany.

Ekholm, Gordon F.

1962 U-Shaped "Ornaments" Identified as Finger-Loops from Atlatls. *American Antiquity* 28: 181–185.

1964 The Problem of Fakes in Pre-Columbian Art. *Curator* 7: 19–32.

n.d. The Birth-Giving Deity in the Bliss Collection. Manuscript on file, Dumbarton Oaks Research Library and Collection, Washington, D.C., September 1963.

Evans, Susan Toby

2004 *Ancient Mexico and Central America: Archaeology and Culture History.* Thames and Hudson, New York.

2008 *Ancient Mexico and Central America: Archaeology and Culture History.* 2nd ed. Thames and Hudson, London and New York.

2009 Tenochtitlan, Aztec City in the Lake. In *The Great Cities in History* (John Julius Norwich, ed.): 150–153. Thames and Hudson, London and New York.

Evans, Susan Toby, and Joanne Pillsbury (eds.)

2004 *Palaces of the Ancient New World.* Dumbarton Oaks Research Library and Collection, Washington, D.C.

Evans, Susan Toby, and David L. Webster (eds.)

2001 *Archaeology of Ancient Mexico and Central America: An Encyclopedia.* Garland, New York.

Fabbri, Dino, and Nicolás J. Gibelli

1965 *El arte en América precolombina, en África y en Oceanía.* Arte/rama 9. Fratelli Fabbri Editori, Milan.

Fash, William L., and Barbara W. Fash

2000 Teotihuacan and the Maya: A Classic Heritage. In *Mesoamerica's Classic Heritage: From Teotihuacan to the Aztecs* (David Carrasco, Lindsay Jones, and Scott Sessions, eds.): 433–462. University Press of Colorado, Boulder.

Feldman, Edmund B.

1982 *The Artist.* Prentice-Hall, Englewood Cliffs, N.J.

Fergus, Charles

2000 *Wildlife of Pennsylvania and the Northeast.* Stackpole Books, Mechanicsburg, Pa.

Fernández de Oviedo y Valdés, Gonzalo

1946 [1526–1549] *Sucesos y diálogo de la Nueva España.* Universidad Nacional Autónoma de México, Mexico City.

Fichner-Rathus, Lois

1989 *Understanding Art.* Prentice-Hall, Englewood Cliffs, N.J.

Fitzhugh, William W., and Susan A. Kaplan

1982 *Inua: Spirit World of the Bering Sea Eskimo.* Smithsonian Institution Press, Washington, D.C.

Flannery, Kent V., and Joyce Marcus

1983 Urban Mitla and Its Rural Hinterland. In *The Cloud People: Divergent Evolution of the Zapotec and Mixtec Civilizations* (Kent V. Flannery and Joyce Marcus, eds.): 295–300. Academic Press, New York.

Florance, Charles A.

1985 Recent Work in the Chupícuaro Region. In *The Archaeology of West and Northwest Mesoamerica* (Michael S. Foster and Phil C. Weigand, eds.): 9–45. Westview Press, Boulder, Colo.

Follett, Prescott H. F.

1932 *War and Weapons of the Maya.* Middle American Research Series Publication 4. Tulane University, New Orleans, La.

Foncerrada de Molina, Marta
1980 Mural Painting in Cacaxtla and Teotihuacán Cosmopolitanism. In *Third Palenque Round Table, 1978—Part 2: Proceedings of the Tercera Mesa Redonda de Palenque, June 11–18, 1978* (Merle Greene Robertson, ed.): 183–198. University of Texas Press, Austin.

Frierman, Jay D. (ed.)
1969 *The Natalie Wood Collection of Pre-Columbian Ceramics from Chupícuaro, Guanajuato, Mexico, at UCLA.* Museum and Laboratories of Ethnic Arts and Technology, University of California, Los Angeles.

Fuente, Beatriz de la
1975 *Arte huaxteco prehispánico.* Artes de México 187. Revista Artes de México, Mexico City.
1980 *Escultura huasteca en piedra: Catálogo.* Universidad Nacional Autónoma de México, Mexico City.
1985 Main Subjects in Huastec Sculpture. In *Fourth Palenque Round Table 1980* (Elizabeth P. Benson, ed.): 303–312. Pre-Columbian Art Research Institute, San Francisco.
1992 The Huastecs. In *Museum of Anthropology of Xalapa* (Beatrice Trueblood, ed., and Anne Hill de Mayagoitia, trans.): 163–191. Government of the State of Veracruz, Xalapa.
1995 Tetitla. In *La pintura mural prehispánica en México.* Vol. 1, *Teotihuacán,* bk. 1: *Catálogo* (Beatriz de la Fuente, ed.): 258–311. Universidad Nacional Autónoma de México, Instituto de Investigaciones Estéticas, Mexico City.

Galindo y Villa, Jesús
1912 *Las ruinas de Cempoala y del Templo del Tajín (Estado de Veracruz): Exploradas por el director del Museo Nacional de Arqueología, Historia y Etnología, en Misíon en Europa, Francisco del Paso y Troncoso.* El Museo, México City.

Gallegos Ruiz, Roberto
1978 *El señor 9 Flor en Zaachila.* Universidad Nacional Autónoma de México, Mexico City.

Gamio, Manuel
1921 Vestigios del Templo Mayor de Tenochtitlan descubiertos recientemente. El Coateocalli. *Ethnos* 1 (8–12): 205–207.

García Cisneros, Florencio
1970 *Maternity in Pre-Columbian Art.* Cisneros Gallery of New York, New York.

García Granados, Rafael
1940–42 Reminiscencias idolatricas en monumentos coloniales. *Anales del Instituto de Investigaciones Estéticas* 2: 54–56.

García Moll, Roberto
1999 Tlatilco prácticas funerarias. *Arqueología mexicana* 7 (40): 20–23.

García Moll, Roberto, and Marcela Salas Cuesta
1998 *Tlatilco: De mujeres bonitas, hombres y dioses.* Consejo Nacional para la Cultura y las Artes, Dirección General de Publicaciones, Mexico City.

García Moll, Roberto, Felipe Solís Olguín, and Jaime Bali
1990 *El tesoro de Moctezuma.* Colección Editorial de Arte Chrysler, Mexico City.

García Moll, Roberto, Daniel Juárez Cossío, Carmen Pijoan Aguade, Ma. Elena Salas Cuesta, and Marcela Salas Cuesta
1991 *Catálogo de entierros de San Luis Tlatilco, México: Temporada IV.* Serie Antropología Física-Arqueología. Instituto Nacional de Antropología e Historia, Mexico City.

García Payón, José
1941 Estudio preliminar de la zona arqueológica de Texmelincan, estado de Guerrero. *El México antiguo* 5: 341–364.
1943 *Interpretación cultural de la zona arqueológica de El Tajín.* Imprenta Universitaria, Mexico City.
1955 *Exploraciones en El Tajín, temporadas 1953 y 1954.* Instituto Nacional de Antropología e Historia, Mexico City.
1957 *El Tajín: Guía oficial.* Instituto Nacional de Antropología e Historia, Mexico City.
1973 *Los enigmas de El Tajín.* Colección científica, Arqueología 3. Instituto Nacional de Antropología e Historia, Mexico City.

García Vega, Agustín
1939 Exploraciones en El Tajín, 1934–1938. *Cuadernos americanos* 27 (2): 78–87.

Garibay, Angel Ma., K. (ed.)
1996 *Teogonía e historia de los mexicanos: Tres opúsculos del siglo XVI.* Colección Sepan Cuantos 37. Editorial Porrúa, Mexico City.

Garza, Mercedes de la

2004 The Harmony between People and Animals in the Aztec World. In *The Aztec Empire: Catalogue of the Exhibition* (Felipe Solís Olguín, ed.): 70–81. Guggenheim Museum Publications, New York.

Gay, Carlos

n.d. Letter to Gordom Ekholm re: PC.B.071. Manuscript on file, Dumbarton Oaks Research Library and Collection, Washington, D.C., 30 June 1963.

Gendrop, Paul, and Iñaki Díaz Balerdi

1994 *Escultura azteca: Una aproximación a su estética*. Editorial Trillas, Mexico City.

Gilboa, R.

1994 *Sun Goddess Crouching: Research of an Enigma*. R. Gilboa in collaboration with Castle Museum, Nottingham.

2009 *And There Was Sculpture: Jacob Epstein's Formative Years (1882–1930)*. Paul Holberton, London.

Gill, Richardson Benedict

2000 *The Great Maya Droughts: Water, Life, and Death*. University of New Mexico Press, Albuquerque.

Glass, John B., in collaboration with Donald Robertson

1975 A Census of Native Middle American Pictorial Manuscripts. In *Guide to Ethnohistorical Sources*, Pt. 3 (Howard F. Cline, ed.): 81–252. *Handbook of Middle American Indians*, Vol. 14 (Robert Wauchope, ed.). University of Texas Press, Austin.

González Licón, Ernesto

1994 *Los zapotecas y mixtecas: Tres mil años de civilización precolombina*. Jaca Book, Milan, and Consejo Nacional para la Cultura y las Artes, Mexico City.

González Licón, Ernesto, and Lourdes Márquez Morfín

1990 Costumbres funerarias en Monte Albán. In *Monte Albán* (Ernesto González Licón, ed.): 53–137. El Equilibrista, Mexico City, and Turner Libros, Madrid.

1994 Rito y ceremonial prehispánico en las Cuevas de la Cañada, Oaxaca. In *Mixteca-Puebla: Discoveries and Research in Mesoamerican Art and Archaeology* (H. B. Nicholson and Eloise Quiñones Keber, eds.): 223–234. Labyrinthos, Culver City, Calif.

Graham, F. Lanier

1997 *Goddesses*. Abbeville, New York.

Graves, Robert

1977 *New Larousse Encyclopedia of Mythology*. Hamlyn, London.

Greenwood, Hugh A.

1942 *Special Exhibit of Latin American Silver*. Pan American Union, Washington, D.C.

Grey, Michael

1978 *Pre-Columbian Art*. St. Martin's Press, New York.

Grosses modernes Lexikon

1982 *Grosses modernes Lexikon*. Lexikothek Verlag, Gütersloh, Germany.

Grossman, Wendy

2008 Man Ray's Lost and Found Photographs: Arts of the Americas in Context. *Journal of Surrealism and the Americas* 2 (1): 114–139.

Grove, David C.

1970 *The Olmec Paintings of Oxtotitlan Cave, Guerrero, Mexico*. Studies in Pre-Columbian Art and Archaeology 6. Dumbarton Oaks, Trustees for Harvard University, Washington, D.C.

Guirand, Félix

1968 *New Larousse Encyclopedia of Mythology*. New ed. Hamlyn, London and New York.

Gump, Richard

1962 *Jade: Stone of Heaven*. Doubleday, Garden City, N.Y.

Gutiérrez Marié, Juan

2000 *Memorias del Totonacapan*. Secretaría de Educación y Cultura, Xalapa.

Gutiérrez Solana, Nelly

1978 Xiuhcoatl tallada en piedra del Museum of Mankind, Londres. *Anales del Instituto de Investigaciones Estéticas* 12 (48): 5–17.

1982 El relieve en el arte mexica. In *Historia del arte mexicano*. Vol. 2, *Arte prehispánico*: 258–273. Salvat, Mexico City.

1983 *Objetos ceremoniales en piedra de la cultura mexica*. Universidad Nacional Autónoma de México, Mexico City.

1987 *Las serpientes en el arte mexica*. Colección de arte 40. Universidad Nacional Autónoma de México, Coordinación de Humanidades, Mexico City.

Gutiérrez Solana, Nelly, and Susan K. Hamilton
1977 *Las esculturas en terracota de El Zapotal, Veracruz*. Universidad Nacional Autónoma de México, Mexico City.

Haags Gemeentemuseum
1959 *Dertig eeuwen Mexicaanse Kunst*. Haags Gemeentemuseum, The Hague.

Hall, Barbara Ann
1997 Spindle Whorls and Cotton Production at Middle Classic Matacapan and in the Gulf Lowlands. In *Olmec to Aztec: Settlement Patterns in the Ancient Gulf Lowlands* (Barbara L. Stark and Philip J. Arnold III, eds.): 115–135. University of Arizona Press, Tucson.

Hamy, Ernest T.
1883 *Note sur une inscription chronographique de la fin de la période aztèque appartenant au Musée du Trocadéro*. Ernest Leroux, Paris.
1899 Commentaire explicatif. In *Codex Borbonicus: Manuscrit mexicain de la Bibliothèque du Palais Bourbon (livre divinatoire et rituel figuré) publié en facsimilé, avec un commentaire explicatif par M.E.-T. Hamy*: 1–24. Ernest Leroux, Paris.
1906 Note sur une statuette mexicaine en wernerite représentant la Desse Ixcuina. *Journal de la Société des Américanistes de Paris* 3: 5.

Hansen, Maren Tonder
1997 *Mother Mysteries*. Random House, New York.

Haus der Kunst München
1958 *Präkolumbische Kunst aus Mexiko und Mittelamerika*. Ausstellungsleitung München e. V. Haus der Kunst, Munich.

Headrick, Annabeth
1999 The Street of the Dead . . . It Really Was: Mortuary Bundles at Teotihuacan. *Ancient Mesoamerica* 10: 69–85.
2007 *The Teotihuacan Trinity: The Sociopolitical Structure of an Ancient Mesoamerican City*. University of Texas Press, Austin.

Heflin, Allen A.
1963 A Rare Type Atlatl Spur from the Valley of Mexico. *Boletín del Centro de Investigaciones Antropológicas de México* 13: 1–4.

Heiniger, Ernst A., and Jean Heiniger (eds.)
1974 *The Great Book of Jewels*. New York Graphic Society, Boston.

Heinken, Siebo
2003 Ein Herz für die Götter. *National Geographic Deutschland* April: 32–44.

Herrera, Hayden
1979 Native Roots: Frida Kahlo's Art. *Artscanada* 230–231: 25–28.

Heyden, Doris
1972 Xiuhtecutli: Investidor de soberanos. *Boletín del Instituto Nacional de Antropología e Historia*, series II, 3: 3–10.

Heyden, Doris, and Luis Francisco Villaseñor
1984 *The Great Temple and the Aztec Gods*. Editorial Minutiae Mexicana, Mexico City.

Hirth, Kenneth G.
2001 Salitron Viejo. In *Archaeology of Ancient Mexico and Central America* (Susan Toby Evans and David L. Webster, eds.): 441–442. Garland, New York.

Hirth, Kenneth G., and Susan Grant Hirth
1992 Objektbeschreibungen: The El Cajón Jades. In *Die Welt der Maya* (Eva Eggebrecht, Arne Eggebrecht, and Nikolai Grube, eds.): 300, 368, 530–551. Verlag Philipp von Zabern, Mainz am Rhein, Germany.
1993 Ancient Currency. In *Pre-Columbian Jade* (Frederick W. Lange, ed.): 173–190. University of Utah Press, Salt Lake City.

Historisches Museum Frankfurt am Main
1960 *Präkolumbische Kunst aus Mexiko und Mittelamerika*. Kuratorium Kulturelles Frankfurt, Frankfurt am Main, Germany.

Holmes, William H.
1897 Onyx Tablet with Engraved Figure of a Deity. In *Archaeological Studies among the Ancient Cities of Mexico*: 304–309. Field Columbian Museum Publication 16, vol. 1, no. 1. Field Columbian Museum, Chicago.
1914 Masterpieces of Aboriginal American Art: Mosaic Work, Minor Examples. *Art and Archaeology* 1 (3): 90–102.

Honan, William H.
2000 History of Medical Art Gets Pre-Columbian Chapter. *New York Times* August 22: D5.

Hosler, Dorothy
1994 *The Sounds and Colors of Power: The Sacred Metallurgical Technology of Ancient West Mexico.* MIT Press, Cambridge, Mass.
2003 Metal Production. In *The Postclassic Mesoamerican World* (Michael E. Smith and Frances F. Berdan, eds.): 159–171. University of Utah Press, Salt Lake City.

Houston, Stephen, and David Stuart
1989 *The Way Glyph: Evidence for "Co-essences" Among the Classic Maya.* Research Reports on Ancient Maya Writing 30. Center for Maya Research, Washington, D.C.

Humboldt, Alexander von
1811 *Essai politique sur le royaume de la Novelle-Espagne.* Chez F. Schoell, Paris.

Ichon, Alain
1973 *La religión de los totonacas de la sierra.* Instituto Nacional Indigenista, Mexico City.

Incas, Mayas, Azteken
2004 Incas, Mayas, Azteken. *Geoepoche: Das Magazin für Geschichte 15.*

Instituto Nacional de Antropología e Historia
1946 *Pre-Spanish Art of Mexico.* Secretaría de Educación Pública, Mexico City.

Ishida, Eiichirō
1962 *Amerika.* Sekai Bijutsu Zenshū 24. Kadokawa Shoten, Tokyo.

Izeki, Mutsumi
2008 *Conceptualization of "Xihuitl": History, Environment, and Cultural Dynamics in Postclassic Mexica Cognition.* BAR International Series 1863. Archaeopress, Oxford.

Jarquín Pacheco, Ana María, and Enrique Martínez Vargas
1982 Las excavaciones en el Conjunto 1D. In *Teotihuacán 80–82: Primeras resultados* (Rubén Cabrera Castro, Ignacio Rodríguez, and Noel Morelos, eds.): 89–126. Instituto Nacional de Antropología e Historia, Mexico City.

Jett, Paul
n.d. Report on PC.B.090. Manuscript on file at Dumbarton Oaks Research Library and Collection, Washington, D.C., 3 December 1992.

Jiménez Moreno, Wigberto, and Salvador Mateos Higuera
1940 *Códice de Yanhuitlán: Edición en facsímile y con un estudio preliminar.* Museo Nacional, Mexico City.

Jiménez Salas, Oscar, Ricardo Sánchez Hernández, and Jasinto Robles Camacho
2000 El Tecali, un tipo de travertino. *Arqueología* 24: 129–143.

Johnson, Harmer
1992 *Guide to the Arts of the Americas.* Rizzoli, New York.

Joyce, Thomas A.
1916 Note on a Fine Tecalli Vase of Ancient Mexican Manufacture. *Man* 16: 33–34.

Kampen, Michael Edwin
1971 *The Sculptures of El Tajín, Veracruz, Mexico.* University of Florida Press, Gainesville.

Kassner, Lily S.
2003 *Tiempo, piedra y barro.* Universidad Nacional Autónoma de México, Mexico City.

Kausch, Michael
1998 Henry Moore—Mensch und Natur. In *Henry Moore, 1898–1986: Eine Retrospektive zum 100. Geburtstag* (Wilfried Seipel, ed.): 15–53. Skira, Milan, and Kunsthistorisches Museum, Vienna.

Kelemen, Pál
1937 *Battlefield of the Gods: Aspects of Mexican History, Art and Exploration.* George Allen & Unwin, London.
1943 *Medieval American Art.* 2 vols. Macmillan, New York.

Kellar, James
1955 *The Atlatl in North America.* Prehistory Research Series 3, no. 3: 280–352. Indiana Historical Society, Indianapolis.

Kelly, Isabel
1947 *Excavations at Apatzingan, Michoacan.* Viking Fund Publications in Anthropology 7. New York.

Kerr, Justin
1989 *The Maya Vase Book: A Corpus of Rollout Photographs of Maya Vases,* Vol. 1. Kerr Associates, New York.
n.d.a Kerr Maya Vase Database. Electronic document, http://research.famsi.famsi.org/kerrmaya.html, accessed November 2005.

n.d.b Kerr Pre-Columbian Portfolio. Electronic document, http://research.famsi.org/kerrportfolio.html, accessed October 2005.

Keys, David

1999 *Catastrophe: An Investigation into the Origins of the Modern World.* Ballantine Books, New York.

Kidder, Alfred V.

1947 *The Artifacts of Uaxactun, Guatemala.* Carnegie Institution of Washington Publication 576. Carnegie Institution of Washington, Washington, D.C.

Kidder, Alfred V., Jesse D. Jennings, and Edward M. Shook

1977 *Excavations at Kaminaljuyu, Guatemala.* Pennsylvania State University Press, University Park. Originally published 1946, Carnegie Institution of Washington Publication 561, Carnegie Institution of Washington, Washington, D.C.

Kirchhoff, Paul

1981 Mesoamerica. In *Ancient Mesoamerica: Selected Readings* (John Graham, ed.): 1–10. Peek Publications, Palo Alto, Calif. Originally published 1943, *Acta Americana* 1: 92–107.

Klein, Cecelia F.

1975 Post-Classic Mexican Death Imagery as a Sign of Cyclical Completion. In *Death and the Afterlife in Pre-Columbian America* (Elizabeth P. Benson, ed.): 69–85. Dumbarton Oaks Research Library and Collection, Washington, D.C.

1993 The Shield Women: Resolution of an Aztec Gender Paradox. In *Current Topics in Aztec Studies* (Alana Cordy-Collins and Douglas Sharon, eds.): 39–64. San Diego Museum Papers 30. San Diego Museum of Man, San Diego, Calif.

2000 The Devil and the Skirt. *Ancient Mesoamerica* 11: 1–26.

Knoblock, Byron W.

1939 *Banner-Stones of the North American Indian.* Byron W. Knoblock, La Grange, Ill.

Kolb, Charles

1987 *Marine Shell Trade and Classic Teotihuacan, Mexico.* BAR International Series 364. B.A.R., Oxford.

Koontz, Rex

n.d. The Iconography of El Tajín, Veracruz, Mexico. Ph.D. dissertation, Department of Art History, University of Texas, Austin, 1994.

Krickeberg, Walter

1969 *Felsbilder Mexicos: als historische, religiöse und Kunstdenkmäler.* Dietrich Reimer, Berlin.

Kubler, George

1954 *The Louise and Walter Arensberg Collection.* Vol. 2, *Pre-Columbian Sculpture.* Philadelphia Museum of Art, Philadelphia, Pa.

1962 *The Art and Architecture of Ancient America: The Mexican, Maya, and Andean Peoples.* Penguin, Baltimore, Md.

1967 *The Iconography of the Art of Teotihuacan.* Studies in Pre-Columbian Art and Archaeology 4. Dumbarton Oaks, Trustees for Harvard University, Washington, D.C.

1972 Jaguars in the Valley of Mexico. In *The Cult of the Feline* (Elizabeth P. Benson, ed.): 19–49. Dumbarton Oaks Research Library and Collection, Washington, D.C.

1984 Ancient American Gods and Their Living Impersonators. *Apollo* 119 (266): 10–20.

Kubler, George (ed.)

1986 *Pre-Columbian Art of Mexico and Central America.* Yale University Art Gallery, New Haven, Conn.

Kunst der Mexikaner

1959 *Kunst der Mexikaner.* Rautenstauch-Joest-Museum, Cologne.

Kunsthaus Zürich

1959 *Kunst der Mexikaner.* Kunsthaus Zürich, Zürich.

Künstlerhaus Wien

1959 *Präkolumbische Kunst aus Mexiko und Mittelamerika, und Kunst der Mexikaner aus späterer Zeit im Wiener Künstlerhaus.* Österreichische Kulturvereinigung, Vienna.

Ladrón de Guevara, Sara

1999 *Imagen y pensamiento en El Tajín.* Universidad Veracruzana, Xalapa, and Instituto Nacional de Antropología e Historia, Mexico City.

Landa, Diego de (Fray)

1959 [1566] *Relación de las cosas de Yucatán.* Editorial Porrúa, Mexico City.

Langley, James C.

1986 *Symbolic Notation of Teotihuacan: Elements of Writing in a Mesoamerican Culture of the Classic Period.* BAR International Series 313. B.A.R., Oxford.

1992 Teotihuacan Sign Clusters. In *Art, Ideology, and the City of Teotihuacan* (Janet Catherine Berlo, ed.): 247–280. Dumbarton Oaks Research Library and Collection, Washington, D.C.

1993 Symbols, Signs, and Writing Systems. In *Teotihuacan: Art from the City of the Gods* (Kathleen Berrin and Esther Pasztory, eds.): 128–139. Fine Arts Museums of San Francisco, San Francisco, and Thames and Hudson, New York.

Laurencich Minelli, Laura

1993 I due antichi atlatl messicani del Museo Nazionale di Antropología e Etnología di Firenze. *Archivio per l'antropologia e la etnología* 133: 391–403.

Lehmann, Walter

1938 Analyse d'un vase mexicain de l'époque précolombienne. *Journal de la Société des Américanistes* 30: 289–298.

Leyenaar, Ted J. J.

1978 *Ulama: The Perpetuation in Mexico of the Pre-Spanish Ball Game Ullamaliztli* (Inez Seeger, trans.). E. J. Brill, Leiden.

1992 Los tres ulamas del siglo XX. In *El juego de pelota en Mesoamérica: Raices y supervivencia* (María Teresa Uriarte, ed.): 357–389. Siglo Veinteuno Editores, Mexico City.

2001 The Modern Ballgames of Sinaloa. In *The Sport of Life and Death: The Mesoamerican Ballgame* (E. Michael Whittington, ed.): 122–129. Thames and Hudson, London.

Liljevalchs Konsthall

1952 *Mexikansk konst från forntid till nutid.* Liljevalchs Konsthall, Stockholm.

Lind, Michael D.

1994 Cholula and Mixteca Polychromes. In *Mixteca-Puebla: Discoveries and Research in Mesoamerican Art and Archaeology* (H. B. Nicholson and Eloise Quiñones Keber, eds.): 79–99. Labyrinthos, Culver City, Calif.

Lindauer, Margaret A.

1999 *Devouring Frida: The Art History and Popular Celebrity of Frida Kahlo.* University Press of New England, Hanover, N.H.

Linné, Sigvald

1956 *Treasures of Mexican Art: Two Thousand Years of Art and Art Handicraft* (Albert Read, trans.). Nordisk Rotogravyr, Stockholm.

2003a *Archaeological Researches at Teotihuacan, Mexico.* University of Alabama Press, Tuscaloosa. Originally published 1934, V. Petterson, Stockholm.

2003b *Mexican Highland Cultures: Archaeological Researches at Teotihuacan, Calpulalpan, and Chalchicomula in 1934–35.* University of Alabama Press, Tuscaloosa. Originally published 1942, Stockholm.

Lino Fábrega, José

1900 *Interpretación del Códice Borgiano.* Museo Nacional de México, Mexico City.

Lippincott, Kristen

1999 *The Story of Time.* Merrell Holberton, London.

Lombardo de Ruíz, Sonia

1995 El estilo teotihuacano en la pintura mural. In *La pintura mural prehispánica en México.* Vol. 1, *Teotihuacán,* bk. 2: *Estudios* (Beatriz de la Fuente, ed.): 3–64. Universidad Nacional Autónoma de México, Instituto de Investigaciones Estéticas, Mexico City.

Lombardo de Ruíz, Sonia, Diana López de Molina, Daniel Molina Feal, Carolyn Baus de Czitrom, and Oscar J. Polaco

1991 *Cacaxtla: El lugar donde muere la lluvia en la tierra.* Gobierno del Estado de Tlaxcala and Instituto Tlaxcalteca de Cultura, Mexico City.

López Austin, Alfredo

1993 *The Myths of the Opossum: Pathways of Mesoamerican Mythology.* University of New Mexico Press, Albuquerque.

1996 *The Rabbit on the Face of the Moon: Mythology in the Mesoamerican Tradition.* University of Utah Press, Salt Lake City.

López Luján, Leonardo

1993 *Las ofrendas del Templo Mayor de Tenochtitlan.* Instituto Nacional de Antropología e Historia, Mexico City.

1995 Xochicalco. In *Xochicalco y Tula* (Leonardo López Luján, Robert Cobean, and Alba Guadalupe Mastache Flores): 15–141. Consejo Nacional para la Cultura y las Artes, Mexico City, and Jaca Book, Milan.

2005 *The Offerings of the Templo Mayor of Tenochtitlan* (Bernard R. Ortiz de Montellano and Thelma Ortiz de Montellano, trans.). University of New Mexico Press, Albuquerque.

2006 *La Casa de las Águilas: Un ejemplo de la arquitectura religiosa de Tenochtitlan.* 2 vols. Consejo Nacional para la Cultura y las Artes, Instituto Nacional de Antropología e Historia, and Fondo de Cultura Económica, Mexico City.

López Mestas, Lorenza, and Jorge Ramos

1998 Excavating the Tomb at Huitzilapa. In *Ancient West Mexico: Art and Archaeology of the Unknown Past* (Richard F. Townsend, ed.): 53–69. Art Institute of Chicago, Chicago, and Thames and Hudson, New York.

López Portillo, José, Miguel León Portilla, and Eduardo Matos Moctezuma

1981 *El Templo Mayor.* Bancomer, Mexico City.

López Portillo, José, Demetrio Sodi, and Fernando Díaz Infante

1982 *Quetzalcoatl: In Myth, Archaeology, and Art.* Continuum, New York.

Lothrop, Samuel Kirkland

1933 *Atitlan: An Archaeological Study of Ancient Remains on the Borders of Lake Atitlan, Guatemala.* Carnegie Institution of Washington Publication 444. Carnegie Institution of Washington, Washington, D.C.

1936 *Zacualpa, a Study of Ancient Quiche Artifacts.* Carnegie Institution of Washington Publication 472. Carnegie Institution of Washington, Washington, D.C.

Louisiana Museum

1987 *Mexicos kunst—før spanierne kom.* Louisiana Revy 28. Louisiana Museum, Humlebæk, Denmark.

Lowe, Lynneth S.

1998 *El salvamento arqueológico de la presa de Mal Paso, Chiapas: Excavaciones menores.* Centro de Estudios Mayas 24. Universidad Nacional Autónoma de México, Mexico City.

Lozano, Luis-Martín, and Juan Rafael Coronel Rivera

2007 *Diego Rivera: Obra Mural Completa.* Taschen, Cologne.

Luke, Christina

2003 Ulúa-Style Marble Vase Project. Report to FAMSI. Electronic document, http://www.famsi.org/reports/02081/index.html, accessed November 2005.

Luke, Christina, Rosemary A. Joyce, John S. Henderson, and Robert H. Tykot

2003 Marble Carving Traditions in Honduras. In *ASMOSIA 6: Interdisciplinary Studies on Ancient Stone* (L. Lazzarini, ed.): 485–496. Bottega d'Erasmo, Padua.

Lumholtz, Carl

1904 *Bland mexikos indianer.* 2 vols. A. Bonnier, Stockholm.

Mahler, Joy

1965 Garments and Textiles of the Maya Lowlands. In *Archaeology of Southern Mesoamerica,* Pt. 2 (Gordon R. Willey, ed.): 581–593. *Handbook of Middle American Indians,* Vol. 3 (Robert Wauchope, ed.). University of Texas Press, Austin.

Márquez, Pietro José

1804 *Du antichi monumenti di architettura messicana illustrati.* Press il Salomoni, Rome.

Marquina, Ignacio

1951 *Arquitectura prehispánica.* Memorias del Instituto Nacional de Antropología e Historia 1. Secretaría de Educación Publica and Instituto Nacional de Antropología e Historia, Mexico City.

Martin, Simon

2001 The Power in the West—The Maya and Teotihuacan. In *Maya: Divine Kings of the Rain Forest* (Nikolai Grube, ed.): 99–111. Könemann, Cologne, Germany.

Martin, Simon, and Nikolai Grube

2000 *Chronicle of the Maya Kings and Queens: Deciphering the Dynasties of the Ancient Maya.* Thames and Hudson, London and New York.

Marx, Gertie F.

1982 "Natural" Childbirth. *AECOM* Spring: 11.

Mason, J. Alden

1958 Review of *Pre-Columbian Art* (1957). *Archaeology* 11 (2): 123–124.

Matos Moctezuma, Eduardo

1990 *Treasures of the Great Temple.* Fundación Universo Veintiuno and ALTI, La Jolla, Calif.

1994 *The Great Temple of the Aztecs.* Thames and Hudson, London and New York.

2003 Embarazo, parto y niñez en el México prehispanico/Las edades del hombre en Mesoamerica. *Arqueología mexicana* 10 (60): 1, 16–21.

Matos Moctezuma, Eduardo, and Felipe Solís Olguin
2002 *Aztecs.* Royal Academy of Arts, London

Mazzetti, Giuseppe
1993 Alcuni dati sulla doratura degli atlatl del Museo Nazionale de Antropologia e Etnologia. Appendix to "I due antichi atlatl messicani del Museo Nazionale di Antropología e Etnología di Firenze," by Laura Laurencich Minelli. *Archivio per l'antropologia e la etnología* 133: 402–403.

McAndrew, John
1965 *The Open-Air Churches of Sixteenth-Century Mexico.* Harvard University Press, Cambridge, Mass.

McBride, Harold W.
1969 The Extent of the Chupícuaro Tradition. In *The Natalie Wood Collection of Pre-Columbian Ceramics from Chupícuaro, Guanajuato, Mexico, at UCLA* (Jay D. Frierman, ed.): 31–49. Museum and Laboratories of Ethnic Arts and Technology, University of California, Los Angeles.

McElvaine, Robert S.
2001 *Eve's Seed: Biology, the Sexes, and the Course of History.* McGraw-Hill, New York.

McEwan, Colin
1994 *Ancient Mexico in the British Museum.* British Museum Press, London.

Medellín Zenil, Alfonso
1960 *Cerámicas del Totonacapan; Exploraciones arqueológicas en el centro de Veracruz.* Instituto de Antropología, Universidad Veracruzana, Xalapa.
1962 El monolito de Maltrata, Veracruz. *La palabra y el hombre* 24: 555–562.
1971 *Monolitos olmecas y otros en el Museo de la Universidad de Veracruz.* Corpus antiquitatum americanensium 5. Instituto Nacional de Antropología e Historia, Mexico City.
1983 *Obras maestras del Museo de Xalapa.* Studio Beatrice Trueblood, Mexico City.

Meeks, Nigel
n.d. Report on the Scientific Examination of the Gilding on an Aztec Spear Thrower. Manuscript on file, Brandeis University, Department of Anthropology, Waltham, Mass., 1992.

Meer, Ron van
n.d. Los procesos inquisitoriales de San Juan Teitipac, Valle de Tlacolula, Oaxaca (1560–1574). Presentación, transcripción y estudio introductorio. Mansucript on file, Brandeis University, Department of Anthropology, Waltham, Mass., 2002.

Mexican Fine Arts Center Museum
1992 *México, la visión del cosmos.* Mexican Fine Arts Center Museum, Chicago.

Miller, Arthur G.
1973 *The Mural Painting of Teotihuacan.* Dumbarton Oaks Research Library and Collection, Washington, D.C.

Miller, Mary Ellen
1986 *The Art of Mesoamerica: From Olmec to Aztec.* Thames and Hudson, New York.
1991 Rethinking the Classic Sculptures of Cerro de las Mesas, Veracruz. In *Settlement Archaeology of Cerro de las Mesas, Veracruz, Mexico* (Barbara L. Stark, ed.): 26–38. Monograph 34. Institute of Archaeology, University of California, Los Angeles.

Miller, Mary Ellen, and Karl Taube
1993 *The Gods and Symbols of Ancient Mexico and the Maya.* Thames and Hudson, New York.

Millon, Clara
1972 The History of Mural Art at Teotihuacan. In *Teotihuacán: Onceava Mesa Redonda,* Vol 2: 1–16. Sociedad Mexicana de Antropología, Mexico City.
1973 Painting, Writing, and Polity in Teotihuacan, Mexico. *American Antiquity* 38: 294–314.
1988 Great Goddess Fragment. In *Feathered Serpents and Flowering Trees: Reconstructing the Murals of Teotihuacán* (Kathleen Berrin, ed.): 226–228. Fine Arts Museums of San Francisco, San Francisco.

Millon, Clara, and Evelyn Rattray
1972 An Extraordinary Teotihuacan Mural. *Muse* 6: 46–48.

Millon, René
1992 Teotihuacan Studies. In *Art, Ideology, and the City of Teotihuacan* (Janet Catherine Berlo, ed.): 339–419. Dumbarton Oaks Research Library and Collection, Washington, D.C.
1993 The Place Where Time Began. In *Teotihuacan: Art from the City of the Gods* (Kathleen Berrin and Esther Pasztory, eds.): 17–43. Fine Arts Museums of San Francisco, San Francisco, and Thames and Hudson, New York.

Millon, René (ed.)
1973 *Urbanization at Teotihuacán, Mexico.* University of Texas Press, Austin.

Mirkin, Dina Comisarenco
1999 Images of Childbirth in Modern Mexican Art. *Woman's Art Journal* 20 (1): 18–24.

Moedano Koer, Hugo
1957 Informe preliminar sobre las exploraciones en San Luis Tlatilco. *Anales del Instituto Nacional de Antropología e Historia* 9: 73–84.

Moholy-Nagy, Hattula, and John M. Ladd
1992 Objects of Stone, Shell, and Bone. In *Artifacts from the Cenote of Sacrifice, Chichen Itza, Yucatán* (Clemency Chase Coggins, ed.): 99–152. Memoirs of the Peabody Museum of Archaeology and Ethnology, Harvard University, Vol. 10, no. 3. Harvard University Press, Cambridge, Mass.

Montolíu, María
1977 Algunos aspectos del venado en la religión de los mayas de Yucatán. *Estudios de cultura maya* 10: 149–172.

Moore, Frank W.
1966 An Excavation at Tetitla, Teotihuacan. *Mesoamerican Notes* 7–8: 69–85.

Morelos García, Noel
1982 Exploraciones en el area central de la Calzada de los Muertos al norte del Río San Juan, dentro del llamado Complejo Calle de los Muertos. In *Memoria del Proyecto Arqueológico Teotihuacán 80–82* (Rubén Cabrera Castro, Ignacio Rodríguez, and Noel Morelos, eds.): 311–314. Instituto Nacional de Antropología e Historia, Mexico City.

Motolinía, Toribio
1950 [1541] *History of the Indians of New Spain* (Elizabeth Andros Foster, ed. and trans.). Cortés Society, Berkeley, Calif.

Mountjoy, Joseph B.
1998 The Evolution of Complex Societies in West Mexico. In *Ancient West Mexico: Art and Archaeology of the Unknown Past* (Richard F. Townsend, ed.): 250–265. Art Institute of Chicago, Chicago, and Thames and Hudson, New York.

Murro, Juan Antonio
2004a Necklace with Decorated Beads. In *The Aztec Empire: Catalogue of the Exhibition* (Felipe Solís Olguín, ed.): 42, cat. no. 181. Guggenheim Museum Publications, New York.
2004b Skull Cup. In *The Aztec Empire: Catalogue of the Exhibition* (Felipe Solís Olguín, ed.): 47, cat. no. 204. Guggenheim Museum Publications, New York.

Musée National d'Art Moderne
1952 *Art mexicain du précolombien á nos jours.* 2nd ed. Presses artistiques, Paris.

Nakagawa, Motoko
2007 A Great Project Named Birth [in Japanese]. In *History of Birth* (Michihiko Oikawa, ed.): 189–197. Heibonsha, Tokyo.

National Geographic Society
1983 *Peoples and Places of the Past: The National Geographic Illustrated Cultural Atlas of the Ancient World.* National Geographic Society, Washington, D.C.

Natural History
1958 A Collection of Pre-Columbian Fine Art. *Natural History* 67 (3): 128–129.

Nebel, Charles
1836 *Voyage pittoresque et archéologique dans la partie la plus interessante du Mexique.* B. Dafour, Paris.

Nichols, Deborah L., and Charles D. Frederick
1993 Irrigation Canals and Chinampas. *Research in Economic Anthropology* Supplement 7: 123–150.

Nichols, Deborah L., Michael W. Spence, and Mark D. Borland
1991 Watering the Fields of Teotihuacan. *Ancient Mesoamerica* 2: 119–129.

Nicholson, H. B.
1971a Major Sculpture in Prehispanic Central Mexico. In *Archaeology of Northern Mesoamerica* (Gordon Ekholm and Ignacio Bernal, eds.): 92–132. *Handbook of Middle American Indians*, Vol. 10 (Robert Wauchope, ed.). University of Texas Press, Austin.
1971b Religion in Pre-Hispanic Central Mexico. In *Archaeology of Northern Mesoamerica* (Gordon Ekholm and Ignacio Bernal, eds.): 395–446. *Handbook of Middle American Indians*, Vol. 10 (Robert Wauchope, ed.). University of Texas Press, Austin.
1973 The Late Pre-Hispanic Central Mexican (Aztec) Iconographic System. In *The Iconography of Middle American Sculpture* (Ignacio Bernal et al., eds.): 72–97. Metropolitan Museum of Art, New York.
1976 Preclassic Mesoamerican Iconography from the Perspective of the Postclassic: Problems in Interpretational Analysis. In *Origins of Religious Art and Iconography in Preclassic Mesoamerica* (H. B. Nicholson, ed.): 157–175. UCLA Latin American Center Publications, Los Angeles.

Nicholson, H. B., with Eloise Quiñones Keber

1983 *Art of Aztec Mexico: Treasures of Tenochtitlan.* National Gallery of Art, Washington, D.C.

Nicholson, Irene

1967 *Mexican and Central American Mythology.* Hamlyn, London.

Niederberger Betton, Christine

2000 Ranked Societies, Iconographic Complexity, and Economic Wealth in the Basin of Mexico toward 122 B.C. In *Olmec Art and Archaeology in Mesoamerica* (John E. Clark and Mary E. Pye, eds.): 168–191. National Gallery of Art, Washington, D.C.

Noguera, Eduardo

1944 Exploraciones en Jiquilpan. *Anales del Museo Michoacano,* series 2, no. 3: 37–54.

Nuttall, Zelia

1891 *The Atlatl or Spear-Thrower of the Ancient Mexicans.* Archaeological and Ethnological Papers of the Peabody Museum, Harvard University 1, no. 3. Harvard University, Cambridge, Mass.

1910 The Island of Sacrificios. *American Anthropologist* 12: 257–295.

Oertwig, Siegfried, and Karl Friese

1960 *Gang durch versunkene Städte: Ein Ausflug ins Reich der Archäologie.* 5th ed. Prisma-Verlag, Leipzig.

Olivier, Guilhem

1997 *Moqueries et métamorphoses d'un dieu aztèque: Tezcatlipoca, le "Seigneur au umant."* Mémoires de l'Institut d'Ethnologie 33. Institut d'Ethnologie, Musée de l'Homme, Paris.

2003 *Mockeries and Metamorphoses of an Aztec God: Tezcatlipoca, "Lord of the Smoking Mirror."* University Press of Colorado, Boulder.

2004 De flechas, dardos y saetas. In *De historiografía lingüística e historia de las lenguas* (Juan M. Lope Blanch, Ignacio Guzmán Betancourt, Pilar Máynez, and Ascensión H. de León-Portilla, eds.): 309–324. Universidad Nacional Autónoma de México and Siglo Veintiuno editores, Mexico City.

Ortiz C., Ponciano, Ma. Del Carmen Rodríguez M., and Alfredo Delgado C.

1997 *Las investigaciones arqueológicas en el Cerro Sagrado Manatí.* Universidad Veracruzana, Xalapa.

Oudijk, Michel

2002 La Toma de Posesión. *Relaciones (Colegio de Michoacán)* 23 (91): 97–131.

Paddock, John

1966 Oaxaca in Ancient Mesoamerica. In *Ancient Oaxaca* (John Paddock, ed.): 83–241. Stanford University Press, Stanford, Calif.

Pahl, Gary

1977 The Iconography of an Engraved Olmec Figurine. In *Pre-Columbian Art History: Selected Readings* (Alana Cordy-Collins and Jean Stern, eds.): 35–42. Peek, Palo Alto, Calif.

Palacio de Bellas Artes

1934 *Exposición de escultura mexicana antigua, 1934.* Palacio de Bellas Artes, Mexico City.

Palacios, Enrique Juan

1926 *Yohualichan y el Tajín, monumentos arqueológicos en Cuetzalán, descubiertos por la Dirección de Arqueología.* Talleres Gráficos de la Nación, Mexico City.

1935 La cintura de serpientes de la Pirámide de Tenayuca. In *Tenayuca: Estudio arqueológico de la piramide de este lugar, hecho por el Departamento de Monumentos de la Secretaría de Educación Pública.* Talleres Gráficos del Museo Nacional de Arqueología, Historia y Etnografía, Mexico City.

Palacios, Enrique Juan, and Enrique Meyer

1932 *La ciudad arqueológica del Tajín.* La Impresora, Mexico City.

Palavicini, Beatriz, and Gilberto Reyes Zepeda

2005 El Museo de Sitio de Cacaxtla, Tlaxcala. *Arqueología mexicana* 13 (75): 72–75.

Palencia, José Servin

1959 Las artes menores. *Esplendor del México antiguo* 1: 407, fig. 20.

Parsons, Lee A.

1969 *Bilbao, Guatemala: An Archaeological Study of the Pacific Coast, Cotzumalhuapa Region,* Vol. 2. Publications in Anthropology 11–12. Milwaukee Public Museum, Milwaukee, Wis.

1980 *Pre-Columbian Art: The Morton D. May and the Saint Louis Art Museum Collections.* Harper and Row, New York.

Parsons, Lee A., John B. Carlson, and Peter D. Joralemon

1988 *The Face of Ancient America: The Wally and Brenda Zollman Collection of Pre-Columbian Art.* Indianapolis Museum of Art and Indiana University Press, Bloomington.

Pasztory, Esther

1974 *The Iconography of the Teotihuacan Tlaloc.* Studies in Pre-Columbian Art and Archaeology 15. Dumbarton Oaks, Trustees for Harvard University, Washington, D.C.

1976 *The Murals of Tepantitla, Teotihuacan.* Garland, New York.

1982 Three Aztec Masks of the God Xipe. In *Falsifications and Misreconstructions of Pre-Columbian Art* (Elizabeth H. Boone, ed.): 77–105. Dumbarton Oaks, Trustees for Harvard University, Washington, D.C.

1983 *Aztec Art.* Harry N. Abrams, New York.

1988a A Reinterpretation of Teotihuacan and Its Mural Painting Tradition. In *Feathered Serpents and Flowering Trees: Reconstructing the Murals of Teotihuacán* (Kathleen Berrin, ed.): 45–77. Fine Arts Museums of San Francisco, San Francisco.

1988b Small Birds with Shields and Spears and Other Fragments. In *Feathered Serpents and Flowering Trees: Reconstructing the Murals of Teotihuacán* (Kathleen Berrin, ed.): 168–183. Fine Arts Museums of San Francisco, San Francisco.

1992 Abstraction and the Rise of a Utopian State at Teotihuacan. In *Art, Ideology, and the City of Teotihuacan* (Janet Catherine Berlo, ed.): 281–320. Dumbarton Oaks Research Library and Collection, Washington, D.C.

1993a Ceramics. In *Teotihuacan: Art from the City of the Gods* (Kathleen Berrin and Esther Pasztory, eds.): 236. Fine Arts Museums of San Francisco, San Francisco, and Thames and Hudson, New York.

1993b Mask. In *Teotihuacan: Art from the City of the Gods* (Kathleen Berrin and Esther Pasztory, eds.): 18–87. Fine Arts Museums of San Francisco, San Francisco, and Thames and Hudson, New York.

1993c Mask. In *Teotihuacan: Art from the City of the Gods* (Kathleen Berrin and Esther Pasztory, eds.): 188. Fine Arts Museums of San Francisco, San Francisco, and Thames and Hudson, New York.

1993d Miniature Mask with Necklace. In *Teotihuacan: Art from the City of the Gods* (Kathleen Berrin and Esther Pasztory, eds.): 193. Fine Arts Museums of San Francisco, San Francisco, and Thames and Hudson, New York.

1993e Teotihuacan Unmasked. In *Teotihuacan: Art from the City of the Gods* (Kathleen Berrin and Esther Pasztory, eds.): 44–63. Fine Arts Museums of San Francisco, San Francisco, and Thames and Hudson, New York.

1997 *Teotihuacan: An Experiment in Living.* University of Oklahoma Press, Norman.

1998a *Pre-Columbian Art.* Cambridge University Press, Cambridge and New York.

1998b Truth in Forgery. *Res* 42: 159–165.

2005 *Thinking with Things: Toward a New Vision of Art.* University of Texas Press, Austin.

Paxson, James J.

1998 The Nether-Faced Devil and the Allegory of Parturition. *Studies in Iconography* 19: 139–176.

Peabody Museum of Archaeology and Ethnology and Fogg Art Museum

1940 *An Exhibition of Pre-Columbian Art.* Fogg Art Museum, Harvard University, Cambridge, Mass.

Pérez Campa, Mario

1998 La Estela de Cuicuilco. *Arqueología mexicana* 5 (30): 37.

Peterson, Frederick

1959 *Ancient Mexico: An Introduction to the Pre-Hispanic Cultures.* Putnam, New York.

Pijoán, José

1946 *Arte precolombiano, mexicano y maya.* Espasa-Calpe, Madrid.

Pillsbury, Joanne

1996 The Thorny Oyster and the Origins of Empire. *Latin American Antiquity* 7: 313–340.

Piña Chán, Román

1958 *Tlatilco.* Serie investigaciones 1–2. Instituto Nacional de Antropología e Historia, Mexico City.

1960 *Mesoamérica: Ensayo histórico cultural.* Memorias 6. Instituto Nacional de Antropología e Historia, Mexico City.

Pleasants, Frederick R.

1940 Pre-Columbian Art at the Fogg. *Magazine of Art* 33 (2): 84–91.

Pohl, Mary

1981 Ritual Continuity and Transformation in Mesoamerica. *American Antiquity* 46: 513–529.

Pollard, Helen Perlstein, and Michael E. Smith

2003 The Aztec/Tarascan Border. In *The Postclassic Mesoamerican World* (Michael E. Smith and Frances F. Berdan, eds.): 87–90. University of Utah Press, Salt Lake City.

Porter [Weaver], Muriel Noë

1953 *Tlatilco and the Pre-Classic Cultures of the New World.* Viking Fund Publications in Anthropology 19. Wenner-Gren Foundation for Anthropological Research, New York.

1956 *Excavations at Chupícuaro, Guanajuato, Mexico.* Transactions of the American Philosophical Society 46, pt. 5. American Philosophical Society, Philadelphia, Pa.

Preble, Duane

1976 *We Create Art, Art Creates Us.* Canfield, San Francisco.

Proskouriakoff, Tatiana

1954 *Varieties of Classic Central Veracruz Sculpture.* Contributions to American Anthropology and History 58: 61–93. Carnegie Institution of Washington, Washington, D.C.

1974 *Jades from the Cenote of Sacrifice, Chichen Itza, Yucatan.* Peabody Museum of Archaeology and Ethnology, Harvard University, Cambridge, Mass.

Quilter, Jeffrey

1989 *Life and Death at Paloma: Society and Mortuary Practices in a Preceramic Peruvian Village.* University of Iowa Press, Iowa City.

2004 *Cobble Circles and Standing Stones: Archaeology at the Rivas Site, Costa Rica.* University of Iowa Press, Iowa City.

2005 *Treasures of the Andes: The Glories of Inca and Pre-Columbian South America.* Duncan Baird, London.

Rademacher, Cay

2004 Azteken. *Geoepoche: Das Magazin für Geschichte* (15): 96–111.

Rands, Robert, L.

1965 Jades of the Maya Lowlands. In *Archaeology of Southern Mesoamerica,* Pt. 2 (Gordon R. Willey, ed.): 561–580. *Handbook of Middle American Indians,* Vol. 3 (Robert Wauchope, ed.). University of Texas Press, Austin.

Rattray, Evelyn Childs

1992 *The Teotihuacan Burials and Offerings: A Commentary and Inventory.* Vanderbilt University Publications in Anthropology 42. Vanderbilt University, Nashville, Tenn.

1997 *Entierros y ofrendas en Teotihuacan.* Universidad Nacional Autónoma de México, Instituto de Investigaciones Antropológicas, Mexico City.

Rautenstrauch-Joest-Museum für Völkerkunde and Wallraf-Richartz-Museum

1959 *Kunst der Mexikaner.* Rautenstrauch-Joest-Museum, Cologne.

Read, Herbert Edward

1956 *The Art of Sculpture.* Pantheon, New York.

Reed, Alma

1966 *The Ancient Past of Mexico.* Crown, New York.

Reents-Budet, Dorie

1994 *Painting the Maya Universe: Royal Ceramics of the Classic Period.* Duke University Press, Durham, N.C.

Rickenbach, Judith (ed.)

1997 *Mexico: Präkolumbische Kulturen am Gulf von Mexiko.* Museum Rietberg, Zurich.

Rivet, Paul

1954 *Mexique précolombien.* Editions ides et calendes, Neuchâtel and Paris.

Robertson, Donald

1959 Review of *Pre-Columbian Art* (1957). *College Art Journal* 19: 106–107.

Rodríguez, Luis Angel

1940 La leyenda de las pirámides. *Zeta* 8: 27–33.

Rodríguez M., María del Carmen, and Ponciano Ortiz C.

1994 *El Manatí: Un espacio sagrado olmeca.* Universidad Veracruzana, Xalapa.

Romano, Arturo

1967 Tlatilco. *Boletín del Instituto Nacional de Antropología e Historia* 30: 38–42.

Romero, Javier

1986 *Catálogo de la colección de dientes mutilados prehispánicos: IV parte.* Instituto Nacional de Antropología e Historia, Mexico City.

Rubín de la Borbolla, Daniel, Marc Jost, and Laboratorios Grupo Roussel (Mexico)

1952 *Medicina pre-cortesiana.* Grupo Roussel, Mexico City.

Ruíz, Diego

1785 Papantla. *Gazeta de México,* 12 July. Mexico City.

Ruíz de Alarcón, Hernando

1984 [1629] *Treatise on the Heathen Superstitions that Live Today among the Indians Native to This New Spain* (J. Richard Andrews and Ross Hassig, trans. and eds.). University of Oklahoma Press, Norman.

Ruíz Gallut, María Elena, Jesús Galindo Trejo, and Daniel Flores Gutiérrez

1996 Implicaciones arqueoastronómicas de pórticos con felinos en Teotihuacan. In *La pintura mural prehispánica en México*. Vol. 1, *Teotihuacán*, bk. 2: *Estudios* (Beatriz de la Fuente, ed.): 343–360. Universidad Nacional Autónoma de México, Instituto de Investigaciones Estéticas, Mexico City.

Sáenz, Cesar

1963 Exploraciones en la Pirámide de las Serpientes Emplumadas, Xochicalco. *Revista mexicana de estudios antropológicos* 19: 7–25.

1964 *Ultimos descubrimientos en Xochicalco*. Instituto Nacional de Antropología e Historia, Mexico City.

Sahagún, Bernardino de

1959 [1569] *The Merchants*. Bk. 9 of *Florentine Codex: General History of the Things of New Spain* (Arthur J. O. Anderson and Charles E. Dibble, trans. and eds.). School of American Research, Santa Fe, N.Mex., and University of Utah, Salt Lake City.

1961 [1569] *The People*. Bk. 10 of *Florentine Codex: General History of the Things of New Spain* (Arthur J. O. Anderson and Charles E. Dibble, trans. and eds.). School of American Research, Santa Fe, N.Mex., and University of Utah, Salt Lake City.

1963 [1569] *Earthly Things*. Bk. 11 of *Florentine Codex: General History of the Things of New Spain* (Arthur J. O. Anderson and Charles E. Dibble, trans. and eds.). School of American Research, Santa Fe, N.Mex., and University of Utah, Salt Lake City.

1969 [1569] *Rhetoric and Moral Philosophy*. Bk. 6 of *Florentine Codex: General History of the Things of New Spain* (Arthur J. O. Anderson and Charles E. Dibble, trans. and eds.). School of American Research, Santa Fe, N.Mex., and University of Utah, Salt Lake City.

1970 [1569] *The Gods*. Bk. 1 of *Florentine Codex: General History of the Things of New Spain* (Arthur J. O. Anderson and Charles E. Dibble, trans. and eds.). School of American Research, Santa Fe, N.Mex., and University of Utah, Salt Lake City.

1978 [1569] *The Origin of the Gods*. Bk. 3 of *Florentine Codex: General History of the Things of New Spain* (Arthur J. O. Anderson and Charles E. Dibble, trans. and eds.). School of American Research, Santa Fe, N.Mex., and University of Utah, Salt Lake City.

1979a [1569] *Kings and Lords*. Bk. 8 of *Florentine Codex: General History of the Things of New Spain* (Arthur J. O. Anderson and Charles E. Dibble, trans. and eds.). School of American Research, Santa Fe, N.Mex., and University of Utah, Salt Lake City.

1979b [1569] *The Omens*. Bk. 5 of *Florentine Codex: General History of the Things of New Spain* (Arthur J. O. Anderson and Charles E. Dibble, trans. and eds.). School of American Research, Santa Fe, N.Mex., and University of Utah, Salt Lake City.

1979c [1569] *The Soothsayers*. Bk. 4 of *Florentine Codex: General History of the Things of New Spain* (Arthur J. O. Anderson and Charles E. Dibble, trans. and eds.). School of American Research, Santa Fe, N.Mex., and University of Utah, Salt Lake City.

Sánchez Sánchez, Jesús

1982a El Conjunto NW del Río San Juan. In *Teotihuacán 80–82: Primeros resultados* (Rubén Cabrera Castro, Ignacio Rodríguez, and Noel Morelos, eds.): 227–246. Instituto Nacional de Antropología e Historia, Mexico City.

1982b Exploraciones en el área SW del Complejo Calle de los Muertos. In *Teotihuacán 80–82: Primeros resultados* (Rubén Cabrera Castro, Ignacio Rodríguez, and Noel Morelos, eds.): 249–270. Instituto Nacional de Antropología e Historia, Mexico City.

Sánchez Scott, Daniel (ed.)

2001 *Tesoros de Oaxaca*. Gobierno Constitucional del Estado de Oaxaca and Instituto Nacional de Antropología e Historia, Mexico City.

Sanders, William T., and Susan Toby Evans

2006 Rulership and Palaces at Teotihuacan. In *Palaces and Power in the Americas: From Peru to the Northwest Coast* (Jessica Joyce Christie and Patricia Joan Sarro, eds.): 256–284. University of Texas Press, Austin.

Santa Barbara Museum of Art

1942 *Ancient American Art, 500 B.C.–A.D. 1500: The Catalog of an Exhibit of the Art of the Pre-European Americas*. Santa Barbara Museum of Art, Santa Barbara, Calif.

Sarro, Patricia Joan

2006 Rising Above: The Elite Acropolis of El Tajín. In *Palaces and Power in the Americas: From Peru to the Northwest Coast* (Jessica Joyce Christie and Patricia Joan Sarro, eds.): 166–188. University of Texas Press, Austin.

Saunders, Nicholas J.

1989 *People of the Jaguar: The Living Spirit of Ancient America*. Souvenir, London.

2001 A Dark Light. *World Archaeology* 33: 220–236.

2002 Mirror or Portable Altar. In *Aztecs* (Eduardo Matos Moctezuma and Felipe Solís Olguin, eds.): 484, cat. no. 335. Royal Academy of Arts, London.

2003 "Catching the Light": Technologies of Power and Enchantment in Pre-Columbian Goldworking. In *Gold and Power in Ancient Costa Rica, Panama, and Colombia* (Jeffrey Quilter and John W. Hoopes, eds.): 15–47. Dumbarton Oaks Research Library and Collection, Washington, D.C.

2004a *Ancient Americas: The Great Civilisations*. Sutton, Stroud, Gloucestershire.

2004b Mirror or Portable Altar. In *The Aztec Empire: Catalogue of the Exhibition* (Felipe Solís Olguín, ed.): 77, cat. no. 362. Guggenheim Museum Publications, New York.

2005 *Peoples of the Caribbean: An Encyclopedia of Caribbean Archaeology and Traditional Culture*. ABC-CLIO, Santa Barbara, Calif.

Saunders, Nicholas J. (ed.)

1998 *Icons of Power: Feline Symbolism in the Americas*. Routledge, London.

Saville, Marshall H.

1899 Exploration of Zapotec Tombs in Southern Mexico. *American Anthropologist* 1: 350–362.

1900 An Onyx Jar from Mexico, in Process of Manufacture. *Bulletin of the American Museum of Natural History* 13: 105–107.

1920 *The Goldsmith's Art in Ancient Mexico*. Indian Notes and Monographs 7. Museum of the American Indian, Heye Foundation, New York.

1925 *The Wood-Carver's Art in Ancient Mexico*. Contributions from the Museum of the American Indian, Heye Foundation 9. Museum of the American Indian, Heye Foundation, New York.

Sawyer, Alan, and John Wise

n.d. Comment about PC.B.092. Manuscript on file, Dumbarton Oaks Research Library and Collection, Washington, D.C.

Scarborough, Vernon L., and David R. Wilcox (eds.)

1991 *The Mesoamerican Ballgame*. University of Arizona Press, Tucson.

Schele, Linda, and Mary Miller

1986 *The Blood of Kings: Dynasty and Ritual in Maya Art*. George Braziller, New York, and Kimbell Art Museum, Fort Worth, Tex.

Schmidt, Peter, Mercedes de la Garza, and Enrique Nalda (eds.)

1998 *Maya*. Bompiani, Venice.

Schulz, Matthias

2008 Gralsburg im Regenwald. *Der Spiegel*, 10 May: 164–167.

Scott, John F.

1999 *Latin American Art: Ancient to Modern*. University Press of Florida, Gainesville.

Seipel, Wilfried (ed.)

1998 *Henry Moore, 1898–1986: Eine Retrospektive zum 100. Geburtstag*, Skira, Milan, and Kunsthistorisches Museum, Vienna.

Séjourné, Laurette

1959 *Un palacio en la ciudad de los dioses, Teotihuacán*. Instituto Nacional de Antropología e Historia, Mexico City.

1962a Interpretación de un jeroglífico teotihuacano. *Cuadernos americanos* 22 (3): 133–181.

1962b *El universo de Quetzalcoatl*. Fondo de Cultura Económica, Mexico City.

1966a *Arquitectura y pintura en Teotihuacán*. Siglo Veintiuno Editores, Mexico City.

1966b *El lenguaje de las formas en Teotihuacán*. Gabriel Mancera, Mexico City.

Seler, Eduard

1991 [1901] Excavations at the Site of the Principal Temple in Mexico. In *Collected Works in Mesoamerican Linguistics and Archaeology*, Vol. 3 (J. Eric S. Thompson, Francis B. Richardson, and Frank E. Comparato, eds.): 114–193. Labyrinthos, Culver City, Calif.

1991 [1904] Ancient Mexican Throwing Sticks. In *Collected Works in Mesoamerican Linguistics and Archaeology by Eduard Seler*, Vol. 2 (J. Eric S. Thompson, Francis B. Richardson, and Frank E. Comparato, eds.): 203–219. Labyrinthos, Culver City, Calif.

1996 [1904] Scenic Pictures on Old Mexican Mosaics. In *Collected Works in Mesoamerican Linguistics and Archaeology by Eduard Seler*, Vol. 5 (J. Eric S. Thompson, Francis B. Richardson, and Frank E. Comparato, eds.): 116–129. Labyrinthos, Culver City, Calif.

Sempowski, Martha L.

1992 Economic and Social Implications of Variations in Mortuary Practices at Teotihuacan. In *Art, Ideology, and the City of Teotihuacan* (Janet Catherine Berlo, ed.): 27–58. Dumbarton Oaks Research Library and Collection, Washington, D.C.

1994 Mortuary Practices at Teotihuacan. In *Mortuary Practices and Skeletal Remains at Teotihuacan* (Martha L. Sempowski and Michael W. Spence): 1–314. University of Utah Press, Salt Lake City.

Sepúlveda y Herrera, María Teresa

1999 *Procesos por idolatría al cacique, gobernadores y sacerdotes de Yanhuitlán, 1544–1546*. Colección científica 396. Instituto Nacional de Antropología e Historia, Mexico City.

Serra Puche, Mari Carmen, and Felipe Solís Olguín (eds.)

1994 *Cristales y obsidiana prehispánicos*. Siglo Veintiuno Editores, Mexico City.

Seymour, Charles

1949 *Tradition and Experiment in Modern Sculpture*. American University Press, Washington, D.C.

Shlain, Leonard

2003 *Sex, Time, and Power: How Women's Sexuality Shaped Human Evolution*. Viking, New York.

Sjöö, Monica, and Barbara Mor

1987 *The Great Cosmic Mother: Rediscovering the Religion of the Earth*. Harper and Row, San Francisco.

Smith, A. Ledyard, and Alfred V. Kidder

1951 *Excavations at Nebaj, Guatemala*. Carnegie Institution of Washington Publication 594. Carnegie Institution of Washington, Washington, D.C.

Smith, Michael E.

1996 *The Aztecs*. Blackwell, Oxford and Cambridge, Mass.

2003 Key Commodities. In *The Postclassic Mesoamerican World* (Michael E. Smith and Frances F. Berdan, eds.): 117–125. University of Utah Press, Salt Lake City.

Solís Olguín, Felipe

1982 The Formal Pattern of Anthropomorphic Sculpture and the Ideology of the Aztec State. In *The Art and Iconography of Late Post-Classic Central Mexico* (Elizabeth H. Boone, ed.): 73–110. Dumbarton Oaks, Trustees for Harvard University, Washington, D.C.

1991 Vase with the Effigy of the God of Death. In *Circa 1492: Art in the Age of Exploration* (Jay A. Levenson, ed.): 546. National Gallery of Art, Washington, D.C., and Yale University Press, New Haven, Conn.

Solís Olguín, Felipe (ed.)

2004 *The Aztec Empire: Catalogue of the Exhibition*. Guggenheim Museum Publications, New York.

Solís Olguín, Felipe, and Martha Carmona Macías

1995 *El oro precolombino de México: Colecciones mixteca y azteca*. Américo Arte Editores, Mexico City.

Solís Olguín, Felipe, and Ted J. J. Leyenaar

2002 *Art Treasures of Ancient Mexico: Journey to the Land of the Gods*. De Nieuwe Kerk and Waanders in association with Lund Humphries, Amsterdam.

Solís Olguin, Felipe, and Roberto Velasco Alonso

2002 Rabbit. In *Aztecs* (Eduardo Matos Moctezuma and Felipe Solís Olguín, eds.): 159, 417, cat. no. 72. Royal Academy of Arts, London.

Solís Olguín, Felipe, Martha Carmona Macías, and Eréndira Camarena Ortiz

1993 *Mobilier funéraire des zapoteèques et mixteques*. Europalia Kredietbank, Brussels.

Sotheby's

1937 *Egyptian, Greek, Roman, Indian and South American Antiquities, Native Art*. [9 June 1937 auction]. London.

Soustelle, Jacques

1967a *Arts of Ancient Mexico*. Viking, New York.

1967b *Mexico*. Nagel, Geneva, Switzerland.

Stark, Barbara L.

2001 Figurines and Other Artifacts. In *Classic Period Mixtequilla, Veracruz, Mexico* (Barbara L. Stark, ed.): 179–226. Institute for Mesoamerican Studies Monograph 12. Institute for Mesoamerican Studies, University at Albany, Albany, N.Y.

Stark, Barbara L., Robert J. Speakman, and Michael D. Glascock

n.d. Inter-Regional and Regional Scale Compositional Variability in Pottery from South-central Veracruz, Mexico. Manuscript on file at MURR Laboratory, University of Missouri, Columbia, 2005.

Steele, Janet F., and Ralph Snavely

1997 Cueva Cheve Tablet. *Journal of Cave and Karst Studies* 59: 26–32.

Stingl, Miloslav

1976 *Indianer vor Kolumbus.* Union, Stuttgart.

Stirling, Matthew

1940 Great Stone Faces of the Mexican Jungle. *National Geographic* 78 (3): 309–334.

1943 *Stone Monuments of Southern Mexico.* Bulletin 138, Bureau of American Ethnology. Government Printing Office, Washington, D.C.

Stresser-Péan, Guy

2005 El volador: Datos históricos y simbolismo de la danza. *Arqueología mexicana* 13 (75): 20–27.

Struble, Stanley L.

2000 *Filth Eater.* Writers Club, San Jose, Calif.

Stuart, Gene S.

1988 *America's Ancient Cities.* National Geographic Society, Washington, D.C.

Stuart, George E.

2003 *Ancient Pioneers: The First Americans.* National Geographic Society, Washington, D.C.

Sugiyama, Saburo

1992 Rulership, Warfare, and Human Sacrifice at the Ciudadela. In *Art, Ideology, and the City of Teotihuacan* (Janet Catherine Berlo, ed.): 205–230. Dumbarton Oaks Research Library and Collection, Washington, D.C.

1998 Termination Programs and Prehispanic Looting at the Feathered Serpent Pyramid in Teotihuacan, Mexico. In *The Sowing and the Dawning: Termination, Dedication, and Transformation in the Archaeological and Ethnographic Record of Mesoamerica* (Shirley Boteler Mock, ed.): 147–164. University of New Mexico Press, Albuquerque.

2005 *Human Sacrifice, Militarism, and Rulership: Materialization of State Ideology at the Feathered Serpent Pyramid, Teotihuacan.* Cambridge University Press, Cambridge and New York.

Sullivan, Thelma D.

1963 Nahuatl Proverbs, Conundrums and Metaphors Collected by Sahagún. *Estudios de cultura náhuatl* 4: 93–178.

1982 Tlazolteotl-Ixcuina: The Great Spinner and Weaver. In *The Art and Iconography of Late Post-Classic Central Mexico* (Elizabeth H. Boone, ed.): 7–35. Dumbarton Oaks, Trustees for Harvard University, Washington, D.C.

Sydow, Eckart von

1923 *Die Kunst der Naturvölker und der Vorzeit.* Propyläen-Kunstgeschichte 1. Propyläen-Verlag, Berlin.

Taft Museum

1950 *Ancient American Gold and Jade: An Exhibition.* Taft Museum, Cincinnati, Ohio.

Tait, Hugh

1967 "The Devil's Looking Glass": The Magical Speculum of Dr. John Dee. In *Horace Walpole: Writer, Politician and Connoisseur* (Warren Hunting Smith, ed.): 195–212. Yale University Press, New Haven, Conn.

Tate Gallery

1953 *Exhibition of Mexican Art from Pre-Columbian Times to the Present Day, Organized under the Auspices of the Mexican Government. Tate Gallery, 4 March to 26 April.* Arts Council, London.

Taube, Karl A.

1983 The Teotihuacan Spider Woman. *Journal of Latin American Lore* 9: 107–189.

1988 A Study of Classic Maya Scaffold Sacrifice. In *Maya Iconography* (Elizabeth P. Benson and Gillett G. Griffin, eds.): 331–351. Princeton University Press, Princeton, N.J.

1992 The Iconography of Mirrors at Teotihuacan. In *Art, Ideology, and the City of Teotihuacan* (Janet Catherine Berlo, ed.): 169–204. Dumbarton Oaks Research Library and Collection, Washington, D.C.

1993 Bilimek Pulque Vessel: Starlore, Calendrics, and Cosmology of Late Postclassic Central Mexico. *Ancient Mesoamerica* 4: 1–15.

2000a The Turquoise Hearth: Fire, Self-Sacrifice, and the Central Mexican Cult of War. In *Mesoamerica's Classic Heritage: From Teotihuacan to the Aztecs* (David Carrasco, Lindsay Jones, and Scott Sessions, eds.): 269–340. University Press of Colorado, Boulder.

2000b *The Writing System of Ancient Teotihuacán.* Ancient America 1. Center for Ancient American Studies, Barnardsville, N.C.

2003 Tetitla and the Maya Presence at Teotihuacan. In *The Maya and Teotihuacan: Reinterpreting Early Classic Interaction* (Geoffrey E. Braswell, ed.): 273–314. University of Texas Press, Austin.

2004a Flower Mountain: Concepts of Life, Beauty, and Paradise among the Classic Maya. *Res* 45: 69–98.

2004b *Olmec Art at Dumbarton Oaks.* Pre-Columbian Art at Dumbarton Oaks 2. Dumbarton Oaks Research Library and Collection, Washington, D.C.

n.d. The Mirrors of Offerings 1 and 2 of Sala 2 in the Palacio Quemado at Tula: An Inconographic Interpretation. Manuscript on file, Brandeis University, Department of Anthropology, Waltham, Mass., 1998.

Taylor, Dicey

2000 A Chocolate Cup for Eternity in the Road of Awe: The Detroit Cylinder Tripod. *Bulletin of the Detroit Institute of Arts* 74 (1/2): 4–19.

Thompson, J. Eric S.

1939 *The Moon Goddess in Middle America, with Notes on Related Deities.* Contributions to American Anthropology and History 29. Carnegie Institution of Washington, Washington, D.C.

Thompson, Lana

1999 *The Wandering Womb: A Cultural History of Outrageous Beliefs about Women.* Prometheus, Amherst, N.Y.

Time

1959 Mexico: Treasure Traffic. *Time,* 30 March.

Tinoco, Becket Lailson

2004a Xiuhtecuhtli Pectoral. In *The Aztec Empire: Catalogue of the Exhibition* (Felipe Solís Olguín, ed.): 38, cat. no. 159. Guggenheim Museum Publications, New York.

2004b Pendant with the Figure of Xiuhtecuhtli. In *The Aztec Empire: Catalogue of the Exhibition* (Felipe Solís Olguín, ed.): 38, cat. no. 160. Guggenheim Museum Publications, New York.

2004c Xiuhtecuhtli Pendant. In *The Aztec Empire: Catalogue of the Exhibition* (Felipe Solís Olguín, ed.): 38, cat. no. 161. Guggenheim Museum Publications, New York.

Tolstoy, Paul

1989a Coapexco and Tlatilco: Sites with Olmec Materials in the Basin of Mexico. In *Regional Perspectives on the Olmec* (Robert J. Sharer and David C. Grove, eds.): 85–121. Cambridge University Press, Cambridge and New York.

1989b Western Mesoamerica and the Olmec. In *Regional Perspectives on the Olmec* (Robert J. Sharer and David C. Grove, eds.): 275–302. Cambridge University Press, Cambridge and New York.

Torquemada, Juan de

1943 [1615] *Monarquía indiana.* 3 vols. S. Chávez Hayhoe, Mexico City.

1975–83 [1615] *Monarquia indiana.* 7 vols. Universidad Nacional Autónoma de México, Instituto de Investigaciones Históricas, Mexico City.

Townsend, Richard F.

2000 *The Aztecs.* 2nd ed. Thames and Hudson, London.

Townsend, Richard F. (ed.)

1998 *Ancient West Mexico: Art and Archaeology of the Unknown Past.* Art Institute of Chicago, Chicago, and Thames and Hudson, New York.

Traxler, Loa P.

2002a Ear-spool. In *Aztecs* (Eduardo Matos Moctezuma and Felipe Solís Olguín, eds.): 448, cat. no. 195. Royal Academy of Arts, London.

2002b Ornament. In *Aztecs* (Eduardo Matos Moctezuma and Felipe Solís Olguín, eds.): 447, cat. no. 192. Royal Academy of Arts, London.

2002c Pendant. In *Aztecs* (Eduardo Matos Moctezuma and Felipe Solís Olguín, eds.): 478, cat. no. 314. Royal Academy of Arts, London.

2002d Pendants. In *Aztecs* (Eduardo Matos Moctezuma and Felipe Solís Olguín, eds.): 443, cat. no. 178. Royal Academy of Arts, London.

2002e Tlazolteotl. In *Aztecs* (Eduardo Matos Moctezuma and Felipe Solís Olguín, eds.): 479, cat. no. 320. Royal Academy of Arts, London.

2004a Fire Serpent (Xiuhcoatl). In *The Aztec Empire: Catalogue of the Exhibition* (Felipe Solís Olguín, ed.): 35, cat. no. 144. Guggenheim Museum Publications, New York.

2004b String of Snail Shaped Beads. In *The Aztec Empire: Catalogue of the Exhibition* (Felipe Solís Olguín, ed.): 42, cat. no. 178. Guggenheim Museum Publications, New York.

2004c Xipe Totec Pendant. In *The Aztec Empire: Catalogue of the Exhibition* (Felipe Solís Olguín, ed.): 51, cat. no. 224. Guggenheim Museum Publications, New York.

Trik, Helen, and Michael E. Kampen

1983 *The Graffiti of Tikal.* Tikal Report 31, University Museum Monograph 57. University Museum, University of Pennsylvania, Philadelphia, Pa.

Turner, Margaret H.

1992 Style in Lapidary Technology: Identifying the Teotihuacan Lapidary Industry. In *Art, Ideology, and the City of Teotihuacan* (Janet Catherine Berlo, ed.): 89–112. Dumbarton Oaks Research Library and Collection, Washington, D.C.

Umberger, Emily

1984 El trono de Moctezuma. *Estudios de cultura nahuatl* 17: 63–87.

1987 Antiques, Revivals, and References to the Past in Aztec Art. *Res* 13: 62–105.

1996 Monumental Sculpture. In *The Dictionary of Art* (Jane Turner, ed.): 21: 217–225. Oxford University Press, New York.

n.d. Notes on the Atlatl in the Bliss Collection. Manuscript on file, Brandeis University, Department of Anthropology, Waltham, Mass.

Urcid, Javier

1999 La lápida grabada de Noriega: Tres rituales en la vida de un noble Zapoteca. *Indiana* 16: 211–264.

2001 *Zapotec Hieroglyphic Writing.* Studies in Pre-Columbian Art and Archaeology 34. Dumbarton Oaks Research Library and Collection, Washington, D.C.

2002 La faz oculta de una misteriosa máscara de piedra. In *Sociedad y patrimonio arqueológico en el valle de Oaxaca* (Nelly M. Robles García, ed.). Consejo Nacional para la Cultura y las Artes and Instituto Nacional de Antropología e Historia, Mexico City.

Uriarte, María Teresa

1982 La escultura mexica. In *Historia del arte mexicano.* Vol. 2: *Arte prehispánico*: 236–257. Salvat, Mexico City.

Urueta Flores, Cecilia

n.d. Presencia del material mixteco dentro del Templo Mayor. B.A. thesis, Escuela Nacional de Antropología e Historia, Mexico City, 1990.

Vaillant, George C.

1930 *Excavations at Zacatenco.* Anthropological Papers of the American Museum of Natural History 32, pt. 1. American Museum of Natural History, New York.

1935 *Early Cultures of the Valley of Mexico: Results of the Stratigraphical Project of the American Museum of Natural History in the Valley of Mexico, 1928–1933.* Anthropological Papers of the American Museum of Natural History 35, pt. 3. American Museum of Natural History, New York.

1962 *Aztecs of Mexico: Origin, Rise, and Fall of the Aztec Nation.* Doubleday, Garden City, N.Y.

Vaillant, Suzannah B., and George C. Vaillant

1934 *Excavations at Gualupita.* Anthropological Papers of the American Museum of Natural History 35, pt. 1. American Museum of Natural History, New York.

Valenzuela, Juan

1945 Las exploraciones efectuadas en Los Tuxtlas, Veracruz. *Talleres Gráficos de la Editorial Stylo,* 5th series 3: 83–107.

Vargas, Ernesto (ed.)

1989 *Las máscaras de la cueva de Santa Ana Teloxtoc.* Serie Antropológica 105. Universidad Nacional Autónoma de México, Mexico City.

Vila Llonch, Elisenda

2008a Portable Altar with Obsidian Plaque. In *Dumbarton Oaks: The Collections* (Gudrun Bühl, ed.): 188–189. Dumbarton Oaks Research Library and Collection, Washington, D.C.

2008b Sculpture of Xiuhcoatl (Fire Serpent). In *Dumbarton Oaks: The Collections* (Gudrun Bühl, ed.): 190–191. Dumbarton Oaks Research Library and Collection, Washington, D.C.

2008c Sculpture of Tezcatlipoca (Smoking Mirror). In *Dumbarton Oaks: The Collections* (Gudrun Bühl, ed.): 192–193. Dumbarton Oaks Research Library and Collection, Washington, D.C.

2008d Head of Xipe Totec (The Flayed One). In *Dumbarton Oaks: The Collections* (Gudrun Bühl, ed.): 194–195. Dumbarton Oaks Research Library and Collection, Washington, D.C.

2008e Atlatl (Spear Thrower). In *Dumbarton Oaks: The Collections* (Gudrun Bühl, ed.): 196–197. Dumbarton Oaks Research Library and Collection, Washington, D.C.

2008f Mural with a Net-Jaguar. In *Dumbarton Oaks: The Collections* (Gudrun Bühl, ed.): 198–199. Dumbarton Oaks Research Library and Collection, Washington, D.C.

2008g Tripod Polychrome Vessel. In *Dumbarton Oaks: The Collections* (Gudrun Bühl, ed.): 200–201. Dumbarton Oaks Research Library and Collection, Washington, D.C.

2008h Stone Mask. In *Dumbarton Oaks: The Collections* (Gudrun Bühl, ed.): 202–203. Dumbarton Oaks Research Library and Collection, Washington, D.C.

2008i Ball Game Yoke. In *Dumbarton Oaks: The Collections* (Gudrun Bühl, ed.): 204–205. Dumbarton Oaks Research Library and Collection, Washington, D.C.

2008j Ball Game Hacha. In *Dumbarton Oaks: The Collections* (Gudrun Bühl, ed.): 206–207. Dumbarton Oaks Research Library and Collection, Washington, D.C.

Villagra Caleti, Agustín

1951 Las pinturas de Atetelco en Teotihuacan. *Cuadernos americanos* 55: 153–162.

1954 Trabajos realizados en Teotihuacan: 1952. *Anales del Instituto Nacional de Antropología e Historia* 6 (34): 69–78.

1971 Mural Painting in Central Mexico. In *Archaeology of Northern Mesoamerica* (Gordon Ekholm and Ignacio Bernal, eds.): 135–156. *Handbook of Middle American Indians*, Vol. 10 (Robert Wauchope, ed.). University of Texas Press, Austin.

Virginia Museum of Fine Arts

1961 *Treasures in America*. Virginia Museum of Fine Arts, Richmond.

Vizcaíno, Antonio

1988 *The Xalapa Museum of Anthropology*. Government of the State of Veracruz, Xalapa.

Von Hagen, Victor Wolfgang

1958 *De Azteken: Geschiedenis en Cultuur*. Van Ditmar, Amsterdam.

1961 *The Ancient Sun Kingdoms of the Americas: Aztec, Maya, Inca*. World, Cleveland, Ind.

Von Winning, Hasso

1961 Teotihuacan Symbols. *Ethnos* 26: 3.

1968a Der Netzjaguar in Teotihuacán, Mexico. *Baessler-Archiv*, new series, 16: 31–46.

1968b *Pre-Columbian Art of Mexico and Central America*. Harry N. Abrams, New York.

1971 Shell Pendants from Jalisco, Mexico. *Masterkey* 45 (1): 20–26.

1977 The Old Fire God and His Symbolism at Teotihuacan. *Indiana* 4: 7–61.

1986a A Monkey Effigy Jar from Ancient Mexico. *Art Bulletin of Victoria* 27: 66–73.

1986b Stone Vase with Zapotec Glyphs. *Mexicon* 8 (6): 119–122.

1987 *La iconografía de Teotihuacan: Los dioses y los signos*. 2 vols. Universidad Nacional Autónoma de México, Mexico City.

Voss, Alexander W., and H. Jürgen Kremer

1998 La estela de Tabi: Un monumento a la Cacería. *Mexicon* 20 (4): 74–79.

Voyages of the Mind

1991 Voyages of the Mind: The AAAS Annual Meeting. *Science* 254 (15 November).

Vuille, Marilène

1998 *Accouchement et douleur: Une étude sociologique*. Editions Antipodes, Lausanne, Switzerland.

Walsh, Jane MacLaren

2003 Máscaras teotihuacanas de Teotihuacan a Filadelfia en 1830. *Arqueología mexicana* 11 (64): 62–64.

2008a The Dumbarton Oaks Tlazolteotl: Looking Beneath the Surface. *Journal de la Société des Américanistes* 94 (1): 7–43.

2008b Legend of the Crystal Skulls. *Archaeology* 61 (3): 36–41.

Washington Post

2003 From the Collection: Washington's Prize Possessions. *Washington Post*, 23 February.

Weiant, Clarence W.

1943 *An Introduction to the Ceramics of Tres Zapotes, Veracruz, Mexico*. Bulletin 139, Bureau of American Ethnology. Government Printing Office, Washington, D.C.

Weigle, Marta

1989 *Creation and Procreation: Feminist Reflections on Mythologies of Cosmogony and Parturition*. University of Pennsylvania Press, Philadelphia.

Die Weltkunst

1959 *Die Weltkunst*, 1 July.

Wenham, Edward

1937 Spanish-American Silverwork, Part 2. *Apollo* 26: 258–265.

Werness, Hope B.

2004 *The Continuum Encyclopedia of Animal Symbolism in Art*. Continuum, New York.

West, Robert C.

1994 Aboriginal Metallurgy and Metalworking in Spanish America: A Brief Overview. In *In Quest of Mineral Wealth: Aboriginal and Colonial Mining and Metallurgy in Spanish America* (Alan K. Craig and Robert C. West, eds.): 5–20. Geoscience and Man 33. Louisiana State University, Baton Rouge.

Westheim, Paul

1956 *La escultura del México antiguo*. Universidad Nacional Autónoma de México, Mexico City.

1977 *Obras maestras del México antiguo*. Ediciones Era, Mexico City.

Whittaker, John

n.d.a Weapon Trials: The Atlatl and Experiments in Hunting Technology. Manuscript on file, Brandeis University, Department of Anthropology, Waltham, Mass., 2004.

n.d.b Atlatl Record Form for the Implement in the British Museum. Manuscript on file, Brandeis University, Department of Anthropology, Waltham, Mass., 2004.

Whittington, E. Michael (ed.)

2001 *The Sport of Life and Death: The Mesoamerican Ballgame*. Thames and Hudson, London.

Widmer, Randolph J.

1997 Especialización económica en Copán. *Yaxkin* 15: 141–160.

Widmer, Randolph J., and Rebecca Storey

1993 Social Organization and Household Structure of a Teotihuacan Apartment Compound: S3W1:33 of the Tlajinga Barrio. In *Prehispanic Domestic Units in Western Mesoamerica* (Robert S. Santley and Kenneth G. Hirth, eds.): 87–104. CAC, Boca Raton, Fla.

Wiener, Norman

n.d.a Letter to Robert Woods Bliss. Manuscript on file, Dumbarton Oaks Research Library and Collection, Washington, D.C., 27 June 1962.

n.d.b Letter to Robert Woods Bliss. Manuscript on file, Dumbarton Oaks Research Library and Collection, Washington, D.C., 29 June 1962.

Wilkerson, S. Jeffrey K.

1971 Un yugo en situ de la región del Tajín. *Boletín* 41: 41–45.

1974 Sub-Culture Areas of Eastern Mesoamerica. In *Primera Mesa Redonda de Palenque: A Conference on the Art, Iconography, and Dynastic History of Palenque* (Merle Greene Robertson, ed.), Pt. II: 89–102. Robert Louis Stevenson School, Pre-Columbian Art Research, Pebble Beach, Calif.

1976 *The Sculptures of El Tajín: A Special Exhibition of Photographs and Drawings, University Gallery, February 15 through March 21, 1976*. College of Fine Arts, University of Florida, Gainesville.

1980 Man's Eighty Centuries in Veracruz. *National Geographic Magazine* 158 (2): 202–231.

1984 In Search of the Mountain of Foam. *Ritual Human Sacrifice in Mesoamerica* (Elizabeth H. Boone, ed.): 101–131. Dumbarton Oaks Research Library and Collection, Washington, D.C.

1987 *El Tajín: A Guide for Visitors*. Universidad Veracruzana, Xalapa.

1988 Cultural Time and Space in Ancient Veracruz. *Ceremonial Sculpture of Ancient Veracruz* (Marilyn M. Goldstein, ed.): 6–17. Hillwood Art Gallery–Long Island University, Brookville, N.Y.

1990 El Tajín: Great Center of the Northeast. *Mexico: Splendors of Thirty Centuries*: 155–181. Metropolitan Museum of Art, New York.

1991 And They Were Sacrificed. In *The Mesoamerican Ballgame* (Vernon L. Scarborough and David R. Wilcox, eds.): 45–72. University of Arizona Press, Tucson.

1993 Escalante's Entrada. *National Geographic Research and Exploration* 9: 12–31.

1994a The Garden City of El Pital. *National Geographic Research and Exploration* 10: 56–71.

1994b Nahua Presence on the Mesoamerican Gulf Coast. In *Chipping Away on Earth: Studies in Prehispanic and Colonial Mexico in Honor of Arthur J. O. Anderson and Charles E. Dibble* (Eloise Quiñones-Keber, ed.): 177–186. Labyrinthos, Culver City, Calif.

1997a Grosswild, frühe Menschen und erste Dörfer im Tiefland Ostmexikos. In *Mexiko: Präkolumbische Kulturen am Golf von Mexiko* (Judith Rickenbach, ed.): 19–23. Museum Rietberg, Zurich.

1997b In Booten über das Meer: die Herkunft der Nahuas, Veracruz-Kultur. In *Mexiko: Präkolumbische Kulturen am Golf von Mexiko* (Judith Rickenbach, ed.): 55–59. Museum Rietberg, Zurich.

1997c El Tajín und der Höhepunkt der Klassischen Veracruz-Kultur. In *Mexiko: Präkolumbische Kulturen am Golf von Mexiko* (Judith Rickenbach, ed.): 61–76. Museum Rietberg, Zurich.

1997d Palmas und das Ballspielritual an der Golfküste, Veracruz-Kultur. In *Mexiko: Präkolumbische Kulturen am Golf von Mexiko* (Judith Rickenbach, ed.): 113–118. Museum Rietberg, Zurich.

1999 Classic Veracruz Architecture: Cultural Symbolism in Time and Space. In *Mesoamerican Architecture as a Cultural Symbol* (Jeff K. Kowalski, ed.): 110–139. Oxford University Press, New York.

2000 Huastec Sculptures: Stone Art of the Northeastern Frontier of Mesoamerica. *Precolombart* 3: 34–52.

2001a Gulf Lowlands. In *Archaeology of Ancient Mexico and Central America: An Encyclopedia* (Susan Toby Evans and David L. Webster, eds.): 323–324. Garland, New York.

2001b Gulf Lowlands: North Central Region. In *Archaeology of Ancient Mexico and Central America: An Encyclopedia* (Susan Toby Evans and David L. Webster, eds.): 324–329. Garland, New York.

2001c Gulf Lowlands: North Region. In *Archaeology of Ancient Mexico and Central America: An Encyclopedia* (Susan Toby Evans and David L. Webster, eds.): 329–334. Garland, New York.

2001d Tajín, El: Art and Artifacts. In *Archaeology of Ancient Mexico and Central America: An Encyclopedia* (Susan Toby Evans and David L. Webster, eds.): 696–698. Garland, New York.

2001e Tajín, El: Religion and Ideology. In *Archaeology of Ancient Mexico and Central America: An Encyclopedia* (Susan Toby Evans and David L. Webster, eds.): 696–698. Garland, New York.

2005 Rivers in the Sea: The Gulf of Mexico as a Cultural Corridor in Antiquity. In *Gulf Coast Archaeology: The Southeastern United States and Mexico* (Nancy White, ed.): 56–67. University Press of Florida, Gainsville.

2008 And the Waters Took Them: Catastrophic Flooding and Civilization on the Mexican Gulf Coast. In *El Niño, Catastrophism, and Culture Change in Ancient America* (Daniel H. Sandweiss and Jeffrey Quilter, eds.): 243–271. Dumbarton Oaks Research Library and Collection, Washington, D.C., and Harvard University Press, Cambridge, Mass.

n.d. Ethnogensis of the Huastecs and Totonacs. Ph.D. dissertation, Department of Anthropology, Tulane University, New Orleans, La., 1972.

Willey, Gordon R.

1966 *An Introduction to American Archaeology.* Vol. 1, *North and Middle America.* Prentice-Hall, Englewood Cliffs, N.J.

William Rockhill Nelson Gallery of Art and Mary Atkins Museum of Fine Arts

1962 *The Imagination of Primitive Man: A Survey of the Arts of the Non-Literate Peoples of the World.* Nelson Gallery and Atkins Museum Bulletin 4, no. 1. The Museum, Kansas City, Mo.

Winter, Marcus C.

1989 From Classic to Post-Classic in Pre-Hispanic Oaxaca. In *Mesoamerica after the Decline of Teotihuacan A.D. 700–900* (Richard A. Diehl and Janet Catherine Berlo, eds.): 123–130. Dumbarton Oaks Research Library and Collection, Washington, D.C.

Winter, Marcus C., and Vicente Marcial Cerqueda (eds.)

2004 Excavaciones arqueológicas en El Carrizal, Ixtepec, Oaxaca. In *Palabras de luz, palabras floridas* (Vicente Marcial Cerque, ed.): 17–48. Universidad del Istmo, Tehuantepec, Mexico.

Wolfman, Dan

1990 Mesoamerican Chronology and Archaeomagnetic Dating, A.D. 1–1200. In *Archaeomagnetic Dating* (Jeffrey L. Eighmy and Robert S. Sternberg, eds.): 261–308. University of Arizona Press, Tucson.

Woodbury, Richard B.

1965 Artifacts of the Guatemala Highlands. In *Archaeology of Southern Mesoamerica,* Pt. 1 (Gordon R. Willey, ed.): 163–179. *Handbook of Middle American Indians,* Vol. 2 (Robert Wauchope, ed.). University of Texas Press, Austin.

Woodbury, Richard B., and Aubrey S. Trik

1953 *The Ruins of Zaculeu, Guatemala.* 2 vols. United Fruit Company, New York.

Young-Sanchez, Margaret

1990 Veneration of the Dead: Religious Ritual on a Pre-Columbian Mirror-Back. *Bulletin of the Cleveland Museum of Art* 77: 326–335.

Younger, Jennifer K.

2004 Pair of Tubular Rounded Beads. In *The Aztec Empire: Catalogue of the Exhibition* (Felipe Solís Olguín, ed.): 43, cat. no. 184. Guggenheim Museum Publications, New York.

Zantwijk, Rudolf van

1983 Aztecs and Mayas. In *An Illustrated History of the World's Religions* (Geoffrey Parrinder, ed.): 69–89. Newnes, Feltham, England.

1985 *The Aztec Arrangement: The Social History of Pre-Spanish Mexico.* University of Oklahoma Press, Norman.

Zenner, Klaus

1974 *Gang durch Versunkene Städte: Ein Ausflug ins Reich der Archäologie.* 9th ed. Prisma-Verlag, Leipzig.

SUSAN TOBY EVANS is a professor of Anthropology at Pennsylvania State University, University Park, Pennsylvania. Her major research interest is Aztec culture, and she has surveyed Aztec settlement systems and excavated the site of Cihuatecpan in the Teotihuacan Valley, Mexico. She is the author of *Ancient Mexico and Central America: Archaeology and Culture History* (2008), winner of the Society for American Archaeology's Book Award. With Joanne Pillsbury she edited *Palaces of the Ancient New World* (2004), and with David Webster she edited *Archaeology of Ancient Mexico and Central America: An Encyclopedia* (2001).

JEFFREY QUILTER is deputy director for Curatorial Affairs and curator for Intermediate Area Archaeology at the Peabody Museum, Harvard University, Cambridge, Mass. He has conducted archaeological fieldwork in Peru and Costa Rica, including recent work at El Brujo in the Chicama Valley, Peru. His publications include *Life and Death at Paloma, Society and Mortuary Practices at a Preceramic Peruvian Village* (1989); *Cobble Circles and Standing Stones: Archaeology at the Rivas Site, Costa Rica* (2004); and *Treasures of the Andes* (2005), as well as journal and book articles on the Moche and other topics in archaeology and art history.

NICHOLAS J. SAUNDERS is reader in Material Culture at University College, London. An archaeologist specializing in the symbolism of Mesoamerican, Andean, and Caribbean material culture, he is especially interested in ideas concerning brilliance and color. He has published *People of the Jaguar* (1989), *Icons of Power* (1998), *Ancient Americas: The Great Civilisations* (2004a), and *Peoples of the Caribbean* (2005), as well as many academic articles.

JAVIER URCID is associate professor of Anthropology at Brandeis University, Waltham, Massachusetts. He received his Ph.D. from Yale University and is an anthropological archaeologist interested in the role of ancient literacy and writing systems. He is the author of *Zapotec Hieroglyphic Writing* (2001). His other interests center on archaeological approaches to ancient political economies and on bio-archaeology, particularly work on the social dimensions of mortuary practices and cultural and/or ritual modifications of human bones.

S. JEFFREY K. WILKERSON directs the Institute for Cultural Ecology of the Tropics and is based in Veracruz, Mexico. For more than 45 years he has undertaken research in the lowlands tropics of Mexico and Central America. He has written extensively on the art, architecture, and archaeology of eastern Mesoamerica, focusing primarily on the pivotal ancient cities of El Tajín, El Pital, and Santa Luisa. Recent publications include "Classic Veracruz Architecture, Cultural Symbolism in Time and Space" (1999), "Huastec Sculptures: Stone Art of the Northeastern Frontier of Mesoamerica" (2000), "Rivers in the Sea: The Gulf of Mexico as a Cultural Corridor in Antiquity" (2005), and "And the Waters Took Them: Catastrophic Flooding and Civilization on the Mexican Gulf Coast" (2008).

INDEX

Italic page numbers indicate plates.

E

F

N

Q

R

S